At Issue

| Military Recruiters

Other Books in the At Issue Series:

At Issue

Military Recruiters

Lauri Harding, Book Editor

GREENHAVEN PRESS
An imprint of Thomson Gale, a part of The Thomson Corporation

THOMSON
GALE

Detroit • New York • San Francisco • New Haven, Conn. • Waterville, Maine • London

Christine Nasso, *Publisher*
Elizabeth Des Chenes, *Managing Editor*

© 2008 The Gale Group.

For more information, contact:
Greenhaven Press
27500 Drake Rd.
Farmington Hills, MI 48331-3535
Or you can visit our Internet site at http://www.gale.com

LIBRARY OF CONGRESS CATALOGING-IN-PUBLICATION DATA

Military recruiters / Lauri Harding, book editor.
   p. cm. -- (At issue)
Includes bibliographical references and index.
ISBN-13: 978-0-7377-3787-5 (hardcover)
ISBN-13: 978-0-7377-3788-2 (pbk.)
1. United States--Armed Forces--Recruiting, enlistment, etc. 2. United States--ArmedForces--Recruiting, enlistment, etc.--Iraq War, 2003- 3. Military service, Voluntary-- United States. 4. Draft--United States. I. Harding, Lauri.
   UB323.M55 2007
   355.2'23620973--dc22

                                                                        2007037478

ISBN-10: 0-7377-3787-5 (hardcover)
ISBN-10: 0-7377-3788-3 (pbk.)

Printed in the United States of America
10 9 8 7 6 5 4 3 2 1

Contents

Introduction

Jessica Faustner was only seventeen years old and a few months short of graduating from Northampton Area High School near Allentown, Pennsylvania when she enlisted in the Pennsylvania Army National Guard in 2005. Described by reporter Lawrence Hardy as a bright but mediocre student who was "more infatuated with boys than schoolwork," Faustner began attending the Guard's monthly drill weekends at Allentown's National Guard Armory, but suddenly stopped before her final required session and went into hiding.

Faustner would later go public with accusations that a Guard recruiter had enticed her into enlisting with an offer of sending her through nursing school before she would be deployed overseas. Through her attorney, she further alleged that the recruiter used other deceptive practices to get her and her parents to sign her enlistment papers. According to Faustner, after enlisting she learned at a meeting of new recruits that she had a 90 percent chance of being deployed to Iraq after basic training. So she went AWOL (absent without leave) instead. "You know, a 17-year-old girl should be thinking about her prom and her graduation, not about going to Iraq. She was just misled all the way around," her attorney, John Roberts, told reporters.

Back in Allentown, a big showdown between Faustner (in hiding and speaking through her attorney) and the National Guard (threatening to prosecute her and compel her to report for duty) dominated the local media for weeks. Captain Cory Angell, a spokesperson for the National Guard, contended that Faustner's assumption of immediate deployment to Iraq was wrong. "She, at minimum, would be non-deployable until her second year of college," Angell commented.

Faustner's allegations of wrongdoing by her recruiter are not uncommon. The war in Iraq created heightened demand for military manpower by 2005. Men and women serving in the active-duty military, the Reserves, and the National Guard could all expect to be sent overseas to fight. With casualties mounting and popular support for the war in decline, military recruiters were under pressure.

In fact, Faustner's complaint coincided with a massive U.S. Army "stand down" (a one-day halt in all recruiting activities) to review recruiting practices used by the military across the nation. This was mostly in response to recurring media reports of fraud and deception, and a measurable rise in claims alleging recruiter misconduct. Between fiscal years 2004 and 2005, the military reviewed more than 11,000 cases of alleged deception, coercion, or other abuse by military recruiters.

In Faustner's case, a full investigation was conducted and a staff judge advocate concluded that her accusations were not substantiated. "Our recruiting command says he [the recruiter] did everything to the letter, to the 'T' perfect," said Angell. But in other cases misunderstandings between military recruiters and their prospective enlistees have been substantiated, and are increasingly common as America's citizens grapple with conflicting notions of honor, duty, patriotism, and their fears of being sent into battle.

There are recruiters deserving of criticism for their role in painting an unrealistic picture of military service, or stoking the fire of patriotism that feeds unrealistic expectations of military conflict and its dangers. Some have gone as far as to intentionally deceive. They have taken the innocent enthusiasm of many and turned it into sour resentment.

On the other hand, honorable and undeserving recruiters have themselves been victims of counter-recruitment extremism (particularly on college campuses) involving ransacked offices, blood thrown through smashed windows, recruiting vehicles set on fire, and office door locks jammed with powerful glue. Other recruiters, lawfully dispatched to set up recruiting booths at local high schools or college campuses, have been met with massive anti-war demonstrations and protests. Students have blocked access to recruiting booths for interested students wanting information, and many recruiters have been falsely charged of wrongful conduct or statement.

Recruiters often serve as "fall guys," taking criticism as the result of unpopular wars, unpopular recruiting policies and practices, and unpopular political administrations or agendas. Many in the general public who oppose recruiters would do so for these reasons even if there were no cases of recruiters behaving improperly.

In the end, most Americans believe that the United States needs a competent and committed military. The all-volunteer force relies on recruiters to make this a reality, therefore protesting them for doing their jobs can be counterproductive. As Ken Harbaugh, a former Navy Pilot and student at Yale Law School, put it in a commentary on *National Public Radio:*

> Every year the law school sends some of its brightest graduates to work in the Justice Department and the State Department. Yale certainly doesn't endorse every practice of those organizations, but it understands that by working with them it is much more likely to influence their policies for the better. . . .

> Imagine if America's elite universities had obstructed recruiting efforts during World War II. God knows there were decent reasons then. Just consider the appalling treatment of blacks in uniform. But Yale and others sent their best to fight and, in doing so, helped improve the character of our armed forces.

It is this conflict that makes military recruiters and recruitment such a controversial issue. Justified or not, military recruiters will continue to face charges of deception and abusive practices so long as they remain the primary means of convincing young Americans to join the armed forces.

1

Military Recruiters Charm Impressionable Youth Into Risky Business

William Ayers

William Ayers is a professor of education and senior university scholar at the University of Illinois at Chicago. He is a published author in the field of education.

Military recruiters influence vulnerable teenagers by taking advantage of their desire to fit in, aggression, and sense of invincibility. The prospect of becoming a member of an identifiable group with a distinctive uniform, combined with a shared mission and grand purpose, is highly attractive to teens. Moreover, the military culture especially appeals to lower-income youths with less opportunity for varied futures. This makes the Junior Reserve Officers' Training Corps (JROTC, the high school version of ROTC) a popular choice in many schools. As a result, high schools have become battlefields for the hearts and minds of our youth.

In her book, *Purple Hearts*, documentary photographer Nina Berman presents 40 photographs—two each of 20 U.S. veterans of the American war in Iraq—plus a couple accompanying paragraphs of commentary from each vet in his or her own words.

Their comments cohere around their service, their sacrifice, their suffering. The Purple Heart binds them together—

William Ayers, "Hearts and Minds: Military Recruitment and the High School Battlefield," *Education Digest*, vol. 71, May 2006, pp. 594–599. Reproduced by permission.

this award is their common experience, this distinction is what they embrace and what embraces them. This is what they live with.

Youthful Stories

Their views on war, on their time in arms, on where they hope they are headed with their lives, are various; their ways of making sense about the U.S. military mission, wildly divergent.

Josh Olson, 24 years old, begins: "We bent over backwards for these people, but they ended up screwing us over, stabbing us in the back. A lot of them, I mean, they're going to have to be killed. . . . As Americans we've taken it upon ourselves to almost cure the world's problems I guess, give everybody else a chance. I guess that's how we're good-hearted." He's missing his right leg now and was presented with his Purple Heart at Walter Reed Military Hospital by President Bush himself. He feels it all—pride, anger, loss.

Jermaine Lewis, 23, grew up in a Chicago neighborhood where "death has always been around." At basic training, "they break you down and then they try to build you up." To him, the "reasons for going to war were bogus, but we were right to go in there."

The vets are all young. Several recall deciding to enlist when much younger still, more innocent, more vulnerable, but feeling somehow invincible. Says Lewis: "I've been dealing with the military since I was a sophomore in high school. They came to the school like six times a year, all military branches. They had a recruiting station like a block from our high school. It was just right there."

Tyson Johnson III, 22, wanted out of the poverty and death he saw all around him. His life was going nowhere, he thought, so he signed on: "And here I am, back here . . . I don't know where it's going to end up." Joseph Mosner enrolled at 19: "There was nothing out there. There was no good jobs so I figured this would have been a good thing." Frederick Allen thought war would be "jumping out of planes." He joined when recruiters came to his high school. "I thought it would be fun."

Add the need to prove oneself to be a macho, strong, tough, capable person, combined with an unrealistic calculus of vulnerability and a constricted sense of options specifically in poor and working-class communities—all of this creates the toxic mix in a young person's head that can be a military recruiter's dream.

Adam Zaremba, 20, also enlisted while still in high school: "The recruiter called the house, he was actually looking for my brother and he happened to get me. I think it was because I didn't want to do homework for a while, and then I don't know, you get to wear a cool uniform. It just went on from there. I still don't even understand a lot about the Army."

His Purple Heart seemed like a good thing from a distance, "but then when it happens you realize that you have to do something, or something has to happen to you in order to get it."

Creating an Appealing Image

Military recruiting in high schools has been a mainstay of the so-called all-volunteer armed forces from the start. High school kids are at an age when being a member of an identifiable group with a grand mission and a shared spirit—and never underestimate a distinctive uniform—is of exaggerated importance, which gang recruiters in big cities note with interest and exploit with skill.

Kathy Dobie (in "AWOL in America," in Harper's, March 2005), quoting a military historian, notes that "basic training has been essentially the same in every army in every age, because it works with the same raw material that's always been there in teenage boys: a fair amount of aggression, a strong tendency to hang around in groups, and an absolute desperate desire to fit in."

Being cool and going along with the crowd are big things. Add the need to prove oneself to be a macho, strong, tough, capable person, combined with an unrealistic calculus of vulnerability and a constricted sense of options specifically in poor and working-class communities—all of this creates the toxic mix in a young person's head that can be a military recruiter's dream.

One of the most effective recruitment tools is Junior Reserve Officers' Training Corps (JROTC), the high school version of ROTC established by an act of Congress in 1916 "to develop citizenship and responsibility in young people." JROTC is now experiencing the most rapid expansion in its history. . . .

There is no doubt that JROTC programs target poor, black, and Latino kids without the widest range of options to begin with.

JROTC and MSCC [Middle School Cadet Corps] defenders claim the goal is leadership and citizen development, dropout prevention or simply the fun of dressing up and parading around. Skeptics note that Pentagon money for these programs provides needed resources for starving public schools and ask why the military has become such an important route to adequate school funding. . . .

Selective Recruiting

There is no doubt that JROTC programs target poor, black, and Latino kids without the widest range of options to begin with. Recruiters know where to go: Whitney Young High School, a large, selective magnet school in Chicago, had seven military recruiter visits last year, compared to 150 from university recruiters; Schurz High School, 80% Hispanic, had nine military and 10 university visits.

Bob Herbert, in the June 16, 2005, *New York Times*, notes that all high schools are not equal to recruiters: "Schools with kids from wealthier families (and a high percentage of college-bound students) are not viewed as good prospects. . . . The kids in those schools are not the kids who fight America's wars." Absent arts and sports programs or a generous array of clubs and activities, JROTC and its accompanying culture of war—militarism, aggression, violence, repression, the demonization of others, and mindless obedience—become the default choice for poor kids attending low-income schools.

The military culture seeps in at all levels and has a more generally corrosive impact on education itself, narrowing curriculum choices and promoting a model of teaching as training and of learning as "just following orders." In reality, good teaching always involves thoughtful and complicated judgments, careful attention to relationships, and complex choices about how to challenge and nurture each student.

Good teachers are not drill instructors. Authentic learning, too, is multidimensional and requires the constant construction and reconstruction of knowledge built on expanding experiences.

The educational model that employs teachers to simply pour imperial gallons of facts into empty vessels—ridiculed by Charles Dickens 150 years ago and discredited as a path to learning by modern psychologists and educational researchers—is making a roaring comeback. The rise of the military in schools adds energy to that.

A vibrant democratic culture requires free people with minds of their own capable of making independent judgments. Education in a democracy resists obedience and conformity for free inquiry and the widest possible exploration. Obedience training may have a place in instructing dogs, but not in educating citizens.

Keeping the Numbers Up

Today, two years into the invasion of Iraq [in 2003], recruiters are consistently failing to meet monthly enlistment quotas, despite deep penetration into high schools, sponsorship of NASCAR and other sporting events, and a $3 billion Pentagon recruitment budget. Recruiters are offering higher bonuses and shortened tours of duty, and violations of ethical guidelines and the military's own putative standards are becoming commonplace: In one highly publicized case, a recruiter was taped coaching a high school kid how to fake a mandatory drug test.

"One of the most common lies told by recruiters," writes Dobie, "is that it's easy to get out of the military if you change your mind. But once they arrive at training, the recruits are told there's no exit period." Although recruiters are known to lie, the number of young people signing up is still plummeting.

The military manpower crisis includes escalating desertions: 4,739 Army deserters in 2001 compared to 1,509 in 1995. An Army study says deserters tend to be "Younger when they enlist, less educated . . . come from 'broken homes,' and [have] 'engaged in delinquent behavior.'"

In war time, desertion tends to spike upward. So, after 9/11, the Army "issued a new policy regarding deserters, hoping to staunch the flow." The new rules return deserters to their units, hoping they can be "integrated back into the ranks"—not a happy circumstance: "I can't afford to babysit problem children everyday," says one commander.

At the end of March 2005, the Pentagon announced the active-duty Army achieved only about two-thirds of its March goal and was 3,973 short for the year; Army Reserve was 1,382 short of its year-to-date goal. 2005 was the toughest recruiting year since 1973, the first year of the all-volunteer Army. Americans don't want to fight this war, and a huge investment in high school recruiting is the military's latest desperate hope.

The Home Front

The high school itself has become a battlefield for hearts and minds. On one side: the power of the federal government; claims (often unsubstantiated) of financial benefits; humvees on school grounds; goody bags filled with donuts, key chains, video games, and T-shirts. Most ominous of all is No Child Left Behind, the controversial omnibus education bill of 2001.

Its Section 9528 reverses policies in many cities keeping organizations that discriminate on the basis of race, gender, or sexual orientation—including the military—out of schools. It mandates that military recruiters have the same access to students as colleges. The bill also requires schools to turn over students' addresses and home phone numbers to the military unless parents expressly opt out.

On the other side: a mounting death toll in Iraq, a growing sense among the citizenry that politicians lied and manipulated us at every turn to wage an aggressive war outside any broad popular interest, and groups of parents mobilizing to oppose high school recruitment.

A front-page story in the *New York Times* reported a "Growing Problem for Military Recruiters: Parents." Resistance to recruiters, says the report, is spreading coast to coast, and "was provoked by the very law that was supposed to make it easier for recruiters to reach students more directly. 'No Child Left Behind' . . . is often the spark that ignites parental resistance."

The military injunction—hierarchy, obedience, conformity, and aggression—stands in stark opposition to the democratic imperative of respect, cooperation, and equality.

And parents, it turns out, can be a formidable obstacle to a volunteer Army. Unlike the universal draft, signing up requires an affirmative act, and parents can and often do exercise a strong negative drag on their kids' stepping forward. A Department of Defense survey from November 2004 found that "only 25% of parents would recommend military service to their children, down from 42% in August 2003."

Herbert focuses attention on an Army publication called "School Recruiting Program Handbook." Its goal is straightforward: "school ownership that can only lead to a greater number of Army enlistments." This means promoting military participation in every feasible dimension, from making classroom presentations to involvement in Hispanic heritage and Black History months.

The handbook recommends that recruiters contact athletic coaches and volunteer to lead calisthenics, get involved with the homecoming committee and organize a presence in the parade, donate coffee and donuts to the faculty on a regular basis, eat in the cafeteria, and target influential students who, while they may not enlist, can refer others who might.

For Adults Only

The military injunction—hierarchy, obedience, conformity, and aggression—stands in stark opposition to the democratic imperative of respect, cooperation, and equality. The noted New Zealand educator Sylvia Ashton-Warner wrote that war and peace—acknowledged or hidden—"wait and vie" in every classroom.

She argued that all human beings are like volcanoes with two vents, one destructive and the other creative. If the creative vent is open, she maintained, then the destructive vent will atrophy and close; on the other hand, if the creative vent is shut down, the destructive will have free rein.

"Creativity in this time of life," she wrote, "when character can be influenced forever, is the solution to the problem of war." She quoted Erich Fromm: "The amount of destructiveness in a child is proportionate to the amount to which the expansiveness of his life has been curtailed. Destructiveness is the outcome of the unlived life."

Herbert, himself a Vietnam combat vet, is deeply troubled by the deceptive and manipulative tactics of recruiters: "Let the Army be honest and upfront in its recruitment," he writes. "War is not child's play, and warriors shouldn't be assembled through the use of seductive sales pitches to youngsters too immature to make an informed decision on matters that might well result in them having to kill others, or being killed themselves."

A little truth-telling, then. War is catastrophic for human beings, and, indeed, for the continuation of life on Earth. With 120 military bases around the globe and the second largest military force ever assembled, the U.S. government is engaged in a constant state of war, and American society is necessarily distorted and disfigured around the aims of war. . . .

Youth Warriors

There are now more than 300,000 child soldiers worldwide. . . .

The United States, which consistently refused to ratify the United Nations Convention on the Rights of the Child, agreed in 2002 to sign on to the "Optional Protocol" to the Convention, covering the involvement of children in armed conflicts. In its "Declarations and Reservations," the U.S. stipulated that the Protocol in no way carries any obligations under the Convention and that "nothing in the Protocol establishes a basis for jurisdiction by any international tribunal, including the International Criminal Court."

It lists several other reservations, including an objection to Article 1 of the Protocol, which states, "Parties shall take all feasible measures to ensure that members of their armed forces who have not attained the age of 18 years do not take direct part in hostilities."

Timely Advice

The U.S. stipulates that "feasible measures" means what is "practical" when taking into account all circumstances, "including humanitarian and military considerations," and that the article does not apply to "indirect participation in hostilities, such as gathering and transmitting military information, transporting weapons, ammunition, or other supplies, or forward deployment."

Because recruiters do lie, because the U.S. steps back from international law and standards, and because the cost of an education for too many poor and working-class kids is constructed as a trip through a minefield and a pact with the devil, teachers should consider Bill Bigelow's advice to critically examine the "Enlistment/Reenlistment Document—Armed Forces of the United States" that recruits sign when they join up. (Copies can be downloaded at rethinking schools.org.)

Among a host of loopholes and disclaimers is this in section 9b: "Laws and regulations that govern military personnel may change without notice to me. Such changes may affect my status, pay, allowances, benefits, and responsibilities as a member of the armed forces regardless of the provisions of this enlistment/reenlistment document."

When Bigelow's students analyzed the entire contract, they concluded it more honest to simply say something like, "Just sign up. . . . Now you belong to us." They advise students; "Read the contract thoroughly. . . . Don't sign unless you're 100% sure, 100% of the time." One of Bigelow's students, who had suffered through the war in Bosnia, recommended students inclined to enlist might "shoot a bird, and then think about whether you can kill a human."

Jermaine Lewis, the 23-year-old vet from Chicago who spoke of the war being "bogus" in Purple Hearts, always wanted to be a teacher but worried about the low pay. Now, with both legs gone, he calculates that a teacher's salary plus disability pay will earn him an adequate income: "So I want to go to college and study education—public school, primarily middle school, sixth to eighth grade." He went through the minefield to get what more privileged kids have access to without asking. It's something.

2

Bad Military Recruiters Are the Exception and Not the Rule

Rod Powers

Rod Powers is a retired U.S. Air Force First Sergeant, public speaker, and military author. His Barron's Guide to Officer Candidate School Tests *was released for publication in October 2006.*

The vast majority of recruiters are hard-working and honest professionals whose reputations can be hurt by the few "bad apples" that can be found in any profession, including the military. The job of a military recruiter is to find a sufficient number of qualified volunteers to fill projected vacancies for the fiscal year. The recruiting system is set up as a numbers game and it is true that recruiters are often judged by their superiors according to the number of recruits signed up. When recruiters stretch the truth, or when prospective recruits selectively listen to answers to their questions, everyone loses.

The vast majority of U.S. Military recruiters are honest, hard-working professionals, completely dedicated to the core values of their service. In fact, few military personnel put in more hours of work per week than recruiters.

The recruiter's job is to find enough qualified volunteers to fill projected vacancies for the fiscal year, for their particular branch of service. While a majority of military recruiters are hard-working, honest, and dedicated, there are some (and I emphasize *some*) recruiters who are tempted to bend the truth, and/or downright lie, and/or blatantly cheat in order to sign up a recruit. It happens often enough where we've all heard "horror stories" about military recruiters.

So, why do some recruiters do this?

It's because of the way the recruiting system is set up. It's a numbers game, pure and simple. Recruiters are judged by their superiors primarily upon the number of recruits they get to sign up. Sign up large numbers, and you're judged to be a good recruiter. Fail to sign up the minimum number assigned to you (known as "making mission"), and you can find your career at a dead-end. This policy pressures *some* recruiters to adopt unethical practices in order to "make mission."

Preventive Measures

So, you ask, "why don't the services put a stop to this?" Easier said, than done. Each of the services has recruiting regulations which make it a crime for recruiters to lie, cheat, or knowingly process applicants that they know are ineligible for enlistment. Recruiters are punished when they are caught violating the standards. However, the key phrase is "when they are caught." Not that easy to do, as there are usually no witnesses. It becomes a "he said/he said" type of deal.

I should also mention here that, in many cases, "lies" told by a recruiter are actually cases of selected listening by recruits. A recruiter may say, "Many of our bases now have single rooms for most people," and the applicant may hear, "You are definitely not going to have a roommate." . . .

As I've said, most recruiters are honest. [My intent] is not to run down military recruiters, but rather inform potential recruits the truth about joining the military; the benefits and disadvantages of joining the military, whether for a four-year enlistment, or a 30-year military career. . . . I spent 23 years in the Air Force and enjoyed every minute of it. My primary profession today is to research/write about the United States Military. Both of my daughters are happily serving in the Air Force (one on active duty, one in the Air National Guard). I love the military and every aspect of it. . . .

Vision vs. Reality

However, the military is not for everyone. Fully 40 percent of recruits who enlist in the military today will not complete their full term of service. While many discharges will be for reasons beyond the recruit's control, such as medical problems that develop after joining the military, as a First Sergeant for 11 years, I found that a significant number of the *involuntary discharges* we imposed on first-term recruits was because they simply stopped trying—they discovered that the military wasn't what they thought it was going to be. Many of them told me that the military wasn't even close to what their recruiters told them it was going to be (either the recruiter lied to them, or they were guilty of "selective listening.") When this happens, everyone loses.

3

Military Recruiters Should Not Have Access to Students' Contact Information

Leah C. Wells

Leah C. Wells is the peace education coordinator for the Nuclear Peace Foundation.

The No Child Left Behind Act opened the door for military recruiters to gain unimpeded access to students' names, addresses, and telephone numbers, making it easy for them to contact youth at home. Combined with the presence of recruiters in schools, this can reinforce the perception that the military is the only option for students who don't succeed academically. But schools should be havens for higher learning, and not fertile fields of students ripe for the picking by military recruiters. The No Child Left Behind Act should serve as a wake-up call for all students to reclaim their privacy and demand more quality in educational rather than in military pursuits.

The No Child Left Behind Act which went into effect last week has some surprising implications for high school students. Buried deep within the funding benefits is Section 9528 which grants the Pentagon access to directories with students' names, addresses and phone numbers so that they may be more easily contacted and recruited for military service. Prior to this provision, one-third of the nation's high schools refused recruiters' requests for students' names or access to campus because they believed it was inappropriate for educational institutions to promote military service.

Leah C. Wells, "No Child Left Alone by Military Recruiters," *Humanist*, vol. 63, March–April 2003. Reproduced by permission of the author.

This portion of the Department of Education's initiative to create better readers, testers and homework-doers is a departure from the previously federally guaranteed privacy protections students have traditionally known. Until now, schools have been explicitly instructed to protect the integrity of students' information—even to guard students' private information from college recruiters. Students must consent to releasing their personal data when they take college entrance exams.

However, since September 11, 2001, educational institutions have slid down the slippery slope in doling out student information when solicited by the FBI and now the Pentagon. Only one university—Earlham in Richmond, Indiana—declined to release student data when approached after the terrorist attacks in the fall of 2001.

Checkpointing Access

The No Child Left Behind Act paves the way for the military to have unimpeded access to underage students who are ripe for solicitation for the military. This blatant contradiction of prior federal law is not only an invasion of students' privacy but an assault on their educational opportunities as well. Too many students are lulled by the siren songs of military service cooing promises of funding for higher education. Too many students have fallen between the cracks due to underfunded educational programs, underresourced schools and underpaid teachers. Such students penalized in their educational opportunities for the systemic failure to put our money where our priorities ought to be: in schools.

It is critical that students, schools and school districts have accurate information regarding this No Child Left Behind Act in preparation for the forthcoming military solicitation. First, the Local Educational Agency (LEA), not individual schools, may grant dissemination of student information. When recruiters approach individual schools, the administration should refer them to the school district office where they are supposed to visit in the first place.

In some cases, the recruiters on site have coerced employees at individual schools to sign previously prepared documents stating that in refusing to release student information, they are out of compliance with the No Child Left Behind Act and risk losing federal funding. All requests for student information should be referred to the school district's office and not left to the discretion of individual school employees. School boards, Parent-Teacher Organizations and Student Council/ASB groups can mobilize to support the administrations who are not willing to distribute private student information.

Second, students or their parents may opt themselves out of this recruitment campaign. So as not to be in violation of the previous federal law which restricts disclosure of student information, the LEA must notify parents of the change in federal policy through an addendum to the student handbook or individual letters sent to students' homes. Parents and students can notify their school administration and district in writing of their desire to have their records kept private.

At the heart of this argument over students' records and privacy is the true purpose and meaning of education.

The San Francisco School District has maintained a policy of non-recruitment by the military and is leading the nation in their efforts to educate parents and students on their right to privacy. As advocates for their students, the district is sending home individual letters to parents outlining their options for protecting their child's information.

Education vs. Solicitation

At the heart of this argument over students' records and privacy is the true purpose and meaning of education. Is the goal of education to provide a fertile field of students ripe for the picking by the military which will send them to the front lines of battle, potentially never to return? Is the essence of education to dichotomize the availability of quality education between those with ample finances and those with no financial mobility?

Students are continually guilted into shouldering the burden of responsibility when they do not succeed in school and all too often accept as inevitable their fate of being sucked into military service.

Or is education meant to develop students' minds, hearts and talents through self-discovery and academic exploration? Does education aim to promote critical thinking skills, empathy for others, understanding of individual roles in community service, and a sense of global connectedness? Was education designed to be an equitable opportunity for all students?

A newspaper from the U.K., *The Scotsman*, recently interviewed a young American woman on an aircraft carrier in the Middle East. Eighteen-year-old Karen de la Rosa said, "I have no idea what is happening. I just hear the planes launching above my head and pray that no one is going to get killed. I keep telling myself I'm serving my country."

But is her country serving her?

The relationship between militarism and education is evident. The current Department of Education budget proposal for 2003 is $56.5 billion. The recently approved Department of Defense budget is $396 billion—nearly seven times what is allocated for education, and more than three times the combined military budgets of Russia, China, Iraq, Iran, North Korea, Libya, Cuba, Sudan and Syria. An escalated war in Iraq [fighting in Iraq began in March 2003, after this article was written] could add more than $200 billion to the defense budget as well.

Students are continually guilted into shouldering the burden of responsibility when they do not succeed in school and all too often accept as inevitable their fate of being sucked into military service. The Leave No Child Behind Act is a wake up call to students to reclaim their privacy, to reinvest their energy into demanding quality education and to remind their leaders that stealing money from education to pay for military is unacceptable.

4

Military Recruiting Exploits the Vulnerability of Teens

Terry J. Allen

Terry J. Allen is a senior editor of In These Times, *a magazine dedicated to informing and analyzing popular movements for social, environmental and economic justice. Her work has appeared in* Harper's, The Nation, New Scientist, *and elsewhere.*

The United States military markets itself to children as young as thirteen. This marketing exploits American youth because they are physically incapable of making such important on-the-spot decisions about their futures. The teenage brain has an underdeveloped impulse control; thus, teens may be easily swayed into joining the military by persistent recruiters, without really giving their decision serious thought. Some recruiters' aggressive tactics further exploit teens by making them or their parents think that military service is mandatory, or by otherwise tricking them into signing enlistment papers.

Almost 600,000 of America's 1 million active and reserve soldiers enlisted as teens. The military lures these physiologically immature kids with a PR machine that would make Joe Camel proud.

While the age of legal and cultural adulthood can vary, science is now able to determine the physiological markers of maturity. A recent study headed by Jay Giedd of the National Institutes of Health using MRI scans shows that the brain of

Terry J. Allen, "Pentagon's Teen Recruiting Methods Would Make Tobacco Companies Proud," www.alternet.org, May 22, 2007. Reproduced by permission of the publsiher, www.inthesetimes.com.

an 18-year-old is not fully developed, with the limbic cortex-brain structures, the cerebellum and prefrontal cortex still undergoing substantial changes.

As of March 31 [2007] the U.S. military included 81,000 teenagers. Its 7,350 17-year-olds needed parental consent to enlist, and only this April were all barred from battle zones.

But the military aims even lower, marketing itself to children as young as 13 with multimedia videos, school visits and cold calls to teens' homes and cell phones. In Junior ROTC, kids get uniforms, win medals, fire real guns and play soldier, while adults trained in psychological manipulation steer them toward the army. The Army's JROTC website lists such motivating activities as "eating at concession stands."

Teens Are Not Mature Enough to Decide to Enlist

A mature prefrontal cortex, "the area of sober second thought," is vital not only to deciding whether to enlist, but also to choices made under the stress of deployment and the terrors of combat. But the prefrontal cortex, "important for controlling impulses, is among the last brain regions to mature," according to Giedd, and doesn't reach "adult dimensions until the early 20s."

Teenagers' brains simply lack the impulse control that can prevent a lifetime of regret, psychological and physical disability, and preventable deaths—their own, their fellow soldiers' and those of civilians.

The child soldier problem is global and so is America's part in it. More than 300,000 children around the world, some as young as seven, serve as soldiers, or, in the case of girls, as military sex slaves. The State Department reports that 10 countries are violating international treaties against child soldiers. Washington provides military assistance to nine of these outlaw nations: Afghanistan, Burundi, Chad, Colombia, Ivory Coast, Democratic Republic of Congo, Sri Lanka, Sudan and Uganda.

The reason the United States and other militaries target children is their need for cannon fodder, coupled with the vulnerability of youth. In 2002, almost half of Marine recruits were 17 or 18. A Pentagon survey found that "for both males and females, propensity [to enlist] is highest among 16- and 17-year-olds." That "propensity" quickly declines with age.

A 2004 Pentagon database listed the number of 16- and 17-year-olds who applied for active service enlistment at 69,000 and 18-year-olds at 73,000. By 19, the count had dropped to 49,000 and by age 24 had plummeted to 9,700.

The Department of Defense (DoD) spends more than $4 billion a year on recruiting with $1.5 billion for advertising and maintaining the recruiting stations staffed by more than 22,000 recruiters. Much of that money goes to convincing children to become soldiers.

Aggressive Tactics Exploit Teens

A recruiters handbook discusses creepy seduction techniques with all the subtlety of predatory stalking. Adult recruiters skilled in "projecting credibility" lurk in snack joints, set up laptops playing action-packed videos, proffer rides and promise friendship and fatherly advice. With blacks particularly skeptical of the war effort, the military is aggressively targeting Hispanics with multimillion dollar marketing campaigns that include chatting up mothers and attending church. Recruiters get non-English speaking parents to sign enlistment papers for 17-year-olds by letting them believe that service is mandatory, or that they were approving blood tests, according to the *New York Times*.

Recruiters also try to win over high school guidance counselors with offers of "extended tours, VIP trips ('A day in the life of a sailor') or workshops."

A DoD training manual instructs recruiters to appropriate the techniques that pharmaceutical salespeople use to convince doctors to prescribe the most profitable drugs: "Pharmaceutical representatives court doctors and provide incentives to them in exchange for listening to a sales pitch and considering their products." DoD advises following the pharma model by offering "personalized incentives in exchange for some of their time (bring food when asking favors.)"

The manual suggests bribing teachers: "Provide lunch for teachers in exchange for information." It quotes an anonymous teacher: "Giving teachers pencils and calendars lets us know that you understand our needs and support us. We, in turn, are more likely to support your efforts in the future."

"Chiefs of warfare reach out to children precisely because they are innocent, malleable, impressionable," says Olara Otunnu, the U.N. Special Representative for Children and Armed Conflict.

The science is clear: Turning children below the age of brain maturity into soldiers, whether in the United States or Sudan, exploits that vulnerability.

5

Military Recruiters Can Provide Youths Many Options Besides Combat

Jorge Correa

Jorge Correa is a staff writer for the Pasadena City College Courier online.

If students will not listen to what recruiters have to say, they will never know of some great programs and opportunities that could be beneficial to them. Just because someone enlists in the military to defend our country does not mean that he or she will be handed a gun and sent to the front lines. There is a need for everything from doctors and x-ray technicians to electronics experts, mechanics, and aviators. And there is no way to estimate the value of all the life experiences one might gain, including overseas travel and just learning how other people live. Young adults should keep an open mind, because a recruiter might just say something that sparks real interest.

It's too bad that knowledge is scant about what a brief military career can offer an individual. And it comes as no surprise when recruiters on campus get completely shunned by the very students they hope to enlist. No one wants to go to Iraq and die, and that seems to be the general argument against joining the military.

Without even making eye contact, one student walked straight past a recruiter and said, "Sorry, I don't feel like dying."

Business major Ko Nishimoto said, "I'll talk to them when they stop me, but I have no desire to join. I'm 26 now and that option has diminished. I don't want to be gone for four years then start school again when I'm 30."

PCC [Pasadena City College] student Sophia Kritselis believes if someone wants to join the military then they should seek them out. "I don't believe they should come to campus or try recruiting people at the mall. If people want to join, then go to them."

There are hundreds of different jobs within each branch to choose from, along with programs that will help you in your education and career.

With four branches to choose from, five if you count the Coast Guard, each one has special programs and opportunities that could be beneficial to students at PCC. But they will never know if they don't take the time to at least hear what recruiters have to say.

I know there are some students who have worked hard for scholarships and grants or some other form of financial aid and have the next four-to-six years planned out. But what about those who don't?

Just because you decide to enlist in the military and defend your country, that doesn't mean you're going to get handed an M-16 and then get sent straight to the frontlines. There are hundreds of different jobs within each branch to choose from, along with programs that will help you in your education and career.

I spent five years working with Navy aircraft, such as the F-18 Super Hornet, the F-14 Tomcat Fighter and MH-60 Night Hawk helicopter. My favorite job was when I was attached to a search and rescue helicopter squadron in Guam and served as a flight deck landing signalman.

I was in the aviation field, but recruits may choose from electronics, administration, medical and more. For example, PCC has a great nursing program, and once equipped with a degree, a graduate can join the military as an officer and work in a base hospital.

It's not just nurses. There's a need for everything from doctors, x-ray technicians, pharmacists and optometrists to man base medical facilities. There are also opportunities in every aspect of dentistry as well.

The most popular program is the Montgomery GI Bill, which is offered by each branch. By giving up $100 a month out of my paycheck for only the first year I served, it has now turned into roughly $36,000 for school.

According to PCC's veterans affair office, our campus currently has just over 300 students who are currently collecting veterans benefits. Sure I did a full five years before I started collecting money, but that doesn't have to be the case. Many active duty personnel now collect their GI Bill money while they are serving.

Where else can you shoot 18 holes of golf on a tropical island that just happens to be in your own backyard, every day before or after work?

Depending on the number of units you have, you can enlist at a higher rank than someone who doesn't have any. I joined as an E-1, the lowest pay grade, and with good conduct it took me nine months to get the next rank. If I had over 60 units, I could have jumped two pay grades and started as an E-3 right away. And do you know what comes with higher rank? A higher pay check.

Besides the GI Bill, each branch offers forms of educational benefits of their own as well. For instance the Army has the Army College Fund which adds more money to the GI Bill, making it worth up to $50,000. The Navy has PACE or

Programs Afloat for a College Education, which allow sailors to earn degrees while aboard a ship. Trust me, I wish I would of done that with my spare time on the ship, instead of becoming a master at Halo.

Although each branch is similar in ways, choosing a branch to enlist in can be difficult, and like most decisions, you have to weigh the ups and downs that are personal to you. The small spaces, long hours, and separation from family and friends for months at a time were not easy to endure. Ship life was hard.

Some branches invest their money in areas that others don't. For example, Air Force recruiter Staff Sergeant Derek Hudson said, "The Army likes to put a lot of their money into advertisement, where the Air Force puts the money into their people. We have a better quality of life."

For instance, Air Force bases are first-rate with more amenities. Although I was Navy enlisted, in Guam I was stationed on Anderson Air Force Base, and this was where I learned to golf. Where else can you shoot 18 holes on a tropical island that just happens to be in your own backyard, every day before or after work?

Also, Air Force barracks are in better shape. I had my own mock-studio apartment, with a full kitchen and my own bathroom. Food on the Air Force base was better too. I would put Anderson's galley food up against Fresno State's dorm food any time.

Bottom line, I would do it again if I had to, in order to be where I am today. Plus, you can't put a price on all the life experiences, like traveling overseas and visiting exotic foreign places. Whether it's attending college, being in the labor force or joining the military, it's what you make of it that counts. So keep in mind that one of these recruiters might say something that sparks your interest.

6

Concerned Citizens Should Take Action Against Military Recruiting in Schools

Ron Jacobs

Ron Jacobs is the author of two books and a regular contributing essayist to the online publication, www.counterpunch.org.

The military is becoming increasingly intrusive in its attempts to recruit college and high school students, using the Solomon Amendment to force schools to provide personal information about students and allow recruiting even if it goes against school policy. Anti-war and anti-recruitment activists have responded in a variety of ways, including petitions, protests, opting out, and lawsuits. These efforts should continue. In addition, the anti-recruitment effort should broaden its campaign to include opposition to defense contractors and others who benefit from war, and by examining the very role of the military.

Recently, most students at the University of Vermont (UVM) in Burlington received an email with the heading ARMY PAYS OFF STUDENT LOANS in their university email box. The general message of the mass mailing was that if a student was nearing graduation and wondering how they were going to pay off the massive debt today's U.S. college students incur, they should join the army. In essence, this email was a college student's version of the poverty draft that entraps so many working class and poor young people into enlisting in

Ron Jacobs, "Let The Pentagon Pay Off Those Loans, Lies Military Recruiters Tell," *CounterPunch*, Weekend Edition, March 5–6, 2005. Reproduced by permission.

the service. The sender was a military recruiter working out of the U.S. Army recruitment office in the Burlington suburb of Williston. Given that the university has a very clear policy forbidding these types of solicitations on their email servers one wonders how the recruiting office was able to obtain the address list. The university administration has been reticent when asked this question by various faculty, students, and parents. It is fair to assume, however, that the email list was released to the recruiter under the compliance sections of the so-called Solomon Amendment. For those unfamiliar with this legislation, it essentially forbids Department of Defense (DOD) funding of schools unless those schools provide military representatives access to their students for recruiting purposes. It is this same law that enables military recruiters to set up shop in high schools across the U.S. and to call students at their homes attempting to entice them into joining the military.

[I]n high schools across the U.S., more students and their parents seem to be opting out of taking the Armed Services Vocational Aptitude Battery (ASVAB), a test given to high school juniors as a method of targeting potential recruits.

At UVM, this email was met with anger and questions, and probably even a few inquiries. The anger is now being organized into a drive to keep military recruiters off the university campus and out of the students' private communications. There is a petition campaign underway that demands that no recruiters for the regular military or the Vermont National Guard be allowed to recruit on campus. Despite this, recruiters do show up unannounced on campus. One assumes that their strategy is designed to prevent student organizers from organizing protests against the recruiters' presence. In addition, there is organizing underway to organize some kind of response to the military and Guard's presence at the University's Spring Career Day on March 8th. (This career day is also the host to recruiters from various corporations from the war industry—General Dynamics foremost among them). Here in Vermont, the Guard recruitment hits close to home, since the state ranks near the top in the number of deaths per capita in Iraq. The likelihood of the university denying these recruiters access is slim, especially in light of the mass email, yet the students involved continue on undaunted. If the petition campaign fails to produce the results they desire, there will likely be some kind of protest.

Other college campuses have already experienced such protests. On January 20, 2005, several hundred students at Seattle Central Community College chased army recruiters from their spot in the Student center. On February 23, campus police arrested a woman student during a picket in front of the military's recruitment table at a job fair at the University of Wisconsin-Madison. A couple days before that, several dozen students chased military recruiters off campus at Southern Connecticut State University (SCSU). In September 2004, more than a hundred students protested the presence of military recruiters at the University of Pennsylvania. On February 22, 2005 several dozen students picketed recruiters at the University of Illinois campus in Chicago. At the USC Law School, recruiters were met with pickets and leafleters demanding that they leave, and at UC Berkeley, a couple dozen students protested the presence of a military recruiter table there. These are but a few of the dozens of protests that have taken place.

Meanwhile, in high schools across the U.S., more students and their parents seem to be opting out of taking the Armed Services Vocational Aptitude Battery (ASVAB), a test given to high school juniors as a method of targeting potential recruits. It is an admissions and placement test for the U.S. military. All persons enlisting in the U.S. military are required to take the ASVAB. Although the military does not usually start turning up the pressure to join the military until students reach their senior year, about 14,000 high schools nationwide give this test to juniors. A recent piece in the *Boston Globe* detailed the troubles one recruiting office in New Hampshire is facing this year. According to ASVAB testing coordinator at the Military Entrance Processing Station in Boston, which handles enlistment processing for Rhode Island, much of New Hampshire and parts of Massachusetts, many parents are writing notes excusing their kids from taking the test. At one high school in Nashua, NH, school administrators opted out of even administering the test this year. This is not an isolated case either; of the thirty schools in the Boston region that administered the test in 2004, only nineteen signed up to do so this year. One wonders how long it will be before the military makes the test mandatory for graduation.

In my mind, the best political strategy is one that challenges the imperial policies of the U.S. and calls into question not just the military's discriminatory recruitment policies, but also the role of the military itself.

Campus antiwar groups that formed in the past three years have called most of the university and college protests. In addition, lesbian and gay organizations and individuals have joined in because of their opposition to the military's "don't ask, don't tell" policy on homosexuality. Of course, many of the latter group also oppose the war in Iraq. According to a federal appeals court ruling made in November 2004, the essentially anti-gay policies of the military do allow universities to deny its recruiters access to their students and property. On top of that ruling, another federal judge in Connecticut found that the government unconstitutionally applied the Solomon Amendment after Yale Law School faculty sued Donald Rumsfeld when he attempted to deny federal funds to Yale because it prevented military recruitment on its campus.

Yale denied the recruiters access because of their discriminatory policies against gays and lesbians.

While this strategy is not necessarily the best political strategy possible to chase recruiters off campus, it is a legal tool counter-recruitment activists should utilize while it exists. In my mind, the best political strategy is one that challenges the imperial policies of the U.S. and calls into question not just the military's discriminatory recruitment policies, but also the role of the military itself. A strategy based on this premise would not only diminish the military's visibility, it would also challenge young people (and the rest of us) to examine for whom and what the military really fights. Additionally, it would allow the organizers of these campaigns to include defense contractors in their campaign. After all, it is these corporations that truly need young men and women to go to war.

7

Colleges Should Not Deny Access to Military Recruiters

Debra Saunders

In FAIR v. Rumsfeld, *126 S.Ct. 1297 (2006), the U.S. Supreme Court unanimously rejected the collective argument of several law schools that they were justified in denying campus access to military recruiters because of the military's anti-gay discrimination policy. The Court basically said if universities cannot accept the "don't ask, don't tell" policy, they are free to reject federal funds for their schools. The academic world has argued that it is hypocrisy to preach against discrimination while allowing recruiters to discriminate against gays. Saunders argues that it is academia that is hypocritical. In a truly free academic environment, students would accept the presence of persons and ideologies different than their own, and respect others' right to express opposing views. This allows the students to choose their associations themselves, as it should be.*

Law schools that challenged the Solomon Amendment, a federal law passed in 1994 that eliminates federal funding to universities that deny equal access to military recruiters, tried to hide behind noble motives. The Forum for Academic and Institutional Rights, for example, claimed that its support of academic freedom and nondiscrimination required law schools to bar military recruiters from campus because of the military's discriminatory "don't ask, don't tell" policy on gays.

This week [March 2006], the U.S. Supreme Court rejected the lawsuit unanimously. As the opinion written by Chief Justice John Roberts noted, the Solomon Amendment doesn't, in any way, limit universities' rights to protest "don't ask, don't tell." If universities cannot abide by the policy, Roberts wrote, they are "free to decline the federal funds."

But you see, this lawsuit was all about letting academia have it both ways. Clearly the law-school litigants believe they have a constitutional right to thumb their nose at military policies, while burning through tax dollars paid by voters who, as a rule, hold those who serve in the military in high esteem—and no doubt respect soldiers more than they respect lawyers.

It's so, well, lawyer-like for academics to argue that they have deeply-held convictions—but that doesn't mean they should have to pay any consequences for them.

Besides, where is the academic freedom in barring recruiters from campus? Freedom should mean that military recruiters have their platform. Students are free to enlist, if they so choose, or not enlist if they do not. Critics are free to protest against Pentagon practices. It's called a free exchange of ideas.

(This may be a good place to mention, I think "don't ask, don't tell" is a foolish policy. I think the military should welcome gays, that it is wrong-headed to assume gay officers will misbehave, and that existing rules can address any wrongful actions of any gay or straight officers.)

In barring the military, law students and faculty are working to marginalize not only recruits, but also any students who support military policy.

Think about it. If the Bushies wanted to bar Muslim recruiting on campus, academics would be hollering—despite Islam's hostility toward homosexuality. The big dif here is that fellow academics have decided who cannot speak freely on campus.

Pentagon rules discriminate against women by barring all women from serving in certain combat positions. I wondered: If ivory-tower elites truly oppose discrimination, why didn't they challenge the Solomon Amendment on military policies that discriminate against all women?

Plaintiff Michael Rooke-Ley, a law prof at Santa Clara University, answered that military recruiters will interview females, but they won't interview gay students. I reply that the military will interview gay law students who don't announce that they are homosexual. Rooke-Ley believes no institution should expect applicants to deny a fundamental fact about themselves. You can't argue that it is acceptable to discriminate against Jews because someone can deny being Jewish, he said. The same goes for homosexuality.

Rooke-Ley sees the lawsuit as a way to fight "hypocrisy on campus"—that law schools can't preach against discrimination, then allow recruiters that discriminate.

I see the suit itself as the height of hypocrisy. In a truly free academic environment, students would accept the presence of those with whom they disagree, while exercising their right to speak against them. In barring the military, law students and faculty are working to marginalize not only recruits, but also any students who support military policy. It's not enough to protest recruiters. Only a solid ban will do to let students interested in military service understand that, in the university, they are the freaks.

They don't care that, to the extent that this is a free country, you can thank the military.

8

Recruiter Denial to College Campuses Would Harm Society and the Military

Sean Aqui

Sean Aqui is the pen name of a regular contributing writer for blogcritics.org. After graduating from college through the ROTC program, he served in the military as a second lieutenant in the armor branch.

The U.S. Supreme Court flatly rejected the free-speech challenge by several law schools that had banned military recruiters from campuses because of the military's policy on homosexuals. Notwithstanding, the schools' argument was not without merit. Why should military recruiters be exempt from discrimination rules that apply to other recruiters or companies that are allowed on campus? Further, allowing recruiters to discriminate against gays might create the appearance that a school might condone such a policy even if it is against the school's own policies. However, at the end of the day, fair is fair. Banning military recruiters from campuses goes too far. Too many bright and talented officers— 70 percent of whom receive their commissions through ROTC— would be lost. This would not only adversely affect national security, but also would further isolate the military from mainstream society. People can publicly protest or declare their support for gays in the military, but derailing the ROTC cripples not only the military, but all of us.

Sean Aqui, "Why Everyone Should Want Military Recruiters On Campus," *Blogcritics Online Magazine*, March 6, 2006. Reproduced by permission.

The Supreme Court has ruled [in *FAIR* v. Rumsfeld, 2006] that colleges that accept federal money must allow military recruiters on campus. The case involved some law schools who had banned the recruiters because the military's policy on homosexuals violates the schools' own policies.

The ruling was unanimous, so there's not a lot of room for interpretation: if you want federal money, military recruiters come with it.

FAIR Is Fair

I sympathize with the schools to some extent. There's a fairness issue: Why should the military be exempt from rules that apply to every other recruiter or company that has access to a given school? In addition, there's the appearance of condoning discrimination.

But I bring another perspective to the case, having been commissioned through ROTC and witnessed the same debate and protests while I was in college in the late 1980s at the University of Minnesota.

If military culture grows too separated from civilian culture we risk a 'Prussification' of the military—an insular society led by elites that have little in common with the people whom they ostensibly serve.

First, let me be clear: I think the military's policy on gays is asinine, the discrimination both unfounded and unnecessary. The military has plenty of rules on conduct and fraternization that would maintain discipline even if soldiers were openly gay, just as they manage to maintain discipline where heterosexual men and women serve alongside each other. And, in an era when the military is having difficulty meeting recruiting goals, turning away thousands of otherwise qualified (in some cases, highly qualified) soldiers makes no sense from a national-security standpoint.

Throwing Out the Baby With the Bathwater

The problem, as I see it, is one of relative weight. Military access to college campuses is simply too important to be derailed by the military's gay policy. Protest? Fine. Work to change minds? Fine. Declare and demonstrate support for military gays? Of course. But banning ROTC and recruiters goes too far, doing real damage to our security and further isolating the military from mainstream society.

When I was in the military, 70 percent of officers received their commissions through ROTC—including some of the brightest and best-educated soldiers. Simply put, that is an irreplaceable source of military leaders. If we ban ROTC and recruiters, we cripple the future of the military—and thus our security.

A second point that opponents should consider is somewhat subversive. Soldiers recruited from college campuses tend to have a broader education and life exposure than those who are educated in the hothouses of service academies and military schools. They bring that with them into the military, forming the main part of what might be considered the "liberal" wing of the military. They help ensure that mainstream American values continue to be represented in military culture.

This is crucial, coming as it does at a time when fewer and fewer people know someone who is in the military. If military culture grows too separated from civilian culture we risk a "Prussification" of the military—an insular society led by elites that have little in common with the people whom they ostensibly serve. That would be a disaster on many levels.

The military must be given access to college students both to maintain our physical security and to save the military from itself.

9

Counter-Recruitment Efforts Are Needed to Save Our Youths

Don Trent Jacobs

Don Trent Jacobs is an author and associate professor in the Educational Leadership Department at Northern Arizona University. He also serves on the faculty of the Educational Leadership and Change College at Fielding Graduate Institute.

Military recruiters are committing a fraud upon our youth. They are luring them into dangerous service in an immoral war with promises of benefits few will receive in full. They have the backing of the government, and an all-out draft could be next. It is up to parents and educators to inform America's youth and save them from the military.

Some think that because I was an officer in the U.S. Marine Corps during the Viet Nam War, I have a special right to challenge military recruitment in public schools. Not so. Every teacher, school administrator, and parent has this right. Moreover, I believe each has the responsibility to do so if and when the recruiting is fraudulent.

Actual Fraud

In law, fraud is understood as an intentional perversion of truth undertaken with the intent to induce another to part with some valuable thing. In this case, the valuable item is a

Don Trent Jacobs, "Reading, Writing, and Counter-Recruiting," *Paths of Learning*, vol. 22, Autumn 2004, pp. 29–30. Reproduced by permission.

teenager's life. The perversion has to do with lies about education and health benefits for veterans; about the value of military training for one's future; about the psychological and physical costs of war; and about the legal and moral issues relating to the rationale for a particular war.

For example, only 35% of veterans will receive any money for college and only 15% will earn a four-year degree. (The government makes more money from the $1200 it receives in the form of non-refundable payroll deductions for future education benefits than it gives out for schooling!) V.A. medical benefits are shockingly inadequate. As for the legality or morality of war, how many of our high-school students are aware of the gross deceptions that brought us into Afghanistan and Iraq?

Moreover, the fraud occurring in our schools with respect to students' joining the military is legislated. Both Section 9528 of the NCLB [No Child Left Behind] law and the National Defense Authorization Act make it mandatory for high schools to provide recruiters with monthly quotas of juniors' and seniors' names, home addresses, and records. Growing numbers of schools now have recruiters on campuses throughout each school day. (If this is not bad enough, JROTC [Junior Reserve Officer Training Corps] programs are increasing, and 2/3 of the cost is paid by the school district!) Yet teachers, counselors, administrators, and parents do very little to teach "the other side" to students. (Ironically, Michael Moore's new film about the Iraq war [*Fahrenheit 9/11*] has been rated "R" so that the same Americans who are subjected to recruitment fraud cannot even watch film footage of the war's truths without being accompanied by an adult. Perhaps even more ironically, Moore's film documents the deceptive tactics used by military recruiters intent on enticing youths to join the military.)

Protecting Our Youths

Although still too few, more and more parents, teachers, and counselors are engaging in counter-recruitment education. Federal district and appellate courts have repeatedly upheld Equal Access Laws that enable students to receive opposing points of view. In fact, if a school district discourages students from having access to this opposing view, the school can be held liable. (For a listing of ways to offer this information, from publishing it in school newspapers to inviting speakers from Veterans for Peace chapters, go to ⟨www.objector.org⟩.)

Hopefully, educators and parents will nonetheless use their critical thinking skills to help them understand the severity of the military recruitment/drafting situation now facing our youth.

In 2003, the government spent 2.7 billion dollars for military recruiting (including 4 million dollars for a U.S. Army-sponsored race car). To save on this expense, legislators have introduced legislation for a draft. Although this pending legislation is highly controversial some think it will pass by July 2005. . . . [I]n addition to parents', teachers', and counselors' engaging in rigorous counter-recruiting efforts NOW, it is essential that all high-school students immediately familiarize themselves with both the requirements for and the difficulties in applying for conscientious objector status. There is no place on draft registration forms to check and, once drafted, one has fewer than ten days to make a claim for conscientious objection. Affidavits, as well as letters from teachers and others that demonstrate moral, ethical, and religious beliefs that preclude killing others or going to war, must be prepared well in advance. Remember, students claiming to be opposed to war on political, sociological, philosophical or personal grounds will be denied C.O. [conscientious objector] status. In other words, the law says that critical thinking is not allowed. Rather, moral or ethical objections must be affiliated with your religious perspective, and only well established religious conviction is taken into account for conscientious objector status. Hopefully, educators and parents will nonetheless use their critical thinking skills to help them understand the severity of the military recruitment/drafting situation now facing our youth. With such an understanding, they can gain or strengthen the conviction that they will need to have and maintain in their valiant counter-recruiting efforts undertaken on behalf of our nation's youth.

10

The Real Motivation for Anti-Recruiting Efforts Is Hatred of the Military

Jamie Weinstein

Jamie Weinstein was an upperclassman in the College of Arts and Sciences at Cornell University when he wrote this article.

Those opposed to recruiting on college campuses often justify their actions by pointing to the military's discriminatory policies toward homosexuals. They may be right that these policies are unfair or counterproductive, but this is not the genuine reason they are trying to stop recruitment efforts. What really motivates anti-recruitment activists is a dislike of the military and opposition to U.S. actions in Iraq. If activists' concerns about discrimination were really their priority, they would be trying to change the military's policy towards homosexuals. Instead they use that issue as a pretext while attempting to force the military off of college campuses, and often use suspect methods in the process.

I guess I overestimated the movement to drive our military off campus. While it is true I believed the motivating force behind it was hatred for our troops, and not "discrimination," I thought that the shameful protesters would at least try to hide this. Evidently not.

Writing in *The Sun*, Professors Moncrieff Cochran and William Trochim, along with students Patrick Young '06 and Bekah Ward grad, revealed their true intentions in trying to

Jamie Weinstein, "The Campus Left's War on ROTC," *FrontPageMagazine*, April 5, 2005, www.frontpagemag.com. Reproduced by permission.

remove the military from the University. After placating the discrimination argument, they turned to their real gripe: the United States military itself. They wrote, "we oppose military recruiter's presence on campus because they are selling a career in killing."

Make no mistake, the discrimination argument is a canard [a fake]. This coalition of radical writers, along with their considerable following, hates our military and our soldiers not because of anything relating to discriminatory practices, but because they consider them killers. Having failed to stop the liberation of Iraq with their rallies and teach-ins, these anti-war radicals have turned to another front to attack the U.S. Armed Forces.

Backstage

Behind the calls of "Support Our Troops—Bring Them Home," lies the belief that the U.S. military is not generally a force of good in the world, but rather a negative one. In their mind, American G.I.'s do not stand for freedom and protecting America, but rather are drones helping further American "imperialism." I'm not pulling this out of thin air. The authors admitted it themselves: "These recruiters further U.S. imperialism. . . ."

Not surprisingly, within this movement there rests no respect for the sacrifices made on a daily basis or the bravery habitually exhibited by the men and women of our Armed Forces. Instead of appreciation, these radicals spout condemnation. Their heroes do not overthrow mass murderers and protect American values, they ransack ROTC offices and spout off silly chants.

So let's get it straight from the start. All this talk about the Solomon Amendment being "illegal"—which in my opinion is nonsense—is just talk. It is merely another front in a continuing battle against the U.S. military by the radical left.

This Much Granted

Truth be told, there are legitimate questions that can be raised about "Don't Ask, Don't Tell." Personally, I'm conflicted over whether it is the right policy. On one hand I understand that permitting homosexuals in the military may create an uncomfortable environment. There are reasons why men and women do not share barracks today, and it is the same reason—or at least a major part of the reason—for the reluctance to allow gays into the service.

If Donald Rumsfeld announced tomorrow that gays would now be allowed in the military, no questions asked, the movement to drive the military off campus would not fade away.

On the other hand, other functioning and active militaries such as Britain and Israel have incorporated homosexuals. Furthermore, I find it counterproductive to dismiss gay translators, especially those who are proficient in Arabic, at a time when there is such a dire need for such linguists. When nine gay linguists were dismissed in 2002, some proficient in Arabic, I questioned if there could be some modification to "Don't Ask, Don't Tell" to allow them to remain.

But this is a question that one should bring to Congress if they were serious about strengthening America and our military. If one felt that barring gays from the military was hurting American interests and the strength of our armed services at a time when we are engaged in a great war, presumably they wouldn't want to take actions to further weaken them, even if they felt it may be following a discriminatory policy. By trying to force ROTC and military recruiters off campus they would be doing just that.

Calling Their Bluff

So clearly, the protesters—at least most of them—aren't demanding that the U.S. military change its position on "Don't

Ask, Don't Tell" so that the U.S. army would be strengthened. If Donald Rumsfeld announced tomorrow that gays would now be allowed in the military, no questions asked, the movement to drive the military off campus would not fade away. It would just adapt. They would have to develop another pretext to fight military recruitment and ROTC training on campus. As I said, the primary motivation is not discrimination, but loathing of the American military itself.

The article by the radical anti-war activists goes on to describe how at a recent Cornell Career Fair, activists bombarded military recruiters, claiming they were interested in joining the military. After wasting the recruiters' time, they proceeded to tell them that they were gay and asked whether that would be a problem.

After getting the answer they expected, the anti-war radicals began filling out bias related reports against the recruiters on campus in the middle of the career fair. The radical coalition of writers described it as follows: "There was an air of excitement, people getting involved and hundreds of supportive passers-by."

While it seems that the protesters had fun playing their anti-war games and stymieing military recruiters from doing their job, it also sounds like some false reports may have been filed. From what I gathered in the article and heard around campus, it sounded like non gay activists also participated in the childish shenanigans and filed bias-related incident reports. If in fact this is true, and I would be willing to bet that it is, in filing the reports the non-gay students would be submitting reports to the Cornell administration that were false. You can't be discriminated against for being gay if you are not, in fact, gay.

After doing some research, it appears that such actions would violate Title III, Section II, Subsection C of the Campus Code of Conduct which states as a violation, "To furnish false information to the University with intent to deceive." The

Judicial Administrator should look into this to see if any false reports were filed, and if so, they should hold the offenders accountable.

11

The National Media Is Biased in Support of Anti-Recruitment Efforts

Warner Todd Huston

Warner Todd Huston is a widely-read columnist who is a regular contributor to many Web sites, including Renew America, Townhall, American Daily, *and* Opinion Editorials. *In addition to writing for several history magazines as well, Huston appears in the book,* Americans on Politics, Policy and Pop Culture.

The national news media goes out of its way to highlight problems with recruiting and gives free publicity to anti-recruitment efforts. It rarely presents the views of recruitment supporters.

With the talk of Charlie Rangel's [a U.S. Representative from New York] second try to get the draft reinstated, it is interesting to take a look at how leftists are attempting to destroy our military and one of the ways the left is trying to undermine our military is by attacking its recruiting base in high schools across the country. Activists are trying to persuade kids of military recruitment age to "opt out" from allowing their schools to provide the student's public information to military sources.

The anti-military left has also found a constant assistant in the MSM [Main Stream Media] toward this goal. Every few months the MSM comes out with articles highlighting military recruiting and invariably they also give free publicity to the anti-[m]ilitary groups trying to stop recruiting.

Warner Todd Huston, "MSM Killing Military Recruiting," *The Conservative Voice*, November 23, 2006. Reproduced by permission.

For example, a recent *USA Today* report, titled "Some opt out of military options," introduces us to a school in northern Illinois where a large number of parents, totaling about half the class, have signed forms to stop the school from sending the military their info—a trend that has grown there since at least 2004.

USA Today helpfully supplies a graphic showing the "Opt out" split in the school body. 2004 saw 2,126 opt outers in a student body of 4,505. 2,802 of 4,573 in 2005 and 2,920 out of 4,472 this school year. This stat shows a pretty steady growth toward the anti-military position.

It almost mirrors the voting trend north of Chicago in Lake County, Illinois, where the school is located.

Lincolnshire, Illinois, a northern suburb of the city of Chicago, is in Lake county. It broke close to even in the 2004 election with 50% going for Bush and 48% going for Kerry. And, while they voted overwhelmingly for Democrat Barack Obama in 2004, the rest of the votes were weighted Republican at least since the 2000 general election. But in this 2006 cycle, the GOP took a hit with Democratic votes gaining for most of the top offices, as it did in many areas of the country.

A Forum for the Left

But, what the *USA Today* article proves most clearly, is that the left is doing what it does best; organize. And they are organizing in an effort to undermine the U.S. military. The article covers several organizations that have organized to fight Military recruiters from having access to school records.

A quick perusal of some of the stories over the last couple of years—since the war in Iraq started—on military recruiting shows a constant drumbeat against the military.

Even cities have taken up the anti-military cause. The school board in San Francisco has recently banned the Junior

Reserve Officers' Training Corps from operating in city high schools, despite complaints from students, over the "don't ask, don't tell" that supposedly discriminates against gays. School board member, Eric Mar, was quoted as saying ". . . in many ways, we're preventing military values on students at the high-school level."

The reason I use this article as an example, though, is in the unusual aspect of it. It gives both sides of the argument where few others do. This article gives space to military spokesmen and gives some info to mitigate the attacks by the anti-military left. The most salient points being that the military isn't asking for any more information than colleges and Universities get from schools and that the military can get the student's info from other sources quite legally, anyway.

Still, we get a pretty detailed listing of several of the anti-military groups formed to mount an attack on the U.S. military's ability to recruit in schools. In that *USA Today* helps the anti-military as much as possible.

As I said, that mirrors the common drift of most of the stories on the issue of recruiting. A quick perusal of some of the stories over the last couple of years—since the war in Iraq started—on military recruiting shows a constant drumbeat against the military. Whether it be a dour report on the military missing its goals or the resistance being mounted in schools to disrupt military recruit efforts, these stories constantly show a heavy bias against the military.

A Few Examples

A writer from the Portland Oregonian gins up a tale about how military recruiter's misconduct "is a growing national problem as the military faces increasing pressure to hit recruiting targets during an unpopular war." (A story the subject of which that I proved to be pure hyperbole since the stats show an extremely low number of such cases. . . .)

The San Francisco Chronicle delighted in reporting that the "U.S. is recruiting misfits for army—felons, racists, gang members fill in the ranks".

The stories show a mounting effort to undermine the U.S. military's recruitment efforts.

A 2005 story informs us that the army is having trouble because "Parents can opt to deny this information to recruiters, and antiwar groups are mounting a national effort to encourage them to do so."

Then there was the 2004 PBS story that highlighted the work of "the head of a local San Diego peace group which has serious problems with military recruitment at high schools."

In 2002, *Mother Jones Magazine* complained that military recruiters access to students "undercuts the authority of some local school districts, including San Francisco and Portland, Oregon, that have barred recruiters from schools on the grounds that the military discriminates against gays and lesbians."

In any case, the inference is clear. The stories show a mounting effort to undermine the U.S. military's recruitment efforts. Sadly, in this time of mounting security risks, one of the most threatening things that recruiters face seem not to be the prospect of new recruits being sent into combat, but teachers and unpatriotic parents telling their kids they don't have any duty to their country.

We have heard the sobriquet of "Greatest Generation" bestowed upon those who fought WWII [World War II]. One wonders what title these kinds of people might be saddled with in the decades to come? Perhaps the "Weakest Generation"? And, it would not be the mantle given to the youngsters who now serve, but their parent's generation, instead.

12

The Military Has Lowered Its Standards to Meet Recruiting Quotas

Fred Kaplan

Fred Kaplan is a regular contributing writer to Slate Magazine, *specifically writing the "War Stories" column for this publication. He is a former reporter and military correspondent for the* Boston Globe, *also serving as its Moscow bureau chief and New York bureau chief, and the author of* The Wizards of Armageddon. *He graduated from Oberlin College and has a PhD in political science from the Massachusetts Institute of Technology.*

Faced with falling short of its recruitment goals, the U.S. Army has been lowering its recruitment standards to improve its numbers. Not only has it been picking up more high school dropouts, it has also been enlisting more and more applicants who score in the lowest third of those taking the armed forces aptitude test. Unfortunately, in the military, intelligence does make a difference. Smarter soldiers means better performance and more lives saved in the field, as well as less monetary expense for the military.

Three months ago, I wrote that the war in Iraq was wrecking the U.S. Army, and since then the evidence has only mounted, steeply. Faced with repeated failures to meet its recruitment targets, the Army has had to lower its standards dramatically. First it relaxed restrictions against high-school drop-outs. Then it started letting in more applicants who score in the lowest third on the armed forces aptitude test—a group, known as Category IV recruits, who have been kept to exceedingly small numbers, as a matter of firm policy, for the past 20 years. (There is also a Category V—those who score in the lowest 10^0 percentile. They have always been ineligible for service in the armed forces and, presumably, always will be.)

The bad news is twofold. First, the number of Category IV recruits is starting to skyrocket. Second, a new study compellingly demonstrates that, in all realms of military activity, intelligence does matter. Smarter soldiers and units perform their tasks better; dumber ones do theirs worse.

Until just last year, the Army had no trouble attracting recruits and therefore no need to dip into the dregs. As late as 2004, fully 92 percent of new Army recruits had graduated high school and just 0.6 percent scored Category IV on the military aptitude test.

Then came the spiraling casualties in Iraq, the diminishing popularity of the war itself, and the subsequent crisis in recruitment.

The Band-Aid Fix

In response to the tightening trends, on Sept. 20, 2005, the Defense Department released *DoD Instruction 1145.01*, which allows 4 percent of each year's recruits to be Category IV applicants—up from the 2 percent limit that had been in place since the mid-1980s. Even so, in October, the Army had such a hard time filling its slots that the floodgates had to be opened; *12 percent* of that month's active-duty recruits were Category IV. November was another disastrous month; Army officials won't even say how many Cat IV applicants they took in, except to acknowledge that the percentage was in "double digits."

(These officials insist that they will stay within the 4 percent limit *for the entire fiscal year*, which runs from October 2005 through September 2006. But given the extremely high percentage of Cat IVs recruited in the fiscal year's first two months, this pledge may be impossible to keep. . . .)

Some may wonder: So what? Can't someone who scores low on an aptitude test, even very low, go on to become a fine, competent soldier, especially after going through boot camp and training? No question. Some college drop-outs also end up doing very well in business and other professions. But in general, in the military no less than in the civilian world, the norm turns out to be otherwise.

In a *RAND Corp. report* commissioned by the office of the secretary of defense and published in 2005, military analyst Jennifer Kavanagh reviewed a spate of recent statistical studies on the various factors that determine military performance—experience, training, aptitude, and so forth—and concluded that aptitude is key. A force "made up of personnel with high AFQT [armed forces aptitude test] scores," Kavanagh writes, "contributes to a more effective and accurate team performance."

The evidence is overwhelming. Take tank gunners. You wouldn't think intelligence would have much effect on the ability to shoot straight, but apparently it does. Replacing a gunner who'd scored Category IV on the aptitude test (ranking in the 10–30 percentile) with one who'd scored Category IIIA (50–64 percentile) improved the chances of hitting targets by 34 percent. . . .

In another study cited by the RAND report, 84 three-man teams from the Army's active-duty signal battalions were given the task of making a communications system operational. Teams consisting of Category IIIA personnel had a 67 percent chance of succeeding. Those consisting of Category IIIB (who'd ranked in the 31–49 percentile on the aptitude test) had a 47 percent chance. Those with Category IV personnel had only a 29 percent chance.

The same study of signal battalions took soldiers who had just taken advanced individual training courses and asked them to troubleshoot a faulty piece of communications gear. They passed if they were able to identify at least two technical problems. Smarts trumped training. Among those who had scored Category I on the aptitude test (in the 93–99 percentile), 97 percent passed. Among those who'd scored Category II (in the 65–92 percentile), 78 percent passed. Category IIIA: 60 percent passed. Category IIIB: 43 percent passed. Category IV: a mere 25 percent passed.

Brains Needed Here

The pattern is clear: The higher the score on the aptitude test, the better the performance in the field. This is true for individual soldiers and for units. Moreover, the study showed that adding one high-scoring soldier to a three-man signals team boosted its chance of success by 8 percent (meaning that adding one low-scoring soldier boosts its chance of failure by a similar margin).

These are the soldiers that the Army has long shut out of its ranks; that it is now recruiting avidly, out of sheer desperation; and that—according to the military's own studies—seriously degrade the competence of every unit they end up joining.

Smarter also turns out to be cheaper. One study examined how many Patriot missiles various Army air-defense units had to fire in order to destroy 10 targets. Units with Category I personnel had to fire 20 missiles. Those with Category II had to fire 21 missiles. Category IIIA: 22. Category IIIB: 23. Category IV: 24 missiles. In other words, to perform the same task, Category IV units chewed up 20 percent more hardware than Category I units. For this particular task, since each *Patriot missile* costs about $2 million, they also chewed up $8 million more of the Army's procurement budget.

Some perspective here: Each year the Army recruits 80,000 new troops—which amount to 16 percent of its 500,000 active-duty soldiers. Even if 12 percent of recruits were Category IV, not just for October but for the entire coming year, they would swell the ranks of Cat IV soldiers *overall* by just 1.9 percent (0.12 x 0.16 = .0192).

Then again, viewed from another angle, this would double the Army's least desirable soldiers. These are the soldiers that the Army has long shut out of its ranks; that it is now recruiting avidly, out of sheer desperation; and that—according to the military's own studies—seriously degrade the competence of every unit they end up joining. No, things haven't gone to hell in a handbasket, but they're headed in that direction. Every Army officer knows this. And that's why many of them want the United States to get out of Iraq.

13

The Draft Is Needed to Maintain Military Superiority

Phillip Carter and Paul Glastris

Phillip Carter and Paul Glastris are both professionally associated with The Washington Monthly. *Carter is an attorney and former Army captain who writes about national security issues. Glastris is the publication's editor-in-chief.*

Iraq is unlike other countries to which the United States came, sponsored elections, and left behind a relatively stable and peaceful democracy (e.g., Germany, Japan, Bosnia, Kosovo). The present volunteer military force may not have the strength to secure peace in such a volatile environment. But that's not to say that America needs a bigger army. Rather, what it needs is a highly-trained active-duty force, backed up with a hefty-sized reserve of soldiers who can readily mobilize and provide massive surge capacity in the event of unpredictable war or unmanageable circumstance. At the end of the day, what America should rely on is a twenty-first-century-style draft of all eligible young persons.

The United States has occupied many foreign lands over the last half century—Germany and Japan in World War II, and, on a much smaller scale, Haiti, Bosnia, and Kosovo in the 1990s. In all these cases, we sponsored elections and handed-off to democratic governments control of countries that were relatively stable, secure, and reasonably peaceful.

In Iraq, we failed to do this, despite heroic efforts by U.S. and coalition troops. The newly-elected Iraqi government inherits a country in which assassinations, kidnappings, suicide bombings, pipeline sabotages, and beheadings of foreigners are daily occurrences. For the last eight months, the ranks of the insurgency have been growing faster than those of the security forces of the provisional Iraqi government—and an alarming number of those government forces are secretly working for the insurgency. American-led combat operations in Ramadi and Fallujah killed large numbers of the enemy, but at the price of fanning the flames of anti-American hatred and dispersing the insurrection throughout Iraq. Despite nearly two years of effort, American troops and civilian administrators have failed to restore basic services to much of the central part of the country where a majority of Iraqis live. The U.S. military has not even been able to secure the 7-mile stretch of highway leading from the Baghdad airport to the Green Zone where America's own embassy and the seat of the Iraqi government are headquartered.

Off to a Bad Start

How we got to this point is by now quite obvious. Even many of the war's strongest supporters admit that the Bush administration grievously miscalculated by invading Iraq with too few troops and then by stubbornly refusing to augment troop numbers as the country descended into violent mayhem after the fall of Saddam.

This analysis, of course, presumes that it was ever possible to invade and quickly pacify Iraq, given the country's religious-ethnic divisions and history of tyranny. But it also presumes that the fault is primarily one of judgment: that the president and key senior military officials made a mistake by accepting Defense Secretary Donald Rumsfeld's theory that a "transformed" American military can prevail in war without great masses of ground troops. That judgment was indeed foolish;

events have shown that, while a relatively modest American force can win a stunning battlefield victory, such a force is not enough to secure the peace.

America has a choice. It can be the world's superpower, or it can maintain the current all-volunteer military, but it probably can't do both.

But there's a deeper problem, one that any president who chose to invade a country the size of Iraq would have faced. In short, America's all-volunteer military simply cannot deploy and sustain enough troops to succeed in places like Iraq while still deterring threats elsewhere in the world. Simply adding more soldiers to the active duty force, as some in Washington are now suggesting, may sound like a good solution. But it's not, for sound operational and pragmatic reasons. America doesn't need a bigger standing army; it needs a deep bench of trained soldiers held in reserve who can be mobilized to handle the unpredictable but inevitable wars and humanitarian interventions of the future. And while there are several ways the all-volunteer force can create some extra surge capacity, all of them are limited.

The only effective solution to the manpower crunch is the one America has turned to again and again in its history: the draft. Not the mass combat mobilizations of World War II, nor the inequitable conscription of Vietnam—for just as threats change and war-fighting advances, so too must the draft. A modernized draft would demand that the privileged participate. It would give all who serve a choice over how they serve. And it would provide the military, on a "just in time" basis, large numbers of deployable ground troops, particularly the peacekeepers we'll need to meet the security challenges of the 21st century.

America has a choice. It can be the world's superpower, or it can maintain the current all-volunteer military, but it probably can't do both. . . .

Five Bad Options

In theory, there are several ways to get out of the military manpower bind we find ourselves in. In reality, there are inherent limits to almost all of them.

The first option—at least the one Democrats and moderate Republicans have talked most about—is to convince other countries to share the burden in Iraq. But that's not likely. Even if the security situation in Iraq improves and the Bush administration begins to share decision-making—something it's so far refused to do—European leaders would be extremely wary of trying to sell their citizens on sending troops to keep the peace in a war they expressly opposed. It may be possible to convince the Europeans and other developed nations to be more willing to contribute troops the next time there's an international need. But that, as we've seen, will require more U.S. troops, not fewer. Nor should it be the policy of the United States to have to rely on other countries' troops. We must be prepared to intervene unilaterally if necessary.

A second solution to the manpower crisis would be to rely more on private military contractors, whose use has exploded in recent years. Currently, more than 10,000 government contractors are on duty in Iraq, working in myriad jobs from security to reconstruction. The advantage of using contractors is that they provide surge capacity; they are hired only for the duration of an engagement. But according to Peter W. Singer, a research fellow at the Brookings Institution, these private armies also create problems. First, all costs considered, they're not necessarily less expensive for the military. Second, private military contractors often compete with the military for personnel, so any growth in these contractors usually results in tension between military retention and contractor recruiting efforts. Third, contractors operate in a legal gray area where their financial and accounting activities are heavily regulated, but their operations are barely looked at. It's one thing to contract for truck drivers; it's another to hire contractors to guard Afghan President Hamid Karzai or work as interrogation linguists in the Abu Ghraib prison because the military has too few commandos or linguists in its own ranks. The military has probably already pushed the contractor concept about as far as it will go; expecting much more surge capacity from private industry is probably unrealistic.

[T]he army is mainly comprised of healthy young people with high school degrees but no college plans. That pool is inherently limited, especially when the economy is heating up and there's a shooting war on.

Transforming Existing Forces

A third possibility might be to follow the advice of several cutting-edge military reformers to radically transform today's military. According to these reformers, today's force was drawn up for a bygone age of massed superpower armies; it does not reflect today's threats. These visionaries would downsize the Navy, scrap some of the Army's mechanized divisions, and in these and other ways free up tens of thousands of troops to be redeployed into "soldier centric" units capable of doing everything along the spectrum from humanitarian relief in Banda Aceh to combat patrols in Baghdad. Under pressure from the Iraq mission, the military has taken some steps in this direction—for instance, by retraining and reequipping some army artillery and air defense units into military police units. But such moves have been incremental in nature thus far; the true scope of the problem is orders of magnitude larger than the Pentagon's current solution. And some day, a war may come which requires all kinds of combat power—from large land-based formations to ships capable of sailing through the Taiwan strait to legions of peacekeepers. The military cannot build additional capability simply by playing a shell game with its personnel; at some point, it must genuinely add more soldiers too, and in large numbers.

A fourth option, and the most obvious one, would be to simply increase the size of the active-duty force. This too has been discussed. During the 2004 campaign, Sen. John Kerry called for increasing the active-duty force by 40,000 troops. More recently, a bipartisan group of hawkish defense intellectuals published an open letter on *The Weekly Standard* Web site calling on Congress to add 25,000 ground troops each year for the next several years. And the Pentagon has announced some money for extra troops in the administration's latest budget. The problem with such proposals is that they underestimate both current manpower needs and the cost of forcing the all-volunteer military to grow.

In theory, one can always lure the next recruit, or retain the next soldier, by offering a marginally higher monetary incentive—but in reality, there are practical limits to such measures. The pool of people who might be convinced to join the Army is mainly comprised of healthy young people with high school degrees but no college plans. That pool is inherently limited, especially when the economy is heating up and there's a shooting war on. Last year, despite signing bonuses in the tens of thousands and other perks, military recruiters had to lower entry standards to meet their enlistment goals. The active force met its recruiting targets for 2004, but the reserves have found themselves increasingly struggling to bring enough soldiers in the door.

But it's the long-term cost issues that most militate against making the all-volunteer force bigger. Generals today are fond of saying that you recruit a soldier, but you retain their families. One reason the Army has resisted Congress' attempts to raise its end strength is that it does not want to embrace all of the costs associated with permanently increasing the size of the military, because it sees each soldier as a 30-year commitment—both to the soldier and his (or her) family. According to the Congressional Budget Office, each soldier costs $99,000 per year—a figure which includes medical care, housing, and family benefits.

When Size Matters

The United States does not necessarily need a massive standing military all the time. What it needs is a highly trained professional force of a certain size—what we have right now is fine—backed by a massive surge capacity of troops in reserve to quickly augment the active-duty force in times of emergency. Sure, right now, the Army is light several hundred thousand deployable ground troops. But over the long term, the demands of Iraq will subside, the need for troops will decline, and it could be another decade or two before another mission that big comes along.

The problem is that under the all-volunteer system it's hard to fix the short-term problem (too few troops now) without creating long-term problems (too many troops later). And so, paying for the salaries and benefits and families of 50,000 or 500,000 extra soldiers on active duty over the course of their careers doesn't, from a military standpoint, make sense. Politically, it would put the senior military leadership in the position of convincing the American people to keep military budgets extremely high to pay for a huge standing army that isn't being used and might not be for years. It might be possible now to convince the public to add another 100,000 soldiers (annual cost: about $10 billion in personnel costs alone, not including equipment and training). But the generals rightly worry that this support will evaporate after Iraq stabilizes. Indeed, Americans have a long tradition dating back to the writing of [the] Constitution, of refusing to support a large standing military unless the need is apparent. (The public paid for a much bigger all-volunteer military in the 1970s and 1980s, but only because of the obvious need to deter a massive Soviet army from threatening Europe; after the Berlin Wall fell, both political parties supported big cuts in troop strength). What we really need is the capability to rapidly mobilize and deploy a half million troops to project U.S. power abroad, and to be able to sustain them indefinitely while maintaining a reserve with which to simultaneously engage other enemies.

A fifth option would be to build this surge capacity into the reserves, instead of the active force. Under this plan, which some military personnel planners are already discussing, the army would radically bump up enlistment bonuses and other incentives to lure vastly more young people directly into the reserves than are being recruited now. Such a plan would have the advantage of creating the surge capacity the nation needs without saddling the nation with a large, standing professional army. But the disadvantages are substantial, too. For such a plan to work, the military would have to make a commitment, which thus far it never has, to fix the legendary resources problems and anemic readiness of the reserves. A great many reservists have gone through the crucible of combat in Afghanistan and Iraq, and yet still cope with vehicles that lack armor, weapons older than they are, and a paucity of training dollars. Also, the army would always (and rightly) insist that signing bonuses for reservists be substantially below those offered to active-duty recruits. And even if bonuses and other renumeration for both the active-duty and the reserves were to rise substantially, it is hard to see how the reserves could lure in a sufficient number of recruits without significantly lowering admissions standards. The real advantage of the all-volunteer force is its quality. If the military tries to recruit so many soldiers that it must substantially lower its entry requirements, then the all-volunteer force will lose its qualitative edge. This decrease in quality will have a cascade effect on discipline within the ranks, degrading combat effectiveness for these units.

A Modern Proposal

That leaves one option left for providing the military with sufficient numbers of high-quality deployable ground forces: conscription. America has nearly always chosen this option to staff its military in times of war. Today, no leading politician in either party will come anywhere near the idea—the draft having replaced Social Security as the third rail of American politics. This will have to change if the United States is to remain the world's preeminent power.

[A]ny American, liberal or conservative, ought to have moral qualms about basing our nation's security on an all-volunteer force drawn disproportionately, as ours is, from America's lower socioeconomic classes.

Traditional conscription has its obvious downsides. On a practical level, draftees tend to be less motivated than volunteers. Because they serve for relatively short periods of time (typically two years), any investment made in their training is lost to the military once the draftees return to civilian life. And despite the current manpower shortage, there's no foreseeable scenario in which all 28 million young Americans currently of draft age would be needed.

Above all else, there's the serious ethical problem that conscription means government compelling young adults to risk death, and to kill—an act of the state that seems contrary to the basic notions of liberty which animate our society.

In practice, however, our republic has decided many times throughout its history that a draft was necessary to protect those basic liberties. Even if you disagreed with the decision to invasion of Iraq, or think the president's rhetoric is demagogic and his policies disastrous, it is hard to argue that Islamic terrorism isn't a threat to freedom and security, at home and abroad. Moreover, any American, liberal or conservative, ought to have moral qualms about basing our nation's security on an all-volunteer force drawn disproportionately, as ours is, from America's lower socioeconomic classes. And the cost of today's war is being borne by an extremely narrow slice of America. Camp Pendleton, Calif., home to the 1st Marine Expeditionary Force, is also home to approximately one-seventh of the U.S. fatalities from Iraq. In theory, our democracy will not fight unpopular wars because the people who must bear the casualties can impose their will on our elected leaders to end a war they do not support. But when such a small fraction of America shoulders the burden—and pays the cost—of America's wars, this democratic system breaks down.

Nor are the practical considerations of a draft impossible to overcome. A draft lottery, of the kind that existed in the peacetime draft of the 1950s, with no exemptions for college students, would provide the military an appropriate and manageable amount of manpower without the class inequities that poisoned the national culture during Vietnam. Such a system, however, would not avoid the problem of flooding the military with less-than-fully-motivated conscripts.

How a Modern Draft Should Function

A better solution would fix the weaknesses of the all-volunteer force without undermining its strengths. Here's how such a plan might work. Instead of a lottery, the federal government would impose a requirement that no four-year college or university be allowed to accept a student, male or female, unless and until that student had completed a 12-month to two-year term of service. Unlike an old-fashioned draft, this 21st-century service requirement would provide a vital element of personal choice. Students could choose to fulfill their obligations in any of three ways: in national service programs like AmeriCorps (tutoring disadvantaged children), in homeland security assignments (guarding ports), or in the military. Those who chose the latter could serve as military police officers, truck drivers, or other non-combat specialists requiring only modest levels of training. (It should be noted that the Army currently offers two-year enlistments for all of these jobs, as well as for the infantry.) They would be deployed as needed for peacekeeping or nation-building missions. They would serve for 12-months to two years, with modest follow-on reserve obligations.

Whichever option they choose, all who serve would receive modest stipends and GI Bill-type college grants. Those who sign up for lengthier and riskier duty, however, would receive higher pay and larger college grants. Most would no doubt pick the less dangerous options. But some would certainly select the military—out of patriotism, a sense of adventure, or to test their mettle. Even if only 10 percent of the one-million young people who annually start at four-year colleges and universities were to choose the military option, the armed forces would receive 100,000 fresh recruits every year. These would be motivated recruits, having chosen the military over other, less demanding forms of service. And because they would all be college-grade and college-bound, they would have—to a greater extent than your average volunteer recruit—the savvy and inclination to pick up foreign languages and other skills that are often the key to effective peacekeeping work.

A 21st-century draft like this would create a cascading series of benefits for society. It would instill a new ethic of service in that sector of society, the college-bound, most likely to reap the fruits of American prosperity. It would mobilize an army of young people for vital domestic missions, such as helping a growing population of seniors who want to avoid nursing homes but need help with simple daily tasks like grocery shopping. It would give more of America's elite an experience of the military. Above all, it would provide the all-important surge capacity now missing from our force structure, insuring that the military would never again lack for manpower. And it would do all this without requiring any American to carry a gun who did not choose to do so.

The war in Iraq has shown us, and the world, many things: the bloody costs of inept leadership; the courage of the average American soldier; the hunger for democracy among some of the earth's most oppressed people. But perhaps more than anything, Iraq has shown that our military power has limits. As currently constituted, the U.S. military can win the wars, but it cannot win the peace, nor can it commit for the long term to the stability and security of a nation such as Iraq. Our enemies have learned this, and they will use that knowledge to their advantage in the next war to tie us down and bleed us until we lose the political will to fight.

If America wishes to retain its mantle of global leadership, it must develop a military force structure capable of persevering under these circumstances. Fortunately, we know how to build such a force. We have done it many times in the past. The question is: Do we have the will to do so again?

14

Only Unjust Wars Require a Draft

Ron Paul

Ron Paul serves as Representative of the Fourteenth District of Texas in the U.S. House of Representatives, and is a 2008 presidential candidate seeking nomination by the Republican Party. During the Vietnam War, he was a flight surgeon in the U.S. Air Force. In Congress, he has served as member of the Committee on International Relations, among others.

War itself is a doubtful necessity at best; a costly waste of life and liberty at worst. U.S. presidents have established a long history of deceiving the public to justify war or garner support for ill-conceived military conflict. This is certainly true of the Iraq war, despite its staggering cost in human casualties and dollars. Few persons readily volunteer for service in an unjust, unnecessary war such as this, therefore the possibility of a military draft looms on the horizon. But conscription is always unfair and discriminatory: it takes our youthful best to fight the wars conceived by politicians who seek the glory of victory without personally paying any price. Conscription is an instrument of tyranny that men of principle should oppose.

The ultimate cost of war is almost always the loss of liberty. True defensive wars and revolutionary wars against tyrants may preserve or establish a free society, as did our war against the British. But these wars are rare. Most wars are unnecessary, dangerous, and cause senseless suffering with little

Ron Paul, "Pro & Con: Congress Reinstating the Military Draft?" *Congressional Digest*, May 2004, pp. 143–147. Reproduced by permission.

being gained. Loss of liberty and life on both sides has been the result of most of the conflicts throughout the ages. The current war in which we find ourselves clearly qualifies as one of those unnecessary and dangerous wars. To get the people to support ill-conceived wars the Nation's leaders employ grand schemes of deception.

A History of Deception

Woodrow Wilson orchestrated our entry into World War I by first promising in the election of 1916 to keep us out of the European conflict, then a few months later pressured and maneuvered the Congress into declaring war against Germany. Whether it was the Spanish-American War before that or all the wars since, U.S. Presidents have deceived the people to gain popular support for ill-conceived military ventures.

Wilson wanted the war and immediately demanded conscription to fight it. He didn't have the guts to even name the program a military draft, and instead in a speech before Congress calling for war advised the army should be "chosen upon the principle of universal liability, to service." Most Americans at the time of the declaration didn't believe actual combat troops would be sent. What a dramatic change from this early perception when the people endorsed the war to the carnage that followed and the later disillusionment with Wilson and his grand scheme for world government under the League of Nations, The American people rejected this gross new entanglement, reflecting a somewhat healthier age than the one in which we find ourselves today.

But when it comes to war, the principle of deception lives on and the plan for "universal liability to serve" once again is raising its ugly head. The dollar cost of the current war is already staggering, yet plans are being made to drastically expand the human cost by forcing conscription on the young men (and maybe women) who have no ax to grind with the Iraqi people and want no part of this fight. Hundreds of

Americans have already been killed and thousands more wounded and crippled while thousands of others will suffer from new and deadly war-related illnesses not yet identified.

We were told we had to support this preemptive war against Iraq because Saddam Hussein had weapons of mass destruction and to confront the al Qaeda. It was said our national security depended on it. But all these dangers were found not to exist in Iraq. It was implied that those who did not support this Iraqi invasion were un-American and unpatriotic.

Since the original reasons for the war never existed, it is now claimed that we're there to make Iraq a Western-style democracy and to spread Western values. And besides, it's argued, it's nice that Saddam Hussein has been removed from power. But does the mere existence of evil somewhere in the world justify preemptive war at the expense of the American people?

Setting the Stage For A Draft

These after-the-fact excuses for invasion and occupation of a sovereign nation direct attention away from the charge that this war was encouraged by the military industrial complex, war profiteering, control of natural resources (oil), and a neo-con agenda of American hegemony with a desire to redraw the borders of the countries of the Middle East.

The inevitable failure of such a seriously flawed foreign policy cannot be contemplated by those who have put so much energy into this occupation. The current quagmire prompts calls from many for escalation with more troops being sent to Iraq. Many of our Reservists and National Guardsmen cannot wait to get out and have no plans to re-enlist.

To get more troops, the draft will likely be reinstituted. The implicit prohibition of "involuntary servitude" by the Thirteenth Amendment to the Constitution has already been ignored many times, so few will challenge the constitutionality of the coming draft. Unpopular wars invite conscription. Volunteers disappear, as well they should. A truly defensive, just war prompts popular support.

A conscripted, unhappy soldier is better off in the long run than the slaves of old since the "enslavement" is only temporary. But in the short run, the draft may well turn out to be more deadly and degrading as one is forced to commit life and limb to a less than worthy cause—like teaching democracy to unwilling and angry Arabs. Slaves were safer in that their owners had an economic interest in protecting their lives. Life endangerment for a soldier is acceptable policy and that's why they are needed. Too often though, our men and women who are exposed to the hostilities of war and welcomed initially are easily forgotten after the fighting ends.

There Is No Justification For A Draft

It is said we go about the world waging war to promote peace, and yet the price paid is rarely weighed against the failed efforts to make the world a better place. But justifying conscription to promote the cause of liberty is one of the most bizarre notions ever conceived by man.

Forced servitude with risk of death and serious injury as a price to live free makes no sense. By what right does anyone have to sacrifice the lives of others for some cause of questionable value?

Without conscription, unpopular wars are much more difficult to fight.

It's said that the 18-year-old owes it to his country. Hogwash. It could just as easily be argued that a 50-year-old chicken-hawk who promotes war and places the danger on the innocent young owes a heck of a lot more to the country than the 18-year-old being denied his liberty for a cause that has no justification.

All drafts are unfair. All 18- and 19-year-olds are never needed. By its very nature, a draft must be discriminatory. All drafts hit the most vulnerable as the elitists learn quickly how to avoid the risks of combat.

The dollar cost of war and the economic hardship is great in all wars and cannot be minimized. War is never economically beneficial except for those in position to profit from war expenditures.

But the great tragedy of war is the careless disregard for civil liberties of our own people. Abuse of German and Japanese Americans in World War I and World War II is well known. But the real sacrifice comes with conscription—forcing a small number of young vulnerable citizens to fight the wars that old men and women, who seek glory in military victory without themselves being exposed to danger, promote. These are wars with neither purpose nor moral justification and too often are not even declared by the Congress.

Choose Liberty, Not Tyranny

Without conscription, unpopular wars are much more difficult to fight. Once the draft was undermined in the 1960s and early 1970s, the Vietnam war came to an end.

But most importantly, liberty cannot be preserved by tyranny. A free society must always resort to volunteers. Tyrants think nothing of forcing men to fight and die in wrongheaded wars; a true fight for survival and defense of one's homeland I'm sure would elicit the assistance of every able-bodied man and woman. This is not the case for wars of mischief far away from home in which we so often have found ourselves in the past century.

One of the worst votes that an elected official could ever cast would be to institute a military draft to fight an illegal war, if that individual himself maneuvered to avoid military service. But avoiding the draft on principle qualifies oneself to work hard to avoid all unnecessary war and oppose the draft for all others.

A government that's willing to enslave a portion of its people to fight an unjust war can never be trusted to protect the liberties of its own citizens. The end can never justify the means, no matter what the neo-cons say.

15

All Americans Should Be Recruited to Serve Society

William A. Galston

William A. Galston is Interim Dean of the University of Maryland's School of Public Policy. He previously served as Deputy Assistant to President Bill Clinton for Domestic Policy. Galston has written several books, including The Practice of Liberal Pluralism.

During the Vietnam War (1959–1975) the draft was widely considered unfair, and this is largely to blame for the present anti-draft sentiment. Despite a good job done by our volunteer forces, the military has created a spectator audience of non-volunteers. This, in turn, creates the much larger question of what each person should do to become a good citizen. The all-volunteer force should include other contributions from non-military citizens. A true democracy involves the equal sharing of burdens in return for an overwhelmingly worthy benefit.

In the wake of September 11, [2001] the United States has undertaken a range of new and expanded military commitments, especially in Central Asia and the Middle East. The military occupation of Iraq is likely to last longer, and require larger forces, than civilian leaders in the Department of Defense had predicted prior to the war. The rising demands on U.S. military personnel, including lengthy overseas deployments and the increased risk of casualties, may well put pres-

William A. Galston, "Thinking About the Draft," *Public Interest*, Winter 2004. Copyright © 2004 by National Affairs, Inc. Reproduced by permission of the author.

sure on current recruitment strategies. This is an appropriate moment, then, to review the military manpower decisions we made a generation ago.

The Vietnam-era military draft was widely regarded as arbitrary and unfair, and it was held responsible for dissension within the military as well as the wider society. In the aftermath of the military failure in Vietnam, the United States made a historic decision to end the draft and institute the All-Volunteer Force (AVF). On one level, it's hard to argue with success. The formula of high-quality volunteers and intensive training plus investment in state-of-the-art equipment has produced by far the most formidable military in history. Evidence suggests that the military's performance, especially since 1990, has bolstered public trust and confidence. For example, a recent Gallup survey of public-opinion trends since the end of the Vietnam War in 1975 indicates that whereas the percentage of Americans expressing confidence in religious leaders fell from 68 to 45, and from 40 to 29 for members of Congress, those expressing confidence in the military rose from under 30 to 78 percent. Among 18-to-29 year-olds, the confidence level rose from 20 percent to 64 percent. These figures reflect public sentiment in late 2002, before the U.S. military victory in Iraq.

Less Palpable Costs

These gains in institutional performance and public confidence are impressive and significant, but they hardly end the discussion. The organization of the military is closely related to larger issues of citizenship and civic life. And here the decision in favor of the AVF has entailed significant costs. First, the AVF reflects, and has contributed to the development of, what I call "optional citizenship," the belief that being a citizen involves rights without responsibilities and that we need do for our country only what we choose to do. Numerous studies have documented the rise of a highly individualistic culture in contemporary America. Many young people today believe that being a good person—decent, kind, caring, and tolerant—is all it takes to be a good citizen. This duty-free understanding of citizenship is comfortable and undemanding; it is also profoundly mistaken.

Second, the AVF contributes to a kind of "spectatorial citizenship"—the premise that good citizens need not be active and can simply allow others to do the public's work on their behalf. This spectatorial outlook makes it possible to decouple the question of whether we as a nation should choose to engage militarily from the question of whether I would participate in such an endeavor.

In a discussion with his students during the Gulf War, Cheyney Ryan, professor of philosophy at the University of Oregon, was struck by "how many of them saw no connection between whether the country should go to war and whether they would . . . be willing to fight in it." A similar disconnection exists today. Young adults have been more supportive of the war in Iraq than any other age group (with more than 70 percent in favor), but recent surveys have found an equal percentage would refuse to participate themselves.

Finally, the AVF has contributed to a widening gap between the orientation and experience of military personnel and that of the citizenry as a whole. This remains a contested issue, but some facts are not in dispute. First, since the inauguration of the AVF, the share of officers identifying themselves as Republican has nearly doubled, from 33 percent to 64 percent. (To be sure, officers were always technically volunteers, but the threat of the draft significantly affected the willingness of young men to volunteer for officer candidacy.) Second, and more significantly, the share of elected officials with military experience has declined sharply. From 1900 through 1975, the percentage of members of Congress who were veterans was always higher than that of their peers in the population at large. Since the mid 1990s, the congressional percentage has been lower than that of the general public, and it continues to fall.

Lack of military experience does not necessarily imply hostility to the military. But it does reflect ignorance of the nature of military service, as well as diminished capacity and confidence to assess critically the claims that military leaders make. It is no accident that of all the post-war presidents, [former general] Dwight Eisenhower was the most capable of saying no to the military's strategic assessments and requests for additional resources.

Responsible Citizenship

For these reasons, among others, I believe that we should review and revise the decision made 30 years ago to institute an all-volunteer armed force. I hasten to add that I do not favor re-instituting anything like the Vietnam-era draft. It is hard to see how a reasonable person could prefer that fatally flawed system to today's arrangements. The question, rather, is whether feasible reforms could preserve the gains of the past 30 years while more effectively promoting an active, responsible citizenship among all Americans.

Everyone who receives the protection of society owes a return for the benefit, and the fact of living in society renders it indispensable that each should be bound to observe a certain line of conduct toward the rest.

My suggestion, however, faces a threshold objection, one that is widely shared by conservatives and liberals alike. Any significant shift back toward a mandatory system of military manpower, it is said, would represent an abuse of state power. In a recent article appearing in the New Republic, Judge Richard Posner enlists John Stuart Mill as an ally in the cause of classical liberalism—a theory of limited government that provides an "unobtrusive framework for private activities." Limited government so conceived, Posner asserts, "has no ideology, no 'projects,' but is really just an association for mutual protection." Posner celebrates the recent emergence of what he calls the "Millian center"—a form of politics that (unlike the socialist Left) embraces economic liberty and (unlike cultural conservatives on the Right) endorses personal liberty, and he deplores modern communitarianism's critique of untrammeled personal liberty in the name of the common good. High on Posner's bill of particulars against many communitarians is their recommendation to reinstitute a draft.

Before engaging Posner's argument, I should note that his attempt to appropriate Mill's *On Liberty* to oppose conscription is deeply misguided. This is clear if one looks at a few of the opening sentences from the fourth chapter, "Of the Limits to the Authority of Society Over the Individual":

> Everyone who receives the protection of society owes a return for the benefit, and the fact of living in society renders it indispensable that each should be bound to observe a certain line of conduct toward the rest. This conduct consists, first, in not injuring the interests of one another, or rather certain interests which, either by express legal provision or by tacit understanding, ought to be considered as rights; and secondly, in each person's bearing his share (to be fixed on some equitable principle) of the labors and sacrifices incurred for defending the society or its members from injury and molestation. These conditions society is justified in enforcing at all costs to those who endeavor to withhold fulfillment.

Clearly, Mill's liberalism has little to do with Posner's "Millian center." Be that as it may, let's take a closer look at Posner's argument. Posner contends that "conscription could be described as a form of slavery, in the sense that a conscript is a person deprived of the ownership of his own labor." If slavery is immoral, runs the argument, so is the draft. In a similar vein, the philosopher Robert Nozick once contended that "taxation of earnings from labor is on a par with forced labor." (If Nozick were right, then the AVF that Posner supports, funded as it is with tax dollars, could also be described as on a par with forced labor.)

Both Posner's and Nozick's arguments prove too much. If each individual's ownership of his or her own labor is seen as absolute, then society as such becomes impossible, because no political community can operate without resources, which must ultimately come from someone. History has proven that no polity of any size can subsist through voluntary contributions alone; the inevitable free-riders must be compelled by law to do their share.

One might object, reasonably enough, that this argument illustrates the difference between taxation and conscription: While a political community is inconceivable without taxation, it is demonstrably sustainable without conscription. It is one thing to restrict self-ownership of labor out of necessity, but a very different matter to restrict it out of choice. The problem is that this argument proves too little. Posner concedes that "there are circumstances in which military service is an obligation of citizenship." But there are no circumstances in which slavery is an obligation of citizenship. Moreover, it is not morally impermissible to volunteer for military service. But it is rightly forbidden to voluntarily place oneself in slavery. Therefore, slavery and military service must differ in kind, not degree. Furthermore, if there are circumstances in which military service is an obligation of citizenship, then the state is justified in enforcing that obligation through conscription. Notwithstanding the libertarian instincts of many Americans, a legitimate government cannot be said to have exceeded its rightful authority by implementing a mandatory system of military recruitment.

Theory vs. Reality

But this is not the end of the argument, for Posner has a broader agenda. He rejects the claim, advanced by Harvard political theorist Michael Sandel and other communitarians, that substituting market for nonmarket services represents a degrading "commodification" of social and civic life. Indeed, Posner celebrates what communitarians deplore. "Commodification promotes prosperity," he informs us, "and prosperity alleviates social ills." Posner also claims that communitarian theory is incapable of drawing a line between matters that rightly belong within the scope of the market and those that do not. Posner's defense of the cash nexus is exposed to precisely the same objection. Let me offer a series of examples designed to help delimit the proper sphere of nonmarket relations, of which military service is one.

Paying people to obey the law: Suppose we offered individuals a "compliance bonus"—a cash payment awarded at the end of each year they were not convicted of a felony or significant misdemeanor. It's not hard to imagine situations in which the benefits of this policy (measured in reduced enforcement costs) would outweigh the outlays for bonuses. What, if anything, is wrong with this? At least two things: First, it alters for the worse the expressive meaning of law. In a legitimate order, criminal law represents an authoritative declaration of the behavior the members of society expect of one another. The authoritativeness of the law is supposed to be a sufficient condition for obeying it, and internalizing the sense of law as authoritative is supposed to be a sufficient motive for obedience. To offer compliance payments is to contradict the moral and motivational sufficiency of the law.

Second, payment for compliance constitutes a moral version of Gresham's law: Lower motives will tend to drive out higher motives, and the more comfortable motives will tend to drive out the more demanding ones. When those who are inclined to obey the law for its own sake see others receiving compensation, they are likely to question the reasonableness of their conduct and to begin demanding payment themselves.

While compensating individuals for mandatory military service is in itself unobjectionable, the AVF sends a misleading message. It suggests that the military is a career like any other, to be chosen on the basis of inclination and reward. Compensation as the key incentive or motive implies, wrongly, that military service is something to be bought and sold in the market, not part of the fundamental social contract.

Paying citizens for jury duty: Consider the analogy (or disanalogy) between national defense and domestic law enforcement. The latter is divided into two subcategories: voluntary service (there is no draft for police officers) and mandatory service (e.g., jury duty). Our current system of military manpower is all "police" and no "jury." If we conducted domestic law enforcement on our current military model, we'd have what might be called the "All-Volunteer Jury," in which we'd essentially buy the number of jurors necessary for the law enforcement system to function.

[I]t is important for all citizens to understand that citizenship is an office, not simply a status. As an office, citizenship entails both rights and duties.

There are two compelling reasons why our jury system is not run on a volunteer basis. First, citizens who self-select for jury duty would be unlikely to be representative of the population as a whole. Individuals who incur high opportunity costs (those who are gainfully employed, for example) would choose not to serve. The same considerations that militate against forced exclusion of racial and ethnic groups from jury pools would weigh equally against voluntary self-exclusion based upon income or employment status. We should ask ourselves why these considerations do not apply to the composition of the military.

Second, it is important for all citizens to understand that citizenship is an office, not simply a status. As an office, citizenship entails both rights and duties. Service on juries is itself simultaneously a right, in the sense that there is a strong presumption against exclusion, and a duty, in the sense that there is a strong presumption against evasion. The same could be said of military service.

Paying foreigners to do our fighting for us: It could be argued that we would do as well or better to hire foreigners (call it the "All-Mercenary Armed Forces") as kings and princes did regularly during the eighteenth century. The cost might well be lower, and the military performance just as high. Besides, if we hire foreigners to pick our grapes, why shouldn't we hire them to do our fighting? There is, of course, a practical problem, discussed by Machiavelli among others: a pure cash nexus would likely encourage opportunistic side-switching when individuals are presented with a better offer. In addition, what Abraham Lincoln called the "last full measure of devotion" would be less likely to be forthcoming from mercenaries.

Beyond these practical considerations lies a moral intuition: Even if a mercenary army were reliable and effective, it would be wrong, even shameful, to use our wealth to bribe noncitizens to do our fighting for us. This is something we ought to do for ourselves, as a self-respecting people. A similar moral principle should apply in the purely domestic sphere, among citizens.

Paying other citizens to do our fighting for us: Consider military recruitment during the Civil War. In April 1861, President Lincoln called for, and quickly received, 75,000 volunteers. But the expectation of a quick and easy Union victory was soon dashed, and the first conscription act was passed in March 1863. The act contained two opt-out provisions: An individual facing conscription could pay a fee of $300 to avoid a specific draft notice; and an individual could avoid service for the entire war by paying a substitute to volunteer for three years.

This law created a complex pattern of individual incentives and unanticipated social outcomes, including anticonscription riots among urban workers. Setting these aside, was there anything wrong in principle with these opt-out provisions? One argument against such provisions was their obvious distributional unfairness: The well-off could afford to avoid military service, while the poor and working classes could not. Historian James McPherson observes that the slogan "a rich man's fight, but a poor man's war" had a powerful impact, particularly among impoverished Irish laborers already chafing against the contempt with which they were regarded by the Protestant elite. Second, even if income and wealth had been more nearly equal, there was something unprincipled in the idea that dollars could purchase exemption from an important civic duty. As McPherson notes, this provision enjoyed a poor reputation after the Civil War, and the designers of the World War I-era Selective Service Act were careful not to repeat it.

Widening the Gap

What is the difference between the use of personal monetary resources to opt out of military service and the impact of such resources on the decision to opt in? In both practical and moral terms the difference is less than the defenders of the current system would have us believe. To begin with, the move to the AVF has had a profound effect on the educational and class composition of the U.S. military. During World War II and the Korean War—indeed, through the early 1960s—roughly equal percentages of high school and college graduates served in the military, and about one-third of college graduates were in the enlisted (that is, non-officer) ranks. Today, enlisted men and women are rarely college graduates, and elite colleges other than the service academies are far less likely to produce military personnel of any rank, officer or enlisted. As a lengthy *New York Times* feature story recently put it, today's military "mirrors a working-class America." Of the first 28 soldiers to die in Iraq, only one came from a family that could be described as well-off.

Many have argued that this income disparity is a positive reflection of a military that extends good career opportunities to young men and women whose prospects are otherwise limited. There is some merit to this argument, of course. But the current system purchases economic mobility at the expense of social integration. Today's privileged young people tend to grow up hermetically sealed off from the rest of society. Episodic volunteering in soup kitchens doesn't really break the seal. Military service is one of the few experiences that can.

The separation is more than economic. The sons and daughters of the middle and upper classes grow up in a cultural milieu in which certain assumptions tend to be taken for granted. Often, college experiences reinforce these views rather than challenging them. Since the Vietnam War, moreover, many elite colleges and universities have held the military at arm's length, ending ROTC curricula and banning campus-based military recruitment. As a Vietnam-era draftee, I can attest to the role military service plays in expanding mutual awareness across cultural lines. This process is not always pleasant or pretty, but it does help to bridge the gap between the privileged and lower classes.

In an evocative letter to his sons, Brookings scholar Stephen Hess reflects on his experiences as a draftee and defends military service as a vital socializing experience for children from fortunate families. His argument is instructive:

> Being forced to be the lowest rank . . . serving for long enough that you can't clearly see "the light at the end of the tunnel," is as close as you will ever come to being a member

of society's underclass. To put it bluntly, you will feel in your gut what it means to be at the bottom of the heap.

It is a matter not just of compassion, but of respect:

> The middle class draftee learns to appreciate a lot of talents (and the people who have them) that are not part of the lives you have known, and, after military duty, will know again for the rest of your lives. This will come from being thrown together with—and having to depend on—people who are very different from you and your friends.

A modern democracy, in short, combines legal equality with economic and social stratification. It is far from inevitable, or even natural, that democratic leaders who are drawn disproportionately from the upper ranks of society will adequately understand the experiences or respect the contributions of those from the lower. Integrative experiences are needed to bring this about. In a society in which economic class largely determines residence and education and in which the fortunate will not willingly associate with the rest, only nonvoluntary institutions cutting across class lines can hope to provide such experiences.

Uncle Sam Wants You

The inference I draw from the foregoing analysis is this: To the extent that circumstances permit, we should move toward a system of universal 18-month service for all high school graduates (and in the case of dropouts, all 18 year-olds) who are capable of performing it. Within the limits of the ceiling on military manpower, those subject to this new system would be assigned to either military or full-time civilian service. (If all military slots were filled, then some form of civilian service would be the only option.) The cost of enacting this proposal (a minimum of $60 billion per year) would certainly slow the pace of implementation and might well set limits on its final scope. The best response to these constraints would be a lottery from which none except those unfit to serve would be exempt.

It might be argued that a program of this sort would have little if any effect on the armed forces, which would continue to draw their manpower from the current stream of volunteers. That may be the case if the military doesn't expand during the next decade. But there are reasons to believe that it will. It is quickly becoming evident that the post-war occupation of Iraq will require more troops and last longer than administration officials had predicted. As an interim response, the military has already moved away from the all-volunteer principle. The U.S. Marine Corps has frozen enlistments for all of the 175,000 personnel currently on active duty. Marines whose period of voluntary enlistment has expired are required to remain in the service, on active duty, until the freeze expires. Other services have imposed similar if more limited freezes. It is possible, moreover, that the prospect of being sent to Iraq as part of a vulnerable long-term occupation force will depress the number of voluntary enlistments, especially in the Army and Marines.

A less purely voluntary system of military and civilian service might well garner popular support. For example, a 2002 survey sponsored by the Center for Information and Research on Civic Learning and Engagement (CIRCLE) found that over 60 percent of Americans across lines of sex, race, ethnicity, partisan affiliation, and ideology would support a plan that allows draftees to choose between civilian and military service. Still, it is plausible that intense opposition on the part of young adults and their parents could stymie such a change. Assuming that this is the case, there are some feasible interim steps that could yield civic rewards.

Former Secretary of the Navy John Lehman has suggested eliminating the current bias of military recruiters who favor career personnel over those willing to serve for shorter periods. As Lehman puts it, we should "actively seek to attract the most talented from all backgrounds with service options that allow them to serve their country . . . without having to commit to six to ten years' active duty." He makes a strong case that this change would markedly increase the number of young men and women from elite colleges and universities who would be willing to undertake military service. Coupled with a more accommodating stance toward the military on the part of academic administrators, this new recruitment strategy could make a real difference.

In a similar vein, the Progressive Policy Institute's Marc Magee has recently proposed reorganizing the current Selective Service registration system into a National Service System that would encourage young Americans to serve their country. Under this proposal, which would include both men and women, individuals who commit to serve in a military or civilian capacity would be exempt from any future draft. To make service more meaningful and attractive, the short-term military enlistment program would be expanded, an enlarged AmeriCorps would be linked more closely to homeland security, and a substantial portion of a scaled-up Peace Corps would be reoriented towards changing the conditions overseas that breed terror.

It would be wrong to oversell the civic benefits that might accrue from the revisions to the AVF that I propose, let alone the more modest steps I have just sketched. Still, enhanced contact between the sorts of young people who provide the bulk of today's volunteers and the sons and daughters of the privileged upper and middle classes would represent real progress. The sacrifices demanded of those who perform military service should be borne more equitably than they currently are. This is especially the case today as the military responsibilities of the United States appear to be on the rise. If reconsidering a decision about military manpower made three decades ago could yield even a fraction of these civic dividends while preserving the military effectiveness of the current system, it would be well worth the effort.

16

Do Not Bring Back the Draft

Rick Jahnkow

Rick Jahnkow is a contributing writer for various liberal Web sites and works for two San Diego-based anti-militarist organizations: the Project on Youth and Non-Military Opportunities, and the Committee Opposed to Militarism and the Draft.

Some among liberals and progressives, long a source of opposition to the draft in particular, have begun agitating to bring back the draft. They argue that a new draft could be more fair than drafts of the past, and that by drafting Americans from all walks of life, the military would be transformed into a more representative organization that would also be more difficult to politically justify sending into battle. These are false beliefs. History has shown that drafts create large standing armies that make it easier to wage war, not harder. Rather than transforming the character of the military, drafts spread military culture into society at large. Furthermore, no matter what the intentions, drafts will always hit the poor and disadvantaged harder than those with greater means. For these reasons any effort to institute a draft should be vigorously opposed.

Ever since House Democrat Charles Rangel introduced his first proposal to bring back the military draft in 2003, it's been amazing to see how much amnesia there is on the subject, especially among some of those who consider themselves liberals or "progressives."

Rick Jahnkow, "Muddled Thinking About Conscription," *Draft Notices*, January–March 2007, published by the Committee Opposed to Militarism and the Draft. Reproduced by permission.

Shaky Premises

Supporters of Rangel's bill (which includes a mandatory civilian service option) make what seems on the surface to be a compelling case. They say one reason our government is so willing to launch aggressive military action is that the children of political leaders and the wealthy elite do not face much risk from combat. They point out that this is because the armed forces are maintained by a system of recruitment that unfairly targets working-class and middle-income people. They also argue that a stronger service ethic is needed, along with more civilian options for performing tasks that would benefit society. The points are valid, and so it seems reasonable when some people conclude that a system of conscription is needed to address such issues.

But the problem with this thinking is that it is far too simplistic and only focuses on limited parts of the picture. It ignores important historical facts and fails to consider an entirely different set of social and political consequences that are inherent in any system of involuntary service.

Whenever we go to war, whether our military is drafted or recruited, socio-economic status is always a factor in determining who is at greatest risk.

One of the forgotten historical facts is that whenever a draft has been employed in the U.S. (which has been infrequently), it has been used to make waging war possible, not as a device to keep our government from entering a conflict. A good example is our most recent experience with conscription during the Vietnam War. The draft that was already in place as the war developed made it easier for presidents Johnson and Nixon to merely open the tap and pour out more bodies to fuel the conflict. As a result, it lasted almost 10 years, took the lives of millions of people and caused massive destruction in Southeast Asia. All of this happened despite the strong anti-war and draft resistance movements that spread across the country.

No Draft Can Be Made Fair

Draft supporters say that in the past, the rules of the Selective Service System favored privileged youths and therefore didn't trigger the kind of opposition from the elite that would have stopped the Vietnam War sooner. But there is no evidence that drafting a few more affluent kids would have made a difference, since initial support for the war was high and was driven by a general Cold War fever that affected almost the entire population.

[A] system that would further militarize the U.S. is the last thing anyone should support.

The claim that a draft could be made fairer today isn't realistic anyway. There will always have to be medical deferments, which are easier to get when you have the money to pay for braces or private medical exams and documentation that are the key to getting disqualified at an Army induction physical. And those with a better education—which is linked to one's socio-economic status—will have a distinct advantage when it comes to successfully wading through the process to secure conscientious objector status. I know how these factors work because as a community college draft counselor during the Vietnam War, I struggled to help low-income students whose limited resources made it harder to gain recognition of legitimate claims for medical deferments and conscientious objector status. It won't be any different under Rangel's proposed draft. Furthermore, affluent individuals who do wind up in the military would still have the advantages of their education and political connections to help avoid combat.

Whenever we go to war, whether our military is drafted or recruited, socio-economic status is always a factor in determining who is at greatest risk. And in a system with a civilian service component like Rangel is proposing, advantages in education, personal wealth and political influence will still be a factor in avoiding the battlefield.

Drafts Militarize Society

Another part of the picture ignored by supporters of Rangel's legislation—one that is especially ironic for those draft advocates who say they are "peace activists"—is the increased militarization that comes with conscription. Because draftees are in the military for only two-year terms instead of four or six, there is a much higher turnover of personnel, and this means that a much larger portion of society is required to go through military training. One of the main functions of this training, especially at boot camp, is to strip the civilian identity from every trainee, instill in him or her the values of military culture, and perform the conditioning needed to produce an obedient soldier who is acclimated to the use of violence.

What many people ignore is that there is no comparable effort made to reverse this process when draftees leave the military. So even though the conditioning doesn't stick in everyone, the net effect over time is to further militarize civilian society, not civilianize the military (which some people have argued). Indeed, this militarization function is one reason why conscription has been so favored by authoritarian states. Examples include Nazi Germany, Imperial Japan, Prussia, and dictators like Napoleon, Stalin and Franco, just to name a few. In today's context of a U.S. government that wages preemptive war, threatens countries that have done nothing to harm us, and assumes police powers that the Constitution disallows, a system that would further militarize the U.S. is the last thing that anyone should support.

Imagine, for a moment, what would have happened if conscription had been in place at the time of 9/11. In that period of emotional nationalism, Bush could have easily gotten away with boosting draft calls and deploying a much larger force to the Middle East. Following the neocon agenda for the region, then, we could have already extended the fighting to Syria and Iran by now, and then moved on to a confrontation with North Korea.

Those Opposed to War Should Oppose A Draft

This leads me to point out a major contradiction in Rangel's rationale for a draft. He and others are arguing that it would help slow down the rush to war (a claim unsupported by any historical facts), while at the same time arguing that we need a draft because our military is exhausted and more troops are required for the mission they've been given. So which is it? Is a draft going to help prevent or end a war, or help wage it? And if it's the latter, then isn't opening up the tap for more troops the last thing that war opponents should want to do? If we really are against military aggression, isn't it better that we stick to demanding that the current mission be cancelled and, simultaneously, do everything we can to cut off the flow of personnel for war?

People who are now advocating a draft need to be challenged to look more closely at the facts and consider the full, global implications of what they are proposing.

If you believe the other part of Rangel's argument, he essentially wants to force a change in foreign policy by holding people's children hostage—which includes the children of people who have been struggling and sacrificing to end the Iraq war. Isn't hostage-taking something we generally condemn in our society, and shouldn't we have serious reservations about supporting such a tactic?

The reality is that popular opposition to bringing back the draft is still overwhelming, and legislators know that it would be political suicide to attempt such a thing at the moment. So why go to the trouble of rebutting pro-draft arguments from liberals or anyone else? The answer is that such efforts to promote conscription can, over time, accustom enough people to the idea of a draft that at a point in the future, in the context of some national emergency pretext, the politicians may then attempt what they now are afraid to do.

People who are now advocating a draft need to be challenged to look more carefully at the facts and consider the full, global implications of what they are proposing. Otherwise, they may eventually get what they are asking for, which would come back to haunt us all.

Organizations to Contact

The editors have compiled the following list of organizations concerned with the issues debated in this book. The descriptions are derived from materials provided by the organizations. All have publications or information available for interested readers. The list was compiled on the date of publication of the present volume; the information provided here may change. Be aware that many organizations take several weeks or longer to respond to inquiries, so allow as much time as possible.

American Civil Liberties Union
125 Broad Street, 18th Floor, New York, NY   10004
(212) 549-2585
Web site: www.aclu.org

The American Civil Liberties Union (ACLU) is a public advocacy organization that works with courts, legislatures, and communities to promote and protect personal liberties and related constitutional rights. Among its many interests is the equal treatment of gays and lesbians under the law. The ACLU opposes the military's policies on homosexuality as unfair and discriminatory. The organization provides press releases, policy and position statements, and/or legal *amicus* briefs (arguments submitted for a court's consideration by persons or entities who are not parties to the litigation, but who have a strong interest or concern in the subject matter at issue) for use in motions and appellate briefs in federal and state courts.

American Friends Service Committee
1501 Cherry Street, Philadelphia, PA   19102
(215) 241-7000 • fax: (215) 241-7275
Web site: www.afsc.org

The American Friends Service Committee (AFSC) is a nonprofit organization originally founded by Quakers in 1917 to provide conscientious objectors with an alternative opportunity to aid civilian war victims. It continues its work to promote service to others, social justice, and peace programs around the world. The "Youth and Militarism" link found at its main Web site features several of its publications, including *Do You Know Enough to Enlist?* and *Questions for Military Recruiters.*

America Supports You
Web site: www.americasupportsyou.mil

American Supports You (ASY) is an organization sponsored by the U.S. Department of Defense that recognizes the support Americans feel for the men and women in the armed forces, and communicates that support to service members serving at home and abroad. Through its Web site, individuals can send messages of support to U.S. servicemen and women. The organization also serves as a resource to service members in need of assistance, directing them to various programs and organizations around the country that can provide them and their family members with resources and advice.

Coalition Against Militarism In Our Schools
P.O. Box 3012, South Pasadena, CA   91031
(626) 799-9118
e-mail: info@militaryfreeschools.org
Web site: www.militaryfreeschools.org

The Coalition Against Militarism In Our Schools (CAMS) is a non-profit program operating under the International Humanities Center, with a stated mission to demilitarize schools by presenting alternatives. CAMS has written a resolution approved by the California Federation of Teachers seeking to eliminate Section 9528 from any reauthorization of No Child Left Behind Act (which provides military access to all schools that accept federal funds) as applicable to California.

Committee Opposed to Militarism and the Draft
P.O. Box 15195, San Diego, CA   92175
(760) 753-7518

e-mail: COMD@comdsd.org
Web site: www.comdsd.org

The Committee Opposed to Militarism and the Draft (COMD) defines itself as an anti-militarism organization "that also challenges the institution of the military, its effect on society, its budget, its role abroad and at home, and the racism, sexism and homophobia that are inherent in the armed forces and Selective Service System." It directs its focus on community education, youth outreach, and direct action. Two of its related publications are *Teach Peace* and *High School Rights*.

National Association for Uniformed Services
5535 Hempstead Way, Springfield, VA   22151
(703) 750-1342 • fax: (703) 354-4380
e-mail: info@naus.org
Web site: www.naus.org

The National Association for Uniformed Services (NAUS) is the only military-affiliated association whose membership is open to all military branches and ranks, active and retired. It provides its members with assistance in all areas of military service, including recruitment, retention, spousal support, and survivorship. It also lobbies and promotes members' interests in Washington. NAUS publishes the *Uniformed Services Journal*.

National Priorities Project
17 New South Street, Northampton, MA   01060
(413) 584-9556 • fax: (413) 586-9647
e-mail: info@nationalpriorities.org
Web site: www.nationalpriorities.org

The National Priorities Project (NPP) is a non-profit research organization that analyzes and clarifies federal data for the general reading public. The organization focuses on issues involving federal budgets and spending, as well as other key policies affecting government at all levels. Military recruiting is one of the topics the group studies. Its publication *Military Recruiting—2006* examines trends in recruiting quantity, quality, and spending.

Project on Youth and Non-Military Opportunities
P.O. Box 230157, Encinitas, CA   92023
(760) 634-3604
e-mail: projyano@aol.com
Web site: www.projectyano.org

Project on Youth and Non-Military Opportunities (Project YANO) works in conjunction with the Committee Opposed to Militarism and the Draft (COMD), both of which are anti-militarist organizations working with schools to provide alternatives to the military for students and other youths. It produces numerous pamphlets on topics related to recruiting, such as "Military Enlistment," "Non-Military Alternatives," and "JROTC."

U.S. Armed Forces
(866) VIEW-NOW
Web site: www.todaysmilitary.com

The U.S. Armed Forces include the four active duty military services—the Army, Marines, Navy, and Air Force—their Reserves, the National Guard, and the Coast Guard. Together they are charged with defending the United States' vital interests at home and abroad. Every branch of the armed forces engages in its own publicity and recruiting activities, including Web sites, phone numbers, and publications. The U.S. Department of Defense maintains the "Today's Military" Web site as a clearinghouse of information on all branches of the armed forces, with the goal of educating "parents, teachers, and others about the opportunities and benefits available to young people in the Military today."

War Resisters League
339 Lafayette St., New York, NY   10012
(212) 228-0450 • fax: (212) 228-6193

e-mail: wrl@warresisters.org
Web site: www.warresisters.org

The War Resisters League (WRL) is a private organization committed to a philosophy of non-violence, democracy, and equality. It maintains a number of programs aimed at reducing or eliminating war and violence. This includes a Youth and Countermilitarism Program, which publishes the *DMZ: A Guide to Taking Your School Back From the Military* booklet.

Bibliography

Books

Beth Asch, Can Du, and Matthias Schonlau
Policy Options for Military Recruiting in the College Market: Results from a National Survey. Santa Monica, CA: RAND, 2004.

Ronald D. Fricker Jr. and C. Christine Fair
Going to the Mines to Look for Diamonds: Experimenting with Recruiting Stations in Malls. Santa Monica, CA: RAND, 2003.

Curtis L. Gilroy, Barbara A. Bicksler, and John T. Warner
The All-Volunteer Force: Thirty Years of Service. College Park, MD: Potomac Books, 2004.

Philip Gold
The Coming Draft: The Crisis in Our Military and Why Selective Service Is Wrong for America. New York: Presidio Press, 2006.

Bill Harris
The Complete Idiot's Guide to Careers in the U.S. Military. Indianapolis, IN: Alpha Publishers, 2002.

Max Hastings
Warriors: Portraits from the Battlefield. New York: Knopf, 2006.

James R. Hosek, et al.
Attracting the Best: How the Military Competes for Information Technology Personnel. Santa Monica, CA: RAND, 2004.

Kaplan   *Kaplan ASVAB, 2007 Ed.: The Armed*
                          Services Vocational Aptitude Battery,
                          rev. ed. New York: Kaplan Education,
                          2006.

J.F. Leahy   *Honor, Courage, Commitment: Navy*
                          Boot Camp. Annapolis, MD: U.S. Na-
                          val Institute Press, 2002.

August T. Murray   *Military Recruiting: How to Build*
                          Recruiting Skills, Get Results, Adapt to
                          the Mission, and Sustain Success.
                          Bloomington, IN: AuthorHouse,
                          2005.

Scott A. Ostrow   *Guide to Joining the Military.*
                          Lawrenceville, NJ: Thomson/ARCO,
                          2004.

Kelly Perdew   *Take Command: 10 Leadership Prin-*
                          ciples I Learned in the Military and
                          Put to Work for Donald Trump. Wash-
                          ington, DC: Regnery Publishing,
                          2006.

Rod Powers and   *ASVAB For Dummies*, 2nd ed. India-
Jennifer Lawler   napolis, IN: Wiley Publishing, 2007.

U.S. Department   *Americas Top Military Careers: Offi-*
of Defense   *cial Guide to Occupations in the*
                          Armed Forces, 4th ed. Indianapolis,
                          IN: Jist Publishing, 2003.

U.S. National Research Council, Committee on the Youth Population and Military Recruitment   *Attitudes, Aptitudes, and Aspirations of American Youth: Implications for Military Recruiting*, Eds. Paul Sacket and Anne Mavor. Washington, DC: National Academy Press, 2003.

Michael C. Volkin   *The Ultimate Basic Training Guidebook: Tips, Tricks, and Tactics for Surviving Boot Camp*, 2nd ed. New York: Savas Beatie, 2005.

Periodicals

Drake Bennet   "Doing Disservice," *American Prospect*, October 2003.

Michael Bronner   "Abuse by Military Recruiters," *Blade* (Toledo, OH), September 26, 2006.

"The Recruiters' War," *Vanity Fair*, September 2005.

Bruce Chapman   "A Bad Idea Whose Time is Past: The Case Against Universal Service," *Brookings Review*, Fall 2002.

Congressional Daily   "Dems Want Hearing on Mounting Recruiting Violations," September 12, 2006.

Brendan Conway   "Elites and the Military," *Washington Times*, September 5, 2006.

Diego Cupolo   "Military Recruiters in High Schools," *Gotham Gazette* (New York, NY), January 2007.

Thomas J. Cutler   "Someone Else's Turn," *U.S. Naval Institute Proceedings*, December 2006.

David Goodman   "NCLB Accesses High-Schoolers for the Military in War Time," *Education Digest*, May 2004.

Ken Harbaugh   "Commentary: Military Recruiters on Campus," *National Public Radio: All Things Considered*, November 25, 2005.

Lawrence Hardy   "Recruiters at School," *American School Board Journal*, October 2005.

Hartford Courant (CT)   "Don't Strong-Arm Recruits," August 28, 2006.

Bob Herbert   "Op-Ed: The Army's Hard Sell," *New York Times*, June 27, 2005.

Karen Houppert   "Who's Next?" *Nation*, September 12, 2005.

Tim Kane   "Who Are the Recruits?: The Demographic Characteristics of U.S. Military Enlistment, 2003–2005," Center for Data Analysis Report no. 06-09, *Heritage Foundation*, October 27, 2006.

Stanley Kurtz   "San Francisco to Army: Drop Dead," *Weekly Standard*, November 28, 2005.

Jorge Mariscal   "The Poverty Draft: Do Military Recruiters Disproportionately Target Communities of Color and the Poor?" *Sojourners*, June 2007.

Meredith May   "De-Recruiter Wins Long Haul Prize," *San Francisco Chronicle*, September 16, 2006.

Renae Merle   "Army Tries Private Pitch for Recruits," *Washington Post*, September 6, 2006.

Jack Minch   "Five Years After 9/11, Military Recruiters Busy," *The Sun* (Lowell, MA), September 15, 2006.

Brian Mockenhaupt   "The Army We Have," *Atlantic Monthly*, June 2007.

Officer   "Military Recruiters Still Face Barriers on Campus," May 2006.

Judy O'Rourke   "Military Recruiters Compete to Lure People," *Daily News* (Los Angeles), October 17, 2006.

Philadelphia Inquirer   "Military Recruiters on Campus: High Court Ruling Is On the Mark," March 8, 2006.

Stephen Phillips   "Let in the Army or Risk Your Funding," *Times Educational Supplement*, July 11, 2003.

James Pinkerton   "Immigrants Find Military a Faster Path to Citizenship," *Houston Chronicle*, September 14, 2006.

Reading Eagle (PA)   "Many Aren't Willing to Even Debate Draft," November 28, 2006.

Thom Shanker   "Army and Other Ground Forces
                    Meet '06 Recruiting Goals," *New York
                    Times*, October 10, 2006.

Barry Strauss   "Reflections on the Citizen-Soldier,"
                    Parameters, Summer 2003.

Stuart Tannock   "Is 'Opting Out' Really an Answer?
                    Schools, Militarism, and the Counter-
                    Recruitment Movement in Post-
                    September 11 United States at War,"
                    Social Justice, vol. 32, no. 3, 2005.

Index

...an Detective Stories

...commissioning editor with the
...ior commissioning editor of *The Oxford*
...He is the editor of *Ghost Stories: An*
Victorian Ghost Stories). He has also
...ilbert).

...a sen...
...niversity Press. H...
...ook of English Ghost Stories* and ...
Oxford Anthology (both with R. A. G...
written a biography of M. R. James.

VICTORIAN DETECTIVE STORIES

An Oxford Anthology

Selected and introduced by
MICHAEL COX

Oxford   New York
OXFORD UNIVERSITY PRESS

Oxford University Press, Walton Street, Oxford OX2 6DP

Oxford New York Toronto
Delhi Bombay Calcutta Madras Karachi
Kuala Lumpur Singapore Hong Kong Tokyo
Nairobi Dar es Salaam Cape Town
Melbourne Auckland Madrid
and associated companies in
Berlin Ibadan

Oxford is a trade mark of Oxford University Press

British Library Cataloguing in Publication Data

Data available

Library of Congress Cataloging in Publication Data
Victorian tales of mystery and detection: an Oxford anthology /
selected and introduced by Michael Cox.
p. cm.
Includes bibliographical references.
1. Detective and mystery stories. English. 2. English
fiction—19th century. I. Cox, Michael, 1948–
PR1309.D4V49 1992 823'.0872090908—dc20 91-46719
ISBN 0-19-283150-X

3 5 7 9 10 8 6 4

Printed in Great Britain by
Biddles Ltd.
Guildford and King's Lynn

ACKNOWLEDGEMENTS

Several people have contributed to the compilation of this anthology with help, advice, and information. I should like to thank in particular: Jack Adrian, for numerous suggestions, and especially for details concerning Harry Blyth, the creator of Sexton Blake; Julian Symons; and Rosemary Herbert. I should also like to pay homage to the sterling bibliographical work performed by George Locke in his Ferret Fantasy catalogues, without which this anthologist's knowledge would be very much the poorer. Finally, my thanks are again due to the staff of the Bodleian Library, Oxford, and the University Library, Cambridge.

CONTENTS

INTRODUCTION

Crime writers, said G. K. Chesterton with typical audacity, are divided into two types: cut-throats and poisoners. The latter are the novelists, 'those authors who prolong the agony of anticipation or bewilderment in the reader through a long series of chapters, leaving the reader writhing on a sick-bed of baffled curiosity, as it were, for weeks on end'. Cut-throats, on the other hand, are those who, 'realizing that the murder story must cut short the life, decide also to cut the story short. It is their pride as artists to deal in daggers; and startle the unfortunate reader with the stabs of the short story.'[1]

This anthology is of the cut-throat variety, its authors dealing uniformly in stilettos rather than nightshade or arsenic. The short-story form has inherent limitations for the writer of detective fiction, but in the most capable hands these can be turned to triumphant effect, with consequent pleasures for the reader that the detective novel, for all its enticements, cannot provide. The establishing of a credible and engaging narrative voice is essential to a successful crime short; flamboyance of invention and a certain leisureliness in the telling must co-exist with economy of style, compression, and a well-paced plot; character must be sketched out swiftly but decisively; every incident must carry its share of relevance to the main idea, which itself needs to be simple and surprising. The art of the short detective story continues to evolve; but all its essential qualities and characteristics were developed in the course of the nineteenth century, particularly in its last two decades. The aim of this collection is to bring together some of the best, as well as some of the most representative (not always the same thing), short stories of crime and detection written, for the most part, during the reign of Queen Victoria. As with its companion volume, *Victorian Ghost Stories*, the selection is not based on a strict definition of the term 'Victorian'. Two stories post-date the official Victorian age; but they are authentically Victorian in tone and ambience, written by authors whose Victorian credentials are indisputable.

Julian Symons rightly observed that 'The first problem facing

---

[1] Introduction to *A Century of Detective Stories* (n.d.).

anybody writing about crime fiction is to stake out the limits of the theme.'[2] This, however, is a notoriously difficult task: is a mystery story necessarily a crime story? When is a mystery story a thriller? Is the detective story a unique category, or merely a variation? And, centrally, does a detective story need a detective? On this last question Cecil Chesterton, writing in the magazine *Temple Bar* in October 1906, had no doubt: 'The detective or mystery story need not, of course, be primarily concerned with detectives... The real distinguishing feature is that the reader should be confronted with a number of mysterious facts of which the explanation is reserved till the end.' On the other hand, modern authorities such as Ellery Queen (the joint pseudonym of Frederic Dannay and Manfred Bennington Lee) and John Carter insist that such stories should have (in Carter's words) 'a proper detective, whether amateur or professional'.[3] In this anthology all the stories are mysteries, but not all are detective stories, either because they lack the central figure of the detective or because no formal process of investigation, deduction, and revelation takes place. But all the stories, in whichever category the purist prefers to place them, are branches of the same tree—the protean genre known in the nineteenth century as sensation fiction, a form of popular literature which, in another of Julian Symons's happy encapsulations, 'has produced a few masterpieces, many good books, and an enormous mass of more or less entertaining rubbish'.[4]

In the beginning—as far as the received history of the short detective story is concerned—there was Edgar Allan Poe. Like its cousin the ghost story, the short detective story has a definable starting-point. The two first short fictional ghost stories worthy of the name were written by Sir Walter Scott and published in the 1820s: the genesis of the detective story similarly can be traced, twenty years later, to the genius of a single author. Poe's 'The Murders in the Rue Morgue' (1841) and the stories that followed, in particular 'The Mystery of Marie Roget' (1842) and 'The Purloined Letter' (1845), in which Poe developed the character of the eccentric but brilliant Chevalier C.

---

[2] *Bloody Murder. From the detective story to the crime novel* (rev. edn., 1985), 13.

[3] John Carter, introduction to *Victorian Detective Fiction. A catalogue of the collection made by Dorothy Glover and Graham Greene, bibliographically arranged by Eric Osborne* (1966).

[4] *Bloody Murder*, 15.

Auguste Dupin, form the indisputable fountain-head of the detective-story tradition. There may have been—there were—antecedents of various kinds, and on these some historians of the subject are wont to dwell. Dorothy Sayers held that the classic tale of detection possessed 'an Aristotelian perfection of beginning, middle and end',[5] which perhaps it does; but in linking it with Aristotle, Sayers was investing the detective story with characteristics and continuities that do not seem much to the point when the genre is taken as a whole, or when faced with authors such as Dick Donovan or Headon Hill.

In the search for historical precedents of the detective story, Sayers invoked stories from the Apocrypha, the *Aeneid*, and Herodotus. Other claimed precursors of detective fiction have included Voltaire (the chapter from *Zadig* [1747] entitled 'Le Chien et le Cheval'), Defoe (e.g. *Jonathan Wild*, 1725), and—more plausibly—William Godwin's *Caleb Williams* (1794). Such anticipatory incunabula undoubtedly deserve notice; more relevant examples of primitive detective fiction, unmentioned by Sayers, might include William Leggett's story 'The Rifle', first published in the United States in 1827 (though dated 1828), the solution of which involves some elementary ballistic evidence. There are other stories—Nathaniel Hawthorne's 'Mr Higginbotham's Catastrophe' (from *Twice-told Tales*, 1837) is a well-known example—in which elements of the detective story can be distinctly traced; and in the novels of Fenimore Cooper techniques of detection, though in a different context, abound. But it is not until Poe that the figure of the detective first shows its potential as a literary type. The seminal story, 'The Murders in the Rue Morgue', first appeared in *Graham's Magazine* in April 1841, and all three Dupin stories were published together in *Tales* (1845)—a volume described by Dannay and Lee in *Queen's Quorum* as 'the first important book of detective stories, the first and the greatest, the cornerstone of cornerstones in any readers' or collectors' guide', and by Dorothy Sayers as '[constituting] in itself almost a complete manual of detective theory and practice'.[6]

The profound, but unintentional, influence of Poe was slow in making itself felt because the Dupin stories, although they form

---

[5] Introduction to *Great Short Stories of Detection, Mystery and Horror* (First Series, 1928).
[6] Ibid.

the basic genetic material of detective fiction, were the work of an essentially aberrant literary figure, a Gothicist whose idiosyncratic romances delineated a fictional world in opposition to the prevailing tide of realism; and in writing short stories at a time when the novel was fast establishing itself as the dominant fictional form, Poe was also going against the contemporary grain, so that it was not until the short story truly came into its own in the later decades of the century—especially with the launch of heavily illustrated monthly magazines aimed at a mass readership in the 1890s—that the potentialities of the Dupin stories began to be realized fully.

Thus Poe's stories in the 1840s did not immediately inspire a wave of imitators in the way that Conan Doyle's did in the 1890s, though they formed the chief of several tributaries that fed into what was to become the mainstream of detective fiction in both its short and long forms. During the four decades that followed the publication of the first Dupin story there was plenty of fiction dealing with crime, and indeed no shortage of 'detectives', if the term is liberally interpreted; but of short detective fiction, as it has been understood in the post-Conan Doyle era, there was relatively little. Poe's detective stories were ratiocinative fantasies in which time and place were only incidental components of the setting, never of its essence. The hints they contained for the future of the short detective story lay largely undeveloped until they could be relocated in a context that accentuated and exploited solid aspects of the real world. Just as ghost stories became domesticated during the middle decades of the nineteenth century and evoked a strong sense of the mundane in order to make the intrusion of the supernatural convincing, so, towards the end of the century, the detective story fixed itself firmly in contemporary life through its settings and characterizations. The world of Sherlock Holmes—for all its improbabilities—is rooted in a sense of the actual; the world of Dupin assuredly is not.

In England, between Godwin and Dickens, no writer of the first rank used the figure of the detective in fiction. Over the same period the detection of real crime was gradually being transformed—first by the formation of the Bow Street Runners in the latter past of the eighteenth century, and then by the passing of Sir Robert Peel's Metropolitan Police Act of 1829, which established the Metropolitan

Police and led to the setting up in 1842 of a special Criminal Investigation Department dedicated to detective work.

These important social developments generated a large body of popular literature from the 1820s onwards, mostly works claiming to be authentic reminiscences of police officers but invariably fictionalized to a greater or lesser degree. Bow Street's most celebrated representation in fiction was *Richmond: or, Scenes in the Life of a Bow Street Officer* (Henry Colburn, 3 vols., 1827), anonymous but generally attributed to Thomas Gaspey. The most influential instance of fiction masquerading as fact, however, was French: the *Mémoires* of François-Eugène Vidocq (1775–1857), published in Paris in 1828–9, with English and American editions in 1828 and 1834. Vidocq was a deserter, forger, and convict who offered his services as an informer and detective to the Paris police, ending up as head of the Sûreté in 1812. His self-congratulatory, highly fictionalized, and probably ghosted Memoirs are important because of the vivacity and definition of their central character: for the first time, the figure of the detective attains memorable individuality. In England, despite some moral aversion to the spectacle of the convict turned detective, the Memoirs found immediate favour with both reviewers and readers and even became the basis of two melodramas, by Douglas Jerrold and John Baldwin Buckstone, with the same title, *Vidocq, the French Police Spy*.

Vidocq's Memoirs had a marked influence on the authentically fictional work of Emile Gaboriau (1832–73), usually labelled as the father of the *roman policier* (and occasionally the Edgar Allan Poe of French literature). Gaboriau began as a *feuilletoniste*, turning out serialized novels of a lurid complexion for daily newspapers. Each episode of a *feuilleton* was written to an exact length and the endings were designed as irresistible lures for the next episode. Gaboriau's *L'Affaire Lerouge*, in which his most famous creation, the Sûreté agent Lecoq, makes his first, though minor, appearance, began its serialization in 1865 and was published in book form in 1868 (in English, as *The Widow Lerouge*, in 1887). With Poe's Dupin, Lecoq shares the distinction of a direct ancestral relationship with Sherlock Holmes. Though the Great Detective himself dismissed the former as 'a very inferior fellow' and the latter as 'a miserable blunderer' (*A Study in Scarlet*), his creator more charitably acknowledged their influence: 'Gaboriau had rather attracted me by the neat dovetailing of his plots, and Poe's masterful detective, M. Dupin, had from boyhood been one of my heroes.'[7]

In England the tradition of police 'reminiscences' was also strongly influenced by Vidocq's Memoirs. The formation of the New Police in 1829 and the Detective Department in 1842 unleashed a tide of fiction posing as genuine memoirs. Of these the 'Recollections of a Police-Officer', first published in *Chamber's Edinburgh Journal* between July 1849 and September 1853, and collected in volume form in 1856 as *Recollections of a Detective Police-Officer*, have established themselves, despite their many and obvious weaknesses, as a sigificant staging-post in the history of short detective fiction. Their author, 'Waters', was not a policeman but a hack writer called William Russell. 'Waters', who takes up police work after a mildly misspent youth, brings worldly experience, rather than exceptional intellect and perspicacity, to bear on his cases. He is particularly prone to assuming disguises (as Sherlock Holmes was to be): in the second story, 'Guilty or Not Guilty?', for instance, he pursues his quarry dressed in a flaxen wig, broad-brimmed hat, green spectacles, 'and a multiplicity of waistcoats and shawls'. Despite the unintentional comic effects of such transformations, the character of the detective in these tales begins to assume distinct individuality—one small step in the evolution of the Great Detective.

The exploits of 'Waters' and others provide ample evidence of the mid-Victorian public's fascination for criminous fiction. Throughout the middle years of the century, however, the short detective story was overshadowed by novel-length fiction dealing with mystery and crime; it was in the novel, not the short story, that the literary stereotype of the detective was defined, and in this process the pivotal figure was Dickens—who, at the same time, was also largely responsible for stimulating popular taste for ghost fiction. Dickens was the first and greatest chronicler of the Scotland Yard detective service and in both his fiction and his journalism fashioned an image of the police detective that persisted throughout the nineteenth century and well into the twentieth. Dickens's interest in crime combined a visceral, boyish delight in villainy and its uncovering with instinctive indignation in the face of an urgent social problem. In *Bleak House*

[7] *Memories and Adventures* (1924), ch. viii.

(1853), in which Dickens introduced Inspector Bucket, the first police detective in English literary fiction, the fusion becomes manifest, making it, in Edmund Wilson's words, 'a detective story which is also a social fable'.[8]

But in its basic plot elements *Bleak House* also exemplified what Ruskin called 'the peculiar tone of the modern novel', by which he meant the kind of writing known as sensation fiction. 'Sensation' was one of the literary catchwords of the mid nineteenth century. Two novels in particular were commonly cited as exemplars of the term: Wilkie Collins's *The Woman in White* (1860) and Mary Elizabeth Braddon's *Lady Audley's Secret* (1862). Its broad characteristics, in the words of a reviewer in the *Athenaeum* of Miss Braddon's *John Marchmont's Legacy* (1863), included 'startling positions, sudden surprises, and a series of incidents causing painful emotions'. H. L. Mansel, writing for the *Quarterly Review* in 1863, isolated 'proximity' (meaning contemporary settings) and 'personality' (meaning the adaptation of actual contemporary events) as being amongst its defining qualities. This modernity—a feature, too, of detective fiction— was a new departure, signalling the form's anti-Gothic temper. Henry James gave Wilkie Collins the credit for having introduced into fiction 'those most mysterious of mysteries, the mysteries which are at our own doors. This innovation was fatal to the authority of Mrs Radcliffe and her everlasting castle in the Appenines. What are the Appenines to us or we to the Appenines? Instead of the terrors of *Udolpho*, we are treated to the terrors of the cheerful country house and the busy London lodgings.'[9] It was within the uniquely Victorian matrix of sensation fiction that the detective story progressed towards maturity. In its key elements—episodic incident, the emphasis on plot rather than character, contemporary settings, the manipulation of actual events, murder, forgery, and robbery, mistaken identity, and formulaic construction—sensation fiction provided the bridge between Poe and the true tale of detection as created by Conan Doyle.

Sensation fiction's link with the tale of detection is clear. Both were manipulative literary forms that depended on the ingenious concoction of riddles and mysteries—on 'the gradual unravelling of a

---

[8] *The Wound and the Bow* (1941), 36.
[9] *The Nation* (9 Nov. 1865).

carefully prepared enigma', as an article in the *Spectator* said of Wilkie Collins in 1861. The method found early and classic expression in Collins's *The Moonstone* (1868), which is usually described as the first full-blown detective novel in English, although Angus Bethune Reach's *Clement Lorimer: or, The Book with the Iron Clasps*, first published in six monthly parts, with illustrations by George Cruikshank, in the *Morning Chronicle* in 1848–9, is also a contender for the title, as is *The Notting Hill Mystery* (1863) by Charles Felix. Even so, it is unlikely that *The Moonstone* will lose its distinguished place in the history of detective fiction. *The Times* saw it as typifying 'the essence and secret of sensational novel-writing'; at the same time, Collins's novel has a purity of design that makes it untypical of the sensation genre as a whole: there are no convoluted subplots. and every detail of the narrative assumes a relationship with a single unifying problem—the theft of Rachel Verinder's diamonds. In *The Moonstone* misperception is of the essence: it permeates character relationships as well as the reader's view of events. The narrative method itself—a series of individual viewpoints—ensures that the reader is constantly denied objectivity: everything is filtered and modified by partiality, misjudgements, uncertainty, and fallibility in each witness, and by the author's controlling influence. This manipulation of perspective was to become a key technique for subsequent writers of detective fiction. But in other respects, too, *The Moonstone* was ahead of its time—for instance in its observance of what Dorothy Sayers called the 'fair-play rule', which demands that no vital clue is withheld from the reader.

The Moonstone contains several detectives, amateur and professional, but one in particular now has a fixed place in the pantheon. Descended from Dickens's Inspector Bucket, the figure of Sergeant Cuff marks a further stage in the development of the fictional police detective. Though conforming in many ways to the conventional image of the detective, Cuff's individuality makes a vivid impression from the moment of his introduction—'a grizzled, elderly man, so miserably lean that he looked as if he had not got an ounce of flesh on his bones in any part of him'. Sergeant Cuff, in T. S. Eliot's view, was 'the perfect detective'.[10] Though brilliant, Cuff is fallible; but the power of his presence looks forward to a long line of individuals

---

[10] Introduction to the World's Classics edition of *The Moonstone* (Oxford, 1928).

whose singularity and force of personality became an essential ingredient in the later success of the short detective story.

Ten years before *The Moonstone* began its serial publication in Dickens's *All the Year Round* Collins had also made a notable contribution to the history of the short detective story. 'Who is the Thief?' ('Extracted from the correspondence of the London Police') was published anonymously in the *Atlantic Monthly* for April 1858 and reprinted as 'The Biter Bit' in *The Queen of Hearts* the following year. Like *The Moonstone*, the story is told through the eyes of the main characters, the narrative consisting of a series of letters between Chief Inspector Theakstone, Sergeant Bulmer (who finally cracks the case), and the cocksure novice Matthew Sharpin. Its humorous intent does not diminish its importance, containing as it does elements such as false clues, procedural details, and the 'Most Unlikely Person' formula that were to become the stock-in-trade of so many later writers.

Gradually, the short story proper—as distinct from self-contained episodes within novels, such as chapters 11–14 of *Out of His Head* (1862) by the American author Thomas Bailey Aldrich—began to develop a momentum of its own. The Anglo-Irish writer J. S. Le Fanu produced a large body of short fiction, tales of crime and mystery as well as his more famous ghost stories, on which he often drew for creating the plot lines of novels. Le Fanu's work, which he liked to think of as part of 'the legitimate school of tragic English romance' whose progenitor was Scott, often lacked the plot control and ingenuity displayed by Collins in *The Moonstone* (even though he could occasionally come up with a clever idea, like the criminal who changes his appearance by means of surgery in the novel *Checkmate* [1870]); but this is less apparent in his short stories and in general he made up the deficiency by exceptional powers of description and an ability to evoke a convincing atmosphere of menace. He was an early exponent of the locked-room mystery, pioneered by Poe in 'The Murders in the Rue Morgue'. The situation forms the basis of the plot in 'Some Account of the Latter Days of the Hon. Richard Marston' (*Dublin University Magazine*, 1848)—later modified as 'The Evil Guest' (in *Ghost Stories and Mysteries*, 1851) and expanded into the novel *A Lost Name* (1868)—and is used again in the story reprinted here, 'The Murdered Cousin'

(1851), and in 'The Room in the Dragon Volant' (*London Society*, 1872; reprinted in *In a Glass Darkly*, 1872). 'The Murdered Cousin' is Victorian mystery fiction at its best: a wicked uncle; a murder in a room that has been double locked on the inside; a threatened heroine; and a setting rich in ominous detail—the half-ruined house of Carrickleigh, with its stagnant fishponds and grass-grown court-yard, surrounded by dark woods.

Le Fanu was a master of effects, not of construction. As a reviewer of his most famous novel, *Uncle Silas* (1864), remarked: 'Mr Le Fanu is too assiduously bent on operating on his reader's nerves, and sending a shiver through his frame, to take much trouble in elaborat-ing details or securing for his narrative strict logical sequence.'[11] For the increasingly sophisticated reading public of the mid-1860s hints and suggestions were not enough: 'They like to follow out the track of crime and mystery with the minuteness and particularity of a detective officer.' The growing demand for mystery and crime fiction was increasingly met by the monthly magazines, which also fed Victorian popular taste for ghost stories. Throughout the 1860s a succession was launched into a rapidly expanding market—*Temple Bar*, *London Society*, *The Argosy*, and *Tinsleys'*, amongst many others. *Belgravia*, which first appeared in November 1866, was owned and edited by Miss Braddon, Queen of the Sensation Novel, and she herself supplied a profusion of serialized novels and short stories to fill its pages. The story included here, 'Levison's Victim' (1870), is a typical Braddonesque concoction of mystery and melodrama in which the detection element, though slight, is decisive for the denouement. Another story from *Belgravia*, Richard Dowling's 'The Going Out of Alessandro Pozzone' (1878), is very different in mood and execution and more than satisfied the criteria of 'minuteness and particularity'. 'Levison's Victim', with its diffuse narrative, is an example of the intermediate stage between the Victorian tale of mystery and the detective story proper; 'Alessandro Pozzone'—an objective record of evidence and circumstance within a circumscribed location, and with a single ingenious idea at its heart—exemplifies the beginnings of a new era.

Throughout the 1880s the market for detective fiction continued to grow steadily. An index of popular taste was Fergus Hume's *The*

[11] *Saturday Review* (4 Feb. 1865).

Mystery of a Hansom Cab (Melbourne, 1886), which became one of the most successful crime novels of all time, though Hume himself—born in England but educated in New Zealand—sold the copyright and made virtually nothing from it. In the same year that Hume's best seller was published Arthur Conan Doyle, a young doctor with literary aspirations, sent a short novel featuring a detective called Sherlock Holmes to James Payn, editor of the *Cornhill Magazine*. Payn turned it down, as did two other publishers, but it eventually found a home with Ward, Lock, & Co. (Like Fergus Hume, Conan Doyle disposed of the copyright.) *A Study in Scarlet* first appeared in *Beeton's Christmas Annual* for 1887 and was published in volume form the following year. Conan Doyle then set about giving his detective 'something else to unravel': *The Sign of Four* appeared in *Lippincott's Montly Magazine* for February 1890, with the first edition being issued by Spencer Blackett later in the year.

Both books were successful; but much more was to come. In April 1892 Doyle's agent, A. P. Watt, sent H. Greenhough Smith, literary editor of the *Strand* magazine, a short tale featuring Sherlock Holmes called 'A Scandal in Bohemia'. An unsigned story by Doyle, 'The Voice of Science', had already appeared in the third issue of the *Strand*, launched in January 1891; but this was something altogether different, and Greenhough Smith immediately recognized its potential. Publication of 'The Adventures of Sherlock Holmes' began in the *Strand* in July and continued every month until June 1892—twelve stories in all. 'That dozen stories being finished,' said Conan Doyle in an interview for *Tit Bits* (owned, like the *Strand*, by George Newnes), 'I determined they should be the end of all Sherlock's doings.' But the British reading public determined otherwise.

It is impossible to exaggerate the impact of the first series of Holmes stories. The launch of the *Strand* had already been a triumph for Newnes—nearly 300,000 copies of the first issue had been sold. But the appearance of Sherlock Holmes confirmed its position as the leading illustrated monthly: at its peak it was selling nearly half a million copies a month, with a readership perhaps four times that number. Conan Doyle himself took his success phlegmatically, even dismissively, though he did concede that the format of his 'police romances' had been an original conception. He had hit on the idea of a serial character, whose adventures could be told in separate, self-contained stories, whilst waiting for patients in his Devonshire Place

consulting-room, where he had set up in practice as an oculist. The
patients never came; luckily, the idea that was to transform his life, as
well as the future course of detective fiction, did.

In Conan Doyle's hands the blueprint created by Poe, and to a
lesser extent by Gaboriau, was developed and extended—'galvanized',
as Dorothy Sayers put it, into life and popularity. The character of
Holmes touches that of the Chevalier Dupin at several points, in
particular his bohemianism and the sense of isolation imposed by his
genius, but always with some additional element that modifies the
bloodline. Holmes inhabits a very different world from Dupin. His
adventures are set in solid contemporary settings, dominated by
London and its surburbs, whilst Holmes himself came increasingly to
articulate, indeed to defend, the values of the broad middle stratum
of English society, of which the *Strand's* readership was largely
composed.

Conan Doyle made his detective the focal point, the essential
energizing centre, of his fiction. He intensified the effect by dispens-
ing with anything that obscured the simple clarity of his two main
characters or inhibited the progress of the plot. For the job it was
intended to do—to provide a powerful focus of interest within a
sequence of self-contained stories—the character of Holmes was
supremely effective; but it was, when all was said and done, a formula
that had to be repeated relentlessly; it could not be varied without
diluting its impact or, the supreme offence for a professional like
Doyle, alienating readers. 'I do not wish to be ungrateful to Holmes,'
wrote Doyle in his memoirs, 'who has been a good friend to me in
many ways. If I have sometimes been inclined to weary of him it is
because his character admits of no light and shade. He is a calculating machine, and anything you add to that simply weakens the
effect.'[12]

As well as dominating each story, Holmes was also a new sort of
sleuth. The stereotype of the police detective that had developed
from Vidocq, Gaboriau, 'Waters', Dickens, and Wilkie Collins was
replaced by a more potent image: the private, or consulting, detective
of independent means—the 'professional amateur'.[13] Brilliance and
eccentric genius took over from native shrewdness; organization and

[12] *Memories and Adventures*, ch. xi.
[13] See T. J. Binyon, *Murder Will Out. The detective in fiction* (Oxford, 1984).

scientific exactness took precedence over raw instinct; and the police detective of humble, or no more than middling, social pretensions became the private agent who is a gentleman by birth and education. All this was new; but the ground had been well prepared over five decades by all manner of prototypes and variations. Sherlock Holmes, it has been well said, was 'a cliché whose time had come'.[14]

Throughout the 1890s and into the early twentieth century the short detective story could not rid itself of the shadow of Baker Street. In many cases, to begin with at least, it had no wish to do so: public appetite appeared to be insatiable and there was no shortage of publishers eager to satisfy it. The *Strand* had its rivals—*Pearson's Magazine, Harmsworth's Magazine*, the *Ludgate Monthly, Cassell's*, the *Royal Magazine*, the *Windsor Magazine*, and others—as well as Sherlock Holmes. The *Strand* itself attempted to complement the success of Sherlock Holmes with a series of stories by Arthur Morrison (author of *A Child of the Jago*, 1896) featuring Martin Hewitt—'a stoutish, clean-shaven man, of middle height, and of a cheerful countenance', with 'as little of the aspect of the conventional detective as may be imagined'. (This deliberate distancing of the detective from the ascetic, hawk-faced image established by Holmes was taken up by many writers.) The Hewitt stories were workmanlike and entertaining, but they lacked the inventiveness—and, finally, the magic—of Sherlock Holmes; the *Strand*, at any rate, had no wish to continue with Hewitt and Morrison took the second series of stories to the *Windsor Magazine*. Nothing, in fact, ever replaced Holmes, despite a plethora of imitations and variants: George Sims's Dorcas Dene and Catherine Pirkis's Loveday Brooke, both lady detectives; M. McDonnell Bodkin's Paul Beck, the 'rule-of-thumb' detective; Victor L. Whitechurch's Thorpe Hazell; Fergus Hume's Hagar Stanley; Miss Cusack, created by the formidably prolific Mrs L. T. Meade and her collaborator Robert Eustace; and Headon Hill's Sebastian Zambra, were a few amongst many.

Like Sherlock Holmes, his successors inhabited a predominantly metropolitan world and many of the stories convey a strong sense of the urban environment of the 1890s—from City banks and suburban

---

[14] Ian Ousby, introduction to *Bloodhounds of Heaven. The detective in English fiction from Godwin to Doyle* (Cambridge, Mass., 1976).

villas to boarding houses and mean back streets. Often, as Hugh Greene pointed out, 'the dividing line between crook and detective is a narrow one'.[15] One fertile variation involved complete inversion, producing a line of rogue heroes, with E. W. Hornung's Raffles at their head, who developed alongside the conventional detective. Examples include Grant Allen's Colonel Clay (whose adventures were collected as *An African Millionaire* in 1897), Arthur Morrison's con-man hero Dorrington, Romney Pringle (the joint creation of R. Austin Freeman and Dr John James Pitcairn), the unscrupulous lawyer Randolph Mason (in *The Strange Schemes of Randolph Mason* [1896] by the American author Melville Davisson Post), Barry Pain's Constantine Dix, and Guy Boothby's Klimo, whose first exploit is reprinted here. Klimo applies his mind, not to the solution of a crime, but to the committing of one: ' "I have cracked a good many hard nuts in my time," he said reflectively, "but never one that seemed so difficult at first sight as this." ' Boothby even gives the inversion a further twist by making Simon Carne devise a crime for himself, as Klimo, to solve—even down to laying false clues: 'To him it was scarcely a robbery he was planning, but an artistic trial of skill, in which he pitted his wits and cunning against the forces of society in general.' Arnold Bennett's Cecil Thorold—a millionaire 'in search of joy'—is a variation on the variation, undertaking crime in order to right wrongs in true Robin Hood fashion.

Another development was the fusion of the detective story with the supernatural. A prototype of the psychic, or occult, detective can be found in the anonymous *Tales of an Antiquary* (1828), in the character of the astrologer Ptolemy Horoscope and his Watsonian servant, Titus Parable; but it was in the immediate post-Holmes era that psychic detection emerged as a sub-genre in its own right with sleuths such as John Bell, in L. T. Meade and Robert Eustace's *A Master of Mysteries* (1898); Flaxman Low, created by the mother-and-son writing team of 'E. and H. Heron', whose adventures began in *Pearson's Magazine* in the same year; and, later, Algernon Blackwood's John Silence and W. Hope Hodgson's 'Carnacki, the Ghost-Finder'.

Detective fiction also naturally lent itself to adaptation for juvenile readers, notably in the Sexton Blake cycle. Dorothy Sayers found this to be a 'curious and interesting development', describing the Blake

---

[15] Introduction to *The Rivals of Sherlock Holmes. Early detective stories* (1970).

stories as 'the Holmes tradition adapted for the reading of the board-school boy and crossed with the Buffalo Bill adventure type'. (Perhaps surprisingly, Sayers found much to admire in these stories.) The first tale featuring Sexton Blake (originally, Frank Blake), 'The Missing Millionaire', was written by the Scottish journalist Harry Blyth and appeared in one of Alfred Harmsworth's weekly papers for boys, the *Halfpenny Marvel*, in December 1893—just under a month after Holmes's 'Final Problem' appeared in the *Strand*; thereafter Blake's adventures were chronicled by a host of different writers— some 200 over a 60-year period. The character was an enormous success, eventually even rivalling Sherlock Holmes (whose 'death' in 1893 had inspired Blake's creation) in popularity, though Blyth— who sold the copyright of the first Blake story and who died of typhoid fever in 1898—reaped none of the material rewards. Included here is a story by Blyth, typical of the kind of fiction enjoyed by young (and not so young) readers of the 1890s, concerning Sexton Blake's French partner, Jules Gervaise.

Like any literary genre, detective fiction also produced its oddities. M. P. Shiel's hashish-smoking Prince Zaleski is a detective of the Decadence, a Russian nobleman who has taken up reclusive residence in England, in a 'vast palace of the older world', after becoming the victim of a 'too importunate, too unfortunate Love, which the fulgor of the throne itself could not abash'. The three stories that make up the volume (*Prince Zaleski*, 1895) build on the approach used by Poe in 'The Mystery of Marie Rogêt', in which Dupin solves the mystery simply by analysing newspaper reports. Likewise, Prince Zaleski, in the most familiar of the three stories, 'The Race of Orven', correctly deduces the truth concerning Lord Pharanx's death through the exercise of pure reason. Less well known is Shiel's story 'The Case of Euphemia Raphash', an extraordinary co-mingling of Gothic fantasy, mystery, and detection. Dr Raphash, who inhabits 'a gloomy half-ruined pile, an ancient place, the home of a race most ancient', is another protagonist in the tradition of Poe. When his sister is murdered he takes on the appearance of 'the man of science turned beast of prey, but retaining the perfect scientific calm; an intensity bordering on lunacy shrouding itself behind the serenity of ocean-depths; the avenging angel *without* the flashing eye and flaming sword'. Except that this avenging angel is not quite what he seems . . .

Shiel apart, detective fiction in the second half of the 1890s continued to adhere closely to the Holmesian pattern, reflecting the conservative tastes of the market for magazine fiction. But with the passing of the century the detective story began to show signs of independence from the Baker Street tradition. Baroness Orczy's 'Old Man in the Corner' stories began in the *Royal Magazine* in May 1901, under the series title 'London Mysteries'. A second series of six stories, called 'Mysteries of Great Cities', followed in April 1902. Though conventional enough in execution, they are notable for the way the detective is subordinate to the *process* of detection. They are concerned, not with the heroic image of the Great Detective, but with the power of reason. Indeed, the central character of the sequence (in the first story he is referred to in a list of dramatis personae simply as 'The Man who tells the story') is a distinctly unheroic figure who sits in the corner of a tea-shop constantly knotting and untying a piece of string—pale, thin, 'with such funny light-coloured hair, brushed very smoothly across the top of a very obviously bald crown'. Like Prince Zaleski he is a static detective, reaching his conclusions at a distance from the crime by the application of intellect: '"Mysteries!" he commented. "There is no such thing as a mystery in connection with any crime, provided intelligence is brought to bear upon its investigation."'

Robert Barr's Eugene Valmont, on the other hand, is an active professional of the classic type who often exhibits a flair that is positively Holmesian. But there the resemblance with the great original ends. Valmont (a possible model for Agatha Christie's Poirot and a conspicuously successful creation) is full of Gallic exuberance— opinionated, extrovert, voluble, contentious, and a cavalier to the core. The stories contained in *The Triumphs of Eugene Valmont* (1906, but published earlier in *Pearson's* and the *Windsor*) match the originality of the central character with ingenious plotting and a vein of genuine, but never obtrusive, humour—generated mostly from the opposition of French and English national characteristics ('I hold a theory', proclaims Valmont in 'The Ghost with the Club Foot', 'that the English people are utterly incomprehensible to the rest of humanity . . .').

It is fitting that the last story in this collection, like the first, should feature a French detective. Between Dupin and Eugene Valmont— just over sixty years—the detective had developed into an established set of literary stereotypes, ranging from the plodding official to the scintillatingly brilliant amateur. Valmont can be seen as marking the end of the first great phase in the history of short detective fiction. Soon new characters emerged—Chesterton's Roman Catholic priest Father Brown, R. Austin Freeman's medical scholar Dr Thorndyke, H. Hesketh Prichard's November Joe (a Canadian backwoodsman), Jacques Futrelle's Professor S. F. X. Van Dusen (the 'Thinking Machine'), and Ernest Bramah's Max Carrados (a blind detective) amongst them—to demonstrate that another, equally fecund, period was beginning.

The heyday of the amateur detective of independent means is over; the professional consulting detective, too, may be a thing of the past. Ironically, given the long dominance of Sherlock Holmes and his imitators, it is the official detective, in print and on the screen (Morse, Wexford, Dalgleish, Columbo, even Dale Cooper), who is once again in the ascendancy. What attractions, then, can detective fiction of a century ago hold for the sophisticated reader of today?

Not the least of the pleasures offered by Victorian mystery and detective fiction is the unstudied evocation of time and place. In these stories, written mostly for an audience whose literary experience was limited, we come right up against the daily atmosphere of the age—its social groupings, its language, topography, and domestic conditions, the sights and sounds of its streets, even its modes of transport. As Hugh Greene, compiler of three pioneering anthologies of late Victorian detective fiction, said: 'there is a twilight world of neglected, but not completely forgotten, writers like Dick Donovan, Bodkin, Mrs Pirkis and Mrs L. T. Meade who wrote the occasional story which deserves to be resurrected, if not for its literary quality, then for some ingenuity of plot, some sudden flash of imagination, some light on the late Victorian and Edwardian world.'[16] The same is true of earlier examples; all the stories in this collection hold up a mirror—in some cases cracked, dirty, or distorting—to the age. Like its relative the ghost story, Victorian crime fiction brings us into contact with the common reader. But whereas the ghost story reprimands human reason for its presumption of supremacy, in the detective story there is *always* an explanation. The ghost story, it may be said, is admonitory in its underlying thrust ('There are more things in heaven and earth . . .') and cautions against too great a faith in

---

[16] Introduction to *The Crooked Counties. Further Rivals of Sherlock Holmes* (1973).

rationalism; the detective story celebrates the human ability to explain and comprehend. In the ghost story men and women are subdued by mysteries and often persecuted by forces they cannot understand. In the detective story understanding is everything and mystery itself, through the godlike powers of the detective, is subdued. In the opposing implications of the two genres can be glimpsed the tension between a belief in human power and the consciousness of human dependence on some greater order that helped form the cultural temper of the Victorian age.

But for most readers, the fiction represented in this anthology will be enjoyed at a more basic level. All the stories have value as examples of the story-teller's art and should remind us that most popular fiction—then as now—is produced by professionals who have constantly to survive in a competitive market. The specifically Victorian qualities of these stories lend them a nostalgic charm; but mystery fiction, in all its forms, is deeply conservative by nature: what fascinated the Victorian reading public fascinates us. The lure of the puzzle remains; the spectacle of the unknown becoming known continues to satisfy; the triumph of reason soothes us still.

Michael Cox

25 October 1991

'Draw your chair up, and hand me my violin, for the only problem which we have still to solve is how to while away these bleak autumnal evenings.'

Sir Arthur Conan Doyle, 'The Adventure of the Noble Bachelor'

The Purloined Letter

EDGAR ALLAN POE

Nil sapientiæ odiosius acumine nimio.   SENECA

At Paris, just after dark one gusty evening in the autumn of 18—, I was enjoying the twofold luxury of meditation and a meerschaum, in company with my friend, C. Auguste Dupin, in his little back library or book-closet, *au troisième*, No. 33 Rue Dunôt, Faubourg St Germain. For one hour at least we had maintained a profound silence; while each, to any casual observer, might have seemed intently and exclusively occupied with the curling eddies of smoke that oppressed the atmosphere of the chamber. For myself, however, I was mentally discussing certain topics which had formed matter for conversation between us at an earlier period of the evening; I mean the affair of the Rue Morgue, and the mystery attending the murder of Marie Rogêt. I looked upon it, therefore, as something of a coincidence, when the door of our apartment was thrown open and admitted our old acquaintance, Monsieur G——, the Prefect of the Parisian police.

We gave him a hearty welcome; for there was nearly half as much of the entertaining as of the contemptible about the man, and we had not seen him for several years. We had been sitting in the dark, and Dupin now arose for the purpose of lighting a lamp, but sat down again, without doing so, upon G.'s saying that he had called to consult us, or rather to ask the opinion of my friend, about some official business which had occasioned a great deal of trouble.

'If it is any point requiring reflection,' observed Dupin, as he forbore to enkindle the wick, 'we shall examine it to better purpose in the dark.'

'That is another of your odd notions,' said the Prefect, who had a fashion of calling everything 'odd' that was beyond his comprehension, and thus lived amid an absolute legion of 'oddities'.

'Very true,' said Dupin, as he supplied his visitor with a pipe, and rolled towards him a comfortable chair.

'And what is the difficulty now?' I asked. 'Nothing more in the assassination way, I hope?'

'Oh, no; nothing of that nature. The fact is, the business is *very* simple indeed, and I make no doubt that we can manage it sufficiently well ourselves; but then I thought Dupin would like to hear the details of it, because it is so excessively *odd*.'

'Simple and odd,' said Dupin.

'Why, yes; and not exactly that, either. The fact is, we have all been a good deal puzzled because the affair *is* so simple, and yet baffles us altogether.'

'Perhaps it is the very simplicity of the thing which puts you at fault,' said my friend.

'What nonsense you *do* talk!' replied the Prefect, laughing heartily.

'Perhaps the mystery is a little *too* plain,' said Dupin.

'Oh, good heavens! who ever heard of such an idea?'

'A little *too* self-evident.'

'Ha! ha! ha!—ha! ha! ha!—ho! ho! ho!' roared our visitor, profoundly amused; 'O Dupin, you will be the death of me yet!'

'And what, after all, *is* the matter on hand?' I asked.

'Why, I will tell you,' replied the Prefect, as he gave a long, steady, and contemplative puff, and settled himself in his chair. 'I will tell you in a few words; but, before I begin, let me caution you that this is an affair demanding the greatest secrecy, and that I should most probably lose the position I now hold, were it known that I confided it to any one.'

'Proceed,' said I.

'Or not,' said Dupin.

'Well, then; I have received personal information, from a very high quarter, that a certain document of the last importance has been purloined from the royal apartments. The individual who purloined it is known; this beyond a doubt; he was seen to take it. It is known, also, that it still remains in his possession.'

'How is this known?' asked Dupin.

'It is clearly inferred,' replied the Prefect, 'from the nature of the document, and from the non-appearance of certain results which would at once arise from its passing *out* of the robber's possession— that is to say, from his employing it as he must design in the end to employ it.'

'Be a little more explicit,' I said.

'Well, I may venture so far as to say that the paper gives its holder a certain power in a certain quarter where such power is immensely valuable.' The Prefect was fond of the cant of diplomacy.

'Still I do not quite understand,' said Dupin.

'No? Well; the disclosure of the document to a third person, who shall be nameless, would bring in question the honour of a personage of most exalted station; and this fact gives the holder of the document an ascendency over the illustrious personage whose honour and peace are so jeopardized.'

'But this ascendancy,' I interposed, 'would depend upon the robber's knowledge of the loser's knowledge of the robber. Who would dare——'

'The thief,' said G., 'is the Minister D——, who dares all things, those unbecoming as well as those becoming a man. The method of the theft was not less ingenious than bold. The document in question—a letter, to be frank—had been received by the personage robbed while alone in the royal boudoir. During its perusal she was suddenly interrupted by the entrance of the other exalted personage from whom especially it was her wish to conceal it. After a hurried and vain endeavour to thrust it in a drawer, she was forced to place it, open as it was, upon a table. The address, however, was uppermost, and, the contents thus unexposed, the letter escaped notice. At this juncture enters the Minister D——. His lynx eye immediately perceives the paper, recognizes the handwriting of the address, observes the confusion of the personage addressed, and fathoms her secret. After some business transactions, hurried through in his ordinary manner, he produces a letter somewhat similar to the one in question, opens it, pretends to read it, and then places it in close juxtaposition to the other. Again he converses, for some fifteen minutes, upon the public affairs. At length, in taking leave, he takes also from the table the letter to which he had no claim. Its rightful owner saw, but, of course, dared not call attention to the act, in the presence of the third personage who stood at her elbow. The Minister decamped, leaving his own letter—one of no importance—upon the table.'

'Here, then,' said Dupin to me, 'you have precisely what you demand to make the ascendancy complete—the robber's knowledge of the loser's knowledge of the robber.'

'Yes,' replied the Prefect; 'and the power thus attained has, for some months past, been wielded, for political purposes, to a very dangerous extent. The personage robbed is more thoroughly convinced, every day, of the necessity of reclaiming her letter. But this, of course, cannot be done openly. In fine, driven to despair, she has committed the matter to me.'

'Than whom,' said Dupin, amid a perfect whirlwind of smoke, 'no more sagacious agent could, I suppose, be desired, or even imagined.'

'You flatter me,' replied the Prefect; 'but it is possible that some such opinion may have been entertained.'

'It is clear,' said I, 'as you observe, that the letter is still in the possession of the Minister; since it is this possession, and not any employment of the letter, which bestows the power. With the employment the power departs.'

'True,' said G.; 'and upon this conviction I proceeded. My first care was to make thorough search of the Minister's hotel; and here my chief embarrassment lay in the necessity of searching without his knowledge. Beyond all things, I have been warned of the danger which would result from giving him reason to suspect our design.'

'But,' said I, 'you are quite *au fait* in these investigations. The Parisian police have done this thing often before.'

'Oh yes; and for this reason I did not despair. The habits of the Minister gave me, too, a great advantage. He is frequently absent from home all night. His servants are by no means numerous. They sleep at a distance from their master's apartment, and, being chiefly Neapolitans, are readily made drunk. I have keys, as you know, with which I can open any chamber or cabinet in Paris. For three months a night has not passed, during the greater part of which I have not been engaged, personally, in ransacking the D—— Hôtel. My honour is interested, and, to mention a great secret, the reward is enormous. So I did not abandon the search until I had become fully satisfied that the thief is a more astute man than myself. I fancy that I have investigated every nook and corner of the premises in which it is possible that the paper can be concealed.'

'But is it not possible,' I suggested, 'that although the letter may be in possession of the Minister, as it unquestionably is, he may have concealed it elsewhere than upon his own premises?'

'This is barely possible,' said Dupin. 'The present peculiar condition of affairs at court, and especially of those intrigues in which D—— is known to be involved, would render the instant availability of the document—its susceptibility of being produced at a moment's notice—a point of nearly equal importance with its possession.'

'Its susceptibility of being produced?' said I.

'That is to say, of being *destroyed*,' said Dupin.

'True,' I observed; 'the paper is clearly then upon the premises. As for its being upon the person of the Minister, we may consider that as out of the question.'

'Entirely,' said the Prefect. 'He has been twice waylaid, as if by footpads, and his person rigorously searched under my own inspection.'

'You might have spared yourself this trouble,' said Dupin. 'D——, I presume, is not altogether a fool, and, if not, must have anticipated these waylayings, as a matter of course.'

'Not *altogether* a fool,' said G.; 'but then he's a poet, which I take to be only one remove from a fool.'

'True,' said Dupin, after a long and thoughtful whiff from his meerschaum, 'although I have been guilty of certain doggerel myself.'

'Suppose you detail,' said I, 'the particulars of your search.'

'Why, the fact is we took our time, and we searched *everywhere*. I have had long experience in these affairs. I took the entire building, room by room; devoting the nights of a whole week to each. We examined, first, the furniture of each department. We opened every possible drawer; and I presume you know that, to a properly trained police agent, such a thing as a *secret* drawer is impossible. Any man is a dolt who permits a "secret" drawer to escape him in a search of this kind. The thing is *so* plain. There is a certain amount of bulk—of space—to be accounted for in every cabinet. Then we have accurate rules. The fiftieth part of a line could not escape us. After the cabinets we took the chairs. The cushions we probed with the fine long needles you have seen me employ. From the tables we removed the tops.'

'Why so?'

'Sometimes the top of a table, or other similarly arranged piece of furniture, is removed by the person wishing to conceal an article; then the leg is excavated, the article deposited within the cavity, and the top replaced. The bottoms and tops of bedposts are employed in the same way.'

'But could not the cavity be detected by sounding?' I asked.

'By no means, if, when the article is deposited, a sufficient wadding of cotton be placed around it. Besides, in our case, we were obliged to proceed without noise.'

'But you could not have removed—you could not have taken to pieces *all* articles of furniture in which it would have been possible to make a deposit in the manner you mention. A letter may be compressed into a thin spiral roll, not differing much in shape or bulk from a large knitting-needle, and in this form it might be inserted into the rung of a chair, for example. You did not take to pieces all the chairs?'

'Certainly not; but we did better—we examined the rungs of every chair in the hotel, and, indeed, the jointings of every description of furniture, by the aid of a most powerful microscope. Had there been any traces of recent disturbance we should not have failed to detect it instantly. A single grain of gimlet-dust, for example, would have been as obvious as an apple. Any disorder in the glueing—any unusual gaping in the joints—would have sufficed to ensure detection.'

'I presume you looked to the mirrors, between the boards and the plates, and you probed the beds and the bedclothes, as well as the curtains and carpets.'

'That of course; and when we had absolutely completed every article of the furniture in this way, then we examined the house itself. We divided its entire surface into compartments, which we numbered, so that none might be missed; then we scrutinized each individual square inch throughout the premises, including the two houses immediately adjoining, with the microscope, as before.'

'The two houses adjoining!' I exclaimed; 'you must have had a great deal of trouble.'

'We had; but the reward offered is prodigious.'

'You include the *grounds* about the houses?'

'All the grounds are paved with brick. They gave us comparatively little trouble. We examined the moss between the bricks, and found it undisturbed.'

'You looked among D——'s papers, of course, and into the books of the library?'

'Certainly; we opened every package and parcel; we not only opened every book, but we turned over every leaf in each volume, not contenting ourselves with a mere shake, according to the fashion of some of our police officers. We also measured the thickness of every book-*cover*, with the most accurate admeasurement, and applied to each the most jealous scrutiny of the microscope. Had any of the bindings been recently meddled with, it would have been utterly impossible that the fact should have escaped observation. Some five or six volumes, just from the hands of the binder, we carefully probed longitudinally, with the needles.'

'You explored the floors beneath the carpets?'

'Beyond doubt. We removed every carpet, and examined the boards with the microscope.'

'And the paper on the walls?'

'Yes.'

'You looked into the cellars?'

'We did.'

'Then,' I said, 'you have been making a miscalculation, and the letter is *not* upon the premises, as you suppose.'

'I fear you are right there,' said the Prefect. 'And now, Dupin, what would you advise me to do?'

'To make a thorough re-search of the premises.'

'That is absolutely needless,' replied G——. 'I am not more sure than I breathe than I am that the letter is not at the hotel.'

'I have no better advice to give you,' said Dupin. 'You have, of course, an accurate description of the letter?'

'Oh yes!' And here the Prefect, producing a memorandum-book, proceeded to read aloud a minute account of the internal, and especially of the external appearance of the missing document. Soon after finishing the perusal of this description, he took his departure more entirely depressed in spirits than I had ever known the good gentleman before.

In about a month afterwards he paid us another visit, and found us occupied very nearly as before. He took a pipe and a chair and entered into some ordinary conversation. At length I said—

'Well, but G——, what of the purloined letter? I presume you have at last made up your mind that there is no such thing as overreaching the Minister?'

'Confound him, say I—yes; I made the re-examination, however, as Dupin suggested—but it was all labour lost, as I knew it would be.'

'How much was the reward offered, did you say?' asked Dupin.

'Why, a very great deal—a *very* liberal reward—I don't like to say how much, precisely; but I *will* say, that I wouldn't mind giving my individual cheque for fifty thousand francs to any one who could obtain me that letter. The fact is, it is becoming of more and more importance every day; and the reward has been lately doubled. If it were trebled, however, I could do no more than I have done.'

'Why, yes,' said Dupin drawlingly, between the whiffs of his meerschaum, 'I really—think, G——, you have not exerted yourself—to the utmost—in this matter. You might—do a little more, I think, eh?'

'How?—in what way?'

'Why—puff, puff—you might—puff, puff—employ counsel in the matter, eh?—puff, puff, puff. Do you remember the story they tell of Abernethy?'

'No; hang Abernethy!'

'To be sure! hang him and welcome. But once upon a time, a certain rich miser conceived the design of sponging upon this Abernethy for a medical opinion. Getting up, for this purpose, an ordinary conversation in a private company, he insinuated his case to the physician, as that of an imaginary individual.

'"We will suppose," said the miser, "that his symptoms are such and such; now, doctor, what would *you* have directed him to take?"'

'"Take!" said Abernethy, "why, take *advice*, to be sure."'

'But,' said the Prefect, a little discomposed, 'I am *perfectly* willing to take advice, and to pay for it. I would *really* give fifty thousand francs to any one who would aid me in the matter.'

'In that case,' replied Dupin, opening a drawer, and producing a cheque-book, 'you may as well fill me up a cheque for the amount mentioned. When you have signed it, I will hand you the letter.'

I was astounded. The Prefect appeared absolutely thunderstricken. For some minutes he remained speechless and motionless, looking incredulously at my friend with open mouth, and eyes that seemed starting from their sockets; then, apparently recovering himself in some measure, he seized a pen, and after several pauses and vacant stares, finally filled up and signed a cheque for fifty thousand francs, and handed it across the table to Dupin. The latter examined it carefully and deposited it in his pocket-book; then, unlocking an escritoire, took thence a letter and gave it to the Prefect. This functionary grasped it in a perfect agony of joy, opened it with a trembling hand, cast a rapid glance at its contents, and then, scrambling and struggling to the door, rushed at length unceremoniously from the room and from the house, without having uttered a syllable since Dupin had requested him to fill up the cheque.

When he had gone, my friend entered into some explanations.

'The Parisian police,' he said, 'are exceedingly able in their way. They are persevering, ingenious, cunning, and thoroughly versed in the knowledge which their duties seem chiefly to demand. Thus, when G—— detailed to us his mode of searching the premises at the Hôtel D——, I felt entire confidence in his having made a satisfactory investigation—so far as his labours extended.'

'So far as his labours extended?' said I.

'Yes,' said Dupin. 'The measures adopted were not only the best of their kind, but carried out to absolute perfection. Had the letter been deposited within the range of their search, these fellows would, beyond a question, have found it.'

I merely laughed—but he seemed quite serious in all that he said.

'The measures, then,' he continued, 'were good in their kind, and well executed; their defect lay in their being inapplicable to the case, and to the man. A certain set of highly ingenious resources are, with the Prefect, a sort of Procrustean bed, to which he forcibly adapts his designs. But he perpetually errs by being too deep or too shallow for the matter in hand; and many a schoolboy is a better reasoner than he. I knew one about eight years of age, whose success at guessing in the game of "even and odd" attracted universal admiration. This game is simple, and is played with marbles. One player holds in his hand a number of these toys, and demands of another whether that number is even or odd. If the guess is right, the guesser wins one; if wrong, he loses one. The boy to whom I allude won all the marbles of the school. Of course he had some principle of guessing; and this lay in mere observation and admeasurement of the astuteness of his opponents. For example, an arrant simpleton is his opponent, and, holding up his closed hand, asks, "Are they even or odd?" Our schoolboy replies "Odd," and loses; but upon the second trial he wins, for he then says to himself, "The simpleton had them even upon the first trial, and his amount of cunning is just sufficient to make him have them odd upon the second; I will therefore guess odd"—he guesses odd, and wins. Now, with a simpleton a degree above the first, he would have reasoned thus: "This fellow finds that in the first instance I guessed odd, and, in the second, he will propose to himself, upon the first impulse, a simple variation from even to odd, as did the first simpleton; but then a second thought will suggest that this is too simple a variation, and finally he will decide upon putting it even as before. I will therefore guess even"—he guesses even, and wins. Now this mode of reasoning in the school-boy, whom his fellows termed "lucky"—what, in its last analysis, is it?'

'It is merely,' I said, 'an identification of the reasoner's intellect with that of his opponent.'

'It is,' said Dupin; 'and upon enquiring of the boy by what means he effected the *thorough* identification in which his success consisted, I received answer as follows: "When I wish to find out how wise, or how stupid, or how good, or how wicked is any one, or what are his thoughts at the moment, I fashion the expression of my face, as accurately as possible, in accordance with the expression of his, and then wait to see what thoughts or sentiments arise in my mind or heart, as if to match or correspond with the expression." This response of the schoolboy lies at the bottom of all the spurious profundity which has been attributed to Rochefoucauld, to La Bougive, to Machiavelli, and to Campanella.'

'And the identification,' I said, 'of the reasoner's intellect with that of his opponent, depends, if I understand you aright, upon the accuracy with which the opponent's intellect is admeasured.'

'For its practical value it depends upon this,' replied Dupin; 'and the Prefect and his cohort fail so frequently, first, by default of his identification, and, secondly, by ill-admeasurement, or rather through non-admeasurement, of the intellect with which they are engaged. They consider only their *own* ideas of ingenuity; and, in searching for anything hidden, advert only to the modes in which *they* would have hidden it. They are right in this much—that their own ingenuity is a faithful representative of that of *the mass*; but when the cunning of the individual felon is diverse in character from their own, the felon foils them, of course. This always happens when it is above their own, and very usually when it is below. They have no variation of prin-ciple in their investigations; at best, when urged by some unusual emergency—by some extraordinary reward—they extend or exagger-ate their old modes of *practice*, without touching their principles. What, for example, in this case of D——, has been done to vary the principle of action? What is all this boring, and probing, and sound-ing, and scrutinizing with the microscope, and dividing the surface of the building into registered square inches—what is it all but an exaggeration *of the application* of the one principle or set of principles of search, which are based upon the one set of notions regarding human ingenuity, to which the Prefect, in the long routine of his duty, has been accustomed? Do you not see he has taken it for granted that *all* men proceed to conceal a letter—not exactly in a gimlet-hole bored in a chair-leg—but, at least, in *some* out-of-the-way hole or corner suggested by the same tenor of thought which would urge a man to secrete a letter in a gimlet-hole bored in a chair-leg? And do you not see also, that such recherchés nooks for concealment are adapted only for ordinary occasions, and would be adopted only by ordinary intellects; for, in all cases of concealment, a disposal of the article concealed—a disposal of it in this recherché manner—is, in the very first instance, presumable and presumed; and thus its discovery depends, not at all upon the acumen, but altogether upon the mere care, patience, and determination of the seekers; and where the case is of importance—or, what amounts to the same thing in the policial eyes, when the reward is of magnitude— the qualities in question have *never* been known to fail. You will now understand what I meant in suggesting that, had the purloined letter been hidden anywhere within the limits of the Prefect's examination— in other words, had the principle of its concealment been com- prehended within the principles of the Prefect—its discovery would have been a matter altogether beyond question. This functionary, however, has been thoroughly mystified; and the remote source of his defeat lies in the supposition that the Minister is a fool, because he has acquired renown as a poet. All fools are poets—this the Prefect *feels*; and he is merely guilty of a *non distributio medii* in thence inferring that all poets are fools.'

'But is this really the poet?' I asked. 'There are two brothers, I know; and both have attained reputation in letters. The Minister, I believe, has written learnedly on the Differential Calculus. He is a mathematician, and no poet.'

'You are mistaken; I know him well; he is both. As poet *and* mathematician, he would reason well; as mere mathematician, he could not have reasoned at all, and thus would have been at the mercy of the Prefect.'

'You surprise me,' I said, 'by these opinions, which have been contradicted by the voice of the world. You do not mean to set at naught the well-digested idea of centuries. The mathematical reason has long been regarded as *the* reason *par excellence*.'

'"*Il y a à parier*,"' replied Dupin, quoting from Chamfort, '"*que toute idée publique, toute convention reçue, est une sottise, car elle a convenue au plus grand nombre.*" The mathematicians, I grant you, have done their best to promulgate the popular error to which you allude, and which is none the less an error for its promulgation as truth. With an art worthy a better cause, for example, they have insinuated the term "analysis" into application to algebra. The French are the originators of this particular deception; but if a term is of any importance—if words derive any value from applicability— then "analysis" conveys "algebra" about as much as, in Latin, "*ambitus*" implies "ambition," "*religio*" "religion," or "*homines honesti*" a set of *honourable* men.'

'You have a quarrel on hand, I see,' said I, 'with some of the algebraists of Paris; but proceed.'

'I dispute the availability, and thus the value, of that reason which is cultivated in any especial form other than the abstractly logical. I dispute, in particular, the reason educed by mathematical study. The mathematics are the science of form and quantity; mathematical reasoning is merely logic applied to observation upon form and quantity. The great error lies in supposing that even the truths of what is called *pure* algebra, are abstract or general truths. And this error is so egregious that I am confounded at the universality with which it has been received. Mathematical axioms are *not* axioms of general truth. What is true of *relation*—of form and quantity—is often grossly false in regard to morals, for example. In this latter science it is very usually *un*true that the aggregated parts are equal to the whole. In chemistry also the axiom fails. In the consideration of motive it fails; for two motives, each of a given value, have not, necessarily, a value when united, equal to the sum of their values apart. There are numerous other mathematical truths which are only truths within the limits of *relation*. But the mathematician argues, from his *finite truths*, through habit, as if they were of an absolutely general applicability—as the world indeed imagines them to be. Bryant, in his very learned "Mythology", mentions an analogous source of error, when he says that "although the Pagan fables are not believed, yet we forget ourselves continually, and make inferences from them as existing realities". With the algebraists, however, who are Pagans themselves, the "Pagan fables" *are* believed, and the inferences are made, not so much through lapse of memory, as through an unaccountable addling of the brains. In short, I never yet encountered the mere mathematician who could be trusted out of equal roots, or one who did not clandestinely hold it as a point of his faith that $x^2 + px$ was absolutely and unconditionally equal to q. Say to one of these gentlemen, by way of experiment, if you please, that you believe occasions may occur where $x^2 + px$ is *not* altogether equal to q, and, having made him understand what you mean, get out of his reach as speedily as convenient, for, beyond doubt, he will endeavour to knock you down.

'I mean to say,' continued Dupin, while I merely laughed at his last observations, 'that if the Minister had been no more than a mathematician, the Prefect would have been under no necessity of giving me this cheque. I knew him, however, as both mathematician and poet, and my measures were adapted to his capacity, with reference to the circumstances by which he was surrounded. I knew him as a courtier, too, and as a bold *intriguant*. Such a man, I considered, could not fail to be aware of the ordinary policial modes of action. He could not have failed to anticipate—and events have proved that he did not fail to anticipate—the waylayings to which he was subjected. He must have foreseen, I reflected, the secret investigations of his premises. His frequent absences from home at night, which were hailed by the Prefect as certain aids to his success, I regarded only as ruses, to afford opportunity for thorough search to the police, and thus the sooner to impress them with the conviction to which G——, in fact, did finally arrive—the conviction that the letter was not upon the premises. I felt, also, that the whole train of thought, which I was at some pains in detailing to you just now, concerning the invariable principle of policial action in searches for articles concealed—I felt that this whole train of thought would necessarily pass through the mind of the Minister. It would imperatively lead him to despise all the ordinary *nooks* of concealment. *He* could not, I´reflected, be so weak as not to see that the most intricate and remote recess of his hotel would be as open as his commonest closets to the eyes, to the probes, to the gimlets, and to the microscopes of the Prefect. I saw, in fine, that he would be driven, as a matter of course, to *simplicity*, if not deliberately induced to it as a matter of choice. You will remember, perhaps, how desperately the Prefect laughed when I suggested, upon our first interview, that it was just possible this mystery troubled him so much on account of its being so *very* self-evident.'

'Yes,' said I, 'I remember his merriment well. I really thought he would have fallen into convulsions.'

'The material world,' continued Dupin, 'abounds with very strict analogies to the immaterial; and thus some colour of truth has been given to the rhetorical dogma, that metaphor, or simile, may be made to strengthen an argument, as well as to embellish a description. The principle of the *vis inertiæ*, for example, seems to be identical in physics and metaphysics. It is not more true in the former, that a large body is with more difficulty set in motion than a smaller one, and that its subsequent momentum is commensurate with this difficulty, than it is, in the latter, that intellects of the vaster capacity, while more forcible, more constant, and more eventful in their movements than those of inferior grade, are yet the less readily moved, and more embarrassed and full of hesitation in the first few steps of their progress. Again, have you ever noticed which of the street signs over the shop-doors are the most attractive of attention?'

'I have never given the matter a thought,' I said.

'There is a game of puzzles,' he resumed, 'which is played upon a map. One party playing requires another to find a given word—the name of town, river, state or empire—any word, in short, upon the motley and perplexed surface of the chart. A novice in the game generally seeks to embarrass his opponents by giving them the most minutely lettered names; but the adept selects such words as stretch, in large characters, from one end of the chart to the other. These, like the over-largely lettered signs and placards of the street, escape observation by dint of being excessively obvious; and here the physical oversight is precisely analogous with the moral inapprehension by which the intellect suffers to pass unnoticed those considerations which are too obtrusively and too palpably self-evident. But this is a point, it appears, somewhat above or beneath the understanding of the Prefect. He never once thought it probable, or possible, that the Minister had deposited the letter immediately beneath the nose of the whole world, by way of best preventing any portion of that world from perceiving it.

'But the more I reflected upon the daring, dashing, and discriminating ingenuity of D——; upon the fact that the document must always have been *at hand*, if he intended to use it to good purpose; and upon the decisive evidence, obtained by the Prefect, that it was not hidden within the limits of that dignitary's ordinary search—the more satisfied I became that, to conceal this letter, the Minister had resorted to the comprehensive and sagacious expedient of not attempting to conceal it at all.

'Full of these ideas, I prepared myself with a pair of green spectacles, and called one fine morning, quite by accident, at the Ministerial hotel. I found D—— at home, yawning, lounging, and dawdling, as usual, and pretending to be in the last extremity of ennui. He is, perhaps, the most really energetic human being now alive—but that is only when nobody sees him.

'To be even with him, I complained of my weak eyes, and lamented the necessity of the spectacles, under cover of which I cautiously and thoroughly surveyed the whole apartment, while seemingly intent only upon the conversation of my host.

'I paid especial attention to a large writing-table near which he sat, and upon which lay confusedly some miscellaneous letters and other papers, with one or two musical instruments and a few books. Here, however, after a long and very deliberate scrutiny, I saw nothing to excite particular suspicion.

'At length my eyes, in going the circuit of the room, fell upon a trumpery filigree card-rack of pasteboard, that hung dangling by a dirty blue ribbon, from a little brass knob just beneath the middle of the mantelpiece. In this rack, which had three or four compartments, were five or six visiting cards and a solitary letter. This last was much soiled and crumpled. It was torn nearly in two, across the middle—as if a design, in the first instance, to tear it entirely up as worthless, had been altered, or stayed, in the second. It had a large black seal, bearing the D—— cipher *very* conspicuously, and was addressed, in a diminutive female hand, to D——, the Minister, himself. It was thrust carelessly, and even, as it seemed, contemptuously, into one of the uppermost divisions of the rack.

'No sooner had I glanced at this letter, than I concluded it to be that of which I was in search. To be sure, it was, to all appearance, radically different from the one of which the Prefect had read us so minute a description. Here the seal was large and black, with the D—— cipher; there it was small and red, with the ducal arms of the S—— family. Here, the address, to the Minister, was diminutive and feminine; there the superscription, to a certain royal personage, was markedly bold and decided; the size alone formed a point of correspondence. But then the *radicalness* of these differences, which was excessive; the dirt; the soiled and torn condition of the paper, so inconsistent with the *true* methodical habits of D——, and so suggestive of a design to delude the beholder into an idea of the worthlessness of the document; these things, together with the hyperobtrusive situation of this document, full in the view of every visitor, and thus exactly in accordance with the conclusions to which I had previously arrived; these things, I say, were strongly corroborative of suspicion, in one who came with the intention to suspect.

'I protracted my visit as long as possible, and, while I maintained a most animated discussion with the Minister, upon a topic which I knew well had never failed to interest and excite him, I kept my attention really riveted upon the letter. In this examination, I committed to memory its external appearance and arrangement in the rack; and also fell, at length, upon a discovery, which set at rest whatever trivial doubt I might have entertained. In scrutinising the edges of the paper, I observed them to be more *chafed* than seemed necessary. They presented the *broken* appearance which is manifested when a stiff paper, having been once folded and pressed with a folder, is refolded in a reversed direction, in the same creases or edges which had formed the original fold. This discovery was sufficient. It was clear to me that the letter had been turned, as a glove, inside out, redirected and resealed. I bade the Minister goodmorning, and took my departure at once, leaving a gold snuff-box upon the table.

'The next morning I called for the snuff-box, when we resumed, quite eagerly, the conversation of the preceding day. While thus engaged, however, a loud report, as if of a pistol, was heard immediately beneath the windows of the hotel, and was succeeded by a series of fearful screams, and the shoutings of a terrified mob. D—— rushed to a casement, threw it open, and looked out. In the meantime, I stepped to the card-rack, took the letter, put it in my pocket, and replaced it by a facsimile (so far as regards externals) which I had carefully prepared at my lodgings—imitating the D—— cipher, very readily, by means of a seal formed of bread.

'The disturbance in the street had been occasioned by the frantic behaviour of a man with a musket. He had fired it among a crowd of women and children. It proved, however, to have been without ball, and the fellow was suffered to go his way as a lunatic or a drunkard. When he had gone, D—— came from the window, whither I had followed him immediately upon securing the object in view. Soon afterwards I bade him farewell. The pretended lunatic was a man in my own pay.'

'But what purpose had you,' I asked, 'in replacing the letter by a facsimile? Would it not have been better, at the first visit, to have seized it openly, and departed?'

'D——,' replied Dupin, 'is a desperate man, and a man of nerve. His hotel, too, is not without attendants devoted to his interests. Had I made the wild attempt you suggest, I might never have left the Ministerial presence alive. The good people of Paris might have heard of me no more. But I had an object apart from these considerations. You know my political prepossessions. In this matter, I act as a partisan of the lady concerned. For eighteen months the Minister has had her in his power. She has now him in hers—since, being unaware that the letter is not in his possession, he will proceed with his exactions as if it was. Thus will he inevitably commit himself, at once, to his political destruction. His downfall, too, will not be more precipitate than awkward. It is all very well to talk about the *facilis descensus Averni*; but in all kinds of climbing, as Catalani said of singing, it is far more easy to get up than to come down. In the present instance I have no sympathy—at least no pity—for him who descends. He is that *monstrum horrendum*, an unprincipled man of genius. I confess, however, that I should like very well to know the precise character of his thoughts, when, being defied by her whom the Prefect terms "a certain personage", he is reduced to opening the letter which I left for him in the card-rack.'

'How? did you put anything particular in it?'

'Why—it did not seem altogether right to leave the interior blank—that would have been insulting. D——, at Vienna once, did me an evil turn, which I told him, quite good-humouredly, that I should remember. So, as I knew he would feel some curiosity in regard to the identity of the person who had outwitted him, I thought it a pity not to give him a clue. He is well acquainted with my MS, and I just copied into the middle of the blank sheet the words:

'"—— Un dessein si funeste,
S'il n'est digne d'Atrée, est digne de Thyeste."

They are to be found in Crébillon's "Atrée."''

The Murdered Cousin

J. S. LE FANU

And they lay wait for their own blood: they lurk privily for their own lives.
So are the ways of every one that is greedy for gain; which taketh away the life of the owner thereof.

This story of the Irish peerage is written, as nearly as possible, in the very words in which it was related by its 'heroine', the late Countess D——, and is therefore told in the first person.

My mother died when I was an infant, and of her I have no recollection, even the faintest. By her death my education was left solely to the direction of my surviving parent. He entered upon his task with a stern appreciation of the responsibility thus cast upon him. My religious instruction was prosecuted with an almost exaggerated anxiety; and I had, of course, the best masters to perfect me in all those accomplishments which my station and wealth might seem to require. My father was what is called an oddity, and his treatment of me, though uniformly kind, was governed less by affection and tenderness, than by a high and unbending sense of duty. Indeed I seldom saw or spoke to him except at mealtimes, and then, though gentle, he was usually reserved and gloomy. His leisure hours, which were many, were passed either in his study or in solitary walks; in short, he seemed to take no further interest in my happiness or improvement, than a conscientious regard to the discharge of his own duty would seem to impose.

Shortly before my birth an event occurred which had contributed much to induce and to confirm my father's unsocial habits; it was the fact that a suspicion of *murder* had fallen upon his younger brother, though not sufficiently definite to lead to any public proceedings, yet strong enough to ruin him in public opinion. This disgraceful and dreadful doubt cast upon the family name, my father felt deeply and bitterly, and not the less so that he himself was thoroughly convinced of his brother's innocence. The sincerity and strength of this conviction he shortly afterwards proved in a manner which produced the catastrophe of my story.

Before, however, I enter upon my immediate adventures, I ought to relate the circumstances which had awakened that suspicion to which I have referred, inasmuch as they are in themselves somewhat curious, and in their effects most intimately connected with my own after-history.

My uncle, Sir Arthur Tyrrell, was a gay and extravagant man, and, among other vices, was ruinously addicted to gaming. This unfortunate propensity, even after his fortune had suffered so severely as to render retrenchment imperative, nevertheless continued to engross him, nearly to the exclusion of every other pursuit. He was, however, a proud, or rather a vain man, and could not bear to make the diminution of his income a matter of triumph to those with whom he had hitherto competed; and the consequence was, that he frequented no longer the expensive haunts of his dissipation, and retired from the gay world, leaving his coterie to discover his reasons as best they might. He did not, however, forego his favourite vice, for though he could not worship his great divinity in those costly temples where he was formerly wont to take his place, yet he found it very possible to bring about him a sufficient number of the votaries of chance to answer all his ends. The consequence was, that Carrickleigh, which was the name of my uncle's residence, was never without one or more of such visitors as I have described. It happened that upon one occasion he was visited by one Hugh Tisdall, a gentleman of loose, and, indeed, low habits, but of considerable wealth, and who had, in early youth, travelled with my uncle upon the Continent. The period of this visit was winter, and, consequently, the house was nearly deserted excepting by its ordinary inmates; it was, therefore, highly acceptable, particularly as my uncle was aware that his visitor's tastes accorded exactly with his own.

Both parties seemed determined to avail themselves of their mutual suitability during the brief stay which Mr Tisdall had promised; the consequence was, that they shut themselves up in Sir Arthur's private room for nearly all the day and the greater part of the night, during the space of almost a week, at the end of which the servant having one morning, as usual, knocked at Mr Tisdall's bedroom door repeatedly, received no answer, and, upon attempting to enter, found that it was locked. This appeared suspicious, and the inmates of the house having been alarmed, the door was forced open, and, on proceeding to the bed, they found the body of its occupant perfectly lifeless, and hanging halfway out, the head downwards, and near the floor. One deep wound had been inflicted upon the temple, apparently with some blunt instrument, which had penetrated the brain, and another blow, less effective—probably the first aimed— had grazed his head, removing some of the scalp. The door had been double locked upon the *inside*, in evidence of which the key still lay where it had been placed in the lock. The window, though not secured on the interior, was closed; a circumstance not a little puzzling, as it afforded the only other mode of escape from the room. It looked out, too, upon a kind of courtyard, round which the old buildings stood, formerly accessible by a narrow doorway and passage lying in the oldest side of the quadrangle, but which had since been built up, so as to preclude all ingress or egress; the room was also upon the second storey, and the height of the window considerable; in addition to all which the stone window-sill was much too narrow to allow of any one's standing upon it when the window was closed. Near the bed were found a pair of razors belonging to the murdered man, one of them upon the ground, and both of them open. The weapon which inflicted the mortal wound was not to be found in the room, nor were any footprints or other traces of the murderer discoverable. At the suggestion of Sir Arthur himself, the coroner was instantly summoned to attend, and an inquest was held. Nothing, however, in any degree conclusive was elicited. The walls, ceiling, and floor of the room were carefully examined, in order to ascertain whether they contained a trapdoor or other concealed mode of entrance, but no such thing appeared. Such was the minuteness of investigation employed, that, although the grate had contained a large fire during the night, they proceeded to examine even the very chimney, in order to discover whether escape by it were possible. But this attempt, too, was fruitless, for the chimney, built in the old fashion, rose in a perfectly perpendicular line from the hearth, to a height of nearly fourteen feet above the roof, affording in its interior scarcely the possibility of ascent, the flue being smoothly plastered, and sloping towards the top like an inverted funnel; promising, too, even if the summit were attained, owing to its great height, but a precarious descent upon the sharp and steep-ridged roof; the ashes, too, which lay in the grate, and the soot, as far as it could be seen, were undisturbed, a circumstance almost conclusive upon the point.

Sir Arthur was of course, examined. His evidence was given with clearness and unreserve, which seemed calculated to silence all suspicion. He stated that, up to the day and night immediately preceding the catastrophe, he had lost to a heavy amount, but that, at their last sitting, he had not only won back his original loss, but upwards of £4,000 in addition; in evidence of which he produced an acknowledgement of debt to that amount in the handwriting of the deceased, bearing date the night of the catastrophe. He had mentioned the circumstance to Lady Tyrrell, and in presence of some of his domestics; which statement was supported by *their* respective evidence. One of the jury shrewdly observed, that the circumstance of Mr Tisdall's having sustained so heavy a loss might have suggested to some ill-minded persons, accidentally hearing it, the plan of robbing him, after having murdered him in such a manner as might make it appear that he had committed suicide; a supposition which was strongly supported by the razors having been found thus displaced and removed from their case. Two persons had probably been engaged in the attempt, one watching by the sleeping man, and ready to strike him in case of his awakening suddenly, while the other was procuring the razors and employed in inflicting the fatal gash, so as to make it appear to have been the act of the murdered man himself. It was said that while the juror was making this suggestion Sir Arthur changed colour. There was nothing, however, like legal evidence to implicate him, and the consequence was that the verdict was found against a person or persons unknown, and for some time the matter was suffered to rest, until, after about five months, my father received a letter from a person signing himself Andrew Collis, and representing himself to be the cousin of the deceased. This letter stated that his brother, Sir Arthur, was likely to incur not merely suspicion but personal risk, unless he could account for certain circumstances connected with the recent murder, and contained a copy of a letter written by the deceased, and dated the very day upon the night of which the murder had been perpetrated. Tisdall's letter contained, among a great deal of other matter, the passages which follow:

I have had sharp work with Sir Arthur: he tried some of his stale tricks, but soon found that *I* was Yorkshire, too; it would not do—you understand me. We went to the work like good ones, head, heart, and soul; and in fact, since I came here, I have lost no time. I am rather fagged, but I am sure to be well paid for my hardship; I never want sleep so long as I can have the music of a dice-box, and wherewithal to pay the piper. As I told you, he tried some of his queer turns, but I foiled him like a man, and, in return, gave him more than he could relish of the genuine *dead knowledge*. In short, I have plucked the old baronet as never baronet was plucked before; I have scarce left him the stump of a quill. I have got promissory notes in his hand to the amount of——; if you like round numbers, say five-and-twenty thousand pounds, safely deposited in my portable strong box, alias, double-clasped pocket-book. I leave this ruinous old rat-hole early on tomorrow, for two reasons: first, I do not want to play with Sir Arthur deeper than I think his security would warrant; and, secondly, because I am safer a hundred miles away from Sir Arthur than in the house with him. Look you, my worthy, I tell you this between ourselves—I may be wrong—but, by ——, I am sure as that I am now living, that Sir A—— attempted to poison me last night. So much for old friendship on both sides. When I won the last stake, a heavy one enough, my friend leant his forehead upon his hands, and you'll laugh when I tell you that his head literally smoked like a hot dumpling. I do not know whether his agitation was produced by the plan which he had against me, or by his having lost so heavily; though it must be allowed that he had reason to be a little funked, whichever way his thoughts went; but he pulled the bell, and ordered two bottles of Champagne. While the fellow was bringing them, he wrote a promissory note to the full amount, which he signed, and, as the man came in with the bottles and glasses, he desired him to be off. He filled a glass for me, and, while he thought my eyes were off, for I was putting up his note at the time, he dropped something slyly into it, no doubt to sweeten it; but I saw it all, and, when he handed it to me, I said, with an emphasis which he might easily understand, 'There is some sediment in it, I'll not drink it.' 'Is there?' said he, and at the same time snatched it from my hand and threw it into the fire. What do you think of that? Have I not a tender bird in hand? Win or lose, I will not play beyond five thousand tonight, and tomorrow sees me safe out of the reach of Sir Arthur's Champagne.

Of the authenticity of this document, I never heard my father express a doubt; and I am satisfied that, owing to his strong conviction in favour of his brother, he would not have admitted it without sufficient inquiry, inasmuch as it tended to confirm the suspicions which already existed to his prejudice. Now, the only point in this letter which made strongly against my uncle, was the mention of the 'double-clasped pocket-book', as the receptacle of the papers likely to involve him, for this pocket-book was not forthcoming, nor anywhere to be found, nor had any papers referring to his gaming transactions been discovered upon the dead man.

But whatever might have been the original intention of this man, Collis, neither my uncle nor my father ever heard more of him; he published the letter, however, in Faulkner's newspaper, which was shortly afterwards made the vehicle of a much more mysterious attack. The passage in that journal to which I allude, appeared about four years afterwards, and while the fatal occurrence was still fresh in public recollection. It commenced by a rambling preface, stating that 'a *certain person* whom *certain* persons thought to be dead, was not so, but living, and in full possession of his memory, and moreover, ready and able to make *great* delinquents tremble': it then went on to describe the murder, without, however, mentioning names; and in doing so, it entered into minute and circumstantial particulars of which none but an *eyewitness* could have been possessed, and by implications almost too unequivocal to be regarded in the light of insinuation, to involve the '*titled gambler*' in the guilt of the transaction.

My father at once urged Sir Arthur to proceed against the paper in an action of libel, but he would not hear of it, nor consent to my father's taking any legal steps whatever in the matter. My father, however, wrote in a threatening tone to Faulkner, demanding a surrender of the author of the obnoxious article; the answer to this application is still in my possession, and is penned in an apologetic tone: it states that the manuscript had been handed in, paid for, and inserted as an advertisement, without sufficient enquiry, or any knowledge as to whom it referred. No step, however, was taken to clear my uncle's character in the judgement of the public; and, as he immediately sold a small property, the application of the proceeds of which were known to none, he was said to have disposed of it to enable himself to buy off the threatened information; however the truth might have been, it is certain that no charges respecting the mysterious murder were afterwards publicly made against my uncle, and, as far as external disturbances were concerned, he enjoyed henceforward perfect security and quiet.

A deep and lasting impression, however, had been made upon the public mind, and Sir Arthur Tyrrell was no longer visited or noticed by the gentry of the county, whose attentions he had hitherto received.

He accordingly affected to despise those courtesies which he no longer enjoyed, and shunned even that society which he might have commanded. This is all that I need recapitulate of my uncle's history, and I now recur to my own.

Although my father had never, within my recollection, visited, or been visited by my uncle, each being of unsocial, procrastinating, and indolent habits, and their respective residences being very far apart— the one lying in the county of Galway, the other in that of Cork—he was strongly attached to his brother, and evinced his affection by an active correspondence, and by deeply and proudly resenting that neglect which had branded Sir Arthur as unfit to mix in society.

When I was about eighteen years of age, my father, whose health had been gradually declining, died, leaving me in heart wretched and desolate, and, owing to his habitual seclusion, with few acquaintances, and almost no friends. The provisions of his will were curious, and when I was sufficiently come to myself to listen to, or comprehend them, surprised me not a little: all his vast property was left to me, and to the heirs of my body, for ever; and, in default of such heirs, it was to go after my death to my uncle, Sir Arthur, without any entail. At the same time, the will appointed him my guardian, desiring that I might be received within his house, and reside with his family, and under his care, during the term of my minority; and in consideration of the increased expense consequent upon such an arrangement, a handsome allowance was allotted to him during the term of my proposed residence. The object of this last provision I at once understood; my father desired, by making it the direct apparent interest of Sir Arthur that I should die without issue, while at the same time he placed my person wholly in his power, to prove to the world how great and unshaken was his confidence in his brother's innocence and honour. It was a strange, perhaps an idle scheme, but as I had been always brought up in the habit of considering my uncle as a deeply injured man, and had been taught, almost as a part of my religion, to regard him as the very soul of honour, I felt no further uneasiness respecting the arrangement than that likely to affect a shy and timid girl at the immediate prospect of taking up her abode for the first time in her life among strangers. Previous to leaving my home, which I felt I should do with a heavy heart, I received a most tender and affectionate letter from my uncle, calculated, if anything could do so, to remove the bitterness of parting from scenes familiar and dear from my earliest childhood, and in some degree to reconcile me to the measure. It was upon a fine autumn day that I approached the old domain of Carrickleigh. I shall not soon forget the impression of sadness and of gloom which all that I saw produced upon my mind; the sunbeams were falling with a rich and melancholy lustre upon the fine old trees, which stood in lordly groups, casting their long sweeping shadows over rock and sward; there was an air of neglect and decay about the spot, which amounted almost to desolation, and mournfully increased as we approached the building itself, near which the ground had been originally more artificially and carefully cultivated than elsewhere, and where consequently neglect more immediately and strikingly betrayed itself.

As we proceeded, the road wound near the beds of what had been formerly two fish-ponds, which were now nothing more than stagnant swamps, overgrown with rank weeds, and here and there encroached upon by the straggling underwood; the avenue itself was much broken; and in many places the stones were almost concealed by grass and nettles; the loose stone walls which had here and there intersected the broad park, were, in many places, broken down, so as no longer to answer their original purpose as fences; piers were now and then to be seen, but the gates were gone; and to add to the general air of dilapidation, some huge trunks were lying scattered through the venerable old trees, either the work of the winter storms, or perhaps the victims of some extensive but desultory scheme of denudation, which the projector had not capital or perseverance to carry into full effect.

After the carriage had travelled a full mile of this avenue, we reached the summit of a rather abrupt eminence, one of the many which added to the picturesqueness, if not to the convenience of this rude approach; from the top of this ridge the grey walls of Carrickleigh were visible, rising at a small distance in front, and darkened by the hoary wood which crowded around them; it was a quadrangular building of considerable extent, and the front, where the great entrance was placed, lay towards us, and bore unequivocal marks of antiquity; the time-worn, solemn aspect of the old building, the ruinous and deserted appearance of the whole place, and the associations which connected it with a dark page in the history of my family, combined to depress spirits already predisposed for the reception of sombre and dejecting impressions. When the carriage drew up in the grass-grown courtyard before the hall-door, two lazy-looking men, whose appearance well accorded with that of the place which they tenanted, alarmed by the obstreperous barking of a great chained dog, ran out from some half-ruinous outhouses, and took charge of the horses; the hall-door stood open, and I entered a gloomy and imperfectly lighted apartment, and found no one within it. However, I had not long to wait in this awkward predicament, for before my luggage had been deposited in the house, indeed before I had well removed my cloak and other muffles, so as to enable me to look around, a young girl ran lightly into the hall, and kissing me heartily and somewhat boisterously exclaimed, 'My dear cousin, my dear Margaret—I am so delighted—so out of breath, we did not expect you till ten o'clock; my father is somewhere about the place, he must be close at hand. James—Corney—run out and tell your master; my brother is seldom at home, at least at any reasonable hour; you must be so tired—so fatigued—let me show you to your room; see that Lady Margaret's luggage is all brought up; you must lie down and rest yourself. Deborah, bring some coffee—up these stairs; we are so delighted to see you—you cannot think how lonely I have been; how steep these stairs are, are not they? I am so glad you are come—I could hardly bring myself to believe that you were really coming; how good of you, dear Lady Margaret.' There was real good nature and delight in my cousin's greeting, and a kind of constitutional confidence of manner which placed me at once at ease, and made me feel immediately upon terms of intimacy with her. The room into which she ushered me, although partaking in the general air of decay which pervaded the mansion and all about it, had, nevertheless, been fitted up with evident attention to comfort, and even with some dingy attempt at luxury; but what pleased me most was that it opened, by a second door, upon a lobby which communicated with my fair cousin's apartment; a circumstance which divested the room, in my eyes, of the air of solitude and sadness which would otherwise have characterized it, to a degree almost painful to one so depressed and agitated as I was.

After such arrangements as I found necessary were completed, we both went down to the parlour, a large wainscotted room, hung round with grim old portraits, and, as I was not sorry to see, containing, in its ample grate, a large and cheerful fire. Here my cousin had leisure to talk more at her ease; and from her I learned something of the manners and the habits of the two remaining members of her family, whom I had not yet seen. On my arrival I had known nothing of the family among whom I was come to reside, except that it consisted of three individuals, my uncle, and his son and daughter, Lady Tyrrell having been long dead; in addition to this very scanty stock of information, I shortly learned from my communicative companion, that my uncle was, as I had suspected, completely retired in his habits, and besides that, having been, so far back as she could well recollect, always rather strict, as reformed rakes frequently become, he had latterly been growing more gloomily and sternly religious than heretofore. Her account of her brother was far less favourable, though she did not say anything directly to his disadvantage. From all that I could gather from her, I was led to suppose that he was a specimen of the idle, coarse-mannered, profligate '*squirearchy*'—a result which might naturally have followed from the circumstance of his being, as it were, outlawed from society, and driven for companionship to grades below his own—enjoying, too, the dangerous prerogative of spending a good deal of money. However, you may easily suppose that I found nothing in my cousin's communication fully to bear me out in so very decided a conclusion.

I awaited the arrival of my uncle, which was every moment to be expected, with feelings half of alarm, half of curiosity—a sensation which I have often since experienced, though to a less degree, when upon the point of standing for the first time in the presence of one of whom I have long been in the habit of hearing or thinking with interest. It was, therefore, with some little perturbation that I heard, first a slight bustle at the outer door, then a slow step traverse the hall, and finally witnessed the door open, and my uncle enter the room. He was a striking looking man; from peculiarities both of person and of dress, the whole effect of his appearance amounted to extreme singularity. He was tall, and when young his figure must have been strikingly elegant; as it was, however, its effect was marred by a very decided stoop; his dress was of a sober colour, and in fashion anterior to any thing which I could remember. It was, however, handsome, and by no means carelessly put on; but what completed the singularity of his appearance was his uncut, white hair, which hung in long, but not at all neglected curls, even so far as his shoulders, and which combined with his regularly classic features, and fine dark eyes, to bestow upon him an air of venerable dignity and pride, which I have seldom seen equalled elsewhere. I rose as he entered, and met him about the middle of the room; he kissed my cheek and both my hands, saying—

'You are most welcome, dear child, as welcome as the command of this poor place and all that it contains can make you. I am rejoiced to see you—truly rejoiced. I trust that you are not much fatigued; pray be seated again.' He led me to my chair, and continued, 'I am glad to perceive you have made acquaintance with Emily already; I see, in your being thus brought together, the foundation of a lasting friendship. You are both innocent, and both young. God bless you—God bless you, and make you all that I could wish.'

He raised his eyes, and remained for a few moments silent, as if in secret prayer. I felt that it was impossible that this man, with feelings manifestly so tender, could be the wretch that public opinion had represented him to be. I was more than ever convinced of his innocence. His manners were, or appeared to me, most fascinating. I know not how the lights of experience might have altered this estimate. But I was then very young, and I beheld in him a perfect mingling of the courtesy of polished life with the gentlest and most genial virtues of the heart. A feeling of affection and respect towards him began to spring up within me, the more earnest that I remembered how sorely he had suffered in fortune and how cruelly in fame. My uncle having given me fully to understand that I was most welcome, and might command whatever was his own, pressed me to take some supper; and on my refusing, he observed that, before bidding me good-night, he had one duty further to perform, one in which he was convinced I would cheerfully acquiesce. He then proceeded to read a chapter from the Bible; after which he took his leave with the same affectionate kindness with which he had greeted me, having repeated his desire that I should consider everything in his house as altogether at my disposal. It is needless to say how much I was pleased with my uncle—it was impossible to avoid being so; and I could not help saying to myself, if such a man as this is not safe from the assaults of slander, who is? I felt much happier than I had done since my father's death, and enjoyed that night the first refreshing sleep which had visited me since that calamity. My curiosity respecting my male cousin did not long remain unsatisfied; he appeared upon the next day at dinner. His manners, though not so coarse as I had expected, were exceedingly disagreeable; there was an assurance and a forwardness for which I was not prepared; there was less of the vulgarity of manner, and almost more of that of the mind, than I had anticipated. I felt quite uncomfortable in his presence; there was just that confidence in his look and tone, which would read encouragement even in mere toleration; and I felt more disgusted and annoyed at the coarse and extravagant compliments which he was pleased from time to time to pay me, than perhaps the extent of the atrocity might fully have warranted. It was, however, one consolation that he did not often appear, being much engrossed by pursuits about which I neither knew nor cared anything; but when he did, his attentions, either with a view to his amusement, or to some more serious object, were so obviously and perseveringly directed to me, that young and inexperienced as I was, even *I* could not be ignorant of their significance. I felt more provoked by this odious persecution than I can express, and discouraged him with so much vigour, that I did not stop even at rudeness to convince him that his assiduities were unwelcome; but all in vain.

This had gone on for nearly a twelvemonth, to my infinite annoyance, when one day, as I was sitting at some needlework with my companion, Emily, as was my habit, in the parlour, the door opened, and my cousin Edward entered the room. There was something, I thought, odd in his manner, a kind of struggle between shame and impudence, a kind of flurry and ambiguity, which made him appear, if possible, more than ordinarily disagreeable.

'Your servant, ladies,' he said, seating himself at the same time; 'sorry to spoil your tête-à-tête; but never mind, I'll only take Emily's place for a minute or two, and then we part for a while, fair cousin. Emily, my father wants you in the corner turret; no shilly, shally, he's in a hurry.' She hesitated. 'Be off—tramp, march, I say,' he exclaimed, in a tone which the poor girl dared not disobey.

She left the room, and Edward followed her to the door. He stood there for a minute or two, as if reflecting what he should say, perhaps satisfying himself that no one was within hearing in the hall. At length he turned about, having closed the door, as if carelessly, with his foot, and advancing slowly, in deep thought, he took his seat at the side of the table opposite to mine. There was a brief interval of silence, after which he said:

'I imagine that you have a shrewd suspicion of the object of my early visit; but I suppose I must go into particulars. Must I?'

'I have no conception,' I replied, 'what your object may be.'

'Well, well,' said he becoming more at his ease as he proceeded, 'it may be told in a few words. You know that it is totally impossible, quite out of the question, that an off-hand young fellow like me, and a good-looking girl like yourself, could meet continually as you and I have done, without an attachment—a liking growing up on one side or other; in short, I think I have let you know as plainly as if I spoke it, that I have been in love with you, almost from the first time I saw you.' He paused, but I was too much horrified to speak. He interpreted my silence favourably. 'I can tell you,' he continued, 'I'm reckoned rather hard to please, and very hard to *hit*. I can't say when I was taken with a girl before, so you see fortune reserved me——.'

Here the odious wretch actually put his arm round my waist: the action at once restored me to utterance, and with the most indignant vehemence I released myself from his hold, and at the same time said:

'I *have*, sir, of course, perceived your most disagreeable attentions; they have long been a source of great annoyance to me; and you must be aware that I have marked my disapprobation, my disgust, as unequivocally as I possibly could, without actual indelicacy.'

I paused, almost out of breath from the rapidity with which I had spoken; and without giving him time to renew the conversation, I hastily quitted the room, leaving him in a paroxysm of rage and mortification. As I ascended the stairs, I heard him open the parlour-door with violence, and take two or three rapid strides in the direction in which I was moving. I was now much frightened, and ran the whole way until I reached my room, and having locked the door, I listened breathlessly, but heard no sound. This relieved me for the present; but so much had I been overcome by the agitation and annoyance attendant upon the scene which I had just passed through, that when my cousin Emily knocked at the door, I was weeping in great agitation. You will readily conceive my distress, when you reflect upon my strong dislike to my cousin Edward, combined with my youth and extreme inexperience. Any proposal of such a nature must have agitated me; but that it should come from the man whom, of all others, I instinctively most loathed and abhorred, and to whom I had, as clearly as manner could do it, expressed the state of my feelings, was almost too annoying to be borne; it was a calamity, too, in which I could not claim the sympathy of my cousin Emily, which had always been extended to me in my minor grievances. Still I hoped that it might not be unattended with good; for I thought that one inevitable and most welcome consequence would result from this painful *éclaircissement*, in the discontinuance of my cousin's odious persecution.

When I arose next morning, it was with the fervent hope that I might never again behold his face, or even hear his name; but such a consummation, though devoutedly to be wished, was hardly likely to occur. The painful impressions of yesterday were too vivid to be at once erased; and I could not help feeling some dim foreboding of coming annoyance and evil. To expect on my cousin's part anything like delicacy or consideration for me, was out of the question. I saw that he had set his heart upon my property, and that he was not likely easily to forego such a prize, possessing what might have been considered opportunities and facilities almost to compel my compliance. I now keenly felt the unreasonableness of my father's conduct in placing me to reside with a family, with all the members of which, with one exception, he was wholly unacquainted, and I bitterly felt the helplessness of my situation. I determined, however, in the event of my cousin's persevering in his addresses, to lay all the particulars before my uncle, although he had never, in kindness or intimacy, gone a step beyond our first interview, and to throw myself upon his hospitality and his sense of honour for protection against a repetition of such annoyances.

My cousin's conduct may appear to have been an inadequate cause for such serious uneasiness; but my alarm was awakened neither by his acts nor by words, but entirely by his manner, which was strange and even intimidating. At the beginning of our yesterday's interview, there was a sort of bullying swagger in his air, which, towards the end, gave place to something bordering upon the brutal vehemence of an undisguised ruffian, a transition which had tempted me into a belief that he might seek, even forcibly, to extort from me a consent to his wishes, or by means still more horrible, of which I scarcely dared to trust myself to think, to possess himself of my property.

I was early next day summoned to attend my uncle in his private room, which lay in a corner turret of the old building; and thither I accordingly went, wondering all the way what this unusual measure might prelude. When I entered the room, he did not rise in his usual courteous way to greet me, but simply pointed to a chair opposite to his own; this boded nothing agreeable. I sat down, however, silently waiting until he should open the conversation.

'Lady Margaret,' at length he said, in a tone of greater sternness than I thought him capable of using, 'I have hitherto spoken to you as a friend, but I have not forgotten that I am also your guardian, and that my authority as such gives me a right to control your conduct. I shall put a question to you, and I expect and will demand a plain, direct answer. Have I rightly been informed that you have contemptuously rejected the suit and hand of my son Edward?'

I stammered forth with a good deal of trepidation:

'I believe, that is, I have, sir, rejected my cousin's proposals; and my coldness and discouragement might have convinced him that I had determined to do so.'

'Madame,' replied he, with suppressed, but, as it appeared to me, intense anger, 'I have lived long enough to know that *coldness and discouragement*, and such terms, form the comon cant of a worthless coquette. You know to the full, as well as I, that *coldness and discouragement* may be so exhibited as to convince their object that he is neither distasteful nor indifferent to the person who wears that manner. You know, too, none better, that an affected neglect, when skilfully managed, is amongst the most formidable of the allurements which artful beauty can employ. I tell you, madame, that having, without one word spoken in discouragement, permitted my son's most marked attentions for a twelvemonth or more, you have no *right* to dismiss him with no further explanation than demurely telling him that you had always looked coldly upon him, and neither your wealth nor *your ladyship* (there was an emphasis of scorn on the word which would have become Sir Giles Overreach himself) can warrant you in treating with contempt the affectionate regard of an honest heart.'

I was too much shocked at this undisguised attempt to bully me into an acquiescence in the interested and unprincipled plan for their own aggrandisement, which I now perceived my uncle and his son had deliberately formed, at once to find strength or collectedness to frame an answer to what he had said. At length I replied, with a firmness that surprised myself:

'In all that you have just now said, sir, you have grossly misstated my conduct and motives. Your information must have been most incorrect, as far as it regards my conduct towards my cousin; my manner towards him could have conveyed nothing but dislike; and if anything could have added to the strong aversion which I have long felt towards him, it would be his attempting thus to frighten me into a marriage which he knows to be revolting to me, and which is sought by him only as a means for securing to himself whatever property is mine.'

As I said this, I fixed my eyes upon those of my uncle, but he was too old in the world's ways to falter beneath the gaze of more searching eyes than mine; he simply said—

'Are you acquainted with the provisions of your father's will?'

I answered in the affirmative; and he continued: 'Then you must be aware that if my son Edward were, which God forbid, the un-principled, reckless man, the ruffian you pretend to think him'— (here he spoke very slowly, as if he intended that every word which escaped him should be registered in my memory, while at the same time the expression of his countenance underwent a gradual but horrible change, and the eyes which he fixed upon me became so darkly vivid, that I almost lost sight of everything else)—'if he were what you have described him, do you think, child, he would have found no shorter way than marriage to gain his ends? A single blow, an outrage not a degree worse than you insinuate, would transfer your property to us!!'

I stood staring at him for many minutes after he had ceased to speak, fascinated by the terrible, serpent-like gaze, until he continued with a welcome change of countenance:

'I will not speak again to you, upon this topic, until one month has passed. You shall have time to consider the relative advantages of the two courses which are open to you. I should be sorry to hurry you to a decision. I am satisfied with having stated my feelings upon the subject, and pointed out to you the path of duty. Remember this day month; not one word sooner.'

He then rose, and I left the room, much agitated and exhausted.

This interview, all the circumstances attending it, but most par-ticularly the formidable expression of my uncle's countenance while he talked, though hypothetically, of *murder*, combined to arouse all my worst suspicions of him. I dreaded to look upon the face that had so recently worn the appalling livery of guilt and malignity. I regarded it with the mingled fear and loathing with which one looks upon an object which has tortured them in a nightmare.

In a few days after the interview, the particulars of which I have just detailed, I found a note upon my toilet-table, and on opening it I read as follows:

My Dear Lady Margaret,

You will be, perhaps, surprised to see a strange face in your room today. I have dismissed your Irish maid, and secured a French one to wait upon you; a step rendered necessary by my proposing shortly to visit the Continent with all my family.

Your faithful guardian,
ARTHUR TYRELL.

On enquiry, I found that my faithful attendant was actually gone, and far on her way to the town of Galway; and in her stead there appeared a tall, raw-boned, ill-looking, elderly Frenchwoman, whose sullen and presuming manners seemed to imply that her vocation had never before been that of a lady's-maid. I could not help regarding her as a creature of my uncle's, and therefore to be dreaded, even had she been in no other way suspicious.

Days and weeks passed away without any, even a momentary doubt upon my part, as to the course to be pursued by me. The allotted period had at length elapsed; the day arrived upon which I was to communicate my decision to my uncle. Although my resolution had never for a moment wavered, I could not shake off the dread of the approaching colloquy; and my heart sank within me as I heard the expected summons. I had not seen my cousin Edward since the occurrence of the grand *éclaircissement*; he must have studiously avoided me; I suppose from policy, it could not have been from delicacy. I was prepared for a terrific burst of fury from my uncle, as soon as I should make known my determination; and I not unreasonably feared that some act of violence or of intimidation would next be resorted to. Filled with these dreary forebodings, I fearfully opened the study door, and the next minute I stood in my uncle's presence. He received me with a courtesy which I dreaded, as arguing a favourable anticipation respecting the answer which I was to give; and after some slight delay he began by saying—

'It will be a relief to both of us, I believe, to bring this conversation as soon as possible to an issue. You will excuse me, then, my dear niece, for speaking with a bluntness which, under other circumstances, would be unpardonable. You have, I am certain, given the subject of our last interview fair and serious consideration; and I trust that you are now prepared with candour to lay your answer before me. A few words will suffice; we perfectly understand one another.'

He paused; and I, though feeling that I stood upon a mine which might in an instant explode, nevertheless answered with perfect composure: 'I must now, sir, make the same reply which I did upon the last occasion, and I reiterate the declaration which I then made, that I never can nor will, while life and reason remain, consent to a union with my cousin Edward.'

This announcement wrought no apparent change in Sir Arthur, except that he became deadly, almost lividly pale. He seemed lost in dark thought for a minute, and then, with a slight effort, said, 'You have answered me honestly and directly; and you say your resolution is unchangeable; well, would it had been otherwise—would it had been otherwise—but be it as it is; I am satisfied.'

He gave me his hand—it was cold and damp as death; under an assumed calmness, it was evident that he was fearfully agitated. He continued to hold my hand with an almost painful pressure, while, as if unconsciously, seeming to forget my presence, he muttered, 'Strange, strange, strange, indeed! fatuity, helpless fatuity!' there was here a long pause. 'Madness *indeed* to strain a cable that is rotten to the very heart; it must break—and then—all goes.' There was again a pause of some minutes, after which, suddenly changing his voice and manner to one of wakeful alacrity, he exclaimed,

'Margaret, my son Edward shall plague you no more. He leaves this country tomorrow for France; he shall speak no more upon this subject—never, never more; whatever events depended upon your answer must now take their own course; but as for this fruitless proposal, it has been tried enough; it can be repeated no more.'

At these words he coldly suffered my hand to drop, as if to express his total abandonment of all his projected schemes of alliance; and certainly the action, with the accompanying words, produced upon my mind a more solemn and depressing effect than I believed possible to have been caused by the course which I had determined to pursue; it struck upon my heart with an awe and heaviness which *will* accompany the accomplishment of an important and irrevocable act, even though no doubt or scruple remains to make it possible that the agent should wish it undone.

'Well,' said my uncle, after a little time, 'we now cease to speak upon this topic, never to resume it again. Remember you shall have no further uneasiness from Edward; he leaves Ireland for France tomorrow; this will be a relief to you; may I depend upon your *honour* that no word touching the subject of this interview shall ever escape you?' I gave him the desired assurance; he said, 'It is well; I am satisfied; we have nothing more, I believe, to say upon either side, and my presence must be a restraint upon you, I shall therefore bid you farewell.' I then left the apartment, scarcely knowing what to think of the strange interview which had just taken place.

On the next day my uncle took occasion to tell me that Edward had actually sailed, if his intention had not been prevented by adverse winds or weather; and two days after he actually produced a letter from his son, written, as it said, *on board*, and despatched while the ship was getting under way. This was a great satisfaction to me, and as being likely to prove so, it was no doubt communicated to me by Sir Arthur.

During all this trying period I had found infinite consolation in the society and sympathy of my dear cousin Emily. I never, in after-life, formed a friendship so close, so fervent, and upon which, in all its progress, I could look back with feelings of such unalloyed pleasure, upon whose termination I must ever dwell with so deep, so yet unembittered a sorrow. In cheerful converse with her I soon recovered my spirits considerably, and passed my time agreeably enough, although still in the utmost seclusion. Matters went on smoothly enough, although I could not help sometimes feeling a momentary, but horrible uncertainty respecting my uncle's character; which was not altogether unwarranted by the circumstances of the two trying interviews, the particulars of which I have just detailed. The unpleasant impression which these conferences were calculated to leave upon my mind was fast wearing away, when there occurred a circumstance, slight indeed in itself, but calculated irrepressibly to awaken all my worst suspicions, and to overwhelm me again with anxiety and terror.

I had one day left the house with my cousin Emily, in order to take a ramble of considerable length, for the purpose of sketching some favourite views, and we had walked about half a mile when I perceived that we had forgotten our drawing materials, the absence of which would have defeated the object of our walk. Laughing at our own thoughtlessness, we returned to the house, and leaving Emily outside, I ran upstairs to procure the drawing-books and pencils which lay in my bedroom. As I ran up the stairs, I was met by the tall, ill-looking Frenchwoman, evidently a good deal flurried; 'Que veut Madame?' said she, with a more decided effort to be polite, than I had ever known her make before. 'No, no—no matter,' said I, hastily running by her in the direction of my room. 'Madame,' cried she, in a high key, 'restez ici s'il vous plaît, votre chambre n'est pas faite.' I continued to move on without heeding her. She was some way behind me, and feeling that she could not otherwise prevent my entrance, for I was now upon the very lobby, she made a desperate attempt to seize hold of my person; she succeeded in grasping the end of my shawl, which she drew from my shoulders, but slipping at the same time upon the polished oak floor, she fell at full length upon the boards. A little frightened as well as angry at the rudeness of this strange woman, I hastily pushed open the door of my room, at which I now stood, in order to escape from her; but great was my amazement on entering to find the apartment preoccupied. The window was open, and beside it stood two male figures; they appeared to be examining the fastenings of the casement, and their backs were turned towards the door. One of them was my uncle; they both had turned on my entrance, as if startled; the stranger was booted and cloaked, and wore a heavy, broad-leafed hat over his brows; he turned but for a moment, and averted his face; but I had seen enough to convince me that he was no other than my cousin Edward. My uncle had some iron instrument in his hand, which he hastily concealed behind his back; and coming towards me, said something as if in an explanatory tone; but I was too much shocked and confounded to understand what it might be. He said something about '*repairs*—window-frames—cold, and safety'. I did not wait, however, to ask or to receive explanations, but hastily left the room. As I went down stairs I thought I heard the voice of the Frenchwoman in all the shrill volubility of excuse, and others uttering suppressed but vehement imprecations, or what seemed to me to be such.

I joined my cousin Emily quite out of breath. I need not say that my head was too full of other things to think much of drawing for that day. I imparted to her frankly the cause of my alarms, but, at the same time, as gently as I could; and with tears she promised vigilance, devotion, and love. I never had reason for a moment to repent the unreserved confidence which I then reposed in her. She was no less surprised than I at the unexpected appearance of Edward, whose departure for France neither of us had for a moment doubted, but which was now proved by his actual presence to be nothing more than an imposture practised, I feared, for no good end. The situation in which I had found my uncle had very nearly removed all my doubts as to his designs; I magnified suspicions into certainties, and dreaded night after night that I should be murdered in my bed. The nervousness produced by sleepless nights and days of anxious fears increased the horrors of my situation to such a degree, that I at length wrote a letter to a Mr Jefferies, an old and faithful friend of my father's, and perfectly acquainted with all his affairs, praying him, for God's sake, to relieve me from my present terrible situation, and communicating without reserve the nature and grounds of my suspicions. This letter I kept sealed and directed for two or three days always about my person, for discovery would have been ruinous, in expectation of an opportunity, which might be safely trusted, of having it placed in the post office; as neither Emily nor I were permitted to pass beyond the precincts of the demesne itself, which was surrounded by high walls formed of dry stone, the difficulty of procuring such an opportunity was greatly enhanced.

At this time Emily had a short conversation with her father, which she reported to me instantly. After some indifferent matter, he had asked her whether she and I were upon good terms, and whether I was unreserved in my disposition. She answered in the affirmative; and he then enquired whether I had been much surprised to find him in my chamber on the other day. She answered that I had been both surprised and amused. 'And what did she think of George Wilson's appearance?' 'Who?' enquired she. 'Oh! the architect,' he answered, 'who is to contract for the repairs of the house; he is accounted a handsome fellow.' 'She could not see his face,' said Emily, 'and she was in such a hurry to escape that she scarcely observed him.' Sir Arthur appeared satisfied, and the conversation ended.

This slight conversation, repeated accurately to me by Emily, had the effect of confirming, if indeed any thing was required to do so, all that I had before believed as to Edward's actual presence; and I naturally became, if possible, more anxious than ever to dispatch the letter to Mr Jefferies. An opportunity at length occurred. As Emily and I were walking one day near the gate of the demesne, a lad from the village happened to be passing down the avenue from the house; the spot was secluded, and as this person was not connected by service with those whose observation I dreaded, I committed the letter to his keeping, with strict injunctions that he should put it, without delay, into the receiver of the town post office; at the same time I added a suitable gratuity, and the man having made many protestations of punctuality, was soon out of sight. He was hardly gone when I began to doubt my discretion in having trusted him; but I had no better or safer means of despatching the letter, and I was not warranted in suspecting him of such wanton dishonesty as a disposition to tamper with it; but I could not be quite satisfied of its safety until I had received an answer, which could not arrive for a few days. Before I did, however, an event occurred which a little surprised me. I was sitting in my bedroom early in the day, reading by myself, when I heard a knock at the door. 'Come in,' said I, and my uncle entered the room. 'Will you excuse me,' said he, 'I sought you in the parlour, and thence I have come here. I desired to say a word to you. I trust that you have hitherto found my conduct to you such as that of a guardian towards his ward should be.' I dared not withhold my assent. 'And,' he continued, 'I trust that you have not found me harsh or unjust, and that you have perceived, my dear niece, that I have sought to make this poor place as agreeable to you as may be?' I assented again; and he put his hand in his pocket, whence he drew a folded paper, and dashing it upon the table with startling emphasis he said, 'Did you write that letter?' The sudden and fearful alteration of his voice, manner, and face, but more than all, the unexpected production of my letter to Mr Jefferies, which I at once recognized, so confounded and terrified me, that I felt almost choking. I could not utter a word. 'Did you write that letter?' he repeated, with slow and intense emphasis. 'You did, liar and hypocrite. You dared to write that foul and infamous libel; but it shall be your last. Men will universally believe you mad, if I choose to call for an inquiry. I can make you appear so. The suspicions expressed in this letter are the hallucinations and alarms of a moping lunatic. I have defeated your first attempt, madam; and by the holy God, if ever you make another, chains, darkness, and the keeper's whip shall be your portion.' With these astounding words he left the room, leaving me almost fainting.

I was now almost reduced to despair; my last cast had failed; I had no course left but that of escaping secretly from the castle, and placing myself under the protection of the nearest magistrate. I felt if this were not done, and speedily, that I should be *murdered*. No one, from mere description, can have an idea of the unmitigated horror of my situation; a helpless, weak, inexperienced girl, placed under the power, and wholly at the mercy of evil men, and feeling that I had it not in my power to escape for one moment from the malignant influences under which I was probably doomed to fall; with a consciousness, too, that if violence, if murder were designed, no human being would be near to aid me; my dying shriek would be lost in void space.

I had seen Edward but once during his visit, and as I did not meet him again, I began to think that he must have taken his departure; a conviction which was to a certain degree satisfactory, as I regarded his absence as indicating the removal of immediate danger. Emily also arrived circuitously at the same conclusion, and not without good grounds, for she managed indirectly to learn that Edward's black horse had actually been for a day and part of a night in the castle stables, just at the time of her brother's supposed visit. The horse had gone, and as she argued, the rider must have departed with it.

This point being so far settled, I felt a little less uncomfortable; when being one day alone in my bedroom, I happened to look out from the window, and to my unutterable horror, I beheld peering through an opposite casement, my cousin Edward's face. Had I seen the evil one himself in bodily shape, I could not have experienced a more sickening revulsion. I was too much appalled to move at once from the window, but I did so soon enough to avoid his eye. He was looking fixedly down into the narrow quadrangle upon which the window opened. I shrunk back unperceived, to pass the rest of the day in terror and despair. I went to my room early that night, but I was too miserable to sleep.

At about twelve o'clock, feeling very nervous, I determined to call my cousin Emily, who slept, you will remember, in the next room, which communicated with mine by a second door. By this private entrance I found my way into her chamber, and without difficulty persuaded her to return to my room and sleep with me. We accordingly lay down together, she undressed, and I with my clothes on, for I was every moment walking up and down the room, and felt too nervous and miserable to think of rest or comfort. Emily was soon fast asleep, and I lay awake, fervently longing for the first pale gleam of morning, and reckoning every stroke of the old clock with an impatience which made every hour appear like six.

It must have been about one o'clock when I thought I heard a slight noise at the partition door between Emily's room and mine, as if caused by somebody's turning the key in the lock. I held my breath, and the same sound was repeated at the second door of my room, that which opened upon the lobby; the sound was here distinctly caused by the revolution of the bolt in the lock, and it was followed by a slight pressure upon the door itself, as if to ascertain the security of the lock. The person, whoever it might be, was probably satisfied, for I heard the old boards of the lobby creak and strain, as if under the weight of somebody moving cautiously over them. My sense of hearing became unnaturally, almost painfully acute. I suppose the imagination added distinctness to sounds vague in themselves. I thought that I could actually hear the breathing of the person who was slowly returning along the lobby.

At the head of the staircase there appeared to occur a pause; and I could distinctly hear two or three sentences hastily whispered; the steps then descended the stairs with apparently less caution. I ventured to walk quickly and lightly to the lobby door, and attempted to open it; it was indeed fast locked upon the outside, as was also the other. I now felt that the dreadful hour was come; but one desperate expedient remained—it was to awaken Emily, and by our united strength, to attempt to force the partition door, which was slighter than the other, and through this to pass to the lower part of the house, whence it might be possible to escape to the grounds, and so to the village. I returned to the bedside, and shook Emily, but in vain; nothing that I could do availed to produce from her more than a few incoherent words; it was a death-like sleep. She had certainly drunk of some narcotic, as, probably, had I also, in spite of all the caution with which I had examined every thing presented to us to eat or drink. I now attempted, with as little noise as possible, to force first one door, then the other; but all in vain. I believe no strength could have affected my object, for both doors opened inwards. I therefore collected whatever movables I could carry thither, and piled them against the doors, so as to assist me in whatever attempts I should make to resist the entrance of those without. I then returned to the bed and endeavoured again, but fruitlessly, to awaken my cousin. It was not sleep, it was torpor, lethargy, death. I knelt down and prayed with an agony of earnestness; and then seating myself upon the bed, I awaited my fate with a kind of terrible tranquillity.

I heard a faint clanking sound from the narrow court which I have already mentioned, as if caused by the scraping of some iron instrument against stones or rubbish. I at first determined not to disturb the calmness which I now experienced, by uselessly watching the proceedings of those who sought my life; but as the sounds continued, the horrible curiosity which I felt overcame every other emotion, and I determined, at all hazards, to gratify it. I, therefore, crawled upon my knees to the window, so as to let the smallest possible portion of my head appear above the sill.

The moon was shining with an uncertain radiance upon the antique grey buildings, and obliquely upon the narrow court beneath; one side of it was therefore clearly illuminated, while the other was lost in obscurity, the sharp outlines of the old gables, with their nodding clusters of ivy, being at first alone visible. Whoever or whatever occasioned the noise which had excited my curiosity, was concealed under the shadow of the dark side of the quadrangle. I placed my hand over my eyes to shade them from the moonlight, which was so bright as to be almost dazzling, and, peering into the darkness, I first dimly, but afterwards gradually, almost with full distinctness, beheld the form of a man engaged in digging what appeared to be a rude hole close under the wall. Some implements, probably a shovel and pickaxe, lay beside him, and to these he every now and then applied himself as the nature of the ground required. He pursued his task rapidly, and with as little noise as possible. 'So,' thought I, as shovelful after shovelful, the dislodged rubbish mounted into a heap, 'they are digging the grave in which, before two hours pass, I must lie, a cold, mangled corpse. I am *theirs*—I cannot escape.' I felt as if my reason was leaving me. I started to my feet, and in mere despair I applied myself again to each of the two doors alternately. I strained every nerve and sinew, but I might as well have attempted, with my single strength, to force the building itself from its foundations. I threw myself madly upon the ground, and clasped my hands over my eyes as if to shut out the horrible images which crowded upon me.

The paroxysm passed away. I prayed once more with the bitter, agonized fervour of one who feels that the hour of death is present and inevitable. When I arose, I went once more to the window and looked out, just in time to see a shadowy figure glide stealthily along the wall. The task was finished. The catastrophe of the tragedy must soon be accomplished. I determined now to defend my life to the last; and that I might be able to do so with some effect, I searched the room for something which might serve as a weapon; but either through accident, or else in anticipation of such a possibility, everything which might have been made available for such a purpose has been removed.

I must then die tamely and without an effort to defend myself. A thought suddenly struck me; might it not be possible to escape through the door, which the assassin must open in order to enter the room? I resolved to make the attempt. I felt assured that the door through which ingress to the room would be effected was that which opened upon the lobby. It was the more direct way, besides being, for obvious reasons, less liable to interruption than the other. I resolved, then, to place myself behind a projection of the wall, the shadow would serve fully to conceal me, and when the door should be opened, and before they should have discovered the identity of the occupant of the bed, to creep noiselessly from the room, and then to trust to Providence for escape. In order to facilitate this scheme, I removed all the lumber which I had heaped against the door; and I had nearly completed my arrangements, when I perceived the room suddenly darkened, by the close approach of some shadowy object to the window. On turning my eyes in that direction, I observed at the top of the casement, as if suspended from above, first the feet, then the legs, then the body, and at length the whole figure of a man present itself. It was Edward Tyrrell. He appeared to be guiding his descent so as to bring his feet upon the centre of the stone block which occupied the lower part of the window; and having secured his footing upon this, he kneeled down and began to gaze into the room. As the moon was gleaming into the chamber, and the bed-curtains were drawn, he was able to distinguish the bed itself and its contents. He appeared satisfied with his scrutiny, for he looked up and made a sign with his hand. He then applied his hands to the window-frame, which must have been ingeniously contrived for the purpose, for with apparently no resistance the whole frame, containing casement and all, slipped from its position in the wall, and was by him lowered into the room. The cold night wind waved the bed-curtains, and he paused for a moment; all was still again, and he stepped in upon the floor of the room. He held in his hand what appeared to be a steel instrument, shaped something like a long hammer. This he held rather behind him, while, with three long, *tip-toe* strides, he brought himself to the bedside. I felt that the discovery must now be made, and held my breath in momentary expectation of the execration in which he would vent his surprise and disappointment. I closed my eyes; there was a pause, but it was a short one. I heard two dull blows, given in rapid succession; a quivering sigh, and the long-drawn, heavy breathing of the sleeper was for ever suspended. I unclosed my eyes, and saw the murderer fling the quilt across the head of his victim; he then, with the instrument of death still in his hand, proceeded to the lobby-door, upon which he tapped sharply twice or thrice. A quick step was then heard approaching, and a voice whispered something from without. Edward answered, with a kind of shuddering chuckle, 'Her ladyship is past complaining; unlock the door, in the devil's name, unless you're afraid to come in, and help me to lift her out of the window.' The key was turned in the lock, the door opened, and my uncle entered the room. I have told you already that I had placed myself under the shade of a projection of the wall, close to the door. I had instinctively shrunk down cowering towards the ground on the entrance of Edward through the window. When my uncle entered the room, he and his son both stood so very close to me that his hand was every moment upon the point of touching my face. I held my breath, and remained motionless as death.

'You had no interruption from the next room?' said my uncle.

'No,' was the brief reply.

'Secure the jewels, Ned; the French harpy must not lay her claws upon them. You're a steady hand, by G—d; not much blood—eh?'

'Not twenty drops,' replied his son, 'and those on the quilt.'

'I'm glad it's over,' whispered my uncle again; 'we must lift the—the *thing* through the window, and lay the rubbish over it.'

They then turned to the bedside, and, winding the bedclothes round the body, carried it between them slowly to the window, and exchanging a few brief words with some one below, they shoved it over the window-sill, and I heard it fall heavily on the ground underneath.

'I'll take the jewels,' said my uncle; 'there are two caskets in the lower drawer.'

He proceeded, with an accuracy which, had I been more at ease, would have furnished me with matter of astonishment, to lay his hand upon the very spot where my jewels lay; and having possessed himself of them, he called to his son:

'Is the rope made fast above?'

'I'm no fool; to be sure it is,' replied he.

They then lowered themselves from the window; and I rose lightly and cautiously, scarcely daring to breathe, from my place of conceal-ment, and was creeping towards the door, when I heard my uncle's voice, in a sharp whisper, exclaim, 'Get up again; G—d d—n you, you've forgot to lock the room door'; and I perceived, by the straining of the rope which hung from above, that the mandate was instantly obeyed. Not a second was to be lost. I passed through the door, which was only closed, and moved as rapidly as I could, consistently with stillness, along the lobby. Before I had gone many yards, I heard the door through which I had just passed roughly locked on the inside. I glided down the stairs in terror, lest, at every corner, I should meet the murderer or one of his accomplices. I reached the hall, and listened, for a moment, to ascertain whether all was silent around. No sound was audible; the parlour windows opened on the park, and through one of them I might, I thought, easily effect my escape. Accordingly, I hastily entered; but, to my consternation, a candle was burning in the room, and by its light I saw a figure seated at the dinner-table, upon which lay glasses, bottles, and the other accompaniments of a drinking party. Two or three chairs were placed about the table, irregularly, as if hastily abandoned by their occupants. A single glance satisfied me that the figure was that of my French attendant. She was fast asleep, having, probably, drank deeply. There was something malignant and ghastly in the calmness of this bad woman's features, dimly illuminated as they were by the flickering blaze of the candle. A knife lay upon the table, and the terrible thought struck me—'Should I kill this sleeping accomplice in the guilt of the murderer, and thus secure my retreat?' Nothing could be easier; it was but to draw the blade across her throat, the work of a second.

An instant's pause, however, corrected me. 'No,' thought I, 'the God who has conducted me thus far through the valley of the shadow of death, will not abandon me now. I will fall into their hands, or I will escape hence, but it shall be free from the stain of blood; His will be done.' I felt a confidence arising from this reflection, an assurance of protection which I cannot describe. There were no other means of escape, so I advanced, with a firm step and collected mind, to the window. I noiselessly withdrew the bars, and unclosed the shutters; I pushed open the casement, and without waiting to look behind me, I ran with my utmost speed, scarcely feeling the ground beneath me, down the avenue, taking care to keep upon the grass which bordered it. I did not for a moment slacken my speed, and I had now gained the central point between the park-gate and the mansion-house. Here the avenue made a wider circuit, and in order to avoid delay, I directed my way across the smooth sward round which the carriage-way wound, intending, at the opposite side of the level, at a point which I distinguished by a group of old birch trees, to enter again upon the beaten track, which was from thence tolerably direct to the gate. I had, with my utmost speed, got about half way across this broad flat, when the rapid tramp of a horse's hoofs struck upon my ear. My heart swelled in my bosom, as though I would smother. The clattering of galloping hoofs approached; I was pursued; they were now upon the sward on which I was running; there was not a bush or a bramble to shelter me; and, as if to render escape altogether desperate, the moon, which had hitherto been obscured, at this moment shone forth with a broad, clear light, which made every object distinctly visible. The sounds were now close behind me. I felt my knees bending under me, with the sensation which unnerves one in a dream. I reeled, I stumbled, I fell; and at the same instant the cause of my alarm wheeled past me at full gallop. It was one of the young fillies which pastured loose about the park, whose frolics had thus all but maddened me with terror. I scrambled to my feet, and rushed on with weak but rapid steps, my sportive companion still galloping round and round me with many a frisk and fling, until, at length, more dead than alive, I reached the avenue-gate, and crossed the stile, I scarce knew how. I ran through the village, in which all was silent as the grave, until my progress was arrested by the hoarse voice of a sentinel, who cried 'Who goes there?' I felt that I was now safe. I turned in the direction of the voice, and fell fainting at the soldier's feet. When I came to myself, I was sitting in a miserable hovel, surrounded by strange faces, all bespeaking curiosity and compassion. Many soldiers were in it also; indeed, as I afterwards found, it was employed as a guard-room by a detachment of troops quartered for that night in the town. In a few words I informed their officer of the circumstances which had occurred, describing also the appearance of the persons engaged in the murder; and he, without further loss of time than was necessary to procure the attendance of a magistrate, proceeded to the mansion-house of Carrickleigh, taking with him a party of his men. But the villains had discovered their mistake, and had effected their escape before the arrival of the military.

The Frenchwoman was, however, arrested in the neighbourhood upon the next day. She was tried and condemned at the ensuing assizes; and previous to her execution confessed that '*she had a hand in making Hugh Tisdall's bed*'. She had been a housekeeper in the castle at the time, and a *chère amie* of my uncle's. She was, in reality, able to speak English like a native, but had exclusively used the French language, I suppose to facilitate her designs. She died the same hardened wretch she had lived, confessing her crimes only, as she alleged, that her doing so might involve Sir Arthur Tyrrell, the great author of her guilt and misery, and whom she now regarded with unmitigated detestation.

With the particulars of Sir Arthur's and his son's escape, as far as they are known, you are acquainted. You are also in possession of their after fate; the terrible, the tremendous retribution which, after long delays of many years, finally overtook and crushed them. Wonderful and inscrutable are the dealings of God with his creatures!

Deep and fervent as must always be my gratitude to heaven for my deliverance, effected by a chain of providential occurrences, the failing of a single link of which must have ensured my destruction, it was long before I could look back upon it with other feelings than those of bitterness, almost of agony. The only being that had ever really loved me, my nearest and dearest friend, ever ready to sympathize, to counsel, and to assist; the gayest, the gentlest, the warmest heart; the only creature on earth that cared for me; *her* life had been the price of my deliverance; and I then uttered the wish, which no event of my long and sorrowful life has taught me to recall, that she had been spared, and that, in her stead, *I* were mouldering in the grave, forgotten, and at rest.

Hunted Down

CHARLES DICKENS

I

Most of us see some romances in life. In my capacity of Chief Manager of a Life Assurance Office, I think I have within the last thirty years seen more romances than the generality of men, however unpromising the opportunity may, at first sight, seem.

As I have retired, and live at my ease, I possess the means that I used to want, of considering what I have seen, at leisure. My experiences have a more remarkable aspect, so reviewed, than they had when they were in progress. I have come home from the Play now, and can recall the scenes of the Drama upon which the curtain has fallen, free from the glare, bewilderment, and bustle of the Theatre.

Let me recall one of these Romances of the real world.

There is nothing truer than physiognomy, taken in connection with manner. The art of reading that book of which Eternal Wisdom obliges every human creature to present his or her own page with the individual character written on it, is a difficult one, perhaps, and is little studied. It may require some natural aptitude, and it must require (for everything does) some patience and some pains. That these are not usually given to it—that numbers of people accept a few stock commonplace expressions of the face as the whole list of characteristics, and neither seek nor know the refinements that are truest—that You, for instance, give a great deal of time and attention to the reading of music, Greek, Latin, French, Italian, Hebrew, if you please, and do not qualify yourself to read the face of the master or mistress looking over your shoulder teaching it to you—I assume to be five hundred times more probable than improbable. Perhaps a little self-sufficiency may be at the bottom of this; facial expression requires no study from you, you think; it comes by nature to you to know enough about it, and you are not to be taken in.

I confess, for my part, that I *have* been taken in, over and over again. I have been taken in by acquaintances, and I have been taken in (of course) by friends; far oftener by friends than by any other class of persons. How came I to be so deceived? Had I quite misread their faces?

No. Believe me, my first impression of those people, founded on face and manner alone, was invariably true. My mistake was in suffering them to come nearer to me, and explain themselves away.

II

The partition which separated my own office from our general outer office in the City was of thick plate glass. I could see through it what passed in the outer office, without hearing a word. I had it put up in place of a wall that had been there for years—ever since the house was built. It is no matter whether I did or did not make the change in order that I might derive my first impression of strangers, who came to us on business, from their faces alone, without being influenced by anything they said. Enough to mention that I turned my glass partition to that account, and that a Life Assurance Office is at all times exposed to be practised upon by the most crafty and cruel of the human race.

It was through my glass partition that I first saw the gentleman whose story I am going to tell.

He had come in without my observing it, and had put his hat and umbrella on the broad counter, and was bending over it to take some papers from one of the clerks. He was about forty or so, dark, exceedingly well dressed in black—being in mourning—and the hand he extended, with a polite air, had a particularly well-fitting black kid glove upon it. His hair, which was elaborately brushed and oiled, was parted straight up the middle; and he presented this parting to the clerk, exactly (to my thinking) as if he had said, in so many words: 'You must take me, if you please, my friend, just as I show myself. Come straight up here, follow the gravel path, keep off the grass, I allow no trespassing.'

I conceived a very great aversion to that man the moment I thus saw him.

He had asked for some of our printed forms, and the clerk was giving them to him and explaining them. An obliged and agreeable smile was on his face, and his eyes met those of the clerk with a sprightly look. (I have known a vast quantity of nonsense talked about bad men not looking you in the face. Don't trust that conventional idea. Dishonesty will stare honesty out of countenance, any day in the week, if there is anything to be got by it.)

I saw, in the corner of his eyelash, that he became aware of my looking at him. Immediately he turned the parting in his hair toward the glass partition, as if he said to me with a sweet smile, 'Straight up here, if you please. Off the grass!'

In a few moments he had put on his hat and taken up his umbrella, and was gone.

I beckoned the clerk into my room, and asked, 'Who was that?'

He had the gentleman's card in his hand. 'Mr Julius Slinkton, Middle Temple.'

'A barrister, Mr Adams?'

'I think not, sir.'

'I should have thought him a clergyman, but for his having no Reverend here,' said I.

'Probably, from his appearance,' Mr Adams replied, 'he is reading for orders.'

I should mention that he wore a dainty white cravat, and dainty linen altogether.

'What did he want, Mr Adams?'

'Merely a form of proposal, sir, and form of reference.'

'Recommended here? Did he say?'

'Yes, he said he was recommended here by a friend of yours. He noticed you, but said that, as he had not the pleasure of your personal acquaintance, he would not trouble you.'

'Did he know my name?'

'Oh yes, sir! He said, "There *is* Mr Sampson, I see!" '

'A well-spoken gentleman, apparently?'

'Remarkably so, sir.'

'Insinuating manners, apparently?'

'Very much so, indeed, sir.'

'Hah!' said I. 'I want nothing at present, Mr Adams.'

Within a fortnight of that day I went to dine with a friend of mine, a merchant, a man of taste, who buys pictures and books; and the first man I saw among the company was Mr Julius Slinkton. There he was, standing before the fire, with good large eyes and an open expression of face; but still (I thought) requiring everybody to come at him by the prepared way he offered, and by no other.

I noticed him ask my friend to introduce him to Mr Sampson, and my friend did so. Mr Slinkton was very happy to see me. Not too happy; there was no overdoing of the matter; happy in a thoroughly well-bred, perfectly unmeaning way.

'I thought you had met,' our host observed.

'No,' said Mr Slinkton. 'I did look in at Mr Sampson's office, on your recommendation; but I really did not feel justified in troubling Mr Sampson himself, on a point in the every-day routine of an ordinary clerk.'

I said I should have been glad to show him any attention on our friend's introduction.

'I am sure of that,' said he, 'and am much obliged. At another time, perhaps, I may be less delicate. Only, however, if I have real business; for I know, Mr Sampson, how precious business time is, and what a vast number of impertinent people there are in the world.'

I acknowledged his consideration with a slight bow. 'You were thinking,' said I, 'of effecting a policy on your life.'

'Oh dear no! I am afraid I am not so prudent as you pay me the compliment of supposing me to be, Mr Sampson. I merely enquired for a friend. But you know what friends are in such matters. Nothing may ever come of it. I have the greatest reluctance to trouble men of business with enquiries for friends, knowing the probabilities to be a thousand to one that the friends will never follow them up. People are so fickle, so selfish, so inconsiderate. Don't you, in your business, find them so every day, Mr Sampson?'

I was going to give a qualified answer; but he turned his smooth, white parting on me, with its 'Straight up here, if you please!' and I answered 'Yes.'

'I hear, Mr Sampson,' he resumed presently, for our friend had a new cook, and dinner was not so punctual as usual, 'that your profession has recently suffered a great loss.'

'In money?' said I.

He laughed at my ready association of loss with money, and replied, 'No, in talent and vigour.'

Not at once following out his allusion, I considered for a moment. '*Has* it sustained a loss of that kind?' said I. 'I was not aware of it.'

'Understand me, Mr Sampson. I don't imagine that you have retired. It is not so bad as that. But Mr Meltham——'

'Oh, to be sure!' said I. 'Yes. Mr Meltham, the young actuary of the "Inestimable".'

'Just so,' he returned in a consoling way.

'He is a great loss. He was at once the most profound, the most original, and the most energetic man I have ever known connected with Life Assurance.'

I spoke strongly; for I had a high esteem and admiration for Meltham; and my gentleman had indefinitely conveyed to me some suspicion that he wanted to sneer at him. He recalled me to my guard by presenting that trim pathway up his head, with its infernal 'Not on the grass, if you please—the gravel.'

'You knew him, Mr Slinkton?'

'Only by reputation. To have known him as an acquaintance, or as a friend, is an honour I should have sought if he had remained in society, though I might never have had the good fortune to attain it, being a man of far inferior mark. He was scarcely above thirty, I suppose?'

'About thirty.'

'Ah!' he sighed in his former consoling way. 'What creatures we are! To break up, Mr Sampson, and become incapable of business at that time of life!—Any reason assigned for the melancholy fact?'

('Humph!' thought I as I looked at him. 'But I won't go up the track and I will go on the grass.')

'What reason have you heard assigned, Mr Slinkton?' I asked point-blank.

'Most likely a false one. You know what Rumour is, Mr Sampson. I never repeat what I hear; it is the only way of paring the nails and shaving the head of Rumour. But, when *you* ask me what reason I have heard assigned for Mr Meltham's passing away from among men, it is another thing. I am not gratifying idle gossip then. I was told, Mr Sampson, that Mr Meltham had relinquished all his avocations and all his prospects, because he was, in fact, brokenhearted. A disappointed attachment, I heard—though it hardly seems probable, in the case of a man so distinguished and so attractive.'

'Attractions and distinctions are no armour against death,' said I.

'Oh, she died? Pray pardon me. I did not hear that. That, indeed, makes it very, very sad. Poor Mr Meltham! She died? Ah, dear me! Lamentable, lamentable!'

I still thought his pity was not quite genuine, and I still suspected an unaccountable sneer under all this, until he said, as we were parted, like the other knots of talkers, by the announcement of dinner:

'Mr Sampson, you are surprised to see me so moved on behalf of a man whom I have never known. I am not so disinterested as you may suppose. I have suffered, and recently too, from death myself. I have lost one of two charming nieces, who were my constant companions. She died young—barely three-and-twenty; and even her remaining sister is far from strong. The world is a grave!'

He said this with deep feeling, and I felt reproached for the coldness of my manner. Coldness and distrust had been engendered in me, I knew, by my bad experiences; they were not natural to me; and I often thought how much I had lost in life, losing trustfulness, and how little I had gained, gaining hard caution. This state of mind being habitual to me, I troubled myself more about this conversation than I might have troubled myself about a greater matter. I listened to his talk at dinner, and observed how readily other men responded to it, and with what a graceful instinct he adapted his subjects to the knowledge and habits of those he talked with. As, in talking with me, he had easily started the subject I might be supposed to understand best, and to be the most interested in, so, in talking with others, he guided himself by the same rule. The company was of a varied character; but he was not at fault, that I could discover, with any member of it. He knew just as much of each man's pursuit as made him agreeable to that man in reference to it, and just as little as made it natural in him to seek modesty for information when the theme was broached.

As he talked and talked—but really not too much, for the rest of us seemed to force it upon him—I became quite angry with myself. I took his face to pieces in my mind, like a watch, and examined it in detail. I could not say much against any of his features separately; I could say even less against them when they were put together. 'Then is it not monstrous,' I asked myself, 'that because a man happens to part his hair straight up the middle of his head, I should permit myself to suspect, and even to detest him?'

(I may stop to remark that this was no proof of my sense. An observer of men who finds himself steadily repelled by some apparently trifling thing in a stranger is right to give it great weight. It may be the clue to the whole mystery. A hair or two will show where a lion is hidden. A very little key will open a very heavy door.)

I took my part in the conversation with him after a time, and we got on remarkably well. In the drawing-room I asked the host how long he had known Mr Slinkton. He answered, not many months; he had met him at the house of a celebrated painter then present, who had known him well when he was travelling with his nieces in Italy for their health. His plans in life being broken by the death of one of them, he was reading with the intention of going back to college as a matter of form, taking his degree, and going into orders. I could not but argue with myself that here was the true explanation of his interest in poor Meltham, and that I had been almost brutal in my distrust on that simple head.

III

On the very next day but one I was sitting behind my glass partition, as before, when he came into the outer office, as before. The moment I saw him again without hearing him, I hated him worse than ever.

It was only for a moment that I had this opportunity; for he waved his tight-fitting black glove the instant I looked at him, and came straight in.

'Mr Sampson, good day! I presume, you see, upon your kind permission to intrude upon you. I don't keep my word in being justified by business, for my business here—if I may so abuse the word—is of the slightest nature.'

I asked, was it anything I could assist him in?

'I thank you, no. I merely called to enquire outside whether my dilatory friend had been so false to himself as to be practical and sensible. But, of course, he has done nothing. I gave him your papers with my own hand, and he was hot upon the intention, but of course he has done nothing. Apart from the general human disinclination to do anything that ought to be done, I dare say there is a speciality about assuring one's life. You find it like will-making. People are so superstitious, and take it for granted they will die soon afterwards.'

'Up here, if you please; straight up here, Mr Sampson. Neither to the right nor to the left.' I almost fancied I could hear him breathe the words as he sat smiling at me, with that intolerable parting exactly opposite the bridge of my nose.

'There is such a feeling sometimes, no doubt,' I replied; 'but I don't think it obtains to any great extent.'

'Well,' said he with a shrug and a smile, 'I wish some good angel would influence my friend in the right direction. I rashly promised his mother and sister in Norfolk to see it done, and he promised them that he would do it. But I suppose he never will.'

He spoke for a minute or two on different topics, and went away.

I had scarcely unlocked the drawers of my writing-table next morning, when he reappeared. I noticed that he came straight to the door in the glass partition, and did not pause a single moment outside.

'Can you spare me two minutes, my dear Mr Sampson?'

'By all means.'

'Much obliged,' laying his hat and umbrella on the table. 'I came early, not to interrupt you. The fact is, I am taken by surprise in reference to this proposal my friend has made.'

'Has he made one?' said I.

'Ye-es,' he answered, deliberately looking at me; and then a bright idea seemed to strike him—'or he only tells me he has. Perhaps that may be a new way of evading the matter. By Jupiter, I never thought of that?'

Mr Adams was opening the morning's letters in the outer office. 'What is the name, Mr Slinkton?' I asked.

'Beckwith.'

I looked out at the door, and requested Mr Adams, if there were a proposal in that name, to bring it in. He had already laid it out of his hand on the counter. It was easily selected from the rest, and he gave it me. Alfred Beckwith. Proposal to effect a policy with us for two thousand pounds. Dated yesterday.

'From the Middle Temple, I see, Mr Slinkton.'

'Yes He lives on the same staircase with me; his door is opposite. I never thought he would make me his reference, though.'

'It seems natural enough that he should.'

'Quite so, Mr Sampson; but I never thought of it. Let me see.' He took the printed paper from his pocket. 'How am I to answer all these questions?'

'According to the truth, of course,' said I.

'Oh, of course!' he answered, looking up from the paper with a smile. 'I meant they were so many. But you do right to be particular. It stands to reason that you must be particular. Will you allow me to use your pen and ink?'

'Certainly.'

'And your desk?'

'Certainly.'

He had been hovering about between his hat and his umbrella for a place to write on. He now sat down in my chair, at my blotting-paper and inkstand, with the long walk up his head in accurate perspective before me, as I stood with my back to the fire.

Before answering each question he ran it over aloud, and discussed it. How long had he known Mr Alfred Beckwith? That he had to calculate by years upon his fingers. What were his habits? No difficulty about them; temperate in the last degree, and took a little too much exercise, if anything. All the answers were satisfactory. When he had written them all, he looked them over, and finally signed them in a very pretty hand. He supposed he had now done with the business. I told him he was not likely to be troubled any further. Should he leave the papers there? If he pleased. Much obliged. Good morning.

I had had one other visitor before him; not at the office, but at my own house. That visitor had come to my bedside when it was not yet daylight, and had been seen by no one else but my faithful confidential servant.

A second reference paper (for we required always two) was sent down into Norfolk, and was duly received back by post. This, likewise, was satisfactorily answered in every respect. Our forms were all complied with; we accepted the proposal, and the premium for one year was paid.

IV

For six or seven months I saw no more of Mr Slinkton. He called once at my house, but I was not at home; and he once asked me to dine with him in the Temple, but I was engaged. His friend's assurance was effected in March. Late in September, or early in October, I was down at Scarborough for a breath of sea air, where I met him on the beach. It was a hot evening; he came toward me with his hat in his hand; and there was the walk I felt so strongly disinclined to take in perfect order again, exactly in front of the bridge of my nose.

He was not alone, but had a young lady on his arm.

She was dressed in mourning, and I looked at her with great

interest. She had the appearance of being extremely delicate, and her face was remarkably pale and melancholy; but she was very pretty. He introduced her as his niece, Miss Niner.

'Are you strolling, Mr Sampson? Is it possible you can be idle?'

It *was* possible, and I *was* strolling.

'Shall we stroll together?'

'With pleasure.'

The young lady walked between us, and we walked on the cool sea-sand, in the direction of Filey.

'There have been wheels here,' said Mr Slinkton. 'And now I look again, the wheels of a hand-carriage! Margaret, my love, your shadow, without doubt!'

'Miss Niner's shadow?' I repeated, looking down at it on the sand.

'Not that one,' Mr Slinkton returned, laughing. 'Margaret, my dear, tell Mr Sampson.'

'Indeed,' said the young lady, turning to me, 'there is nothing to tell—except that I constantly see the same invalid old gentleman at all times, wherever I go. I have mentioned it to my uncle, and he calls the gentleman my shadow.'

'Does he live in Scarborough?' I asked.

'He is staying here.'

'Do you live in Scarborough?'

'No, I am staying here. My uncle has placed me with a family here, for my health.'

'And your shadow?' said I, smiling.

'My shadow,' she answered, smiling too, 'is—like myself—not very robust, I fear; for I lose my shadow sometimes, as my shadow loses me at other times. We both seem liable to confinement to the house. I have not seen my shadow for days and days; but it does oddly happen, occasionally, that wherever I go, for many days together, this gentleman goes. We have come together in the most unfrequented nooks on this shore.'

'Is this he?' said I, pointing before us.

The wheels had swept down to the water's edge, and described a great loop on the sand in turning. Bringing the hoop back towards us, and spinning it out as it came, was a hand-carriage, drawn by a man.

'Yes,' said Miss Niner, 'this really is my shadow, uncle.'

As the carriage approached us, and we approached the carriage, I saw within it an old man, whose head was sunk on his breast, and who was enveloped in a variety of wrappers. He was drawn by a very quiet but very keen-looking man, with iron-grey hair, who was slightly lame. They had passed us, when the carriage stopped, and the old gentleman within, putting out his arm, called to me by my name. I went back, and was absent from Mr Slinkton and his niece for about five minutes.

When I rejoined them Mr Slinkton was the first to speak. Indeed he said to me in a raised voice, before I came up with him:

'It is well you have not been longer, or my niece might have died of curiosity to know who her shadow is, Mr Sampson.'

'An old East India Director,' said I. 'An intimate friend of our friend's, at whose house I first had the pleasure of meeting you. A certain Major Banks. You have heard of him?'

'Never.'

'Very rich, Miss Niner; but very old, and very crippled. An amiable man, sensible—much interested in you. He has just been expatiating on the affection that he has observed to exist between you and your uncle.'

Mr Slinkton was holding his hat again, and he passed his hand up the straight walk, as if he himself went up it serenely after me.

'Mr Sampson,' he said, tenderly pressing his niece's arm in his, 'our affection was always a strong one, for we have had but few near ties. We have still fewer now. We have associations to bring us together, that are not of this world, Margaret.'

'Dear uncle!' murmured the young lady, and turned her face aside to hide her tears.

'My niece and I have such remembrances and regrets in common, Mr Sampson,' he feelingly pursued, 'that it would be strange indeed if the relations between us were cold or indifferent. If I remember a conversation we once had together, you will understand the reference I make. Cheer up, dear Margaret. Don't droop, don't droop. My Margaret! I cannot bear to see you droop!'

The poor young lady was very much affected, but controlled herself. His feelings, too, were very acute. In a word, he found himself under such great need of a restorative, that he presently went away, to take a bath of sea-water, leaving the young lady and me sitting by a point of rock, and probably presuming—but that you will say was a pardonable indulgence in a luxury—that she would praise him with all her heart.

She did, poor thing! With all her confiding heart, she praised him to me, for his care of her dead sister, and for his untiring devotion in her last illness. The sister had wasted away very slowly, and wild and terrible fantasies had come over her toward the end, but he had never been impatient with her, or at a loss; had always been gentle, watchful, and self-possessed. The sister had known him, as she had known him, to be the best of men, the kindest of men, and yet a man of such admirable strength of character, as to be a very tower for the support of their weak natures while their poor lives endured.

'I shall leave him, Mr Sampson, very soon,' said the young lady; 'I know my life is drawing to an end; and, when I am gone, I hope he will marry and be happy. I am sure he has lived single so long, only for my sake, and for my poor, poor sister's.'

The little hand-carriage had made another great loop on the damp sand, and was coming back again, gradually spinning out a slim figure of eight, half a mile long.

'Young lady,' said I, looking around, laying my hand upon her arm, and speaking in a low voice, 'time presses. You hear the gentle murmur of that sea?'

She looked at me with the utmost wonder and alarm, saying: 'Yes!'

'And you know what a voice is in it when the storm comes?' 'Yes!'

'You see how quiet and peaceful it lies before us, and you know what an awful sight of power without pity it might be, this very night?' 'Yes!'

'But if you had never heard or seen it, or heard of it in its cruelty, could you believe that it beats every inanimate thing in its way to pieces without mercy, and destroys life without remorse?'

'You terrify me, sir, by these questions!'

'To save you, young lady, to save you! For God's sake, collect your strength and collect your firmness! If you were here alone, and hemmed in by the rising tide on the flow to fifty feet above your head, you could not be in greater danger than the danger you are now to be saved from.'

The figure on the sand was spun out, and straggled off into a crooked little jerk that ended at the cliff very near us.

'As I am, before, Heaven and the Judge of all mankind, your friend, and your dead sister's friend, I solemnly entreat you, Miss

Niner, without one moment's loss of time, to come to this gentleman with me!'

If the little carriage had been less near to us, I doubt if I could have got her away; but it was so near that we were there before she had recovered the hurry of being urged from the rock. I did not remain there with her two minutes. Certainly within five, I had the inexpressible satisfaction of seeing her—from the point we had sat on, and to which I had returned—half supported and half carried up some rude steps notched in the cliff, by the figure of an active man. With that figure beside her I knew she was safe anywhere.

I sat alone on the rock, awaiting Mr Slinkton's return. The twilight was deepening and the shadows were heavy, when he came round the point, with his hat hanging at his buttonhole, smoothing his wet hair with one of his hands, and picking out the old path with the other and a pocket-comb.

'My niece not here, Mr Sampson?' he said, looking about.

'Miss Niner seemed to feel a chill in the air after the sun was down, and has gone home.'

He looked surprised, as though she were not accustomed to do anything without him; even to originate so slight a proceeding.

'I persuaded Miss Niner,' I explained.

'Ah!' said he. 'She is easily persuaded—for her good. Thank you, Mr Sampson; she is better within doors. The bathing-place was further than I thought, to say the truth.'

'Miss Niner is very delicate,' I observed.

He shook his head and drew a deep sigh. 'Very, very, very. You may recollect my saying so. The time that has since intervened has not strengthened her. The gloomy shadow that fell upon her sister so early in life seems, in my anxious eyes, to gather over her, ever darker, ever darker. Dear Margaret, dear Margaret? But we must hope.'

The hand-carriage was spinning away before us at a most indecorous pace for an invalid vehicle, and was making most irregular curves upon the sand. Mr Slinkton, noticing it after he had put his handkerchief to his eyes, said:

'If I may judge from appearances, your friend will be upset, Mr Sampson.'

'It looks probable, certainly,' said I.

'The servant must be drunk.'

'The servants of old gentlemen will get drunk sometimes,' said I.

'The major draws very light, Mr Sampson.'

'The major does draw light,' said I.

By this time the carriage, much to my relief, was lost in the darkness. We walked on for a little, side by side over the sand, in silence. After a short while he said, in a voice still affected by the emotion that his niece's state of health had awakened in him:

'Do you stay here long, Mr Sampson?'

'Why, no. I am going away tonight.'

'So soon? But business always holds you in request. Men like Mr Sampson are too important to others, to be spared to their own need of relaxation, and enjoyment.'

'I don't know about that,' said I. 'However, I am going back.'

'To London?'

'To London.'

'I shall be there, too, soon after you.'

I knew that as well as he did. But I did not tell him so. Any more than I told him what defensive weapon my right hand rested on in my pocket, as I walked by his side. Any more than I told him why I did not walk on the sea side of him with the night closing in.

We left the beach, and our ways diverged. We exchanged goodnight, and had parted indeed, when he said, returning:

'Mr Sampson, *may* I ask? Poor Meltham, whom we spoke of— dead yet?'

'Not when I last heard of him; but too broken a man to live long, and hopelessly lost to his old calling.'

'Dear, dear, dear!' said he with great feeling. 'Sad, sad, sad! The world is a grave!' And so went his way.

It was not his fault if the world were not a grave; but I did not call that observation after him, any more than I had mentioned those other things just now enumerated. He went his way, and I went mine with all expedition. This happened, as I have said, either at the end of September or beginning of October. The next time I saw him, and the last time, was late in November.

V

I had a very particular engagement to breakfast in the Temple. It was a bitter north-easterly morning, and the sleet and slush lay inches deep in the streets. I could get no conveyance, and was soon wet to the knees; but I should have been true to that appointment, though I had to wade to it up to my neck in the same impediments.

The appointment took me to some chambers in the Temple. They were at the top of a lonely corner house overlooking the river. The name, MR ALFRED BECKWITH, was painted on the outer door. On the door opposite, on the same landing, the name MR JULIUS SLINKTON. The doors of both sets of chambers stood open, so that anything said aloud in one set could be heard in the other.

I had never been in those chambers before. They were dismal, close, unwholesome, and oppressive: the furniture, originally good, and not yet old, was faded and dirty; the rooms were in great disorder; there was a strong prevailing smell of opium, brandy, and tobacco; the grate and fire-irons were splashed all over with unsightly blotches of rust; and on a sofa by the fire, in the room where breakfast had been prepared, lay the host, Mr Beckwith, a man with all the appearances of the worst kind of drunkard, very far advanced upon his shameful way to death.

'Slinkton is not come yet,' said this creature, staggering up when I went in; 'I'll call him.—Halloa! Julius Cæsar! Come and drink!' As he hoarsely roared this out, he beat the poker and tongs together in a mad way, as if that were his usual manner of summoning his associate.

The voice of Mr Slinkton was heard through the clatter from the opposite side of the staircase, and he came in. He had not expected the pleasure of meeting me. I have seen several artful men brought to a stand, but I never saw a man so aghast as he was when his eyes rested on mine.

'Julius Cæsar,' cried Beckwith, staggering between us, 'Mist' Sampson! Mist' Sampson, Julius Cæsar! Julius, Mist' Sampson, is the friend of my soul. Julius keeps me plied with liquor, morning, noon, and night. Julius is a real benefactor. Julius threw the tea and coffee out of window when I used to have any. Julius empties all the water-jugs of their contents, and fills them with spirits. Julius winds me up and keeps me going.—Boil the brandy, Julius!'

There was a rusty and furred saucepan in the ashes—the ashes looked like the accumulation of weeks—and Beckwith, rolling and staggering between us as if he were going to plunge headlong into the fire, got the saucepan out, and tried to force it into Slinkton's hand.

'Boil the brandy, Julius Cæsar! Come! Do your usual office. Boil the brandy!'

He became so fierce in his gesticulations with the saucepan, that I expected to see him lay open Slinkton's head with it. I therefore put out my hand to check him. He reeled back to the sofa, and sat there panting, shaking, and red-eyed, in his rags of dressing-gown, looking at us both. I noticed then that there was nothing to drink on the table but brandy, and nothing to eat but salted herrings, and a hot, sickly, highly peppered stew.

'At all events, Mr Sampson,' said Slinkton, offering me the smooth gravel path for the last time, 'I thank you for interfering between me and this unfortunate man's violence. However you came here, Mr Sampson, or with whatever motive you came here, at least I thank you for that.'

'Boil the brandy,' muttered Beckwith.

Without gratifying his desire to know how I came there, I said quietly, 'How is your niece, Mr Slinkton?'

He looked hard at me, and I looked hard at him.

'I am sorry to say, Mr Sampson, that my niece has proved treacherous and ungrateful to her best friend. She left me without a word of notice or explanation. She was misled, no doubt, by some designing rascal. Perhaps you may have heard of it?'

'I did hear that she was misled by a designing rascal. In fact, I have proof of it.'

'Are you sure of that?' said he.

'Quite.'

'Boil the brandy,' muttered Beckwith. 'Company to breakfast, Julius Cæsar. Do your usual office—provide the usual breakfast, dinner, tea, and supper. Boil the brandy!'

The eyes of Slinkton looked from him to me, and he said, after a moment's consideration:

'Mr Sampson, you are a man of the world, and so am I. I will be plain with you.'

'Oh no, you won't!' said I, shaking my head.

'I tell you, sir, I will be plain with you.'

'And I tell you you will not,' said I. 'I know all about you. *You* plain with any one? Nonsense, nonsense!'

'I plainly tell you, Mr Sampson,' he went on, with a manner almost composed, 'that I understand your object. You want to save your funds, and escape from your liabilities; these are old tricks of trade with you Office gentlemen. But you will not do it, sir; you will not succeed. You have not an easy adversary to play against, when you play against me. We shall have to enquire, in due time, when and how Mr Beckwith fell into his present habits. With that remark, sir, I put this poor creature, and his incoherent wanderings of speech, aside, and wish you a good morning and a better case next time.'

While he was saying this, Beckwith had filled a half-pint glass with brandy. At this moment, he threw the brandy at his face, and threw the glass after it. Slinkton put his hands up, half blinded with the spirit, and cut with the glass across the forehead. At the sound of the breakage, a fourth person came into the room, closed the door, and stood at it. He was a very quiet, but very keen-looking man, with iron-grey hair, and slightly lame.

Slinkton pulled out his handkerchief, assuaged the pain in his smarting eyes, and dabbled the blood on his forehead. He was a long time about it, and I saw that in the doing of it a tremendous change came over him, occasioned by the change in Beckwith—who ceased to pant and tremble, sat upright, and never took his eyes off him. I never in my life saw a face in which abhorrence and determination were so forcibly painted as in Beckwith's then.

'Look at me, you villain,' said Beckwith, 'and see me as I really am! I took these rooms to make them a trap for you. I came into them as a drunkard, to bait the trap for you. You fell into the trap, and you will never leave it alive. On the morning when you last went to Mr Sampson's office, I had seen him first. Your plot has been known to both of us all along and you have been counter-plotted all along. What! Having been cajoled into putting that prize of two thousand pounds in your power, I was to be done to death with brandy, and, brandy not proving quick enough, with something quicker? Have I never seen you, when you thought my senses gone, pouring from your little bottle into my glass? Why, you Murderer and Forger, alone here with you in the dead of night, as I have so often been, I have had my hand upon the trigger of a pistol, twenty times, to blow your brains out!'

This sudden starting up of the thing that he had supposed to be his imbecile victim into a determined man, with a settled resolution to hunt him down and be the death of him, mercilessly expressed from head to foot, was, in the first shock, too much for him. Without any figure of speech, he staggered under it. But there is no greater mistake than to suppose that a man who is a calculating criminal is, in any phase of his guilt, otherwise than true to himself, and perfectly consistent with his whole character. Such a man commits murder, and murder is the natural culmination of his course; such a man has to outface murder, and will do it with hardihood and effrontery. It is a sort of fashion to express surprise that any notorious criminal, having such crime upon his conscience, can so brave it out. Do you think that if he had it on his conscience at all, or had a conscience to have it upon, he would ever have committed the crime?

Perfectly consistent with himself, as I believe all such monsters to be, this Slinkton recovered himself, and showed a defiance that was sufficiently cold and quiet. He was white, he was haggard, he was changed; but only as a sharper who had played for a great stake, and had been outwitted and had lost the game.

'Listen to me, you villain,' said Beckwith, 'and let every word you hear me say be a stab in your wicked heart. When I took these rooms, to throw myself in your way and lead you on to the scheme that I knew my appearance and supposed character and habits would suggest to such a devil, how did I know that? Because you were no stranger to me. I knew you well. And I knew you to be the cruel wretch who, for so much money, had killed one innocent girl while she trusted him implicitly, and who was by inches killing another.'

Slinkton took out a snuff-box, took a pinch of snuff, and laughed.

'But see here,' said Beckwith, never looking away, never raising his voice, never relaxing his face, never unclenching his hand. 'See what a dull wolf you have been, after all! The infatuated drunkard who never drank a fiftieth part of the liquor you plied him with, but poured it away, here, there, everywhere—almost before your eyes; who bought over the fellow you set to watch him and to ply him, by outbidding you in his bribe, before he had been at his work three days—with whom you have observed no caution, yet who was so bent on ridding the earth of you as a wild beast, that he would have defeated you if you had been ever so prudent—that drunkard whom you have, many a time, left on the floor of this room, and who has even let you go out of it, alive and undeceived, when you have turned him over with your foot—has, almost as often, on the same night, within an hour, within a few minutes, watched you awake, had his hand at your pillow when you were asleep, turned over your papers, taken samples from your bottles and packets of powder, changed their contents, rifled every secret of your life!'

He had had another pinch of snuff in his hand, but had gradually let it drop from between his fingers to the floor: where he now smoothed it out with his foot, looking down at it the while.

'That drunkard,' said Beckwith, 'who had free access to your rooms at all times, that he might drink the strong drinks that you left in his way, and be the sooner ended, holding no more terms with you than he would hold with a tiger, has had his master key for all your locks, his tests for all your poisons, his clue to your cipher-writing. He can tell you, as well as you can tell him, how long it took to complete that deed, what doses there were, what intervals, what signs of gradual decay upon mind and body; what distempered fancies were produced, what observable changes, what physical pain. He can tell you, as well as you can tell him, that all this was recorded day by day, as a lesson of experience for future service. He can tell you, better than you can tell him, where that journal is at this moment.'

Slinkton stopped the action of his foot, and looked at Beckwith.

'No,' said the latter, as if answering a question from him. 'Not in the drawer of the writing-desk that opens with a spring; it is not there, and it never will be there again.'

'Then you are a thief!' said Slinkton.

Without any change whatever in the inflexible purpose, which it was quite terrific even to me to contemplate, and from the power of which I had always felt convinced it was impossible for this wretch to escape, Beckwith returned:

'And I am your niece's shadow, too.'

With an imprecation Slinkton put his hand to his head, tore out some hair, and flung it to the ground. It was the end of the smooth walk; he destroyed it in the action, and it will soon be seen that his use for it was past.

Beckwith went on: 'Whenever you left here, I left here. Although I understood that you found it necessary to pause in the completion of that purpose, to avert suspicion, still I watched you close, with the poor confiding girl. When I had the diary, and could read it word by word—it was only about the night before your last visit to Scarborough—you remember the night? you slept with a small flat vial tied to your wrist—I sent to Mr Sampson, who was kept out of view. This is Mr Sampson's trusty servant standing by the door. We three saved your niece among us.'

Slinkton looked at us all, took an uncertain step or two from the place where he had stood, returned to it, and glanced about him in a very curious way—as one of the meaner reptiles might, looking for a hole to hide in. I noticed, at the same time, that a singular change took place in the figure of the man—as if it collapsed within his clothes, and they consequently became ill-shapen and ill-fitting.

'You shall know,' said Beckwith, 'for I hope the knowledge will be bitter and terrible to you, why you have been pursued by one man, and why, when the whole interest that Mr Sampson represents would have expended any money in hunting you down, you have been tracked to death at a single individual's charge. I hear you have had the name of Meltham on your lips sometimes?'

I saw, in addition to those other changes, a sudden stoppage come upon his breathing.

'When you sent the sweet girl whom you murdered (you know with what artfully made-out surroundings and probabilities you sent her) to Meltham's office, before taking her abroad to originate the transaction that doomed her to the grave, it fell to Meltham's lot to see her and to speak with her. It did not fall to his lot to save her, though I know he would freely give his own life to have done it. He admired her—I would say he loved her deeply, if I thought it possible that you could understand the word. When she was sacrificed, he was thoroughly assured of your guilt. Having lost her, he had but one object left in life, and that was to avenge her and destroy you.'

I saw the villain's nostrils rise and fall convulsively; but I saw no moving at his mouth.

'That man Meltham,' Beckwith steadily pursued, 'was as absolutely certain that you could never elude him in this world, if he devoted himself to your destruction with his utmost fidelity and earnestness, and if he divided the sacred duty with no other duty in life, as he was certain that in achieving it he would be a poor instrument in the hands of Providence, and would do well before Heaven in striking you out from among living men. I am that man, and I thank God that I have done my work!'

If Slinkton had been running for his life from swift-footed savages, a dozen miles, he could not have shown more emphatic signs of being oppressed at heart and labouring for breath than he showed now, when he looked at the pursuer who had so relentlessly hunted him down.

'You never saw me under my right name before; you see me under my right name now. You shall see me once again in the body when you are tried for your life. You shall see me once again in the spirit, when the cord is round your neck, and the crowd are crying against you!'

When Meltham had spoken these last words, the miscreant suddenly turned away his face, and seemed to strike his mouth with his open hand. At the same instant, the room was filled with a new and powerful odour, and, almost at the same instant, he broke into a crooked run, leap, start—I have no name for the spasm—and fell, with a dull weight that shook the heavy old doors and windows in their frames.

That was the fitting end of him.

When we saw that he was dead, we drew away from the room, and Meltham, giving me his hand, said, with a weary air:

'I have no more work on earth, my friend. But I shall see her again elsewhere.'

It was in vain that I tried to rally him. He might have saved her, he said; he had not saved her, and he reproached himself; he had lost her, and he was broken-hearted.

'The purpose that sustained me is over, Sampson, and there is nothing now to hold me to life. I am not fit for life; I am weak and spiritless; I have no hope and no object; my day is done.'

In truth, I could hardly have believed that the broken man who then spoke to me was the man who had so strongly and so differently impressed me when his purpose was before him. I used such entreaties with him as I could; but he still said, and always said, in a patient, undemonstrative way—nothing could avail him—he was broken-hearted.

He died early in the next spring. He was buried by the side of the poor young lady for whom he had cherished those tender and unhappy regrets; and he left all he had to her sister. She lived to be a happy wife and mother; she married my sister's son, who succeeded poor Meltham; she is living now, and her children ride about the garden on my walking-stick when I go to see her.

Levison's Victim

MARY ELIZABETH BRADDON

'Have you seen Horace Wynward?'

'No. You don't mean to say that he is here?'

'He is indeed. I saw him last night; and I think I never saw a man so much changed in so short a time.'

'For the worse?'

'Infinitely for the worse. I should scarcely have recognized him but for that peculiar look in his eyes, which I daresay you remember.'

'Yes; deep-set grey eyes, with an earnest penetrating look that seems to read a man up as he talks to him. I'm very sorry to hear of this change in him. We were at Oxford together, you know; and his place is near my father's in Buckinghamshire. We have been fast friends for a long time; but I lost sight of him about two years ago, before I went on my Spanish rambles, and I've heard nothing of him since. Do you think he has been leading a dissipated life—going the pace a little too violently?'

'I don't know what he has been doing; but I fancy he must have been travelling during the last year or two, for I've never come across him in London.'

'Did you speak to him last night?'

'No; I wanted very much to get hold of him for a few minutes' chat, but couldn't manage it. It was in one of the gambling-rooms I saw him, on the opposite side of the table. The room was crowded. He was standing looking on at the game over the heads of the players. You know how tall he is, and what a conspicuous figure anywhere. I saw him one minute, and in the next he had disappeared. I left the rooms in search of him, but he was not to be seen anywhere about.'

'I shall try and hunt him up tomorrow. He must be stopping at one of the hotels. There can't be much difficulty in finding him.'

The speakers were two young Englishmen; the scene a little lamplit grove of trees outside the Kursaal of a German spa. The elder, George Theobald, was a barrister of the Inner Temple; the younger, Francis Lorrimore, son and heir of a Buckinghamshire squire, and gentleman at large.

'What was the change that struck you so painfully, George?' Lorrimore asked between the puffs of his cigar; 'you couldn't have seen much of Wynward in that look across the gaming-table.'

'I saw quite enough. His face has a worn haggard expression—he looks like a man who never sleeps; and there's a fierceness about the eyes—a contraction of the brows, a kind of restless searching look— as if he were on the watch for some one or some thing. In short, the poor fellow seemed to me altogether queer—the sort of man one would expect to hear of in a madhouse, or committing suicide, or something bad of that kind.'

'I shall certainly hunt him out, George.'

'It would be only a kindness to do so, old fellow, as you and he have been intimate. Stay!' exclaimed Mr Theobald, pointing suddenly to a figure in the distance. 'Do you see that tall man under the trees yonder? I've a notion it's the very man we're talking of.'

They rose from the bench on which they had been sitting smoking their cigars for the last half-hour, and walked in the direction of the tall figure pacing slowly under the pine-trees. There was no mistaking that muscular frame—six feet two, if an inch—and the peculiar carriage of the head. Frank Lorrimore touched his friend lightly on the shoulder, and he turned round suddenly and faced the two young men, staring at them blankly without a sign of recognition.

Yes, it was indeed a haggard face, with a latent fierceness in the deep-set grey eyes overshadowed by strongly marked black brows, but a face which, seen at its best, must needs have been very handsome.

'Wynward,' said Frank, 'don't you know me?'

He held out both his hands. The other took one of them slowly, looking at him like a man suddenly awakened from sleep.

'Yes,' he said, 'I know you well enough now, Frank; but you startled me just this moment. I was thinking. How well you're looking, old fellow!—What, you here too, Theobald!'

'Yes; I saw you in the rooms last night,' answered George Theobald as they shook hands; 'but you were gone before I could get a chance of speaking to you. Where are you staying?'

'At the Hotel des Etrangers. I shall be off tomorrow.'

'Don't run away in such a hurry, Horace,' said Frank; 'it looks as if you wanted to cut us.'

'I'm not very good company just now; you'd scarcely care to see much of me.'

'You are not looking very well, Horace, certainly. Have you been ill?'

'No, I am never ill; I am made of iron, you know.'

'But there's something wrong, I'm afraid.'

'There is something wrong, but nothing that talk or friendship can mend.'

'Don't say that, Horace. Come to breakfast with me tomorrow, and tell me your troubles.'

'It's a common story enough; I shall only bore you.'

'I think you ought to know me better than that.'

'Well, I'll come, if you like,' Horace Wynward answered in a softer tone; 'I'm not very much given to confide in friendship, but you were once a kind of younger brother of mine, Frank. Yes, I'll come. How long have you been here?'

'I only came yesterday. I am at the Couronne d'Or, where I discovered my friend Theobald, happily for me, at the table d'hôte. I am going back to Buckinghamshire next week. Have you been at Crofton lately?'

'No; Crofton has been shut up for the last two years. The old housekeeper is there, of course, and there are men to keep the gardens in order. I shouldn't like the idea of my mother's flower-gardens being neglected; but I doubt if I shall ever live at Crofton.'

'Not when you marry, Horace?'

'Marry? Yes, when that event occurs, I may change my mind,' he answered with a scornful laugh.

'Ah, Horace, I see there is a woman at the bottom of your trouble!'

He did not answer this, but began to talk of indifferent subjects.

The three young men walked for some time under the pines, smoking and talking in a fragmentary manner. Horace Wynward had an absent-minded way, which was not calculated to promote a lively style of conversation; but the others indulged his humour, and did not demand much from him. It was late when they shook hands and separated.

'At ten o'clock tomorrow, Horace?' said Frank.

'I shall be with you at ten. Good-night.'

Mr Lorrimore ordered an excellent breakfast, and a little before ten o'clock awaited his friend in a pretty sitting-room overlooking the gardens of the hotel. He had been dreaming of Horace all night, and was thinking of him as he walked up and down the room waiting his arrival. As the little clock on the mantelpiece struck the hour, Mr Wynward was announced. His dress was dusty, and he had a tired look even at that early hour. Frank welcomed him heartily.

'You look as if you had been walking, Horace,' he said, as they sat down to breakfast.

'I have been on the hills since five o'clock this morning.'

'So early?'

'Yes; I am a bad sleeper. It is better to walk than to lie tossing about hour after hour, thinking the same thoughts with maddening repetition.'

'My dear boy, you will make yourself ill with this kind of life.'

'Don't I tell you that I am never ill? I never had a day's illness in my life. I suppose when I die, I shall go down at a shot—apoplexy or heart-disease. Men of my build generally do.'

'I hope you may have a long life.'

'Yes, a long life of emptiness.'

'Why shouldn't it be a useful happy life, Horace?'

'Because it was shipwrecked two years ago. I set sail for a given port, Frank, with a fair wind in my favour; and my ship went down in sight of land, on a summer's day, without a moment's warning. I can't rig another boat, and make for another harbour, as some men can. All my world's wealth was adventured in this one argosy. That sounds tall talk, doesn't it? but you see there is such a thing as passion in the world, and I've so much faith in your sympathy, that I'm not ashamed to tell you what a fool I have been, and still am. You were such a romantic fellow five years ago, Frank; and I used to laugh at your sentimental notions.'

'Yes, I was obliged to stand a good deal of ridicule from you.'

'Let those laugh who win. It was in the last long vacation before I left Oxford that I went to read, at a quiet little village on the Sussex coast, with a retired tutor, an eccentric old fellow, but a miracle of learning. He had three daughters, the eldest of them, to my mind, the loveliest girl that ever the sun shone upon. I'm not going to make a long story of it. I think it was a case of love at sight. I know that before I had been a week in the humdrum sea-coast village, I was

over head and ears in love with Laura Daventry; and at the end of a
month was happy in the belief that my love was returned. She was the
dearest, brightest of girls, with a happy disposition that won her
friends in every direction; and a man must have had a dull un-
impressionable nature who could have withstood her charm. I was
free to make my own choice, rich enough to marry a penniless girl;
and before I went back to Oxford I made her an offer. It was
accepted; and I returned to the University the happiest of men.'

He drank a cup of coffee, and rose from the table to walk up and
down the room.

'Well, Frank, you would imagine that nothing could arise to interfere with our happiness after this. In worldly circumstances I was
what would be considered an excellent match for Miss Daventry, and
I had every reason to believe that she loved me. She was very young,
not quite eighteen; and I was the first man who had ever proposed to
her. I left her, with the most entire confidence in her good faith; and
to this hour I believe in her.'

There was a pause, and then he went on again.

'We corresponded, of course. Laura's letters were charming; and I
had no greater delight than in receiving and replying to them. I had
promised her to work hard for my degree, and for her sake I kept my
promise, and won it. My first thought was to carry her the news of my
success; and directly the examinations were over, I ran down to
Sussex. I found the cottage empty. Mr Daventry was in London; the
two younger girls had gone to Devonshire, to an aunt who kept a
school there. About Miss Daventry the neighbours could give me no
positive information. She had left a few days before her father, but no
one knew where she had gone. When I pressed them more closely,
they told me that it was rumoured in the village that she had gone
away to be married. A gentleman from the Spanish colonies, a Mr
Levison, had been staying at the cottage for some weeks, and had
disappeared about the same time as Miss Laura.'

'And you believe that she had eloped with him?'

'To this day I am ignorant as to the manner of her leaving. Her last
letters were only a week old. She had told me of this Mr Levison's
residence in their household. He was a prosperous merchant, a
distant relation of her father's, and was staying in Sussex for his
health. This was all she had said of him. Of their approaching
departure she had not given me the least hint. No one in the vil-

lage could tell me Mr Daventry's London address. The cottage, a furnished one, had been given up to the landlord, and every debt paid. I went to the post office; but the people there had received no directions as to the forwarding of letters, nor had any come as yet for Mr Daventry.'

'The girls in Devonshire—you applied to them, I suppose?'

'I did; but they could tell me nothing. I wrote to Emily, the eldest girl, begging her to send me her sister's address. She answered my letter immediately. Laura had left home with her father's full knowledge and consent, she said, but had not told her sisters where she was going. She had seemed very unhappy. The whole affair had been sudden, and her father had also appeared much distressed in mind. This was all I could ascertain. I put an advertisement in *The Times*, addressed to Mr Daventry, begging him to let me know his whereabouts; but nothing came of it. I employed a man to hunt London for him, and hunted myself; but without avail. I wasted months in this futile search, now on one false track, now on another.'

'And you have long ago given up all hope, I suppose?' I said, as he paused, walking up and down the room with a moody face.

'Given up all hope of seeing Laura Levison alive? Yes; but not of tracking her destroyer.'

'Laura Levison! Then you think she married the Spanish merchant?'

'I am sure of it. I had been more than six months on the look-out for Mr Daventry, and had begun to despair of finding him, when the man I employed came to me and told me that he had found the registry of a marriage between Michael Levison and Laura Daventry, at an obscure church in the City, where he had occasion to make researches for another client. The date of the marriage was within a few days of Laura's departure from Sussex.'

'Strange!'

'Yes, strange that a woman could be so fickle, you would say. I felt convinced that there had been something more than girlish inconstancy at work in this business—some motive-power strong enough to induce this girl to sacrifice herself in a loveless marriage. I was confirmed in this belief, when, within a very short time of the discovery of the registry, I came suddenly upon old Daventry in the street. He would fain have avoided me; but I insisted on a conversation with him, and he reluctantly allowed me to accompany him to his lodging, a wretched place in Southwark. He was very ill, with the stamp of death upon his face, and had a craven look that convinced me it was to him I was indebted for my sorrow. I told him that I knew of his daughter's marriage, when and where it had taken place, and boldly accused him of having brought it about.'

'How did he take your accusation?'

'Like a beaten hound. He whimpered piteously, and told me that the marriage had been no wish of his. But Levison had possession of secrets which made him the veriest slave. Little by little I wrung from him the nature of these secrets. They related to forged bills of exchange, in which the old man had made free with his kinsman's name. It was a transaction of many years ago; but Levison had used this power in order to induce Laura to marry him; and the girl, to save her father from utter ruin, as she believed, had consented to become his wife. Levison had promised to do great things for the old man, but had left England immediately after his marriage, without settling a shilling on his father-in-law. It was altogether a most wretched business: the girl had been sacrificed to her father's weakness and folly. I asked him why he had not appealed to me, who could no doubt have extricated him from his difficulty; but he could give me no clear answer. He evidently had an overpowering dread of Michael Levison. I left him, utterly disgusted with his imbecility and selfishness; but for Laura's sake I took care that he wanted for nothing during the remainder of his life. He did not trouble me long.'

'And Mrs Levison?'

'The old man told me that the Levisons had gone to Switzerland. I followed post-haste, and traced them from place to place, closely questioning the people at all the hotels. The accounts I heard were by no means encouraging. The lady did not seem happy. The gentleman looked old enough to be her father, and was peevish and fretful in his manner, never letting his wife out of his sight, and evidently suffering torments of jealousy on account of the admiration which her beauty won for her from every one they met. I traced them stage by stage, through Switzerland into Italy, and then suddenly lost the track. I concluded that they had returned to England by some other route; but all my attempts to discover traces of their return were useless. Neither by land nor by sea passage could I hear of the yellow-faced trader and his beautiful young wife. They were not a couple to be overlooked easily; and this puzzled me. Disheartened and dispirited, I halted in Paris, where I spent a couple of months in hopeless idleness—a state of utter stagnation, from which I was aroused abruptly by a communication from my agent, a private detective—a very clever fellow in his way, and well in with the police of civilized Europe. He sent me a cutting from a German newspaper, which described the discovery of a corpse in the Tyrol. It was supposed, from the style of the dress, to be the body of an English-woman; but no indication of a name or address had been found, to give a clue to identity. Whether the dead woman had been the victim of foul play, or whether she had met her death from an accidental fall, no one had been able to decide. The body had been found at the bottom of a mountain gorge, the face disfigured by the fall from the height above. Had the victim been a native of the district, it might have been easily supposed that she had lost her footing on the mountain-path; but that a stranger should have travelled alone by so unfrequented a route seemed highly improbable. The spot at which the body was found lay within a mile of a small village; but it was a place rarely visited by travellers of any description.'

'Had your agent any reason to identify this woman with Mrs Levison?'

'None; except the fact that Mrs Levison was missing, and his natural habit of suspicion. The paragraph was nearly a month old when it reached me. I set off at once for the place named; saw the village authorities, and visited the Englishwoman's grave. They showed me the dress she had worn; a black silk, very simply made. Her face had been too much disfigured by the fall, and the passage of time that had occurred before the finding of the body, for them to give me any minute description of her appearance. They could only tell me that her hair was dark auburn, the colour of Laura's, thick and long; and that her figure was that of a young woman.

'After exhausting every possible enquiry, I pushed on to the next village, and there received confirmation of my worst fears. A gentle-man and his wife—the man of foreign appearance, but talking English; the woman young and beautiful—had stopped for a night at the chief inn of the place, and had left the next morning without a guide. The gentleman, who talked German perfectly, told the land-lady that his travelling-carriage and servants were to meet him at the nearest stage on the home journey. He knew every inch of the country, and wished to walk across the mountain, in order to show his wife a prospect which had struck him particularly upon his last expedition a few years before. The landlady remembered that, just before setting out, he asked his wife some question about her watch, took it from her to regulate it, and then, after some peevish exclamation about her carelessness, put it into his waistcoat pocket. The lady was very pale and quiet, and seemed unhappy. The description which the woman gave me was only too like the woman I was looking for.'

'And you believe there had been foul play?'

'As certainly as I believe in my own existence. This man Levison had grown tired of a wife whose affection had never been his; nay more, I have reason to know that his unresting jealousy had intensified into a kind of hatred of her some time before the end. From the village in the Tyrol, which they left together on the bright October morning, I tracked their footsteps stage by stage back to the point at which I had lost them on the Italian frontier. In the course of my wanderings I met with a young Austrian officer who had seen them at Milan, and had ventured to pay the lady some frivolous harmless attentions. He told me that he had never seen anything so appalling as Levison's jealousy; not an open fury, but a concentrated silent rage, which gave an almost devilish expression to the man's parchment face. He watched his wife like a lynx, and did not allow her a moment's freedom from his presence. Every one who met them pitied the beautiful girlish wife, whose misery was so evident; every one loathed her tyrant. I found that the story of the servants and the travelling-carriage was a lie. The Levisons had been attended by no servants at any of the hotels where I heard of them, and had travelled always in public or in hired vehicles. The ultimate result of my enquiries left me little doubt that the dead woman was Laura Levison; and from that hour to this I have been employed more or less in the endeavour to find the man who murdered her.'

'And you have not been able to discover his whereabouts?' asked Frank Lorrimore.

'Not yet. I am looking for him.'

'A useless quest, Horace. What would be the result of your finding him? you have no proof to offer of his guilt. You would not take the law into your own hands?'

'By the heaven above me, I would!' answered the other fiercely. 'I would shoot that man down with as little compunction as I would kill a mad dog.'

'I hope you may never meet him,' said Frank solemnly.

Horace Wynward gave a short impatient sigh, and paced the room for some time in silence. His share in the breakfast had been a mere pretence. He had emptied his coffee-cup, but had eaten nothing.

'I am going back to London this afternoon, Frank.'

'On the hunt for this man?'

'Yes. My agent sent me a description of a man calling himself Lewis, a bill-discounter, who has lately set up an office in the City, and whom I believe to be Michael Levison.'

The office occupied by Mr Lewis, the bill-discounter, was a dismal place enough, consisting of a second-floor in a narrow alley called St Guinevere's Lane. Horace Wynward presented himself at this office about a week after his arrival in London, in the character of a gentleman in difficulties.

He found Mr Lewis exactly the kind of man he expected to see; a man of about fifty, with small crafty black eyes shining out of a sallow visage that was as dull and lifeless as a parchment mask, thin lips with a cruel expression, and a heavy jaw and bony chin that betokened no small amount of power for evil.

Mr Wynward presented himself under his own name; on hearing which the bill-discounter looked up at him suddenly with an exclamation of surprise.

'You know my name?' said Horace.

'Yes; I have heard your name before. I thought you were a rich man.'

'I have a good estate, but I have been rather imprudent, and am short of ready-money. Where and when did you hear my name, Mr Lewis?'

'I don't remember that. The name sounds familiar to me, that is all.'

'But you have heard of me as a rich man, you say?'

'I had an impression to that effect. But the circumstances under which I heard the name have quite escaped my memory.'

Horace pushed the question no further. He played his cards very carefully, leading the usurer to believe that he had secured a profitable prey. The preliminaries of a loan were discussed, but nothing fully settled; and before leaving, Horace Wynward invited Mr Lewis to dine with him at his lodgings, in the neighbourhood of Piccadilly, on the following evening. After a few minutes' reflection Lewis accepted the invitation.

He made his appearance at the appointed hour, dressed in a suit of shabby black, in which his sallow complexion looked more than usually parchment-like and ghastly. The door was opened by Horace Wynward in person, and the money-lender was surprised to find himself in an almost empty house. In the hall and on the staircase there were no signs of occupation whatever; but in the dining-room, to which Horace immediately ushered his guest, there was a table ready laid for dinner, a couple of chairs, and a dumb-waiter loaded with the appliances of the meal. The room was dimly lighted by four wax candles in a tarnished candelabrum.

Mr Lewis, the money-lender, looked round him with a shudder; there was something sinister in the aspect of the room.

'It's rather a dreary-looking place, I'm afraid,' said Horace Wynward. 'I've only just taken the house, you see, and have had in a few sticks of hired furniture to keep me going till I make arrangements with an upholsterer. But you'll excuse all shortcomings, I'm sure—bachelor fare, you know.'

'I thought you said you were in lodgings, Mr Wynward.'

'Did I?' asked the other absently; 'a mere slip of the tongue. I took this house on lease a week ago, and am going to furnish it as soon as I am in funds.'

'And are you positively alone here?' enquired Mr Lewis rather suspiciously.

'Well, very nearly so. There is a charwoman somewhere in the depths below, as deaf as a post and almost as useless. But you needn't be frightened about your dinner; I had it in from a confectioner in Piccadilly.'

He lifted the cover of the soup tureen as he spoke. The visitor seated himself at the table with rather a nervous air, and glanced more than once in the direction of the shutters closely fastened with heavy bars. He began to think there was something alarmingly eccentric in the conduct and manner of his host, and was inclined to repent having accepted the invitation, profitable as his new client promised to be.

The dinner was excellent, the wines of the first quality; and after drinking somewhat freely, Mr Lewis began to be better reconciled to his position. He was a little disconcerted, however, in perceiving that his host scarcely touched either the viands or the wine, and that those deep-set grey eyes were lifted every now and then to his face with a strangely observant look. When dinner was over, Mr Wynward heaped the dishes on the dumb-waiter, wheeled it into the next room with his own hands, and came back to his seat at the table opposite the bill-discounter, who sat meditatively sipping his claret.

Horace filled his glass, but remained for some time silent, without once lifting it to his lips. His companion watched him nervously, every moment more impressed with the belief that there was something wrong in his new client's mind, and bent on making a speedy escape. He finished his claret, looked at his watch, and rose hastily.

'I think I must wish you good-night, Mr Wynward. I am a man of early habits, and have some distance to go. My lodging is at Brompton, more than an hour's ride from here.'

'Stay,' said Horace, 'we have not begun business yet. It's only nine o'clock. I want an hour's quiet talk with you—Mr Levison.'

The bill-discounter's face changed. It was almost impossible for that pallid mask of parchment to grow paler, but a sudden ghastliness came over the man's evil countenance.

'My name is Lewis,' he said, with an artificial grin.

'Lewis, or Levison. Men of your trade have as many names as they please. When you were travelling in Switzerland two years ago, your name was Levison; when you married Laura Daventry, your name was Levison.'

'You are under some absurd mistake, sir. The name of Levison is strange to me.'

'Is the name of Daventry strange to you too? You recognized my name yesterday. When you first heard it, I was a happy man, Michael Levison. The blight upon me is your work. O, I know you well enough, and am provided with ample means for your identification. I have followed you step by step upon your travels—tracked you to the inn from which you set out one October morning, nearly a year ago, with a companion who was never seen alive by mortal eyes after that date. You are a good German scholar, Mr Levison; read that.'

Horace Wynward took out of his pocket-book the paragraph cut from the German paper, and laid it before his visitor. The bill-discounter pushed it away after a hasty glance at its contents.

'What has this to do with me?' he asked.

'A great deal, Mr Levison. The hapless woman described in that paragraph was once your wife: Laura Daventry, the girl I loved, and who returned my love; the girl whom you basely stole from me by trading on her natural affection for a weak unworthy father, and whose life you made wretched, until it was foully ended by your cruel hand. If I had stood behind you upon that lonely mountain pathway in the Tyrol, and had seen you hurl your victim to destruction, I could not be more convinced than I am that your arm did the deed; but such crimes as these are difficult—in this case perhaps impossible—to prove, and I fear you will escape the gallows. There are other circumstances in your life, however, more easily brought to light; and by the aid of a clever detective I have made myself master of some curious secrets in your past existence. I know the name you bore some fifteen years ago, before you settled in Trinidad as a merchant. You were at that time called Michael Lucas, and you fled from this country with a large sum of money, embezzled from your employers, Messrs Harwell and Oliphant, sugar-brokers in St Nicholas Lane. You have been "wanted" a long time, Mr Levison; but you would most likely have gone scot-free to the end, had I not set my man to hunt you and your antecedents.'

Michael Levison rose from his seat hastily, trembling in every limb. Horace rose at the same moment, and the two men stood face to face—one the very image of craven fear, the other cool and self-possessed.

'This is a tissue of lies!' gasped Levison, wiping his lips nervously with a handkerchief that fluttered in his tremulous fingers. 'Have you brought me here to insult me with this madman's talk?'

'I have brought you here to your doom. There was a time when I thought that if you and I ever stood face to face, I should shoot you down like a dog; but I have changed my mind. Such carrion as you are not worth the stain of guilt upon an honest man's hand. It is useless to tell you how I loved the girl you murdered. Your savage nature would not comprehend any but the basest and most selfish passion. Don't stir another step—I have a loaded revolver within reach, and shall make an end of you if you attempt to leave this room. The police are on the watch for you outside, and you will leave this place for a gaol. Hark! what is that?'

It was a footstep on the stairs outside, a woman's footstep, and the rustling of a silk dress. The dining-room door was ajar, and the sounds were very audible in the bare empty house. Michael Levison made for the door, availing himself of this momentary diversion, with some vague hope of escape, but within a few paces of the door he recoiled suddenly with a hoarse gasping cry.

The door was pushed wide open by a light hand, and a figure stood upon the threshold—a girlish figure dressed in black silk, a pale sad face framed by dark-auburn hair.

'The dead returned to life!' cried Levison. 'Hide her, hide her! I can't face her! Let me go!'

He made for the other door, leading into the inner room, but found it locked, and then sank cowering down into his chair, covering his eyes with his skinny hands. The girl came softly into the room, and stood by Horace Wynward.

'You have forgotten me, Mr Levison,' she said; 'and you take me for my sister's ghost. I was always like her, and they say I have grown more so within the last two years. We had a letter from you a month ago, posted from Trinidad, telling us that my sister Laura was well and happy there with you—yet you mistake me for the shadow of the dead!'

The frightened wretch did not look up. He had not yet recovered from the shock produced by his sister-in-law's sudden appearance. The handkerchief which he held to his lips was stained with blood. Horace Wynward went quietly to the outer door and opened it, returning presently with two men, who came softly into the room and approached Levison. He made no attempt to resist them as they slipped a pair of handcuffs on his bony wrists, and led him away. There was a cab standing outside ready to convey him to prison.

Emily Daventry sank into a chair as he was taken from the room.

'O Mr Wynward,' she said, 'I think there can be little doubt of my sister's wretched fate. The experiment which you proposed has succeeded only too well.'

Horace had been down to Devonshire to question the two girls about their sister. He had been struck by Emily's likeness to his lost love, and had brought her up to London with him, in order to identify Levison by her means, and to test the effect which her appearance might produce upon the nerves of the suspected assassin.

The police were furnished with a complicated mass of evidence against Levison in his character of clerk, merchant, and bill-discounter; but the business was of a nature that entailed much delay, and after several adjourned examinations the prisoner fell desperately ill of a heart-disease from which he had suffered for years, but which grew much worse during his imprisonment. Finding his death certain, he sent for Horace Wynward, and to him confessed his crime, boasting of his wife's death with a fiendish delight in the deed, which he called an act of vengeance against his rival.

'I knew you well enough when you came home, Horace Wynward,' he said, 'and I thought it would be my happy lot to compass your ruin. You trapped me, but to the last you have the worst of it. The girl you loved is dead. She dared to tell me that she loved you; defied my anger; told me that she had sold herself to me to save her father from disgrace, and confessed that she hated, and had always hated me. From that hour she was doomed. Her white face was a constant reproach to me. I was goaded to madness by her tears. She used to say your name in her sleep. I wonder I did not cut her throat as she lay there with the name upon her lips. But I must have swung for that. So I was patient, and waited till I could have her alone with me upon the mountains. It was only a push, and she was gone. I came home alone, free from the worry and fever of her presence: except in my dreams. She has haunted them with her pale face and the one long shriek that went up to the sky as she fell.'

He died within a few days of this interview; and before his final trial could take place. Time, that heals almost all griefs, brought peace by and by to Horace Wynward. He furnished the house in Mayfair, and for some time led a misanthropical life there; but on paying a second visit to Devonshire, where the two Daventry girls lived their simple industrious life in their aunt's school, he discovered that Emily's likeness to her sister made her very dear to him, and in the following year he brought a mistress to Crofton in the person of that young lady. Together they paid a mournful visit to that lonely spot in the Tyrol where Laura Levison had perished, and stayed there while a white marble cross was erected above her grave.

The Mystery at Number Seven

MRS HENRY WOOD

'Let us go and give her a turn,' cried the Squire.

Tod laughed. 'What, all of us?' said he.

'To be sure. All of us. Why not? We'll start tomorrow.'

'Oh dear!' exclaimed Mrs Todhetley, dismay in her mild tone. 'Children and all?'

'Children and all: and take Hannah to see to them,' said the Squire. 'You don't count, Joe: you will be off elsewhere.'

'We could never be ready,' said the Mater, looking the image of perplexity. 'Tomorrow's Friday. Besides, there would be no time to write to Mary.'

'*Write to her!*' cried the Squire, turning sharply on his heel as he paced the room in his nankeen morning coat. 'And who do you suppose is going to write to her? Why, it would cause her to make all sorts of preparation; put her to no end of trouble. A pretty conjurer you'd make! We will take her by surprise: that's what we will do.'

'But, if, when we got there, we should find her rooms are let, sir?' said I, the doubt striking me.

'Then we'll go into others, Johnny. A spell at the seaside will be a change for us.'

This conversation, and the Squire's planning-out, arose, through a letter we had just received from Mary Blair—poor Blair's widow, if you have not forgotten him, who went to his end through that gazette of Jerry's. After a few ups and downs, trying at this thing for a living, trying at that, Mrs Blair had now settled in a house at the seaside and opened a day-school. She hoped to get on in it in time, she wrote, especially if she could be so fortunate as to let her drawing-room to visitors. The Squire, always impulsive and good-hearted, at once cried out that *we* would go and take it.

'It will be doing her a good turn, you see,' he ran on, 'and when we leave I daresay she'll find other people to go in. Let's see'—picking up the letter to refer to the address: 'No. 6, Seabord Terrace, Montpellier-by-Sea. Whereabouts is Montpellier-by-Sea?'

'Never heard of it in my life,' cried Tod. 'Don't believe there is such a place.'

'Be quiet, Joe. I fancy it lies somewhere towards Saltwater.'

Tod flung back his head. 'Saltwater! A nice common place that is!'

'Hold your tongue, sir. Johnny, fetch me the railway guide.'

Upon looking at the guide, it was found there, 'Montpellier-by-Sea,' the last station before getting to Saltwater. As to Saltwater, it might be common, as Tod said; for it was crowded by all sorts of people, but it was lively and healthy.

Not on the next day, Friday, for it was impossible to get ready in such a heap of a hurry, but on the following Tuesday we started. Tod had left on the Saturday for Gloucestershire. His own mother's relatives lived there, and they were always inviting him.

'Montpellier-by-Sea?' cried the railway clerk in a doubting tone as we were getting the tickets. 'Let's see? Where is that?'

Of course that set the Squire exploding: what right had clerks to pretend to issue tickets unless they knew their business? The clerk in question coolly ran his finger down the railway list he had turned to, and then gave us the tickets.

'It is a station not much frequented, you see,' he civilly observed, 'Travellers mostly go on to Saltwater.'

But for the train being due, and our having to make a rush for the platform, the Squire would have waited to give the young man a piece of his mind. 'Saltwater, indeed!' said he, 'I wonder the fellow does not issue his edict as to where people shall go and where they sha'n't.'

We arrived in due time at our destination. It was written up as large as life on a white board, 'Montpellier-by-Sea'. A small roadside station, open to the country around; no signs of sea or of houses to be seen; a broad rural district, apparently given over entirely to agriculture. On went the whistling train, leaving the group of us standing by our luggage on the platform. The Squire was staring about him doubtfully.

'Can you tell me where Seabord Terrace is?'

'Scabord Terrace?' repeated the station-master. 'No, sir, I don't know it. There's no terrace of that name hereabouts. For that matter there are no terraces at all; no houses, in fact.'

The Squire's face was a picture. He saw that (save a solitary farm homestead or two) the country was bare of dwelling places.

'This is Montpellier-by-Sea?' he questioned at last.

'Sure enough it is, sir. Munpler, it's called down here.'

'Then Seabord Terrace must be *somewhere* in it—somewhere about. What a strange thing!'

'Perhaps the gentlefolks want to go to Saltwater?' spoke up one of the two porters employed at the little station. 'There's lots of terraces there. Here, Jim!'—calling to his fellow—'come here a minute. He'll know, sir; he comes from Saltwater.'

Jim approached, and settled the doubt at once. He knew Seabord Terrace very well indeed: it was at Saltwater; just out at the eastern end of it.

Yes, it was at Saltwater. And there were we, more than two miles off it, on a broiling hot day when walking was impracticable, with all our trunks about us, and no fly to be had, or other means of getting on. The Squire went into one of his passions, and demanded why people living at Saltwater should give their address as Montpellier-by-Sea.

He had hardly patience to listen to the station-master's explanation—who acknowledged that we were not the first travelling party that had been deluded in like manner. Munpler (as he and the rest of the natives persisted in calling it) was an extensive, straggling, rural parish, filled with farm lands; an arm of it extended as far as Saltwater, and the new buildings at that end of Saltwater had rechristened themselves Montpellier-by-Sea, deeming it more aristocratic than the common old name. Had the Squire been able to transport the new buildings, builders and all, he had surely done it on the spot.

Well, we got on to Saltwater in the evening by another train, and to No. 6, Seaboard Terrace. Mary Blair was just delighted.

'If I had but known you were coming, if you had but written to me, I would have explained that it was Saltwater Station you must get out at, not Montpellier,' she cried in deprecation.

'But, my dear, why on earth do you give in to a deceit?' stormed the Squire. 'Why call your place Montpellier when it's Saltwater?'

'I do what other people do,' she sighed; 'I was told it was Montpellier when I came here. Generally speaking, I have explained when writing to friends, that it is really Saltwater, in spite of its fine name: I suppose I forgot it when writting to you—I had so much to say. The people really to blame are those who named it so.'

'And that's true, and they ought to be shown up,' said the Squire.

Seabord Terrace consisted of seven houses, built in front of the sea a little beyond the town. The parlours had bay windows; the drawing-rooms had balconies and verandahs. The two end houses, Nos. 1 and 7, were double houses, large and handsome, each of them being inhabited by a private family; the middle houses were smaller, most of them being let out in lodgings in the season. Mary Blair began talking that first evening as we sat together about the family who lived in the house next door to her, No. 7. Their name was Peahern, she said, and they had been so very, very kind to her since she took her house in March. Mr Peahern had interested himself for her and got her several pupils; he was much respected at Saltwater. 'Ah, he is a good man,' she added; 'but——'

'I'll call and thank him,' interrupted the Squire. 'I am proud to shake hands with such a man as that.'

'You cannot,' she said; 'he and his wife are gone abroad. A great misfortune has lately befallen them.'

'A great misfortune! what was it?'

I noticed a kind of cloud pass over Mary Blair's face, a hesitation in her manner before she replied. Mrs Todhetley was sitting by her on the sofa; the Squire was in the armchair opposite them, and I at the table, as I had sat at our tea-dinner.

'Mr Peahern was in business once; a wholesale druggist, I believe; but he made a good fortune, and retired some years ago,' began Mary. 'Mrs Peahern has poor health and is a little lame. She was very kind to me also; very good and kind indeed. They had one son; no other children; I think he was studying for the Bar; I am not sure; but he lived in London and came down here occasionally. My young maid-servant, Susan, got acquainted with their servants, and she gathered from their gossip that he, Edmund Peahern, a very handsome young man, was in some way a trouble to his parents. He was down at Easter, and stayed three weeks; and in May he came down again. What happened I don't know; I believe there was some scene with his father the day he arrived; anyway, Mr Peahern was heard talking angrily to him: and that night he—he died.'

She had dropped her voice to a low whisper. The Squire spoke.

'Died! Was it a natural death?'

'No. A jury decided that he was insane; and he was buried here in the churchyard. Such a heap of claims and debts came to light, it was said. Mr Peahern left his lawyer to pay them all, and went abroad with his poor wife for change of scene. It has been a great grief to me. I feel so sorry for them.'

'Then, is the house shut up?'

'No. Two servants are left in it; the two housemaids. The cook, who had lived with them five-and-twenty years and was dreadfully affected at the calamity, went with her mistress. Nice, good-natured young women, are these two that are left, running in most days to ask if they can do anything for me.'

'It is good to have such neighbours,' said the Squire. 'And I hope you'll get on, my dear. How came you at this place at all?'

'It was through Mr Lockett,' she answered: the clergyman who had been so much with her husband before he died, and who had kept up a correspondence with her. Mr Lockett's brother was in practice as a doctor at Saltwater, and they thought she might perhaps do well if she came to it. So Mary's friends had screwed a point or two to put her into the house, and gave her besides a ten-pound note to start with.

'I tell you what it is, young Joe: if you run and reve yourself into that scarlet heat, you sha'n't come here with me again.'

'But I like to race with the donkeys,' replied young Joe. 'I can run a'most as fast as they, Johnny. I like to see the donkeys.'

'Wouldn't it be better to ride a donkey, lad?'

He shook his head. 'I have never had a ride but once,' he answered: 'I've no sixpences for it. That once Matilda treated me. She brings me on the sands.'

'Who is Matilda?'

'Matilda at No. 7: Mr Peahern's.'

'Well, if you are a good boy, young Joe, and stay by me, you shall have a ride as soon as the donkeys come back.'

They were fine sands. I sat down on a bench with a book; little Joe strained his eyes to look after the donkeys in the distance, cantering off with some young shavers like himself on their backs, their nursemaids walking quickly after them. Poor little Joe!—he had the gentlest, meekest face in the world, with his thoughtful look and nice eyes—waited and watched in silent patience. The sands were crowded with people this afternoon; organs were playing, dancing dolls exhibiting; and vessels with their white sails spread glided smoothly up and down on the sparkling sea.

'And will you really pay the sixpence?' asked the little fellow presently. 'They won't let me get on for less.'

'Really and truly, Joe. I'll take you for a row in a boat some calm day, if mamma will allow you to go.'

Joe looked grave. 'I don't *much* like the water, please,' said he, timidly. 'Alfred Dale went on it in a boat and fell in, and was nearly drowned. He comes to mamma's school.'

'Then we'll let the boats alone, Joe. There's Punch! He is going to set himself up yonder: wouldn't you like to run and see him?'

'But I might miss the donkeys,' answered Joe.

He stood by me quietly, gazing in the direction taken by the donkeys: evidently they made his primary attraction. The other child, Mary, who was a baby when her father died (poor Baked Pie, as we boys used to call him at Frost's), was in Wales with Mrs Blair's people. They had taken the child for a few months, until she saw whether she should get along at Saltwater.

But we thought she would get along. Her school was a morning school for little boys of good parentage, all of whom paid liberal terms: and she would be able to let her best rooms for at least six months in the year.

'There's Matilda! Oh, there's Matilda!'

It was quite a loud shout for little Joe. Looking up, I saw him rush to a rather good-looking young woman, neatly dressed in a black-and-white print gown and small shawl of the same, with black ribbons crossed on her straw bonnet. Servants did not dress fine enough to set the Thames on fire in those days. Joe pulled her triumphantly up to me. She was one of the housemaids at No. 7.

'It's Matilda,' he said: and the young woman curtsied. 'And I am going to have a donkey-ride, Matilda: Mr Johnny Ludlow's going to give the sixpence for me!'

'I know you by sight, sir,' observed Matilda to me. 'I have seen you go in and out of No. 6.'

She had a pale olive complexion, with magnificent, melancholy dark eyes. Many persons would have called her handsome. I took a sort of liking for the girl—if only for her kindness to poor little fatherless Joe. In manner she was particularly quiet, subdued, and patient.

'You had a sad misfortune at your house not long ago,' I observed to her, at a loss for something to say.

'Oh sir, don't talk of it, please!' she answered with a sob of the breath. 'I seem to have the shivers at times ever since. It was me that found him.'

Up cantered the donkeys: and presently away went Joe on the back of one, Matilda attending him. The ride was just over and Joe beginning to enlarge on its delights to me, when another young woman, dressed precisely similar to Matilda, even to the zigzag white running pattern on the print gown, and the black cotton gloves, was seen making her way towards us. She was nice looking also in a different way; fair, with blue eyes, and a laughing, arch face.

'Why, there's Jane Cross!' exclaimed Matilda. 'What in the world have you come out for, Jane? Have you left the house safe?'

'As if I should leave it unsafe!' lightly retorted the one they had called Jane Cross. 'The back door's locked, and here's the key of the front—showing a huge key. Why shouldn't I go out if you do?— come, Matilda! The house is none so lively a one now, to stop in all alone.'

'And that's true enough,' was Matilda's quiet answer. 'Little master Joe's here: he has been having a donkey-ride.'

The two servants, fellow-housemaids, strolled off towards the sea, taking Joe with them. At the edge of the beach they encountered Hannah, who had just come on with our two children, Hugh and Lena. The maids sat down for a gossip, while the children took off their shoes and stockings to dabble in the gently rising tide.

And that was my introductory acquaintanceship with the servant maids at No. 7. Unfortunately it did not end there.

Twilight was coming on. We had been out and about all day, had dined as usual at one o'clock (not to give unnecessary trouble) and had just finished tea in Mrs Blair's parlour. It was where we generally took tea, and supper also. The Squire liked to sit in the open bay window and watch the passers-by as long as ever a glimmer of daylight lasted: and he could not see then so well in the drawing-room above. I was at the other corner of the bay window. The Mater and Mary Blair were on their favourite seat, the sofa, at the end of the room, both knitting. In the room at the back, Mary held her morning school.

I sat facing towards the end house, No. 7. And I must here say that during the last two or three weeks I had met the house maids several times on the sands and so had become quite at home with each of them. Both appeared to be thoroughly well-conducted, estimable young women; but, of the two, I liked Jane Cross best, she was always so lively and pleasant-mannered. One day, she told me why No. 7 generally called her by her two names—which I had thought rather odd. It appeared that when she entered her place two years before, the other housemaid was named Jane, so they took to call her by her full name, Jane Cross. That housemaid had left in about a twelve-month, and Matilda had entered in her place. The servants were regarded as equals in the house, not one above the other, as is the case in many places. These details will probably be thought unnecessary and uncalled for, but you will soon see why I mention them. This was Monday. On the morrow we should have been three weeks at Saltwater, and the Squire did not yet talk of leaving. He was enjoying the free-and-easy life, and was as fond as a child of picking up shells, on the sands and looking at Punch and the dancing dolls.

Well, we sat this evening in the bay window as usual, I facing No. 7. Thus sitting, I saw Matilda cross the strip of garden with a jug in her hand, and come out of the gate to fetch the beer for supper.

'There goes Jane Cross,' cried the Squire, as she passed the window. 'Is it not, Johnny?'

'No sir, it's Matilda.' But the mistake was a very natural one, for the girls were about the same height and size, and were usually dressed alike, the same mourning having been supplied to both of them.

Ten minutes, or so, had elapsed when Matilda came back: she liked a gossip with the landlady of the Swan. She had her pint jug full of beer, and shut the iron gate of No. 7 after her. Putting my head as far out at the window as it would go, to watch her indoors, for no earthly reason but that I had nothing else to do, I saw her try the front door, and then knock at it. This knock she repeated three times over at intervals, each knock being louder than the last.

'Are you shut out, Matilda?' I called out.

'Yes, sir, it seems like it,' she called back again, without turning her head. 'Jane Cross must be gone to sleep.'

Had she been a footman with a carriage full of ladies in court trains behind him, she could not have given a louder or longer knock than she gave now. There was no bell to the front door at No. 7. But the knock remained unanswered and the door unopened.

'Matilda at No. 7 is locked out,' I said, laughing, bringing in my head and speaking to the parlour generally. 'She has been to fetch the supper beer and can't get in again.'

'The supper beer,' repeated Mrs Blair. 'They generally go out, at the back gate to fetch that, Johnny.'

'Anyhow, she took the front way to tonight. I saw her come out.'

Another tremendous knock. The Squire put his good old nose round the window-post; two boys and a lady, passing by, halted a minute to look on. It was getting exciting, and I ran out. She was still at the door, which stood in the middle of the house, between the sitting-rooms on each side.

'So you have got the key of the street, Matilda!'

'I can't make it out,' she said: 'what Jane Cross can be about, or why the door should be closed at all. I left it on the latch.'

'Somebody has slipped in to make love to her. Your friend, the milkman, perhaps.'

Evidently Matilda did not like the allusion to the milkman: catching a glimpse of her face by the street gas-lamp, I saw it had turned white. The milkman was supposed to be paying court at No. 7: but to which of the two maids gossip did not decide. Mrs Blair's Susan, who knew them well, said it was Matilda.

'Why don't you try the back way?' I asked, after more waiting.

'Because I know the outer door is locked, sir. Jane Cross locked it just now, and that's why I came out this front way. I can try it.'

She went round to the road that ran by the side of the house, and tried the door in the garden wall. It was fastened, as she had said. Seizing the bell-handle, she gave a loud peal. Another, and another.

'I say, it seems odd, though,' I cried, beginning to find it so. 'Do you think she can have gone out?'

'I'm sure I don't know, sir. But—no; it's not likely, Master Johnny. I left her laying the cloth for our supper.'

'Was she in the house alone?'

'We are always alone, sir; we don't have visitors. Anyway, none have been with us this evening.'

I looked at the upper windows of the house. No light was to be seen in any of them, no sign of Jane Cross. The lower windows were hidden from view by the wall—which was high.

'I think she must have dropped asleep, Matilda. Suppose you come in through Mrs Blair's and get over the wall?'

I ran round to tell the news to our people. Matilda followed me slowly; I thought, reluctantly. Even in the dim twilight, as she stood at our gate in hesitation, I could see how white her face was.

'What are you afraid of?' I asked her, going out again to where she stood.

'I hardly know, Master Johnny. Jane Cross used to have fits. Perhaps she has been frightened into one.'

'What should frighten her?'

The girl looked round in a scared manner before replying. Just then I found my jacket sleeve wet. Her trembling hands had shaken some drops of the ale upon it.

'If she—should have seen Mr Edmund?' the girl brought out in a horrified whisper.

'Seen Mr Edmund! Mr Edmund who?—Mr Edmund Peahern? Why! You don't surely mean his ghost?'

Her face was growing whiter. I stared at her in surprise.

'We have always been afraid of seeing something, she and me, since last May: we haven't liked the house at night-time. It has often been quite a scuffle which of us should fetch the beer, so as not to be the one left alone. Many a time I have stood right out at the back door while Jane Cross has gone for it.'

I began to think her an idiot. If Jane Cross was another, why perhaps she had scared herself into a fit. All the more reason that somebody should see after her.

'Come along, Matilda, don't be foolish: we'll get over the wall.'

It was a calm, still summer evening, nearly dark now. All the lot of us went out to the back garden, I whispering to them what the girl had said to me.

'Poor thing!' said Mrs Todhetley, who had a kind of fellow-feeling for ghosts. 'It has been very lonely for the young women: and if Jane Cross is subject to fits, she may be lying in one.'

The wall between the gardens was nothing like as high as the outer one. Susan brought out a chair, and Matilda could have got over easily. But when she reached the top she stuck there.

'I can't go on by myself; I dare not,' she said, turning her scared face towards us. 'If Mr Edmund is there——'

'Don't thee be a goose, girl!' interrupted the Squire, in doubt whether to laught or scold. 'Here, I'll go with you. Get on down. Hold the chair tight for me, Johnny.'

We hoisted him over without damage. I leaped after him, and Susan, grinning with delight, came after me. She supposed that Jane Cross had slipped out somewhat during Matilda's absence.

The door faced the garden, and the Squire and Susan were the first to enter. There seemed to be no light anywhere, and the Squire went gingerly, picking his way. I turned round to look for Matilda, who had hung back, and found her with her hand on the trellis work of the porch, and the beer shaking over.

'I say, look here, Matilda: you must be a regular goose, as the Squire says, to put yourself into this fright before you know whether there's any cause for it. Susan says she has only stepped out somewhere.'

She put up her hand and touched my arm, panting like mad. Her lips were the colour of chalk.

'Only last night that ever was, Mr Johnny, as we were going up the staircase to bed, we heard a sound in the room as we passed it. It was just like a groan. Ask Jane Cross, else, sir.'

'What room?'

'Mr Edmund's: where he did it. She has heard him tonight, or seen him, or something, and has got a fit.'

The kitchen was on the right of the passage. Susan, knowing the ways of the house, soon lighted a candle. On a small round table was spread a white cloth, some bread and cheese, and two tumblers. A knife or two had seemingly been flung on it at random.

'Jane Cross! Jane Cross!' shouted the Squire, going forward towards the front hall, Susan following with the candle. It was a good-sized hall; I could see that; with a handsome well-staircase at this end of it.

'Halloa! What's this? Johnny! Susan!—all of you come here. Here's somebody lying here. It must be the poor girl. Goodness bless my heart! Johnny, help me to raise her.'

Still and white she was lying, underneath the opening of the staircase. Upon lifting her head, it fell back in a curious manner. We both backed a little. Susan held the candle nearer. As its light fell on the upturned face, the girl shrieked.

'She has got a fit,' cried Matilda.

'God help her!' whispered the Squire. 'I fear this is something worse than a fit. We must have a doctor.'

Susan thrust the candlestick into my hand and ran out at the back door, saying she'd fetch Mr Lockett. Back she came in a moment: the garden gate was locked and the key not in it.

'There's the front door, girl,' stuttered the Squire in a passion, angry with her for returning, though it was no fault of hers. He was like one off his head, and his nose and cheeks had turned blue.

But there could be no more egress by the front door than the back. It was locked, and the key gone. Who had done these things? what strange mystery was here? Locking the poor girl in the house to kill her!

Matilda, who had lighted another candle, found the key of the back gate lying on the kitchen dresser. Susan caught it up, and flew away. It was a most uncomfortable moment: there lay Jane Cross, pale and motionless, and it seemed that we were helpless to aid her.

'Ask that stupid thing to bring a pillow or a cushion, Johnny. Ghosts, indeed! The idiots that women are!'

'What else has done it?—what else was there to hurt her?' remonstrated Matilda, bringing up the second candle. 'She'd not go into a fit for nothing, sir.'

And now that more light was present, we began to see other features of the scene. Nearly close to Jane Cross lay a work-basket, overturned: a flat open basket, a foot and a half square. Reels of cotton, scissors, tapes, small bundles of work tied up, and such like things, lay scattered around.

The Squire looked at these, and then at the opening above. 'Can she have fallen down the well?' he asked, in a low tone. And Matilda, catching the words, gave a great cry of dismay, and burst into tears.

'A pillow, girl. A pillow, or a cushion.'

She went into one of the sitting-rooms and brought out a thick sofa cushion. The Squire, going down on his knees, for he was not good at stooping, told me to slip it under while he raised the head.

A sound of stalking feet, a sudden flash of light from a bull's-eye, and a policeman came upon the scene. The man was quietly passing on his beat when met by Susan. In her excitement she told him what had happened, and sent him in. We knew the man, whose beat lay at this end of Saltwater; a civil man, named Knapp. He knelt down where the Squire had just been kneeling, touching Jane Cross here and there.

'She's dead, sir,' he said. 'There can be no mistake about that.'

'She must have fallen down the well of the staircase, I fear,' observed the Squire.

'Well—yes; perhaps so,' assented the man in a doubtful tone. 'But what of this?'

He flung the great light on the front of poor Jane Cross's dress. A small portion of the gown-body, where it fastened in front, had been torn away; as well as one of the sleeve wristbands.

'It's no fall,' said the man. 'It is foul play—as I think.'

'Goodness bless me!' gasped the Squire. 'Some villains must have got in. This comes of that other one's having left the front door on the latch.' But I am not sure that any of us, including himself, believed she could be really dead.

Susan returned with speed, and was followed by Mr Lockett. He was a young man, thirty perhaps, pale and quiet, and much like what I remembered of his brother. Poor Jane Cross was certainly dead, he said: had been dead, he thought, an hour.

But this could scarcely have been—as we knew. It was not, at the very utmost, above twenty-five minutes since Matilda went out to fetch the beer, leaving her alive and well. Mr Lockett looked again, but thought he was not mistaken. When a young doctor takes up a crotchet, he likes to hold to it.

A nameless sensation of awe fell upon us all. Dead! In that sudden manner! The Squire rubbed up his head like a helpless lunatic; Susan's eyes were round with horror; Matilda had thrown her apron over her face to hide its grief and tears.

Leaving her for the present where she was, we turned to go upstairs. I stooped to pick up the overturned basket, but the policeman sharply told me to let all things stay as they were until he had time to look into them.

The first thing the man did, on reaching the landing above, was to open the room doors one by one, and throw his bull's-eye light into them. They were all right; unoccupied, straight and tidy. On the landing of the upper floor lay one or two articles, which seemed to indicate that some kind of struggle had taken place there. A thimble here, a bodkin there; also the bit that had been torn out of the girl's gown in front and the wristband from the sleeve. The balustrades were very handsome but very low; on this upper landing, dangerously low. These bedrooms were all in order; the one in which the two servants slept, alone showing signs of occupation.

Downstairs went Knapp again, carrying with him the torn-out pieces, to compare them with the gown. It was the print gown I had often seen Jane Cross wear: a black gown with white zigzag lines running down it. Matilda was wearning the fellow to it now. The pieces fitted in exactly.

'The struggle must have taken place upstairs: not here,' observed the doctor.

Matilda, questioned and cross-questioned by the policeman, gave as succinct an account of the evening as her distressed state allowed. We stood round the kitchen while she told it.

Neither she nor Jane Cross had gone out at all that day. Monday was rather a busy day with them, for they generally did a bit of washing. After tea, which they took between four and five o'clock, they went up to their bedroom, it being livelier there than in the kitchen, the window looking down the side road. Matilda sat down to write a letter to her brother, who lived at a distance; Jane Cross sat at the window doing a job of sewing. They sat there all the evening, writing, working, and sometimes talking. At dusk, Jane remarked that it was getting Blindman's holiday, and that she should go on down-stairs and put the supper. Upon that, Matilda finished her letter quickly, folded and directed it, and followed her down. Jane had not yet laid the cloth, but was then taking it out of the drawer. 'You go and fetch the beer, Matilda,' she said: and Matilda was glad to do so. 'You can't go that way: I have locked the gate,' Jane called out, seeing Matilda turning towards the back; accordingly she went out at the front door, leaving it on the latch. Such was her account; and I have given it almost verbatim.

'On the latch,' repeated the policeman, taking up the words. 'Does that mean that you left it open?'

'I drew it quite to, so that it looked as if it were shut; it was a heavy door, and would keep so,' was Matilda's answer. 'I did it, not to give Jane the trouble to open it to me. When I got back I found it shut and could not get in.'

The policeman mused. 'You say it was Jane Cross who locked the back door in the wall?'

'Yes,' said Matilda. 'She had locked it before I got downstairs. We liked to lock that door early, because it could be opened from the outside—while the front door could not be.'

'And she had not put these things on the table when you went out for the beer?'—pointing to the dishes.

'No: she was only then putting the cloth. As I turned round from taking the beer-jug from its hook, the fling she gave the cloth caused the air of it to whiffle in my face like a wind. She had not begun to reach out the dishes.'

'How long were you away?'

'I don't know exactly,' she answered, with a moan. 'Rather longer than usual, because I took my letter to the post before going to the Swan.'

'It was about ten minutes,' I interposed. 'I was at the window next door, and saw Matilda go out and come back.'

'Ten minutes!' repeated the policeman. 'Quite long enough for some ruffian to come in and fling her over the stairs.'

'But who would do it?' asked Matilda, looking up at him with her poor pale face.

'Ah, that's the question; that's what we must find out,' said Knapp. 'Was the kitchen just as it was when you left it?'

'Yes—except that she had put the bread and cheese on the table. And the glasses, and knives,' added the girl, looking round at the said table, which remained as we had found it, 'but not the plates.'

'Well now, to go to something else: Did she bring her work-basket downstairs with her from the bedroom when she remarked to you that she would go and put the supper on?'

'No, she did not.'

'You are sure of that?'

'Yes. She left the basket on the chair in front of her where it had been standing. She just got up and shook the threads from off her gown, and went on down. When I left the room the basket was there; I saw it. And I think,' added the girl, with a great sob, 'I think that while putting the supper she must have gone upstairs again to fetch the basket, and must have fallen against the banisters with fright, and overbalanced herself.'

'Fright at what?' asked Knapp.

Matilda shivered. Susan whispered to him that they were afraid at night of seeing the ghost of Mr Edmund Peahern.

The man glanced keenly at Matilda for a minute. 'Did you ever see it?' he asked.

'No,' she shuddered. 'But there are strange noises, and we think it is in the house.'

'Well,' said Knapp, coughing to hide a comical smile, 'ghosts don't tear pieces out of gowns—that ever I heard of. I should say it was something worse than a ghost that has been here tonight. Had this poor girl any sweetheart?'

'No,' said Matilda.

'Have you one?'

'No.'

'Except Owen the milkman.'

A scarlet streak flashed into Matilda's cheeks. I knew Owen: he was Mrs Blair's milkman also.

'I think Owen must be your sweetheart or hers,' went on Knapp. 'I've seen him, often enough, talking and laughing with you both when bringing the afternoon's milk round. Ten minutes at a stretch he has stayed in this garden, when he need not have been as many moments.'

'There has been no harm: and it's nothing to anybody,' said Matilda.

The key of the front door was searched for, high and low; but it could not be found. Whoever locked the door, must have made off with the key. But for that, and for the evidences of the scuffle above and the pieces torn out of the gown, we should have thought Matilda's opinion was correct: that Jane Cross had gone upstairs for her basket, and through some wretched accident had pitched over the balustrades. Matilda could not relinquish the notion.

'It was only a week ago that ever was; a week ago this very day; that Jane Cross nearly fell over there. We were both running upstairs, trying in sport which should get first into our bedroom; and, in jostling one another on the landing, she all but overbalanced herself. I caught hold of her to save her. It's true—if it were the last word I had to speak.'

Matilda broke down, with a dreadful fit of sobbing. Altogether she struck me as being about as excitable a young woman as one could meet in a summer day's journey.

Nothing more could be made out of it this evening. Jane Cross had met her death, and some evil or other must have led to it. The police took possession of the house for the night: and Matilda, out of compassion, was brought to ours. To describe the Mater's shock and Mary Blair's, when they heard the news, would be beyond me.

All sorts of conjectures arose in the neighbourhood. The most popular belief was that some person must have perceived the front door open, and, whether with a good or an ill intention, entered the house; that he must have stolen upstairs, met Jane Cross on the top landing, and flung her down in a scuffle. That he must then have let himself out at the front door and locked it after him.

Against this theory there were obstacles. From the time of Matilda's leaving the house till her return, certainly not more than ten minutes had elapsed, perhaps not quite as much, and this was a very short space of time for what had been done in it. Moreover, the chances were that I, sitting at the next window, should have seen anyone going in or out; though it was not of course certain. I had got up once to ring the bell, and stayed a minute or two away from the window, talking with Mary Blair and the Mater.

Some people thought the assassin (is it too much to call him so?) had been admitted by Jane Cross herself; or he might have been in hiding in the garden before she locked the door. In short, the various opinions would fill a volume.

But suspicion fell chiefly upon one person—and that was Thomas Owen the milkman. Though, perhaps, 'suspicion' is too strong a word to give to it—I ought rather to say 'doubt'. These Owens were originally from Wales, very respectable people. The milk business was their own; and, since the father's death, which happened only a few months before, the son had carried it on in conjunction with his mother. He was a young man of three or four-and-twenty, with a fresh colour and open countenance, rather superior in his manners and education. The carrying out the milk himself was a temporary arrangement, the boy employed for it being ill. That he had often lingered at No. 7, laughing with the two young women, was well known; he had also been seen to accost them in the street. Only the previous day, he and Matilda had stayed talking in the churchyard after morning service when everybody else had left it; and he had walked up nearly as far as Seabord Terrace with Jane Cross in the evening. A notion existed that he had entered the house on the

Monday evening, for who else was it likely to have been, cried everybody. Which was, of course, logic. At last a rumour arose— arose on the Tuesday—that Owen had been *seen* to leave the house at dusk on the fatal evening; that this could be proved. If so, it looked rather black. I was startled, for I had liked the man.

The next day, Wednesday, the key was found. A gardener who did up the gardens of the other end house, No. 1, every Wednesday, was raking the ground underneath some dwarf pines that grew close against the front railings, and raked out a big door-key. About fifteen people came rushing off with it to No. 7.

It was the missing key. It fitted into the door at once, locked and unlocked it. When the villain had made his way from the house after doing the mischief, he must have flung the key over amidst the pines, thinking no doubt it would lie hidden there.

The coroner and jury assembled; but they could not make more of the matter than we had made. Jane Cross had died of the fall down the well staircase, which had broken her neck; and it was pretty evident she had been flung down. Beyond the one chief and fatal injury, she was not harmed in any way; not by so much as a scratch. Matilda, whose surname turned out to be Valentine, having got over the first shock, gave her testimony with subdued composure. She was affected at parts of it, and said she would have saved Jane Cross's life with her own: and no one could doubt that she spoke the truth. She persisted in asserting her opinion that there had been no scuffle, in spite of appearances; but that the girl had been terrified in some way and had accidentally fallen over.

When Matilda was done with, Thomas Owen took her place. He was all in black, having dressed himself to come to the inquest and wearing mourning for his father; and I must say, looking at him now, you'd never have supposed he carried out milk-pails.

Yes, he had known the poor young woman in question, he readily said in answer to questions; had been fond of chaffing with the two girls a bit, but nothing more. Meant nothing by it, nothing serious. Respected both of them; regarded them as perfectly well-conducted young women. Was either of them his sweetheart? Certainly not. Had not courted either of them. Never thought of either of them as his future wife: should not consider a servant eligible for that position— at least, his mother would not. Of the two, he had liked Jane Cross the best. Did not know anything whatever of the circumstances attending the death; thought it a most deplorable calamity, and was never more shocked in his life than when he heard of it.

'Is there any truth in the report that you were at the house on Monday evening?' asked the coroner.

'There is no truth in it.'

'I see him come out o' No. 7: I see him come out o' the side door in the garden wall,' burst forth a boy's earnest voice from the back of the room.

'You saw me *not* come out of it,' quietly replied Thomas Owen, turning round to see who it was that had spoken. 'Oh, it is you, is it, Bob Jackson! Yes, you came running round the corner just as I turned from the door.'

'You *were* there then?' cried the coroner.

'No, sir. At the door, yes; that's true enough; but I was not inside it. What happened was this: on Monday I had some business at a farmhouse near Munpler, and set out to walk over there early in the evening. In passing down the side road by No. 7, I saw the two maids at the top window. One of them—I think it was Jane Cross—called out to ask me in a joking of way whether I was about to pay them a visit; I answered, not then, but I would as I came back if they liked. Accordingly, in returning, I rang the bell. It was not answered, and I rang again with a like result. Upon that, I went straight home to my milk books, and did not stir out again, as my mother can prove. That is the truth, sir, on my oath; and all the truth.'

'What time was this?'

'I am not quite sure. It was getting dusk.'

'Did you see anything of the young women this second time?'

'Not anything.'

'Or hear anything?—Any noise?'

'None whatever. I supposed that they would not come to the door to me because it was late: I thought nothing else. I declare, sir, that this is all I know of the matter.'

There was a pause when he concluded. Knapp, the policeman, and another one standing by his side, peered at Owen from under their eyebrows, as if they did not put implicit faith in his words: and the coroner recalled Matilda Valentine.

She readily confirmed the statement of his having passed along the side road, and Jane Cross's joking question to him. But she denied having heard him ring on his return, and said the door-bell had not rung at all that night. Which would seem to prove that Owen must have rung during the time she had gone out for the beer.

So, you perceive, the inquest brought forth no more available light, and had to confess itself baffled.

'A fine termination this is to our pleasure,' cried the Squire, gloomily. 'I don't like mysteries, Johnny. And of all the mysteries I have come across in my life, the greatest mystery is this at No. 7.'

It was a grand sea: one of the grandest that we had seen at Saltwater. The waves were dancing and sparkling like silver; the blue of the sky was deeper than a painter's ultramarine. But to us, looking on it from Mrs Blair's house in Seabord Terrace, its brightness and beauty were dimmed.

Matilda was to be pitied. The two young women had cared a good deal for one another, and the shock to Matilda was serious. The girl, now staying in our house, had worn a half-dazed look since, and avoided No. 7 as though it had the plague. Superstition in regard to the house had already been rife in both the servants' minds, in consequence of the unhappy death in it of their master's son, Edmund Peahern, some weeks back: and if Matilda had been afraid of seeing one ghost before (as she had been) she would now undoubtedly expect to see two of them.

On this same morning, as I stood with the Squire looking at the sea from the drawing-room window of No. 6, Matilda came in. Her large dark eyes had lost their former sparkle, her clear olive skin its freshness. She asked leave to speak to Mrs Todhetley: and the Mater—who sat at the table adding up some bills, for our sojourn at Saltwater was drawing towards its close—told her, in a kind tone, to speak on.

'I am making bold to ask you, ma'am, whether you could help me to find a place in London,' began Matilda, standing between the door and the table in her black dress. 'I know, ma'am, you don't live in London, but a long way off it; Mrs Blair has told me so, Master Johnny Ludlow also: but I thought perhaps you knew people there, and might be able to hear of something.'

The Mater looked at Matilda without answering, and then round at us. Rather strange it was, a coincidence in a small way, that we had had a letter from London from Miss Deveen that morning, which had concluded with these lines of postscript: 'Do you chance to know of any nice, capable young woman in want of a situation? One of my housemaids is going to leave.'

Naturally this occurred to the Mater's mind when Matilda spoke. 'What kind of situation do you wish for?' she asked.

'As housemaid, ma'am, or parlour-maid. I can do my duty well in either.'

'But now, my girl,' spoke up the Squire, turning from the window, 'why need you leave Saltwater? You'd never like London after it. This is a clear, fresh, health-giving place, with beautiful sands and music on them all day; London is nothing but smoke and fogs.'

Matilda shook her head. 'I could not stay here, sir.'

'Nonsense, girl. Of course what has happened *has* happened, and it's very distressing; and you, of all people, must feel it so: but you will forget it in time. If you don't care to go back to No. 7 before Mr and Mrs Peahern come home——'

'I can never go back to No. 7, sir,' she interrupted, a vehemence that seemed born of terror in her subdued voice. 'Never in this world. I would rather die.'

'Stuff and nonsense!' said the Squire, impatiently. 'There's nothing the matter with No. 7. What has happened in it won't happen again.'

'It is an unlucky house, sir; a haunted house,' she contended with suppressed emotion. 'And it's true that I would rather die outright than go to live in it; for the terror of being there would slowly kill me. And so, ma'am,' she added quickly to Mrs Todhetley, evidently wishing to escape the subject, 'I should like to go away altogether from Saltwater; and if you can help me to hear of a place in London, I shall be very grateful.'

'I will consider of it, Matilda,' was the answer. And when the girl had left the room the Mater asked us what we thought about recommending her to Miss Deveen. We saw no reason against it—not but what the Squire put the girl down as an idiot on the subject of haunted houses—and Miss Deveen was written to.

The upshot was, that on the next Saturday, Matilda bade farewell to Saltwater and departed for Miss Deveen's, the Squire sarcastically assuring her that *that* house had no ghosts in it. We should be leaving, ourselves, the following Tuesday.

But, before that day came, it chanced that I saw Owen, the

milkman. It was on the Sunday afternoon. I had taken little Joe Blair for a walk across the fields as far as Munpler (their Montpellier-by-Sea, you know), and in returning met Thomas Owen. He wore his black Sunday clothes, and looked a downright fine fellow, as usual. There was something about the man I could not help liking, in spite of the doubt attaching to him.

'So Matilda Valentine is gone, sir,' he observed, after we had exchanged a few sentences.

'Yes, she went yesterday,' I answered, putting my back against the field fence, while young Joe went careering about in chase of a yellow butterfly. 'And for my part, I don't wonder at the girl's not liking to stay at Saltwater. At least, in Seabord Terrace.'

'I was told this morning that Mr and Mrs Peahern were on their road home,' he continued.

'Most likely they are. They'd naturally want to look into the affair for themselves.'

'And I hope with all my heart they will be able to get some light out of it,' returned Owen, warmly. 'I mean to do *my* best to bring out the mystery, sir; and I sha'n't rest till it's done.'

His words were fair, his tone was genuine. If it was indeed himself who had been the chief actor in the tragedy, he carried it off well. I hardly knew what to think. It is true I had taken a bit of a fancy to the man, according to my customary propensity to take a fancy, or the contrary; but I did not know much of him, and not anything of his antecedents. As he spoke to me now, his tone was marked, rather peculiar. It gave me a notion that he wanted to say more.

'Have you any idea that you will be able to trace it out?'

'For my own sake I should like to get the matter cleared up,' he added, not directly answering my question. 'People are beginning to turn the cold shoulder my way: one woman asked me to my face yesterday whether I did it. No, I told her, I did not it, but I'd try and find out who did.'

'You are sure you heard and saw nothing suspicious that night when you rang at the bell and could not get in, Owen?'

'Not then, sir; no. I saw no light in the house and heard no noise.'

'You have not any clue to go by, then?'

'Not much, sir, yet. But I can't help thinking somebody else has.'

'Who is that?'

'Matilda.'

'Matilda!' I repeated, in amazement. 'Surely you can't suspect that she—that she was a party to any deed so cruel and wicked!'

'No, no, sir, I don't mean that; the young women were too good friends to harm one another: and whatever took place, took place while Matilda was out of the house. But I can't help fancying that she knows, or suspects, more of the matter than she will say. In short, that she is screening some one.'

To me it seemed most unlikely. 'Why do you judge so, Owen?'

'By her manner, sir. Not by much else. But I'll tell you something that I saw. On the previous Wednesday when I left the afternoon milk at that tall house just beyond Seabord Terrace, the family lodging there told me to call in the evening for the account, as they were leaving the next day. Accordingly I went; and was kept waiting so long before they paid me that it was all but night when I came out. Just as I was passing the back door at No. 7, it was suddenly drawn open from the inside, and a man stood in the opening, whispering with one of the girls. She was crying, for I heard her sobs, and he kissed her and came out, and the door was hastily shut. He was an ill-looking man; so far at least as his clothes went; very shabby. His face I did not see, for he pulled his slouching round hat well over his brows as he walked away rapidly, and the black beard he wore covered his mouth and chin.'

'Which of the maids was it?'

'I don't know, sir. The next day I chaffed them a bit about it, but they both declared that nobody had been there but the watchmaker, Mr Renninson, who goes every Wednesday to wind up the clocks, and that it must have been him that I saw, for he was late that evening. I said no more; it was no business of mine; but the man I saw go out was just about as much like Renninson as he was like me.'

'And do you fancy——'

'Please wait a minute, sir,' he interrupted, 'I haven't finished. Last Sunday evening, upon getting home after service, I found I had left my prayer-book in church. Not wishing to lose it, for it was the one my father always used, I went back for it. However, the church was shut, so I could not get in. It was a fine evening, and I took a stroll round the churchyard. In the corner of it, near to Mr Edmund Peahern's tomb, they had buried poor Jane Cross but two days before—you know the spot, sir. Well, on the flat square of earth that covers her grave, stood Matilda Valentine, the greatest picture of distress you can imagine, tears streaming down her cheeks. She dried her eyes when she saw me, and we came away together. Naturally I fell to talking of Jane Cross and the death. "I shall do as much as lies in my power to bring it to light," I said to Matilda; "or people may go on doubting me to the end. And I think the first step must be to find out who the man was that called in upon you the previous Wednesday night." Well, sir, with that, instead of making any answering remark as a Christian would, or a rational being, let us say, Matilda gives a smothered, sobbing shriek, and darts away out of the churchyard. I couldn't make her out; and all in a minute a conviction flashed over me, though I hardly know why, that she knew who was the author of the calamity, and was screening him; or at any rate that she had her suspicions, if she did not actually know. And I think so still, sir.'

I shook my head, not seeing grounds to agree with Owen. He resumed:

'The next morning, between nine and ten, I was in the shop, putting a pint of cream which had been ordered into a can, when to my surprise Matilda walked in, cool and calm. She said she had come to tell me that the man I had seen leave the house was her brother. He had fallen into trouble through having become security for a fellow workman, had had all his things sold up, including his tools, and had walked every step of the way—thirty miles—to ask her if she could help him. She did help him as far as she could, giving him what little money she had by her, and Jane Cross had added ten shillings to it. He had got in only at dusk, she said, had taken some supper with them, and left again afterwards, and that she was letting him out at the gate when I must have been passing it. She did not see me, for her eyes were dim with crying: her heart felt like to break in saying farewell. That was the truth, she declared, and that her brother had had no more to do with Jane's death than she or I had; he was away again out of Saltwater the same night he came into it.'

'Well? Did you not believe her?'

'No, sir,' answered Owen, boldly. 'I did not. If this was true, why should she have gone off into that smothered shriek in the churchyard when I mentioned him, and rush away in a fright?'

I could not tell. Owen's words set me thinking.

'I did not know which of the two girls it was who let the man out that Wednesday night, for I did not clearly see; but, sir, the impression on my mind at the moment was, that it was Jane Cross. Jane Cross, and not Matilda. If so, why does she tell me this tale about her brother, and say it was herself?'

'And if it was Jane Cross?'

Owen shook his head. 'All sorts of notions occur to me, sir. Sometimes I fancy that the man might have been Jane's sweetheart, that he might have been there again on the Monday night, and done the mischief in a quarrel; and that Matilda is holding her tongue because it is her brother. Let the truth be what it will, Matilda's manner convinces me of one thing: that there's something she is concealing, and that it is half frightening her wits out of her.—— You are going to leave Saltwater, I hear, sir,' added the young man in a different tone, 'and I am glad to have the opportunity of saying this, for I should not like you to carry away any doubt of me. I'll bring the matter to light if I can.'

Touching his hat, he walked onwards, leaving my thoughts all in a whirligig.

Was Owen right in drawing these conclusions?—or was he purposely giving a wrong colouring to facts, and seeking craftily to throw suspicion off himself? It was a nice question, one I could make neither top nor tail of. But, looking back to the fatal evening, weighing this point, sifting that, I began to see that Matilda showed more anxiety, more terror, than she need have shown *before* she knew that any ill had happened. Had she a prevision, as she stood at the door with the jug of ale in her hand, that some evil might have chanced? Did she leave some individual in the house with Jane Cross when she went to the Swan to get the ale?—and was it her brother? Did she leave Owen in the house, and was she screening him?

'Why, Matilda! Is it you?'

It was fourteen months later, and autumn weather, and I had just arrived in London at Miss Deveen's. My question to Matilda, who came into my dressing-room with some warm water to wash off the travelling dust, was not made in surprise at seeing *her*, for I supposed she was still in service at Miss Deveen's, but at seeing the change in her. Instead of the healthy and, so to say, handsome girl known at Saltwater, I saw a worn, weary, anxious-looking shadow, with a feverish fire in her wild dark eyes.

'Have you been ill, Matilda?'

'No, sir, not at all. I am quite well.'

'You have grown very thin.'

'It's the London air, sir. I think everybody must get thin that lives in it.'

Very civilly and respectfully, but yet with an unmistakable air of reticence, spoke she. Somehow the girl was changed, and greatly changed. Perhaps she had been grieving after Jane Cross? Perhaps the secret of what had happened (if in truth Matilda knew it) lay upon her with too heavy a weight?

'Do you find Matilda a good servant?' I asked of Miss Deveen, later, she and I being alone together.

'A very good servant, Johnny. But she is going to leave me.'

'Is she? Why?'

Miss Deveen only nodded, in answer to the first query, passing over the last. I supposed she did not wish to say.

'I think her so much altered.'

'In what way, Johnny?'

'In looks: looks and manner. She is just a shadow. One might say she had passed through a six months' fever. And what a curious light there is in her eyes!'

'She has always impressed me with the idea of having some great care upon her. None can mistake that she is a sorrowful woman. I hear that the other servants accuse her of having been "crossed in love"', added Miss Deveen, with a smile.

'She is thinner even than Miss Cattledon.'

'And that, I daresay you think, need not be, Johnny! Miss Cattledon, by the way, is rather hard upon Matilda just now: calls her a "demon".'

'A demon! Why does she?'

'Well, I'll tell you. Though it is but a little domestic matter, one that perhaps you will hardly care to hear. You must know (to begin with) that Matilda has never made herself sociable with the other servants here; in return they have become somewhat prejudiced against her, and have been ready to play her tricks, tease her, and what not. But you must understand, Johnny, that I knew nothing of the state of affairs below; such matters rarely reach me. My cook, Hall, was especially at war with Matilda: in fact, I believe there was no love lost between the two. The girl's melancholy—for at times she does seem very melancholy—was openly put down by the rest to the assumption that she must have had some love affair in which the swain had played her false. They were continually plaguing her on this score, and it no doubt irritated Matilda; but she rarely retorted, preferring rather to leave them and take refuge in her room.'

'Why could they not let her alone?'

'People can't let one another alone, as I believe, Johnny. If they did, the world would be pleasanter to live in.'

'And I suppose Matilda got tired at last, and gave warning?'

'No. Some two or three weeks back it appears that, by some means or other, Hall obtained access to a small trunk; one that Matilda keeps her treasures in, and has cautiously kept locked. If I thought Hall had opened this trunk with a key of her own, as Matilda accuses her of doing, I would not keep the woman in my house another day. But she declares to me most earnestly—for I had her before me here to question her—that Matilda, called suddenly out of her chamber, left the trunk open there, and the letter, of which I am about to tell you, lying, also open, by its side. Hall says that she went into the room—it adjoins her own—for something she wanted, and that all she did—and she admits this much—was to pick up the letter, carry it downstairs, read it to the other servants, and make fun over it.'

'What letter was it?'

'Strictly speaking, it was only part of a letter: one begun but not concluded. It was in Matilda's own hand, apparently written a long while ago, for the ink was pale and faded, and it began "Dearest Thomas Owen. The——"'

'Thomas Owen!' I exclaimed, starting in my chair. 'Why, that is the milkman at Saltwater.'

'I'm sure I don't know who he is, Johnny, and I don't suppose it matters. Only a few lines followed, three or four, speaking of some private conversation that she had held with him on coming out of church the day before, and of some reproach that she had then made to him respecting Jane Cross. The words broke suddenly off there, as if the writer had been interrupted. But why Matilda did not complete the letter and send it, and why she should have kept it by her all this while, must be best known to herself.'

'Jane Cross was her fellow-servant at Mr Peahern's. She who was killed by falling down the staircase.'

'Yes, poor thing, I remembered the name. But, to go on. In the evening, after the finding of this letter, I and Miss Cattledon were startled by a disturbance in the kitchen. Cries and screams, and loud, passionate words. Miss Cattledon ran down; I stayed at the top of the stairs. She found Hall, Matilda, and one of the others there, Matilda in a perfect storm of fury, attacking Hall like a maniac. She tore handfuls out of her hair, she bit her thumb until her teeth met in it: Hall, though by far the bigger person of the two, and I should have thought the stronger, had no chance against her; she seemed to be as a very reed in her hands, passion enduing Matilda with a strength perfectly unnatural. George, who had been out on an errand, came in at the moment, and by his help the women were parted. Cattledon maintains that Matilda, during the scene, was nothing less than a demon; quite mad. When it was over, the girl fell on the floor utterly exhausted, and lay like a dead thing, every bit of strength, almost of life, gone ot her.'

'I never could have believed it of Matilda.'

'Nor I, Johnny. I grant that the girl had just cause to be angry. How should we like to have our private places rifled, and their contents exhibited to and mocked at by the world; contents which to us seem sacred? But to have put herself into that wild rage was both unseemly and unaccountable. Her state then, and her state immediately afterwards, made me think—I speak it with all reverence, Johnny—of the poor people in holy writ from whom the evil spirits were cast out.'

'Ay. It seems to be just such a case, Miss Deveen.'

'Hall's thumb was so much injured that a doctor had to come daily to it for nine or ten days,' continued Miss Deveen. 'Of course, after this climax, I could not retain Matilda in my service; neither would she have remained in it. She indulged a feeling of the most bitter hatred to the women servants, to Hall especially—she had not much liked them before, as you may readily guess—and she said that nothing would induce her to remain with them, even had I been willing to keep her. So she has obtained a situation with some acquaintances of mine who live in this neighbourhood, and goes to it next week. That is why Matilda leaves me, Johnny.'

In my heart I could not help being sorry for her, and said so. She looked so truly, sadly unhappy!

'I am very sorry for her,' assented Miss Deveen. 'And had I known the others were making her life here uncomfortable, I should have taken means to stop their pastime. Of the actual facts, with regard to the letter, I cannot be at any certainty—I mean in my own mind. Hall is a respectable servant, and I have never had cause to think her untruthful during the three years she has lived with me: and she most positively holds to it that the little trunk was standing open on the table and the letter lying open beside it. Allowing that it was so, she had, of course, no right to touch either trunk or letter, still less to take the letter downstairs and exhibit it to the others, and I don't defend her conduct: but yet it is different from having rifled the lock of the trunk and filched the letter out.'

'And Matilda accuses her of doing that?'

'Yes: and, on her side, holds to it just as positively. What Matilda tells me is this: On that day it chanced that Miss Cattledon had paid the women servants their quarter's wages. Matilda carried hers to her chamber, took this said little trunk out of her large box, where she keeps it, unlocked it, and put the money into it. She disturbed nothing in the trunk; she says she had wrapt the sovereigns in a bit of paper, and she just slipped them inside, touching nothing else. She was shutting down the lid when she heard herself called to by me on the landing below. She waited to lock the box but not to put it up, leaving it standing on the table. I quite well remembered calling to the girl, having heard her run upstairs. I wanted her in my room.'

Miss Deveen paused a minute, apparently thinking.

'Matilda has assured me again and again that she is quite sure she locked the little trunk, that there can be no mistake on that point. Moreover, she asserts that the letter in question was lying at the bottom of the trunk beneath other things, and that she had not taken it from thence or touched it for months and months.'

'And when she went upstairs again—did she find the little trunk open or shut?'

'She says she found it shut: shut and locked just as she had left it; and she replaced it in her large box, unconscious that anybody had been to it.'

'Was she long in your room, Miss Deveen?'

'Yes, Johnny, the best part of an hour. I wanted a little sewing done in a hurry, and told her to sit down there and then and do it. It was during this time that the cook, going upstairs herself, saw the trunk, and took the opportunity to do what she did do.'

'I think I should feel inclined to believe Matilda. Her tale sounds the more probable.'

'I don't know that, Johnny. I can hardly believe that a respectable woman, as Hall undoubtedly is, would deliberately unlock a fellow-servant's box with a false key. Whence did she get the key to do it? Had she previously provided herself with one? The lock is of the most simple description, for I have seen the trunk since, and Hall might possess a key that would readily fit it: but if so, as the woman herself says, how could she know it? In short, Johnny, it is one woman's word against another's: and, until this happened, I had deemed each of them to be equally credible.'

To be sure there was reason in that. I sat thinking.

'Were it proved to have been as Matilda says, still I could not keep her,' resumed Miss Deveen. Mine is a peaceable, well-ordered household, and I should not like to know that one, subject to insane fits of temper, was a member of it. Though Hall in that case would get her discharge also.'

'Do the people where Matilda is going know why she leaves?'

'Mrs and Miss Soames. Yes. I told them all about it. But I told them at the same time, what I had then learnt—that Matilda's temper had doubtlessly been much tried here. It would not be tried in their house, they believed, and took her readily. She is an excellent servant, Johnny, let who will get her.'

I could not resist the temptation of speaking to Matilda about it, an opportunity offering that same day. She came into the room with some letters just left by the postman.

'I thought my mistress was here, sir,' she said, hesitating with the tray in her hand.

'Miss Deveen will be here in a minute: you can leave the letters. So you are going to take flight, Matilda! I have heard all about it. What a silly thing you must be to put yourself into that wonderful tantrum!'

'She broke into my box, and turned over its contents, and stole my letter to mock me,' retorted Matilda, her fever-lighted eyes taking a momentary fierceness. 'Who, put in my place, would not have gone into a tantrum, sir?'

'But she says she did not break into it.'

'As surely as that is heaven's sun above us, she *did it*, Mr Johnny. She has been full of spite towards me for a long time, and she thought she would pay me out. I did but unlock the box, and slip the little paper of money in, and I locked it again instantly and brought the key away with me: I can never say anything truer than that, sir: to make a mistake about it is not possible.'

No pen could convey the solemn earnestness with which she spoke. Somehow it impressed me. I hoped Hall would get served out.

'Yes, the wrong has triumphed for once. As far as I can see, sir, it often does triumph. Miss Deveen thinks great things of Hall, but she is deceived in her; and I daresay she will find her out sometime. It was Hall who ought to have been turned away instead of me. Not that I would stay here longer if I could.'

'But you like Miss Deveen?'

'Very much indeed, sir; she is a good lady and a kind mistress. She spoke very well indeed of me to the new family where I am going, and I daresay I shall do well enough there.—Have you been to Saltwater lately, sir?' she added, abruptly.

'Never since. Do you get news from the place?'

She shook her head. 'I have never heard a word from any soul in it. I have written to nobody, and nobody has written to me.'

'And nothing more has come out about poor Jane Cross. It is still a mystery.'

'And likely to be one,' she replied, in a low tone.

'Perhaps so. Do you know what Owen the milkman thought?'

She had been speaking the last sentence or two with her eyes bent, fiddling with the silver waiter. Now they were raised quickly.

'Owen thought that you could clear up the mystery if you liked, Matilda. At least, that you possessed some clue to it. He told me so.'

'Owen as good as said the same to me before I left,' she replied, after a pause. 'He is wrong, sir: but he must think it if he will. Is he—is he at Saltwater still?'

'For all I know to the contrary. This letter, that the servants here got at, was one you were beginning to write to Owen. Did——'

'I would rather not talk of that letter, Mr Johnny: my private affairs concern myself only,' she interrupted—and went out of the room like a shot.

Had anyone told me that during this short visit of mine in London I should fall across the solution of the mystery of that tragedy enacted at No. 7, I might have been slow to credit it. Nevertheless, it was to be so.

Have you ever noticed, in going through life, that events seem to carry a sequence in themselves almost as though they bore in their own hands the guiding thread that connects them from beginning to end? For a time this thread will seem to be lost; to lie dormant, as though it had snapped, and the course of affairs it was holding to have disappeared for good. But lo! up peeps a little end when least expected, and we catch hold of it, and soon it grows into a handful; and what we had thought lost is again full of activity, and gradually works itself out. Not a single syllable, good or bad, had we heard of that calamity at Saltwater during the fourteen months which had passed since. The thread of it lay dormant. At Miss Deveen's it began to steal up again: Matilda, and her passion, and the letter she had commenced to Thomas Owen were to the fore: and before that visit of mine came to an end, the thread had, strange to say, unwound itself.

I was a favourite of Miss Deveen's: you may have gathered that from past papers. One day, when she was going shopping, she asked me to accompany her and not Miss Cattledon: which made that rejected lady's face all the more like vinegar. So we set off in the carriage.

'Are we going to Regent Street, Miss Deveen.'

'Not today, Johnny. I like to encourage my neighbouring trades-people, and shall buy my new silk here. We have excellent shops not far off.'

After a few intricate turning and windings, the carriage stopped before a large linendraper's, which stood amidst a colony of shops nearly a mile from Miss Deveen's. George came round to open the door.

'Now what will you do, Johnny?' said Miss Deveen. 'I daresay I shall be half an hour in here, looking at silks and calico; and I won't inflict that penalty on you. Shall the carriage take you for a short drive the while, or will you wait in it?—or walk about?'

'I will wait in the street here,' I said, 'and come in to you when I am tired. I like looking at shops.' And I do like it.

The next shop to the linendraper's was a carver and gilder's: he had some nice pictures displayed in his window; at any rate, they looked nice to me: and there I took up my station to begin with.

'How do you do, sir? Have you forgotten me?'

The words came from a young man who stood at the next door, close to me, causing me to turn quickly to him from my gaze at the pictures. No, I had not forgotten him. I knew him instantly. It was Owen, the milkman.

After a few words had passed, I went inside. It was a spacious shop, well fitted up with cans and things pertaining to a milkman's business. The window-board was prettily set off with moss, ferns, a bowl containing gold and silver fish, a miniature fountain, and a rush basket of fresh eggs. Over the door was his own name, Thomas Owen.

'You are living here, Owen?'

'Yes, sir.'

'But why have you left Saltwater?'

'Because, Mr Johnny, the place looked askance at me. People, in their own minds, set down that miserable affair at No. 7 to my credit. Once or twice I was hooted at by the street boys, asking what I had done with Jane Cross. My mother couldn't stand that, and I couldn't stand it, so we just sold our business at Saltwater, and bought this one here. And a good change it has been, in a pecuniary point of view: this is an excellent connection, and grows larger every day.'

'I'm sure I am glad to hear it.'

'At first, mother couldn't bear London: she longed for the pure country air and the green fields: but she is reconciled to it now. Perhaps she'll have an opportunity soon of going back to see her own old Welsh mountains, and of staying there if it pleases her.'

'Then I should say you are going to be married, Owen.'

He laughed and nodded. 'You'll wish me good luck, won't you, sir? She's the only daughter at the next door, the grocer's.'

'That I will. Have you discovered any more of that mysterious business, Owen?'

'At Saltwater? No, sir: not anything at all that could touch the matter itself. But I have heard a good bit that bears upon it.'

'Do you still suspect that Matilda could tell if she chose?'

'I suspect more than that, sir?'

The man's words were curiously significant. He had a bit of fern in his hand, and his fresh, open, intelligent face was bent downwards, as if he wanted to see what the leaf was made of.

'I am not sure, sir. It is but suspicion at the best: but it's an uncommonly strong one.'

'Won't you tell me what you mean? You may trust me.'

'Yes, I am sure I may,' he said, promptly. 'And I think I will tell you—though I have never breathed it to mortal yet. I think Matilda did it herself.'

Backing away from the counter in my surprise, I upset an empty milk-can.

'Matilda!' I exclaimed, picking up the can.

'Mr Johnny, with all my heart I believe it to have been so. I have believed it for some time now.'

'But the girls were too friendly to harm one another. I remember you said so yourself, Owen.'

'And I thought so then, sir. No suspicion of Matilda had occurred to me, but rather of the man I had seen there on the Wednesday. I think she must have done it in a sudden passion; not of deliberate purpose.'

'But now, what are your reasons?'

'I told you, sir, as I daresay you can recall to mind, that I should do what lay in my power to unravel the mystery—for it was not at all agreeable to have it laid at my door. I began, naturally, with tracing out the doings of that night as connected with No. 7. Poor Jane Cross had not been out of doors that night, and so far as I knew had spoken to no one, save to me from the window; therefore of her there seemed nothing to be traced: but of Matilda there was. Enquiring here and there, I, bit by bit, got a few odds and ends of facts together. I traced out the exact time, almost to a minute, that I rang twice at the doorbell at No. 7, and was not answered; and the time that Matilda entered the Swan to get the supper beer. Pretty nearly half an hour had elapsed between the first time and the second.'

'Half an hour!'

'Not far short of it. Which proved that Matilda must have been indoors when I rang, though she denied it before the coroner, and it was taken for granted that I had rung during her absence to fetch the beer. And you knew, sir, that her absence did not exceed ten minutes. Now why did not Matilda answer my ring? Why did she not candidly say that she had heard the ring, but did not choose to answer it? Well, sir, that gave rise to the first faint doubt of her: and when I recalled and dwelt on her singular manner, it appeared to me that the doubt might pass into grave suspicion. Look at her superstitious horror of No. 7. She never would go into the house afterwards!'

I nodded.

'Two or three other little things struck me, all tending to strengthen my doubts, but perhaps they are hardly worth naming. Still, make the worst of it, it was only suspicion, not certainty, and I left Saltwater, holding my tongue.'

'And is this all, Owen?'

'Not quite, sir. Would you be so good as to step outside, and just look at the name over the grocer's door?'

I did so, and read Valentine. 'John Valentine'. The same name as Matilda's.

'Yes, sir, it is,' Owen said, in answer to me. 'After settling here we made acquaintance with the Valentines, and by and by learnt that they are cousins of Matilda's. Fanny—my wife that is to be—has often talked to me about Matilda; they were together a good bit in early life; and by dint of mentally sifting what she said, and putting that and that together, I fancy I see daylight.'

'Yes. Well?'

'Matilda's father married a Spanish woman. She was of a wild, ungovernable temper, subject to fits of frenzy; in one of which fits she died. Matilda has inherited this temper; she is liable to go into frenzies that can only be compared to insanity. Fanny has seen her in two only; they occur but at rare intervals; and she tells me that she truly believes that girl is mad—mad, Mr Johnny—during the few minutes that they last.'

The history I had heard of her mad rage at Miss Deveen's flashed over me. Temporarily insane they had thought her there.

'I said to Fanny one day when we were talking of her,' resumed Owen, 'that a person in that sort of uncontrollable passion, might commit any crime; a murder, or what not. "Yes," Fanny replied, "and not unlikely to do it, either: Matilda has more than once said that she should never die in her bed." Meaning——'

'Meaning what?' I asked, for he came to a pause.

'Well, sir, meaning, I suppose, that she might sometime lay violent hands upon herself, or upon another. I can't help thinking that something must have put her into one of these rages with Jane Cross, and that she pushed or flung the poor girl over the stairs.'

Looking back, rapidly recalling signs and tokens, I thought it might have been so. Owen interrupted me.

'I shall come across her sometime, Mr Johnny. These are things that don't hide themselves for ever: at least, not often. And I shall tax her with it to her face.'

'But—don't you know where she is?'

'No, I don't, sir. I wish I did. It was said that she came up to take a situation in London, and perhaps she is still in it. But London's a large place, I don't know what part of it she was in, and one might as well look for a needle in a bundle of hay. The Valentines have never heard of her at all since she was at Saltwater.'

How strange it seemed;—that she and they were living so near one another, and yet not to be aware of it. Should I tell Owen? Only for half a moment did the question cross me. *No*: most certainly not. It might be as he suspected; and, with it all, I could only pity Matilda. Of all unhappy women, she seemed the unhappiest.

Miss Deveen's carriage bowled past the door to take her up at the linendraper's. Wishing Owen good-day, I was going out, but drew back to make room for two people who were entering: an elderly woman in a close bonnet, and a young one with a fair, pretty, and laughing face.

'My mother and Fanny, sir,' he whispered.

'She is very pretty, very nice, Owen,' I said, impulsively. 'You'll be sure to be happy with her.'

'Thank you, sir; I think shall. I wish you had spoken a word or two to her, Mr Johnny: you'd have seen how nice she is.'

'I can't stay now, Owen. I'll come again.'

Not even to Miss Deveen did I speak of what I had heard. I kept thinking of it as we drove round Hyde Park, and she told me I was unusually silent.

The thread was unwinding itself more and more. Once it had set on a lengthening, I suppose it could not stop. Accident led to an encounter between Matilda and Thomas Owen. Accident? No, it was this same thread of destiny. There's no such thing as accident in the world.

During the visit to the linendraper's, above spoken of, Miss Deveen bought a gown for Matilda. Feeling in her own heart sorry for the girl, thinking she had been somewhat hardly done by in her house, what with Hall and the rest of them, she wished to make her a present on leaving, as a token of her goodwill. But the quantity of stuff bought proved not to be sufficient: Miss Deveen had had her doubts upon the point when it was cut off, and she told Matilda to go herself and get two yards more. This it was, this simple incident, that led to the meeting with Owen. And I was present at it.

The money-order office of the district was situated amidst this colony of shops. In going down there one afternoon to cash an order, I overtook Matilda. She was on her way to buy the additional yards of stuff.

'I suppose I am going right, sir?' she said to me. 'I don't know much about this neighbourhood.'

'Not know much about it! What, after having lived in it more than a year!'

'I have hardly ever gone out; except to church on a Sunday,' she answered. 'And what few articles I've wanted in the dress line, I have mostly bought at the little draper's shop round the corner.'

Hardly had the words left her lips, when we came face to face with Thomas Owen. Matilda gave a kind of smothered cry, and stood stock still, gazing at him. What they said to one another in that first moment, I did not hear. Matilda had a scared look, and was whiter than death. Presently we were all walking together towards Thomas Owen's, he having invited Matilda to go and see his home.

But there was another encounter first. Standing at the grocer's door was pretty Fanny Valentine. She and Matilda recognized each other, and clasped hands. It appeared to me that Matilda did it with suppressed reluctance, as though it gave her no pleasure to meet her relatives. She must have known how near they lived to Miss Deveen's, and yet she had never sought them out. Perhaps the very fact of not wishing to see them had kept her from the spot.

They all sat down in the parlour behind the shop—a neat room. Mrs Owen was out; her son produced some wine. I stood up by the bookcase, telling them I must be off the next minute to the post office. But the minutes passed, and I stayed on.

How he led up to it, I hardly know; but, before I was prepared for anything of the kind, Thomas Owen had plunged wholesale into the subject of Jane Cross, recounting the history of that night, in all its minute details, to Fanny Valentine. Matilda, sitting back on the far side of the room in an armchair, looked terror-stricken: her face seemed to be turning into stone.

'Why do you begin about that, Thomas Owen?' she demanded, when words at length came to her. 'It can have nothing to do with Fanny.'

'I have been wishing to tell it her for some little time, and this seems to be a fitting opportunity,' he answered, coolly resolute. 'You, being better acquainted with the matter than I, can correct me if I make any blunders. I don't care to keep secrets from Fanny: she is going to be my wife.'

Matilda's hands lifted themselves with a convulsive movement and fell again. Her eyes flashed fire.

'*Your wife?*'

'If you have no objection,' he replied. 'My dear old mother goes into Wales next month, and Fanny comes here in her place.'

With a cry, faint and mournful as that of a wounded dove, Matilda put her hands before her face and leaned back in her chair. If she had in truth loved Thomas Owen, if she loved him still, the announcement must have caused her cruel pain.

He resumed his narrative; assuming as facts what he had in his own mind conceived to have been the case, and by implication, but not directly, charging Matilda with the crime. It had a dreadful effect upon her; her agitation increased with every word. Suddenly she rose up in the chair, her arms lifted, her face distorted. One of those fits of passion had come on.

We had a dreadful scene. Owen was powerful, I of not much good, but we could not hold her. Fanny ran sobbing into her own door and sent in two of the shopmen.

It was the climax in Matilda Valentine's life. One that perhaps might have been always looked for. From that hour she was an insane woman, her ravings being interspersed with lucid intervals. During one of these, she disclosed the truth.

She had loved Thomas Owen with a passionate love. Mistaking the gossip and the nonsense that the young man was fond of chattering to her and Jane Cross, she believed her love was returned. On the day preceding the tragedy, when talking with him after morning service, she had taxed him with paying more attention to Jane Cross than to herself. Not a bit of it, he had lightly answered; he would take her for a walk by the sea-shore that evening if she liked to go. But, whether he had meant it, or not, he never came, though Matilda dressed herself to be in readiness. On the contrary, he went to church, met Jane there, and walked the best part of the way home with her. Matilda jealously resented this; her mind was in a chaos; she began to suspect that it was Jane Cross he liked, not herself. She said a word or two upon the subject to Jane Cross on the next day, Monday; but Jane made sport of it—laughed if off. So the time went on to the evening, when they were upstairs together, Jane sewing, Matilda writing. Suddenly Jane Cross said that Thomas Owen was coming along, and Matilda ran to the window. They spoke to him as he passed, and he said he would look in as he returned from Munpler. After Matilda's letter to her brother was finished, she began a note to Thomas Owen, intending to reproach him with not keeping his promise to her and for joining Jane Cross instead. It was the first time she had ever attempted to write to him; and she stuck her work-box with the lid open behind the sheet of paper that Jane Cross might not see what she was doing. When it got dusk, Jane Cross remarked that it was blind man's holiday and that she would go on down and put the supper. In crossing the room, work-basket in hand, she passed behind Matilda, glanced at her letter, and saw the first words of it, 'Dearest Thomas Owen.' In sport, she snatched it up, read the rest where her own name was mentioned, and laughingly began, probably out of pure fun, to plague Matilda. 'Thomas Owen your sweetheart!' she cried, running out on the landing. 'Why, he is mine. He cares more for my little finger than for——' Poor girl! She never finished her sentence. Matilda, fallen into one of those desperate fits of passion, had caught her up and was clutching her like a tiger-cat, tearing her hair, tearing pieces out of her gown. The scuffle was but brief: almost in an instant Jane Cross was falling headlong down the well of the staircase, pushed over the very low balustrades by Matilda, who threw the work-basket after her.

The catastrophe sobered her passion. For a while she lay on the landing in a sort of faint, all strength and power taken out of her as usual by the frenzy. Then she went down to look after Jane Cross.

Jane was dead. Matilda, not unacquainted with the aspect of death, saw that at once, and her senses pretty nearly deserted her again with remorse and horror. She had never thought to kill Jane Cross, hardly to harm her, she liked her too well: but in those moments of frenzy she had not the slightest control over her actions. Her first act was to run and lock the side door in the garden wall, lest anyone should come in. How she lived through the next half hour, she never knew. Her superstitious fear of seeing the dead Edmund Peahern in the house was strong—and now there was another one! But, with all her anguish and her fear, the instinct of self-preservation was making itself heard. What must she do? How could she throw the suspicion off herself? She could not run out of the house and say, 'Jane Cross has fallen accidentally over the stairs; come and look to her'—for no one would have believed it to be an accident. And there were the pieces, too, she had clutched out of the gown! While thus deliberating, the gate bell rang, putting her into a state of the most intense terror. It rang again. Trembling, panting, Matilda stood cowering in the kitchen, but it did not ring a third time. This was, of course, Thomas Owen.

Necessity is the mother of invention. Something she *must* do, and her brain hastily concocted the plan she should adopt. Putting the cloth and the bread-and-cheese on the table, she took the jug and went out at the front door to fetch the usual pint of ale. A moment or two she stood at the front door, peering up and down the road to make sure that no one was passing. Then she slipped out, locking the door softly; and, carrying the key concealed in the hollow of her hand, she threw it amidst the shrubs at No. 1. *Now* she could not get into the house herself; she would not have entered it alone for the world: people must break it open. All along the way to the post office, to which she really did go, and then to the Swan, she was mentally rehearsing her tale. And it succeeded in deceiving us all, as the reader knows. With regard to the visit of her brother on the Wednesday, she had told Thomas Owen the strict truth; though, when he first alluded to it in the churchyard, her feelings were wrought up to such a pitch that she could only cry out and escape. But how poor Matilda contrived to live on and carry out her invented story, how she bore the inward distress and repentance that lay upon her, we shall never know. A distress, remorse, repentance that never quitted her, night or day; and which no doubt contributed to gradually unhinge her mind, and to throw it finally off its balance.

Such was the true history of the affair at No. 7, which had been so great a mystery to Saltwater. The truth was never made public, save to the very few who were specially interested in it. Matilda Valentine is in the asylum, and likely to remain there for life; while Thomas Owen and his wife flourish in sunshine, happy as a summer's day.

The Going Out of Alessandro Pozzone

RICHARD DOWLING

Granthorne Avenue is a short turning off the Dulwich Road. On each side of the Avenue are a dozen houses or so; the houses are detached, and let for forty-five pounds a year. Each house has in front a pretty little piece of garden, and at the back a considerable piece of ground. At the end of the ground, to the rear, is a small green gate, opening upon a narrow private lane. This lane is for the exclusive use of the houses in Granthorne Avenue, there being no other buildings close to the lane on either side. At one end of Granthorne Avenue runs the Dulwich Road; at the other rises a black plank fence six feet high, cutting off the road from fields beyond, where in summer-time well-conditioned cows lie in the rich long grass. The ground at the backs of the houses is not cut up into beds, but each house owns a nice smooth grass-plot large enough for a modest croquet party, and skirted on both sides by a gravel path, at the bottom of the right-hand one of which stands the small green door into the lane.

It was the beginning of June. The month had come in with all the violence of March and all the inconsistency of April; the fourth of the month had been a remarkably inclement day. It blew a gale from the south, accompanied by occasional brilliant sunshine and deluging showers. As night drew on, the wind abated, but the rain was still heavy and frequent.

At ten o'clock the wind sprung up again, and blew steadily from the west, wailing and soughing through the trees at the back of Granthorne Avenue. At eleven o'clock a terrific shower fell. Most of the lights in Granthorne Avenue were now on the upper floors: the people were going to bed. The sound of the rain was positively alarming, and many persons came to their bedroom windows, drew up the blinds and curtains, and looked out. The rain beat into the fronts of the houses on the left-hand side of the Avenue.

All the basements and the ground-floor windows were dark on the right-hand side of the Avenue. On the left-hand side a light burned in the hall of No. 17, and upon the Venetian blinds of the drawing-room on the ground floor of No. 7 shone a bright cheerful light, and from behind it came the sound of music, a piano and a man's voice, a high tenor flat voice; the tune and song were 'Robin Adair'.

The shower lasted no longer than ten minutes. The wind and the music outlasted the shower, and at a quarter past eleven the bedroom windows were deserted, and Granthorne Avenue was going to bed.

At a quarter to twelve, Mr Frederick Morley and Mr Charles Bell stepped out of a first-class smoking compartment of a train from town at the Herne Hill Station, and walked arm-in-arm to the end of Granthorne Avenue. While they stood a moment at the end of the Avenue, Mr Bell said, 'I go in the back way when I am late.' Heavy drops began to fall, 'Another shower. What weather for June! Let's get in quickly or we shall be wet through. Good-night.'

'I go in the front way,' said Mr Morley, adding, 'Good-night,' as he hastened up the Avenue in the rain, now once more falling in torrents, and beating noisily on the windows of the left-hand side of the way.

From the corner of the Avenue to its first house, extended about fifty yards of blank wall, enclosing the garden at the back of the house on the main road. When Mr Morley reached the door of No. 8, which was his house, he glittered all over with wet in the light of a lamp just opposite his door. In No. 7, at the other side, the light shone through the blind. Mr Morley fumbled in his pockets, muttered something to himself, then half aloud, 'Confound it, I've left my latch key behind me. I shall have to knock them up.' He rang and knocked, and drawing himself within the shelter of the porch patiently awaited the result.

Through the beating of the rain and the soughing of the wind in the trees, he heard the music from the cheerfully lighted drawing-room of No. 7 opposite. Partly to beguile the time and partly that those in the house might recognize his voice and be not alarmed, he caught up the tune from No. 7 and commenced humming 'Robin Adair'.

For two or three minutes Mr Morley waited, but heard no stir within. Then he dropped his humming, knocked and rang again, and resumed 'Robin Adair' in a louder tone, keeping time with the instrument over the way.

He heard the bell in the servant's room ring. 'Now it's all right,' he muttered; 'but Matilda is so very nice in her notions, and so very slow in her movements, that she'll keep me here a good five minutes yet.'

After two or three minutes he grew a little impatient, and, to cool his haste, set up a whistling accompaniment to the music from No. 7, remarking, before he started, 'By Jove, our foreign friend opposite does stick to poor Robin!'

He had been in all about five minutes at his door, when suddenly he threw up his head and listened with a look of alarm on his face, as it glittered with rain in the lamplight.

He listened intently. 'No, no. That was no low of a cow in her sleep. It was a human sound, a human groan.'

There again! There it was again! Confound the rain and the piano. Something wrong at the back of the opposite row of houses. It must have been a loud groan to carry so far. Confound that foreigner and his wretched piano and his everlasting 'Robin Adair'! Could anything have happened to Bell?

Without any more hesitation Mr Morley set off at a run down Granthorne Avenue, into the Dulwich Road, and turned up the lane at the back of the houses.

Here he shortened his stick in his hand, shook it to see that it and his arm were trustworthy, and advanced more slowly.

He reached the backs of the houses. All was very quiet and very dark. He passed one, two, three doors, and here was four, No. 7, and that interminable 'Robin Adair' wheezing through the window and the rain! But nothing noteworthy or suspicious.

Five, six, seven, eight, nine. This ought to be the back of No. 17, Bell's house. Yes, no doubt.

Bell's door ajar! And, O God! what is this? A dead or stunned man across the threshold, as though he had fallen the moment he entered!

'Help here! Lights, I say! Help! Murder!'

For a moment all was silent save the rain and the wind, and the instrument now faintly heard by Morley. Soon after his cry the tune ceased, the back door of No. 7 opened, a man stepped out and asked in a foreign accent, 'What noise is this? Who called? There is no one hurt, I hope!'

Morley heard the voice and called out, 'Yes, come here, sir, and help me. I fear he is dead.'

'Where are you?'

'At Mr Bell's back gate. Come and knock his people up. For heaven's sake come. I won't leave him lest the villains come back. I can feel the blood. Feel, it is warm and—salt.'

By this time the foreigner was by the side of Mr Morley. 'Blood,' said the foreigner, 'hot and salt. Leave me to mind him. I do not know his people. You go tell them of this sadness. No fear of anyone coming back. It seems to be his head that is hurt. Poor man, hot and salt. So it is. You are right, sir. Go at once, I will stay. Go with speed.'

In a short time Mr Bell's household, consisting of a son and daughter and maid-servant, were aroused, the wounded man was carried into the house by Mr Morley, Sig. Cordella, the foreigner, and Mr John Bell, son of the victim. A little later came surgeons and the police. The doctors gave little hope; the junior of the two sat up all night; and in the morning, at six o'clock, Mr Charles Bell passed away without having had one moment of consciousness.

Next day, that is on June 6, the inquest was opened, and the facts disclosed were briefly these:

Mr Morley, the last person known to have seen the deceased before he had received the fatal blow, swore that he had known the late Mr Bell about five years. Had became acquainted with him in a railway carriage, soon after deceased came to live at Granthorne Avenue. They both went into town by the same train every morning. So they had grown to be quite intimate. Rarely came out with deceased in the evening or at night. Witness usually got home about 7 p.m., and, he understood, deceased not until nine or ten usually; and often not until midnight: the deceased had told him this. On only two or three previous occasions had he and deceased come home together so late as on the night of the 4th. His memory was quite clear on every event connected with that night. Witness then described his parting from the murdered man at the end of the Avenue, the wind and rain, the delay at his own door; how free from all suspicion of danger to his friend he was, for, while waiting for his door to be opened, he caught up the tune his neighbour Sig. Cordella was playing, and was whistling it, when his attention was attracted by the groan. How he ran round to be back lane, found the injured man, knew Sig. Cordella was up and called for help. How the Signore came and supported the injured man until further help arrived, and they carried the dying man into the house.

Next came Sig. Roberto Cordella, of No. 7, a native of Italy, who swore that towards midnight on the 4th, he being then enjoying some music, heard a cry from the back of the houses, and going out found matters as described by the former witness. Sig. Cordella had lived only a few months, about five, in Granthorne Avenue, during which time he had had no intercourse of any kind with deceased. Witness was a retired music master. Did not remember ever seeing deceased. This was partly explained by the fact that, as a rule, Mr Bell came home late of nights, and, as the last witness swore, usually went in the back way, as on the night of the murder. The witness said he had been greatly shocked and shaken by the melancholy occurrence. Being a foreigner he knew little of such legal proceedings as the present; and in conclusion he asked the coroner if he were now free to retire. The coroner told him he might go down; and, although there was no great likelihood of his being required further, still he had better remain within hearing; there was no knowing but they might have to recall him. Sig. Cordella bowed and stepped down.

The medical evidence was simplicity itself. Deceased had died from injuries to the back of the skull. Two blows had been inflicted. One apparently as the deceased was entering the garden gate; the other as he lay on the ground. The former had smashed in the poll, and would have been quite sufficient to cause death. The second had battered in the right temple and cheek-bone, leaving on the wet earth the impression of the left side of the face. The injuries from which the man died were, no doubt, inflicted by the stone produced by the police. [The stone was a piece of flag eighteen inches long, six inches wide, and three inches deep.] On the stone human hair, human blood, and particles of flesh corresponding with wants in the head of deceased were to be seen. All the organs in deceased's body were healthy, and he had been a powerful man notwithstanding that he must have been past sixty years of age.

The evidence of the police followed:

The stone produced by them was one of many similar in the lane. They had found nothing else of any consequence. There were upon the clothes of Mr Morley and Sig. Cordella such blood-stains as would be accounted for by the succour they had given the deceased. No suspicious people or person had been seen lurking about the place. Supposing the assassin had run from the back door of No. 17

to the Dulwich Road end of the lane, starting at the same moment as Mr Morley from his house, Mr Morley would surely have seen him, as the Road was quite straight, well lighted, and at this point afforded no shelter or means of concealment.

Mr Morley: 'I saw no one.'

It was true that from the back of No. 17 to the board fence at the field end of the lane was a less distance than from the same point to the Road, and that the murderer would have had time to reach that fence, scale it, and drop into the field at the other side before Mr Morley could have come round the other end of the lane.

Up to this point the whole inquiry had gone on without exciting any exceptional interest, and the majority of people present seemed to have made up their minds that the criminal, having given the fatal blows, had run down the lane, scaled the fence, and escaped through the fields. The further evidence of the police produced a profound sensation, bordering upon dismay; and those closely connected with the case began to regard one another half in suspicion, half in fear. The officer continued:

But it was quite certain that neither on the night of the murder nor the day before it had anyone crossed the fence; the reasons for thinking so were conclusive. On 3 June ten cart-loads of fine building sand had been backed against that wooden fence on the field side, and on the morning of the 5th no trace whatever of footsteps or disturbance could be found in this sand. The walls of the lane were of smooth brick and high, thirteen feet, for wall-fruit, and no man could possibly reach their summit without a ladder; and not only was no ladder found, but not the smallest fresh scratch upon the walls, the surface of which was soft from moisture and would show the scratch of even a thumb-nail. On the field side, the sand, intended for a wall to be built in place of the wooden fence, overlapped the end of the lane many feet. Through interstices between the planking of this black plank fence some sand had percolated into the lane and lay in a fine smooth mat, four feet wide from the planking. From this sand the rain falling at the time of the murder might obliterate, or at least deaden, footmarks; but the sand in the lane was examined with lamps in less than an hour after the fatal blow was struck, and when the rain had been falling only about ten minutes after the blow, and yet no footmarks had been found. The sand at the other side of the lane was sheltered by two large chestnuts and showed perfect shovel marks of the day before, but no trace of footsteps whatever. No arrests had been made yet.

The son of the deceased was next called. He had not much to tell; such as it was the substance is as follows:

His father had passed his sixty-third year. Had been at one time an outdoor officer of Customs; last stationed at Avonford. About fifteen years ago he had been obliged to leave the Customs owing to a severe rheumatic affection contracted while on duty. At that time and for many years afterwards, witness, who was now seven-and-thirty years of age, was in Australia and did not know details. After retiring from the Customs, deceased came from Avonford to London, and set up a grocery business in Baroda Street, Oxford Street. The business had been prosperous; and some years ago deceased had taken his present house, where deceased, being a widower, lived with his daughter and a maid-servant until now. Witness upon coming home on leave last year joined his father's household and had lived at No. 17 ever since.

Evidently the disquieting discovery of the police caused the coroner to proceed with much more care and deliberation than he had employed in the earlier stage of the inquiry, and he examined the son with great fullness and most minutely. In answer to further interrogation the son went on:

On the morning of the 4th, Mr Bell left home for town at the usual hour, half-past eight. He ate a hearty breakfast and seemed in excellent spirits. The last words witness heard his father utter were said just as deceased was leaving: 'Don't wait up. I shall be late tonight. Leave the dining-room door open.' The last sentence referred to the door from the dining-room into the back garden. This door opened on a little exterior landing which communicated by means of a flight of steps with the garden. By 'Leave the dining-room door open,' deceased meant on the latch or spring lock, for which deceased had a key. It was deceased's habit when he returned late to come in by the door, bolt it, eat a little supper, have a glass of grog and a smoke before going to bed. On the night in question, witness went to bed as usual at a little after eleven, fell asleep, and was soon roused by Mr Morley knocking at the kitchen door and calling for help. Witness got up, put on some clothes hastily, and came down. That was all he could say of the whole affair. The police had found his father's purse and watch upon the person of the injured man. Didn't think his father had a personal enemy in the world. As far as witness knew not a soul but he himself would benefit by his father's untimely death. His sister would be a loser by it.

The maid-servant and the daughter of deceased were briefly examined as to the events on the night of the murder and dismissed; and, it being then evening, the inquiry was adjourned for a week to give the police an opportunity of investigating the case further. Before rising, the coroner made an order for the interment of the body.

Next day John Bell was busy about the funeral. Many of the friends and acquaintances of the deceased made visits of condolence and all the neighbourhood was full of horror at the awful deed, regret for the pleasant inoffensive man who had been done to death, and sympathy for the son and daughter.

It was midnight before John Bell found himself alone. He was a tall, powerful man, with red-brown beard, brown eyes, a bronzed face, and brown strong hands. When at rest in ordinary times his face had a stern expression. You could see he was not a man to be trifled with. In movement he was slow, ponderous. No matter what he did it seemed as though he had fully considered it before commencing to move; once action begun, there was such an evidence of the means to the end that few would think of trying to stand between him and his object. As he sat in the hideous stiffness of his new black clothes, a cruel smile played upon his features alternately with a look of profound and passionless thought. He sat by the open dining-room door through which Mr Morley, Sig. Cordella, and himself had carried the dying man on the night of the 4th. This night there was neither wind nor rain. The houses all round were still, and Nature slept like a weary child, without a cry or a sigh.

The police had carefully examined Mr Bell's house in the hope of getting a clue to the murderer. They had asked to see Mr Bell's private papers, and these had been shown to them. They had read some of the documents, and, having made notes, felt no further need of the papers, and gave them back to Mr John Bell. These letters, diaries, memoranda, etc., were now lying in a confused heap on the dining-room table. For an hour John Bell had been sitting at the open window in a profound reverie. He now aroused himself, turned up the gas fully (it had been half turned down), drew a chair close to the table, and commenced turning over the papers, now reading one through, now merely glancing at another. At last he came to one which seemed to interest and excite him greatly.

It was a lengthy document in his father's writing, and was battered a good deal and showed signs of wear and tear and age. He did not wait to finish reading it, but got up hastily, left the room, went into the hall, pulled out the drawer in the hall table, took from the drawer a small slip of paper on which were written a few words, came back to the room, held the slip of paper and the document he had been reading, one in each hand, under the gaslight, and compared one line of the old document with the slip; then lct both fall from his hands, shivered, covered his face with his hands, and sank down into a chair.

He remained for half an hour absolutely motionless, save for the regular rising and falling of his broad back. At the end of that time he rose, finished the reading of the sheets of old paper, folded them up, put them in his breast pocket, and placed the small slip which he had taken from the drawer in his watch pocket. When this was done he put his hand under his coat-tails for a moment, as if to tighten the back strap of his waistcoat, did not tighten the strap, went and got his hat, descended the steps from the dining-room into the garden, opened the garden gate, and went out into the lane.

It was then about half-past one in the morning.

The place was still as death; the trees stood up silently in the darkness; the dark violet vault of heaven hung spread with myriads of pale stars overhead. John Bell looked warily up and down the lane. 'It is very dark and very late,' he thought, as he closed the garden door behind him, 'but it will be darker and later before the dawn.'

He turned towards the Dulwich Road, and walked very slowly down the lane. He reached the end of the lane, turned to his left, and again to his left. He was now in the Avenue, and taking the left-hand footway he commenced ascending the Avenue. He passed by the blank wall and the houses 1, 3, and 5. These were all dark. In the drawing-room window of No. 7 there was a light. Not a ray in any other house in the Avenue. John Bell drew back the bolt on the garden gate, entered the garden, went up the steps, and knocked very softly. In a few seconds the door was unchained, unlocked, and unbolted, and Sig. Cordella, recognizing him at once, cried, 'Ah, Mr Bell, is it you? There is nothing more wrong, I hope?'

'There is nothing new wrong,' answered the visitor; adding, 'I know this is a most extraordinary time for making a call on a comparative stranger, but seeing your light burning, and being greatly troubled and disturbed in my mind, I ventured to knock.'

'Come in,' said the foreigner, 'come in. I always sit up late. Come in and rest with me for some time.' He led the way into the drawing-room.

The room was furnished in good taste. The colours were all cool and grey, rather French than Italian. There were no pictures on the pearl-grey walls. The drapery and upholstery were of a delicate shade of deep fawn; the carpet a dull amber. Against one wall stood a cottage piano, on which lay a guitar. In a corner was a violin case, and upon a table opposite the door a large musical box and a silver flute. A couch was drawn halfway across the window, and at the foot of the couch stood a small inlaid table. Scattered about were a few ordinary drawing chairs, and at the table one easy-chair. Upon the inlaid table were placed cigars, a tobacco jar, a cigarette book, an ashtray, and a box of matches. Although the room was a small one, three gas jets were at their full height, and John Bell was compelled to shade his eyes for a moment.

'You will sit down?' said the Italian, waving his hand to the chair by the table and sinking softly on the couch himself.

Bell hesitated a moment, looked slowly round the room, and then said, 'I will.'

The Italian rolled up a cigarette, lighted it, and threw himself into the arm of the couch. He was a low-sized man of about five-and-forty years of age, bald, dark-skinned, black-bearded, black-eyed, with black heavy eyebrows—not at all a pleasant face. Although there was always a faint smile on the features, it seemed a smile the motive for which had passed away, and that the smile itself ought to have passed away too. It was the fag end of a stale smile, and the face would have been much improved if it had been swept off altogether. Notwithstanding this unpleasant smile the Italian's face was handsome, eminently handsome.

John Bell was evidently a little perplexed, for he paused awhile before even attempting to offer an explanation or apology for his late visit. At last he spoke:

'As you may fancy, Mr Cordella, nothing but a matter of great importance could induce me to intrude upon you at this time of night.'

'Pray, no apology. I know how troubled you must be in your mind. I sympathize with you; I sympathize with you out of my heart, indeed, Mr Bell. In your trouble you no doubt could find no sleep, so you come out for a walk, for fresh air, and you see my light, a neighbour's light, and you come in. Make nothing of it. I always sit up till late—these times till daylight. Will you smoke?'

'I will smoke, thank you. But, Mr Cordella, it was not accident brought me here tonight; I came on purpose. I came on most important business. I owe you thanks for your great kindness on that awful night—I have come now to make but a poor return. I am sorry to say that I find it absolutely necessary to ask you some questions which, though they may seem impertinent at the outset, are of vital consequence to me. You will answer me without taking offence for what must seem an unpardonable and outrageously ill-timed intrusion and an unwarrantable inquisitiveness.'

'Indeed you may ask, and indeed I will answer,' said the Italian, waving his hand softly through the smoke of his cigarette.

'Remember before I begin that I will ask you no question which is not of importance, and that I have excellent cause to risk seeming impertinent in order to get the information I require.'

Speaking through a veil of smoke the Italian answered: 'I have told you, Mr John Bell, that I will answer you. What is it that I have to conceal?'

'Nothing, no doubt, about yourself, but I am not come to speak about yourself. I want to ask you some questions about another. First and foremost, you and I are in this room; who else is in this house?'

The Italian took his cigarette slowly from his lips with his left hand, emerged from the smoke, and leaned towards John Bell until his left elbow rested on the couch. Then thrusting his right hand softly between his waistcoat and shirt at the breast he looked up into John Bell's face with an expression of playful surprise. 'Why?'

John Bell took his cigar from his mouth and moved only his eyes towards the other. For a moment the two men regarded one another as though neither had the faintest clue to what was in the mind of the other, and each was very desirous to get some insight into the thought of the other before proceeding further. Said Bell, 'That is not a very clear answer to my question, is it?'

'No; but you come to me telling me you are curious to know some things. You come at two o'clock in the morning; that is strange. Then you ask me a strange question; that, too, is strange. You make me feel, like yourself, curious. You must not feel angry with me if I feel curious, and ask you why do you want to know who else is in this house?'

'You are quite right,' said John Bell. 'I was most unreasonable in expecting that I, who am almost a complete stranger to you, had any right to question you about your household without giving ample reason. I'll give you the reason now, and repeat the question when I have done so.'

'It is so kind of you,' said the Italian, drawing his hand out from under his waistcoat, and gently resuming his old pose in the arm of the couch. As he lay back he touched his chest, and said with an apologetic smile, 'I have the heart disease, and any shock or thing gives me, ah! such great pain. When you asked me that strange question I thought I should die. You will pardon me; your father's sad fate has quite unnerved me for a moment. Ah! you will pardon me! I feared—well, I feared you wished to know whether—cannot you understand?' He closed his eyes and drew back his lips from his teeth, and inhaled painfully through his set teeth.

'I am very sorry that you suffer from heart disease, and I am very sorry I have caused you pain. I can now see my question in another light, and that it was equal to an enquiry into your means of defence. I am sorry I was so abrupt. I hope you will forgive me and hear me out, Mr Cordella?'

The Italian opened his eyes with an expression of pain and effort, answering very gently, 'Do not make any further apologies, Mr Bell; please go on. I am quite able and most willing to listen.' He closed his eyes again and gradually grew paler.

John Bell shook himself back into his chair. 'It will take some time,' he said, 'and I shall have to go back to the 4th of June. My father left home as usual at half-past eight. You may remember on that day in the forenoon a particular letter was dropped in the box of No. 17, my father's house. That letter was not for anyone we knew, being addressed to' (here John Bell took the slip of paper out of his watch-pocket and read from it) 'Sig. Alessandro Pozzone, 17 Granthorne Avenue, Dulwich, Londra.' 'Knowing that you were an Italian, and being ignorant of your name, and seeing how easily the mistake between 7 and 17 might arise, and finding the post-mark of "Torino" on the envelope, I wrote a line to "The Owner of No. 7," enclosing the foreign letter and asking you if it were for you.'

'You were most thoughtful.'

'To my note I signed my name. You returned a verbal message, saying that the foreign letter was not for you; that you knew nothing whatever of the person, Alessandro Pozzone, to whom it was addressed; and that you yourself would return it to the postman when next he called. You gave your message verbally, accompanied by your card. This was about noon. By your card and from your evidence at the inquest I learned that your name is Roberto Cordella. You will, I hope, pardon my great minuteness, but all this is really of prime importance.'

The Italian was rolling up another cigarette; he paused, opened his half-closed eyes, and signified by a gracious gesture that he was paying attention and held himself completely at the disposal of the other.

'At twelve o'clock that night my father was murdered.'

'Yes,' through a dense cloud of tobacco smoke.

'About an hour ago I came on a document which I will now take the liberty of reading to you. It is in my father's handwriting and relates to an event in his own experience—I fear I'd better stop. Your heart seems to trouble you again.'

'It is nothing; pressing it thus relieves it. Please go on.'

John Bell drew the paper out of his breast coat pocket and began to read. When the foreigner saw the document he nestled still more cosily into the arm of the couch, rolled up another cigarette and, when it was closed, replaced his hand over his heart.

'This paper,' began Bell, 'is apparently the rough draft of a report, to whom furnished it does not say. It is dated Avonford, 18 September 1865:

Sir,—At the earliest moment my health will allow I hasten to furnish you with a report of the events connected with the loss of the customs boat, *Swift* and two men on the 14th ult.

On the afternoon of the 13th ult., the Italian barque *San Giovanni Batista* being then cleared out and hauled out into the tide-way ready for sea, I received information that the customs officer in charge was in some way or other to be tampered with, the seals on the ship's stores broken, and the twenty-six thousand cigars under seal run ashore as soon as it was dark. I immediately ordered four men—namely, James Archer, John Brown, William Flynn, and John Plucknett—into the *Swift* and pulled down to the *San Giovanni*, myself steering; and she being then about a mile to the westward of Dockyard point with her anchor hove short ready to trip before she tended on the first of the ebb.

It was dark before we made her out; the night was clear with a new moon but not much light. The wind was then pretty much up and down the mast, but any little air there was being off the land. All the barque's sails were hanging loose. As soon as we got within half a mile or so we heard the windlass going. I stood up to watch her. I saw her head come up with a jerk and then I saw her veer when the anchor hung free. They began setting the sails, and the wind freshening a little the canvas commenced to fill, and she began to forge ahead. But I knew we could overhaul her, hand over hand, and we were overhauling her, for we were pulling two feet to her one.

We were coming up on her starboard quarter, and I saw a boat (not one of her own, they were all painted white, and this one was black and British built) by the starboard main-chains. 'The cigars are in that boat,' I thought, and I said to the men, 'Give way, men, give way with a will.'

My men gave way with a will, and I kept the *Swift* heading for the starboard mizen chains of the barque. There was fair steerage way on the barque now.

When we were about three cables' length astern I hailed the barque. She did not answer. A man came and looked over the taffarel and I heard an order given on deck. Upon the order being given the barque ported her helm until her head looked two points to port, then there was another order and the barque steadied her helm and kept on. This brought us right astern of the barque. The sails were now beginning to draw better every stroke we pulled, and as I did not like to lose any time I kept head on to her stern, although I did not a bit like her manœuvre.

As soon as we were about a cable's length off I hailed again. Still no answer. When we were half a cable's length I sang out once more. Said we were revenue officers and told them to come round and let us board.

'What do you want the ship to stop for?' asked the man at the tafferel whom I now knew quite well and who was not one of the crew of the *San Giovanni Batista*.

'Whose boat is that alongside?'

'The Vice-Consul's.'

'Send the customs' officer in charge aft.'

'He's gone ashore in the pilot's boat.'

'It's not time for either pilot or the customs' officer to go ashore yet. Who's taking the vessel out?'

'The channel pilot.'

'Come round, I say, I must board. I must see the captain and I must see the Vice-Consul's boat go ashore before I leave the ship.'

We were now only a couple of boats length from the stern post, dead astern. I did not like to yaw the boat to get round to the mizen chains, as it was easier to keep in the back water of the wake, and beside the barque had got more legs under her by this time, and I could do little more than keep up to her.

Foot by foot we drew up on the barque until at last we were right under the stern. I sang out again:

'If you won't come about heave us a line.'

'Ay, ay!' cried the man on the taffarel.

For a moment I saw him rise up, standing on the taffarel; he leaned forward with a heavy three-tackle block in his hand—I saw the moonlight through the block—and then dropped the block into the *Swift*. It came aboard on the foremost bow thwart, broke it in two, and stove out the bottom of the boat.

Before we could do anything the boat was full of water and turned bottom up. As long as we could we shouted. The barque kept her course until we could not even see her, and there was no other vessel in sight. James Archer, John Plucknett, and I clung on the bottom of the boat until morning, when the fishing boat *Toby* of Avonford saw us and took us off.

After the boat filled and turned over I never saw either John Brown or William Flynn alive. I saw the body of William Flynn when it was washed ashore next morning.

John Bell stopped reading, folded up the paper and replaced it in his breast pocket. As he did so he glanced at the recumbent Italian. The attitude of the latter was unchanged. Still the right hand thrust between the waistcoat and the breast of the shirt in the region of the heart; still the luxurious pose in the soft arm of the chair; still the everlasting cigarette and the cloud of ascending blue smoke. The foreigner now spoke in a voice of one who suffered not a little, and caught his breath uneasily.

'I have not the least dislike to tell you the answer to the question which I did not answer a while ago. There is at present none in this house but you, I, and the old woman, my servant and housekeeper. I am a bachelor, and there is no relative or friend or guest of mine under this roof now. Having answered you so far, and, as far as you have shown, answered you without knowing how the painful history you have read may be connected with your question, will you permit me to say that it is very late, and that I am far from well. I am most ill.'

'I am exceedingly sorry you should feel so poorly. I will not intrude much longer if you will permit me to explain.'

The Italian smiled languidly, signified that the other might proceed, and closed his eyes with an expression of great pain and exhaustion.

'I shall soon be done. The man who murdered the two men in the boat that night was interpreter to the Vice-Consul at Avonford. He was never found to answer for that crime. My father knew that this man was to endeavour to run the cigars. Next day the Vice-Consul's boat with the cigars untouched was found in a bight of the Avon bay. But the Vice-Consul's interpreter, the murderer, was never found. The barque, bound to Callao, never arrived in any port; it is believed she foundered in mid-ocean.

'Now this Vice-Consul's clerk or interpreter, knew my father well by name and appearance, often had business intercourse with my father. On the night of the 4th of this month my father was murdered by this self-same Vice-Consul's clerk. As sure as I live here he murdered my poor father, Mr Cordella.'

'Why are you so sure of that? and what can I do for you in this sad case?' demanded the foreigner, in a tone so languid and so faint that John Bell was compelled to draw near and bend low in order to hear.

'In the forenoon of the 4th that letter came to No. 17, misaddressed, intended to be left for Alessandro Pozzone at No. 7. You, Mr Cordella, forwarded my note to Pozzone with his own one; he recognized the name Bell, found out who my father was, lay in wait for my father and killed him before my poor father could get home and recognize the name of the man who fifteen years ago failed to do for him—for that Vice-Consul's clerk who let fall the block was Alessandro Pozzone.'

'I am completely prostrated by the news you tell me,' whispered the reclining man. 'Get me a little wine from the chiffonier. Since this matter is so dreadful I will now admit that I know Pozzone well. He represented to me his dangers were political, and I was sworn to divulge nothing about him.'

John Bell put an arm under the other man; from the fingers of the foreigner dropped the end of the half-smoked cigarette.

Bell held the wine to the recumbent man's lips. He drank a little and then whispered, 'Put down the wine. I can swallow no more. I am better—I am better, thank you; I shall be all right soon.' His right hand fell out of his breast, and lay upon the floor. 'Go on,' he whispered, 'I am most anxious to hear what you want me to do.'

'Tell me where Pozzone is.'

'I can, and I will. It is only right you should know, and at once. I will place him in your grasp in less than an hour. Ah! Ah, my breath once more—I am suffocating! Put your two strong arms round me and raise me.'

John Bell did as he was requested.

'Wait a second,' said the Italian, resting his two arms on the shoulders of the other.

'I can speak once more,' whispered the Italian. 'Your ear now. So. Now I will tell you where Pozzone is—In your arms! Now I will tell you where his knife is—In your heart!'

The Englishman drew himself up with a powerful effort, shook himself clear of his assailant, slipped his hand beneath his waistcoat as though to loose its strap, drew out the hand—

Bang!

But Pozzone had seen his action, and, suspecting it, dashed the hand aside. The ball struck the musical box, and with a loud crash smashed off the brake-end, the barrel began to revolve, and the teeth to vibrate—'Robin Adair'!

A superstitious fear seemed to seize upon Pozzone, and he whispered through his white lips, 'I played that air on the piano, and then I set the box to it and went out—'

Bang!

This time Pozzone staggered to his feet and steadied himself for an instant. He raised his hand to his forehead. His hand grew suddenly red.

'Warm and salt,' he cried; 'I set the box to "Robin Adair" and—went out. Curse it! What's this? Ah you'll never lift that revolver again, John Bell. Bell! Bell! "Robin Adair". I set the—there's "Robin Adair" again! Am I never to hear anything else here or in—— I set it to "Robin Adair" and went out—I am going out again! Am I to be always going out to the tune of "Robin Adair," here and in—hell?'

Who Killed Zebedee?

WILKIE COLLINS

A FIRST WORD FOR MYSELF

Before the Doctor left me one evening, I asked him how much longer I was likely to live. He answered: 'It's not easy to say; you may die before I can get back to you in the morning, or you may live to the end of the month.'

I was alive enough on the next morning to think of the needs of my soul, and (being a member of the Roman Catholic Church) to send for the priest.

The history of my sins, related in confession, included blameworthy neglect of a duty which I owed to the laws of my country. In the priest's opinion—and I agreed with him—I was bound to make public acknowledgement of my fault, as an act of penance becoming to a Catholic Englishman. We concluded, thereupon, to try a division of labour. I related the circumstances, while his reverence took the pen, and put the matter into shape.

Here follows what came of it:

I

When I was a young man of five-and-twenty, I became a member of the London police force. After nearly two years' ordinary experience of the responsible and ill-paid duties of that vocation, I found myself employed on my first serious and terrible case of official inquiry—relating to nothing less than the crime of Murder.

The circumstances were these:

I was then attached to a station in the northern district of London—which I beg permission not to mention more particularly. On a certain Monday in the week, I took my turn of night duty. Up to four in the morning, nothing occurred at the station-house out of the ordinary way. It was then springtime, and, between the gas and the fire, the room became rather hot. I went to the door to get a breath of fresh air—much to the surprise of our Inspector on duty, who was constitutionally a chilly man. There was a fine rain falling; and a nasty damp in the air sent me back to the fireside. I don't suppose I had sat down for more than a minute when the swinging-door was violently pushed open. A frantic woman ran in with a scream, and said: 'Is this the station-house?'

Our Inspector (otherwise an excellent officer) had, by some perversity of nature, a hot temper in his chilly constitution. 'Why, bless the woman, can't you *see* it is?' he says. 'What's the matter now?'

'Murder's the matter!' she burst out. 'For God's sake come back with me. It's at Mrs Crosscapel's lodging-house, number 14, Lehigh Street. A young woman has murdered her husband in the night! With a knife, sir. She says she thinks she did it in her sleep.'

I confess I was startled by this; and the third man on duty (a sergeant) seemed to feel it too. She was a nice-looking young woman, even in her terrified condition, just out of bed, with her clothes huddled on anyhow. I was partial in those days to a tall figure—and she was, as they say, my style. I put a chair for her; and the sergeant poked the fire. As for the Inspector, nothing ever upset *him*. He questioned her as coolly as if it had been a case of petty larceny.

'Have you seen the murdered man?' he asked.

'No, sir.'

'Or the wife?'

'No, sir. I didn't dare go into the room; I only heard about it!'

'Oh? And who are You? One of the lodgers?'

'No, sir. I'm the cook.'

'Isn't there a master in the house?'

'Yes, sir. He's frightened out of his wits. And the housemaid's gone for the Doctor. It all falls on the poor servants, of course. Oh, why did I ever set foot in that horrible house?'

The poor soul burst out crying, and shivered from head to foot. The Inspector made a note of her statement, and then asked her to read it, and sign it with her name. The object of this proceeding was to get her to come near enough to give him the opportunity of smelling her breath. 'When people make extraordinary statements,' he afterwards said to me, 'it sometimes saves trouble to satisfy yourself that they are not drunk. I've known them to be mad—but not often. You will generally find *that* in their eyes.'

She roused herself, and signed her name—'Priscilla Thurlby.' The Inspector's own test proved her to be sober; and her eyes—of a nice light blue colour, mild and pleasant, no doubt, when they were not staring with fear, and red with crying—satisfied him (as I supposed) that she was not mad. He turned the case over to me, in the first instance. I saw that he didn't believe in it, even yet.

'Go back with her to the house,' he says. 'This may be a stupid hoax, or a quarrel exaggerated. See to it yourself, and hear what the Doctor says. If it *is* serious, send word back here directly, and let nobody enter the place or leave it till we come. Stop! You know the form if any statement is volunteered?'

'Yes, sir. I am to caution the persons that whatever they say will be taken down, and may be used against them.'

'Quite right. You'll be an Inspector yourself one of these days. Now, Miss!' With that he dismissed her, under my care.

Lehigh Street was not very far off—about twenty minutes' walk from the station. I confess I thought the Inspector had been rather hard on Priscilla. She was herself naturally angry with him 'What does he mean,' she says, 'by talking of a hoax? I wish he was as frightened as I am. This is the first time I have been out at service, sir—and I did think I had found a respectable place.'

I said very little to her—feeling, if the truth must be told, rather anxious about the duty committed to me. On reaching the house the door was opened from within, before I could knock. A gentleman stepped out, who proved to be the Doctor. He stopped the moment he saw me.

'You must be careful, policeman,' he says. 'I found the man lying on his back, in bed, dead—with the knife that had killed him left sticking in the wound.'

Hearing this, I felt the necessity of sending at once to the station. Where could I find a trustworthy messenger? I took the liberty of asking the Doctor if he would repeat to the police what he had already said to me. The station was not much out of his way home. He kindly granted my request.

The landlady (Mrs Crosscapel) joined us while we were talking. She was still a young woman; not easily frightened, as far as I could see, even by a murder in the house. Her husband was in the passage behind her. He looked old enough to be her father; and he so trembled with terror that some people might have taken him for the guilty person. I removed the key from the street door, after locking it; and I said to the landlady: 'Nobody must leave the house, or enter the house, till the Inspector comes. I must examine the premises to see if anyone has broken in.'

'There is the key of the area gate,' she said, in answer to me. 'It's always kept locked. Come downstairs, and see for yourself.' Priscilla went with us. Her mistress set her to work to light the kitchen fire. 'Some of us,' says Mrs Crosscapel, 'may be the better for a cup of tea.' I remarked that she took things easy, under the circumstances. She answered that the landlady of a London lodging-house could not afford to lose her wits, no matter what might happen.

I found the gate locked, and the shutters of the kitchen window fastened. The back kitchen and back door were secured in the same way. No person was concealed anywhere. Returning upstairs, I examined the front parlour window. There again, the barred shutters answered for the security of that room. A cracked voice spoke through the door of the back parlour. 'The policeman can come in,' it said, 'if he will promise not to look at me.' I turned to the landlady for information. 'It's my parlour lodger, Miss Mybus,' she said, 'a most respectable lady.' Going into the room, I saw something rolled up perpendicularly in the bed curtains. Miss Mybus had made herself modestly invisible in that way. Having now satisfied my mind about the security of the lower part of the house, and having the keys safe in my pocket, I was ready to go upstairs.

On our way to the upper regions I asked if there had been any visitors on the previous day. There had been only two visitors, friends of the lodgers—and Mrs Crosscapel herself had let them both out. My next enquiry related to the lodgers themselves. On the ground floor there was Miss Mybus. On the first floor (occupying both rooms) Mr Barfield, an old bachelor, employed in a merchant's office. On the second floor, in the front room, Mr John Zebedee, the murdered man, and his wife. In the back room, Mr Deluc; described as a cigar agent, and supposed to be a Creole gentleman from Martinique. In the front garret, Mr and Mrs Crosscapel. In the back garret, the cook and the housemaid. These were the inhabitants, regularly accounted for. I asked about the servants. 'Both excellent characters,' says the landlady, 'or they would not be in my service.'

We reached the second floor, and found the housemaid on the

watch outside the door of the front room. Not as nice a woman, personally, as the cook, and sadly frightened of course. Her mistress had posted her, to give the alarm in the case of an outbreak on the part of Mrs Zebedee, kept locked up in the room. My arrival relieved the housemaid of further responsibility. She ran downstairs to her fellow-servant in the kitchen.

I asked Mrs Crosscapel how and when the alarm of the murder had been given.

'Soon after three this morning,' says she, 'I was woke by the screams of Mrs Zebedee. I found her out here on the landing, and Mr Deluc, in great alarm, trying to quiet her. Sleeping in the next room, he had only to open his door, when her screams woke him. "My dear John's murdered! I am the miserable wretch—I did it in my sleep!" She repeated those frantic words over and over again, until she dropped in a swoon. Mr Deluc and I carried her back into the bedroom. We both thought the poor creature had been driven distracted by some dreadful dream. But when we got to the bedside—don't ask me what we saw; the Doctor has told you about it already. I was once a nurse in a hospital, and accustomed, as such, to horrid sights. It turned me cold and giddy, notwithstanding. As for Mr Deluc, I thought *he* would have had a fainting fit next.'

Hearing this, I enquired if Mrs Zebedee had said or done any strange things since she had been Mrs Crosscapel's lodger.

'You think she's mad?' says the landlady. 'And anybody would be of your mind, when a woman accuses herself of murdering her husband in her sleep. All I can say is that, up to this morning, a more quiet, sensible, well-behaved little person than Mrs Zebedee I never met with. Only just married, mind, and as fond of her unfortunate husband as a woman could be. I should have called them a pattern couple, in their own line of life.'

There was no more to be said on the landing. We unlocked the door and went into the room.

II

He lay in bed on his back as the Doctor had described him. On the left side of his nightgown, just over his heart, the blood on the linen told its terrible tale. As well as one could judge, looking unwillingly at a dead face, he must have been a handsome young man in his lifetime. It was a sight to sadden anybody—but I think the most painful sensation was when my eyes fell next on his miserable wife.

She was down on the floor, crouched up in a corner—a dark little woman, smartly dressed in gay colours. Her black hair and her big brown eyes made the horrid paleness of her face look even more deadly white than perhaps it really was. She stared straight at us without appearing to see us. We spoke to her, and she never answered a word. She might have been dead—like her husband—except that she perpetually picked at her fingers, and shuddered every now and then as if she was cold. I went to her and tried to lift her up. She shrank back with a cry that well-nigh frightened me—not because it was loud, but because it was more like the cry of some animal than of a human being. However quietly she might have behaved in the landlady's previous experience of her, she was beside herself now. I might have been moved by a natural pity for her, or I might have been completely upset in my mind—I only know this, I could not persuade myself that she was guilty. I even said to Mrs Crosscapel, 'I don't believe she did it.'

While I spoke, there was a knock at the door. I went downstairs at once, and admitted (to my great relief) the Inspector, accompanied by one of our men.

He waited downstairs to hear my report, and he approved of what I had done. 'It looks as if the murder had been committed by some-body in the house.' Saying this, he left the man below, and went up with me to the second floor.

Before he had been a minute in the room, he discovered an object which had escaped my observation.

It was the knife that had done the deed.

The Doctor had found it left in the body—had withdrawn it to probe the wound—and had laid it on the bedside table. It was one of those useful knives which contain a saw, a corkscrew, and other like implements. The big blade fastened back, when open, with a spring. Except where the blood was on it, it was as bright as when it had been purchased. A small metal plate was fastened to the horn handle, containing an inscription, only partly engraved, which ran thus: '*To John Zebedee, from*——' There it stopped, strangely enough.

Who or what had interrupted the engraver's work? It was im-possible even to guess. Nevertheless, the Inspector was encouraged.

'This ought to help us,' he said—and then he gave an attentive ear (looking all the while at the poor creature in the corner) to what Mrs Crosscapel had to tell him.

The landlady having done, he said he must now see the lodger who slept in the next bedchamber.

Mr Deluc made his appearance, standing at the door of the room, and turning away his head with horror from the sight inside.

He was wrapped in a splendid blue dressing-gown, with a golden girdle and trimmings. His scanty brownish hair curled (whether artificially or not, I am unable to say) in little ringlets. His complexion was yellow; his greenish-brown eyes were of the sort called 'goggle'—they looked as if they might drop out of his face, if you held a spoon under them. His moustache and goat's beard were beautifully oiled; and, to complete his equipment, he had a long black cigar in his mouth.

'It isn't insensibility to this terrible tragedy,' he explained. 'My nerves have been shattered, Mr Policeman, and I can only repair the mischief in this way. Be pleased to excuse and feel for me.'

The Inspector questioned this witness sharply and closely. He was not a man to be misled by appearances; but I could see that he was far from liking, or even trusting, Mr Deluc. Nothing came of the examination, except what Mrs Crosscapel had in substance already mentioned to me. Mr Deluc returned to his room.

'How long has he been lodging with you?' the Inspector asked, as soon as his back was turned.

'Nearly a year,' the landlady answered.

'Did he give you a reference?'

'As good a reference as I could wish for.' Thereupon, she mentioned the names of a well-known firm of cigar merchants in the City. The Inspector noted the information in his pocket-book.

I would rather not relate in detail what happened next: it is too distressing to be dwelt on. Let me only say that the poor demented woman was taken away in a cab to the station-house. The Inspector possessed himself of the knife, and of a book found on the floor, called *The World of Sleep*. The portmanteau containing the luggage was locked—and then the door of the room was secured, the keys in both cases being left in my charge. My instructions were to remain in the house, and allow nobody to leave it, until I heard again shortly from the Inspector.

III

The coroner's inquest was adjourned; and the examination before the magistrate ended in a remand—Mrs Zebedee being in no condition to understand the proceedings in either case. The surgeon reported her to be completely prostrated by a terrible nervous shock. When he was asked if he considered her to have been a sane woman before the murder took place, he refused to answer positively at that time.

A week passed. The murdered man was buried; his old father attending the funeral. I occasionally saw Mrs Crosscapel, and the two servants, for the purpose of getting such further information as was thought desirable. Both the cook and the housemaid had given their month's notice to quit; declining, in the interest of their characters, to remain in a house which had been the scene of a murder. Mr Deluc's nerves led also to his removal; his rest was now disturbed by frightful dreams. He paid the necessary forfeit-money, and left without notice. The first-floor lodger, Mr Barfield, kept his rooms, but obtained leave of absence from his employers, and took refuge with some friends in the country. Miss Mybus alone remained in the parlours. 'When I am comfortable,' the old lady said, 'nothing moves me, at my age. A murder up two pairs of stairs is nearly the same thing as a murder in the next house. Distance, you see, makes all the difference.'

It mattered little to the police what the lodgers did. We had men in plain clothes watching the house night and day. Everybody who went away was privately followed; and the police in the district to which they retired were warned to keep an eye on them, after that. As long as we failed to put Mrs Zebedee's extraordinary statement to any sort of test—to say nothing of having proved unsuccessful, thus far, in tracing the knife to its purchaser—we were bound to let no person living under Mrs Crosscapel's roof, on the night of the murder, slip through our fingers.

IV

In a fortnight more, Mrs Zebedee had sufficiently recovered to make the necessary statement—after the preliminary caution addressed to persons in such cases. The surgeon had no hesitation, now, in reporting her to be a sane woman.

Her station in life had been domestic service. She had lived for four years in her last place as lady's-maid, with a family residing in Dorsetshire. The one objection to her had been the occasional infirmity of sleep-walking, which made it necessary that one of the other female servants should sleep in the same room, with the door locked and the key under her pillow. In all other respects the lady's-maid was described by her mistress as 'a perfect treasure'.

In the last six months of her service, a young man named John Zebedee entered the house (with a written character) as footman. He soon fell in love with the nice little lady's-maid, and she heartily returned the feeling. They might have waited for years before they were in a pecuniary position to marry, but for the death of Zebedee's uncle, who left him a little fortune of two thousand pounds. They were now, for persons in their station, rich enough to please themselves; and they were married from the house in which they had served together, the little daughters of the family showing their affection for Mrs Zebedee by acting as her bridesmaids.

The young husband was a careful man. He decided to employ his small capital to the best advantage, by sheep-farming in Australia. His wife made no objection; she was ready to go wherever John went.

Accordingly they spent their short honeymoon in London, so as to see for themselves the vessel in which their passage was to be taken. They went to Mrs Crosscapel's lodging-house because Zebedee's uncle had always stayed there when he was in London. Ten days were to pass before the day of embarkation arrived. This gave the young couple a welcome holiday, and a prospect of amusing themselves to their hearts' content among the sights and shows of the great city.

On their first evening in London they went to the theatre. They were both accustomed to the fresh air of the country, and they felt half stifled by the heat and the gas. However, they were so pleased with an amusement which was new to them that they went to another theatre on the next evening. On this second occasion, John Zebedee found the heat unendurable. They left the theatre, and got back to their lodgings towards ten o'clock.

Let the rest be told in the words used by Mrs Zebedee herself. She said:

We sat talking for a little while in our room, and John's headache got worse and worse. I persuaded him to go to bed, and I put out the candle (the fire giving sufficient light to undress by), so that he might the sooner fall asleep. But he was too restless to sleep. He asked me to read him something. Books always made him drowsy at the best of times.

I had not myself begun to undress. So I lit the candle again, and I opened the only book I had. John had noticed it at the railway bookstall by the name of *The World of Sleep*. He used to joke with me about my being a sleep-walker; and he said, 'Here's something that's sure to interest you'—and he made me a present of the book.

Before I had read to him for more than half an hour he was fast asleep. Not feeling that way inclined, I went on reading to myself.

The book did indeed interest me. There was one terrible story which took a hold on my mind—the story of a man who stabbed his own wife in a sleep-walking dream. I thought of putting down my book after that, and then changed my mind again and went on. The next chapters were not so interesting; they were full of learned accounts of why we fall asleep, and what our brains do in that state, and such like. It ended in my falling asleep, too, in my armchair by the fireside.

I don't know what o'clock it was when I went to sleep. I don't know how long I slept, or whether I dreamed or not. The candle and the fire had both burned out, and it was pitch dark when I woke. I can't even say why I woke—unless it was the coldness of the room.

There was a spare candle on the chimney-piece. I found the matchbox, and got a light. Then, for the first time, I turned round towards the bed; and I saw——

She had seen the dead body of her husband, murdered while she was unconsciously at his side—and she fainted, poor creature, at the bare remembrance of it.

The proceedings were adjourned. She received every possible care and attention; the chaplain looking after her welfare as well as the surgeon.

I have said nothing of the evidence of the landlady and the servants. It was taken as a mere formality. What little they knew proved nothing against Mrs Zebedee. The police made no discoveries that supported her first frantic accusation of herself. Her master and mistress, where she had been last in service, spoke of her in the highest terms. We were at a complete deadlock.

It had been thought best not to surprise Mr Deluc, as yet, by citing him as a witness. The action of the law was, however, hurried in this case by a private communication received from the chaplain.

After twice seeing, and speaking with, Mrs Zebedee, the reverend gentleman was persuaded that she had no more to do than himself with the murder of her husband. He did not consider that he was justified in repeating a confidential communication—he would only recommend that Mr Deluc should be summoned to appear at the next examination. This advice was followed.

The police had no evidence against Mrs Zebedee when the inquiry was resumed. To assist the ends of justice she was now put into the witness-box. The discovery of her murdered husband, when she woke in the small hours of the morning, was passed over as rapidly as possible. Only three questions of importance were put to her.

First, the knife was produced. Had she ever seen it in her husband's possession? Never. Did she know anything about it? Nothing whatever.

Secondly: Did she, or did her husband, lock the bedroom door when they returned from the theatre? No. Did she afterwards lock the door herself? No.

Thirdly: Had she any sort of reason to give for supposing that she had murdered her husband in a sleep-walking dream? No reason, except that she was beside herself at the time, and the book put the thought into her head.

After this the other witnesses were sent out of court. The motive for the chaplain's communication now appeared. Mrs Zebedee was asked if anything unpleasant had occurred between Mr Deluc and herself.

Yes. He had caught her alone on the stairs at the lodging-house; had presumed to make love to her; and had carried the insult still further by attempting to kiss her. She had slapped his face, and had declared that her husband should know of it, if his misconduct was repeated. He was in a furious rage at having his face slapped; and he said to her: 'Madam, you may live to regret this.'

After consultation, and at the request of our Inspector, it was decided to keep Mr Deluc in ignorance of Mrs Zebedee's statement for the present. When the witnesses were recalled, he gave the same evidence which he had already given to the Inspector—and he was then asked if he knew anything of the knife. He looked at it without any guilty signs in his face, and swore that he had never seen it until that moment. The resumed inquiry ended, and still nothing had been discovered.

But we kept an eye on Mr Deluc. Our next effort was to try if we could associate him with the purchase of the knife.

Here again (there really did seem to be a sort of fatality in this case) we reached no useful result. It was easy enough to find out the wholesale cutlers, who had manufactured the knife at Sheffield, by the mark on the blade. But they made tens of thousands of such knives, and disposed of them to retail dealers all over Great Britain—to say nothing of foreign parts. As to finding out the person who had engraved the imperfect inscription (without knowing where, or by whom, the knife had been purchased) we might as well have looked for the proverbial needle in the bundle of hay. Our last resource was to have the knife photographed, with the inscribed side uppermost, and to send copies to every police station in the kingdom.

At the same time we reckoned up Mr Deluc—I mean that we made investigations into his past life—on the chance that he and the murdered man might have known each other, and might have had a quarrel, or a rivalry about a woman, on some former occasion. No such discovery rewarded us.

We found Deluc to have led a dissipated life, and to have mixed with very bad company. But he had kept out of reach of the law. A man may be a profligate vagabond; may insult a lady; may say threatening things to her, in the first stinging sensation of having his face slapped—but it doesn't follow from these blots on his character that he has murdered her husband in the dead of the night.

Once more, then, when we were called upon to report ourselves, we had no evidence to produce. The photographs failed to discover the owner of the knife, and to explain its interrupted inscription. Poor Mrs Zebedee was allowed to go back to her friends, on entering into her own recognizance to appear again if called upon. Articles in the newspapers began to enquire how many more murderers would succeed in baffling the police. The authorities at the Treasury offered a reward of a hundred pounds for the necessary information. And the weeks passed, and nobody claimed the reward.

Our Inspector was not a man to be easily beaten. More enquiries and examinations followed. It is needless to say anything about them. We were defeated—and there, so far as the police and the public were concerned, was an end of it.

The assassination of the poor young husband soon passed out of notice, like other undiscovered murders. One obscure person only was foolish enough, in his leisure hours, to persist in trying to solve the problem of Who Killed Zebedee? He felt that he might rise to the highest position in the police force if he succeeded where his elders and betters had failed—and he held to his own little ambition, though everybody laughed at him. In plain English, I was the man.

V

Without meaning it, I have told my story ungratefully.

There were two persons who saw nothing ridiculous in my resolution to continue the investigation, single-handed. One of them was Miss Mybus; and the other was the cook, Priscilla Thurlby.

Mentioning the lady first, Miss Mybus was indignant at the resigned manner in which the police accepted their defeat. She was a little bright-eyed wiry woman; and she spoke her mind freely.

'This comes home to me,' she said. 'Just look back for a year or two. I can call to mind two cases of persons found murdered in London—and the assassins have never been traced. I am a person too; and I ask myself if my turn is not coming next. You're a nice-looking fellow—and I like your pluck and perseverance. Come here as often as you think right; and say you are my visitor, if they make any difficulty about letting you in. One thing more! I have nothing particular to do, and I am no fool. Here, in the parlours, I see everybody who comes into the house or goes out of the house. Leave me your address—I may get some information for you yet.'

With the best intentions, Miss Mybus found no opportunity of helping me. Of the two, Priscilla Thurlby seemed more likely to be of use.

In the first place, she was sharp and active, and (not having succeeded in getting another situation as yet) was mistress of her own movements.

In the second place, she was a woman I could trust. Before she left home to try domestic service in London, the parson of her native parish gave her a written testimonial, of which I append a copy. Thus it ran:

I gladly recommend Priscilla Thurlby for any respectable employment which she may be competent to undertake. Her father and mother are infirm old people, who have lately suffered a diminution of their income; and they have a younger daughter to maintain. Rather than be a burden on her parents, Priscilla goes to London to find domestic employment, and to devote her earnings to the assistance of her father and mother. This circumstance speaks for itself. I have known the family many years; and I only regret that I have no vacant place in my own household which I can offer to this good girl.

(Signed)

HENRY DERRINGTON, Rector of Roth.

After reading those words, I could safely ask Priscilla to help me in reopening the mysterious murder case to some good purpose.

My notion was that the proceedings of the persons in Mrs Crosscapel's house, had not been closely enough enquired into yet. By way of continuing the investigation, I asked Priscilla if she could tell me anything which associated the housemaid with Mr Deluc. She was unwilling to answer. 'I may be casting suspicion on an innocent person,' she said. 'Besides, I was for so short a time the housemaid's fellow servant——'

'You slept in the same room with her,' I remarked; 'and you had opportunities of observing her conduct towards the lodgers. If they had asked you, at the examination, what I now ask, you would have answered as an honest woman.'

To this argument she yielded. I heard from her certain particulars which threw a new light on Mr Deluc, and on the case generally. On that information I acted. It was slow work, owing to the claims on me of my regular duties; but with Priscilla's help, I steadily advanced towards the end I had in view.

Besides this, I owed another obligation to Mrs Crosscapel's nice-looking cook. The confession must be made sooner or later—and I may as well make it now. I first knew what love was, thanks to Priscilla. I had delicious kisses, thanks to Priscilla. And, when I asked if she would marry me, she didn't say No. She looked, I must own, a little sadly, and she said: 'How can two such poor people as we are ever hope to marry?' To this I answered: 'It won't be long before I lay my hand on the clue which my Inspector has failed to find. I shall be in a position to marry you, my dear, when that time comes.'

At our next meeting we spoke of her parents. I was now her promised husband. Judging by what I had heard of the proceedings of other people in my position, it seemed to be only right that I should be made known to her father and mother. She entirely agreed with me; and she wrote home that day, to tell them to expect us at the end of the week.

I took my turn of night-duty, and so gained my liberty for the greater part of the next day. I dressed myself in plain clothes, and we took our tickets on the railway for Yateland, being the nearest station to the village in which Priscilla's parents lived.

VI

The train stopped, as usual, at the big town of Waterbank. Supporting herself by her needle, while she was still unprovided with a situation, Priscilla had been at work late in the night—she was tired and thirsty. I left the carriage to get her some soda-water. The stupid girl in the refreshment room failed to pull the cork out of the bottle, and refused to let me help her. She took a corkscrew, and used it crookedly. I lost all patience, and snatched the bottle out of her hand. Just as I drew the cork, the bell rang on the platform. I only waited to pour the soda-water into a glass—but the train was moving as I left the refreshment room. The porters stopped me when I tried to jump on to the step of the carriage. I was left behind.

As soon as I had recovered my temper, I looked at the timetable. We had reached Waterbank at five minutes past one. By good luck, the next train was due at forty-four minutes past one, and arrived at Yateland (the next station) ten minutes afterwards. I could only hope that Priscilla would look at the timetable too, and wait for me. If I had attempted to walk the distance between the two places, I should have lost time instead of saving it. The interval before me was not very long; I occupied it in looking over the town.

Speaking with all due respect to the inhabitants, Waterbank (to other people) is a dull place. I went up one street and down another—and stopped to look at a shop which struck me; not from anything in itself, but because it was the only shop in the street with the shutters closed.

A bill was posted on the shutters, announcing that the place was to let. The out-going tradesman's name and business, announced in the customary painted letters, ran thus: *James Wycomb, Cutler, etc.*

For the first time, it occurred to me that we had forgotten an obstacle in our way, when we distributed our photographs of the knife. We had none of us remembered that a certain proportion of cutlers might be placed, by circumstances, out of our reach—either by retiring from business or by becoming bankrupt. I always carried a copy of the photograph about me; and I thought to myself, 'Here is the ghost of a chance of tracing the knife to Mr Deluc!'

The shop door was opened, after I had twice rung the bell, by an old man, very dirty and very deaf. He said: 'You had better go upstairs, and speak to Mr Scorrier—top of the house.'

I put my lips to the old fellow's ear-trumpet, and asked who Mr Scorrier was.

'Brother-in-law to Mr Wycomb. Mr Wycomb's dead. If you want to buy the business apply to Mr Scorrier.'

Receiving that reply, I went upstairs, and found Mr Scorrier engaged in engraving a brass door-plate. He was a middle-aged man, with a cadaverous face and dim eyes. After the necessary apologies, I produced my photograph.

'May I ask, sir, if you know anything of the inscription on that knife?' I said.

He took his magnifying glass to look at it.

'This is curious,' he remarked quietly. 'I remember the queer name—Zebedee. Yes, sir; I did the engraving, as far as it goes. I wonder what prevented me from finishing it?'

The name of Zebedee, and the unfinished inscription on the knife, had appeared in every English newspaper. He took the matter so coolly, that I was doubtful how to interpret his answer. Was it possible that he had not seen the account of the murder? Or was he an accomplice with prodigious powers of self-control?

'Excuse me,' I said, 'do you read the newspapers?'

'Never! My eyesight is failing me. I abstain from reading, in the interests of my occupation.'

'Have you not heard the name of Zebedee mentioned— particularly by people who do read the newspapers?'

'Very likely; but I didn't attend to it. When the day's work is done, I take my walk. Then I have my supper, my drop of grog, and my pipe. Then I go to bed. A dull existence you think, I dare say! I had a miserable life, sir, when I was young. A bare subsistence, and a little rest, before the last perfect rest in the grave—that is all I want. The world has gone by me long ago. So much the better.'

The poor man spoke honestly. I was ashamed of having doubted him. I returned to the subject of the knife.

'Do you know where it was purchased, and by whom?' I asked.

'My memory is not so good as it was,' he said; 'but I have got something by me that helps it.'

He took from a cupboard a dirty old scrap-book. Strips of paper, with writing on them, were pasted on the pages, as well as I could see. He turned to an index, or table of contents, and opened a page. Something like a flash of life showed itself on his dismal face.

'Ha! now I remember,' he said. 'The knife was bought of my late brother-in-law, in the shop downstairs. It all comes back to me, sir. A person in a state of frenzy burst into this very room, and snatched the knife away from me, when I was only half way through the inscription!'

I felt that I was now close on discovery. 'May I see what it is that has assisted your memory?' I asked.

'Oh yes. You must know, sir, I live by engraving inscriptions and addresses, and I paste in this book the manuscript instructions which I receive, with marks of my own on the margin. For one thing, they serve as a reference to new customers. And for another thing, they do certainly help my memory.'

He turned the book towards me, and pointed to a slip of paper which occupied the lower half of a page.

I read the complete inscription, intended for the knife that killed Zebedee, and written as follows:

'To John Zebedee. From Priscilla Thurlby.'

VII

I declare that it is impossible for me to describe what I felt, when Priscilla's name confronted me like a written confession of guilt. How long it was before I recovered myself in some degree, I cannot say. The only thing I can clearly call to mind is, that I frightened the poor engraver.

My first desire was to get possession of the manuscript inscription. I told him I was a policeman, and summoned him to assist me in the discovery of a crime. I even offered him money. He drew back from my hand. 'You shall have it for nothing,' he said, 'if you will only go away and never come here again.' He tried to cut it out of the page—but his trembling hands were helpless. I cut it out myself, and attempted to thank him. He wouldn't hear me. 'Go away!' he said, 'I don't like the look of you.'

It may be here objected that I ought not to have felt so sure as I did of the woman's guilt, until I had got more evidence against her. The knife might have been stolen from her, supposing she was the person who had snatched it out of the engraver's hands, and might have been afterwards used by the thief to commit the murder. All very true. But I never had a moment's doubt in my own mind, from the time when I read the damnable line in the engraver's book.

I went back to the railway without any plan in my head. The train by which I had proposed to follow her had left Waterbank. The next train that arrived was for London. I took my place in it—still without any plan in my head.

At Charing Cross a friend met me. He said, 'You're looking miserably ill. Come and have a drink.'

I went with him. The liquor was what I really wanted; it strung me up, and cleared my head. He went his way, and I went mine. In a little while more, I determined what I would do.

In the first place, I decided to resign my situation in the police, from a motive which will presently appear. In the second place, I took a bed at a public house. She would no doubt return to London, and she would go to my lodgings to find out why I had broken my appointment. To bring to justice the one woman whom I had dearly loved was too cruel a duty for a poor creature like me. I preferred leaving the police force. On the other hand, if she and I met before time had helped me to control myself, I had a horrid fear that I might turn murderer next, and kill her then and there. The wretch had not only all but misled me into marrying her, but also into charging the innocent housemaid with being concerned in the murder.

The same night I hit on a way of clearing up such doubts as still harassed my mind. I wrote to the rector of Roth, informing him that I was engaged to marry her, and asking if he would tell me (in consideration of my position) what her former relations might have been with the person named John Zebedee.

By return of post I got this reply:

Sir,—Under the circumstances, I think I am bound to tell you confidentially ~~t~~ the friends and well-wishers of Priscilla have kept secret, for her sake. ~~Z~~ebedee was in service in this neighbourhood. I am sorry to say it, of a ~~m~~an who has come to such a miserable end—but his behaviour to Priscilla proves him to have been a vicious and heartless wretch. They were engaged—and, I add with indignation, he tried to seduce her under a promise of marriage. Her virtue resisted him, and he pretended to be ashamed of himself. The banns were published in my church. On the next day Zebedee disappeared, and cruelly deserted her. He was a capable servant; and I believe he got another place. I leave you to imagine what the poor girl suffered under the outrage inflicted on her. Going to London, with my recommendation, she answered the first advertisement that she saw, and was unfortunate enough to begin her career in domestic service in the very lodging house, to which (as I gather from the newspaper report of the murder) the man Zebedee took the person whom he married, after deserting Priscilla. Be assured that you are about to unite yourself to an excellent girl, and accept my best wishes for your happiness.

It was plain from this that neither the rector nor the parents and friends knew anything of the purchase of the knife. The one miserable man who knew the truth, was the man who had asked her to be his wife.

I owed it to myself—at least so it seemed to me—not to let it be supposed that I, too, had meanly deserted her. Dreadful as the prospect was, I felt that I must see her once more, and for the last time.

She was at work when I went into her room. As I opened the door she started to her feet. Her cheeks reddened, and her eyes flashed with anger. I stepped forward—and she saw my face. My face silenced her.

I spoke in the fewest words I could find.

'I have been to the cutler's shop at Waterbank,' I said. 'There is the unfinished inscription on the knife, completed in your handwriting. I could hang you by a word. God forgive me—I can't say the word.'

Her bright complexion turned to a dreadful clay-colour. Her eyes were fixed and staring, like the eyes of a person in a fit. She stood before me, still and silent. Without saying more, I dropped the inscription into the fire. Without saying more, I left her.

I never saw her again.

VIII

But I heard from her a few days later.

The letter has been long since burnt. I wish I could have forgotten it as well. It sticks to my memory. If I die with my senses about me, Priscilla's letter will be my last recollection on earth.

In substance it repeated what the rector had already told me. Further, it informed me that she had bought the knife as a keepsake for Zebedee, in place of a similar knife which he had lost. On the Saturday, she made the purchase, and left it to be engraved. On the Sunday, the banns were put up. On the Monday, she was deserted; and she snatched the knife from the table while the engraver was at work.

She only knew that Zebedee had added a new sting to the insult inflicted on her, when he arrived at the lodgings with his wife. Her duties as cook kept her in the kitchen—and Zebedee never discovered that she was in the house. I still remember the last lines of her confession:

The devil entered into me when I tried their door, on my way up to bed, and found it unlocked, and listened awhile, and peeped in. I saw them by the dying light of the candle—one asleep on the bed, the other asleep by the fireside. I had the knife in my hand, and the thought came to me to do it, so that they might hang *her* for the murder. I couldn't take the knife out again, when I had done it. Mind this! I did really like you—— I didn't say Yes, because you could hardly hang your own wife, if you found out who killed Zebedee.

Since that past time I have never heard again of Priscilla Thurlby; I don't know whether she is living or dead. Many people may think I deserve to be hanged myself for not having given her up to the gallows. They may, perhaps, be disappointed when they see this confession, and hear that I have died decently in my bed. I don't blame them. I am a penitent sinner. I wish all merciful Christians goodbye for ever.

A Circumstantial Puzzle

R. E. FRANCILLON

I

The almost insuperable difficulty of telling a story with even a grain
of truth in it is this—or, I should rather say, the two insuperable
difficulties are these: firstly, there is never the faintest dramatic point
about really true stories; secondly, if they are worth telling at all, they
are almost always incredible. And the truer they are, the more point-
less and the more incredible they are. The story I am going to tell
is neither dramatic nor probable. And yet it seems to me worth
telling—independently of its inherent curiosity—as an instance of
those extraordinary freaks of psychology which now and again throw
out of gear altogether the everyday experience of practical men,
among whom I have some claim to be reckoned. It has also a yet
more important bearing upon the manner of making delicate investigations which, if I remember to do so, I may perhaps take occasion
to point out before I have done. As when I sent you my last contribution to your museum of professional curiosities, I will merge my own
proper personality in that of my informant, the solicitor who played so
leading and, for a time, so uncomfortable a part in the affair. For all
purposes it is more convenient to translate 'he' into 'I', when one is
telling another man's story. Indeed, it is almost essential to the
process of telling the tale as it was told to me.

I, then, early one forenoon, received a visit from my very best
client, Mr John Buller.

Mr John Buller was a gentleman who, still hardly past the prime of
life, had made a considerable fortune as a builder and contractor.
Altogether there must have been something out of the common about
him, for he had become the wealthy man he certainly was seemingly
in defiance of all established precedents and rules. He was not what
is commonly—and often very mistakenly—called a 'good man of

business'; he always had more irons in the fire than he could possibly attend to personally, or even superintend generally, and he placed such implicit trust in all who served him or dealt with him as to amount to credulity. Nevertheless, I am by no means sure myself of its being really singular that his many irons should have taken excellent care of themselves, and that he very rarely indeed, at least to my knowledge, found himself seriously deceived. I need hardly say that, like all men of such a temper, to be found out in deceiving him in the smallest trifle was to lose his confidence irrevocably and for ever; so that not only were moderately honourable men put upon their honour to an unusual degree in their relations towards one who trusted them so completely, but the dishonourable were by experience taught to fear injuring one from whom everything was to be gained but pardon. He certainly was not one of those who hold that in business a man should have no enemies and no friends. All men were his friends until, as sometimes would happen, they became his enemies. And yet one might know him for years without suspecting that he had any sort of temper at all. Doubtless it was the consciousness on his own part of having one, and the suspicion that it might be a weakness or a failing, that made him seem needlessly hard and reserved. On the whole, I incline to ascribe his success in life less to courage and over-confidence than to a yet more unbusiness-like habit of always doing his work a little better than his contract required. I would pay ten per cent higher rent, any day, to live in a house that I knew to have been built by John Buller. I should know that everything about that house was better than it seemed. And that is the chief reason why I set out by speaking of him as a gentleman. For he had risen from the lower rounds of the ladder, and, so far as he might be called a diamond, was decidedly an unpolished one. He was, I believe, a seriously religious man; he was an unquestionably generous and charitable one; not highly educated, but with plenty of intelligence and openness of mind. I should add that he had never been married; was without known relations; and lived alone in thoroughly respectable comfort, without pretence of any kind. The nature of his business, by no means confined to the limits of the northern town where we both lived, took him about a great deal, and no doubt largely helped him to ～ without much society at home. For that matter, he was, socially ᴇaking, above one-half the place and below the other; so, though ﹍niversally respected, he must, on the whole, have lived almost too much alone. But in this matter, as in all things, habit is everything; and so busy a man had little time to feel dull.

'Mr Standish,' he began, in the broad north-country speech, which I shall make no pretence of reproducing, 'something mortal queer has happened, that I can't make head or tail o'. It's not the money's-worth, though fifty pound is fifty pound; but—Look here!'

'Your cheque for fifty pounds, cashed by the Redport branch of the County Bank, and returned to you in the regular course. Well, what's wrong?'

'Do you see anything queer about that cheque, Mr Standish—anything out of the way?'

'No. It's drawn to yourself or order by yourself; endorsed by you; and nothing wrong about date or anything else that I can see.'

'And if you'd been a clerk at Redport, you'd have cashed that over the counter without any bones?'

'Of course I should; as I suppose from this you have an account there.'

'And that's just what was done, then. And all the same, that cheque was no more filled up, nor signed, nor backed by me than it was by you.'

'You mean to say it's forged? By Jove, that's a serious thing! Do you mean to say that some rascal has been clever enough to fill up and sign a whole cheque in your handwriting, even down to the least turn of the smallest stroke of the pen? I'd have sworn to this being your own handwriting before a jury.'

'Ay, Mr Standish; and so would I, if I didn't know. But I do know; and that's no more my cheque than it's yours. And I'm hanged if I know what to do.'

'You've seen the bank manager here? What does he say?'

'No, I haven't. I haven't seen a soul; and what's more, I don't mean to, unless I'm driven. And it's to get out of being driven I'm come to you. This cheque isn't the first of 'em, Mr Standish—no, nor the second, nor yet the third. There's four cheques of fifty pounds apiece; and I've not drawn one!'

'And you haven't found it out till now?'

'I've found out nothing, Mr Standish, mark that—not one word. Nothing's found out till it's proved. I want to know what I can do.'

That premature question was the only sign of precipitancy or impatience I had ever seen in John Buller. I began to see that he was disturbed by something beyond the loss, to himself or the bank, of two hundred pounds, or by the always detestable necessity of being mixed up in what looked like a criminal matter. So I made no answer, which is always the best way of getting quickly at the bottom of a story.

'I'm putting up the new row of villas on the esplanade at Redport,' said he. 'It's a biggish job in a small way, and it's very much on my own account; and what with the hands, and one thing and another, there's a goodish lot of cash floating about from week to week— going out, anyhow, though of course none to speak of coming in. So, to save a lot of bother, I've had for some time an account with the branch at Redport. You don't know the place, I believe?'

'I've never been over there yet; but I must run over some day, when I can get a holiday. Well?'

'It's been main through me that the place has got on well enough to make it worth the Bank's while to have a branch there; and if I was to draw for five times what's to my credit, I don't suppose they'd make any bother, looking to my credit at the main branch here. So this game might go on any time before I heard I'd overdrawn. As far as I'm concerned, a cheque on the branch at Redport's much the same as one on the bank here.'

'Well?'

'You see, though that job's middling big, I've got too many bigger on hand to bother in person with Redport. It's two months since I've been near the place, and may be it'll be another month before I can get over there again. So I've got a clerk of the works in an office in one of the villas, and he comes over to me here every Friday to report and take any new orders, and I give him cheques on the Redport branch for what's wanted—he brings me his accounts and vouchers, of course, and I settle that way whatever has to be paid running. And some of the cheques I receive I send over by him to be paid in there.'

'Excuse me,' said I, 'but doesn't this seem rather a loose and rough way of doing things? In the first place, I don't see why you should make any payments through the Redport branch at all; and certainly I don't see how all this concerns these forgeries.'

'I'll tell you why I do it, and how it concerns these—forgeries, too. ...nt to keep as much cash knocking about in Redport as I can, and ...eep as little from going out; that's the way to push a new place on. ...d, for the same reason, I don't want those branch clerks to find they've got too little to do. My clerk comes to me at four o'clock every Friday afternoon. First of all, I give him a cheque for the men's week's wages. Then we go through the accounts, and for any that I want to settle off-hand I either draw separate cheques in favour of the different parties, or else I give him another lump cheque for him to cash and pay out in gold. In fact, there's all sorts of things to be paid in all sorts of ways. If the account seems running low, it's easier for me to pay in a few cheques than to bother the bank here. Anyhow, it saves me a bushel of bother, and don't oblige me to give more than an hour a week to Redport—and even an hour's too much at times.'

'Just tell me precisely everything that happens, please. We're rather vague, where we are. He comes to you at four every Friday, and you give him all these cheques—whatever he asks for—and then he goes back at once to Redport by rail?'

John Buller glanced at me sharply. By those words 'whatever he asks for' I had trodden upon what is always the most sensitive of an over-trustful man's corns: I had hinted at the want of worldly prudence which such a man, far more than any other, hates to be suspected of lacking.'

'I'm not quite a born fool,' said he. 'We go through the accounts, and he stays for supper and a bed. By breakfast-time next morning I've found a half hour to examine the accounts and to write the cheques. I give him the whole lot in a leather case, and he goes back to Redport; and it's his duty, before he goes to the office, to go to the Redport Bank and pay in and draw out whatever's required.'

I did not see how this made matters any better from a prudential point of view; but I did not venture again upon what I felt to be rather dangerous ground.

'Then all your transactions with the branch bank at Redport,' I asked, 'are confined to ten o'clock on Saturday morning? *This* cheque is stamped as cashed on the 15th, which *would* be a Saturday. Of course we shall learn from your passbook, or from the cheques themselves, if that was so with the others. If so, the false cheques must either have been presented together with the others, or by somebody who knew your system. Also, it is clear they were drawn, judging from this, by somebody who had exceptional means of knowing your handwriting, and of practising it at leisure—and, if I may say so, how little likely you were, with such a system of business as yours, to detect fraud very soon. Also, by somebody to whom your cheque-book was accessible, in one way or another. Are these cheques taken from your cheque-book, or can the thief have got hold of some other?'

I could see that John Buller began to look strangely troubled.

'From mine!' said he, in a curiously defiant tone.

'And the counterfoils? Cut out, I suppose? That's the usual way.'

'No; every man Jack filled up in a way that would take the very devil in. And yet, Mr Standish, those cheques are no more my drawing than they're yours. I keep a private account of every cheque I draw; and it stands to reason that when four cheques that you know you didn't draw are alone missing out of an account of fifty that you know you *did* draw, then you can't be mistaken. That's as clear as day.'

'All right, Mr Buller; it *is* as clear as day. And though criminal business is very much out of my line, we'll have that forger beyond the seas in, comparatively speaking, the twinkling of an eye. What's the fellow's name?'

'His name? And how the deuce, sir, should *I* know his name?'

'Not know the name of your own clerk of the works at Redport? By Jove, Mr Buller, I *shall* begin to think you a queer sort of a business man!'

'We're at crooked answers, Mr Standish, it seems to me,' he said, wiping his forehead hard, though the weather was unusually cold. 'My clerk at Redport is Adam Brown.'

'Then it's lucky Mr Adam Brown didn't live when forgers were hanged,' said I. 'You won't be able to recover from the bank, I'm afraid; such forgeries as those defy even extraordinary care to detect them. A bank clerk is expected to be a great deal; but nobody expects him to be a conjurer. But'—

To my amazement, John Buller sprang up in a towering rage.

'And you—you dare to hint that—that—that poor lad, who's as honest as the day, would steal one farthing from me—a young man I'd trust with untold gold—the orphan of the best woman that ever touched God's earth! I won't hear it, sir! I didn't come to *you* to hear slander against *her* son, that I've looked after for *her* sake, and who'd no more touch a farthing rushlight that belonged to me than you would yourself, sir! If there's one man who's as guiltless as the babe unborn, it's Adam Brown!'

'I honour your confidence in your *employés*, sir,' said I. 'Trust makes Trustworthy nine times out of ten. But look here. Here is a man whom you trust implicitly on your own showing. There is your cheque-book for one night every week under the same roof with him, the place where you keep it probably known to him. That man knows your writing, and how you fill up your cheques and your counterfoils. That man transacts *all* your business with the bank at Redport. That man, it seems, may account to you or not account to you just in what form he will. Nobody else in your employ seems open to suspicion; no stranger could act in such a way without instant detection. Think what any jury would say to such a state of things. We've as yet got no direct proof; but, with such circumstantial evidence to start with, direct proof is absolutely sure to come. Why, he might hope to carry on such a game as that safely for many years; at any rate, till he had restored what he had taken, as all those young rascals always "mean" to do some day when some impossible horse wins some impossible Derby. And I'm afraid, previous good character in such cases always goes against a man. It doubles the guilt of his downfall, and is, indeed, the very means and cause of his being able to fall. Adam Brown is the man.'

John Buller's anger passed suddenly, as if ashamed of itself; and there was no mistaking the profound grief and distress of the tone in which he answered me.

'You'll excuse me,' said he. 'It was because I saw all this just as well as you do that I came here, hoping you, as a practical and unprejudiced man, would help me to see t'other side of things. And I was disappointed you didn't, and that was what made me fly. Don't you go to mistake me for being any softer than my neighbours. If you can prove to me the man who's been tampering with my cheque-book is Adam Brown, I'll treat him like a viper, Mr Standish—that I will! I'd sooner cut my own throat than throw a crust to my own son, if I had one, if I couldn't trust him as my own right hand. And, if you'll believe it, sir, Adam Brown has been more to me than if he was my own son. For he's the orphan boy of the only woman I ever wanted to marry, or ever shall. I don't suspect him for one moment—not I. But for that very reason I want you to show me how to put him above the suspicion of any outside man, such as you. Take my word for it, it's not Adam Brown. If it was, I'd have done his business for him pretty quick, without bothering myself to come to you. But make as if I thought it was: you prove the innocence of an innocent lad, and, by Jingo, you'll take off my mind the biggest load of bricks that ever was on.'

The speech was inconsistent enough. But one thing was plain from it—John Buller was determined to disbelieve the clear evidence of his own reason. He had not come to me to find out a thief, but to get me to prove to his own satisfaction that the thief was an innocent man; and, at the same time, to acquit him in his own eyes of intentional self-deception. He knew how he would have to act if he found his trust deceived, and the severity which he thought his duty in such cases frightened him, lest he should feel compelled to exercise it towards Adam Brown. I could not help smiling at the openness of the workings of his mind, or being touched by them, too. I had never suspected my substantial client of having been the victim of a romance since I had first gone down from London to Carcester.

'Then,' I asked again, a little hypocritically, 'you are convinced in your own mind, from your previous knowledge of his character, that Adam Brown is *not* the man?'

'I'm just as certain he's not as that I stand here. And, more for his sake than my own, I mean to know who *is* the man.'

'Have you spoken about it to Adam Brown?'

'Not I. I'd as soon speak to you, Mr Standish, on the supposition that it might have been *you*.'

'Very good. If Adam Brown—'

'*If*, sir?'

'Since Adam Brown is innocent, we can very soon put him beyond the reach of any sort of suspicion, and without bringing the people at the bank into the affair—at least, not in any way that would make them think anything was seriously wrong in any particular direction. In the first place, arrange with them, both here and at Redport, not to cash any cheque of yours not bearing a certain private mark (which you will keep secret from all your *employés*) without forthwith advertising you of the person by whom it was presented. This will have the effect of narrowing matters very considerably. What had better be done further I think we will wait and see.'

'You quite understand, Mr Standish, that whatever you do will find out who was the real man—not young Adam Brown? I—I doubt if I quite like to do that about the private mark after all. It seems a bit mean-like to my mind.'

'It's the best way of clearing Adam Brown if—since he's innocent, it seems to me,' said I.

'You think that? Well, you're right, I suppose. And, by Jingo, as he is innocent why should I be afraid? If he wasn't—if I wasn't as sure of it as I'm alive—but it can't be! I'd sooner doubt my own right hand! I will. I'll settle about the private mark this very day.'

Of course I had not the faintest doubt in my own mind about the identity of this ingenious and systematic forger with Mr Adam Brown. I had already given my reasons to John Buller; and they are so perfectly obvious, under all the circumstances, that I need not repeat them here. I could quite understand why John Buller, since he had a more than common interest in his clerk of the works at Redport, should be very anxious to be convinced that his belief in the latter's innocence was not inconsistent with the common sense proper to a shrewd man of the world, whose pride in never being 'done' is always the greater in proportion as it is unjustified. Men who are really sharp and shrewd know too well that they are always and inevitably being 'done' to bother their heads about their share in a universal doom.

I knew Adam Brown pretty well by sight, and a little by reputation. He was a good-looking, pleasant young fellow, certainly too young for his over-responsible place in John Buller's service, but well up to his work, and very popular with the young men of his own class in Carcester. His father had been an unsuccessful commission agent, and, as I had today learned for the first time, the successful rival in love of John Buller. I must leave it to others wholly to understand why the beaten suitor, whom nobody suspected of having a grain of sentiment in his composition, should have made himself a second father to this young man—in a reserved and wholly undemonstrative way, that is; for I feel certain now that Adam Brown looked upon himself simply as an ordinary *employé*, and did not fancy that the place he held in John Buller's business was due to the place in John Buller's heart of his dead mother. I daresay that little romance might prove worth writing for its own sake in the hands of a sentimental author. But this story is *not* a sentimental one.

So I was really rather sorry that circumstances pointed so clearly to Adam Brown as the guilty man, though of course I felt also that John Buller's eyes ought to be opened, and that such ungrateful crime ought to be punished as openly and as richly as it deserved. I had not the least intention of helping my client to persuade himself of the innocence of a guilty man. On the contrary, I fully meant to expose the young rascal before he could do worse harm; and for that purpose the plan of privately marked cheques seemed the best that, upon the spur of the moment, I could hit on. It would satisfy John Buller by avoiding immediate scandal, and no doubt convict the forger just as well as any more open way.

But the explosion was to come more sharply and swiftly than I had planned.

On the following Saturday morning the spirit moved me to take John Buller's house on my way to my own office, for I was not particularly busy at the moment. I thought it advisable to see with my own eyes something of that curious weekly despatch of cheques and bills to Redport, and I wanted also to make more particular acquaintance with the physiognomy of Mr Adam Brown. I believed in physiognomy in those days. I need hardly say that I no longer now do anything of the kind, beyond knowing when a man eats too much and drinks too often. I have seen such saintly faces in the dock, and men on whom Nature has stamped blackguard, or even murderer, have been among the best whom she has made. Adam Brown, who had finished his breakfast and was just on the eve of starting for Redport, fell into neither of these extreme classes, and might easily have belonged to either side of the broad band between them where good is inextricably and undecipherably mixed up and often confused with harm. As I have said, he was young and good-looking; and he had a good face too, like a lad's who comes of good people and has been brought up well. And, what was better, it was not a weak one, nor a stupid one. But, at the same time, it wasn't a happy one, and gloomy rather than merely grave. His eyes, instead of looking bright or open, as a young man's should always be in the morning, were dull and red, as if he had either slept but little or were in the habit of taking something stronger than tea or coffee for breakfast when at home in his Redport lodgings. In such cases, the eye and the hand are one; and his hand was not quite so steady as he held out his hand for the leather cheque-case, so I thought at least, as it ought to have been.

'I've only dropped in to see if you've made your arrangements about marking today's cheques,' said I, as soon as Adam Brown had closed the street-door. 'You've found nothing new, I suppose?'

'No. I wish to Heaven the thing was out and over; it worries me more than I try to say. There's nothing so horrible as having somebody about that you can't trust and you don't know who. And you're a married man, Standish; you don't know what it means to swallow all your own worries yourself, with nobody to give the least bit of 'em to. But—holloa! Hi, Adam!' he called out, throwing up the window and calling down the street. 'Just to show you how things bother me,' he said to me, 'I've left out of the case just the very cheque from Archer & Company that I wanted to have paid in at Redport this very day. Hi, Adam! Ah, here you are! I was afraid you were out of earshot; but you're in lots of time for the train. There's something I wanted to say to you, and Mr Standish coming in just now—'

There was nothing in the sudden recall, however unusual, to frighten an honest man. But I could not mistake my eyes—there are some cases in which we can't help reading faces, ay, and in believing what we read. If ever fright turned a man's face red and pale, it turned Adam Brown's now.

'Here's a cheque of Archer's,' said John Buller, noticing nothing, 'that I want paid in at Redport this morning, and I forgot it when Mr Standish came in. Put it in the case with the others. Here it is. Three hundred and eighty-eight pounds nine.'

Adam Brown held out his hand for the cheque; but a sudden inspiration, prompted by the young man's unmistakable confusion, made me say,

'Yes; there's plenty of time for the train, but not for me. There's something I must say to you, Mr Buller, before I go on to the office, and I've only allowed myself a minute to spare. Would you mind leaving us alone for one minute, Mr Brown? You can leave the case here; Mr Buller can put in the cheque while he's listening to me to save time.'

I watched the young man while I spoke, and what I saw made me feel more sure than ever. I held out my hand for the case, to pass it to John Buller, and felt Adam's fingers tremble as they touched mine. And yet not a word had been said that could alarm a perfectly innocent man, who has no secrets from his employer or even from his employer's attorney.

'Wait a bit,' I said to John Buller, as soon as Adam had left the room. 'Before putting in that cheque, just see if the others are as they ought to be.'

'The others? Of course they are. What do you mean?'

'Why, as you made one mistake, you might by chance have made another, you know. Well, while you're overhauling, I only just wanted to say—'

There was nothing I wanted to say, but I had no need to think of a pretext. I had my eye on John Buller, and before 'say' was off my lips—

'Good God!' cried he. 'Look here! Brown!' he shouted, 'Adam Brown—'

'Don't frighten him,' said I, rising and opening the door, knowing what John Buller had found in the case as well as if I had seen it with my very eyes. 'Mr Brown, you may come in now.'

He came in, as a detected criminal comes before a judge, trembling and pale. I wondered he had been able to remain in the hall all alone for that terrible moment, during which, as he must have known, he was being tried, found guilty, and condemned.

To my surprise, John Buller, whom I had thought in the first stage of a passion, sat still, in front of his detected clerk, without a word. But I should not like to have been in Adam Brown's shoes during that silent pause. There was no sign or thought of anger in the long look of mingled sorrow and scorn—more of sorrow than of scorn—with which John Buller regarded the young man to whom he had tried to be a second father. I had done my duty, I suppose; but I could not help pitying both, and I know whom I pitied the most of the two. It was not the younger man.

I looked steadfastly at the fifth forged cheque for fifty pounds which John Buller had found, just as I had expected, in the leather case, and the preparation of which was quite enough to account for the sleepless look of the young man's eyes. It seemed to me that the imitation was even better than before.

'Adam Brown,' said John Buller at last, in a voice full of sadness, and yet of the double pathos which comes alone from more dignified firmness than I should have expected from such a man—'Adam Brown, I know well enough that you see your deceit discovered, and I won't add to your wrongdoing by tempting you to tell a lie. I knew your mother—long ago—and for her sake I first gave you work, and bread to work for. But it was for your own sake I trusted you, even as she might have trusted me; and the end is that I shall never be able to trust man, woman, or child again. That is the injury *you* have done to *me*; and there's none greater that man can do man. I fought hard against the belief of my own eyes—for weeks I've fought against it; but I know now. Don't be afraid. I'm not going to have you—your mother's son—put in the dock as a felon. But there's nothing I can do *for* a man—a boy—that—that—Go; and never cross my path again.'

The culprit tried to lift his eyes, but failed.

'Sir,' he began, 'I do not defend—I do not excuse—I never intended—'

'I am sorry for myself. Do not make me despise *you*. A man does as he intends. I'm wrong not to prosecute you; it's what I should do to any other man who did as—as you have done. Go. I give you the chance to redeem yourself, if you can; but not with me. Go.'

Without one attempt to defend or excuse his guilt, far less to deny it, the young man was gone.

'I do *not* thank you for this, Mr Standish,' said John Buller. The tears came into his voice as he turned away.

II

The more I thought things over, the less displeased I was with myself for the way in which they had gone. The more anybody thinks about it, the more finished a rogue, in spite of his years, will Adam Brown appear to be. His plan was as clear as daylight now. Obviously, he had easily found where his employer kept his cheque-book for the bank at Redport, and spent the better part of Friday night in filling up one of its forms, and manipulating the counterfoil so as to produce an exact facsimile of a cheque drawn and signed by John Buller. On my life, I believe he might, so perfect was his process, have got a jury to acquit him on the ground that some strange accident must have been his enemy, and that the cheque was really John Buller's after all; for the best men of business may be guilty of mistake or error now and then. Yes, but then you see that defence would not have done after all, seeing that here was the sixth cheque forged in six weeks; and that John Buller not only had never had occasion to draw these, and knew he never had drawn them, but had kept a perfectly complete and accurate account, inaccurate in no slightest particular, of all he had had occasion to draw and remembered drawing. Mistake—if the reader will think for one instant—was thus rendered absolutely impossible. And not only was the matter clenched now by conduct on Adam Brown's part amounting to confession, without so much as an appeal for mercy, but *every cheque in the case bore the private mark except this alone.* And the packet had been in no hands but those of Adam Brown.

Of course it was natural that John Buller, like all men of his temper when they met with such everyday things as ingratitude and breach of trust, should feel misanthropical, and as if confidence in his fellow-creatures was henceforth dead in him. But very few men indeed are Timons. We mostly return to our original nature: instinctive trust is happily a fine hardy growth that requires a great deal of killing. In a little while, no doubt, John Buller would trust the next stranger rather more implicitly than if he had been his own brother, and be all the better for being rid of such an exceptionally clever rogue, a man with a positive genius for forgery, as his ex-clerk of the works at Redport. Perhaps, even, his experience would have a wholesome effect upon him by teaching him that the son of a woman we have loved in our youth is not, solely for that rather sentimental reason, bound to be better than all other sons of Eve in general. Young men who have had mothers have also had fathers; and Mr Brown, the commission agent, had not borne altogether the highest of characters while alive.

I did not see, or hear from, John Buller for the next few days; which was rather singular, as he nearly always had a good deal of business on hand which required the help of a solicitor, and as two or three important agreements to which he was party were just then passing through my hands. But I heard in various incidental ways of young Brown. A clerk of mine was an acquaintance of his; and he told me—without knowing any of the circumstances—that Brown had suddenly left John Buller and had gone up to London to find another situation; which, without any sort of character (for John Buller was incapable of giving a false or even a misleading one to anybody), I imagined he would find it hard to do, except as active partner in a firm of forgers. From another source I heard he had had a fortune left him, and was going to live on a fine estate in the country. Anyhow, he left both Redport and Carcester without leaving behind him a guess as to the true reason of his departure.

It was not, indeed, till the following Friday afternoon that I next received a visit from John Buller. I thought him looking fagged and harassed, and I told him so.

_'I'm afraid you keep too many irons in the fire,' said I.

'Not a bit of it. One keeps the other warm. If you was as much by yourself as I am, you'd want a bit more work than you could manage, just to keep you and yourself from quarrelling.'

'Have you heard anything more of young Brown?'

'Young Who?'

'Young Brown.'

'I've forgotten his name. And you won't remind me of it, if you and me's to keep friends. There's no such name. Talking of not looking well—it's you that don't look yourself, it seems to me. You want a day's holiday, and I've looked in to ask you to be so kind as to take one.'

'You're very kind, I'm sure; but—'

'"But" be hanged! Look here, Mr Standish. Today's Friday; and there's the usual business of paying in and drawing out to be done over at Redport tomorrow. I can't do it myself, as I've got to be in three other places at once by the first train; and I'm not such an ass as to trust any of my people here with the value of sevenpence-halfpenny. Once bit, twice shy. I've done with trusting for the rest of *my* days. At the rate of fifty pound a week, it don't pay. You've never been over at Redport; and, though I say it that shouldn't, the place is worth seeing, as a specimen of what places can be made to grow. You take a day's run over there tomorrow—you and Mrs Standish too. I'll give you a pass on the line, and telegraph to the Star to treat you like princes and princesses. All you'll have to do will be to hand my cheque-case over the bank counter, which won't take you two minutes, or fifty yards out of your way to the new pier; and then you can make a Saturday-to-Monday of it, if you please. I want you to see Redport before it grows out of all knowing. Say yes, and I'll have the cheques and things ready for you to pick up at my house on your way to the train.'

I was not particularly anxious for a holiday; and certainly no wish to spend one *en prince* at the Star. But, at the same time, I had no sort of objection to an idle day, and it was almost necessary, as a matter of business, to see the neighbouring town which was becoming every day more and more an office word. So, though more to please my best client than for any other reason, I agreed, only bargaining that I should be left free from the special attentions of the Star. John Buller thanked me for my promise to go as if I had done him some extraordinary favour.

'Well, if you won't let me telegraph, when you do ask for lunch at the Star, mention my name. You won't see much going on in the building line just now; one of the things I've got to be away for tomorrow is to get another scoundrel—till *he's* found out, like the rest of 'em—in the place of poor young—of that young blackguard whose name I'll never remember again, if I live for a thousand years.'

Now I don't want to have it supposed for a moment that my going over to Redport alone—that is to say, without my wife—was due to any fault or neglect of mine. If I could have foreseen that my day of idleness was to be one of solitude also, I should probably not quite so readily have consented to take a holiday. As it happened, however, I found, when I got home from the office, that Mrs Standish had almost that very moment received an urgent summons to the sick-bed of her sister, who lived at the other end of England, which obliged her to take the very next train from Carcester and to travel all night through. Naturally, until I had seen her off, I did not think again of my promised visit to Redport. So, as it was too late to back out of going, I decided to run over in the morning, do my business at the bank, and get back as early in the afternoon as the then infrequent trains between Redport and Carcester allowed.

So next morning, having told my clerks to close the office at the usual hour which on Saturday was always an early one, I went to John Buller's house, and from his hands received the cheque-case which he had ready for me. Knowing his feelings about the matter, I refrained from making any sort of allusion to it, and even made a point, while receiving the case, of speaking carelessly about in-different things. I put the case, otherwise untouched, in my breast-pocket, and there it remained till I reached the counter of the bank at Redport.

'Where's Mr Brown?' asked the clerk, as he took the leather case. 'It doesn't seem like Saturday morning without seeing Brown.'

'He's away just at present,' said I. 'Mr Buller asked me to give you this. All right, I suppose?'

There was no need to lessen my dignity in Redport as Mr Buller's legal adviser, or to give Adam Brown the reputation he deserved, by explaining why I was doing the work of a builder's clerk and messenger on this occasion.

'All right,' said the clerk, turning over the cheques and duly noticing whether they were properly endorsed, and so on. 'Quite right. By the way, there's a message or something the manager wants to send to Mr Buller. I believe. I was to tell Brown so when he called. I suppose you'll do just the same?'

'I can take any message for Mr Buller,' said I. 'Anyhow, I shall be seeing him on Monday if that will do.'

'I daresay it will. Would you mind stepping this way?'

I followed the clerk into an inner room, where I for the first time met the manager of the Redport branch of the County Bank, hitherto known to me as Mr George Richards by name only. We bowed, and he offered me a seat politely.

'You are my friend Mr Buller's new clerk of the works, I presume?' asked he.

'No,' said I. 'I have no business in Redport, except to cash and pay in these papers for Mr Buller, while passing by. But if there is any message I can give him—'

'I don't know. You are not leaving Redport immediately, I suppose?'

'Well, as to that, I am. In fact, by the very next train.'

'By the next train? H'm!' Mr Richards was a very young man for his place, and I began to fancy there was something I did not like in his manner. 'Going back to Carcester anyhow, I suppose?' he asked again.

'Yes,' I answered shortly. 'And I believe the train starts in half an hour. So if you can tell me what you want said to Mr Buller I shall be glad, as I haven't much time to lose.'

'Yes—of course—certainly. But there is a little matter: would you mind telling me if you received these cheques straight from Mr Buller?'

'Certainly I did. Is there anything wrong?'

'You received them just as they are now?'

'Exactly as they are now. What is it, Mr Richards? I am really in a hurry—'

'I'm very sorry. But you see, I am in a responsible position, and one can't be too careful in these days. I have already sent a messenger to telegraph to Mr Buller; would you mind waiting here till he comes?'

'The messenger?'

'No, till Mr Buller can come over. I daresay it is all right, but—'

'But I can't wait, Mr Richards. May I ask you what you mean? I can tell you that Mr Buller is not in Carcester, and will not get your telegram till Monday, if then.'

'That's awkward, by Jove, if it *is* so. But that we shall see.'

'But meanwhile I must wish you good-day. If there's anything wrong you must settle it with Mr Buller. I can't wait now.'

'No? Well, then, Mr—Mr—I must frankly tell you that I must ask you to wait, even if it's till Monday, till Mr Buller can come over here. It's an awkward situation I'm placed in, but—and I daresay Mr Buller is *not* at Carcester, as you say; but—well: whether you're—it's, all right or all wrong, you see, in your own interest that I must ask you to remain. You see here's a cheque here that I daren't cash without special instructions from Mr Buller.'

'Don't cash it, then. Good-day—'

'Quite so. But I'd advise you not to be in quite such a hurry to be off, all the same. In fact, it's my unpleasant duty to ask you to stay here at the bank until the fact of *this*, cheque being in your hands can be more fully explained.'

'I have explained it,' I began rather angrily. 'I received it from Mr Buller, if it came out with the rest from that case lying before you. Why should you venture to speak, even to a stranger, as if you had any reason to doubt his word? I don't understand this at all.'

'For this reason: I have the best reason for believing that this cheque was never drawn by Mr Buller. And now you see how it becomes my unpleasant duty—'

'Nonsense! As if I hadn't received every one of those cheques straight from his hands! You talk as if you took me for a forger. Well, I suppose I must excuse you, on the ground of over-zeal.'

'It is most improbable that this cheque was drawn by—well, never mind why. I'm bound to tell you that if you refuse to wait here for Mr Buller's arrival of your own free will, and in your own interest, I shall have to call upon the police to assist me in the execution of my duty towards the bank and its customers and the public at large.'

'Why,' I began, my anger half losing itself in amusement, 'this is something too absurd. You can't call in a constable unless you can give him good reason to suspect me of felony. I have half a mind to let you try, for the fun of the thing. Only it would be wasting my own time. So I'll put an end to your scruples about the public at large by telling you at once that my name is Standish, and that I am solicitor to Mr Buller, and live at Carcester. And the next time I advise you, as a lawyer, to be more careful how you treat people who come to your bank.'

'You are Mr Buller's solicitor? Indeed? Of course that *is* important—very important; and no doubt you can send for somebody in Redport who knows you? No—we can't be too careful in these days.'

'I don't know a soul in Redport.'

'No? H'm! Well, Mr Buller will know you—when he comes.'

'But I tell you he won't get your telegram for at least two days. This is monstrous!' I broke out, my amusement turning back into anger again.

'Monstrous or not—Well then, perhaps, as you feel safe from being brought face to face with—I should say, as you are convinced Mr Buller is not at home, I suppose you have friends or clerks in Carcester who could give evidence as to who you say you are—are, I ought no doubt to say? The telegraph's as open to you as to me.'

'You positively are so insane as to say you will forcibly detain me—*me*—in Redport unless I can convince you that I am myself? And for no reason—'

'You must make up your mind to it. I know what law is,' said Mr Richards; 'and—well, not to mince matters, I've already got our police sergeant waiting in the next room. A messenger from the bank can dispatch any summons to any of your friends, if you'll write it down. Yes—it *is* in my power to give you into custody on suspicion of having forged a cheque which you yourself admit has passed through the hands of no third parties—a cheque of £50, signed John Buller. And as to why I have particular reasons for my belief, I don't mind telling you it's because the bank here has had special notice from the chief branch at Carcester to cash no cheques signed 'John Buller' till we've communicated with the drawer, and to detain the person presenting them, whoever he may be—unless the cheques bear a certain private sign. There's reason for that, you may be sure. And there is the sign on every one of these cheques—except the one for £50.'

'You mean to say that this cheque for £50 is the only one unmarked?'

'The only one.'

'Let me see it, if you please.'

He held it so that I might see it, taking care that I should have no chance of wresting it from his hands. I certainly could not blame him any longer for over-zeal, seeing it was on my own advice he was acting. But what room could I find for a single thought, save that an unmarked cheque, as like those presented by Adam Brown as a cheque could be, *had been received straight from John Buller's very own hands by my very own?* Surely it looked more like witchcraft than forgery.

And yet Adam's effective confession of guilt, and the regularity with which the undoubtedly forged cheques had been presented—I could not make head or tail of it at all. I must have been bewildered; I must have seemed confused, as if with guilt or fright, for I was confused in reality. I could not even affect the indignation of injured honesty; I was not indignant with Mr Richards for being suspicious of what might be witchcraft, but certainly had all the air of a forgery—I, Charles Standish, being the forger!

'It is utterly unintelligible,' said I, using the common phrase of people who won't, rather than can't, explain things that seem going against them. 'But I am sure of one thing—Charles Standish of Carcester I am. And I don't want to stay in Redport till Monday. I will telegraph, as you say. I'll send word to my wife to—but no; *she's* not in Carcester either just now. I must send for one of the clerks at the office, I'm afraid, and make everybody wonder at what I can have been doing at Redport to need proof of my identity. Give me a form, and I'll write a message for my clerk—'

For my own credit's sake, and out of justice to Mr Richards's zeal, I chose to wait in an inner office of the bank till somebody whom I knew should come. I need hardly say that Mr Buller, being away from getting telegrams, never came. But it was not till hours had passed that I began to realize that it was Saturday afternoon—and that my idle dogs of clerks had of course taken advantage of my absence to close the office and go off to play at an exceptionally early hour. Closing time for the bank itself (also earlier than usual on Saturdays) had come when I saw in my mind, as clearly and truly as with my eyes, my telegram lying unopened on my clerk's desk at Carcester—and tomorrow was Sunday.

All I could do was to send off six telegrams to six different people, in the bare hope that one of them might bring over to Redport some respectable citizen of Carcester before the very last train. Not one brought a soul. And I could see what Mr Richards thought of the result of my telegrams when I had, perforce, to put up with the accommodation of the police station instead of the hotel, there to remain until John Buller himself should come and set me free.

In effect, I was a prisoner on suspicion of Forgery—and I had in truth presented an unquestionably forged cheque that had been through no hands but my own! It was the most unaccountable mystery I had ever known; and it kept me from sleeping, even more than the discomfort of my cell, as much as if I were really a conscious sharer in the villanies of Adam Brown. This could not be his doing— and what then of the rest, and of his admitted guilt concerning them? Not even sleep, when it came in an uncomfortable shape at last, let me dream of a possible way through such a mystery.

It was not till Monday afternoon that I received the welcome news that John Buller was on his way to see me at the police station in company with Mr Richards. I must say that I had become more anxious now about getting home as fast as I could than about anything else in the world. It is not an amusing thing to be treated in a strange place as a suspected felon; and I have held very strong views about the treatment of unconvicted prisoners ever since that Redport Sunday.

'Here he is, sir,' said Mr Richards. 'This is the—the gentleman who presented that cheque on Saturday morning. I hope and trust it's all right; but in these times, you see, one can't be too—'

'Thank Heaven, at last!' said I, springing from my seat, and holding out my hand. 'I've never passed so long a day since I was born; but I certainly don't complain of Mr Richards—he's been zealous enough, anyhow; and I only wish *my* clerks would simply do what they're bid, and give up that confounded habit of thinking for themselves. If you ever have to leave the Company's service, Mr Richards, for want of thinking-power, never mind; I'll take you into mine. Well, Mr Buller, you must have slipped into drawing *one* unmarked cheque, after all?'

'No, sir!' said John Buller, with strange vehemence, for him. 'No—I did *not* draw that cheque—with or without a sign. I drew no cheque for fifty pounds at all. And if you're the rascal that has been up to these games, and got it all on poor young Adam's shoulders, I'm glad I see you here; I'm glad of it, with all my heart and soul. I'm hanged if I didn't know I was right, all along. Adam Brown, if a letter can find him, poor lad, goes back to my works at Redport this very hour!'

Could I believe my ears?

'You—John Buller—*you* believe *me* guilty of having forged cheques, and tried to throw the guilt of it upon Adam Brown? Think for one least moment of what you are saying—'

'Think? Thinking's plain enough, it seems to me—a mile too plain by the longest chalks you can draw. It's likelier anybody would be a rogue than the orphan lad I'd brought up as my own son. I daresay, like enough, he was too taken aback by such a charge to say a word. I wonder he didn't double his fist, and knock me down. But I hope I'm a just man if I'm a bit of a hasty one. I'm not going to be hasty with *you*. If you can explain what's at best an ugly business, say it out like a man.'

'If I didn't respect an old client, and an old friend—But I can't forget how you've been worrying about this business. Explain? I will, though I don't see how you and I can ever be friends again. You know as well as I do that I never cashed a cheque for you in my life before, or ever was at Redport till the day before yesterday—'

'Ay; so you say.'

'So I *do* say. And you know that I received that case of cheques and bills—whatever they were, for I never looked at them—from your own hands on Saturday morning.'

'Did you? That's my cheque-case, sure enough. But suppose you did, what then? Because something comes out of it, it doesn't follow it was I who put it in. No, no. I never drew that cheque. You present it to be cashed, and it purports to be drawn, signed, and endorsed by me. You say you received it from me. I say you didn't. And I ought to know; for you couldn't have received a cheque that never was drawn. Justice is justice. Adam Brown goes back to my works; and you'll go to the country's, whoever you are. I don't know what's the right way to start a prosecution, but that's easy known. I'll see Standish this very day.'

'You'll see Standish?'

'Ay, Standish of Carcester, my lawyer. Criminal business isn't his line, he says; but he'll do it for me.'

'You mean I'm to prosecute myself? Well, it all seems queer enough. Perhaps I don't know who I am. Do you?'

'No, sir, I don't, I'm happy to say. Forgers aren't in *my* line.'

'Good Heaven! Do you mean to deny that *I* am Mr Standish of Carcester?'

I saw a very decided smile come over the face of Mr Richards. And it was not pleasant to see. For if John Buller, as he was quite capable of doing, chose to prosecute me for forgery—well, I should be acquitted, of course, but my character would be gone for ever and a day. The names of ladies are not more delicate than those of professional men.

'Come, none of that nonsense,' said John Buller, 'you're no more Standish than I am the Duke of Wellington. It does aggravate me to hear a man talk in that way. If you choose to deny that you're the Duke of Wellington, when I say you are, we'll have a wager upon that, and toss up for the winner. You come and dine with me at the Star, both of you, and I'll treat you like princes. We'll eat cheques for fifty pound apiece between slices of brown bread-and-butter cut thin, with lemon and cayenne. Its very odd, but I took a fancy to you the first minute I saw you. There's something about you puts me in mind of somebody or other—I never could remember names. But it's all one whoever we are. We're the sparks that fly upwards; and by Jingo, we'll have a jolly good fly . . . Who are *you*?' he called out at the top of his voice to Richards. 'You're a murderer, sir, and a forger, and a fool. Come and dine with me at the Star. . . .'

I need not continue the talk of poor John Buller, whom overwork, and loss of faith in the one human being who was dear to him, had driven out of his mind. It was an overwhelming relief when my managing-clerk arrived, and when sufficient explanations were obtained to allow of my return home in company with my poor friend. Even to the zealous Mr Richards the state of things was as clear as day, so far as he knew.

III

It was not hard for me, now, to see how John Buller, once assured against his will of Adam's treachery in the first instance, had brooded over the shock, with an already overlonely and overburdened mind, till, as sure as Friday night came round, he, possessed by the demon of monomania—which simply means the abnormal growth of a natural and normal idea—drew the cheque which haunted and fascinated him. If my readers cannot follow the chain of mental association, with its manifold links of time, place, person, and occasion, in which his disturbed brain became tangled and coiled, I fear I cannot hope to make it very clear. But there are very few who have not met with the most extraordinary cases of monomania in some form, and noticed how consistent they are with all outward appearance of sanity. Are there very many of us who have not felt some form of it ourselves in some slight degree? But, fortunately, few of us live altogether alone; few of us are overtrustful or, therefore, half maddened when deceived; most of us have more, if not much more, self-control than was evidently possessed by John Buller. And yet he must have had a great deal. Only the insane can tell the very torture of self-suppression they have to undergo when they feel monomania slowly broadening into a wider, if not deeper, mode of lunacy. For, conscious of its own state every diseased brain must be when that state first begins.

And yet—*could* this be all? The madness of John Buller did not account for the more than apparent guilt of Adam Brown.

It was not till years afterwards—not till my poor old friend had left all his troubles behind him; not till I had long ago given up puzzling my head about the matter—that I one day received a letter bearing an Australian postmark, and addressed to myself in a strange hand. There was nothing curious in that; but, as I read, the story I have been trying to tell came back to me as freshly as if it had all happened yesterday. For thus the letter ran:

Sir,—It will doubtless surprise you to receive this from me; for I cannot suppose that you will remember so much as my name. But you will remember—I fear only too well—a clerk in the service of Mr John Buller, who was dismissed from his service for embezzlement. I am that man; and my reason for calling myself to your remembrance is, that I have at last found myself able to repay the sums that I abstracted wrongfully, and for which only Mr Buller's kindness saved me from being sent to gaol. I do not, moreover, want him to think me always such a hopelessly ungrateful and treacherous scoundrel as he must be thinking me. I got into bad ways, knowing them bad all the time. I wanted more money than I could get honestly, and I had to pay it. I needn't tell *that* story; it's over now, and no harm done to anybody but me.

I was tempted, by what I called to myself need and weakness, to 'borrow', I called it then—to steal, that is to say—some of the money I drew from

Redport bank. I had complete control of the accounts at Redport, and I suppose it was all so easy that at first it didn't so much feel like stealing, and so I went on and on. I used to take sometimes more than fifty pounds together. I've sent you a statement of all I took; and I hope it's correct, for of course I had to muddle up all the accounts. You see, sir, Mr Buller, always used to give me a fifty-pound cheque over and above what I asked for, meaning, I suppose, to keep plenty of ready-money in the works for the week; and I never told him it was more than was wanted, for the reasons I've written. The only excuse I had is this—I never knew how much I owed to Mr Buller. I thought I was nothing more to him, and rather less, than any other man. That's no reason I should rob him, but it makes me a bit less of a thorough blackguard. He ought to have had me sent to gaol. And when he didn't, but just as much as told me to go and do no more wrong, as if I had been his own son—well, sir, it did go to the bottom of all the heart I've got, and I'd like him just to know that he wasn't foolish in being kind. If I ever did another wrong, or mean, or dishonest thing, I should have been the biggest cur on earth. I got a chance in New Zealand, and I should like him to know that his words made a man of me. This is a poor sort of a letter, but I can't say what I feel, and I won't try.—Trusting to hear from you per return, yours respectfully,

ADAM BROWN.

And that is the not wholly unsatisfactory end of a sad story. I suppose that the *first* cheque must have been some sort of a blunder; and that an obstinate man's supposition that forgery on somebody else's part was more probable than a blunder on his own, resulted in—what we have seen. I intended, when I set out, to point a good number of morals, legal and otherwise. But I will content myself with two. One is, that justice has even queerer ways of going to work than law—as when it punishes a man for a fault that hasn't been found out by finding him guilty of one that he has never committed. The other is, that trust, even if carried to the pitch of insanity, is not by any means so mad a thing as it seems. John Buller's over-trust sent him out of his own mind, but it saved another man.

The Mystery of Essex Stairs

SIR GILBERT CAMPBELL

It was a bright moonlight night, the stars were shining clearly, and scarcely a breath of wind was stirring, as Police Constable X924 walked slowly down Essex Street, whistling to himself softly as he did so. His tour of duty was nearly over, and he was feeding his mind on the anticipations of a snug supper, with a comfortable pipe afterwards, when he heard a deep groan and a heavy fall, succeeded almost immediately by the rapid patter of footsteps, as though someone had made away at the top of his speed. These sounds appeared to come from the foot of the flight of stone steps, with which Essex Street terminates at one end. 'There's something wrong there,' muttered the constable, as he abruptly ceased his whistling and quickened his pace, descending the timeworn stairs with as much celerity as was compatible with safety.

When, however, he reached the bottom, he could not at first see anything to account for the sounds which had alarmed him, until glancing into the dark street on the right of the steps, he saw a shapeless mass extended on the pavement, whilst a smaller object close by was struggling with quick, uncertain movements. Just as the constable flashed his bull's-eye on the recumbent figure, and had discovered that the struggling creature was a black poodle, the creature, by a sudden exertion, succeeded in emancipating itself, and, with a bark of triumph, tore away round the corner and along the embankment in the direction of the Temple Station.

'It ain't no good my following that cretur,' thought Constable X924; 'there seems to me to be something more important here.'

The constable was right, for the recumbent form was that of a man lying with his face in a pool of blood, which was still flowing from a terrible wound in the neck.

Constable X924 was a prudent man, and had an intense horror of responsibility, and therefore the shrill notes of his whistle soon brought a couple of his comrades upon the scene.

They raised up the fallen man, who was still breathing, but it was evident to all the constables that the little life which still lingered in him would speedily have fled. There was a terrified look in his eyes, and his lips moved eagerly, though no sound issued from between them. Robbery had evidently been the object of the murder, for coat and waistcoat were torn open, and no sign of a watch-chain was visible.

'He's going,' remarked one of the new arrivals. 'Where's the nearest doctor?'

'In Norfolk Street,' answered Constable X924; 'if you fellows will stand by I will run and fetch him.'

'Stop!' exclaimed the third man, as the constable was about to make a start; 'look here, the poor fellow has been trying to write something on the pavement in his blood.'

The light of the lantern showed the letters 'J. A.' roughly scrawled in the crimson fluid, then came something like an incomplete half circle, and after that a dash, as if the writer's strength had failed.

'Is that meant for the name of the fellow that hurt you?' demanded one of the constables, bending over the wounded man, who made a movement of his hand, which might have been taken either for assent or negation, and then lapsed into a state of unconsciousness.

Police Constable X924 hurried off, but the medical man was unfortunately not at home, and the policeman was standing disconsolately on the embankment, wondering what he should do next, when he was startled by seeing the identical black poodle, which had escaped from the grasp of the injured man, jumping and whining round a figure seated upon one of the seats.

The constable at once walked up to the bench, and perceived that the person with whom the dog appeared to be on such intimate terms was a young man, with a fair moustache and a pleasant cast of features. He was very shabbily dressed, and had on a much worn light overcoat.

'That dog seems precious fond of you,' remarked Constable X924; addressing the young man.

'He ought to be,' was the reply, 'for he has been with me five years, and shared good and evil fortune with me, principally the latter, during that period.'

'Oh, and so the dog is yours, is he?' asked the constable, a little suspiciously.

'Of course he is,' replied the young man; 'but fool that I am, what am I thinking of? Besotted fool that I am, I have parted with him, and my curse upon the juggling fiend who tempted me. Scrub, where is your new master?'

'That is a question you will have to answer, as well as to account for those blood stains on the sleeve of your coat,' replied the constable.

'So I will, whenever you like,' returned the late master of Scrub, 'but not now; any time after nine this morning I will come where you like, but I have an appointment at that hour, and am only resting here because I have no money to pay for a bed.'

'Gammon,' replied the constable; 'a fine chance I should have of meeting you again if I let you out of my sight. Come along,' and he seized him roughly by the collar.

The young man made a violent resistance, but he was weak and unable to cope with the stalwart constable, and though Scrub utterly ruined Constable X924's pantaloons by a sudden attack on his rear, both he and his late master were eventually overpowered and marched off to the police station.

When the prisoner, who gave the name of John Maynard, was brought before the magistrate, the case seemed very black against him, and he was remanded for a week.

When he was brought up again, the coroner's inquest had delivered a verdict of wilful murder against him, and a well-known barrister had been instructed by the Treasury to prosecute.

The prisoner, John Maynard, who was in a terribly depressed state of mind, would have been without legal assistance had not a young barrister, who had become interested in the case, volunteered his services. Arthur Medlecott had been called to the bar about three years; he was a quiet, studious young man, and though he had not as yet received many briefs, had won golden opinions in those cases in which he had been engaged.

Something seemed to tell him that there was some mystery in this affair, and the further he went into it the deeper interest he felt. The unhappy man who had been found at the foot of Essex Stairs, and who had died whilst being conveyed to the hospital, was identified as a certain Reuben Blatchley, a betting man, who bore rather an equivocal reputation. There was no money save a few coppers found on the body, though it was well known the deceased had been in possession of a comparatively large sum of money before his death.

Before obtaining the assistance of the young barrister, the prisoner had made a statement to the following effect. His name was John Maynard, aged twenty-eight, and he earned his living by exhibiting his trained dog, Scrub, at various music halls of inferior stamp. For the past two years his mother had been suffering from a painful and incurable disease, the expense of which took away every farthing he made. He had an acquaintance with the dead man, Reuben Blatchley, who had for some months been desirous of purchasing the poodle Scrub. At length, crushed down by adverse circumstances, Maynard had consented to sell the faithful animal for ten pounds, which sum Blatchley had paid him at a public house on the night of the murder. He confessed that he had been very angry at the time, and had accused the deceased of putting pressure upon him, but he had no hand in his death. He had parted with him outside the door of the public house, and after placing Scrub's lead in his hand, had seen him turn toward the Temple, with the dog whining and struggling to get free. Police Constable James Morgan, X924, deposed to finding the dying man, and also to seeing the dog escape. He arrested the prisoner, who made considerable resistance.

Cross-examined by Mr Medlecott. 'Did he not say that he would come at ten o'clock and explain matters?'

Witness, smiling, 'Yes, but I did not put any faith in him.'

Inspector Frederick Hailes deposed that the prisoner had been brought to the police station, and that he noticed blood on his coat sleeves. Two five-pound notes were found in his pocket, each of which had two small punctures as though made by the point of a pin.

Question by counsel for the defence. 'Did not the prisoner say that he was waiting for daylight in order to take the money, which was the price of his dog, to his mother?'

Answer. 'He did make such a statement.'

Gregory Marlton, publican, deposed that the prisoner and deceased were in his house on the night of the murder, and that prisoner was speaking very angrily to the dead man, but at the time he did not pay much attention, as he was accustomed to hear people quarrel. He heard deceased call the prisoner 'Jack'. Deceased had given him a fifty-pound note early in the day, requesting him to get it changed. He would swear to the notes found on the prisoner as forming a portion of the money he had handed to deceased, because he had pinned the notes together, and the holes were still apparent. Prisoner had a black poodle with him, and he and deceased left the house together.

By Mr Medlecott. 'Did you hear anything said about the sale of a dog?'

Witness. 'No, I did not.'

'Did deceased pay prisoner any money?'

'Not as far as I saw; he bundled the notes into his breast pocket and went on jawing. He was a little gone, I think.'

'And you will swear that he and the prisoner went out together?'

'Yes, I will swear to that.'

William Hallock was next sworn. He said that he was at the 'Bunch of Grapes' on the night in question, and heard the prisoner call deceased a mean-spirited devil, who would take advantage of a man's necessities, and that he would repent of it sooner than he fancied. Prisoner's manner was threatening, but deceased was conciliatory, and called him 'Jack, old fellow', offering to stand him a drink. He saw deceased receive money from the landlord. He left the house before deceased or prisoner. He had no acquaintance with either of them.

By Mr Medlecott. 'What is your business?'

Witness. 'I haven't any; I do odd jobs.'

'Have you ever been in trouble?'

'I got into a mess a year ago about a gentleman's watch, but it was all a mistake.'

'However, mistake or not, you got six months' hard labour.'

'Yes; the witnesses were all prejudiced; it was a cruel shame.'

'You were drinking in the "Bunch of Grapes"; where did you get your money from?'

The witness, insolently. 'I don't see that I have any call to tell you that, gov'nor.'

'When the clerk gave you the testament you put out your wrong hand; are you left-handed?'

'There is no harm if I am, is there?'

'I ask you again if you are left-handed?'

Witness. 'Well, for the matter of that, I am.'

Police Constable Robert Dicker, Z834, who had been summoned to the spot, deposed that he had discovered the handwriting on the flagstone, and said that the facsimile of it produced in court was perfectly correct.

By Mr Medlecott. 'You assisted in placing the deceased on the ambulance for conveyance to the hospital?'

Answer. 'I did.'

'Did you notice his hands?'

Witness. 'I do not understand what you mean.'

Mr Medlecott. 'Were there any bloodstains upon them?'

Witness. 'No, they were perfectly clean.'

Mr Medlecott. 'If there was no stain on his fingers how do you account for his having written the letters "J. A." in his blood?'

Witness, hesitatingly. 'I cannot account for it at all.'

Dr Andrew Macalister, MD, was then called, and deposed that he was house-surgeon at St Gengulphus' Hospital, and that the deceased when brought in was quite dead. The witness then proceeded to state that death had been caused by an incised wound in the throat, and that it could not have been self-inflicted.

By Mr Medlecott. 'Would it have been possible for the deceased to have written the letters which have been produced in court after having received a mortal wound?'

Dr Macalister. 'Quite possible, though I do not think, after such a shock to the system as deceased received, he would have had sufficient presence of mind to have given such a clue to his murderer.'

No further evidence was brought forward on behalf of the prosecution, and the magistrate was about to commit the prisoner for trial at the approaching sessions, when Mr Medlecott interposed, saying that he had further evidence which he wished to bring forward for the defence.

Peter Romney, of Beech Place, Peckham, deposed that he was well acquainted with the deceased, and acted as his 'penciller' at all race meetings.

The magistrate. 'What do you mean by "penciller"?'

The witness. 'His clerk, your worship. I entered the bets he made, and kept his accounts generally. He had plenty of money, but used to drink a bit, at times.'

The magistrate. 'Really, Mr Medlecott, I cannot see that this evidence has any bearing on the case.'

Mr Medlecott. 'One moment, sir, and I think you will see that I am not wasting the time of the court.'

To the witness. 'Had you any particular reason for acting as clerk to the murdered man?'

Witness, with a laugh. 'He had a precious good reason for engaging me, for if it had been to save his life, he couldn't have written a single letter of the alphabet.'

Sensation in the court.

Mr Medlecott. 'Thank you, that will do. Please call Mr Erasmus Urswick.'

Erasmus Urswick stepped into the witness box, and made the following statement. 'I am a professional expert in handwriting, and I have examined the facsimile of the marks made in blood on the flagstone, which were supplied to me by the police authorities. The letters "J. A.", and the unfinished semicircle, have certainly been traced by someone using their left hand; of this there can be no doubt—'

The magistrate. 'I should really be unwilling, Mr Urswick, to challenge the professional opinion of a gentleman who has now such a reputation as you have, but do you not think that you are going a little too far?'

Mr Urswick. 'In what way, your worship?'

The magistrate. 'In so decidedly stating that the writing must have been executed with the left hand.'

Mr Urswick. 'The caligraphy of the right hand differs in the most wonderful and marked manner, and there are very few persons whose handwritings are alike; but in the course of my experience, I have invariably found that the writing executed by the left hand has almost invariably the same characteristics. I produce, for the inspection of the court, a sheet of paper, upon which I have obtained a dozen copies of the letters "J. A." Not copies, for they have not seen the facsimiles in the hands of the police. They were all effected in the same manner—by dipping the forefinger in blacking—and your worship will observe the marked resemblance between the various attempts. I am now going to make a further statement, which may seem even more incredible than my first one, and that is, that if the letters were written with the left hand, they were never written by the dead man.'

The magistrate. 'That is a bold assertion, Mr Urswick, and I shall be glad to hear how you will prove it.'

'I was brought up, your worship, for the medical profession, and took my degree in due course, but I, after a time, abandoned it—I am sure Dr Macalister will pardon me—for a less precarious position. I examined the left hand of the murdered man, and I find that the middle finger is wanting, doubtless the result of some accident, and the forefinger and the one next to it are stiff and unbendable, so that by no possibility could they have been used to inscribe the letters "J. A." I appeal to Dr Macalister to know whether I am, or am not, right.'

Dr Macalister, rising and bowing. 'You are perfectly right, Mr Urswick.'

Renewed sensation in the court.

The magistrate. 'Then what is your argument, Mr Medlecott?'

Mr Medlecott. 'That it would be absurd to suppose that my client would have inscribed the two first letters of his Christian name had he been the actual murderer, and that "J. A." was written by the real criminal in order to throw the blame upon an innocent party.'

'You forget the blood upon the coat, and the two five-pound notes, which have been identified as having been in possession of the deceased on the night of the murder, and which were found upon the prisoner.'

'The notes, my client has asserted, were given him in payment for the poodle, which the police constable, who discovered the body, saw escaping from the dying man's grasp; and the blood is easily accounted for by a wound which the dog received when the murderer made his first attack, and with which he would have stained his master's coat in his joy at finding him again.'

'Let the dog be brought into court,' said the magistrate; 'I should like to examine the wound myself.'

Within five minutes after this order had been given, a sudden tumult arose at the door of the court. The barking and snarling of a dog was mingled with the oaths and vociferations of a man, and a confused murmur from the officials.

Above it all rose the tones of a man, pronouncing these words, clearly and distinctly: 'You infernal brute, are you not content with having bitten my leg nearly through for the accidental slash I gave you at the foot of Essex Street, but you must make for me again.'

'There is the end of my case for the defence, your worship,' remarked Mr Medlecott. 'Scrub, the poodle, has put in the finishing link of evidence, and if you want the real murderer, why, there he stands, self-confessed, in the person of William Hallock, the left-handed villain who, with his fingers dipped in his victim's blood, traced the lying letters which have almost thrust an innocent man's neck into the hangman's noose.'

Taken by surprise, and feeling that there was no retracting the admission he had made, Hallock sulkily confessed his crime. The remainder of the stolen notes were found in the lining of his coat, and Scrub's mark was visible on the calf of his leg. He confessed that he had seen the notes handed over to Blatchley and heard the quarrel between the two men. The idea of the crime had flashed suddenly upon him, and waiting outside, he had dogged the betting man, after he had parted with Maynard, until a convenient spot was reached, when, springing upon him, he had cut his throat with a razor which he had in his pocket. The dog had received a chance cut in the struggle, and had retaliated after the manner of his kind with his teeth. He had then robbed the dying man, and traced the letters 'J. A.' on the flagstone near, as if the expiring efforts of the victim had been to give a clue to his murderer. He had then run off at full speed and hurled the bloodstained weapon into the Thames.

In due time William Hallock expiated his crime on the gallows, whilst John Maynard, whom Scrub had quietly followed out of court, was lucky enough to obtain a good engagement for his canine protégé at one of the leading music halls, where his sensational story became known through the medium of the press, and so to supply his mother in her last days with every comfort.

The Adventure of the Blue Carbuncle

SIR ARTHUR CONAN DOYLE

I had called upon my friend Sherlock Holmes upon the second morning after Christmas, with the intention of wishing him the compliments of the season. He was lounging upon the sofa in a purple dressing-gown, a pipe-rack within his reach upon the right, and a pile of crumpled morning papers, evidently newly studied, near at hand. Beside the couch was a wooden chair, and on the angle of the back hung a very seedy and disreputable hard felt hat, much the worse for wear, and cracked in several places. A lens and a forceps lying upon the seat of the chair suggested that the hat had been suspended in this manner for the purpose of examination.

'You are engaged,' said I; 'perhaps I interrupt you.'

'Not at all. I am glad to have a friend with whom I can discuss my results. The matter is a perfectly trivial one' (he jerked his thumb in the direction of the old hat), 'but there are points in connection with it which are not entirely devoid of interest, and even of instruction.'

I seated myself in his armchair, and warmed my hands before his crackling fire, for a sharp frost had set in, and the windows were thick with the ice crystals. 'I suppose,' I remarked, 'that, homely as it looks, this thing has some deadly story linked on to it—that it is the clue which will guide you in the solution of some mystery, and the punishment of some crime.'

'No, no. No crime,' said Sherlock Holmes, laughing. 'Only one of those whimsical little incidents which will happen when you have four million human beings all jostling each other within the space of a few square miles. Amid the action and reaction of so dense a swarm of humanity, every possible combination of events may be expected to take place, and many a little problem will be presented which may be striking and bizarre without being criminal. We have already had experience of such.'

'So much so,' I remarked, 'that, of the last six cases which I have added to my notes, three have been entirely free of any legal crime.'

'Precisely. You allude to my attempt to recover the Irene Adler papers, to the singular case of Miss Mary Sutherland, and to the adventure of the man with the twisted lip. Well, I have no doubt that this small matter will fall into the same innocent category. You know Peterson, the commissionaire?'

'Yes.'

'It is to him that this trophy belongs.'

'It is his hat.'

'No, no; he found it. Its owner is unknown. I beg that you will look upon it, not as a battered billycock, but as an intellectual problem. And, first, as to how it came here. It arrived upon Christmas morning, in company with a good fat goose, which is, I have no doubt, roasting at this moment in front of Peterson's fire. The facts are these. About four o'clock on Christmas morning, Peterson, who, as you know, is a very honest fellow, was returning from some small jollification, and was making his way homewards down Tottenham Court Road. In front of him he saw, in the gaslight, a tallish man, walking with a slight stagger, and carrying a white goose slung over his shoulder. As he reached the corner of Goodge Street, a row broke out between this stranger and a little knot of roughs. One of the latter knocked off the man's hat, on which he raised his stick to defend himself, and, swinging it over his head, smashed the shop window behind him. Peterson had rushed forward to protect the stranger from his assailants, but the man, shocked at having broken the window, and seeing an official-looking person in uniform rushing towards him, dropped his goose, took to his heels, and vanished amid the labyrinth of small streets which lie at the back of Tottenham Court Road. The roughs had also fled at the appearance of Peterson, so that he was left in possession of the field of battle, and also of the spoils of victory in the shape of this battered hat and a most unimpeachable Christmas goose.'

'Which surely he restored to their owner?'

'My dear fellow, there lies the problem. It is true that "For Mrs Henry Baker" was printed upon a small card which was tied to the bird's left leg, and it is also true that the initials "H. B." are legible upon the lining of this hat; but, as there are some thousands of Bakers, and some hundreds of Henry Bakers in this city of ours, it is not easy to restore lost property to any one of them.'

'What, then, did Peterson do?'

'He brought round both hat and goose to me on Christmas morning, knowing that even the smallest problems are of interest to me. The goose we retained until this morning, when there were signs that, in spite of the slight frost, it would be well that it should be eaten without unnecessary delay. Its finder has carried it off, therefore, to fulfil the ultimate destiny of a goose, while I continue to retain the hat of the unknown gentleman who lost his Christmas dinner.'

'Did he not advertise?'

'No.'

'Then, what clue could you have as to his identity?'

'Only as much as we can deduce.'

'From his hat?'

'Precisely.'

'But you are joking. What can you gather from this old battered felt?'

'Here is my lens. You know my methods. What can you gather yourself as to the individuality of the man who has worn this article?'

I took the tattered object in my hands, and turned it over rather ruefully. It was a very ordinary black hat of the usual round shape, hard, and much the worse for wear. The lining had been of red silk, but was a good deal discoloured. There was no maker's name; but, as Holmes had remarked, the initials 'H. B.' were scrawled upon one side. It was pierced in the brim for a hat-securer, but the elastic was missing. For the rest, it was cracked, exceedingly dusty, and spotted in several places, although there seemed to have been some attempt to hide the discoloured patches by smearing them with ink.

'I can see nothing,' said I, handing it back to my friend.

'On the contrary, Watson, you can see everything. You fail, however, to reason from what you see. You are too timid in drawing your inferences.'

'Then, pray tell me what it is that you can infer from this hat?'

He picked it up, and gazed at it in the peculiar introspective fashion which was characteristic of him. 'It is perhaps less suggestive than it might have been,' he remarked, 'and yet there are a few inferences which are very distinct, and a few others which represent at least a strong balance of probability. That the man was highly intellectual is of course obvious upon the face of it, and also that he was fairly well-to-do within the last three years, although he has now fallen upon evil days. He had foresight, but has less now than formerly, pointing to a moral retrogression, which, when taken with the decline of his fortunes, seems to indicate some evil influence, probably drink, at work upon him. This may account also for the obvious fact that his wife has ceased to love him.'

'My dear Holmes!'

'He has, however, retained some degree of self-respect,' he continued, disregarding my remonstrance. 'He is a man who leads a sedentary life, goes out little, is out of training entirely, is middle-aged, has grizzled hair which he has had cut within the last few days, and which he anoints with lime-cream. These are the more patent facts which are to be deduced from his hat. Also, by the way, that it is extremely improbable that he has gas laid on in his house.'

'You are certainly joking, Holmes.'

'Not in the least. Is it possible that even now when I give you these results you are unable to see how they are attained?'

'I have no doubt that I am very stupid; but I must confess that I am unable to follow you. For example, how did you deduce that this man was intellectual?'

For answer Holmes clapped the hat upon his head. It came right over the forehead and settled upon the bridge of his nose. 'It is a question of cubic capacity,' said he; 'a man with so large a brain must have something in it.'

'The decline of his fortunes, then?'

'This hat is three years old. These flat brims curled at the edge came in then. It is a hat of the very best quality. Look at the band of ribbed silk, and the excellent lining. If this man could afford to buy so expensive a hat three years ago, and has had no hat since, then he has assuredly gone down in the world.'

'Well, that is clear enough, certainly. But how about the foresight, and the moral retrogression?'

Sherlock Holmes laughed. 'Here is the foresight,' said he, putting his finger upon the little disc and loop of the hat-securer. 'They are never sold upon hats. If this man ordered one, it is a sign of a certain amount of foresight, since he went out of his way to take this precaution against the wind. But since we see that he has broken the elastic, and has not troubled to replace it, it is obvious that he has less foresight now than formerly, which is a distinct proof of a weakening nature. On the other hand, he has endeavoured to conceal some of these stains upon the felt by daubing them with ink, which is a sign that he has not entirely lost his self-respect.'

'Your reasoning is certainly plausible.'

'The further points, that he is middle-aged, that his hair is grizzled, that it has been recently cut, and that he uses lime-cream, are all to be gathered from a close examination of the lower part of the lining. The lens discloses a large number of hair ends, clean cut by the scissors of the barber. They all appear to be adhesive, and there is a distinct odour of lime-cream. This dust, you will observe, is not the gritty, grey dust of the street, but the fluffy brown dust of the house, showing that it has been hung up indoors most of the time; while the marks of moisture upon the inside are proof positive that the wearer perspired very freely, and could, therefore, hardly be in the best of training.'

'But his wife—you said that she had ceased to love him.'

'This hat has not been brushed for weeks. When I see you, my dear Watson, with a week's accumulation of dust upon your hat, and when your wife allows you to go out in such a state, I shall fear that you also have been unfortunate enough to lose your wife's affection.'

'But he might be a bachelor.'

'Nay, he was bringing home the goose as a peace-offering to his wife. Remember the card upon the bird's leg.'

'You have an answer to everything. But how on earth do you deduce that the gas is not laid on in his house?'

'One tallow stain, or even two, might come by chance; but, when I see no less than five, I think that there can be little doubt that the individual must be brought into frequent contact with burning tallow—walks upstairs at night probably with his hat in one hand and a guttering candle in the other. Anyhow, he never got tallow stains from a gas jet. Are you satisfied?'

'Well, it is very ingenious,' said I, laughing; 'but, since, as you said just now, there has been no crime committed, and no harm done save the loss of a goose, all this seems to be rather a waste of energy.'

Sherlock Holmes had opened his mouth to reply, when the door flew open, and Peterson the commissionaire rushed into the apartment with flushed cheeks and the face of a man who is dazed with astonishment.

'The goose, Mr Holmes! The goose, sir!' he gasped.

'Eh? What of it, then? Has it returned to life, and flapped off through the kitchen window?' Holmes twisted himself round upon the sofa to get a fairer view of the man's excited face.

'See here, sir! See what my wife found in its crop!' He held out his hand, and displayed upon the centre of the palm a brilliantly scintillating blue stone, rather smaller than a bean in size, but of such purity and radiance that it twinkled like an electric point in the dark hollow of his hand.

Sherlock Holmes sat up with a whistle. 'By Jove, Peterson!' said he, 'this is treasure trove indeed. I suppose you know what you have got?'

'A diamond, sir! A precious stone! It cuts into glass as though it were putty.'

'It's more than a precious stone. It's *the* precious stone.'

'Not the Countess of Morcar's blue carbuncle!' I ejaculated.

'Precisely so. I ought to know its size and shape, seeing that I have read the advertisement about it in *The Times* every day lately. It is absolutely unique, and its value can only be conjectured, but the reward offered of a thousand pounds is certainly not within a twentieth part of the market price.'

'A thousand pounds! Great Lord of mercy!' The commissionaire plumped down into a chair, and stared from one to the other of us.

'That is the reward, and I have reason to know that there are sentimental considerations in the background which would induce the Countess to part with half her fortune, if she could but recover the gem.'

'It was lost, if I remember aright, at the Hotel Cosmopolitan,' I remarked.

'Precisely so, on the twenty-second of December, just five days ago. John Horner, a plumber, was accused of having abstracted it from the lady's jewel case. The evidence against him was so strong that the case has been referred to the Assizes. I have some account of the matter here, I believe.' 'He rummaged amid his newspapers, glancing over the dates, until at last he smoothed one out, doubled it over, and read the following paragraph:

Hotel Cosmopolitan Jewel Robbery. John Horner, 26, plumber, was brought up upon the charge of having upon the 22nd inst. abstracted from the jewel case of the Countess of Morcar the valuable gem known as the blue carbuncle. James Ryder, upper-attendant at the hotel, gave his evidence to the effect that he had shown Horner up to the dressing-room of the Countess of

Morcar upon the day of the robbery, in order that he might solder the second bar of the grate, which was loose. He had remained with Horner some little time, but had finally been called away. On returning, he found that Horner had disappeared, that the bureau had been forced open, and that the small morocco casket in which, as it afterwards transpired, the Countess was accustomed to keep her jewel was lying empty upon the dressing-table. Ryder instantly gave the alarm, and Horner was arrested the same evening; but the stone could not be found either upon his person or in his rooms. Catherine Cusack, maid to the Countess, deposed to having heard Ryder's cry of dismay on discovering the robbery, and to having rushed into the room, where she found matters as described by the last witness. Inspector Bradstreet, B division, gave evidence as to the arrest of Horner, who struggled frantically, and protested his innocence in the strongest terms. Evidence of a previous conviction for robbery having been given against the prisoner, the magistrate refused to deal summarily with the offence, but referred it to the Assizes. Horner, who had shown signs of intense emotion during the proceedings, fainted away at the conclusion, and was carried out of court.

'Hum! So much for the police-court,' said Holmes, thoughtfully, tossing aside the paper. 'The question for us now to solve is the sequence of events leading from a rifled jewel case at one end to the crop of a goose in Tottenham Court Road at the other. You see, Watson, our little deductions have suddenly assumed a much more important and less innocent aspect. Here is the stone; the stone came from the goose, and the goose came from Mr Henry Baker, the gentleman with the bad hat and all the other characteristics with which I have bored you. So now we must set ourselves very seriously to finding this gentleman, and ascertaining what part he has played in this little mystery. To do this, we must try the simplest means first, and these lie undoubtedly in an advertisement in all the evening papers. If this fail, I shall have recourse to other methods.'

'What will you say?'

'Give me a pencil, and that slip of paper. Now, then: "Found at the corner of Goodge Street, a goose and a black felt hat. Mr Henry Baker can have the same by applying at 6.30 this evening at 221B, Baker Street." That is clear and concise.'

'Very. But will he see it?'

'Well, he is sure to keep an eye on the papers, since, to a poor man, the loss was a heavy one. He was clearly so scared by his mischance in breaking the window, and by the approach of Peterson, that he thought of nothing but flight; but since then he must have bitterly regretted the impulse which caused him to drop his bird. Then, again, the introduction of his name will cause him to see it, for everyone who knows him will direct his attention to it. Here you are, Peterson, run down to the advertising agency, and have this put in the evening papers.'

'In which, sir.'

'Oh, in the *Globe, Star, Pall Mall, St James's, Evening News, Standard, Echo,* and any others that occur to you.'

'Very well, sir. And this stone?'

'Ah, yes, I shall keep the stone. Thank you. And, I say, Peterson, Just buy a goose on your way back, and leave it here with me, for we must have one to give to this gentleman in place of the one which your family is now devouring.'

When the commissionaire had gone, Holmes took up the stone and held it against the light. 'It's a bonny thing,' said he. 'Just see how it glints and sparkles. Of course it is a nucleus and focus of crime. Every good stone is. They are the devil's pet baits. In the larger and older jewels every facet may stand for a bloody deed. This stone is not yet twenty years old. It was found in the banks of the Amoy River in Southern China, and is remarkable in having every characteristic of the carbuncle, save that it is blue in shade, instead of ruby red. In spite of its youth, it has already a sinister history. There have been two murders, a vitriol-throwing, a suicide, and several robberies brought about for the sake of this forty-grain weight of crystallized charcoal. Who would think that so pretty a toy would be a purveyor to the gallows and the prison? I'll lock it up in my strong box now, and drop a line to the Countess to say that we have it.'

'Do you think that this man Horner is innocent?'

'I cannot tell.'

'Well, then, do you imagine that this other one, Henry Baker, had anything to do with the matter?'

'It is, I think, much more likely that Henry Baker is an absolutely innocent man, who had no idea that the bird which he was carrying was of considerably more value than if it were made of solid gold. That, however, I shall determine by a very simple test, if we have an answer to our advertisement.'

'And you can do nothing until then?'

'Nothing.'

'In that case I shall continue my professional round. But I shall come back in the evening at the hour you have mentioned, for I should like to see the solution of so tangled a business.'

'Very glad to see you. I dine at seven. There is a woodcock, I believe. By the way, in view of recent occurrences, perhaps I ought to ask Mrs Hudson to examine its crop.'

I had been delayed at a case, and it was a little after half-past six when I found myself in Baker Street once more. As I approached the house I saw a tall man in a Scotch bonnet, with a coat which was buttoned up to his chin, waiting outside in the bright semicircle which was thrown from the fanlight. Just as I arrived, the door was opened, and we were shown up together to Holmes' room.

'Mr Henry Baker, I believe,' said he, rising from his armchair, and greeting his visitor with the easy air of geniality which he could so readily assume. 'Pray take this chair by the fire, Mr Baker. It is a cold night, and I observe that your circulation is more adapted for summer than for winter. Ah, Watson, you have just come at the right time. Is that your hat, Mr Baker?'

'Yes, sir, that is undoubtedly my hat.'

He was a large man, with rounded shoulders, a massive head, and a broad, intelligent face, sloping down to a pointed beard of grizzled brown. A touch of red in nose and cheeks, with a slight tremor of his extended hand, recalled Holmes' surmise as to his habits. His rusty black frock coat was buttoned right up in front, with the collar turned up, and his lank wrists protruded from his sleeves without a sign of cuff or shirt. He spoke in a slow staccato fashion, choosing his words with care, and gave the impression generally of a man of learning and letters who had had ill-usage at the hands of fortune.

'We have retained these things for some day,' said Holmes, 'because we expected to see an advertisement from you giving your address. I am at a loss to know now why you did not advertise.'

Our visitor gave a rather shamefaced laugh. 'Shillings have not been so plentiful with me as they once were,' he remarked. 'I had no doubt that the gang of roughs who assaulted me had carried off both my hat and the bird. I did not care to spend more money in a hopeless attempt at recovering them.'

'Very naturally. By the way, about the bird, we were compelled to eat it.'

'To eat it!' Our visitor half rose from his chair in his excitement.

'Yes, it would have been no use to anyone had we not done so. But

I presume that this other goose upon the sideboard, which is about the same weight and perfectly fresh, will answer your purpose equally well?'

'Oh, certainly, certainly!' answered Mr Baker, with a sigh of relief.

'Of course, we still have the feathers, legs, crop, and so on of your own bird, so if you wish——'

The man burst into a hearty laugh. 'They might be useful to me as relics of my adventure,' said he, 'but beyond that I can hardly see what use the *disjecta membra* of my late acquaintance are going to be to me. No, sir, I think that, with your permission, I will confine my attentions to the excellent bird which I perceive upon the sideboard.'

Sherlock Holmes glanced sharply across at me with a slight shrug of his shoulders.

'There is your hat, then, and there your bird,' said he. 'By the way, would it bore you to tell me where you got the other one from? I am somewhat of a fowl fancier, and I have seldom seen a better-grown goose.'

'Certainly, sir,' said Baker, who had risen and tucked his newly gained property under his arm. 'There are a few of us who frequent the "Alpha" Inn, near the Museum—we are to be found in the Museum itself during the day, you understand. This year our good host, Windigate by name, instituted a goose club, by which, on consideration of some few pence every week, we were each to receive a bird at Christmas. My pence were duly paid, and the rest is familiar to you. I am much indebted to you, sir, for a Scotch bonnet is fitted neither to my years nor my gravity.' With a comical pomposity of manner he bowed solemnly to both of us, and strode off upon his way.

'So much for Mr Henry Baker,' said Holmes, when he had closed the door behind him. 'It is quite certain that he knows nothing whatever about the matter. Are you hungry, Watson?'

'Not particularly.'

'Then I suggest that we turn our dinner into a supper, and follow up this clue while it is still hot.'

'By all means.'

It was a bitter night, so we drew on our ulsters and wrapped cravats about our throats. Outside, the stars were shining coldly in a cloudless sky, and the breath of the passers-by blew out into smoke like so many pistol shots. Our footfalls rang out crisply and loudly as we swung through the Doctors' quarter, Wimpole Street, Harley Street, and so through Wigmore Street into Oxford Street. In a quarter of an hour we were in Bloomsbury at the 'Alpha' Inn, which is a small public house at the corner of one of the streets which runs down into Holborn. Holmes pushed open the door of the private bar, and ordered two glasses of beer from the ruddy-faced, white-aproned landlord.

'Your beer should be excellent if it is as good as your geese,' said he.

'My geese!' The man seemed surprised.

'Yes. I was speaking only half an hour ago to Mr Henry Baker, who was a member of your goose-club.'

'Ah! yes, I see. But you see, sir, them's not *our* geese.'

'Indeed! Whose, then?'

'Well, I got the two dozen from a salesman in Covent Garden.'

'Indeed! I know some of them. Which was it?'

'Breckinridge is his name.'

'Ah! I don't know him. Well, here's your good health, landlord, and prosperity to your house. Good-night!'

'Now for Mr Breckinridge,' he continued, buttoning up his coat, as we came out into the frosty air. 'Remember, Watson, that though we have so homely a thing as a goose at one end of this chain, we have at the other a man who will certainly get seven years' penal servitude, unless we can establish his innocence. It is possible that our inquiry may but confirm his guilt; but, in any case, we have a line of investigation which has been missed by the police, and which a singular chance has placed in our hands. Let us follow it out to the bitter end. Faces to the south, then, and quick march!'

We passed across Holborn, down Endell Street, and so through a zigzag of slums to Covent Garden Market. One of the largest stalls bore the name of Breckinridge upon it, and the proprietor, a horsey-looking man, with a sharp face and trim side-whiskers, was helping a boy to put up the shutters.

'Good evening. It's a cold night,' said Holmes.

The salesman nodded, and shot a questioning glance at my companion.

'Sold out of geese, I see,' continued Holmes, pointing at the bare slabs of marble.

'Let you have five hundred tomorrow morning.'

'That's no good.'

'Well, there are some on the stall with the gas flare.'

'Ah, but I was recommended to you.'

'Who by?'

'The landlord of the "Alpha." '

'Oh, yes; I sent him a couple of dozen.'

'Fine birds they were, too. Now where did you get them from?'

To my surprise the question provoked a burst of anger from the salesman.

'Now, then, mister,' said he, with his head cocked and his arms akimbo, 'what are you driving at? Let's have it straight, now.'

'It is straight enough. I should like to know who sold you the geese which you supplied to the "Alpha".'

'Well, then, I sha'n't tell you. So now!'

'Oh, it is a matter of no importance; but I don't know why you should be so warm over such a trifle.'

'Warm! You'd be as warm, maybe, if you were as pestered as I am. When I pay good money for a good article there should be an end of the business; but it's "Where are the geese?" and "Who did you sell the geese to?" and "What will you take for the geese?" One would think they were the only geese in the world, to hear the fuss that is made over them.'

'Well, I have no connection with any other people who have been making enquires,' said Holmes, carelessly. 'If you won't tell us the bet is off, that is all. But I'm always ready to back my opinion on a matter of fowls, and I have a fiver on it that the bird I ate is country bred.'

'Well, then you've lost your fiver, for it's town bred,' snapped the salesman.

'It's nothing of the kind.'

'I say it is.'

'I don't believe it.'

'D'you think you know more about fowls than I, who have handled them ever since I was a nipper? I tell you, all those birds that went to the "Alpha" were town bred.'

'You'll never persuade me to believe that.'

'Will you bet, then?'

'It's merely taking your money, for I know that I am right. But I'll have a sovereign on with you, just to teach you not to be obstinate.'

The salesman chuckled grimly. 'Bring me the books, Bill,' said he.

The small boy brought round a small thin volume and a great greasy-backed one, laying them out together beneath the hanging lamp.

'Now then, Mr Cocksure,' said the salesman, 'I thought that I was out of geese, but before I finish you'll find that there is still one left in my shop. You see this little book?'

'Well?'

'That's the list of the folk from whom I buy. D'you see? Well, then, here on this page are the country folk, and the numbers after their names are where their accounts are in the big ledger. Now, then! You see this other page in red ink? Well, that is a list of my town suppliers. Now, look at that third name. Just read it out to me.'

'Mrs Oakshott, 117, Brixton Road—249,' read Holmes.

'Quite so. Now turn that up in the ledger.'

Holmes turned to the page indicated. 'Here you are, "Mrs Oakshott, 117, Brixton Road, egg and poultry supplier".'

'Now, then, what's the last entry?'

'"December 22. Twenty-four geese at 7s. 6d."'

'Quite so. There you are. And underneath?'

'"Sold to Mr Windigate of the "Alpha" at 12s."'

'What have you to say now?'

Sherlock Holmes looked deeply chagrined. He drew a sovereign from his pocket and threw it down upon the slab, turning away with the air of a man whose disgust is too deep for words. A few yards off he stopped under a lamp-post, and laughed in the hearty, noiseless fashion which was peculiar to him.

'When you see a man with whiskers of that cut and the "pink 'un" protruding out of his pocket, you can always draw him by a bet,' said he. 'I dare say that if I had put a hundred pounds down in front of him that man would not have given me such complete information as was drawn from him by the idea that he was doing me on a wager. Well, Watson, we are, I fancy, nearing the end of our quest, and the only point which remains to be determined is whether we should go on to this Mrs Oakshott tonight, or whether we should reserve it for tomorrow. It is clear from what that surly fellow said that there are others besides ourselves who are anxious about the matter, and I should——'

His remarks were suddenly cut short by a loud hubbub which broke out from the stall which we had just left. Turning round we saw a little rat-faced fellow standing in the centre of the circle of yellow light which was thrown by the swinging lamp, while Breckinridge the salesman, framed in the door of his stall, was shaking his fists fiercely at the cringing figure.

'I've had enough of you and your geese,' he shouted. 'I wish you were all at the devil together. If you come pestering me any more with your silly talk I'll set the dog at you. You bring Mrs Oakshott here and I'll answer her, but what have you to do with it? Did I buy the geese off you?'

'No; but one of them was mine all the same,' whined the little man.

'Well, then, ask Mrs Oakshott for it.'

'She told me to ask you.'

'Well, you can ask the King of Proosia for all I care. I've had enough of it. Get out of this!' He rushed fiercely forward, and the enquirer flitted away into the darkness.

'Ha, this may save us a visit to Brixton Road,' whispered Holmes. 'Come with me, and we will see what is to be made of this fellow.' Striding through the scattered knots of people who lounged round the flaring stalls, my companion speedily overtook the little man and touched him upon the shoulder. He sprang round, and I could see in the gaslight that every vestige of colour had been driven from his face.

'Who are you, then? What do you want?' he asked in a quavering voice.

'You will excuse me,' said Holmes blandly, 'but I could not help overhearing the questions which you put to the salesman just now. I think that I could be of assistance to you.'

'You? Who are you? How could you know anything of the matter?'

'My name is Sherlock Holmes. It is my business to know what other people don't know.'

'But you can know nothing of this?'

'Excuse me, I know everything of it. You are endeavouring to trace some geese which were sold by Mrs Oakshott, of Brixton Road, to a salesman named Breckinridge, by him in turn to Mr Windigate, of the "Alpha", and by him to his club, of which Mr Henry Baker is a member.'

'Oh, sir, you are the very man whom I have longed to meet,' cried the little fellow, with outstretched hands and quivering fingers. 'I can hardly explain to you how interested I am in this matter.'

Sherlock Holmes hailed a four-wheeler which was passing. 'In that case we had better discuss it in a cosy room rather than in this windswept market-place,' said he. 'But pray tell me, before we go further, who it is that I have the pleasure of assisting.'

The man hesitated for an instant. 'My name is John Robinson,' he answered, with a sidelong glance.

'No, no; the real name,' said Holmes, sweetly. 'It is always awkward doing business with an *alias*.'

A flush sprang to the white cheeks of the stranger. 'Well, then,' said he, 'my real name is James Ryder.'

'Precisely so. Head attendant at the Hotel Cosmopolitan. Pray step into the cab, and I shall soon be able to tell you everything which you would wish to know.'

The little man stood glancing from one to the other of us with half-frightened, half-hopeful eyes, as one who is not sure whether he is on the verge of a windfall or of a catastrophe. Then he stepped into the cab, and in half an hour we were back in the sitting-room at Baker Street. Nothing had been said during our drive, but the high thin breathing of our new companion, and the claspings and unclaspings of his hands spoke of the nervous tension within him.

'Here we are!' said Holmes, cheerily, as we filed into the room. 'The fire looks very seasonable in this weather. You look cold, Mr Ryder. Pray take the basket chair. I will just put on my slippers before we settle this little matter of yours. Now, then! You want to know what became of those geese?'

'Yes, sir.'

'Or rather, I fancy, of that goose. It was one bird, I imagine, in which you were interested—white, with a black bar across the tail.'

Ryder quivered with emotion. 'Oh, sir, he cried, 'can you tell me where it went to?'

'It came here.'

'Here?'

'Yes, and a most remarkable bird it proved. I don't wonder that you should take an interest in it. It laid an egg after it was dead—the bonniest, brightest little blue egg that ever was seen. I have it here in my museum.'

Our visitor staggered to his feet, and clutched the mantelpiece with his right hand. Holmes unlocked his strong box, and held up the blue carbuncle, which shone out like a star, with a cold, brilliant, many-pointed radiance. Ryder stood glaring with a drawn face, uncertain whether to claim or to disown it.

'The game's up, Ryder,' said Holmes, quietly. 'Hold up, man, or you'll be into the fire. Give him an arm back into his chair, Watson. He's not got blood enough to go in for felony with impunity. Give him a dash of brandy. So! Now he looks a little more human. What a shrimp it is, to be sure!'

For a moment he had staggered and nearly fallen, but the brandy brought a tinge of colour into his cheeks, and he sat staring with frightened eyes at his accuser.

'I have almost every link in my hands, and all the proofs which I could possibly need, so there is little which you need tell me. Still that little may as well be cleared up to make the case complete. You had heard, Ryder, of this blue stone of the Countess of Morcar's?'

'It was Catherine Cusack who told me of it,' said he, in a crackling voice.

'I see. Her ladyship's waiting maid. Well, the temptation of sudden wealth so easily acquired was too much for you, as it has been for better men before you; but you were not very scrupulous in the means you used. It seems to me, Ryder, that there is the making of a very pretty villain in you. You knew that this man Horner, the plumber, had been concerned in some such matter before, and that suspicion would rest the more readily upon him. What did you do, then? You made some small job in my lady's room—you and your confederate Cusack—and you managed that he should be the man sent for. Then, when he had left, you rifled the jewel case, raised the alarm, and had this unfortunate man arrested. You then——'

Ryder threw himself down suddenly upon the rug, and clutched at my companion's knees. 'For God's sake, have mercy!' he shrieked. 'Think of my father! Of my mother! It would break their hearts. I never went wrong before! I never will again. I swear it. I'll swear it on a Bible. Oh, don't bring it into court! For Christ's sake, don't!'

'Get back into your chair!' said Holmes, sternly. 'It is very well to cringe and crawl now, but you thought little enough of this poor Horner in the dock for a crime of which he knew nothing.'

'I will fly, Mr Holmes. I will leave the country, sir. Then the charge against him will break down.'

'Hum! We will talk about that. And now let us hear a true account of the next act. How came the stone into the goose, and how came the goose into the open market? Tell us the truth, for there lies your only hope of safety.'

Ryder passed his tongue over his parched lips. 'I will tell you it just as it happened, sir,' said he. 'When Horner had been arrested, it seemed to me that it would be best for me to get away with the stone at once, for I did not know at what moment the police might not take it into their heads to search me and my room. There was no place about the hotel where it would be safe. I went out, as if on some commission, and I made for my sister's house. She had married a man named Oakshott, and lived in Brixton Road, where she fattened fowls for the market. All the way there every man I met seemed to me to be a policeman or a detective, and for all that it was a cold night, the sweat was pouring down my face before I came to the Brixton Road. My sister asked me what was the matter, and why I was so pale; but I told her that I had been upset by the jewel robbery at the hotel. Then I went into the backyard, and smoked a pipe, and wondered what it would be best to do.

'I had a friend once called Maudsley, who went to the bad, and has just been serving his time in Pentonville. One day he had met me, and fell into talk about the ways of thieves and how they could get rid of what they stole. I knew that he would be true to me, for I knew one or two things about him, so I made up my mind to go right on to Kilburn, where he lived, and take him into my confidence. He would show me how to turn the stone into money. But how to get to him in safety. I thought of the agonies I had gone through in coming from the hotel. I might at any moment be seized and searched, and there would be the stone in my waistcoat pocket. I was leaning against the wall at the time, and looking at the geese which were waddling about round my feet, and suddenly an idea came into my head which showed me how I could beat the best detective that ever lived.

'My sister had told me some weeks before that I might have the pick of her geese for a Christmas present, and I knew that she was always as good as her word. I would take my goose now, and in it I would carry my stone to Kilburn. There was a little shed in the yard, and behind this I drove one of the birds, a fine big one, white with a barred tail. I caught it, and, prizing its bill open, I thrust the stone down its throat as far as my finger could reach. The bird gave a gulp, and I felt the stone pass along its gullet and down into its crop. But the creature flapped and struggled, and out came my sister to know what was the matter. As I turned to speak to her the brute broke loose, and fluttered off among the others.

'"Whatever were you doing with that bird, Jem?" says she.

'"Well," said I, "you said you'd give me one for Christmas, and I was feeling which was the fattest."

'"Oh," says she, "we've set yours aside for you. Jem's bird, we call it. It's the big, white one over yonder. There's twenty-six of them, which makes one for you, and one for us, and two dozen for the market.'

'"Thank you, Maggie," says I; "but if it is all the same to you I'd rather have that one I was handling just now."

'"The other is a good three pound heavier," said she, "and we fattened it expressly for you."

'"Never mind. I'll have the other, and I'll take it now," said I.

'"Oh, just as you like," said she, a little huffed. "Which is it you want, then?"

'"That white one, with the barred tail, right in the middle of the flock."

'"Oh, very well. Kill it and take it with you."

'Well, I did what she said, Mr Holmes, and I carried the bird all the way to Kilburn. I told my pal what I had done, for he was a man that it was easy to tell a thing like that to. He laughed until he choked, and we got a knife and opened the goose. My heart turned to water, for there was no sign of the stone, and I knew that some terrible mistake had occurred. I left the bird, rushed back to my sister's, and hurried into the backyard. There was not a bird to be seen there.

'"Where are they all, Maggie?" I cried.

'"Gone to the dealer's, Jim."

'"Which dealer's?"

'"Breckinridge, of Covent Garden."

'"But was there another with a barred tail?" I asked, "the same as the one I chose?"

'"Yes, Jem, there were two barred-tailed ones, and I could never tell them apart."

'Well, then, of course, I saw it all, and I ran off as hard as my feet would carry me to this man Breckinridge; but he had sold the lot at once, and not one word would he tell me as to where they had gone. You heard him yourselves tonight. Well, he has always answered me like that. My sister thinks that I am going mad. Sometimes I think that I am myself. And now—and now I am myself a branded thief, without ever having touched the wealth for which I sold my character. God help me! God help me!' He burst into convulsive sobbing, with his face buried in his hands.

There was a long silence, broken only by his heavy breathing, and by the measured tapping of Sherlock Holmes' fingertips upon the edge of the table. Then my friend rose, and threw open the door.

'Get out!' said he.

'What, sir! Oh, heaven bless you!'

'No more words. Get out!'

And no more words were needed. There was a rush, a clatter upon the stairs, the bang of a door, and the crisp rattle of running footfalls from the street.

'After all, Watson,' said Holmes, reaching up his hand for his clay pipe, 'I am not retained by the police to supply their deficiencies. If Horner were in danger it would be another thing, but this fellow will not appear against him, and the case must collapse. I suppose that I am committing a felony, but it is just possible that I am saving a soul. This fellow will not go wrong again. He is too terribly frightened. Send him to gaol now, and you make him a gaol-bird for life. Besides, it is the season of forgiveness. Chance has put in our way a most singular and whimsical problem, and its solution is its own reward. If you will have the goodness to touch the bell, Doctor, we will begin another investigation, in which also a bird will be the chief feature.'

The Great Ruby Robbery

GRANT ALLEN

I

Persis Remanet was an American heiress. As she justly remarked, this was a commonplace profession for a young woman nowadays; for almost everybody of late years has been an American and an heiress. A poor Californian, indeed, would be a charming novelty in London society. But London society, so far, has had to go without one.

Persis Remanet was on her way back from the Wilcoxes' ball. She was stopping, of course, with Sir Everard and Lady Maclure at their house at Hampstead. I say 'of course' advisedly; because if you or I go to see New York, we have to put up at our own expense (five dollars a day, without wine or extras) at the Windsor or the Fifth Avenue; but when the pretty American comes to London (and every American girl is *ex officio* pretty, in Europe at least; I suppose they keep their ugly ones at home for domestic consumption) she is invariably the guest either of a dowager duchess or of a Royal Academician, like Sir Everard, of the first distinction. Yankees visit Europe, in fact, to see, among other things, our art and our old nobility; and by dint of native persistence they get into places that you and I could never succeed in penetrating, unless we devoted all the energies of a long and blameless life to securing an invitation.

Persis hadn't been to the Wilcoxes with Lady Maclure, however. The Maclures were too really great to know such people as the Wilcoxes, who were something tremendous in the City, but didn't buy pictures; and Academicians, you know, don't care to cultivate City people—unless they're customers. ('Patrons', the Academicians more usually call them; but I prefer the simple business word myself, as being a deal less patronizing.) So Persis had accepted an invitation from Mrs Duncan Harrison, the wife of the well-known member for the Hackness Division of Elmetshire, to take a seat in her carriage to and from the Wilcoxes. Mrs Harrison knew the habits and manners of American heiresses too well to offer to chaperon Persis; and indeed, Persis, as a free-born American citizen, was quite as well able to take care of herself, the wide world over, as any three ordinary married Englishwomen.

Now, Mrs Harrison had a brother, an Irish baronet, Sir Justin O'Byrne, late of the Eighth Hussars, who had been with them to the Wilcoxes, and who accompanied them home to Hampstead on the back seat of the carriage. Sir Justin was one of those charming, ineffective, elusive Irishmen whom everybody likes and everybody disapproves of. He had been everywhere, and done everything—except to earn an honest livelihood. The total absence of rents during the sixties and seventies had never prevented his father, old Sir Terence O'Byrne, who sat so long for Connemara in the unreformed Parliament, from sending his son Justin in state to Eton, and afterwards to a fashionable college at Oxford. 'He gave me the education of a gentleman,' Sir Justin was wont regretfully to observe; 'but he omitted to give me also the income to keep it up with.'

Nevertheless, society felt O'Byrne was the sort of man who must be kept afloat somehow; and it kept him afloat accordingly in those mysterious ways that only society understands, and that you and I, who are not society, could never get to the bottom of if we tried for a century. Sir Justin himself had essayed Parliament, too, where he sat for a while behind the great Parnell without for a moment forfeiting society's regard even in those earlier days when it was held as a prime article of faith by the world that no gentleman could possibly call himself a Home-Ruler. 'Twas only one of O'Byrne's wild Irish tricks, society said, complacently, with that singular indulgence it always extends to its special favourites, and which is, in fact, the correlative of that unsparing cruelty it shows in turn to those who happen to offend against its unwritten precepts. If Sir Justin had blown up a Czar or two in a fit of political exuberance, society would only have regarded the escapade as 'one of O'Byrne's eccentricities'. He had also held a commission for a while in a cavalry regiment, which he left, it was understood, owing to a difference of opinion about a lady with the colonel; and he was now a gentleman-at-large on London society, supposed by those who know more about everyone than one knows about oneself, to be on the look-out for a nice girl with a little money.

Sir Justin had paid Persis a great deal of attention that particular evening; in point of fact, he had paid her a great deal of attention from the very first, whenever he met her; and on the way home from the dance he had kept his eyes fixed on Persis's face to an extent that was almost embarrassing. The pretty Californian leaned back in her place in the carriage and surveyed him languidly. She was looking her level best that night, in her pale pink dress, with the famous Remanet rubies in a cascade of red light setting off that snowy neck of hers. 'Twas a neck for a painter. Sir Justin let his eyes fall regretfully more than once on the glittering rubies. He liked and admired Persis, oh! quite immensely. Your society man who has been through seven or eight London seasons could hardly be expected to go quite so far as falling in love with any woman; his habit is rather to look about him critically among all the nice girls trotted out by their mammas for his lordly inspection, and to reflect with a faint smile that this, that, or the other one might perhaps really suit him—if it were not for—and there comes in the inevitable *But* of all human commendation. Still, Sir Justin admitted with a sigh to himself that he liked Persis ever so much; she was so fresh and original! and she talked so cleverly! As for Persis, she would have given her eyes (like every other American girl) to be made 'my lady'; and she had seen no man yet, with that auxiliary title in his gift, whom she liked half so well as this delightful wild Irishman.

At the Maclures' door the carriage stopped. Sir Justin jumped out and gave his hand to Persis. You know the house well, of course; Sir Everard Maclure's; it's one of those large new artistic mansions, in red brick and old oak, on the top of the hill; and it stands a little way back from the road, discreetly retired, with a big wooden porch, very convenient for leave-taking. Sir Justin ran up the steps with Persis to ring the bell for her; he had too much of the irrepressible Irish blood in his veins to leave that pleasant task to his sister's footman. But he didn't ring it at once; at the risk of keeping Mrs Harrison waiting outside for nothing, he stopped and talked a minute or so with the pretty American. 'You looked charming tonight, Miss Remanet,' he said, as she threw back her light opera wrap for a moment in the porch and displayed a single flash of that snowy neck with the famous rubies; 'those stones become you so.'

Persis looked at him and smiled. 'You think so?' she said, a little tremulous, for even your American heiress, after all, is a woman. 'Well, I'm glad you do. But it's goodbye tonight, Sir Justin, for I go next week to Paris.'

Even in the gloom of the porch, just lighted by an artistic red and blue lantern in wrought iron, she could see a shade of disappointment pass quickly over his handsome face as he answered, with a little gulp, 'No! you don't mean that? Oh, Miss Remanet, I'm so sorry!' Then he paused and drew back: 'And yet ... after all,' he continued, 'perhaps——,' and there he checked himself.

Persis looked up at him hastily. 'Yet, after all, what?' she asked, with evident interest.

The young man drew an almost inaudible sigh. 'Yet, after all— nothing,' he answered, evasively.

'That might do for an Englishwoman,' Persis put in, with American frankness, 'but it won't do for me. You must tell me what you mean by it.' For she reflected sagely that the happiness of two lives might depend upon those two minutes; and how foolish to throw away the chance of a man you really like (with a my-ladyship to boot), all for the sake of a pure convention!

Sir Justin leaned against the woodwork of that retiring porch. She was a beautiful girl. He had hot Irish blood. . . . Well, yes; just for once—he would say the plain truth to her.

'Miss Remanet,' he began, leaning forward, and bringing his face close to hers, 'Miss Remanet—Persis—shall I tell you the reason why? Because I like you so much. I almost think I love you!'

Persis felt the blood quiver in her tingling cheeks. How handsome he was—and a baronet!

'And yet you're not altogether sorry,' she said, reproachfully, 'that I'm going to Paris!'

'No, not altogether sorry,' he answered, sticking to it; 'and I'll tell you why, too, Miss Remanet. I like you very much, and I think you like me. For a week or two, I've been saying to myself, "I really believe I *must* ask her to marry me." The temptation's been so strong I could hardly resist it.'

'And why do you want to resist it?' Persis asked, all tremulous.

Sir Justin hesitated a second; then with a perfectly natural and instinctive movement (though only a gentleman would have ventured to make it) he lifted his hand and just touched with the tips of his fingers the ruby pendants on her necklet. '*This* is why,' he answered simply, and with manly frankness. 'Persis, you're so rich! I never dare ask you.'

'Perhaps you don't know what my answer would be,' Persis murmured very low, just to preserve her own dignity.

'Oh, yes; I think I do,' the young man replied, gazing deeply into her dark eyes. 'It isn't that; if it were only that, I wouldn't so much mind it. But I think you'd take me.' There was moisture in her eye. He went on more boldly: 'I know you'd take me, Persis, and that's why I don't ask you. You're a great deal too rich, and *these* make it impossible.'

'Sir Justin,' Persis answered, removing his hand gently, but with the moisture growing thicker, for she really liked him, 'it's most unkind of you to say so; either you oughtn't to have told me at all, or else—if you did——' She stopped short. Womanly shame overcame her.

The man leaned forward and spoke earnestly. 'Oh, don't say that!' he cried, from his heart. 'I couldn't bear to offend you. But I couldn't bear, either, to let you go away—well—without having ever told you. In that case you might have thought I didn't care at all for you, and was only flirting with you. But, Persis, I've cared a great deal for you—a great, great deal—and had hard work many times to prevent myself from asking you. And I'll tell you the plain reason why I haven't asked you. I'm a man about town, not much good, I'm afraid, for anybody or anything; and everybody says I'm on the look-out for an heiress—which happens not to be true; and if I married you, everybody'd say, "Ah, there! I told you so!" Now, I wouldn't mind that for myself; I'm a man, and I could snap my fingers at them; but I'd mind it for *you*, Persis, for I'm enough in love with you to be very, very jealous, indeed, for your honour. I couldn't bear to think people should say, "There's that pretty American girl, Persis Remanet that was, you know; she's thrown herself away upon that good-for-nothing Irishman, Justin O'Byrne, a regular fortune-hunter, who's married her for her money." So for your sake, Persis, I'd rather not ask you; I'd rather leave you for some better man to marry.'

'But *I* wouldn't,' Persis cried aloud. 'Oh, Sir Justin, you must believe me. You must remember——'

At that precise point, Mrs Harrison put her head out of the carriage window and called out rather loudly:

'Why, Justin, what's keeping you? The horses'll catch their deaths of cold; and they were clipped this morning. Come back at once, my dear boy. Besides, you know, *les convenances*!'

'All right, Nora,' her brother answered; 'I won't be a minute. We can't get them to answer this precious bell. I believe it don't ring! But I'll try again, anyhow.' And half forgetting that his own words weren't strictly true, for he hadn't yet tried, he pressed the knob with a vengeance.

'Is that your room with the light burning, Miss Remanet?' he went on, in a fairly loud official voice, as the servant came to answer. 'The one with the balcony, I mean? Quite Venetian, isn't it? Reminds one of Romeo and Juliet. But most convenient for a burglary, too! Such nice low rails! Mind you take good care of the Remanet rubies!'

'I don't want to take care of them,' Persis answered, wiping her dim eyes hastily with her lace pocket-handkerchief, 'if they make you feel as you say, Sir Justin. I don't mind if they go. Let the burglar take them!'

And even as she spoke, the Maclure footman, immutable, sphinx-like, opened the door for her.

II

Persis sat long in her own room that night before she began undressing. Her head was full of Sir Justin and these mysterious hints of his. At last, however, she took her rubies off, and her pretty silk bodice. 'I don't care for them at all,' she thought, with a gulp, 'if they keep from me the love of the man I'd like to marry.'

It was late before she fell asleep; and when she did, her rest was troubled. She dreamt a great deal; in her dreams, Sir Justin, and dance music, and the rubies, and burglars were incongruously mingled. To make up for it, she slept late next morning; and Lady Maclure let her sleep on, thinking she was probably wearied out with much dancing the previous evening—as though any amount of excitement could ever weary a pretty American! About ten o'clock she woke with a start. A vague feeling oppressed her that somebody had come in during the night and stolen her rubies. She rose hastily and went to her dressing-table to look for them. The case was there all right; she opened it and looked at it. Oh, prophetic soul! the rubies were gone, and the box was empty!

Now, Persis had honestly said the night before the burglar might take her rubies if he chose, and she wouldn't mind the loss of them. But that was last night, and the rubies hadn't then as yet been taken. This morning, somehow, things seemed quite different. It would be rough on us all (especially on politicians) if we must always be bound by what we said yesterday. Persis was an American, and no American is insensible to the charms of precious stones; 'tis a savage taste which the European immigrants seem to have inherited obliquely from their Red Indian predecessors. She rushed over to the bell and rang it with feminine violence. Lady Maclure's maid answered the summons, as usual. She was a clever, demure-looking girl, this maid of Lady Maclure's; and when Persis cried to her wildly, 'Send for the police at once, and tell Sir Everard my jewels are stolen!' she answered 'Yes, miss,' with such sober acquiescence that Persis, who was American, and therefore a bundle of nerves, turned round and stared at her as an incomprehensible mystery. No Mahatma could have been more unmoved. She seemed quite to expect those rubies would be stolen, and to take no more notice of the incident than if Persis had told her she wanted hot water.

Lady Maclure, indeed, greatly prided herself on this cultivated imperturbability of Bertha's: she regarded it as the fine flower of English domestic service. But Persis was American, and saw things otherwise; to her, the calm repose with which Bertha answered, 'Yes, miss; certainly, miss; I'll go and tell Sir Everard,' seemed nothing short of exasperating.

Bertha went off with the news, closing the door quite softly; and a few minutes later Lady Maclure herself appeared in the Californian's room, to console her visitor under this severe domestic affliction. She found Persis sitting up in bed, in her pretty French dressing jacket (pale blue with *revers* of fawn colour), reading a book of verses. 'Why, my dear!' Lady Maclure exclaimed, 'then you've found them again, I suppose? Bertha told us you'd lost your lovely rubies!'

'So I have, dear Lady Maclure,' Persis answered, wiping her eyes; 'they're gone. They've been stolen. I forgot to lock my door when I came home last night, and the window was open; somebody must have come in, this way or that, and taken them. But whenever I'm in trouble, I try a dose of Browning. He's splendid for the nerves. He's so consoling, you know; he brings one to anchor.'

She breakfasted in bed; she wouldn't leave the room, she declared, till the police arrived. After breakfast she rose and put on her dainty Parisian morning wrap—Americans have always such pretty bedroom things for these informal receptions—and sat up in state to await the police officer. Sir Everard himself, much disturbed that such a mishap should have happened in his house, went round in person to fetch the official. While he was gone, Lady Maclure made a thorough search of the room, but couldn't find a trace of the missing rubies.

'Are you sure you put them in the case, dear?' she asked, for the honour of the household.

And Persis answered: 'Quite confident, Lady Maclure: I always put them there the moment I take them off; and when I came to look for them this morning, the case was empty.'

'They were *very* valuable, I believe?' Lady Maclure said, enquiringly.

'Six thousand pounds was the figure in your money, I guess,' Persis answered, ruefully. 'I don't know if you call that a lot of money in England, but we do in America.'

There was a moment's pause, and then Persis spoke again:

'Lady Maclure,' she said, abruptly, 'do you consider that maid of yours a Christian woman?'

Lady Maclure was startled. That was hardly the light in which she was accustomed to regard the lower classes.

'Well, I don't know about that,' she said, slowly; 'that's a great deal, you know, dear, to assert about *anybody*, especially one's maid. But I should think she was honest, quite decidedly honest.'

'Well, that's the same thing, about, isn't it?' Persis answered, much relieved. 'I'm glad you think that's so; for I was almost half afraid of her. She's too quiet for my taste, somehow; so silent, you know, and inscrutable.'

'Oh, my dear,' her hostess cried, 'don't blame her for silence; that's just what I like about her. It's exactly what I chose her for. Such a nice, noiseless girl; moves about the room like a cat on tiptoe; knows her proper place, and never dreams of speaking unless she's spoken to.'

'Well, you may like them that way in Europe,' Persis responded, frankly: 'but in America, we prefer them a little bit human.'

Twenty minutes later the police officer arrived. He wasn't in uniform. The inspector, feeling at once the gravity of the case, and recognizing that this was a Big Thing, in which there was glory to be won, and perhaps promotion, sent a detective at once, and advised that if possible nothing should be said to the household on the subject for the present, till the detective had taken a good look round the premises. That was useless, Sir Everard feared, for the lady's-maid knew; and the lady's-maid would be sure to go down, all agog with the news, to the servants' hall immediately. However, they might try; no harm in trying; and the sooner the detective got round to the house, of course, the better.

The detective accompanied him back—a keen-faced, close-shaven, irreproachable-looking man, like a vulgarized copy of Mr John Morley. He was curt and businesslike. His first question was, 'Have the servants been told of this?'

Lady Maclure looked enquiringly across at Bertha. She herself had been sitting all the time with the bereaved Persis, to console her (with Browning) under this heavy affliction.

'No, my lady,' Bertha answered, ever calm (invaluable servant, Bertha!), 'I didn't mention it to anybody downstairs on purpose, thinking perhaps it might be decided to search the servants' boxes.'

The detective pricked up his ears. He was engaged already in glancing casually round the room. He moved about it now, like a conjurer, with quiet steps and slow. 'He doesn't get on one's nerves,' Persis remarked, approvingly, in an undertone to her friend; then she added, aloud: 'What's your name, please, Mr Officer?'

The detective was lifting a lace handkerchief on the dressing-table at the side. He turned round softly. 'Gregory, madam,' he answered, hardly glancing at the girl, and going on with his occupation.

'The same as the powders!' Persis interposed, with a shudder. 'I used to take them when I was a child. I never could bear them.'

'We're useful, as remedies,' the detective replied, with a quiet smile; 'but nobody likes us.' And he relapsed contentedly into his work once more, searching round the apartment.

'The first thing we have to do,' he said, with a calm air of superiority, standing now by the window, with one hand in his pocket, 'is to satisfy ourselves whether or not there has really, at all, been a robbery. We must look through the room well, and see you haven't left the rubies lying about loose somewhere. Such things often happen. We're constantly called in to investigate a case, when it's only a matter of a lady's carelessness.'

At that Persis flared up. A daughter of the great republic isn't accustomed to be doubted like a mere European woman. 'I'm quite sure I took them off,' she said, 'and put them back in the jewel case. Of that I'm just confident. There isn't a doubt possible.'

Mr Gregory redoubled his search in all likely and unlikely places. 'I should say that settles the matter,' he answered, blandly. 'Our experience is that whenever a lady's perfectly certain, beyond the possibility of doubt, she put a thing away safely, it's absolutely sure to turn up where she says she didn't put it.'

Persis answered him never a word. Her manners had not that repose that stamps the caste of Vere de Vere; so, to prevent an outbreak, she took refuge in Browning.

Mr Gregory, nothing abashed, searched the room thoroughly, up and down, without the faintest regard to Persis's feelings; he was a detective, he said, and his business was first of all to unmask crime, irrespective of circumstances. Lady Maclure stood by, meanwhile, with the imperturbable Bertha. Mr Gregory investigated every hole and cranny, like a man who wishes to let the world see for itself he performs a disagreeable duty with unflinching thoroughness. When he had finished, he turned to Lady Maclure. 'And now, if you please,' he said, blandly, 'we'll proceed to investigate the servants' boxes.'

Lady Maclure looked at her maid. 'Bertha,' she said, 'go downstairs, and see that none of the other servants come up, meanwhile, to their bedrooms.' Lady Maclure was not quite to the manner born, and had never acquired the hateful aristocratic habit of calling women servants by their surnames only.

But the detective interposed. 'No, no,' he said, sharply. 'This young woman had better stop here with Miss Remanet—strictly under her eye—till I've searched the boxes. For if I find nothing there, it may perhaps be my disagreeable duty, by-and-by, to call in a female detective to search her.'

It was Lady Maclure's turn to flare up now. 'Why, this is my own maid,' she said, in a chilly tone, 'and I've every confidence in her.'

'Very sorry for that, my lady,' Mr Gregory responded, in a most official voice; but our experience teaches us that if there's a person in the case whom nobody ever dreams of suspecting, that person's the one who has committed the robbery.'

'Why, you'll be suspecting myself next!' Lady Maclure cried, with some disgust.

'Your ladyship's just the last person in the world I should think of suspecting,' the detective answered, with a deferential bow—which, after his previous speech, was to say the least of it equivocal.

Persis began to get annoyed. She didn't half like the look of that girl Bertha, herself: but still, she was there as Lady Maclure's guest, and she couldn't expose her hostess to discomfort on her account.

'The girl shall *not* be searched,' she put in, growing hot. 'I don't care a cent whether I lose the wretched stones or not. Compared to human dignity, what are they worth? Not five minutes' consideration.'

'They're worth just seven years,' Mr Gregory answered, with professional definiteness. 'And as to searching, why, that's out of your hands now. This is a criminal case. I'm here to discharge a public duty.'

'I don't in the least mind being searched.' Bertha put in obligingly, with an air of indifference. 'You can search me if you like—when you've got a warrant for it.'

The detective looked up sharply; so also did Persis. This ready acquaintance with the liberty of the subject in criminal cases impressed her unfavourably. 'Ah! we'll see about that,' Mr Gregory answered, with a cool smile. 'Meanwhile, Lady Maclure, I'll have a look at the boxes.'

III

The search (strictly illegal) brought out nothing. Mr Gregory returned to Persis's bedroom, disconsolate. 'You can leave the room,' he said to Bertha; and Bertha glided out. 'I've set another man outside to keep a constant eye on her,' he added in explanation.

By this time Persis had almost made her mind up as to who was the culprit; but she said nothing overt, for Lady Maclure's sake, to the detective. As for that immovable official, he began asking questions—some of them, Persis thought, almost bordering on the personal. Where had she been last night? Was she sure she had really worn the rubies? How did she come home? Was she certain she took them off? Did the maid help her undress? Who came back with her in the carriage?

To all these questions, rapidly fired off with cross-examining acuteness, Persis answered in the direct American fashion. She was sure she had the rubies on when she came home to Hampstead, because Sir Justin O'Byrne, who came back with her in his sister's carriage, had noticed them the last thing, and had told her to take care of them.

At mention of that name the detective smiled meaningly. (A meaning smile is stock-in-trade to a detective.) 'Oh, Sir Justin O'Byrne!' he repeated, with quiet self-constraint. '*He* came back with you in the carriage, then? And did he sit the same side with you?'

Lady Maclure grew indignant (that was Mr Gregory's cue). 'Really, sir,' she said, angrily, 'if you're going to suspect gentlemen in Sir Justin's position, we shall none of us be safe from you.'

'The law,' Mr Gregory replied, with an air of profound deference, 'is no respecter of persons.'

'But it ought to be of characters,' Lady Maclure cried, warmly. 'What's the good of having a blameless character, I should like to know, if—if——'

'If it doesn't allow you to commit a robbery with impunity?' the detective interposed, finishing her sentence his own way. 'Well, well, that's true. That's per-fectly true—but Sir Justin's character, you see, can hardly be called blameless.'

'He's a gentleman,' Persis cried, with flashing eyes, turning round upon the officer; 'and he's quite incapable of such a mean and despicable crime as you dare to suspect him of.'

'Oh, I see,' the officer answered, like one to whom a welcome ray of light breaks suddenly through a great darkness. 'Sir Justin's a friend of yours! Did he come into the porch with you?'

'He did,' Persis answered, flushing crimson; 'and if you have the insolence to bring a charge against him——'

'Calm yourself, madam,' the detective replied, coolly. 'I do nothing of the sort—at this stage of the proceedings. It's possible there may have been no robbery in the case at all. We must keep our minds open for the present to every possible alternative. It's—it's a delicate matter to hint at; but before we go any further—do you think, perhaps, Sir Justin may have carried the rubies away by mistake, entangled in his clothes?—say, for example, his coat-sleeve?'

It was a loophole of escape; but Persis didn't jump at it.

'He had never the opportunity,' she answered, with a flash. 'And I know quite well they were there on my neck when he left me, for the last thing he said to me was, looking up at this very window: "That balcony's awfully convenient for a burglary. Mind you take good care of the Remanet rubies." And I remembered what he'd said when I took them off last night; and that's what makes me so sure I really had them.'

'*And* you slept with the window open!' the detective went on, still smiling to himself. 'Well, here we have all the materials, to be sure, for a first-class mystery!'

IV

For some days more, nothing further turned up of importance about the Great Ruby Robbery. It got into the papers, of course, as everything does nowadays, and all London was talking of it. Persis found herself quite famous as the American lady who had lost her jewels. People pointed her out in the park; people stared at her hard through their opera-glasses at the theatre. Indeed, the possession of the celebrated Remanet rubies had never made her half so conspicuous in the world as the loss of them made her. It was almost worth while losing them, Persis thought, to be so much made of as she was in society in consequence. All the world knows a young lady must be somebody when she can offer a reward of five hundred pounds for the recovery of gewgaws valued at six thousand.

Sir Justin met her in the Row one day. 'Then you don't go to Paris for awhile yet—until you get them back?' he enquired very low.

And Persis answered, blushing, 'No, Sir Justin; not yet; and—I'm almost glad of it.'

'No, you don't mean that!' the young man cried, with perfect boyish ardour. 'Well, I confess, Miss Remanet, the first thing I thought myself when I read it in *The Times* was just the very same: "Then, after all, she won't go yet to Paris!"'

Persis looked up at him from her pony with American frankness. 'And I,' she, said, quivering, 'I found anchor in Browning. For what do you think I read?

> And learn to rate a true man's heart
> Far above rubies.

The book opened at the very place; and *there* I found anchor!'

But when Sir Justin went round to his rooms that same evening his servant said to him, 'A gentleman was enquiring for you here this afternoon, sir. A close-shaven gentleman. Not very prepossessin'. And it seemed to me somehow, sir, as if he was trying to pump me.'

Sir Justin's face was grave. He went to his bedroom at once. He knew what that man wanted; and he turned straight to his wardrobe, looking hard at the dress coat he had worn on the eventful evening. Things may cling to a sleeve, don't you know—or be entangled in a cuff—or get casually into a pocket! Or someone may put them there.

V

For the next ten days or so Mr Gregory was busy, constantly busy. Without doubt, he was the most active and energetic of detectives. He carried out so fully his own official principle of suspecting everybody, from China to Peru, that at last poor Persis got fairly mazed with his web of possibilities. Nobody was safe from his cultivated and highly trained suspicion—not Sir Everard in his studio, nor Lady Maclure in her boudoir, nor the butler in his pantry, nor Sir Justin O'Byrne in his rooms in St James's. Mr Gregory kept an open mind against everybody and everything. He even doubted the parrot, and had views as to the intervention of rats and terriers. Persis got rather tired at last of his perverse ingenuity; especially as she had a very shrewd idea herself who had stolen the rubies. When he suggested various doubts, however, which seemed remotely to implicate Sir Justin's honesty, the sensitive American girl 'felt it go on her nerves', and refused to listen to him, though Mr Gregory never ceased to enforce upon her, by precept and example, his own pet doctrine that the last person on earth one would be likely to suspect is always the one who turns out to have done it.

A morning or two later, Persis looked out of her window as she was dressing her hair. She dressed it herself now, though she was an American heiress, and, therefore, of course, the laziest of her kind; for she had taken an unaccountable dislike, somehow, to that quiet girl Bertha. On this particular morning, however, when Persis looked out, she saw Bertha engaged in close, and apparently very intimate, conversation with the Hampstead postman. This sight disturbed the unstable equilibrium of her equanimity not a little. Why should Bertha go to the door to the postman at all? Surely it was no part of the duty of Lady Maclure's maid to take in the letters! And why should she want to go prying into the question of who wrote to Miss Remanet? For Persis, intensely conscious herself that a note from Sir Justin lay on top of the postman's bundle—she recognized it at once, even at that distance below, by the peculiar shape of the broad rough envelope—jumped to the natural feminine conclusion that Bertha must needs be influenced by some abstruse motive of which she herself, Persis, was, to say the very least, a component element. We're all of us prone to see everything from a personal standpoint; indeed, the one quality which makes a man or woman into a possible novelist, good, bad, or indifferent, is just that special power of throwing himself or herself into a great many people's personalities alternately. And this is a power possessed on average by not one in a thousand men or not one in ten thousand women.

Persis rang the bell violently. Bertha came up, all smiles: 'Did you want anything, Miss?' Persis could have choked her. 'Yes,' she answered, plainly, taking the bull by the horns; 'I want to know what you were doing down there, prying into other people's letters with the postman?'

Bertha looked up at her, ever bland; she answered at once, without a second's hesitation: 'The postman's my young man, miss; and we hope before very long now to get married.'

'Odious thing!' Persis thought. 'A glib lie always ready on the tip of her tongue for every emergency.'

But Bertha's full heart was beating violently. Beating with love and hope and deferred anxiety.

A little later in the day Persis mentioned the incident casually to Lady Maclure—mainly in order to satisfy herself that the girl had been lying. Lady Maclure, however, gave a qualified assent:

'I *believe* she's engaged to the postman,' she said. 'I *think* I've heard so; though I make it a rule, you see, my dear, to know as little as I can of these people's love affairs. They're so very uninteresting. But Bertha certainly told me she wouldn't leave me to get married for an indefinite period. That was only ten days ago. She said her young man wasn't just yet in a position to make a home for her.'

'Perhaps,' Persis suggested, grimly, 'something has occurred meanwhile to better her position. Such strange things crop up. She may have come into a fortune!'

'Perhaps so,' Lady Maclure replied, languidly. The subject bored her. 'Though, if so, it must really have been very sudden; for I think it was the morning before you lost your jewels she told me so.'

Persis thought that odd, but she made no comment.

Before dinner that evening she burst suddenly into Lady Maclure's room for a minute. Bertha was dressing her lady's hair. Friends were coming to dine—among them Sir Justin. 'How do these pearls go with my complexion, Lady Maclure?' Persis asked rather anxiously; for she specially wished to look her best that evening, for one of the party.

'Oh, charming!' her hostess answered, with her society smile. 'Never saw anything suit you better, Persis.'

'Except my poor rubies!' Persis cried rather ruefully, for coloured gewgaws are dear to the savage and the woman. 'I wish I could get them back! I wonder that man Gregory hasn't succeeded in finding them.'

'Oh! my dear,' Lady Maclure drawled out, 'you may be sure by this time they're safe at Amsterdam. That's the only place in Europe now to look for them.'

'Why to Amsterdam, my lady?' Bertha interposed suddenly, with a quick side-glance at Persis.

Lady Maclure threw her head back in surprise at so unwonted an intrusion. 'What do you want to know that for, child?' she asked, somewhat curtly. 'Why, to be cut, of course. All the diamond-cutters in the world are concentrated in Amsterdam; and the first thing a thief does when he steals big jewels is to send them across, and have them cut in new shapes so that they can't be identified.'

'I shouldn't have thought,' Bertha put in, calmly, 'they'd have known who to send them to.'

Lady Maclure turned to her sharply. 'Why, these things,' she said, with a calm air of knowledge, 'are always done by experienced thieves, who know the ropes well, and are in league with receivers the whole world over. But Gregory has his eye on Amsterdam, I'm sure, and we'll soon hear something.'

'Yes, my lady,' Bertha answered, in her acquiescent tone, and relapsed into silence.

VI

Four days later, about nine at night, that hard-worked man, the posty on the beat, stood loitering outside Sir Everard Maclure's house, openly defying the rules of the department, in close conference with Bertha.

'Well, any news?' Bertha asked, trembling over with excitement, for she was a very different person outside with her lover from the demure and imperturbable model maid who waited on my lady.

'Why, yes,' the posty answered, with a low laugh of triumph. 'A letter from Amsterdam! And I think we've fixed it!'

Bertha almost flung herself upon him. 'Oh, Harry!' she cried, all eagerness, 'this is too good to be true! Then in just one other month we can really get married!'

There was a minute's pause, inarticulately filled up by sounds unrepresentable through the art of the typefounder. Then Harry spoke again. 'It's an awful lot of money!' he said, musing. 'A regular fortune! And what's more, Bertha, if it hadn't been for your cleverness we never should have got it!'

Bertha pressed his hand affectionately. Even ladies'-maids are human.

'Well, if I hadn't been so much in love with you,' she answered, frankly, 'I don't think I could ever have had the wit to manage it. But, oh! Harry, love makes one do or try anything!'

If Persis had heard those singular words, she would have felt no doubt was any longer possible.

VII

Next morning, at ten o'clock, a policeman came round, post haste, to Sir Everard's. He asked to see Miss Remanet. When Persis came down, in her morning wrap, he had but a brief message from head quarters to give her: 'Your jewels are found, Miss. Will you step-round and identify them?'

Persis drove back with him, all trembling. Lady Maclure accompanied her. At the police station they left their cab, and entered the ante-room.

A little group had assembled there. The first person Persis distinctly made out in it was Sir Justin. A great terror seized her. Gregory had so poisoned her mind by this time with suspicion of everybody and everything she came across, that she was afraid of her own shadow. But next moment she saw clearly he wasn't there as prisoner, or even as witness; merely as spectator. She acknowledged him with a hasty bow, and cast her eye round again. The next person she definitely distinguished was Bertha, as calm and cool as ever, but in the very centre of the group, occupying as it were the place of honour which naturally belongs to the prisoner on all similar occasions. Persis was not surprised at that; she had known it all along; she glanced meaningly at Gregory, who stood a little behind, looking by no means triumphant. Persis found his dejection odd; but he was a proud detective, and perhaps someone else had effected the capture!

'These are your jewels, I believe,' the inspector said, holding them up; and Persis admitted it.

'This is a painful case,' the inspector went on. 'A very painful case. We grieve to have discovered such a clue against one of our own men; but as he owns to it himself, and intends to throw himself on the mercy of the Court, it's no use talking about it. He won't attempt to defend it; indeed, with such evidence, I think he's doing what's best and wisest.'

Persis stood there, all dazed. 'I—I don't understand,' she cried, with a swimming brain. 'Who on earth are you talking about?'

The inspector pointed mutely with one hand at Gregory; and then for the first time Persis saw he was guarded. She clapped her hand to her head. In a moment it all broke in upon her. When she had called in the police, the rubies had never been stolen at all. It was Gregory who stole them!

She understood it now, at once. The real facts came back to her. She had taken her necklet off at night, laid it carelessly down on the dressing-table (too full of Sir Justin), covered it accidentally with her lace pocket-handkerchief, and straightway forgotten all about it. Next day she missed it, and jumped at conclusions. When Gregory came, he spied the rubies askance under the corner of the handkerchief— of course, being a woman, she had naturally looked everywhere except in the place where she laid them—and knowing it was a safe case he had quietly pocketed them before her very eyes, all unsuspected. He felt sure nobody could accuse him of a robbery which was committed before he came, and which he had himself been called in to investigate.

'The worst of it is,' the inspector went on, 'he had woven a very ingenious case against Sir Justin O'Byrne, whom we were on the very point of arresting today, if this young woman hadn't come in at the eleventh hour, in the very nick of time, and earned the reward by giving us the clue that led to the discovery and recovery of the jewels. They were brought over this morning by an Amsterdam detective.'

Persis looked hard at Bertha. Bertha answered her look. 'My young man was the postman, miss,' she explained, quite simply; 'and after what my lady said, I put him up to watch Mr Gregory's delivery for a letter from Amsterdam. I'd suspected him from the very first; and when the letter came, we had him arrested at once, and found out from it who were the people at Amsterdam who had the rubies.'

Persis gasped with astonishment. Her brain was reeling. But Gregory in the background put in one last word:

'Well, I was right, after all,' he said, with professional pride. 'I told you the very last person you'd dream of suspecting was sure to be the one that actually did it.'

Lady O'Byrne's rubies were very much admired at Monte Carlo last season. Mr Gregory has found permanent employment for the next seven years at Her Majesty's quarries on the Isle of Portland. Bertha and her postman have retired to Canada with five hundred pounds to buy a farm. And everybody says Sir Justin O'Byrne has beaten the record, after all, even for Irish baronets, by making a marriage at once of money and affection.

The Sapient Monkey

HEADON HILL

I would advise every person whose duties take him into the field of 'private enquiry' to go steadily through the daily papers the first thing every morning. Personally I have found the practice most useful, for there are not many *causes célèbres* in which my services are not enlisted on one side or the other, and by this method I am always up in my main facts before I am summoned to assist. When I read the account of the proceedings at Bow Street against Franklin Gale in connection with the Tudways' bank robbery, I remember thinking that on the face of it there never was a clearer case against a misguided young man.

Condensed for the sake of brevity, the police-court report disclosed the following state of things:

Franklin Gale, clerk, aged twenty-three, in the employment of Messrs Tudways, the well-known private bankers of the Strand, was brought up on a warrant charged with stealing the sum of £500—being the moneys of his employers. Mr James Spruce, assistant cashier at the bank, gave evidence to the effect that he missed the money from his till on the afternoon of July 22. On making up his cash for the day he discovered that he was short of £300 worth of notes and £200 in gold. He had no idea how the amount had been abstracted. The prisoner was an assistant bookkeeper at the bank, and had access behind the counter. Detective-sergeant Simmons said that the case had been placed in his hands for the purpose of tracing the stolen notes. He had ascertained that one of them—of the value of £5—had been paid to Messrs Crosthwaite & Co., tailors, of New Bond Street, on July 27th, by Franklin Gale. As a result, he had applied for a warrant, and had arrested the prisoner. The latter was remanded for a week, at the end of which period it was expected that further evidence would be forthcoming.

I had hardly finished reading the report when a telegram was put into my hands demanding my immediate presence at 'Rosemount',

Twickenham. From the address given, and from the name of 'Gale' appended to the despatch, I concluded that the affair at Tudways' Bank was the cause of the summons. I had little doubt that I was to be retained in the interests of the prisoner, and my surmise proved correct.

'Rosemount' was by no means the usual kind of abode from which the ordinary run of bank clerks come gaily trooping into the great City in shoals by the early trains. There was nothing of cheap gentility about the 'pleasant suburban residence standing in its own grounds of an acre', as the house-agent would say—with its lawns sloping down to the river, shaded by mulberry and chestnut trees, and plentifully garnished with the noble flower which gave it half its name. 'Rosemount' was assuredly the home either of some prosperous merchant or of a private gentleman, and when I crossed its threshold I did so quite prepared for the fuller enlightenment which was to follow. Mr Franklin Gale was evidently not one of the struggling genus bank clerk, but must be the son of well-to-do people, and not yet flown from the parent nest. When I left my office I had thought that I was bound on a forlorn hope, but at the sight of 'Rosemount'—my first real 'touch' of the case—my spirits revived. Why should a young man living amid such signs of wealth want to rob his employers? Of course I recognized that the youth of the prisoner precluded the probability of the place being his own. Had he been older, I should have reversed the argument. 'Rosemount' in the actual occupation of a middle-aged bank clerk would have been prima-facie evidence of a tendency to outrun the constable.

I was shown into a well-appointed library, where I was received by a tall, silver-haired old gentleman of ruddy complexion, who had apparently been pacing the floor in a state of agitation. His warm greeting towards me—a perfect stranger—had the air of one who clutches at a straw.

'I have sent for you to prove my son's innocence, Mr Zambra,' he said. 'Franklin no more stole that money than I did. In the first place, he didn't want it; and, secondly, if he had been ever so pushed for cash, he would rather have cut off his right hand than put it into his employer's till. Besides, if these thick-headed policemen were bound to lock one of us up, it ought to have been me. The five-pound note with which Franklin paid his tailor was one—so he assures me, and I believe him—which I gave him myself.'

'Perhaps you would give me the facts in detail?' I replied.

'As to the robbery, both my son and I are as much in the dark as old Tudway himself,' Mr Gale proceeded. 'Franklin tells me that Spruce, the cashier, is accredited to be a most careful man, and the very last to leave his till to take care of itself. The facts that came out in evidence are perfectly true. Franklin's desk is close to the counter, and the note identified as one of the missing ones was certainly paid by him to Crosthwaite & Co., of New Bond Street, a few days after the robbery. It bears his endorsement, so there can be no doubt about that.

'So much for their side of the case. Ours is, I must confess, from a legal point of view, much weaker, and lies in my son's assertion of innocence, coupled with the knowledge of myself and his mother and his sisters that he is incapable of such a crime. Franklin insists that the note he paid to Crosthwaite & Co., the tailors, was one that I gave him on the morning of the 22nd. I remember perfectly well giving him a five-pound note at breakfast on that day, just before he left for town, so that he must have had it several hours before the robbery was committed. Franklin says that he had no other banknotes between the 22nd and 27th, and that he cannot, therefore, be mistaken. The note which I gave him I got fresh from my own bankers a day or two before, together with some others; and here is the most unfortunate point in the case. The solicitor whom I have engaged to defend Franklin has made the necessary enquiries at my bankers, and finds that the note paid to the tailors is *not one of those* which I drew from the bank.'

'Did not your son take notice of the number of the note you gave him?' I asked.

'Unfortunately, no. He is too much worried about the numbers of notes at his business, he says, to note those which are his own property. He simply sticks to it that he knows it must be the same note because he had no other.'

In the slang of the day, Mr Franklin Gale's story seemed a little too thin. There was the evidence of Tudways that the note paid to the tailor was one of those stolen from them, and there was the evidence of Mr Gale, senior's, bankers that it was not one of those handed to their client. What was the use of the prisoner protesting in the face of this that he had paid his tailor with his father's present? The notes stolen from Tudways were, I remembered reading, consecutive ones of a series, so that the possibility of young Gale having at the bank changed his father's gift for another note, which was subsequently stolen, was knocked on the head. Besides, he maintained that it was the *same* note.

'I should like to know something of your son's circumstances and position,' I said, trying to divest the question of any air of suspicion it might have implied.

'I am glad you asked me that,' returned Mr Gale, 'for it touches the very essence of the whole case. My son's circumstances and position are such that were he the most unprincipled scoundrel in creation he would have been nothing less than an idiot to have done this thing. Franklin is not on the footing of an ordinary bank clerk, Mr Zambra. I am a rich man, and can afford to give him anything in reason, though he is too good a lad ever to have taken advantage of me. Tudway is an old friend of mine, and I got him to take Franklin into the bank with a view to a partnership. Everything was going on swimmingly towards that end: the boy had perfected himself in his duties, and made himself valuable; I was prepared to invest a certain amount of capital on his behalf; and, lastly, Tudway, who lives next door to me here, got so fond of him that he allowed Franklin to become engaged to his daughter Maud. Would any young man in his senses go and steal a paltry £500 under such circumstances as that?'

I thought not, but I did not say so yet.

'What are Mr Tudways' views about the robbery?' I asked.

'Tudway is an old fool,' replied Mr Gale. 'He believes what the police tell him, and the police tell him that Franklin is guilty. I have no patience with him. I ordered him out of this house last night. He had the audacity to come and offer not to press the charge if the boy would confess.'

'And Miss Tudway?'

'Ah! she's a brick. Maud sticks to him like a true woman. But what is the use of our sticking to him against such evidence?' broke down poor Mr Gale, impotently. 'Can you, Mr Zambra, give us a crumb of hope?'

Before I could reply there was a knock at the library door, and a tall, graceful girl entered the room. Her face bore traces of weeping, and she looked anxious and dejected; but I could see that she was naturally quick and intelligent.

'I have just run over to see if there is any fresh news this morning,' she said, with an enquiring glance at me.

'This is Mr Zambra, my dear, come to help us,' said Mr Gale; 'and this,' he continued, turning to me, 'is Miss Maud Tudway. We are all enlisted in the same cause.'

'You will be able to prove Mr Franklin Gale's innocence, sir?' she exclaimed.

'I hope so,' I said; 'and the best way to do it will be to trace the robbery to its real author. Has Mr Franklin any suspicions on that head?'

'He is as much puzzled as we are,' said Miss Tudway. 'I went with Mr Gale here to see him in that horrible place yesterday, and he said there was absolutely no one in the bank he cared to suspect. But he *must* get off the next time he appears. My evidence ought to do that. I saw with my own eyes that he had only one £5 note in his purse on the 25th—that is two days before he paid the tailor, and three days after the robbery.'

'I am afraid that won't help us much,' I said. 'You see, he might easily have had the missing notes elsewhere. But tell me, under what circumstances did you see the £5 note?'

'There was a garden party at our house,' replied Miss Tudway, 'and Franklin was there. During the afternoon a man came to the gate with an accordion and a performing monkey, and asked permission to show the monkey's tricks. We had the man in, and after the monkey had done a lot of clever things the man said that the animal could tell a good banknote from a "flash" one. He was provided with spurious notes for the purpose, would any gentlemen lend him a good note for a minute, just to show the trick? The man was quite close to Franklin, who was sitting next to me. Franklin, seeing the man's hand held out towards him, took out his purse and handed him a note, at the same time calling my attention to the fact that it was his only one, and laughingly saying that he hoped the man was honest. The sham note and the good one were placed before the monkey, who at once tore up the bad note and handed the good one back to Franklin.'

'This is more important than it seems,' I said, after a moment's review of the whole case. 'I must find that man with the monkey, but it bids fair to be difficult. There are so many of them in that line of business.'

Miss Tudway smiled for the first time during the interview.

'It is possible that I may be of use to you there,' she said. 'I go in for amateur photography, and I thought that the man and his monkey made so good a "subject" that I insisted on taking him before he left. Shall I fetch the photograph?'

'By all means,' I said. 'Photography is of the greatest use to me in my work. I generally arrange it myself, but if you have chanced to take the right picture for me in this case so much the better.'

Miss Tudway hurried across to her father's house and quickly returned with the photograph. It was a fair effort for an amateur, and portrayed an individual of the usual seedy stamp, equipped with a huge accordion and a small monkey secured by a string. With this in my hand it would only be a matter of time before I found the itinerant juggler who had presented himself at the Tudways' garden party, and I took my leave of old Mr Gale and Miss Maud in a much more hopeful frame of mind. Every circumstance outside the terrible array of actual evidence pointed to my client's innocence, and if this evidence had been manufactured for the purpose, I felt certain that the 'monkey man' had had a hand in it.

On arriving at my office I summoned one of my assistants—a veteran of doubtful antecedents—who owns to no other name than 'Old Jemmy'. Old Jemmy's particular line of business is a thorough knowledge of the slums and the folk who dwell there; and I knew that after an hour or two on Saffron Hill my ferret, armed with the photograph, would bring me the information I wanted. Towards evening Old Jemmy came in with his report, to the effect that the 'party' I was after was to be found in the top attic of 7 Little Didman's Fields, Hatton Garden, just recovering from the effects of a prolonged spree.

'He's been drunk for three or four days, the landlord told me,' Old Jemmy said. 'Had a stroke of luck, it seems, but he is expected to go on tramp tomorrow, now his coin has given out. His name is Pietro Schilizzi.'

I knew I was on the right scent now, and that the 'monkey man' had been made the instrument of *changing* the note which Franklin Gale had lent him for one of the stolen ones. A quick cab took me to Little Didman's Fields in a quarter of an hour, and I was soon standing inside the doorway of a pestilential apartment on the top floor of No. 7, which had been pointed out to me as the abode of Pietro Schilizzi. A succession of snores from a heap of rags in a corner told me the whereabouts of the occupier. I went over, and shaking him roughly by the shoulder, said in Italian:

'Pietro, I want you to tell me about that little juggle with a banknote at Twickenham the other day. You will be well rewarded.'

The fellow rubbed his eyes in half-drunken astonishment, but there certainly was no guilty fear about him as he replied:

'Certainly, signor; anything for money. There was nothing wrong about the note, was there? Anyhow, I acted innocently in the matter.'

'No one finds fault with you,' I said; 'but see, here is a five-pound note. It shall be yours if you will tell me exactly what happened.'

'I was with my monkey up at Highgate the other evening,' Mr Schilizzi began, 'and was showing Jacko's trick of telling a good note from a bad one. It was a small house in the Napier Road. After I had finished, the gentleman took me into a public house and stood me a drink. He wanted me to do something for him, he said. He had a young friend who was careless, and never took the number of notes, and he wanted to teach him a lesson. He had a bet about the number of a note, he said. Would I go down to Twickenham next day to a house he described, where there was to be a party, and do my trick with the monkey? I was to borrow a note from the young gentleman, and then, instead of giving him back his own note after the performance, I was to substitute one which the Highgate gentleman gave me for the purpose. He met me at Twickenham next day, and came behind the garden wall to point out the young gentleman to me. I managed it just as the Highgate gentleman wanted, and he gave me a couple of pounds for my pains. I have done no wrong; the note I gave back was a good one.'

'Yes,' I said, 'but it happens to have been stolen. Put on your hat and show me where this man lives in Highgate.'

The Napier Road was a shabby street of dingy houses, with a public house at the corner. Pietro stopped about half-way down the row and pointed out No. 21.

'That is where the gentleman lives,' he said.

We retraced our steps to the corner public house.

'Can you tell me who lives at No. 21?' I asked of the landlord, who happened to be in the bar.

'Certainly,' was the answer; 'it is Mr James Spruce—a good customer of mine, and the best billiard player hereabouts. He is a cashier at Messrs Tudways' bank, in the Strand, I believe.'

It all came out at the trial—not of Franklin Gale, but of James

Spruce, the fraudulent cashier. Spruce had himself abstracted the notes and gold entrusted to him, and his guilty conscience telling him that he might be suspected, he had cast about for a means of throwing suspicion on some other person. Chancing to witness the performance of Pietro's monkey, he had grasped the opportunity for foisting one of the stolen notes on Franklin Gale, knowing that sooner or later it would be traced to him. The other notes he had intended to hold over till it was safe to send them out of the country; but the gold was the principal object of his theft.

Mr Tudway, the banker, was, I hear, so cut up about the false accusation that he had made against his favourite that he insisted on Franklin joining him as a partner at once, and the marriage is to take place before very long. I am also told that the photograph of the 'monkey man', handsomely enlarged and mounted, will form one of the mural decorations of the young couple.

Cheating the Gallows

ISRAEL ZANGWILL

They say that a union of opposites makes the happiest marriage, and perhaps it is on the same principle that men who chum together are always so oddly assorted. You shall find a man of letters sharing diggings with an auctioneer, and a medical student pigging with a stockbroker's clerk. Perhaps each thus escapes the temptation to talk 'shop' in his hours of leisure, while he supplements his own experiences of life by his companion's.

There could not be an odder couple than Tom Peters and Everard G. Roxdal—the contrast began with their names, and ran through the entire chapter. They had a bedroom and a sitting-room in common, but it would not be easy to find what else. To his landlady, worthy Mrs Seacon, Tom Peters's profession was a little vague, but everybody knew that Roxdal was the manager of the City and Suburban Bank, and it puzzled her to think why a bank manager should live with such a seedy-looking person, who smoked clay pipes and sipped whisky and water all the evening when he was at home. For Roxdal was as spruce and erect as his fellow-lodger was round-shouldered and shabby; he never smoked, and he confined himself to a small glass of claret at dinner.

It is possible to live with a man and see very little of him. Where each of the partners lives his own life in his own way, with his own circle of friends and external amusements, days may go by without the men having five minutes together. Perhaps this explains why these partnerships jog along so much more peaceably than marriages, where the chain is drawn so much tighter, and galls the partners rather than links them. Diverse, however, as were the hours and habits of the chums, they often breakfasted together, and they agreed in one thing—they never stayed out at night. For the rest Peters sought his diversions in the company of journalists, and frequented debating rooms, where he propounded the most iconoclastic views; while Roxdal had highly respectable houses open to him in the suburbs, and was, in fact, engaged to be married to Clara Newell, the charming daughter of a retired corn merchant, a widower with no other child.

Clara naturally took up a good deal of Roxdal's time, and he often dressed to go to the play with her, while Peters stayed at home in a faded dressing-gown and loose slippers. Mrs Seacon liked to see gentlemen about the house in evening dress, and made comparisons not favourable to Peters. And this in spite of the fact that he gave her infinitely less trouble than the younger man. It was Peters who first took the apartments, and it was characteristic of his easy-going temperament that he was so openly and naïvely delighted with the view of the Thames obtainable from the bedroom window, that Mrs Seacon was emboldened to ask twenty-five per cent more than she had intended. She soon returned to her normal terms, however, when his friend Roxdal called the next day to inspect the rooms, and over-whelmed her with a demonstration of their numerous shortcomings. He pointed out that their being on the ground floor was not an advantage, but a disadvantage, since they were nearer the noises of the street—in fact, the house being a corner one, the noises of two streets. Roxdal continued to exhibit the same finicking temperament in the petty details of the ménage. His shirt fronts were never sufficiently starched, nor his boots sufficiently polished. Tom Peters, having no regard for rigid linen, was always good-tempered and satisfied, and never acquired the respect of his landlady. He wore blue check shirts and loose ties even on Sundays. It is true he did not go to church, but slept on till Roxdal returned from morning service, and even then it was difficult to get him out of bed, or to make him hurry up his toilette operations. Often the mid-day meal would be smoking on the table while Peters would smoke in the bed, and Roxdal, with his head thrust through the folding doors that separated the bedroom from the sitting-room, would be adjuring the sluggard to arise and shake off his slumbers, and threatening to sit down without him, lest the dinner be spoilt. In revenge, Tom was usually up first on weekdays, sometimes at such unearthly hours that Polly had not yet removed the boots from outside the bedroom door, and would bawl down to the kitchen for his shaving water. For Tom, lazy and indolent as he was, shaved with the unfailing regularity of a man to whom shaving has become an instinct. If he had not kept fairly regular hours, Mrs Seacon would have set him down as an actor, so clean-shaven was he. Roxdal did not shave. He wore a full beard, and, being a fine figure of a man to boot, no uneasy investor could look upon him without being reassured as to the stability of the bank he managed so successfully. And thus the two men lived in an economical comradeship, all the firmer, perhaps, for their mutual incongruities.

It was on a Sunday afternoon in the middle of October, ten days after Roxdal had settled in his new rooms, that Clara Newell paid her first visit to him there. She enjoyed a good deal of liberty, and did not mind accepting his invitation to tea. The corn merchant, himself indifferently educated, had an exaggerated sense of the value of culture, and so Clara, who had artistic tastes without much actual talent, had gone in for painting, and might be seen, in pretty toilettes, copying pictures in the Museum. At one time it looked as if she might be reduced to working seriously at her art, for Satan, who finds mischief still for idle hands to do, had persuaded her father to embark the fruits of years of toil in bubble companies. However, things turned out not so bad as they might have been, a little was saved from the wreck, and the appearance of a suitor, in the person of Everard G. Roxdal, ensured her a future of competence, if not of the luxury she had been entitled to expect. She had a good deal of affection for Everard, who was unmistakably a clever man, as well as a good-looking one. The prospect seemed fair and cloudless. Nothing presaged the terrible storm that was about to break over these two lives. Nothing had ever for a moment come to vex their mutual contentment, till this Sunday afternoon. The October sky, blue and sunny, with an Indian summer sultriness, seemed an exact image of her life, with its aftermath of a happiness that had once seemed blighted.

Everard had always been so attentive, so solicitous, that she was as much surprised as chagrined to find that he had apparently forgotten the appointment. Hearing her astonished interrogation of Polly in the passage, Tom shambled from the sitting-room in his loose slippers and his blue check shirt, with his eternal clay pipe in his mouth, and informed her that Roxdal had gone out suddenly earlier in the afternoon.

'G-g-one out,' stammered poor Clara, all confused. 'But he asked me to come to tea.'

'Oh, you're Miss Newell, I suppose,' said Tom.

'Yes, I am Miss Newell.'

'He has told me a great deal about you, but I wasn't able honestly to congratulate him on his choice till now.'

Clara blushed uneasily under the compliment, and under the ardour of his admiring gaze. Instinctively she distrusted the man. The very first tones of his deep bass voice gave her a peculiar shudder. And then his impoliteness in smoking that vile clay was so gratuitous.

'Oh, then you must be Mr Peters,' she said in return. 'He has often spoken to me of you.'

'Ah!' said Tom, laughingly, 'I suppose he's told you all my vices. That accounts for your not being surprised at my Sunday attire.'

She smiled a little, showing a row of pearly teeth. 'Everard ascribes to you all the virtues,' she said.

'Now that's what I call a friend!' he cried, ecstatically. 'But won't you come in? He must be back in a moment. He surely would not break an appointment with *you*.' The admiration latent in the accentuation of the last pronoun was almost offensive.

She shook her head. She had a just grievance against Everard, and would punish him by going away indignantly.

'Do let *me* give you a cup of tea,' Tom pleaded. 'You must be awfully thirsty this sultry weather. There! I will make a bargain with you! If you will come in now, I promise to clear out the moment Everard returns, and not spoil your tête-à-tête.' But Clara was obstinate; she did not at all relish this man's society, and besides, she was not going to throw away her grievance against Everard. 'I know Everard will slang me dreadfully when he comes in if I let you go,' Tom urged. 'Tell me at least where he can find you.'

'I am going to take the bus at Charing Cross, and I'm going straight home,' Clara announced determinedly. She put up her parasol in a pet, and went up the street into the Strand. A cold shadow seemed to have fallen over all things. But just as she was getting into the 'bus, a hansom dashed down Trafalgar Square, and a well-known voice hailed her. The hansom stopped, and Everard got out and held out his hand.

'I'm so glad you're a bit late,' he said. 'I was called out unexpectedly, and have been trying to rush back in time. You wouldn't have found me if you had been punctual. But I thought,' he added, laughing, 'I could rely on you as a woman.'

'I *was* punctual,' Clara said angrily. 'I was not getting out of this 'bus, as you seem to imagine, but into it, and was going home.'

'My darling!' he cried remorsefully. 'A thousand apologies.' The regret on his handsome face soothed her. He took the rose he was wearing in the buttonhole of his fashionably cut coat and gave it to her.

'Why were you so cruel?' he murmured, as she nestled against him in the hansom. 'Think of my despair if I had come home to hear you had come and gone. Why didn't you wait a moment?'

A shudder traversed her frame. 'Not with that man, Peters!' she murmured.

'Not with that man, Peters!' he echoed sharply. 'What is the matter with Peters?'

'I don't know,' she said. 'I don't like him.'

'Clara,' he said, half sternly, half cajolingly, 'I thought you were above these feminine weaknesses; you are punctual, strive also to be reasonable. Tom is my best friend. From boyhood we have been always together. There is nothing Tom would not do for me, or I for Tom. You must like him, Clara; you must, if only for my sake.'

'I'll try,' Clara promised, and then he kissed her in gratitude and broad daylight.

'You'll be very nice to him at tea, won't you?' he said anxiously. 'I shouldn't like you two to be bad friends.'

'I don't want to be bad friends,' Clara protested; 'only the moment I saw him a strange repulsion and mistrust came over me.'

'You are quite wrong about him—quite wrong,' he assured her earnestly. 'When you know him better, you'll find him the best of fellows. Oh, I know,' he said suddenly, 'I suppose he was very untidy, and you women go so much by appearances!'

'Not at all,' Clara retorted. ''Tis you men who go by appearances.'

'Yes, you do. That's why you care for me,' he said, smiling.

She assured him it wasn't, and she didn't care for him so much as he plumed himself, but he smiled on. His smile died away, however, when he entered his rooms and found Tom nowhere.

'I daresay you've made him run about hunting for me,' he grumbled.

'Perhaps he knew I'd come back, and went away to leave us together,' she answered. 'He said he would when you came.'

'And yet you say you don't like him!'

She smiled reassuringly. Inwardly, however, she felt pleased at the man's absence.

If Clara Newell could have seen Tom Peters carrying on with Polly in the passage, she might have felt justified in her prejudice against him. It must be confessed, though, that Everard also carried on with Polly. Alas! it is to be feared that men are much of a muchness where women are concerned; shabby men and smart men, bank managers and journalists, bachelors and semi-detached bachelors. Perhaps it was a mistake after all to say the chums had nothing patently in common. Everard, I am afraid, kissed Polly rather more often than Clara, and although it was because he respected her less, the reason would perhaps not have been sufficiently consoling to his affianced wife. For Polly was pretty, especially on alternate Sunday afternoons, and when at ten p.m. she returned from her outings, she was generally met in the passage by one or other of the men. Polly liked to receive the homage of real gentlemen, and set her white cap at all indifferently. Thus, just before Clara knocked on that memorable Sunday afternoon, Polly, being confined to the house by the unwritten code regulating the lives of servants, was amusing herself by flirting with Peters.

'You *are* fond of me a little bit,' the graceless Tom whispered, 'aren't you?'

'You know I am, sir,' Polly replied.

'You don't care for anyone else in the house?'

'Oh no, sir, and never let anyone kiss me but you. I wonder how it is, sir?' Polly replied ingenuously.

'Give me another,' Tom answered.

She gave him another, and tripped to the door to answer Clara's knock.

And that very evening, when Clara was gone and Tom still out, Polly turned without the faintest atom of scrupulosity, or even jealousy, to the more fascinating Roxdal, and accepted his amorous advances. If it would seem at first sight that Everard had less excuse for such frivolity than his friend, perhaps the seriousness he showed in this interview may throw a different light upon the complex character of the man.

'You're quite sure you don't care for anyone but me?' he asked earnestly.

'Of course not, sir!' Polly replied indignantly. 'How could I?'

'But you care for that soldier I saw you out with last Sunday?'

'Oh no, sir, he's only my young man,' she said apologetically.

'Would you give him up?' he hissed suddenly.

Polly's pretty face took a look of terror. 'I couldn't, sir! He'd kill me. He's such a jealous brute, you've no idea.'

'Yes, but suppose I took you away from here?' he whispered eagerly. 'Somewhere where he couldn't find you—South America, Africa, somewhere thousands of miles across the seas.'

'Oh, sir, you frighten me!' whispered Polly, cowering before his ardent eyes, which shone in the dimly lit passage.

'Would you come with me?' he hissed. She did not answer; she shook herself free and ran into the kitchen, trembling with a vague fear.

One morning, earlier than his earliest hour of demanding his shaving water, Tom rang the bell violently and asked the alarmed Polly what had become of Mr Roxdal.

'How should I know, sir?' she gasped. 'Ain't he been in, sir?'

'Apparently not,' Tom answered anxiously. 'He never remains out. We have been here three weeks now, and I can't recall a single night he hasn't been home before twelve. I can't make it out.' All enquiries proved futile. Mrs Seacon reminded him of the thick fog that had come on suddenly the night before.

'What fog?' asked Tom.

'Lord! didn't you notice it, sir?'

'No, I came in early, smoked, read, and went to bed about eleven. I never thought of looking out of the window.'

'It began about ten,' said Mrs Seacon, 'and got thicker and thicker. I couldn't see the lights of the river from my bedroom. The poor gentleman has been and gone and walked into the water.' She began to whimper.

'Nonsense, nonsense,' said Tom, though his expression belied his words. 'At the worst I should think he couldn't find his way home, and couldn't get a cab, so put up for the night at some hotel. I daresay it will be all right.' He began to whistle as if in restored cheerfulness. At eight o'clock there came a letter for Roxdal, marked 'immediate', but as he did not turn up for breakfast, Tom went round personally to the City and Suburban Bank. He waited half-an-hour there, but the manager did not make his appearance. Then he left the letter with the cashier and went away with anxious countenance.

That afternoon it was all over London that the manager of the City and Suburban had disappeared, and that many thousand pounds of gold and notes had disappeared with him.

Scotland Yard opened the letter marked 'immediate', and noted that there had been a delay in its delivery, for the address had been obscure, and an official alteration had been made. It was written in a feminine hand and said: 'On second thoughts I cannot accompany you. Do not try to see me again. Forget me. I shall never forget you.'

There was no signature.

Clara Newell, distracted, disclaimed all knowledge of this letter. Polly deposed that the fugitive had proposed flight to her, and the routes to Africa and South America were especially watched. Some months passed without result. Tom Peters went about overwhelmed with grief and astonishment. The police took possession of all the missing man's effects. Gradually the hue and cry dwindled, died.

'At last we meet!' cried Tom Peters, while his face lit up in joy. 'How *are* you, dear Miss Newell?' Clara greeted him coldly. Her face had an abiding pallor now. Her lover's flight and shame had prostrated her for weeks. Her soul was the arena of contending instincts. Alone of all the world she still believed in Everard's innocence, felt that there was something more than met the eye, divined some devilish mystery behind it all. And yet that damning letter from the anonymous lady shook her sadly. Then, too, there was the deposition of Polly. When she heard Peters's voice accosting her all her old repugnance resurged. It flashed upon her that this man—Roxdal's boon companion—must know far more than he had told to the police. She remembered how Everard had spoken of him, with what affection and confidence! Was it likely he was utterly ignorant of Everard's movements? Mastering her repugnance, she held out her hand. It might be well to keep in touch with him; he was possibly the clue to the mystery. She noticed he was dressed a shade more trimly, and was smoking a meerschaum. He walked along at her side, making no offer to put his pipe out.

'You have not heard from Everard?' he asked. She flushed. 'Do you think I'm an accessory after the fact?' she cried.

'No, no,' he said soothingly. 'Pardon me, I was thinking he might have written—giving no exact address, of course. Men do sometimes dare to write thus to women. But, of course, he knows you too well—you would have put the police on his track.'

'Certainly,' she exclaimed, indignantly. 'Even if he is innocent he must face the charge.'

'Do you still entertain the possibility of his innocence?'

'I do,' she said boldly, and looked him full in the face. His eyelids drooped with a quiver. 'Don't you?'

'I have hoped against hope,' he replied, in a voice faltering with emotion. 'Poor old Everard! But I am afraid there is no room for doubt. Oh, this wicked curse of money—tempting the noblest and the best of us.'

The weeks rolled on. Gradually she found herself seeing more and more of Tom Peters, and gradually, strange to say, he grew less repulsive. From the talks they had together, she began to see that there was really no reason to put faith in Everard; his criminality, his faithlessness, were too flagrant. Gradually she grew ashamed of her early mistrust of Peters; remorse bred esteem, and esteem ultimately ripened into feelings so warm, that when Tom gave freer vent to the love that had been visible to Clara from the first, she did not repulse him.

It is only in books that love lives for ever. Clara, so her father thought, showed herself a sensible girl in plucking out an unworthy affection and casting it from her heart. He invited the new lover to his house, and took to him at once. Roxdal's somewhat supercilious manner had always jarred upon the unsophisticated corn merchant. With Tom the old man got on much better. While evidently quite as well informed and cultured as his whilom friend, Tom knew how to impart his superior knowledge with the accent on the knowledge rather than on the superiority, while he had the air of gaining much information in return. Those who are most conscious of defects of early education are most resentful of other people sharing their consciousness. Moreover, Tom's *bonhomie* was far more to the old fellow's liking than the studied politeness of his predecessor, so that on the whole Tom made more of a conquest of the father than of the daughter. Nevertheless, Clara was by no means unresponsive to Tom's affection, and when, after one of his visits to the house, the old man kissed her fondly and spoke of the happy turn things had taken, and how, for the second time in their lives, things had mended when they seemed at their blackest, her heart swelled with a gush of gratitude and joy and tenderness, and she fell sobbing into her father's arms.

Tom calculated that he made a clear five hundred a year by occasional journalism, besides possessing some profitable investments which he had inherited from his mother, so that there was no reason for delaying the marriage. It was fixed for May Day, and the honeymoon was to be spent in Italy.

But Clara was not destined to happiness. From the moment she had promised herself to her first love's friend old memories began to rise up and reproach her. Strange thoughts stirred in the depths of her soul, and in the silent watches of the night she seemed to hear Everard's accents, charged with grief and upbraiding. Her uneasiness increased as her wedding day drew near. One night, after a pleasant afternoon spent in being rowed by Tom among the upper reaches of the Thames, she retired to rest full of vague forebodings. And she dreamt a terrible dream. The dripping form of Everard stood by her bedside, staring at her with ghastly eyes. Had he been drowned on the passage to his land of exile? Frozen with horror, she put the question.

'I have never left England!' the vision answered.

Her tongue clove to the roof of her mouth.

'Never left England?' she repeated, in tones which did not seem to be hers.

The wraith's stony eyes stared on, but there was silence.

'Where have you been then?' she asked in her dream.

'Very near you,' came the answer.

'There has been foul play then!' she shrieked.

The phantom shook its head in doleful assent.

'I knew it!' she shrieked. 'Tom Peters—Tom Peters has done away with you. Is it not he? Speak!'

'Yes, it is he—Tom Peters—whom I loved more than all the world.'

Even in the terrible oppression of the dream she could not resist saying, woman-like:

'Did I not warn you against him?'

The phantom stared on silently and made no reply.

'But what was his motive?' she asked at length.

'Love of gold—and you. And you are giving yourself to him,' it said sternly.

'No, no, Everard! I will not! I will not! I swear it! Forgive me!'

The spirit shook its head sceptically.

'You love him. Women are false—as false as men.'

She strove to protest again, but her tongue refused its office.

'If you marry him, I shall always be with you! Beware!'

The dripping figure vanished as suddenly as it came, and Clara awoke in a cold perspiration. Oh, it was horrible! The man she had learnt to love, the murderer of the man she had learnt to forget! How her original prejudice had been justified! Distracted, shaken to her depths, she would not take counsel even of her father, but informed the police of her suspicions. A raid was made on Tom's rooms, and lo! the stolen notes were discovered in a huge bundle. It was found that he had several banking accounts, with a large, recently paid amount in each bank. Tom was arrested. Attention was now concentrated on the corpses washed up by the river. It was not long before the body of Roxdal came to shore, the face distorted almost beyond recognition by long immersion, but the clothes patently his, and a pocket-book in the breast-pocket removing the last doubt: Mrs Seacon and Polly and Clara Newell all identified the body. Both juries returned a verdict of murder against Tom Peters, the recital of Clara's dream producing a unique impression in the court and throughout the country. The theory of the prosecution was that Roxdal had brought home the money, whether to fly alone or to divide it, or whether even for some innocent purpose, as Clara believed, was immaterial. That Peters determined to have it all, that he had gone out for a walk with the deceased, and, taking advantage of the fog, had pushed him into the river, and that he was further impelled to the crime by love for Clara Newell, as was evident from his subsequent relations with her. The judge put on the black cap. Tom Peters was duly hung by the neck till he was dead.

Brief Résumé of the Culprit's Confession

When you all read this I shall be dead and laughing at you. I have been hung for my own murder. I am Everard G. Roxdal. I am also Tom Peters. We two were one. When I was a young man my moustache and beard wouldn't come. I bought false ones to improve my appearance. One day, after I had become manager of the City and Suburban Bank, I took off my beard and moustache at home, and then the thought crossed my mind that nobody would know me without them. I was another man. Instantly it flashed upon me that if I ran away from the Bank, that other man could be left in London, while the police were scouring the world for a non-existent fugitive. But this was only the crude germ of the idea. Slowly I matured my plan. The man who was going to be left in London must be known to a circle of acquaintance beforehand. It would be easy enough to masquerade in the evenings in my beardless condition, with other disguises of dress and voice. But this was not brilliant enough. I conceived the idea of living with him. It was Box and Cox reversed. We shared rooms at Mrs Seacon's. It was a great strain, but it was only for a few weeks. I had trick clothes in my bedroom like those of quick-change artistes; in a moment I could pass from Roxdal to Peters and from Peters to Roxdal. Polly had to clean two pairs of boots a morning, cook two dinners, etc., etc. She and Mrs Seacon saw one or the other of us every moment; it never dawned upon them they never saw us *both together*. At meals I would not be interrupted, ate off two plates, and conversed with my friend in loud tones. At other times we dined at different hours. On Sundays he was supposed to be asleep when I was in church. There is no landlady in the world to whom the idea would have occurred that one man was troubling himself to be two (and to pay for two, including washing). I worked up the idea of Roxdal's flight, asked Polly to go with me, manufactured that feminine letter that arrived on the morning of my disappearance. As Tom Peters I mixed with a journalistic set. I had another room where I kept the gold and notes till I mistakenly thought the thing had blown over. Unfortunately, returning from here on the night of my disappearance, with Roxdal's clothes in a bundle I intended to drop into the river, it was stolen from me in the fog, and the man into whose possession it ultimately came appears to have committed suicide. What, perhaps, ruined me was my desire to keep Clara's love, and to transfer it to the survivor. Everard told her I was the best of fellows. Once married to her, I would not have had much fear. Even if she had discovered the trick, a wife cannot give evidence against her husband, and often does not want to. I made none of the usual slips, but no man can guard against a girl's nightmare after a day up the river and a supper at the Star and

Garter. I might have told the judge he was an ass, but then I should have had penal servitude for bank robbery, and that is worse than death. The only thing that puzzles me, though, is whether the law has committed murder or I suicide.

Drawn Daggers

C. L. PIRKIS

'I admit that the dagger business is something of a puzzle to me, but as for the lost necklace—well, I should have thought a child would have understood that,' said Mr Dyer irritably. 'When a young lady loses a valuable article of jewellery and wishes to hush the matter up, the explanation is obvious.'

'Sometimes,' answered Miss Brooke calmly, 'the explanation that is obvious is the one to be rejected, not accepted.'

Off and on these two had been, so to speak, 'jangling' a good deal that morning. Perhaps the fact was in part to be attributed to the biting east wind, which had set Loveday's eyes watering with the gritty dust, as she had made her way to Lynch Court, and which was, at the present moment, sending the smoke, in aggravating gusts, down the chimney into Mr Dyer's face. Thus it was, however. On the various topics that had chanced to come up for discussion that morning between Mr Dyer and his colleague, they had each taken up, as if by design, diametrically opposite points of view.

His temper altogether gave way now.

'If,' he said, bringing his hand down with emphasis on his writing-table, 'you lay it down as a principle that the obvious is to be rejected in favour of the abstruse, you'll soon find yourself landed in the predicament of having to prove that two apples added to two other apples do not make four. But there, if you don't choose to see things from my point of view, that is no reason why you should lose your temper!'

'Mr Hawke wishes to see you, sir,' said a clerk, at that moment entering the room.

It was a fortunate diversion. Whatever might be the differences of opinion in which these two might indulge in private, they were careful never to parade those differences before their clients.

Mr Dyer's irritability vanished in a moment.

'Show the gentleman in,' he said to the clerk. Then he turned to Loveday. 'This is the Revd Anthony Hawke, the gentleman at whose house I told you Miss Monroe is staying temporarily. He is a clergyman of the Church of England, but gave up his living some twenty years ago when he married a wealthy lady. Miss Monroe has been sent over to his guardianship from Peking by her father, Sir George Monroe, in order to get her out of the way of a troublesome and undesirable suitor.'

The last sentence was added in a low and hurried tone, for Mr Hawke was at that moment entering the room.

He was a man close upon sixty years of age, white-haired, clean shaven, with a full, round face, to which a small nose imparted a somewhat infantine expression. His manner of greeting was urbane but slightly flurried and nervous. He gave Loveday the impression of being an easy-going, happy-tempered man who, for the moment, was unusually disturbed and perplexed.

He glanced uneasily at Loveday. Mr Dyer hastened to explain that this was the lady by whose aid he hoped to get to the bottom of the matter now under consideration.

'In that case there can be no objection to my showing you this,' said Mr Hawke; 'it came by post this morning. You see my enemy still pursues me.'

As he spoke he took from his pocket a big, square envelope, from which he drew a large-sized sheet of paper.

On this sheet of paper were roughly drawn, in ink, two daggers, about six inches in length, with remarkably pointed blades.

Mr Dyer looked at the sketch with interest.

'We will compare this drawing and its envelope with those you previously received,' he said, opening a drawer of his writing-table and taking thence a precisely similar envelope. On the sheet of paper, however, that this envelope enclosed, there was drawn one dagger only.

He placed both envelopes and their enclosures side by side, and in silence compared them. Then, without a word, he handed them to Miss Brooke, who, taking a glass from her pocket, subjected them to a similar careful and minute scrutiny.

Both envelopes were of precisely the same make, and were each addressed to Mr Hawke's London address in a round, schoolboyish, copy-book sort of hand—the hand so easy to write and so difficult to bring home to any writer on account of its want of individuality. Each envelope likewise bore a Cork and a London postmark.

Loveday laid down her glass.

'The envelopes,' she said 'have, undoubtedly, been addressed by the same person, but these last two daggers have not been drawn by the hand that drew the first. Dagger number one was, evidently, drawn by a timid, uncertain and inartistic hand—see how the lines wave and how they have been patched here and there. The person who drew the other daggers, I should say, could do better work: the outline, though rugged, is bold and free. I should like to take these sketches home with me and compare them again at my leisure.'

'Ah, I felt sure what your opinion would be!' said Mr Dyer complacently.

Mr Hawke seemed much disturbed.

'Good gracious!' he ejaculated; 'you don't mean to say I have two enemies pursuing me in this fashion! What does it mean? Can it be—is it possible, do you think, that these things have been sent to me by the members of some Secret Society in Ireland—under error, of course—mistaking me for someone else? They can't be meant for me; I have never, in my whole life, been mixed up with any political agitation of any sort.'

Mr Dyer shook his head. 'Members of secret societies generally make pretty sure of their ground before they send out missives of this kind,' he said. 'I have never heard of such an error being made. I think, too, we mustn't build any theories on the Irish postmark: the letters may have been posted in Cork for the whole and sole purpose of drawing off attention from some other quarter.'

'Will you mind telling me a little about the loss of the necklace?' here said Loveday, bringing the conversation suddenly round from the daggers to the diamonds.

'I think,' interposed Mr Dyer, turning towards her, 'that the episode of the drawn daggers—drawn in a double sense—should be treated entirely on its own merits, considered as a thing apart from the loss of the necklace. I am inclined to believe that when we have gone a little further into the matter we shall find that each circumstance belongs to a different group of facts. After all, it is possible that these daggers may have been sent by way of a joke—a rather foolish one, I admit—by some harum-scarum fellow bent on causing a sensation.'

Mr Hawke's face brightened. 'Ah! now, do you think so—really think so?' he ejaculated. 'It would lift such a load from my mind if you could bring the thing home, in this way, to some practical joker. There are a lot of such fellows knocking about the world. Why, now I come to think of it, my nephew, Jack, who is a good deal with us just now, and is not quite so steady a fellow as I should like him to be, must have a good many such scamps among his acquaintances.'

'A good many such scamps among his acquaintances,' echoed Loveday; 'that certainly gives plausibility to Mr Dyer's supposition. At the same time, I think we are bound to look at the other side of the case, and admit the possibility of these daggers being sent in right-down sober earnest by persons concerned in the robbery, with the intention of intimidating you and preventing full investigation of the matter. If this be so, it will not signify which thread we take up and follow. If we find the sender of the daggers we are safe to come upon the thief; or, if we follow up and find the thief, the sender of the daggers will not be far off.'

Mr Hawke's face fell once more.

'It's an uncomfortable position to be in,' he said slowly. 'I suppose, whoever they are, they will do the regulation thing, and next time will send an instalment of three daggers, in which case I may consider myself a doomed man. It did not occur to me before, but I remember now that I did not receive the first dagger until after I had spoken very strongly to Mrs Hawke, before the servants, about my wish to set the police to work. I told her I felt bound, in honour to Sir George, to do so, as the necklace had been lost under my roof.'

'Did Mrs Hawke object to your calling in the aid of the police?' asked Loveday.

'Yes, most strongly. She entirely supported Miss Monroe in her wish to take no steps in the matter. Indeed, I should not have come round as I did last night to Mr Dyer if my wife had not been suddenly summoned from home by the serious illness of her sister. At least,' he corrected himself, with a little attempt at self-assertion, 'my coming to him might have been a little delayed. I hope you understand, Mr Dyer; I do not mean to imply that I am not master in my own house.'

'Oh, quite so, quite so,' responded Mr Dyer. 'Did Mrs Hawke or Miss Monroe give any reasons for not wishing you to move in the matter?'

'All told, I should think they gave about a hundred reasons—I can't remember them all. For one thing, Miss Monroe said it might necessitate her appearing in the police courts, a thing she would not consent to do; and she certainly did not consider the necklace was worth the fuss I was making over it. And that necklace, sir, has been valued at over nine hundred pounds, and has come down to the young lady from her mother.'

'And Mrs Hawke?'

'Mrs Hawke supported Miss Monroe in her views in her presence. But privately to me afterwards she gave other reasons for not wishing the police called in. Girls, she said, were always careless with their jewellery, she might have lost the necklace in Peking, and never have brought it to England at all.'

'Quite so,' said Mr Dyer. 'I think I understood you to say that no one had seen the necklace since Miss Monroe's arrival in England. Also, I believe it was she who first discovered it to be missing?'

'Yes. Sir George, when he wrote apprising me of his daughter's visit, added a postscript to his letter, saying that his daughter was bringing her necklace with her, and that he would feel greatly obliged if I would have it deposited with as little delay as possible at my bankers', where it could be easily got at if required. I spoke to Miss Monroe about this two or three times, but she did not seem at all inclined to comply with her father's wishes. Then my wife took the matter in hand—Mrs Hawke, I must tell you, has a very firm, resolute manner—she told Miss Monroe plainly that she would not have the responsibility of those diamonds in the house, and insisted that there and then they should be sent off to the bankers'. Upon this Miss Monroe went up to her room, and presently returned, saying that her necklace had disappeared. She herself, she said, had placed it in her jewel-case and the jewel-case in her wardrobe, when her boxes were unpacked. The jewel-case was in the wardrobe right enough, and no other article of jewellery appeared to have been disturbed, but the little padded niche in which the necklace had been deposited was empty. My wife and her maid went upstairs immediately, and searched every corner of the room, but, I'm sorry to say, without any result.'

'Miss Monroe, I suppose, has her own maid?'

'No, she has not. The maid—an elderly native woman—who left Peking with her, suffered so terribly from seasickness that, when they reached Malta, Miss Monroe allowed her to land and remain there in charge of an agent of the P. and O. Company till an outward-bound packet could take her back to China. It seems the poor woman thought she was going to die, and was in a terrible state of mind because she hadn't brought her coffin with her. I dare say you know the terror these Chinese have of being buried in foreign soil. After her departure, Miss Monroe engaged one of the steerage passengers to act as her maid for the remainder of the voyage.'

'Did Miss Monroe make the long journey from Peking accompanied only by this native woman?'

'No; friends escorted her to Hong Kong—by far the roughest part of the journey. From Hong Kong she came on in the *Colombo*, accompanied only by her maid. I wrote and told her father I would meet her at the docks in London; the young lady, however, preferred landing at Plymouth, and telegraphed to me from there that she was coming on by rail to Waterloo, where, if I liked, I might meet her.'

'She seems to be a young lady of independent habits. Was she brought up and educated in China?'

'Yes; by a succession of French and American governesses. After her mother's death, when she was little more than a baby, Sir George could not make up his mind to part with her, as she was his only child.'

'I suppose you and Sir George Monroe are old friends?'

'Yes; he and I were great chums before he went out to China—now about twenty years ago—and it was only natural, when he wished to get his daughter out of the way of young Danvers's impertinent attentions, that he should ask me to take charge of her till he could claim his retiring pension and set up his tent in England.'

'What was the chief objection to Mr Danvers's attentions?'

'Well, he is only a boy of one-and-twenty, and has no money into the bargain. He has been sent out to Peking by his father to study the language, in order to qualify for a billet in the customs, and it may be a dozen years before he is in a position to keep a wife. Now, Miss Monroe is an heiress—will come into her mother's large fortune when she is of age—and Sir George, naturally, would like her to make a good match.'

'I suppose Miss Monroe came to England very reluctantly?'

'I imagine so. No doubt it was a great wrench for her to leave her home and friends in that sudden fashion and come to us, who are, one and all, utter strangers to her. She is very quiet, very shy, and reserved. She goes nowhere, sees no one. When some old China friends of her father's called to see her the other day, she immediately found she had a headache and went to bed. I think, on the whole, she gets on better with my nephew than with any one else.'

'Will you kindly tell me of how many persons your household consists at the present moment?'

'At the present moment we are one more than usual, for my nephew, Jack, is home with his regiment from India, and is staying with us. As a rule, my household consists of my wife and myself, butler, cook, housemaid, and my wife's maid, who just now is doing double duty as Miss Monroe's maid also.'

Mr Dyer looked at his watch.

'I have an important engagement in ten minutes' time,' he said, 'so I must leave you and Miss Brooke to arrange details as to how and when she is to begin her work inside your house, for, of course, in a case of this sort we must, in the first instance at any rate, concentrate attention within your four walls.'

'The less delay the better,' said Loveday. 'I should like to attack the mystery at once—this afternoon.'

Mr Hawke thought for a moment.

'According to present arrangements,' he said, with a little hesitation, 'Mrs Hawke will return next Friday, that is the day after tomorrow, so I can only ask you to remain in the house till the morning of that day. I'm sure you will understand that there might be some—some little awkwardness in——'

'Oh, quite so,' interrupted Loveday. 'I don't see at present that there will be any necessity for me to sleep in the house at all. How would it be for me to assume the part of a lady house decorator in the employment of a West End firm, and sent by them to survey your house and advise upon its redecoration? All I should have to do, would be to walk about your rooms with my head on one side, and a pencil and notebook in my hand. I should interfere with no one, your family life would go on as usual, and I could make my work as short or as long as necessity might dictate.'

Mr Hawke had no objection to offer to this. He had, however, a request to make as he rose to depart, and he made it a little nervously.

'If,' he said, 'by any chance there should come a telegram from

Mrs Hawke, saying she will return by an earlier train, I suppose—I hope, that is, you will make some excuse, and—and not get me into hot water, I mean.'

To this, Loveday answered a little evasively that she trusted no such telegram would be forthcoming, but that, in any case, he might rely upon her discretion.

Four o'clock was striking from a neighbouring church clock as Loveday lifted the old-fashioned brass knocker of Mr Hawke's house in Tavistock Square. An elderly butler admitted her and showed her into the drawing-room on the first floor. A single glance round showed Loveday that if her role had been real instead of assumed, she would have found plenty of scope for her talents. Although the house was in all respects comfortably furnished, it bore unmistakably the impress of those early Victorian days when aesthetic surroundings were not deemed a necessity of existence; an impress which people past middle age, and growing increasingly indifferent to the accessories of life, are frequently careless to remove.

'Young life here is evidently an excrescence, not part of the home; a troop of daughters turned into this room would speedily set going a different condition of things,' thought Loveday, taking stock of the faded white and gold wall paper, the chairs covered with lilies and roses in cross-stitch, and the knick-knacks of a past generation that were scattered about on tables and mantelpiece.

A yellow damask curtain, half-festooned, divided the back drawing-room from the front in which she was seated. From the other side of this curtain there came to her the sound of voices— those of a man and a girl.

'Cut the cards again, please,' said the man's voice. 'Thank you. There you are again—the queen of hearts surrounded with diamonds, and turning her back on a knave. Miss Monroe, you can't do better than make that fortune come true. Turn your back on the man who let you go without a word and——'

'Hush!' interrupted the girl with a little laugh: 'I heard the next room door open—I'm sure someone came in.'

The girl's laugh seemed to Loveday utterly destitute of that echo of heartache that in the circumstances might have been expected.

At this moment Mr Hawke entered the room, and almost simultaneously the two young people came from the other side of the yellow curtain and crossed towards the door.

Loveday took a survey of them as they passed.

The young man—evidently 'my nephew, Jack'—was a good-looking young fellow, with dark eyes and hair. The girl was small, slight, and fair. She was perceptibly less at home with Jack's uncle than she was with Jack, for her manner changed and grew formal and reserved as she came face to face with him.

'We're going downstairs to have a game of billiards,' said Jack, addressing Mr Hawke, and throwing a look of curiosity at Loveday.

'Jack,' said the old gentleman, 'what would you say if I told you I was going to have the house redecorated from top to bottom, and that this lady had come to advise on the matter?'

This was the nearest (and most anglice) approach to a fabrication that Mr Hawke would allow to pass his lips.

'Well,' answered Jack promptly, 'I should say, "Not before it's time." That would cover a good deal.'

Then the two young people departed in company.

Loveday went straight to her work.

'I'll begin by surveying at the top of the house, and at once, if you please,' she said. 'Will you kindly tell one of your maids to show me through the bedrooms? If it is possible, let that maid be the one who waits on Miss Monroe and Mrs Hawke.'

The maid who responded to Mr Hawke's summons was in perfect harmony with the general appearance of the house. In addition, however, to being elderly and faded, she was also remarkably sour-visaged, and carried herself as if she thought that Mr Hawke had taken a great liberty in thus commanding her attendance.

In dignified silence she showed Loveday over the topmost story, where the servants' bedrooms were situated, and, with a somewhat supercilious expression of countenance, watched her making various entries in her notebook.

In dignified silence, also, she led the way down to the second floor, where were the principal bedrooms of the house.

'This is Miss Monroe's room,' she said, as she threw back a door of one of these rooms, and then shut her lips with a snap, as if they were never going to open again.

The room that Loveday entered was like the rest of the house, furnished in the style that prevailed in the early Victorian period. The bedstead was elaborately curtained with pink-lined upholstery; the toilet table was befrilled with muslin and tarlatan out of all likeness to a table. The one point, however, that chiefly attracted Loveday's attention was the extreme neatness that prevailed throughout the apartment—a neatness, however, that was carried out with so strict an eye to comfort and convenience that it seemed to proclaim the hand of a first-class maid. Everything in the room was, so to speak, squared to the quarter of an inch, and yet everything that a lady could require in dressing lay ready to hand. The dressing-gown lying on the back of a chair had footstool and slippers beside it. A chair stood in front of the toilet table, and on a small Japanese table to the right of the chair were placed hairpin box, comb and brush, and hand mirror.

'This room will want money spent upon it,' said Loveday, letting her eyes roam critically in all directions. 'Nothing but Moorish woodwork will take off the squareness of those corners. But what a maid Miss Monroe must have! I never before saw a room so orderly and, at the same time, so comfortable.'

This was so direct an appeal to conversation that the sour-visaged maid felt compelled to open her lips.

'I wait on Miss Monroe, for the present,' she said snappishly; 'but, to speak the truth, she scarcely requires a maid. I never before in my life had dealings with such a young lady.'

'She does so much for herself, you mean—declines much assistance.'

'She's like no one else I ever had to do with.' (This was said even more snappishly than before.) 'She not only won't be helped in dressing, but she arranges her room every day before leaving it, even to placing the chair in front of the looking-glass.'

'And to opening the lid of the hairpin box, so that she may have the pins ready to her hand,' added Loveday, for a moment bending over the Japanese table, with its toilet accessories.

Another five minutes were all that Loveday accorded to the inspection of this room. Then, a little to the surprise of the dignified maid, she announced her intention of completing her survey of the bedrooms some other time, and dismissed her at the drawing-room door, bidding her tell Mr Hawke that she wished to see him before leaving.

Mr Hawke, looking much disturbed and with a telegram in his hand, quickly made his appearance.

'From my wife, to say she'll be back tonight. She'll be at Waterloo in about half an hour from now,' he said, holding up the brown envelope. 'Now, Miss Brooke, what are we to do? I told you how much Mrs Hawke objected to the investigation of this matter, and she is very—well—firm when she once says a thing, and—and——'

'Set your mind at rest,' interrupted Loveday; 'I have done all I wished to do within your walls, and the remainder of my investigation can be carried on just as well at Lynch Court or at my own private rooms.'

'Done all you wished to do?' echoed Mr Hawke in amazement; 'why, you've not been an hour in the house, and do you mean to tell me you've found out anything about the necklace or the daggers?'

'Don't ask me any questions just yet; I want you to answer one or two instead. Now, can you tell me anything about any letters Miss Monroe may have written or received since she has been in your house?'

'Yes, certainly. Sir George wrote to me very strongly about her correspondence, and begged me to keep a sharp eye on it, so as to nip in the bud any attempt to communicate with Danvers. So far, however, she does not appear to have made any such attempt. She is frankness itself over her correspondence. Every letter that has come addressed to her, she has shown either to me or to my wife, and they have one and all been letters from old friends of her father's, wishing to make her acquaintance now that she is in England. With regard to letter-writing, I am sorry to say she has a marked and most peculiar objection to it. Every one of the letters she has received, my wife tells me, remain unanswered still. She has never once been seen, since she came to the house, with a pen in her hand. And if she wrote on the sly, I don't know how she would get her letters posted—she never goes outside the door by herself, and she would have no opportunity of giving them to any of the servants to post except Mrs Hawke's maid, and she is beyond suspicion in such a matter. She has been well cautioned, and, in addition, is not the sort of person who would assist a young lady in carrying on a clandestine correspondence.'

'I should imagine not! I suppose Miss Monroe has been present at the breakfast table each time that you have received your daggers through the post—you told me, I think, that they had come by the first post in the morning?'

'Yes; Miss Monroe is very punctual at meals, and has been present each time. Naturally, when I received such unpleasant missives, I made some sort of exclamation and then handed the thing round the table for inspection and Miss Monroe was very much concerned to know who my secret enemy could be.'

'No doubt. Now, Mr Hawke, I have a very special request to make to you, and I hope you will be most exact in carrying it out.'

'You may rely upon my doing so to the very letter.'

'Thank you. If, then, you should receive by post tomorrow morning one of those big envelopes you already know the look of, and find that it contains a sketch of three, not two, drawn daggers——'

'Good gracious! what makes you think such a thing likely?' exclaimed Mr Hawke, greatly disturbed. 'Why am I to be persecuted in this way? Am I to take it for granted that I am a doomed man?'

He began to pace the room in a state of great excitement.

'I don't think I would if I were you,' answered Loveday calmly. 'Pray let me finish. I want you to open the big envelope that may come to you by post tomorrow morning just as you have opened the others—in full view of your family at the breakfast table—and to hand round the sketch it may contain for inspection to your wife, your nephew, and to Miss Monroe. Now, will you promise me to do this?'

'Oh, certainly; I should most likely have done so without any promising. But—but—I'm sure you'll understand that I feel myself to be in a peculiarly uncomfortable position, and I shall feel so very much obliged to you if you'll tell me—that is, if you'll enter a little more fully into an explanation.'

Loveday looked at her watch. 'I should think Mrs Hawke would be just at this moment arriving at Waterloo; I'm sure you'll be glad to see the last of me. Please come to me at my rooms in Gower Street tomorrow at twelve—here is my card. I shall then be able to enter into fuller explanations, I hope. Good-bye.'

The old gentleman showed her politely downstairs, and, as he shook hands with her at the front door, again asked, in a most emphatic manner, if she did not consider him to be placed in a 'peculiarly unpleasant position'.

Those last words at parting were to be the first with which he greeted her on the following morning when he presented himself at her rooms in Gower Street. They were, however, repeated in a considerably more agitated manner.

'Was there ever a man in a more miserable position!' he exclaimed, as he took the chair that Loveday indicated. 'I not only received the three daggers for which you prepared me, but I got an additional worry, for which I was totally unprepared. This morning, immediately after breakfast, Miss Monroe walked out of the house all by herself, and no one knows where she has gone. And the girl has never before been outside the door alone. It seems the servants saw her go out, but did not think it necessary to tell either me or Mrs Hawke, feeling sure we must have been aware of the fact.'

'So Mrs Hawke has returned?' said Loveday. 'Well, I suppose you will be greatly surprised if I inform you that the young lady, who has so unceremoniously left your house, is at the present moment to be found at the Charing Cross Hotel, where she has engaged a private room in her real name of Miss Mary O'Grady.'

'Eh! What! Private room! Real name O'Grady! I'm all bewildered!'

'It is a little bewildering; let me explain. The young lady whom you received into your house as the daughter of your old friend, was in reality the person engaged by Miss Monroe to fulfil the duties of her maid on board ship, after her native attendant had been landed at Malta. Her real name as I have told you is Mary O'Grady, and she has proved herself a valuable coadjutor to Miss Monroe in assisting her to carry out a programme, which she must have arranged with her lover, Mr Danvers, before she left Peking.'

'Eh! what!' again ejaculated Mr Hawke. 'How do you know all this? Tell me the whole story.'

'I will tell you the whole story first, and then explain to you how I came to know it. From what has followed, it seems to me that Miss Monroe must have arranged with Mr Danvers that he was to leave Peking within ten days of her so doing, travel by the route by which she came, and land at Plymouth, where he was to receive a note from her, apprising him of her whereabouts. So soon as she was on board ship, Miss Monroe appears to have set her wits to work with great energy; every obstacle to the carrying out of her programme she appears to have met and conquered. Step number one was to get rid of her native maid, who, perhaps, might have been faithful to her master's interests and have proved troublesome. I have no doubt the poor woman suffered terribly from seasickness, as it was her first voyage, and I have equally no doubt that Miss Monroe worked on her fears, and persuaded her to land at Malta, and return to China by the next packet. Step number two was to find a suitable person, who, for a consideration, would be willing to play the part of the Peking heiress among the heiress's friends in England, while the young lady herself arranged her private affairs to her own liking. That person was quickly found among the steerage passengers of the *Colombo* in Miss Mary O'Grady, who had come on board with her mother at Ceylon, and who, from the glimpse I had of her, must, I should conjecture, have been absent many years from the land of her birth. You know how cleverly this young lady has played her part in your house—how, without attracting attention to the matter, she has shunned the society of her father's old Chinese friends, who might be likely to involve her in embarrassing conversations; how she has avoided the use of pen and ink lest ——'

'Yes, yes,' interrupted Mr Hawke; 'but, my dear Miss Brooke, wouldn't it be as well for you and me to go at once to the Charing Cross Hotel, and get all the information we can out of her respecting Miss Monroe and her movements—she may be bolting, you know?'

'I do not think she will. She is waiting there patiently for an answer to a telegram she dispatched more than two hours ago to her mother, Mrs O'Grady, at 14 Woburn Place, Cork.'

'Dear me! dear me! How is it possible for you to know all this?'

'Oh, that last little fact was simply a matter of astuteness on the part of the man whom I have deputed to watch the young lady's movements today. Other details, I assure you, in this somewhat intricate case, have been infinitely more difficult to get at. I think I have to thank those "drawn daggers", that caused you so much consternation, for having, in the first instance, put me on the right track.'

'Ah—h,' said Mr Hawke, drawing a long breath; 'now we come to the daggers! I feel sure you are going to set my mind at rest on that score.'

'I hope so. Would it surprise you very much to be told that it was I who sent to you those three daggers this morning?'

'You! Is it possible?'

'Yes; they were sent by me, and for a reason that I will presently explain to you. But let me begin at the beginning. Those roughly drawn sketches, that to you suggested terrifying ideas of blood-shedding and violence, to my mind were open to a more peaceful and commonplace explanation. They appeared to me to suggest the

Herald's Office rather than the armoury; the cross fitchée of the knight's shield rather than the poniard with which the members of secret societies are supposed to render their recalcitrant brethren familiar. Now, if you will look at these sketches again, you will see what I mean.' Here Loveday produced from her writing-table the missives which had so greatly disturbed Mr Hawke's peace of mind. 'To begin with, the blade of the dagger of common life is, as a rule, at least two-thirds of the weapon in length; in this sketch, what you would call the blade does not exceed the hilt in length. Secondly, please note the absence of guard for the hand. Thirdly, let me draw your attention to the squareness of what you considered the hilt of the weapon, and what, to my mind, suggested the upper portion of a crusader's cross. No hand could grip such a hilt as the one outlined here. After your departure yesterday, I drove to the British Museum, and there consulted a certain valuable work on heraldry, which has more than once done me good service. There I found my surmise substantiated in a surprising manner. Among the illustrations of the various crosses borne on armorial shields, I found one that had been taken by Henri d'Anvers from his own armorial bearings, for his crest when he joined the Crusaders under Edward I, and which has since been handed down as the crest of the Danvers family. This was an important item of information to me. Here was some one in Cork sending to your house, on two several occasions, the crest of the Danvers family; with what object it would be difficult to say, unless it were in some sort a communication to some one in your house. With my mind full of this idea. I left the Museum and drove next to the office of the P. and O. Company, and requested to have given me the list of the passengers who arrived by the *Colombo*. I found this list to be a remarkably small one; I suppose people, if possible, avoid crossing the Bay of Biscay during the Equinoxes. The only passengers who landed at Plymouth besides Miss Monroe, I found, were a certain Mrs and Miss O'Grady, steerage passengers, who had gone on board at Ceylon on their way home from Australia. Their name, together with their landing at Plymouth, suggested the possibility that Cork might be their destination. After this I asked to see the list of the passengers who arrived by the packet following the *Colombo*, telling the clerk who attended to me that I was on the look-out for the arrival of a friend. In that second list of arrivals I quickly found my friend—William Wentworth Danvers by name.'

'No! The effrontery! How dared he! In his own name, too!'

'Well, you see, a plausible pretext for leaving Peking could easily be invented by him—the death of a relative, the illness of a father or mother. And Sir George, though he might dislike the idea of the young man going to England so soon after his daughter's departure, and may, perhaps, write to you by the next mail on the matter, was utterly powerless to prevent his so doing. This young man, like Miss Monroe and the O'Gradys, also landed at Plymouth. I had only arrived so far in my investigation when I went to your house yesterday afternoon. By chance, as I waited a few minutes in your drawing-room, another important item of information was acquired. A fragment of conversation between your nephew and the supposed Miss Monroe fell upon my ear, and one word spoken by the young lady convinced me of her nationality. That one word was the monosyllable "Hush."'

'No! You surprise me!'

'Have you never noted the difference between the "hush" of an Englishman and that of an Irishman? The former begins his "hush" with a distinct aspirate, the latter with as distinct a W. That W is a mark of his nationality which he never loses. The unmitigated "whist" may lapse into a "whish" when he is transplanted to another soil, and the "whist" may in course of time pass into a "whush", but to the distinct aspirate of the English "hush" he never attains. Now Miss O'Grady's was as pronounced a "whush" as it was possible for the lips of a Hibernian to utter.'

'And from that you concluded that Mary O'Grady was playing the part of Miss Monroe in my house?'

'Not immediately. My suspicions were excited, certainly; and when I went up to her room, in company with Mrs Hawke's maid, those suspicions were confirmed. The orderliness of that room was something remarkable. Now, there is the orderliness of a lady in the arrangement of her room, and the orderliness of a maid, and the two things, believe me, are widely different. A lady who has no maid, and who has the gift of orderliness, will put things away when done with, and so leave her room a picture of neatness. I don't think, however, it would for a moment occur to her to put things so as to be conveniently ready for her to use the next time she dresses in that room. This would be what a maid, accustomed to arrange a room for her mistress's use, would do mechanically. Now the neatness I found

in the supposed Miss Monroe's room was the neatness of a maid—
not of a lady, and I was assured by Mrs Hawke's maid that it was a
neatness accomplished by her own hands. As I stood there, looking at
that room, the whole conspiracy—if I may so call it—little by little
pieced itself together, and became plain to me. Possibilities quickly
grew into probabilities, and these probabilities once admitted, brought
other suppositions in their train. Now, supposing that Miss Monroe
and Mary O'Grady had agreed to change places, the Peking heiress,
for the time being, occupying Mary O'Grady's place in the humble
home at Cork and vice versa, what means of communicating with
each other had they arranged? How was Mary O'Grady to know
when she might lay aside her assumed role and go back to her
mother's house? There was no denying the necessity for such communication; the difficulties in its way must have been equally obvious
to the two girls. Now, I think we must admit that we must credit
these young women with having hit upon a very clever way of meeting
those difficulties. An anonymous and startling missive sent to you
would be bound to be mentioned in the house, and in this way a code
of signals might be set up between them that could not direct
suspicion to them. In this connection, the Danvers crest, which it is
possible that they mistook for a dagger, suggested itself naturally, for
no doubt Miss Monroe had many impressions of it on her lover's
letters. As I thought over these things, it occurred to me that possibly
dagger (or cross) number one was sent to notify the safe arrival of
Miss Monroe and Mrs O'Grady at Cork. The two daggers or crosses
you subsequently received were sent on the day of Mr Danvers's
arrival at Plymouth, and were, I should say, sketched by his hand.
Now, was it not within the bounds of likelihood that Miss Monroe's
marriage to this young man, and the consequent release of Mary
O'Grady from the onerous part she was playing, might be notified to
her by the sending of three such crosses or daggers to you? The idea
no sooner occurred to me than I determined to act upon it, forestall
the sending of this latest communication, and watch the result.
Accordingly, after I left your house yesterday, I had a sketch made of
three daggers or crosses exactly similar to those you had already
received, and had it posted to you so that you would get it by the first
post. I told off one of our staff at Lynch Court to watch your house,
and gave him special directions to follow and report on Miss
O'Grady's movements throughout the day. The results I anticipated

quickly came to pass. About half-past nine this morning the man sent a telegram to me saying that he had followed Miss O'Grady from your house to the Charing Cross Hotel, and furthermore had ascertained that she had since dispatched a telegram which (possibly by following the hotel servant who carried it to the telegraph office), he had overheard was addressed to Mrs O'Grady, at Woburn Place, Cork. Since I received this information an altogether remarkable cross-firing of telegrams has been going backwards and forwards along the wires to Cork.'

'A cross-firing of telegrams! I do not understand.'

'In this way. So soon as I knew Mrs O'Grady's address I telegraphed to her, in her daughter's name, desiring her to address her reply to 115A Gower Street, not to Charing Cross Hotel. About three-quarters of an hour afterwards I received in reply this telegram, which I am sure you will read with interest.'

Here Loveday handed a telegram—one of several that lay on her writing-table—to Mr Hawke.

He opened it and read aloud as follows:

Am puzzled. Why such hurry? Wedding took place this morning. You will receive signal as agreed tomorrow. Better return to Tavistock Square for the night.

'"The wedding took place this morning,"' repeated Mr Hawke blankly. 'My poor old friend! It will break his heart.'

'Now that the thing is done past recall we must hope he will make the best of it,' said Loveday. 'In reply to this telegram,' she went on, 'I sent another, asking as to the movements of the bride and bridegroom, and got in reply this.'

Here she read aloud as follows:

They will be at Plymouth tomorrow night; at Charing Cross Hotel the next day, as agreed.

'So, Mr Hawke,' she added, 'if you wish to see your old friend's daughter and tell her what you think of the part she has played, all you will have to do will be to watch the arrival of the Plymouth trains.'

'Miss O'Grady has called to see a lady and gentleman,' said a maid at that moment entering.

'Miss O'Grady!' repeated Mr Hawke in astonishment.

'Ah, yes, I telegraphed to her, just before you came in, to come here to meet a lady and gentleman, and she, no doubt thinking that she would find here the newly married pair, has, you see, lost no time in complying with my request. Show the lady in.'

'It's all so intricate—so bewildering,' said Mr Hawke, as he lay back in his chair. 'I can scarcely get it all into my head.'

His bewilderment, however, was nothing compared with that of Miss O'Grady, when she entered the room and found herself face to face with her late guardian, instead of the radiant bride and bridegroom whom she had expected to meet.

She stood silent in the middle of the room, looking the picture of astonishment and distress.

Mr Hawke also seemed a little at a loss for words, so Loveday took the initiative.

'Please sit down,' she said, placing a chair for the girl. 'Mr Hawke and I have sent for you in order to ask you a few questions. Before doing so, however, let me tell you that the whole of your conspiracy with Miss Monroe has been brought to light, and the best thing you can do, if you want your share in it treated leniently, will be to answer our questions as fully and truthfully as possible.'

The girl burst into tears. 'It was all Miss Monroe's fault from beginning to end,' she sobbed. 'Mother didn't want to do it—I didn't want to—to go into a gentleman's house and pretend to be what I was not. And we didn't want her hundred pounds——'

Here sobs checked her speech.

'Oh,' said Loveday contemptuously, 'so you were to have a hundred pounds for your share in this fraud, were you?'

'We didn't want to take it,' said the girl, between hysterical bursts of tears; 'but Miss Monroe said if we didn't help her some one else would, and so I agreed to——'

'I think,' interrupted Loveday, 'that you can tell us very little that we do not already know about what you agreed to do. What we want you to tell us is what has been done with Miss Monroe's diamond necklace—who has possession of it now?'

The girl's sobs and tears redoubled. 'I've had nothing to do with the necklace—it has never been in my possession,' she sobbed. 'Miss Monroe gave it to Mr Danvers two or three months before she left Peking, and he sent it on to some people he knew in Hong Kong, diamond merchants, who lent him money on it. Decastro, Miss Monroe said, was the name of these people.'

'Decastro, diamond merchant, Hong Kong. I should think that would be sufficient address,' said Loveday, entering it in a ledger; 'and I suppose Mr Danvers retained part of that money for his own use and travelling expenses, and handed the remainder to Miss Monroe to enable her to bribe such creatures as you and your mother, to practise a fraud that ought to land both of you in jail.'

The girl grew deadly white. 'Oh, don't do that—don't send us to prison!' she implored, clasping her hands together. 'We haven't touched a penny of Miss Monroe's money yet, and we don't want to touch a penny, if you'll only let us off! Oh, pray, pray, pray be merciful!'

Loveday looked at Mr Hawke.

He rose from his chair. 'I think the best thing you can do,' he said, 'will be to get back home to your mother at Cork as quickly as possible, and advise her never to play such a risky game again. Have you any money in your purse? No—well, then, here's some for you, and lose no time in getting home. It will be best for Miss Monroe—Mrs Danvers I mean—to come to my house and claim her own property there. At any rate, there it will remain until she does so.'

As the girl, with incoherent expressions of gratitude, left the room, he turned to Loveday.

'I should like to have consulted Mrs Hawke before arranging matters in this way,' he said a little hesitatingly; 'but still, I don't see that I could have done otherwise.'

'I feel sure Mrs Hawke will approve what you have done when she hears all the circumstances of the case,' said Loveday.

'And,' continued the old clergyman, 'when I write to Sir George, as, of course, I must immediately, I shall advise him to make the best of a bad bargain, now that the thing is done. "Past cure should be past care," eh, Miss Brooke? And, think! what a narrow escape my nephew, Jack, has had!'

The Greenstone God and the Stockbroker

FERGUS HUME

As a rule, the average detective gets twice the credit he deserves. I am not talking of the pictorial miracle-monger, but of the flesh and blood reality who is liable to err, and frequently proves such liability. You can take it as certain that a detective who sets down a clean run and no hitch as entirely due to his astucity is young in years, and still younger in experience. Older men, who have been bamboozled a hundred times by the craft of criminality, recognize the influence of Chance to make or mar. There you have it! Nine times out of ten, Chance does more in clinching a case than all the dexterity and mother-wit of the man in charge. The exception must be engineered by an infallible apostle. Such a one is unknown to me—out of print.

This opinion, based rather on collective experience than on any one episode, can be substantiated by several incontrovertible facts. In this instance, one will suffice. Therefore, I take the Brixton case to illustrate Chance as a factor in human affairs. Had it not been for that Maori fetich—but such rather ends than begins the story, therefore it were wise to dismiss it for the moment. Yet that piece of greenstone hanged—a person mentioned hereafter.

When Mr and Mrs Paul Vincent set up housekeeping at Ulster Lodge they were regarded as decided acquisitions to Brixton society. She, pretty and musical; he, smart in looks, moderately well off, and an excellent tennis player. Their antecedents, who were known as his father and her mother (both since deceased), had lived a life of undoubted middle-class respectability. The halo thereof still environed their children, who were, in consequence of such inherited grace and their own individualisms, much sought after by genteel Brixtonians. Moreover, this popular couple were devoted to each other, and even after three years of marriage still posed as lovers. This was as it should be, and by admiring friends and relations the Vincents were regarded as paragons of matrimonial perfection.

Vincent was a stockbroker, and therefore passed most of his time in the City.

Judge, then, of the commotion, when pretty Mrs Vincent was discovered in the study, stabbed to the heart. So aimless a crime were scarce imaginable. She had many friends, no known enemies, yet came to this tragic end. Closer examination revealed that the escritoire had been broken into, and Mr Vincent declared himself the poorer by two hundred pounds. Primarily, therefore, robbery was the sole object, but, by reason of Mrs Vincent's interference, the thief had been converted into a murderer.

So excellently had the assassin chosen his time, that such choice argued a close acquaintance with the domestic economy of Ulster Lodge. The husband was detained in town till midnight; the servants (cook and housemaid), on leave to attend wedding festivities, were absent till eleven o'clock. Mrs Vincent was therefore absolutely alone in the house for six hours, during which period the crime was committed. The servants discovered the body of their unfortunate mistress, and at once raised the alarm. Later on Vincent arrived, to find his wife dead, his house in possession of the police, and the two servants in hysterics. For that night nothing could be done, but at dawn a move was made towards elucidating the mystery. At this point I come into the story.

Instructed at nine to take charge of the case, by ten o'clock I was on the spot noting details and collecting evidence. Beyond removal of the body, nothing had been disturbed, and the study was in precisely the same condition as when the crime was discovered. I carefully examined the apartment, and afterwards interrogated the cook, the housemaid, and, lastly, the master of Ulster Lodge. The result gave me slight hope of securing the assassin.

The room (a fair-sized one looking out on a lawn between house and road) was furnished in cheap bachelor fashion. An old-fashioned desk placed at right angles to the window, a round table reaching nigh the sill, two armchairs, three of the ordinary cane-seated kind, and on the mantelpiece an arrangement of pipes, pistols, boxing gloves, and foils. One of these latter was missing.

A single glimpse showed how terrible a struggle had taken place before the murderer had overpowered his victim. The tablecloth lay disorderly on the floor, two of the lighter chairs were overturned, and the desk, with several drawers open, was considerably hacked about.

No key was in the door-lock facing the escritoire, and the window-snick was securely fastened.

Further search resulted in the following discoveries:

1. A hatchet used for chopping wood (found near the desk).
2. A foil with the button broken off (lying under the table).
3. A greenstone idol (edged under the fender).

The cook (defiantly courageous by reason of brandy) declared that she had left the house at four o'clock on the previous day, and had returned close on eleven. The back door (to her surprise) was open. With the housemaid she went to inform her mistress of this fact, and found the body lying midway between door and fireplace. At once she called in the police. Her master and mistress were a most attached couple, and (so far as she knew) had no enemies.

Similar evidence was obtained from the housemaid, with the additional information that the hatchet belonged to the wood-shed. The other rooms were undisturbed.

Poor young Vincent was so broken down by the tragedy that he could hardly answer my questions with calmness. Sympathizing with his natural grief, I interrogated him as delicately as was possible, and am bound to admit that he replied with remarkable promptitude and clearness.

'What do you know of this unhappy affair?' I asked, when we were alone in the drawing-room. He refused to stay in the study, as was surely natural under the circumstances.

'Absolutely nothing,' he replied. 'I went to the City yesterday at ten in the morning, and, as I had business to do told my wife I would not return till midnight. She was full of health and spirits when I last saw her, but now——' incapable of further speech he made a gesture of despair. Then, after a pause, added, 'Have you any theory on the subject?'

'Judging from the wrecked condition of the desk I should say robbery——'

'Robbery?' he interrupted, changing colour. 'Yes, that was the motive. I had two hundred pounds locked up in the desk.'

'In gold or notes?'

'The latter. Four fifties. Bank of England.'

'You are sure they have gone?'

'Yes! The drawer in which they were placed is smashed to pieces.'

'Did anyone know you had placed two hundred pounds therein?'

'No! Save my wife, and yet—ah!' he said, breaking off abruptly, 'that is impossible.'

'What is impossible?'

'I shall tell you when I hear your theory!'

'You got that notion out of novels of the shilling sort,' I answered dryly; 'every detective doesn't theorize on the instant. I haven't any particular theory that I know of. Whomsoever committed this crime must have known your wife was alone in the house, and that there was two hundred locked up in that desk. Did you mention these two facts to anyone?'

Vincent pulled his moustache in some embarrassment. I guessed by the action he had been indiscreet.

'I don't wish to get an innocent person into trouble,' he said at length, 'but I did mention it—to a man called Roy.'

'For what reason?'

'It is a bit of a story. I lost two hundred to a friend at cards, and drew four fifties to pay him. He went out of town, so I locked the money up in my desk for safety. Last night Roy came to me at the club, much agitated, and asked me to loan him a hundred. Said it meant ruin else. I offered him a cheque, but he wanted cash. I then told him I had left two hundred at home, so could not possibly lend it. He asked if he could not go to Brixton for it, but I said the house was empty, and——'

'But it wasn't empty,' I interrupted.

'I believed it would be! I knew the servants were going to that wedding, and thought my wife, instead of spending a lonely evening, would stay out and see a friend.'

'Well, and after you told Roy that the house was empty?'

'He went away, looking awfully cut up, and swore he must have the money at any price. But it is quite impossible he could have anything to do with this.'

'I don't know. You told him where the money was, and that the house was unprotected, as you thought. What was more probable than that he should have come down with the intention of stealing the money? If so, what follows? Entering by the back door, he takes the hatchet from the wood-shed to open the desk. Your wife, hearing a noise, discovers him in the study. In a state of frenzy, he snatches a foil from the mantelpiece, and kills her. Then decamps with the money. There is your theory, and a mighty bad one—for Roy.'

'You don't intend to convict him?' asked Vincent, quickly.

'Not on insufficient evidence! If he committed the crime and stole the money it is certain that, sooner or later, he will change the notes. Now if I had the numbers——'

'Here are the numbers,' said Vincent, producing his pocket-book. 'I always take the numbers of such large notes. But surely,' he added, as I copied them down—'surely you don't think Roy guilty?'

'I don't know. I should like to know his movements on that night.'

'I cannot tell you. He saw me at the Chestnut Club about seven o'clock, and left immediately afterwards. I kept my business appointment, went to the Alhambra, and then returned home.'

'Give me Roy's address, and describe his personal appearance?'

'He is a medical student, and lodges at No.——, Gower Street. Tall, fair-haired, a good-looking young fellow.'

'And his dress last night?'

'He wore evening dress, concealed by a fawn-coloured overcoat.'

I duly noted these particulars, and was about to take my leave when I recollected the greenstone idol. It was so strange an object to find in prosaic Brixton that I could not help thinking it must have come there by accident.

'By the way, Mr Vincent,' said I, producing the monstrosity, 'is this greenstone god your, property?'

'I never saw it before,' replied he, taking it in his hand. 'Is it—ah!' he added, dropping the idol, 'there is blood on it.'

''Tis the blood of your wife, sir. If it does not belong to you, it does to the murderer. From the position in which this was found I fancy it slipped out of his breast-pocket as he stood over his victim. As you see, it is stained with blood. He must have lost his presence of mind, else he would not have left behind so damning a piece of evidence. This idol, sir, will hang the assassin of Mrs Vincent.'

'I hope so, but, unless you are sure of Roy, do not mar his life by accusing him of this crime.'

'I certainly shall not convict him without sufficient proof,' I answered promptly, and so took my departure.

Vincent showed up very well in this preliminary conversation. Much as he desired to punish the criminal, yet he was unwilling to subject Roy to possibly unfounded suspicions. Had I not forced the club episode out of him I doubt whether he would have told it. As it was, the information gave me the necessary clue. Roy alone knew that the notes were in the escritoire, and imagined (owing to the mistake of Vincent) that the house was empty. Determined to have the money at any price (his own words), he but intended robbery, till the unexpected appearance of Mrs Vincent merged the lesser in the greater crime.

My first step was to advise the Bank that four fifty pound notes, numbered so and so were stolen, and that the thief or his deputy would probably change them within a reasonable period. I did not say a word about the crime, and kept all special details out of the newspapers; as the murderer would probably read up the reports, so as to shape his course by the action of the police, I judged it wiser that he should know as little as possible. Those minute press notices do more harm than good. They gratify the morbid appetite of the public, and put the criminal on his guard. Thereby the police work in the dark, but he—thanks to the posting up of special reporters— knows the doings of the law, and baffles it accordingly.

The greenstone idol worried me considerably. I wanted to know how it had got into the study of Ulster Lodge. When I knew that, I could nail my man. But there was considerable difficulty to overcome before such knowledge was available. Now a curiosity of this kind is not a common object in this country. A man who owns one must have come from New Zealand, or have obtained it from a New Zealand friend. He could not have picked it up in London. If he did, he would not carry it constantly about with him. It was therefore my idea that the murderer had received the idol from a friend on the day of the crime. That friend, to possess such an idol, must have been in communication with New Zealand. The chain of thought is some- what complicated, but it began with curiosity about the idol, and ended in my looking up the list of steamers going to the Antipodes. Then I carried out a little design which need not be mentioned at this moment. In due time it will fit in with the hanging of Mrs Vincent's assassin. Meanwhile, I followed up the clue of the banknotes, and left the greenstone idol to evolve its own destiny. Thus I had two strings to my bow.

The crime was committed on the twentieth of June, and on the twenty-third two fifty-pound notes, with numbers corresponding to those stolen, were paid into the Bank of England. I was astonished at the little care exercised by the criminal in concealing his crime, but still more so when I learned that the money was banked by a very respectable solicitor. Furnished with the address, I called on this gentleman. Mr Maudsley received me politely, and had no hesitation in telling me how the notes had come into his possession. I did not state my primary reason for the enquiry.

'I hope there is no trouble about these notes,' said he, when I explained my errand. 'I have had sufficient already.'

'Indeed, Mr Maudsley, and in what way?'

For answer he touched the bell, and when it was answered, 'Ask Mr Ford to step this way,' he said. Then, turning to me, 'I must reveal what I hoped to keep silent, but I trust the revelation will remain with yourself.'

'That is as I may decide after hearing it. I am a detective, Mr Maudsley, and, you may be sure, do not make these enquiries out of idle curiosity.'

Before he could reply, a slender, weak-looking young man, nervously excited, entered the room. This was Mr Ford, and he looked from me to Maudsley with some apprehension.

'This gentleman,' said Maudsley, not unkindly, 'comes from Scotland Yard about the money you paid me two days ago.'

'It is all right, I hope,' stammered Ford, turning red and pale and red again.

'Where did you get the money?' I asked, parrying this question.

'From my sister.'

I started when I heard this answer, and with good reason. My enquiries about Roy had revealed that he was in love with a hospital nurse whose name was Clara Ford. Without doubt she had obtained the notes from Roy, after he had stolen them from Ulster Lodge. But why the necessity of the robbery?

'Why did you get a hundred pounds from your sister?' I asked Ford.

He did not answer, but looked appealingly at Maudsley. That gentleman interposed.

'We must make a clean breast of it, Ford,' he said, with a sigh; 'if you have committed a second crime to conceal the first, I cannot help you. This time matters are not at my discretion.'

'I have committed no crime,' said Ford desperately, turning to me.

'Sir, I may as well admit that I embezzled one hundred pounds from Mr Maudsley to pay a gambling debt. He kindly and most generously consented to overlook the delinquency if I replaced the money. Not having it myself I asked my sister. She, a poor hospital nurse, had not the amount. Yet, as non-payment meant ruin to me, she asked a Mr Julian Roy to help her. He at once agreed to do so, and gave her two fifty-pound notes. She handed them to me, and I gave them to Mr Maudsley, who paid them into the bank.'

This, then, was the reason of Roy's remark. He did not refer to his own ruin, but to that of Ford. To save this unhappy man, and for love of the sister, he had committed the crime. I did not need to see Clara Ford, but at once made up my mind to arrest Roy. The case was perfectly clear, and I was fully justified in taking this course. Meanwhile, I made Maudsley and his clerk promise silence, as I did not wish Roy to be put on his guard by Miss Ford, through her brother.

'Gentlemen,' I said, after a few moments' pause, 'I cannot, at present, explain my reasons for asking these questions, as it would take too long, and I have no time to lose. Keep silent about this interview till tomorrow, and by that time you shall know all.'

'Has Ford got into fresh trouble?' asked Maudsley, anxiously.

'No, but someone else has.'

'My sister,' began Ford faintly, when I interrupted him at once.

'Your sister is all right, Mr Ford. Pray trust in my assistance; no harm shall come to her or to you, if I can help it—but, above all, be silent.'

This they readily promised, and I returned to Scotland Yard, quite satisfied that Roy would get no warning. The evidence was so clear that I could not doubt the guilt of Roy. Else how had he come into possession of the notes? Already there was sufficient proof to hang him, yet I also hoped to clinch the certainty by proving his ownership of the greenstone idol. It did not belong to Vincent, or to his dead wife, yet someone must have brought it into the study. Why not Roy, who, to all appearances, had committed the crime, the more so as the image was splashed with the victim's blood? There was no difficulty in obtaining a warrant, and with this I went off to Gower Street.

Roy loudly protested his innocence. He denied all knowledge of the crime and of the idol. I expected the denial, but was astonished at the defence he put forth. It was very ingenious, but so manifestly absurd that it did not shake my belief in his guilt. I let him talk himself out—which was perhaps wrong—but he would not be silent, and then took him off in a cab.

'I swear I did not commit the crime,' he said, passionately; 'no one was more astonished than I at the news of Mrs Vincent's death.'

'Yet you were at Ulster Lodge on the night in question?'

'I admit it,' he replied, frankly; 'were I guilty I would not do so. But I was there at the request of Vincent.'

'I must remind you that all you say now will be used in evidence against you.'

'I don't care! I will defend myself. I asked Vincent for a hundred pounds, and——'

'Of course you did, to give to Miss Ford.'

'How do you know that?' he asked, sharply.

'From her brother, through Maudsley. He paid the notes supplied by you into the bank. If you wanted to conceal your crime you should not have been so reckless.'

'I have committed no crime,' retorted Roy, fiercely. 'I obtained the money from Vincent, at the request of Miss Ford, to save her brother from being convicted for embezzlement.'

'Vincent denies that he gave you the money!'

'Then he lies. I asked him at the Chestnut Club for one hundred pounds. He had not that much on him, but said that two hundred were in his desk at home. As it was imperative that I should have the money on the night, I asked him to let me go down for it.'

'And he refused!'

'He did not. He consented, and gave me a note to Mrs Vincent, instructing her to hand me over a hundred pounds. I went to Brixton, got the money in two fifties, and gave them to Miss Ford. When I left Ulster Lodge, between eight and nine, Mrs Vincent was in perfect health, and quite happy.'

'An ingenious defence,' said I, doubtfully, 'but Vincent absolutely denies that he gave you the money.'

Roy stared hard at me to see if I were joking. Evidently the attitude of Vincent puzzled him greatly.

'That is ridiculous,' said he, quietly; 'he wrote a note to his wife instructing her to hand me the money.'

'Where is that note?'

'I gave it to Mrs Vincent.'

'It cannot be found,' I answered; 'if such a note were in her possession it would now be in mine.'

'Don't you believe me?'

'How can I against the evidence of those notes and the denial of Vincent?'

'But he surely does not deny that he gave me the money?'

'He does.'

'He must be mad,' said Roy, in dismay; 'one of my best friends, and to tell so great a falsehood. Why, if——'

'You had better be silent,' I said, weary of this foolish talk; 'if what you say is true, Vincent will exonerate you from complicity in the crime. If things occurred as you say, there is no sense in his denial.'

This latter remark was made to stop the torrent of his speech. It was not my business to listen to incriminating declarations, or to ingenious defences. All that sort of thing is for judge and jury; therefore I ended the conversation as above, and marched off my prisoner. Whether the birds of the air carry news I do not know, but they must have been busy on this occasion, for next morning every newspaper in London was congratulating me on my clever capture of the supposed murderer. Some detectives would have been gratified by this public laudation—I was not. Roy's passionate protestations of innocence made me feel uneasy, and I doubted whether, after all, I had the right man under lock and key. Yet the evidence was strong against him. He admitted having been with Mrs Vincent on the fatal night, admitted possession of two fifty pound notes. His only defence was the letter of the stockbroker, and this was missing—if, indeed, it had ever been written.

Vincent was terribly upset by the arrest of Roy. He liked the young man, and had believed in his innocence so far as was possible. But in the face of such strong evidence, he was forced to believe him guilty; yet he blamed himself severely that he had not lent the money, and so averted the catastrophe.

'I had no idea that the matter was of such moment,' he said to me, 'else I would have gone down to Brixton myself and given him the money. Then his frenzy would have spared my wife, and himself a death on the scaffold.'

'What do you think of his defence?'

'It is wholly untrue. I did not write a note, nor did I tell him to go to Brixton. Why should I, when I fully believed no one was in the house?'

'It was a pity you did not go home, Mr Vincent, instead of to the Alhambra.'

'It was a mistake,' he assented, 'but I had no idea Roy would attempt the robbery. Besides, I was under engagement to go to the theatre with my friend Dr Monson.'

'Do you think that idol belongs to Roy?'

'I can't say, I never saw it in his possession. Why?'

'Because I firmly believe that if Roy had not the idol in his pocket on that fatal night he is innocent. Oh, you look astonished, but the man who murdered your wife owns that idol.'

The morning after this conversation a lady called at Scotland Yard, and asked to see me. Fortunately, I was then in the neighbourhood, and, guessing who she was, afforded her the interview she sought. When all left the room she raised her veil, and I saw before me a noble-looking woman, somewhat resembling Mr Maudsley's clerk. Yet, by some contradiction of nature, her face was the more virile of the two.

'You are Miss Ford?' I said, guessing her identity.

'I am Clara Ford,' she answered quietly. 'I have come to see you about Mr Roy.'

'I am afraid nothing can be done to save him.'

'Something must be done,' she said passionately. 'We are engaged to be married, and all a woman can do to save her lover I will do. Do you believe him guilty?'

'In the face of such evidence, Miss Ford——'

'I don't care what evidence is against him,' she retorted; 'he is as innocent of the crime as I am. Do you think a man fresh from the committal of a crime would place the money won by that crime in the hands of the woman he professes to love? I tell you he is innocent.'

'Mr Vincent doesn't think so.'

'Mr Vincent!' said Miss Ford, with scornful emphasis. 'Oh, yes! I quite believe he would think Julian guilty.'

'Surely not if it were possible to think otherwise! He is, or rather was, a staunch friend to Mr Roy.'

'So staunch that he tried to break off the match between us. Listen to me, sir. I have told no one before, but I tell you now. Mr Vincent is a villain. He pretended to be the friend of Julian, and yet dared to make proposals to me—dishonourable proposals, for which I could have struck him. He, a married man, a pretended friend, wished me to leave Julian and fly with him.'

'Surely you are mistaken, Miss Ford. Mr Vincent was most attentive to his wife.'

'He did not care at all for his wife,' she replied, steadily. 'He was in love with me. To save Julian annoyance I did not tell him of the insults offered to me by Mr Vincent. Now that Julian is in trouble by an unfortunate mistake, Mr Vincent is delighted.'

'It is impossible. I assure you Vincent is very sorry to——'

'You do not believe me,' said she, interrupting. 'Very well, I shall give you proof of the truth. Come to my brother's rooms in Bloomsbury. I shall send for Mr Vincent, and if you are concealed you shall hear from his own lips how glad he is that my lover and his wife are removed from the path of his dishonourable passion.'

'I shall come, Miss Ford, but I think you are mistaken in Vincent.'

'You shall see,' she replied, coldly. Then, with a sudden change of tone, 'Is there no way of saving Julian? I am sure he is innocent. Appearances are against him, but it was not he who committed the crime. Is there no way—no way?'

Moved by her earnest appeal, I produced the greenstone idol, and told her all I had done in connection with it. She listened eagerly, and readily grasped at the hope thus held out to her of saving Roy. When in possession of all the facts she considered in silence for some two minutes. At the end of that time she drew down her veil and prepared to take her departure.

'Come to my brother's rooms in Alfred Place, near Tottenham Court Road,' said she, holding out her hand. 'I promise you that there you shall see Mr Vincent in his true character. Good-bye till Monday at three o'clock.'

From the colour in her face and the bright light in her eye, I guessed she had some scheme in her head for the saving of Roy. I think myself clever, but after that interview at Alfred Place I declare I am but a fool compared to this woman. She put two and two together, ferreted out unguessed-of evidence, and finally produced the most wonderful result. When she left me at this moment the greenstone idol was in her pocket. With that she hoped to prove the innocence of her lover and the guilt of another person. It was the cleverest thing I ever saw in my life.

The inquest on the body of Mrs Vincent resulted in a verdict of wilful murder against some person or persons unknown. Then she was buried, and all London waited for the trial of Roy. He was brought up and charged with the crime, reserved his defence, and in due course was committed for trial. Meantime I called on Miss Ford at the appointed time, and found her alone.

'Mr Vincent will be here shortly,' she said, calmly. 'I see Julian is committed for trial.'

'And has reserved his defence.'

'I will defend him,' said she, with a strange look in her face; 'I am not afraid for him now. He saved my unhappy brother. I am going to save him.'

'Have you discovered anything?'

'I have discovered a good deal. Hush! That is Mr Vincent,' she added, as a cab drew up to the door. 'Hide yourself behind this curtain, and do not appear until I give you the signal.'

Wondering what she was about to do, I concealed myself as directed. The next moment Vincent was in the room, and then ensued one of the strangest of scenes. She received him coldly, and motioned him to a seat. Vincent was nervous, but she might have been of stone, so little emotion did she display.

'I have sent for you, Mr Vincent,' she said, 'to ask your help in releasing Julian.'

'How can I help you,' he answered, in amazement—'willingly would I do so, but it is out of my power.'

'I don't think it is!'

'I assure you, Clara,' he began eagerly, when she cut him short.

'Yes, call me Clara! Say that you love me! Lie, like all men, and yet refuse to do what I wish.'

'I am not going to help Julian to marry you,' declared he, sullenly. 'You know that I love you—I love you dearly, I wish to marry you——'

'Is not that declaration rather soon after the death of your wife?'

'My wife is gone, poor soul, let her rest.'

'Yet you loved her?'

'I never loved her,' he said, rising to his feet. 'I love you! From the first moment I saw you I loved you. My wife is dead! Julian Roy is in prison on a charge of murdering her. With these obstacles removed there is no reason why we should not marry.'

'If I marry you,' she said, slowly, 'will you help Julian to refute this charge?'

'I cannot! The evidence is too strong against him!'

'You know he is innocent, Mr Vincent.'

'I do not! I believe he murdered my wife.'

'You believe he murdered your wife,' she reiterated, coming a step nearer and holding out the greenstone idol—'do you believe that he dropped this in the study when his hand struck the fatal blow?'

'I don't know!' he said, coolly glancing at the idol, 'I never saw it before.'

'Think again, Mr Vincent—think again. Who was it that went to the Alhambra at eight o'clock with Dr Monson, and met there the captain of a New Zealand steamer with whom he was acquainted?'

'It was I,' said Vincent, defiantly, 'and what of that?'

'This!' she said, in a loud voice. 'This captain gave you the greenstone idol at the Alhambra, and you stuffed it into your breast-pocket. Shortly afterwards you went down to Brixton, after the man whose death you had plotted. You repaired to your house, killed your unhappy wife, who received you in all innocence, took the balance of the money, hacked the desk, and then dropped by accident this idol which convicted you of the crime.'

During this speech she advanced step by step towards the wretched man, who, pale and anguished, retreated before her fury. He came right to my hiding place, and almost fell into my arms. I had heard enough to convince me of his guilt, and the next moment was struggling with him.

'It is a lie! a lie!' he said hoarsely, trying to escape.

'It is true!' said I, pinning him down. 'From my soul I believe you guilty.'

During the fight his pocket-book fell on the floor, and the papers therein were scattered. Miss Ford picked up one spotted with blood.

'The proof!' she said, holding it before us. 'The proof that Julian spoke the truth. There is the letter written by you which authorized your unhappy wife to give him one hundred pounds.'

Vincent saw that all was against him, and gave in without further struggles, like the craven he was.

'Fate is too strong for me,' he said, when I snapped the handcuffs on his wrists. 'I admit the crime. It was for love of you that I did it. I hated my wife, who was a drag on me, and I hated Roy, who loved you. In one sweep I thought to rid myself of both. His application for that money put the chance into my hand. I went to Brixton, found that my wife had given the money as directed, and then killed her with the foil snatched from the wall. I smashed the desk and over-turned the chair, to favour the idea of the robbery, and then left the house. Driving to a higher station than Brixton, I caught a train and was speedily back at the Alhambra. Monson never suspected my absence, thinking I was in a different corner of the house. I had thus an alibi ready. Had it not been for that letter, which I was fool enough to keep, and that infernal idol that dropped out of my pocket, I would have hanged Roy and married you. As it turns out the idol has betrayed me. And now, sir,' he added, turning to me, 'you had better take me to gaol.'

I did so there and then. After the legal formalities were gone through Julian Roy was released, and ultimately married Miss Ford. Vincent was hanged, as he well deserved to be, for so cowardly a crime. My reward was the greenstone god, which I keep as a memento of a very curious case. Some weeks later Miss Ford told me the way in which she had laid the trap.

'When you revealed your suspicions about the idol,' she said, 'I was convinced that Vincent had something to do with the crime. You mentioned Dr Monson as having been with him at the Alhambra. He is one of the doctors at the hospital in which I am employed. I asked him about the idol, and showed it to him. He remembered it being given to Vincent by the captain of the *K*——. The curious look of the thing had impressed itself on his memory. On hearing this I went to the docks and saw the captain. He recognized the idol, and remembered giving it to Vincent. From what you told me I guessed the way in which the plot was carried out, so spoke to Vincent as you heard. Most of it was guesswork, and only when I saw that letter was I absolutely sure of his guilt. It is due to the greenstone god.'

So I think, but also to Chance. But for the accident of it dropping out of Vincent's pocket, Roy would have been hanged for a crime of which he was innocent. Therefore do I say that in nine cases out of ten Chance does more in clinching a case than all the dexterity of the man in charge.

The Arrest of Captain Vandaleur

L. T. MEADE and ROBERT EUSTACE

One soft spring day in April I received a hurried message from Miss Cusack asking me to see her immediately.

It was a Sunday, I remember, and the trees were just putting on their first green. I arrived at the house in Kensington Park Gardens between four and five o'clock, and was admitted at once into the presence of my hostess. I found her in her library, a large room on the ground floor fitted with books from wainscot to ceiling, and quite unlike the ordinary boudoir of a fashionable lady.

'It is very good of you to come, Dr Lonsdale, and if it were not that my necessities are pressing, you may be sure I would not ask you to visit me on Sunday.'

'I am delighted to render you any assistance in my power,' I answered; 'and Sunday is not quite such a busy day with me as others.'

'I want you to see a patient for me.'

'A patient?' I cried.

'Yes; his name is Walter Farrell, and he and his young wife are my special friends; his wife has been my friend since her school-days. I want you to see him and also Mrs Farrell. Mrs Farrell is very ill—another doctor might do for her what you can do, but my real reason for asking you to visit her is in the hope that you may save the husband. When you see him you may think it strange of me to call him a patient, for his disease is more moral than mental, and is certainly not physical. His wife is very ill, and he still loves her. Low as he has sunk, I believe that he would make an effort, a gigantic effort, for her sake.'

'But in what does the moral insanity consist?' I asked.

'Gambling,' she replied, leaning forward and speaking eagerly. 'It is fast ruining him body and soul. The case puzzles me,' she continued. 'Mr Farrell is a rich man, but if he goes on as he is now doing he will soon be bankrupt. The largest fortune could not stand the drain he puts upon it. He is deliberately ruining both himself and his wife.'

'What form does his gambling take?' I asked.

'Horse racing.'

'And is he losing money?'

'He is now, but last year he unfortunately won large sums. This fact seems to have confirmed the habit, and now nothing, as far as we can tell, will check his downward career. He has become the partner of a bookmaker, Mr Rashleigh—they call themselves "Turf Commission Agents". They have taken a suite of rooms in Pall Mall, and do a large business. Disaster is, of course, inevitable, and for the sake of his wife I want to save him, and I want you to help me.'

'I will do what I can, of course, but I am puzzled to know in what way I can be of service. Men affected with moral diseases are quite out of an ordinary doctor's sphere.'

'All the same it is in your power to do something. But listen, I have not yet come to the end of my story. I have other reasons, and oddly enough they coincide. I know the history of the man whom Walter Farrell is in partnership with. I know it, although at present I am powerless to expose him. Mr Rashleigh is a notorious swindler. He has been in some mysterious way making enormous sums of money by means of horse-racing, and I have been asked to help the Criminal Investigation Department in the matter. The fact of poor Walter Farrell being in his power has given me an additional incentive to effect his exposure. Had it not been for this I should have refused to have anything to do with the matter.'

'What are Rashleigh's methods of working?' I asked.

'I will tell you. I presume you understand the principles of horse-racing?'

'A few of them,' I answered.

'Mr Rashleigh's method is this: He poses as a bookmaker in want of capital. He has had several victims, and Mr Farrell is his last. In past cases, when he secured his victim, he entered into partnership with him, took a place in the West End, and furnished it luxuriously. One of the Exchange Telegraph Company's tape machines which record the runners, winners, and the starting prices of the horses was introduced. As a matter of course betting men arrived, and for a time everything went well, and the firm made a good business. By degrees, however, they began to lose—time after time the clients backed winners for large sums, and Rashleigh and his partner finally failed. They were both apparently ruined, but after a time Rashleigh re-appeared again, got a fresh victim, and the whole thing went on as before. His present victim is Walter Farrell, and the end is inevitable.'

'But what does it mean?' I said. 'Are the clients who back the horses really conspirators in league with Rashleigh? Do you mean to imply that they make large sums and then share the profits with Rashleigh afterwards?'

'I think it highly probable, although I know nothing. But here comes the gist of the problem. In all the cases against this man it has been clearly proved that one client in particular wins to an extraordinary extent. Now, how in the name of all that is marvellous does this client manage to get information as to what horse will win for certain? and if this were possible in one case, why should he not go and break the ring at once?'

'You are evidently well up in turf affairs,' I replied, laughing, 'but frauds on the turf are so abundant that there is probably some simple explanation to the mystery.'

'But there is not,' she replied, somewhat sharply. 'Let me explain more fully, and then you will see that the chances of fraud are well-nigh at the vanishing point. I was at the office myself one afternoon. Walter Farrell took me in, and I closely watched the whole thing.

'It was the day of the Grand National, and about a dozen men were present. The runners and jockeys were sent through, and were called out by Mr Farrell, who stood by the tape machine; then he drew the curtain across. I made some small bets to excuse my presence there. The others all handed in their slips to him with the names of the horses they wished to back. The machine began clicking again, the curtain was drawn round it, and I will swear no one could possibly have seen the name of the winner as it was being printed on the tape. Just at the last moment, one of the men, a Captain Vandaleur—I know of him well in connection with more than one shady affair—went to the table with a slip, and handed it in. His was the last bet.

'The curtain was drawn back, and on Captain Vandaleur's slip was the name of the winning horse backed for five hundred pounds. The price was six to one, which meant a clear loss to Walter Farrell and Mr Rashleigh of three thousand pounds. The whole transaction was apparently as fair and square as could be, but there is the fact; and as the flat-racing season is just beginning, if this goes on Walter Farrell will be ruined before Derby Day.'

'You say, Miss Cusack, that no communication from outside was possible?'

'Certainly, no one entered or left the room. Communication from without is absolutely out of the question.'

'Could the sound of the clicking convey any meaning?'

She laughed.

'Absolutely none. I had at first an idea that an old trick was being worked—that is, by collusion with the operator at the telegraph office, who waited for the winner before sending through the runners and then sent the winning horse and jockey last on the list. But it is not so—we have made enquiries and had the clerks watched. It is quite incomprehensible. I am, I confess, at my wits' end. Will you help me to save Walter Farrell?'

'I will try, but I am afraid my efforts will be useless; he would resent my interference, and very naturally.'

'His wife is ill; I have told her that you will call on her. She knows that I hope much by your influence over her husband.'

'I will certainly visit Mrs Farrell, but only as an ordinary doctor goes to see a patient.'

'I believe you will do the rest when the time comes,' she answered. I made no reply. She took out her watch.

'The Farrells live not ten doors from here,' she said. 'Will you visit Mrs Farrell now? Walter will in all probability be at home as it is Sunday afternoon. Ask to see Mrs Farrell; I will write my name on your card, and you will be admitted immediately.'

'And am I to come back and tell you the result?' I asked.

'As you please. I shall be very glad to see you. Much depends on what you do.'

I saw by the expression on Miss Cusack's face how intensely in earnest she was. Her enthusiasm fired mine.

'I will go at once,' I said, 'and hope that luck may be with me.'

I left the house, and a few moments later was ringing the bell of No. 15 in the same road. A butler in livery opened the door, and on enquiring for Mrs Farrell I was admitted immediately. I sent up my card, and a moment later a quiet-looking woman tripped downstairs, came to my side, and said in a gentle, suppressed sort of voice—

'My mistress is in bed, doctor, but she will be pleased to see you. Will you follow me? Come this way, please.'

I followed the maid upstairs, we passed the drawing-room floor, and went up to the next storey. Here I was ushered into a large and luxuriously furnished bedroom. In a bed drawn near one of the windows where she could see the setting sun and some of the trees in Kensington Gardens, lay the pretty girl whom I was asked to visit. She could not have been more than nineteen years of age. Her brown hair lay tossed about the pillow, and her small, smooth, unlined face made her look more child than woman. A hectic spot burned on each of her cheeks, and when I touched her hand I knew at once that she was in a feverish and almost dangerous condition.

'So Florence Cusack has sent you, Dr Lonsdale,' was her remark to me.

'I am Dr Lonsdale. What can I do for you, Mrs Farrell?'

'Give me back my strength.'

The maid withdrew to a distant part of the room. I made the ordinary examination of the patient. I asked her what her symptoms were. She described them in a few words.

'I have no pain,' she said, 'but this intolerable weakness increases day by day. It has come on most gradually, and no medicines give me the least relief. A month ago I was well enough to go out, and even walk; then I found myself too tired even to drive in a carriage, then I was too weary to come downstairs, then too prostrate to sit up. Now I stay in bed, and it tires me even to speak. Oh! I am tired of everything,' she added; 'tired of life, tired of—' her eyes filled with tears—'tired of misery, of misery.'

To my dismay she burst into weak, hysterical crying.

'This will never do,' I said; 'you must tell me all, Mrs Farrell. As far as I can see, you have no active disease of any sort. What is the matter with you? What is consuming your life?'

'Trouble,' she said, 'and it is hopeless.'

'You must try to tell me more.'

She looked at me, dashed away her tears, and said, with a sudden spurt of spirit which I had scarcely given her credit for—

'But has not Florence Cusack told you?'

'She has certainly said something.'

'Ah, then you do know all; she said she would speak to you. My husband is downstairs in the smoking-room: go and see him—do what you can for him. Oh! he will be ruined, ruined body and soul. Save him! do save him if you can.'

'Do not excite yourself,' I said. I rose as I spoke, and laid my hand with a slight pressure on hers. 'You need not say any more. Between Miss Cusack and me your husband shall be saved. Now rest in that thought. I would not tell you a thing of this kind lightly.'

'Oh! God bless you,' murmured the poor girl.

I turned to the maid, who now came forward.

'I will write a prescription for your mistress,' I said, 'something to strengthen and calm her at the same time. You must sit up with her tonight, she is very weak.'

The maid promised. I left the room. The bright eyes of the almost dying girl followed me to the door. As I stood on the landing I no longer wondered at Miss Cusack's attitude in the matter. Surely such a case must stir the depths of the most callous heart.

I went downstairs, and unannounced entered the smoking-room. A man was lying back in a deep leather chair, near one of the windows. He was a dark, thin man, with features which in themselves were refined and handsome; but now, with the haggard lines round the mouth, in the deeply set, watchful, and somewhat narrow eyes, and in a sort of recklessness which was characterized by his untidy dress, by the very set of his tie, I guessed too surely that Miss Cusack had not exaggerated the mental condition of Mr Walter Farrell in the very least. With a few words I introduced myself.

'You must pardon this intrusion, Mr Farrell. I am Dr Lonsdale. Miss Cusack has asked me to call and see your wife. I have just seen her; I want to say a few words to you about her.'

He looked anxious just for a moment when I mentioned his wife's name, but then a sleepy indifference crept into his eyes. He was sufficiently a gentleman, however, to show me the ordinary politeness, and motioned me to a chair. I sat down and looked full at him.

'How old is Mrs Farrell?' I said, abruptly.

He stared as if he rather resented the question; then said, in a nonchalant tone—

'My wife is very young, she is not twenty yet.'

'Quite a child,' I said.

'Do you think so?'

'Yes, little more than a child—just on the verge of life. It seems very sad when the young must die.'

I would not have made use of this expression to an ordinary man, but I wanted to rouse and startle Farrell. I did so effectually. A veil seemed to drop from his eyes; they grew wide awake, restless, and agonized. He drew his chair close to mine, and bent forward.

'What do you mean? Surely there is not much the matter with Laura?'

'No active disease, and yet she is dying. I am sorry to tell you that, unless a complete change takes place immediately, she can scarcely live another week.'

Farrell sprang to his feet.

'You don't mean that!' he cried, 'my wife in danger! Dr Lonsdale, you are talking nonsense; she has no cough, she complains of nothing. She is just a bit lazy—that is what I tell her.'

'She has no strength, Mr Farrell, and without strength we cannot live. Something is eating into her life and draining it away. I will be perfectly frank with you, for in a case of life and death there is no time, nor is it right, to stand on ceremony. Your wife is dying because her heart is broken. It remains with you to save her; the case is in your hands.'

'Now what do you mean?'

'You know what I mean. She is unhappy about you. You must understand me.'

He turned very white.

'And yet I am doing all that man can for her,' he said. 'She expects me to smile always and live as a butterfly. Men have troubles and anxieties, and mine are—'

'Pretty considerable, I should say,' I continued.

'They are. Has Florence Cusack been talking to you about me?'

'I am not at liberty to answer your question.'

'You have answered it by not denying it. Florence and Laura are a pair of fools, the greatest fools that ever walked the earth.'

'You do not really think that.'

'I do think it. They want a man to do the impossible—they want a man to withdraw when—— There, Dr Lonsdale, you are a man and I can talk to you. I cannot do what they want.'

'Then your wife will die.'

He began to pace up and down the room.

'I suppose you know all about my connection with Rashleigh?' he said, after a moment.

I nodded.

'Well, then you see how I am placed. Rashleigh is hard up just now; I cannot desert him in a moment like the present. We hope to recoup ourselves this very week, and as soon as such is the case I will withdraw from the business. Will that content you?'

'Why not withdraw at once?'

'I cannot; nothing will induce me to do so. It is useless our prolonging this discussion.'

I saw that I should do harm instead of good if I said anything further, and, asking for a sheet of paper, I wrote a prescription for his wife. I then left the house to return to Miss Cusack.

The moment I entered her library she came eagerly to meet me.

'Well?' she said.

'You are right,' I answered, speaking now with great impulse and earnestness. 'I am altogether with you in this matter. I have seen Mrs Farrell and I have had an interview with Farrell. The wife is dying. Nay, do not interrupt me. She is dying unless relief comes soon. I had a long talk with Farrell and put the case plainly to him. He promises to withdraw from Rashleigh's firm, but not until after this week. He sticks to this resolve, thinking that he is bound in honour to support Rashleigh, whose affairs he believes are in a critical condition. In all probability before the week is up Mrs Farrell will die. What is to be done?'

'There is only one thing to be done, Dr Lonsdale—we must open Walter Farrell's eyes. We must show him plainly that he is Mr Rashleigh's dupe.'

'How can we do that?'

'Ah! there comes the crux of the whole situation. The further I go, the more mysterious the whole thing appears. The ordinary methods which have served me before have failed. Look here.'

She pointed to a page in the book of newspaper cuttings which lay by her side.

'Through channels I need not detail, I have learned that this is a communication of one of the gang to another.'

I took the book from her hands, and read the following words:

'*No mistake. Sea Foam. Jockey Club.*'

'Gibberish!' I said, laying the paper on the table.

'Apparently,' she answered; 'but Sea Foam is Captain Halliday's horse entered for the City and Suburban race to be run on the 21st—that is next Wednesday—at Epsom. For five continuous hours

I have worked at those few words, applying to them what I already know of this matter. It has been of no good.'

'I am scarcely surprised to hear you say so. One would want second sight to put meaning into words like those.'

'Something must be done, and soon,' she said. 'We must expose this matter on Wednesday. I know that Walter Farrell has lost heavily this month. There is not an hour to be lost in trying to save Laura. We must keep up her courage until Wednesday. On Wednesday the whole fraud must be discovered, and her husband liberated. You will help me?'

'Certainly.'

'Then on Wednesday we will go together to Mr Rashleigh's office. You must bet a little to allay suspicion—a few sovereigns only. You will then see him for yourself, and—who knows?—you may be able to solve the mystery.'

I agreed to this, and soon afterwards took my leave.

I received a note from Miss Cusack on Tuesday evening, asking me to lunch with her on the following day. I went. The moment I entered her presence I was struck, and almost startled, by her manner. An extraordinary exaltation seemed to possess her. The pupils of her eyes were largely dilated, and glowed as if some light were behind them. Her face was slightly flushed, and her conversation was marked by an unusual vivacity and sparkle.

'I have been very busy since I saw you last,' she said, 'and I have now every hope that I shall succeed. I fully believe that I shall save Walter Farrell today from the hands of one of the cleverest scoundrels in London,' she said, as we crossed the hall, 'and consign the latter to penal servitude.'

I could not help being much impressed by the matter-of-fact sangfroid with which Miss Cusack spoke the last words. How was she going to obtain such big results?

'Have you no fear of personal rudeness or violence?' I asked.

'None whatever—I have made all arrangements beforehand. You will soon see for yourself.'

We partook of lunch almost in silence. As I was returning to Miss Cusack's library afterwards I saw, seated in the hall, a short, squarely built, but well-dressed man.

'I shall be ready in a few moments, Mr Marling,' she said to him. 'Is everything prepared?'

'Everything, miss,' he replied.

Very soon afterwards we took our seats in Miss Cusack's brougham, and she explained to me that our companion was Inspector Marling, of Scotland Yard, that he was coming with us in the role of a new client for Messrs Rashleigh and Farrell, and that he had made all necessary preparations.

We drove rapidly along Knightsbridge, and, going into Piccadilly, turned down St James's Street. We stopped at last opposite a house in Pall Mall, which was to all appearance a private one. On either side of the door were brass plates bearing names, with the floor of the occupant engraved beneath. On one of the plates were the words, 'Rashleigh and Farrell, Third Floor.' Miss Cusack pressed the bell corresponding to this plate, and in a few moments a quietly dressed man opened the door. He bowed to Miss Cusack as if he knew her, looked at Marling and me with a penetrating glance, and then admitted us. We went upstairs to the third landing, though before we reached it the deep voices of men in the commission agent's suite of rooms fell on our ears. Here we rang again, and after what seemed a long delay the door, which was hung with a heavy velvet curtain on the inner side, was slowly opened. Farrell stood before us.

'I thought it must be you,' he said, the colour mounting into his thin face. 'Come inside; we are rather a large party, as it is an important race day.'

As I entered I looked round curiously. The room was thronged with a smartly dressed crowd of men and women who were lounging about in easy-chairs and on couches. The carpet was a rich Turkey pile, and the decorations were extravagantly gorgeous. At one side of the room near the wall stood a table upon which was a small gas lamp, several slips of paper, and a *Ruff's Racing Guide*. At the further end of the room, set back in a recess, stood the tape machine, which intermittently clicked and whirred while a long strip of paper, recording news automatically, unrolled from the little wheel and fell in serpentine coils into a wastepaper basket beneath.

At one glance I saw that, when the curtain that hung from a semicircular rod above it was drawn, no one in the room could possibly read what the wheel was printing on the tape.

'Let me introduce you to Captain Vandaleur, Dr Lonsdale,' said Miss Cusack's voice behind me.

I turned and bowed to a tall, clean-shaven man, who returned my salutation with a pleasant smile.

'You are, I presume, interested in racing?' he said.

'I am in this particular race,' I answered, 'the City and Suburban. I am anxious to make a small investment, and Miss Cusack has kindly introduced me to Mr Rashleigh for the purpose.'

'What particular horse do you fancy?' he asked.

'Lime-Light,' I replied, at a venture.

'Ha! an outsider; well, you'll get twenties,' and he turned away, for at that moment the runners for the first race began to come through. Farrell stood by the tape and called them out. Several of the men present now went to the table and wrote their fancies on the slips of paper and handed them to Farrell. Vandaleur did not bet.

I watched the whole proceeding carefully, and certainly fraud of any kind seemed out of the question.

Miss Cusack was evidently to all appearance evincing the keenest interest in the proceedings, and betted pretty heavily herself, although the horse she selected did not turn out the winner. Another race followed, and then at 3.30 the runners and jockeys for the great race came through. Heavy bets were made on all sides, and at 3.40 came the magic word 'Off', to signify that the race had started.

Farrell now instantly drew the curtain round the glass case of the instrument, while the bets continued to be made. Some were very heavy, running to hundreds of pounds. In a few moments the machine began clicking and whirring again, probably announcing the name of the winning horse.

'Have you all made your bets, gentlemen?' said Farrell.

'One moment,' cried Vandaleur, going to the table and writing out a slip. 'It's a poor chance, I know; but nothing venture, nothing win. Here goes for a monkey each way Sea Foam—and chance it.'

He crossed the room and handed Farrell the slip.

'All right, Vandaleur,' he replied, 'plunging heavily as usual. Now then, anyone else want to bet? I am going to draw back the curtain.'

No one answered. Farrell's face was pale, and an unmistakable air of nervousness pervaded him. Everyone pressed eagerly forward in order to be as close as possible to the instrument. Each man craned and peered over the other's shoulder. Farrell snatched back the curtain, and a shout of 'Sea Foam first!' rang through the room.

I looked at Miss Cusack. She was still standing by the table, and bending over the chimney of the gas-lamp. At this instant she turned and whispered a few words to Inspector Marling. He left the room quietly and unnoticed in the buzz of conversation that ensued.

Sea Foam's price was twenty to one, and Vandaleur had therefore scored £12,500.

I went up to Farrell, who was standing near the tape machine. I saw drops of perspiration on his forehead, and his face was like death.

'I am afraid this is a heavy blow to you,' I said.

He laughed with an assumption of nonchalance, then he looked me in the face and said slowly, 'It is. Vandaleur is invariably lucky.'

He had scarcely spoken the words before Inspector Marling reappeared. His face betrayed that something exciting was about to happen. What it was I could not guess. The next moment he had crossed the room, and going straight up to Vandaleur laid his hand on his shoulder, and said in a loud voice that rang through the room—

'Captain Vandaleur, I arrest you for conspiracy, and for fraudulently obtaining money by means of a trick.'

If a thunderbolt had fallen it could hardly have caused greater consternation.

Vandaleur started back.

'Who are you? What do you mean?' he cried.

'I am Inspector Marling, of Scotland Yard. Your game is up; you had better come quietly.'

The room was now in the utmost confusion. Two other men had made a dash for the door, only to fall into the arms of two officers who were waiting for them outside. Farrell, with an ashen face, stood like one struck dumb.

'For God's sake explain it all,' he said at last.

'Certainly,' answered Miss Cusack; 'it is simply this: You have been a dupe in one of the most daring and subtle frauds ever conceived. Come this way, I will show you everything.'

As she spoke she led the way from the room and up the stairs which led to the fourth floor. We all followed her and entered a room which was over the one we had just left. It was barely furnished as an office, and to our utter surprise it contained another tape machine, which was working like the one below.

'Dr Lonsdale,' said Miss Cusack, 'you remember the advertisement? "No mistake. Sea Foam. Jockey Club."'

'Perfectly,' I answered.

'When Jockey Club is mentioned in connection with horse-racing, one would naturally suppose that *the* Jockey Club was meant,' she continued. 'That was what puzzled me so long. But there is another kind of Jockey Club. Look here.' She pointed to an open box containing several small bottles, and took one out. Removing the glass stopper, she handed it to me.

'Do you recognize that scent?' she asked, as I sniffed at it.

'Perfectly,' I replied. 'Jockey Club, isn't it? Still, I feel in utter bewilderment.'

'Now I will explain what it means, and you will all, gentlemen, see how abilities can be used for the purposes of crime.'

She went across to a little square deal table that stood in the corner, and moved it aside. Behind one of the legs which had effectually concealed it was what appeared to be an ordinary piece of gas-pipe that passed through the floor. The upper end of it was open and was fitted with a screw for a nut.

'Now see, all of you,' she cried, 'this pipe communicates with the lamp on the table in the room below. When the gas is turned off downstairs there is a free passage. The man who keeps this office, and who, I fear, has contrived to escape, is in league with Captain Vandaleur, and both are, or rather were, in league with Rashleigh. These three scoundrels had a code, and this was their code. As soon as the winner came through, and the machine up here communicated the fact to the man in this room, a certain scent corresponding to a certain horse was sent down through the gas-pipe.

'In this case Jockey Club corresponded to Sea Foam. By means of this spray pump the vapour of the scent was passed down through the pipe to the lamp in the room below. Captain Vandaleur had only to bend over the chimney to get the scent, and write out the name of the horse which it corresponded to.'

To express our unbounded astonishment and our admiration for Miss Cusack's clever solving of the mystery would require more space than I have at my disposal. As to poor Farrell, his eyes were completely opened; he looked at us all with a wild stare, and the next moment I heard him dashing downstairs.

'But how did you discover it? What made you think of it?' I said to Miss Cusack some hours later.

'Ah! that is my secret. That I cannot explain to you, at least not yet,' was her reply.

Rashleigh and Vandaleur have been arrested, and both are now undergoing the punishment they so richly deserve. Farrell has learned his lesson: he has given up horse racing, and Mrs Farrell has recovered her strength, and also her youth and beauty.

The Accusing Shadow

HARRY BLYTH

'Ah, yes, my friend, success in our profession has its joys, but when one becomes my age, and has seen as much as I have of tragedy and evilness, fraud and generosity, dark plottings, and the grimmest of humour, repose offers delights which, in my younger years, were undreamed of by me. So it comes that now I say gladly, let my good partner, Sexton Blake, take the rewards and the honours, while I sit peacefully under my vine, and cultivate my garden.'

'In other words, Jules Gervaise, the most astute of cosmopolitan detectives, the expertest unraveller of mysteries, and the most profound of observers, will cease to be a terror to evil-doers, and those who seek his sage counsel and quick action will seek in vain.'

'That, my dear Saul Lynn, is precisely my determination. Unfortunately I have not quite settled where my vine shall grow, or in which particular part of Europe I shall raise my cabbages. Like most men who are at home in any part of the world. I have had no real home anywhere, so I have a wide choice before me.'

These two men—Jules Gervaise, of Paris, thin, wiry, alert, and wonderfully keen-eyed, and Saul Lynn, a stout, florid man, with rubicund, unwrinkled face, and short white hair, which stood up like bristles on a short brush—sat together in the latter's dining-room in a small comfortable house in the neighbourhood of Kennington Oval.

It was a heavy, gloomy afternoon, in the dreariest autumn London had known for some years, which is a great deal to allow; and both men regarded the fire which glowed in the grate with encouraging appreciation.

'In a few days I shall be pretty much in the same position as yourself, said Mr Lynn. 'When my dear daughter Daisy is married, I shall stand alone in the world, without chick or child. Two lone men might do worse than rent a house between them.'

'Indeed, yes,' replied Gervaise, without enthusiasm. 'Although we have not seen much of one another, our acquaintanceship dates from some years back. But, tell me, my friend, is your daughter's prospected union satisfactory to you both, and especially to her?'

'Bless me, yes! It is a most desirable match from every point of view. George Roach is older than Daisy, that is true, but he is a steady, generous man, wonderfully well off, and devoted to her. What more can any parent desire?'

'And the young lady returns his affection?'

'Of course. There had been some foolish flirtation between her and a young fellow named Rupert Peel, one of Mr Roach's clerks; but it was nothing worth speaking about, and when Mr Roach himself appeared on the scene, Rupert very properly ceased his visits. A worthy young man he is, but, unfortunately, poor.'

'This Mr Roach has been a very great friend to you, I suppose?'

'He literally saved me from ruin. Nothing but misfortune dogged me during all my business efforts in the City. But for the generous offices of Mr Roach, I should not now have a roof over my head, and my name would be stained with a very unsatisfactory bankruptcy. He was my principal creditor, and he proved at the critical moment to be my only friend. He got me out of the tangle. By his help my business was set on its legs again, and now he is soon to become my son-in-law, all indebtedness between us will be wiped out.'

'I see,' said Gervaise drily, shooting a keen glance at his companion. 'Your daughter's wedding will include that rare combination of a love-match enveloping a business necessity.'

Up to this moment the famous criminal investigator had spoken carelessly—lazily; but now his interest was aroused, for he was a man peculiarly solicitous about the happiness of young people. Often had he declared that it gave him more satisfaction to attend a funeral than to witness a marriage which did not promise real happiness to the bride and bridegroom. He came from a country where loveless unions were, alas! too common.

'Not a necessity, my dear Gervaise,' objected Saul Lynn, with a smile. 'Under no circumstances would Mr Roach have pressed his claims against me.'

'Such generous creditors are rare. Is it possible that I may be honoured with an introduction to your future son-in-law?

'Undoubtedly. In the ordinary way you would have seen him this evening, for he gives us a call nearly every night. Yesterday, however, he was summoned hurriedly to Glasgow. He left St Pancras by the night express. We have been expecting a telegram from him all day, announcing his safe arrival in Scotland. He is generally most particular about wiring to Daisy when he is away. He must be terribly busy not to have done so this time. I suppose we shall not hear now until the morning. Hullo! There's a knock at the front door. It's a telegraph boy, I'll be bound! They don't hesitate to give a double rat-tat, with all the confidence of a duke's footman. Dear me! it's Rupert Peel's voice. Something very strange must have happened to bring him here. Daisy has run to admit him. No doubt the poor child is anxious for news of George Roach.'

Mr Lynn's further reflections were cut short by the entrance of the two young people he had named.

Daisy was a fair, sunny creature, all grace and vivacity, with dazzling hair and bright eyes, in which the detective discerned more affection for her companion, Rupert Peel, than her father had any suspicion of. The young clerk himself was tall, lithe, with deep black locks, and strikingly large and luminous orbs, while his cheeks were peculiar for their perfect whiteness. His was a striking face, darkly handsome, but not altogether an alluring one, until he smiled, when a great light shone in it.

'We are anxious at the office about Mr Roach,' he explained to Saul Lynn. 'We have received a message from his Glasgow friends saying he has not called on them, and desiring to know the reason. We have wired to the manager of the hotel where he always stays, and he has not been there. On the other hand, it is quite certain Mr Roach arrived at St Pancras with his luggage in ample time for the train. It is also plain that while ten through tickets for Glasgow were issued for that express, only nine have been given up. So far this is all we are able to ascertain. I thought it just possible that you might be able to throw some light on this erratic behaviour of our principal. We know that he often thinks more of writing to you that to the office.'

'Indeed, I can give you no assistance. We have been very much surprised and disappointed at receiving no message from him. It's a strange business, Mr Peel. What do you make of it?'

As Mr Saul Lynn put this question, he looked more anxious than anyone there.

Jules Gervaise would have been singularly unobserving had be failed to note how absolutely unconcerned Daisy appeared to be.

'Really, sir, I have no suggestion at all to make,' returned Rupert Peel, 'and our Mr Felix Sark—he is our cashier, and the oldest servant in the firm—says that no doubt our principal changed his mind at the last moment, and, for some good reason, with which his employees have nothing to do. "Mr Roach is not a baby," says the cashier, "and no doubt he is safe enough." At any rate, it's not our business to tell him when he should communicate with us. He will let us know where he is in good time.'

'I quite agree with Mr Sark,' said Daisy decisively. 'Mr Roach is a well-travelled man, and if any accident had befallen him we should have heard of it. There is no occasion for alarm.'

'I am sure, my dear, I am glad to see you treat the matter so coolly,' said Saul Lynn, regarding his daughter with some displeasure. 'I am sure that something very unusual has occurred to our friend, or he would have written to you. However, I suppose we can do nothing but wait, and see what the morning brings forth.'

Just then someone called to see Mr Lynn on a small matter of business. He went into another room to have his interview with his visitor, and Daisy busied herself in preparing tea, to which Mr Rupert Peel had been invited, so the latter gentleman and Jules Gervaise were left together for a little.

'How are you progressing with your lessons in French, Mr Peel?' the detective asked, as carelessly as possible.

The clerk started slightly, and red spots burned in his white cheeks.

'How did you know I was learning French?'

'That is a simple matter enough. Whenever an Englishman determines to conquer the Parisian accent, he, quite unconsciously, gives a peculiar intonation to his native words, which he never gets in any other way. Yes, my friend, you are studying French, and because you contemplate taking a visit to Paris—Paris, the beautiful! Paris, the gay! Ah, yes!' Gervaise added, with that pathetic touch with which old men, so often tinge their recollections, 'I also have loved my Paris.'

'Your surmises are correct, sir. I have been studying your language. Mr Roach promised me a holiday while he was on his honeymoon, and I have resolved on seeking the distractions of the French capital, in the hope of forgetting there many things it is pain to remember here.'

'There is no forgetting,' declared the detective sagely. 'We cannot bring back a yesterday, because it lives eternally. Though we may not find it at the moment we want it, nevertheless it is stored up in one of those millions of secretive cells which go towards making up what we call brain, mind, memory. Now, be quite free with me, and tell me what you think of this coming wedding. I judge that George Roach is quite an old man—eh?'

'He is forty-eight. Daisy—Miss Lynn—is only nineteen.'

'What a gulf between! Now, had it been yourself——'

'Well, sir, to be quite frank with you, I had a true and honest affection for Miss Lynn. I believe I was not distasteful to her. I should have asked her in marriage from her father, had not Mr Roach informed me, in quite a casual way, that it was in his power to make Mr Lynn a beggar, and drive his daughter into the world to earn her bread. On that hint I ceased my visits. How could I have looked my darling confidently in the face, if she knew it was through me her father was going hungry? My income is small, and though I might have supported Daisy, I could not possibly have kept her father.'

'So,' said the detective, with a pleasant smile, 'if it should turn out that anything very serious has overtaken George Roach, our friend Saul Lynn will be relieved from his oppression, and you may yet be free to marry Daisy?'

'That is true,' said Rupert, with some hesitation, 'but I had never reckoned on my master's death.'

'Bah!' ejaculated Gervaise, 'a lover thinks of everything, and risks his life's happiness on a chance. You are inwardly praying now that George Roach may never be heard of again.'

'It is not in human nature for a man to be anxious for the success of his rival,' was the quiet, and even dignified, declaration of Rupert. 'But,' he added, 'at present there is no reason for supposing that anything at all out of the way has occurred to the gentleman who is so soon to call Daisy his wife.'

'Surely, my young friend, after having your waistcoat washed you have put it on before it was properly dry! See how it smokes before the blaze of the fire!'

'Really, sir!' protested the clerk, his white face crimsoning all over, 'your comments are uncommonly personal, and scarcely free from insolence. It is surely my own affair whether I have my waistcoat washed or not.'

'Certainly. But that material is not made to wash. It is two-thirds cotton, and all shoddy. It crinkles up as it dries. You will never be able to wear it again. If you listen to me you will put it into the first convenient fire you can use, and you will be careful to see that it is all consumed. There, there! do not fly into a temper. You will soon want my help and advice. Never forget that the smell of wet blood drying has an unmistakable odour to those who have even once known it.'

'You are a miracle—a wizard!' exclaimed Rupert, gazing aghast at the detective, and swaying before him with his fierce, inward agitation.

'Hush!' cried Gervaise, 'Saul Lynn is coming. I am neither of the things you call me. I am simply YOUR FRIEND!'

'The fellow who just called on me,' said Mr Lynn, as he reentered the room, his face more ruddy, and again beaming, 'came from the confectioner's, to arrange about the wedding-breakfast. I shall have a marquee erected in our back garden—indeed, I assure you, Gervaise, I am going to make this marriage quite a stylish thing—absolutely a function. Why, Mr Peel, do you want to leave us so suddenly? I quite understood you were going to remain for tea? Oh! well, if you remember you must go back to the office, I'll not detain you. Business before anything—especially Mr Roach's business. I do hope all is well with him,' he continued fervently, as he followed the clerk to the door, and let him out into the street, with an ill-disguised sigh of relief. 'I don't suppose there is any real cause for anxiety about my future son-in-law. Do you, Gervaise?' added Saul, as he once more returned to the room.

'I cannot tell,' was the grave answer. 'I shall be at St Pancras Station before eight tomorrow morning. The guard who took the Scotch express out of St Pancras last night will probably be returning from St Enoch to London tonight. If I see him he will be able to tell me whether Mr Roach was among his passengers or not.'

'Thank goodness you are so interested in my affairs!' cried Saul Lynn half-incredulously. 'But only an hour ago you declared you had cast all professional work aside. You were sure you would never more busy yourself with the concerns of others. Is the old instinct too strong for you? Must you for ever remain the detective?'

'No, no, my friend,' declared Gervaise gently. 'I hope not. I pray it may not be so. But your daughter is young; she is fair to gaze on. An atmosphere of goodness surrounds her. I should not like to see her stricken down by a great sorrow. Such enquiries as I may make in this affair shall be for Daisy's sake—for her sake only.'

'Of course I know Mr George Roach, sir,' said the guard of the Scotch express, whom the detective interviewed early on the following morning. 'He has often travelled to Glasgow with me. We know our "through" passengers, and they know us. I remember quite well seeing that gentleman's portmanteau and handbag, his rug, and his newspapers in the carriage which I had selected for him. I did not miss him until we reached Leicester. When I discovered that he was not in the train I took the gentleman's traps into my own van, and left them in the cloakroom at Glasgow when we arrived there. I thought he had stayed a little too long at Bedford, our first stopping-place, and so had missed us. Bless you, sir, some of our "regulars" often do that! Under such circumstances a gentleman does not bother much about his luggage, especially by the night train. He knows his things are safe enough in our hands. I did ask a question or two about Mr Roach when I was at Bedford this morning, and when I found he had not got out there I came to one very natural conclusion.'

'And what was that, pray?' asked Gervaise.

'Why, sir, that he did not travel with us. At the last moment something must have happened to make Mr Roach change his mind, and he abandoned our train before it left St Pancras. It's quite plain,' added the guard, 'folks don't disappear out of railway carriages, except in books. If your friend had committed suicide, we should have heard of the body by this time. Take my word for it, sir, he never started by that train at all.'

'My friend,' said Gervaise, as solemnly as though he was reading a funeral oration, 'you are gifted with monumental sense. I am quite sure Mr Roach never did leave London. It is quite refreshing for me to meet with such a piece of living sanity as yourself, but it is odd I should have to go to the guard of a Scotch express to find it. Ah!' added the detective to himself as he walked very thoughtfully along the Euston Road. 'I am glad I have no Sexton Blake with me. He would inevitably ride a bicycle, plunge into a stream, or stop an engine in full career, before he got to the end of this business. I must do my acrobatic feats in my head, and on the ground. Poor Daisy Lynn! I fear much there are some heavy revelations in store for her.'

Then, as though struck by a sudden thought, he walked into
Gower Street Station.

In following closely on Jules Gervaise's heels, in his steps to unravel
the desperate mystery which was soon to confront him, we shall find
it necessary to omit many touching interviews which he had with
Daisy, and also many of his conferences with her less unselfish
father. It will be sufficient if we give the salient features of the
celebrated detective's investigations.

In that labyrinth of narrow streets, with towering buildings, which
lies between Fore Street and Cheapside, where railway vans for ever
block the road, and great bales of 'soft' goods monopolize the pavement, might be found the warehouse of George Roach and Co.,
wholesale dealers in Manchester goods. It appeared to have been
accidentally jammed in between two larger buildings, and it wore a
constant look of pain, as though suffering from the tightness of the
squeeze.

It was one of those dark places where the gas is never extinguished
till the last stroke of business has struck, and there was so much
hurrying to and fro, and shouting out of marks and figures, that the
clerks gave one the idea of being in a perpetual state of altercation.

It was in the midst of this atmosphere, thick with commerce and
cotton-dust, that Jules Gervaise soon found himself enquiring for Mr
Felix Sark, the firm's cashier and oldest servant.

He proved to be a somewhat meagre individual, but sinewy withal.
The bottoms of his trousers showed a marked tendency to creep up
to his knees, while his sleeves were absolutely eager to get about his
neck.

He had a hairless, parchment-like face, and his eyes might have
been of glass for all the expression there was in them.

'No, sir,' he said, in answer to the detective's question, and regarding that worthy gentleman with scant favour, 'we have not received
any letter from Mr Roach this morning, but I have no doubt that our
principal will communicate with us in his own time. I trust you will
tell Mr Saul Lynn what I say. Mr Roach is not a baby, to be tied to
the coat-tails of his future father-in-law, and I may assure you, sir,
that when he knows that a stranger has been fussing round here
about his absence, he will be vastly indignant. Jules Gervaise is, if I
do not err, the name of a detective. That is so, eh? Very good, then. I

may tell you, sir, that you will not be paid for your meddling by this side. And, as for Mr Saul Lynn, if you expect anything from him I advise you to get it in advance. I have the pleasure of wishing you a very good-morning.'

'Good-day, my friend,' returned Gervaise, smiling blandly on the cashier. 'I look forward with great pleasure to meeting you again.'

As Jules was leaving the place he met Rupert Peel entering it. The young man's face expressed no pleasure at the encounter. With a cold 'Good morning', he would have passed on.

'There is still no news of Mr Roach,' said the detective, stopping him.

'So I believe,' was the indifferent answer. 'But at present there is no need for alarm,' Peel continued, 'and I am sure the governor will be very cross when he hears that Mr Lynn has engaged you to come down to the warehouse making enquiries about him. Mr Roach is a very passionate man, and such a liberty as he will judge your behaviour to be may be sufficient to make him break off the match.'

'Ah!' said Gervaise, with a dry smack of his lips, fixing the clerk with his keen eyes, 'Don't you think that Death may have already done that?'

'Really, Mr Gervaise, I have not the time nor the inclination to discuss the subject with you.'

He, too, hastened away from the detective, who still smiled blandly.

'I shall get no help there,' he murmured, 'and I am glad it is so. Their aid would be misleading, while their dislike to my interference is significant.'

'It is ridiculous for Mr Sark and young Peel to feel so confident that all is well with George Roach,' declared Saul Lynn, when Gervaise next saw him. 'I am convinced that something very serious has occurred. I know of nothing that would prevent him from writing to Daisy. As he seems never to have gone by that train, the mystery becomes deeper and more alarming. Thank goodness, my dear child does not realize all that his strange silence may mean.'

'I should like you to take me to his home—the place where he lived,' said Gervaise.

'That is easily done. Being a bachelor, he occupied furnished apartments in a good house, situated in Highbury Park. We will go there at once, my dear Gervaise, if you are willing.'

'Mr Roach gave up his rooms more than a week ago,' declared

Mrs Ballard, the landlady of the handsome villa at which they called and enquired about the missing man. 'Of course, you know, Mr Lynn, that he has taken a large, old-fashioned house in Canonbury, for your daughter to be mistress of. Well, he has furnished it from cellar to attic, and very beautifully, too, I believe. Latterly he has become nervous lest, as the place is empty, thieves should break into it, and so he determined to sleep there himself.'

'Alone?' asked Gervaise.

'Quite alone.'

'What a remarkable thing to do,' declared Mr Lynn. 'I suppose he said nothing to us for fear of alarming Daisy. Of course, we knew all about the house, and he was very anxious for my daughter to go over it. But the child has a superstitious notion that she must not enter her future home until she does so as its mistress.'

'I presume you found Mr Roach regular in his habits,' asked the detective.

'Most regular,' answered the lady. 'Had he been set by clockwork he could not have gone about his affairs more methodically. No club kept him out till early in the morning, though, of course, since he has been visiting at Mr Lynn's, we have not seen him home so early. I don't think, though, that he was a very happy man, for he used to be subject to long and silent fits of depression. Oh! by the way, Mr Lynn, he left an old scrapbook behind him. It's of no value to anyone but the owner, as the saying is, and not much to him, I should say. Perhaps you'll take it, sir, and give it to Mr Roach when he does make his reappearance?'

'I must enter that house at Canonbury,' said the detective, as he walked away with Saul Lynn.

'Well, so you shall, but I don't see how we can do it today. If George Roach has been sleeping there, he probably has the keys with him. I should not care to break into the place on my own responsibility. I must get some authority from the office before I will do that, so we must wait until tomorrow, at least. The worst part of this business is that no one has any legal right to set the law in motion to find our lost friend.'

The detective returned to Kennington with Mr Lynn, and there he interested himself in examining the pages of the scrapbook.

He found it to consist exclusively of extracts from the public journals, describing the almost innumerable exploits of a notorious adventuress, whose real name was Julia Barretti, but whose aliases were to be counted by the score.

She had been guilty of every variety of fraud, and had suffered various terms of imprisonment, long and short. Her beauty of face and figure was said to rival her deformity of character. She was a complete marvel of grace and wickedness.

Jules Gervaise wondered what peculiar fascination the sordid character of such a creature could have for a steady-going City merchant like Mr George Roach, till his brightened eyes lit on the following paragraph, when all his wonder vanished.

It ran as follows:

THE NOTORIOUS JULIA BARRETTI IN A NEW CHARACTER.—In our yesterday's issue we gave the trial of, and sentence passed on, this most expert and dangerous swindler, the more to be feared because of her extreme fascination of manner and appearance. We now learn that three days before her last arrest she had succeeded in luring into matrimony a well-to-do City merchant, named George Roach. The lady's capture by the police brought the honeymoon to an abrupt termination, and Mr Roach is to be congratulated on his escape from the clutches of such a designing harpy. The fact that she has another husband still living has been proved beyond a doubt; so the Court will have no hesitation in releasing the too-confiding City man from his bonds.'

'And that was sixteen years ago!' mused Gervaise. 'It is no wonder that George Roach sometimes looked pensive. This was the skeleton he had in his cupboard. It is more than possible I now hold a clue to the mystery of his disappearance.

When the notion of making a search in the house the missing man had taken in Canonbury was put before Mr Felix Sark, he very promptly, and with great decision, washed his hands of the matter.

'Do as you please, gentlemen,' he said, with a shrug of his lean shoulders, 'but I will be no party to such a desecration of what will yet prove to be my employer's happy and sacred home.'

Rupert Peel also begged to be excused from taking any part in the contemplated proceedings, on the plea that he was sure it was the last thing Mr Roach would care for him to do.

'Of course, Mr Roach has the keys of the house with him,' said Mr Lynn, 'so we shall have to break into it.'

'As for the keys,' answered Felix Sark, with an ugly laugh, 'they are hanging up over Mr Peel's desk.'

'I did not know that,' exclaimed Rupert, with a scared look. 'The master must have put them there before he started for Scotland.'

'If neither of you gentlemen will accompany us yourselves, perhaps there will be no objection to me asking some of the others engaged in the warehouse to do so?'

As Mr Lynn asked this question he took the keys from Rupert Peel's trembling hands, and wondered why that young man looked so faint and ill.

'Do as you please about that,' answered Mr Sark. 'Two of our travellers are on the premises now, and, as a traveller's time always seems to be his own, doubtless they will be glad of the outing. As for me, I have to keep strictly to my time. I am never late coming in nor early in leaving.'

'A very treasure of a cashier,' said Jules Gervaise, with his bland smile.

The gentlemen Mr Sark had alluded to were quite willing to accompany the detective and Saul Lynn to the old Gothic house in Canonbury, which they found to be standing in a goodly piece of ground, well hidden from the roadway by tall, umbrageous trees and rotund shrubs. But neither of the 'bagmen' appeared to merit the disparaging comments of the cashier. One, indeed, was so intent on his business that he carried his account-book with him, and utilized such spare moments as fell to him during the journey in making entries therein, and casting up accounts.

'This place could not be more silent or seemingly more remote were it in the midst of the Black Forest,' said Gervaise. 'My friends!' he cried, with sudden excitement, 'you must, if you please, refrain from mounting these steps leading to the front door. I see, impressed on the green mould which clothes them, the forms of three pairs of boots. These imprints may prove to be of splendid help to us, and they must not be disturbed or confused until we have photographs of them. Stay a few moments here, and I will admit you by the back way.'

The detective himself climbed up the left-hand parapet, which ran by the side of the steps to the main entrance. He sat on it while he bent down and turned the key in the lock. Then, having thrown the door open, he sprang into the house, landing on the mat in the hall, never once letting his feet touch the outside stone landing and steps.

His desire, born of professional pride, to be the first to enter that house, and to enter alone, was gratified.

He closed the door carefully and struck a light, for the vestibule was in darkness.

Nothing there attracted his attention, save the fact that, when he turned on the burner of the gas pendant, the illuminant issued freely from it, showing that it was not off at the meter. He went into a large room on the left-hand side, mainly because its door was wide open. Here he was sufficiently surprised to see that, though the blinds were drawn down, the shutters had not been closed.

'A man who is afraid of thieves breaking into his place does not leave it so unprotected, especially when he is going on a journey,' reflected the detective, as he lit the gas. 'Ah! what is this? The return half of a double ticket between Paris and London, issued by the tourist agents, Thomas Lock and Co. I will keep it. It should prove a valuable piece of paper. In the grate there are ashes of burned paper—stiff, clayey paper, like the pages of account-books. I will put this little cloth over the fireplace, so that those precious remains may not be blown away. Now I must admit my friends, or they will fancy I am committing crimes myself.'

Making his way to the back of the house, he let his companions in by the tradesmen's entrance, at the side of the building.

'There are evidences of a great struggle having taken place in one of the rooms of the hall,' he said. 'I think it will repay us to examine every part of this house very carefully.'

In the apartment which the detective had first entered there was every proof of a desperate conflict having taken place. Chairs were overturned, some vases broken, the hearthrug heeled up, and other unmistakable signs of disorder. There was some blood, too, on the fender, and on the edge of the table. All the other rooms were locked. They opened readily to the call of the keys the detective had with him. In no other part was there any sign of disturbance, or of recent occupation.

'Now, gentlemen, we will see what the basement has to tell us,' said Gervaise.

Every cupboard and cranny was carefully examined, by the detective, at least, but he found nothing which added to his existing knowledge, or which was even suggestive.

Presently they came to a great iron door let into the wall. It evidently guarded a strong-room, built in the house—a place in which former residents had stored their plate and jewels, perchance.

None of the others would have thought it worth while looking into this, but Jules Gervaise did.

'It is odd,' said he, 'that this bunch contains a key for the meanest cupboard in the house; yet the one to open this strong-room is not on the ring. Possibly it is not locked.'

He seized the big knob which stood out in the centre of the ponderous door, and, putting some strength into the attempt, managed to swing it slowly back, disclosing an iron-clad recess, into which the sun streamed through a small, heavily barred window, which looked out from the receptacle on to the bush-covered ground outside.

The four men thronged to the narrow opening, and, looking within, saw, to their horror, the mangled form of a dead man, whose name in life had been George Roach!

Natural it was that this ghastly discovery should produce more effect on Saul Lynn than on any of the others, though each one of them was inexpressibly shocked. But Saul had been the dead man's familiar friend, and, besides, the death of the merchant meant the shattering of Saul's hopes.

The detective was cool and scarcely surprised. His bland countenance was in queer contrast with the blank faces round him.

'Gentlemen,' he said gravely, 'it is not necessary for me to tell you that this is a case of murder—brutal and determined murder!'

'We must lose no time in informing the police!' cried one of the travellers, who was obviously a very excitable man.

'Of course, the police must know of this,' agreed Jules coolly, 'there is no help for it. But, first, I will see what the poor man has left in his pockets. Aha! Here are another set of keys belonging to the house. On this bunch is a key for the door of this strong-room. A significant and suggestive fact.'

'And observe,' said Mr Lynn, 'his rings are on his fingers, his watch and chain are untouched, and now you have found his purse with money in it. So robbery did not prompt this dreadful crime.'

'One may plunder a man, yet not condescend to pick his pockets,' declared Jules. 'Mr Roach's money does not amount to six pounds, all told. It is less than one would expect a man in his position to have with him when he contemplates a journey. There is no cheque-book here. Now, sir,' added Gervaise, to the excitable individual, 'since you are so anxious to see the police, perhaps you will walk round as far as the station and summon them.'

While Mr Lynn and the other traveller were asking one another, in fearful whispers, who could have done this fell deed, and their other companion set about the errand Jules had suggested to him, the detective very carefully gathered together the ashes he had seen in the grate in the room upstairs. He made a little box of brown paper for them, and this he put inside his hat. After this he busied himself in making a minute examination of the grounds at the back of the house, until the inspector at the station, with two of his men, made his appearance.

To him Jules Gervaise explained what had occurred. Nor did he fail to point out to these gentlemen the importance of not disturbing the footprints he had detected impressed on the green mould which covered the steps leading to the entrance-hall. But, even as he spoke, there came a fierce knocking at the front door, and it was soon seen that three other constables had followed their chief, and had come blundering up the marble ascent, to the utter destruction of those imprints which might have proved of such invaluable help in tracking down the assassin.

'Come,' said Gervaise to Saul Lynn, 'we can do no more good here. I want to return to Mr Roach's warehouse.'

'May Providence help me!' murmured Lynn, 'but this terrible tragedy leaves me a ruined man! I had counted too much on my daughter's marriage. Never was a man so doomed to misfortune as I am.'

'Let me forget how wretchedly selfish you are,' said the detective. 'Your losses are nothing compared with the misery this crime will cause others.'

'It will be a blow to my daughter, of course,' said Lynn, 'but she is young, and will soon get over it, whereas I am old. I need my little comforts, Jules! I need them very much!'

Jules smiled grimly.

'Poor human nature,' he muttered to himself, 'what a ragged thing you are at the core! It savours of madness for me to pursue this case, for I shall not get even the husks of thanks for my pains. But there is poor little Daisy! It would be wicked of me not to put out a hand to save her.'

When Mr Felix Sark heard this distressing news, his face took an expression of such profound consternation and grief that it did not seem possible it could be feigned.

'Gentlemen,' he declared, 'I have dreaded this news all along. It has been my waking fear, and the horror of my dreams. I appeared indifferent to you only because I did not want to have my shocking presentiment realized. Poor Mr Roach! Poor Mr Roach! No better employer ever lived. And then Rupert Peel—a mere boy—so amiable! so well-intentioned! so exact to his time! Think of him! I have loved him as a father might his son! It is too awful to dwell on!'

'What has happened to Rupert Peel?' asked Jules sternly.

'My dear sir, who can possibly have committed this monstrous crime but that most unhappy of young men? Driven insane by love; love and jealousy have done it. Mr Roach had not another enemy in the world, and poor Rupert did not hate him till he took Miss Lynn from him. You don't know how he loved Miss Daisy, sir,' he added, addressing Saul, 'you never would know! I am convinced he would not have survived her wedding-day. But, dear me! how much better for him to have died himself than to have slain his master. Oh! the misery of it! And what a disgrace to our firm!'

'You are quicker than the law will be in your condemnation!' said Gervaise sharply. 'What right have you to say that Rupert Peel is guilty of this murder?'

The old, quiet, sinister look came back to the cashier's face, as he replied:

'What I say to you, gentlemen—as friends taking an interest in my late employer—need not go any further, but I may tell you that since you were here this morning I have discovered in Peel's desk a key which belongs to the door of a safe or strong-room. It is still clammy with the dried blood which stains it. It is a sad piece of evidence against him, but of course, I must not hide it from the police. Would you advise me to do so, Mr Gervaise?'

'Certainly not,' replied Jules; 'but don't forget to tell them that you found it. I think it better for the police to discover such things for themselves. Is Mr Peel here now?'

'No. He went out soon after handing that bunch of keys to you. He has not come back. It is my impression that he never will.'

'I wonder if Sark is right,' said Saul Lynn, in a musing kind of way, as he and the detective elbowed their way through the narrow thoroughfare in which stood the premises of the late George Roach. 'I never thought that Rupert Peel had the pluck to kill a rabbit, much less a man. It's a horrible business altogether.'

'Yes,' answered Gervaise, in an abstracted way with the air of a man who is deeply pondering some problem. 'I want you to go at once to Rupert's house,' he added, with sudden life. 'If you find that he is preparing for flight be sure and make him see me before he takes that step or any other. I will go straight to Kennington, and break the news to Daisy. I will wait there for you. If you do manage to bring Rupert with you, all the better; but I fear that you are already too late—too late!'

'I suppose I must do as you wish,' said Lynn grumblingly, 'but, upon my word, I don't see why I should bother about young Peel.'

By this time they had reached Cheapside, and Jules put an effective stop to any further discussion on the subject by jumping into a passing cab, the driver of which he directed to take him to Saul's house at Kennington, leaving that gentleman to either look up Rupert Peel or follow on as he might choose, or as he best could.

Daisy listened to the horrible story the detective very gently broke to her with blanched cheeks. All its terribleness was reflected in her large, frightened eyes; but her voice was firm and clear, and she displayed no tendency to tears or towards any hysterical symptoms.

'It is very awful! very awful indeed! If it does not quite strike me down, helpless and broken, it is only because I never loved Mr Roach, and I looked with horror towards the day which was to see me his wife. He knew I did not love him. He was well aware that I agreed to marry him to save my father from ruin. This is the truth, my good friend, and it may be told now.'

'It is not news to me, any more than the fact that you do love Rupert Peel.'

'Ah, yes!' sighed the girl, burying her face in her hands. 'And I shall love him to the end of my days, as he will love me.'

'It is odd that he should have relinquished you so readily?'

'Not at all, Mr Gervaise. In the first place, he would not see my father a pauper, and myself reduced to such humble means as he is gaining; and, again, there is some mystery connected with his own father which compels him to say he will not marry anyone until his parent is dead. Ours was a hopeless case, you see, so there was little credit to me in resolving to do my duty to my father, and accept George Roach's offer.'

'Tell me, Daisy, tell me truthfully'—the voice of Jules Gervaise was most convincing and tender as he spoke—'tell me, without fear or hesitation, whether you think it possible that, driven to frenzy by the thought of the sacrifice you contemplated, made savage and reckless by the prospect of losing you for ever, Rupert Peel can have committed this crime?'

'It is impossible!' she declared, standing up, and elevating her hands to heaven, as though imploring the azure dome beyond the clouds to bear witness to her truth. 'It is absolutely impossible! There does not live a man less likely to spill human blood than Rupert. And yet—and yet!' she cried sinking again on to her chair, 'he knew that if anything did befall George Roach he would be accused of having done the mischief!'

'Did he tell you this?' asked Jules, with a slight start.

'Oh, yes. He told Mr Sark, too, and Mr Sark quite agreed with him. He was very frightened of you, though I did try to persuade him that you would prove his friend.'

'It will be more than he deserves, if I do,' said the detective sharply. 'Ah! here is your father; back at last. You may speak freely, Mr Lynn,' added the detective, as Saul, looking very flurried, entered the room. 'Your daughter knows all about the wretched tragedy.'

'Well,' said Mr Lynn, 'my news is startling enough, but I don't see that it helps us at all. Rupert Peel has undoubtedly made a clean bolt of it. A warrant has already been issued for his apprehension, and the evening papers are all alive with more or less imaginary accounts of the crime. But, what is more extraordinary, Rupert Peel's father lies dead in his house, and his head is battered about pretty much the same as is poor George Roach's.'

'Well, well,' said the imperturbable Jules, 'this is a rare complication. I must go away now. It may be some days ere you see me again. Keep up your heart, little one,' he said to Daisy, 'if your Rupert is innocent he shall not suffer.'

'Never mind Rupert!' cried Saul angrily. 'Where are you going to, Jules?'

'To Paris, my friend. I shall leave by tonight's express. If I am not mistaken, Mr Sark will call on you presently. It may be wise to welcome him.' He nodded to Daisy as he made this remark. 'There! that short, snappy, half-defiant, half-hesitating knock at the door must be directed by Sark's hand, and by no other.'

The detective's guess proved to be a correct one. The two men passed one another in the hall. Felix Sark was much better pleased to see Jules leave the house than the detective was to observe the cashier entering it.

It will be remembered that the kind-hearted detective had picked up, in the house where the luckless merchant lay murdered, the return portion of a ticket available between the capitals of England and France; and it scarcely need be told that he did not use it on his journey to Paris.

His first care, on his arrival in that city, was to call on the tourist agents who had issued it. As it bore their imprint, and their own number, he was hopeful that Thomas Lock and Company might be able to give him some clue as to the identity of the original purchaser.

'Ah, sir!' cried the clerk, when questioned, 'I have indeed cause for remembering that ticket from us. It was no less celebrated a personage than Madame Ollivier, the magnificence of whose receptions is the wonder and delight of our metropolis. Her superb equipage honoured our office by remaining outside it while she herself paid for the ticket.'

'Tell me,' said Jules, 'is this Madame Ollivier very beautiful?'

'She is incomparable! But, after all, it is not so much her face as the exquisite grace of her manner.'

'And, of course, a Frenchwoman?'

'Ah! Who can tell? I am told she can converse in all languages with equal charm and facility.'

The detective made his way to the offices of the secret police.

'My dear Jules Gervaise, I am delighted to see you,' cried the chief of the secret police, as he grasped our detective's hand with genuine warmth. 'And not the less so because you want information concerning that brilliant but mysterious woman, Madame Ollivier. Our positions are precisely similar. We also are most anxious to learn all we can about the lady, because, though she has succeeded in attracting some of the best people in France, we are convinced she is merely an adventuress. Her residence is the nest of a crowd of conspirators; and there they hatch their nefarious schemes against our Government.

'We want to put an end to these plots,' continued the chief, 'break up for ever these intrigues, and drive Madame Ollivier out of Paris. Now, Jules, you are the very man for our purpose. By helping us you will gain all the information you desire for yourself. You know quite well that, were we against you, it would be as well for you to return to England at once. It is a bargain, then? Very good. Now let us devise some good scheme that will enable you to enter Madame Ollivier's house this very night as a welcome and unsuspected guest.'

In one of the most fashionable quarters of Paris, standing in its own tastefully arranged grounds, hidden from the gaze of the vulgar by high walls and more lofty trees, stood the ornate building wherein Madame Ollivier had made her sumptuous home.

Here by the lavishness of her hospitality, and the brilliancy of her receptions, she had succeeded in capturing, dazzling, and alluring many of the most renowned men and women of the famous city. On this particular night, carriage after carriage had rolled to her gates, depositing on the rich carpet, which ran to the very gravel, its glittering occupant.

Light streamed from every window, while inside all was colour, movement, and melody. The very air seemed rich with delight and harmony.

But, even when the decorous revelry was at its height, the fascinating hostess, the much-applauded Madame Ollivier, withdrew from the crush of the distinguished guests, and, seating herself in a small, deserted ante-chamber, she sighed wearily. There was that pained expression about her features, too, which told how much relief her feelings would experience could she but let tears loosen the mental strain which made her temples throb.

'Do you think the English lord will come tonight?' she asked a swart, heavy-browed man, who followed her into this retreat.

But for the glamour of his surroundings, and the elegance of his apparel, he might very easily have passed for a common cut-throat, or for one of the meaner kind of brigands who infest Greece.

'He is late, but I do not yet despair of him,' answered Den Lockier. 'Oppression sits on my sister's brow, and the smile has fled from her lips.'

'It is no wonder,' answered Madame Ollivier sharply. 'Unless the big collection is made tonight, all our great schemes fall to the ground, and we must fly from Paris like hunted game, the laughing-stock of those who now drink our wine. Our tradesmen clamour for money, and nothing less than gold will now stop their demands. The day for promises has passed.'

'It is even as you say,' agreed the man, smiling sardonically, 'but the grand collection shall be made tonight. Gold shall replenish our coffers, and then, with our princely fortune, another country shall provide us with grateful ease. All our friends are here, my sister.'

'Except the English nobleman, and his purse is richer than all the others put together.'

'Ah! If I am not mistaken, he has this moment entered the house. Let us approach him. Surely it is he. Though I have never seen him, I could swear that he is the wealthy lord.'

'He is the only stranger we expect here tonight, so no doubt he is the one we have been so anxiously looking for. Welcome, my Lord Sellford, to Paris, and to my poor house,' she added, addressing an elaborately attired old gentleman, who had taken very obvious care to disguise his wrinkles, and to appear young.

'I presume I have the pleasure to address Madame Ollivier,' said he, adjusting his eye-glass, and surveying her with a look of unqualified approval. 'Delighted to make the acquaintance of so charming a lady. And this gentleman?'

'My brother.'

'Entirely at your service, my lord,' said the man, with a profound bow.

'That is very good of you, I am sure. I am afraid, madame, I have made a mistake in the night,' continued his lordship, lowering his voice. 'I understood that some trusty friends were to meet here in secret conclave tonight, to decide when the final and decisive blow at existing authority should be struck, but I find your house thronged with merry-makers.'

'Ah!' said madame, smiling sweetly on him, 'many a deep conspiracy has been hatched under the cloak of gay deception. While the music plays and the dance proceeds, our friends meet in a private part of the mansion. The fateful decision will be arrived at while the spies, who are everywhere, have their suspicions lulled by soft sounds and choice wines.'

'It is now the appointed hour,' said Den Lockier. 'If your lordship will condescend to follow me, I will lead the way.'

They passed through many effulgent rooms and strangely silent corridors, till they stood in the grounds, and the revelry within was no more than a low, faint murmur in the air.

'So the meeting place is not actually in your own house, madame?' said Lord Sellford, looking about him as well as the darkness would allow.

'It is not in the main building,' answered the lady, 'but it stands in my own grounds. We have to be very careful. Discovery would mean at least ruin to our friends, if not death.'

'Indeed, yes,' added Den Lockier, 'so the sooner we strike the blow the safer it will be for us all. Some of our contrivances are very cunning,' he went on. 'There does not appear to be any outlet from this garden, save through the house we have just left. A high, strong wall surrounds us. But do you see that huge tree which grows against the stonework at the end of the grounds? Its trunk is hollow. Its front bark slides back like a semicircular door. Observe! You see there is room for one person to pass at a time through the tree to an opening in the wall beyond, where steps lead into a building which looks out on to quite another street from the one my sister's house is in.'

'Capital!' chuckled his lordship.

'Yes.' agreed the other man, 'it is rather good. You see we could keep a man imprisoned for years in that building, and he would never be found.'

'Exactly! A most brilliant notion. But surely your friends are of more use to you free than in confinement.'

'Undoubtedly. But I was thinking how we could serve a traitor or a spy. Let me show your lordship the way in, or you may stumble. The light from the lantern shall guide you.'

Having ascended a few steps, the English aristocrat found himself in a long room, hung from floor to ceiling with black velvet. If there were any windows in the place this heavy drapery effectually concealed them. The carpet was also of a deep dark colour, and so thick and soft, that one's feet sank into it as into feathers, and it deadened all sound.

A large oval table stood in the middle of the room, and round this a number of men were gravely seated. At each end was an empty chair, and another one at the side. In the centre of the table stood a large, heavy-looking silver bowl.

'Lord Sellford!' said Madame Ollivier, in a low tone, as she entered the room, and presented his lordship.

The twelve guests rose, and bowed solemnly to the new arrival. He was motioned to take the vacant seat at the side, while madame arranged herself at what was presumably the head of the table; her brother took the chair at the other end, and facing her.

A few minutes passed in absolute and oppressive silence. Then Den Lockier rose, with much dignity, and addressed them in a most impressive manner.

'Gentlemen of the campaign,' said he, 'I need not at this late day recapitulate our aims or our fervent hopes. We are all in accord. The plan of our warfare has been agreed on. My Lord Sellford, who has missed the pleasure of our nightly conferences, has been advised of the progress we have made, and of the determination we have come to. That he approves of our resolves, and is willing to assist our efforts in the most practical way possible, is proved by his presence here now. One cannot, as we all know, initiate a conflict without those golden sinews of war which every nation finds to be of more importance than even its cannon or its soldiery. So, gentlemen, we have met tonight to contribute, each one of us, as much as we individually can towards the furtherance of the campaign we are pledged to support. We have each been furnished with a similar envelope. Into that envelope each gentleman will put his contribution, and cast it into the open bowl which is on the table. So no one will know what the other has given. But we are men of honour, and we shall be sure that each one has given to his utmost. Gentlemen, I cast my portion into the bowl, and my heart with it.'

With these words, and with dramatic action, he threw a well-filled envelope into the silver basin.

'My fortune follows my brother's!' cried Madame Ollivier, rising, and drawing from her bosom a packet similar to her brother's. As she dropped it into the receptacle she appeared to be overcome with emotion. With a sudden effort she snatched the diamond bracelet from her wrist, she plucked a magnificent spray of precious stones from her hair, and a glittering circle of gems from her throat. 'Let them all go!' she exclaimed grandly, dropping them on the top of the little parcel.

A light shone in madame's eyes which lit fires in the hearts of the hitherto impassive conspirators. This, combined with her emotional declamation, made them start to their feet as one man. Each one of them produced his packet.

'Hold!' cried a small, weazened-faced man. 'Hold! I beseech you!'

A dead silence followed this intimation. Anxious faces were turned on the speaker.

'Gentlemen,' he continued, with most grave mien, 'I am pained to have to tell you that we are BETRAYED!'

'Betrayed!' repeated the conspirators,' and each one replaced his contribution in his most secret pocket.

'Yes, gentlemen,' continued the little old man, 'betrayed!'

'By whom? By whom?'

Each man now felt stealthily for his revolver, and friend eyed friend with suspicion.

Lord Sellford, the English nobleman, is not with us!' screamed the little gentleman, and every eye was turned on his lordship, who had remained in his seat calm—imperturbable.

'That man who has taken his name, who has adopted his mincing airs, who has personified his lordship to the life, is a spy—a friend of the secret police! His disguise is good, clever, complete! But I see through it. He is JULES GERVAISE, THE NOTORIOUS DETECTIVE!'

Each man showed his weapon now, and furious looks were thrown on Jules.

Had Madame Ollivier been struck by a bullet, she could not have sunk into her chair with a more lifeless expression of face or with a keener cry of pain.

'Jules Gervaise, eh?' sneered Den Lockier, showing his teeth. 'Gentlemen, we need not let this incident disturb us. Surely we know what to do with a detective.'

'There is only one fate possible for him,' said madame, in a low tone. 'He must die. If he lives not one of us will be safe. It is a sad necessity,' she added, shedding her bright eyes first on one and then on the other, 'but it is the law of man that one should suffer rather than many.'

'Gentlemen,' said her brother, in his matter-of-fact way, 'a spy has been discovered among us. Our oath compels us to take the life of any of our comrades who prove traitors. Shall we show more mercy to a mere creature of the police? Such a thing cannot be. There are thirteen of you round the table. It is a significant number for a spy.

The detective is naturally debarred from voting on the subject of his own funeral. As I hope to have the honour of being his executioner, I, also, will remain passive. As you number a dozen and one, equal voting is impossible. Those who are in favour of the swift "removal" of Jules Gervaise, the detective, will signify their wishes by placing their right hands on the table.'

'I would not condemn him to death to save myself,' said one gentleman, 'but, while he lives, the cause is not safe, and the cause must be above every other consideration.'

Then sixty white fingers showed themselves on the sombre cloth, and, last of all, madame placed her delicate palm on it. So the sentence of execution was pronounced!

'I shall give him such a tap as will render him insensible.' said the self-constituted executioner complacently. 'Then we will weight him with shot, and drop him into the Seine, the close mistress of so many secrets! Bah! It will be but one detective the less, and such rats can be easily spared. I promise you, gentlemen, that Jules Gervaise shall not trouble you again.'

The speaker resumed his seat, an acid smile of triumph making his evil face look more revolting than before.

Jules Gervaise—for the so-called Lord Sellford was no other than he—rose quietly to his feet, and addressed that assembly for the first time. Had he been proposing an after-dinner health he could not have been more calm or more at his ease.

'My friends,' said he, 'I perceive that you are gentlemen—too much men of honour to deny to me the privilege which is accorded to the most atrocious criminal in every Court of the civilized world and that is the right to say some words in my own defence. If I am to speak at all, it is obvious I must do so before my execution, for you will not be able to hear me afterwards.'

Every face was fixed on the detective's. A grim smile moved their anxious lips, as he uttered this bit of bitter sarcasm.

'It is a long time since I severed my connection with the French police,' he added, 'and I have ceased to take any active interest in the government of France. I have made my home in England, and I have for ever washed my hands of the internal intrigues of Paris. Believe me, gentlemen, I do not know even the name of your society. I am unacquainted with your pass-words, I can only guess at your aims! You may laugh scornfully. You may ask how it comes that I am here if I am no traitor; but still, I will show you that I am your friend, and not your foe. A lucky chance threw me in the way of the true Lord Sellford. It is by his permission that I am here, in his name. It is by his wish that I appear among you to save your fortunes, your persons, maybe your very lives, as I have preserved his!'

'You are here to save us?' many cried at once. 'What mean you?'

Madame gazed at the detective, as though fixed and fascinated by him. Her brother's face blazed fiercely.

'I am here, gentlemen, to save you from being the dupes of two outrageous swindlers—this so-called Madame Ollivier and her cut-throat brother. That woman,' cried Gervaise, directing his finger at their quivering hostess, his voice growing in volume and scorn as he spoke, 'is not the patriot she pretends to be. She has neither the birth nor the wealth she claims to have, and she is as destitute of truth as she is of either. That woman, I say, who would have decamped with all your fortunes to-morrow morning, and have had you all arrested into the bargain, is no other than the infamous English adventuress Julia Barretti, now wanted for the murder of George Roach at Canonbury, London!'

A low wail came from between madame's parched lips, while her brother hissed defiantly:

'It is a lie—an infamous lie! He will tell you a tale to save his life!'

'It is no lie,' replied Jules firmly, casting an illustrated paper on the table before them. 'There is a picture of Julia Barretti, and a detailed account of many of her crimes. See, gentlemen! See for yourselves that Julia Barretti, the ex-convict, and the grand Madame Ollivier, are one, even to the small mole which shows behind her ear.'

'You are a fiend in your malice!' shouted Den Lockier, livid with passion. 'You libel my sister, and you must die!'

He fired his revolver straight at Jules, but it chanced that the gentleman standing next to the latter bent forward at the critical moment, and he received the bullet in his ear. With a deep groan he sank to the floor.

'Wretch!' cried an aristocratic-looking man on the other side of the table, 'you have killed my dearest friend. Let your own life answer for the deed!'

Very deliberately he shot the villain through the heart—dead.

'For heaven's sake, gentlemen, do not let us lose our senses! Calmness is essential.' The speaker was one whose voice commanded instant attention. 'It is quite plain that Jules Gervaise has told us the truth. We are in a den of thieves, and the sooner we escape from it the better. Our friend still lives. Pray help me to carry him to my carriage, and in my own house he shall have every attention. Den Lockier well deserves his doom. Madame has gone off in a dead swoon. But Jules Gervaise is a clever man, and he will know what to do with the corpse and the unconscious lady. Let us leave them both to him.'

A few minutes later the detective was the only conscious person in that black and mournful room.

'I save them their money and their liberty, and this is their gratitude,' growled Jules, as he gloomily watched the last conspirator disappear behind the arras. 'But if they do not close the opening through the tree, I shall be all right. I have only to make the call, and the police will be here to help me.'

Gervaise ran down the steps, and to his infinite joy found himself in the garden.

In reply to his signal, two men issued from among the shrubs.

'This has been a busy night,' cried one. 'There is not one of us who, is not engaged in shadowing someone. It is a splendid time for us all. Ah! Jules Gervaise, you bring the best of luck with you. But you disappeared like magic. We searched the walls for a secret door, but we never thought of that fraudulent old tree. We will attend to the lady, who is alive, and to the conspirator, who is dead. Come and see his excellency the chief tomorrow, and discuss matters further. You have done well—very well indeed.'

'Do not let the woman escape,' said Jules.

'You can trust us,' the men laughed.

A little later, Jules turned into his well-aired bed in a near hotel, and slept as soundly as a philosopher should.

The morning came, and Jules Gervaise was closeted with his friend the chief of the secret police.

'The rascal's death is no loss to the world,' said the chief of the police smilingly. 'We have the name of each of the conspirators, and can put our hands on them whenever we feel inclined. But they were more dupes than knaves, and as, thanks to you, we have broken up the combination, I do not propose to take any further action in the matter, unless some further indiscretion is committed. But I think they have had a lesson sufficiently sharp to last them a lifetime. As for Madame Ollivier—Julia Barretti, as you will call her—I leave her in your hands, on condition that you take her out of the country. I cannot very well prosecute her, without bringing out the whole pretended conspiracy, and it is not our policy to encourage gossip about political plots. Take her, and, if you can contrive to have her hanged in England, I shall be infinitely obliged to you.'

'You are too kind to me,' declared Gervaise. 'You know I am not invested with any power to arrest her. In charging her with the murder of George Roach, I was but following out one of the theories I have formed concerning that crime. If I succeed in getting her to accompany me to England, it must be by diplomacy.'

'And you are a born diplomat. You will find the lady in the adjoining room.'

Gervaise discovered Julia Barretti, deadly pale, and with such dark rims round her large eyes as suggested that the latter and sleep had been strangers for a long time. Yet she was as calm as though no emotion had ever stirred her dark and secret heart.

'You accuse me of the murder of George Roach, who once called me his wife,' said she, in cold, steady tones to the detective. 'How you obtained any information to warrant you in making such a charge is entirely beyond my comprehension. It is possible that you may be able to make out so strong a case against me that I shall be hanged for the crime; but I tell you, Jules Gervaise, that I am as innocent of spilling that man's blood as you are. My past record has been a bad one, yet I, Julia Barretti, the adventuress, can on occasions speak the truth, and I declare it now!'

'Madame,' answered Jules gravely, 'you were in George Roach's house in Canonbury on the night of this murder.'

'That is true,' she replied quietly, 'but I had no hand in the deed.'

'Then you have but to say who the murderer was to escape from the accusation which now confronts you.'

'Alas! that I cannot do.'

'That is one of those misfortunes which will probably cost you your life.'

For a brief space there was silence between them. The woman appeared to be in deep thought.

Suddenly she said:

'I will tell you my story. You are a clever detective, a shrewd man of the world, surely you will be able to judge clearly whether I speak the truth or not.'

Gervaise motioned to her to proceed.

'A few months back, when I was in London, accident made me acquainted with a young man, named Rupert Peel.'

'Ah!' muttered the detective.

'He took me to be a great lady—a countess at the very least—and he regarded me as a possible wealthy patroness, who would procure for him a lucrative appointment in France, when he had once acquired the language, which he set about learning. You may well ask me why I amused myself with so unimportant a person, but I had discovered that he was in the employ of George Roach, who had once married me, and I was curious to learn all about the doings of that man, often thinking that the information might, some day, prove of pecuniary value to me. Not only did I know when George Roach took that house in Canonbury, but, after much trouble, I persuaded Rupert Peel to "borrow" the keys, and take me all over it. He was very nervous lest it should ever be discovered that he had done this.'

'That fact may possibly account for his confusion when he handed the keys to us,' thought Gervaise.

'My visits to London were occasional ones,' continued Julia Barretti. 'As the day fixed for the marriage of Mr Roach and Daisy Lynn grew nearer and nearer, I became more deeply and more terribly pressed for money. Then, when we were every day threatened with a crisis in our affairs, I resolved to see whether I could not frighten George Roach into paying me a couple of thousand pounds. In many matters he was a most nervous man, and I judged he would rather part with this money than have me appear before his affianced wife, and relate to her my story. Of course, he could prove that he had been the wronged and injured one, but this would take time; besides, if people considered how easily they could repel a false accusation, there would be an end to blackmailing as a profitable industry altogether. I wrote to George Roach on the day he should have started for Glasgow. In my letter I declared that if he did not meet me at his house in Canonbury at ten o'clock that same night, and agree to my demands, I would, late though it might be, proceed at once to Miss Lynn's residence at Kennington, and expose him. I relied very much on my intimate knowledge of his private affairs, drawn from the well-intentioned Rupert Peel, to add terrors to my threats. My letter was posted so as to reach him in the evening, and, from all I have since gleaned, I judge that it was put into his hand as he was starting for St Pancras Station. Thinking it was some ordinary communication, I believe, he thrust it into his pocket, and did not again think of it until he had taken his place in the railway carriage, and his train was on the point of starting. Then he opened it, and, terrified at the thought of the pain I might cause Miss Lynn, he jumped from the train, and made for Canonbury with all possible haste.'

'So far, I believe, you have not wandered from the truth,' said Gervaise. 'From my point of view, I think it in your favour that you have not attempted to excuse your own wicked part in this bad business.'

'I shall make no attempt to play on your credulity, monsieur. I believe that when Mr Roach reached his house he found someone already in possession of it.'

'Indeed?'

'Yes. I arrived there rather after my time. A light burned in one of the front rooms. I saw a form distinctly shadowed on the blind, but it was not the figure of my husband. I found the front door open, as though Mr Roach, on putting his key into the lock, had heard someone moving about inside, and had made a dash in to secure the trespasser. When I entered the room, Roach stood facing me. Another man faced him. The latter swung a bar of iron over his head to bring down on George's skull, but I, being just behind, was struck by it, and rendered unconscious. How long I remained so I cannot tell. I have a dim recollection of a fierce voice whispering in my ear these words:

'"Do not dare to breathe a word of what you have seen tonight, or I will take care that you are found guilty of having committed the deed." For a considerable period I remained dazed, and too weak to move. When at last I was able to crawl from that place I did, hoping I should never again be reminded of the fearful experience I had gone through. When I reflected on my past history, on the object of my errand, and, as I remembered that even then he might bear on his slaughtered body the threatening letter I had sent him, I realized how easy it would be to persuade a jury that I had been guilty of bringing about his death. Yes, yes, Jules Gervaise, you, at any rate, will readily understand why I resolved to keep my lips sealed regarding that dark night's work!'

'Well, madame,' said Jules drily, 'if you are innocent of the crime you should not have any difficulty in identifying the assassin, when he is brought before you?'

'Indeed, that I cannot do. When I entered the room his back was towards me, and I was rendered insensible before I could notice even that particularly. But I should know his shadow. The shadow which I saw thrown on the blind of that house at Canonbury is indelibly printed on my brain. I could swear to that shadow, if it ever met my eyes again.'

'Come!' said Gervaise cheerfully, 'that is something. I suppose you are aware that Rupert Peel is at present in prison on suspicion of having committed this murder?'

'I am sorry to hear it,' was the quiet reply. 'He regarded his master with acute bitterness. They were rivals in love. Perhaps Peel did kill him. I could tell you if I saw his shadow.'

This reply was unexpected by the detective. It was a view he was not at all disposed to take.

'Well,' he said sharply, 'will you come with me willingly to England, and help me to prove Rupert Peel innocent or guilty, or do you prefer to go as a prisoner, as which, I candidly confess, you will be of no use to me in establishing the truth of the theory I have formed?'

'I will go with you, and loyally help you as far as I am able. But, remember, I cannot speak to the murderer's tones or to his appearance. I can recognize nothing about him but his shadow.'

'So be it,' said Gervaise 'I shall not be the first detective who has set out in chase of such airy and unsubstantial nothings. We will leave for London tonight.'

'I shall be glad to get away from Paris,' was the woman's answer.

'I am placing more confidence in you than your previous record warrants,' said Gervaise severely to Julia Barretti, as he left her in a quiet private hotel he had selected for her in the neighbourhood of the central London squares, 'but you know quite well that the Continent is closed to you, and if you manage to slip me here I shall soon find you.'

'I have no desire to break faith with you,' was her cold reply. 'I believe it is not unusual for even criminals to keep their word to detectives.'

'That woman is a born rogue,' Gervaise muttered to himself, as he made his way to Holloway Prison, for he was already armed with a permit to interview Rupert Peel, who was in confinement there. 'She pursues crime as a legitimate profession. What can you do with such people but keep them under lock and key?'

At first, Rupert Peel was somewhat shy of his visitor, who had been working so hard on his behalf, but when Jules Gervaise explained to him who the French lady Rupert had regarded with such awe really was, the young man threw aside all reserve, and spoke quite freely.

'Truly,' said the unhappy young man, 'I cannot suggest to you the name of anyone who is likely to have done this terrible deed. I recognize myself that theoretically I am the one most likely to have been guilty of the murder. And,' he added, 'if the whole truth were known about that woman, what a horribly strong case might be established against both of us! Perhaps the woman did it after all!' he added musingly, 'What a fool I was to have ever taken her into that house!'

'She thinks you may be guilty,' said Jules slowly.

'She is not alone in that opinion,' returned the young man bitterly. 'But, Jules Gervaise, I am an innocent man!'

Rupert spoke with calm, convincing earnestness; and, though the detective made no comment on the young man's declaration, he was not inclined to disbelieve him. All he said was:

'It will be well for you if you can account for every minute of your time on the night on which the murder must have taken place.'

'Ah!' sighed Rupert. 'That sounds an easy thing to do, but it is impossible in my case. The only man who could help me in that way is dead. I mean my father.'

'Tell me about him,' said Jules.

'My life has been a very unhappy one,' said the young man, after a pause. 'My mother died when I was very young, and my father fell into the hands of some low-class betting men. His smooth temper and unsuspicious disposition made him an easy prey to their wiles. To make my painful story short, I will say at once that I have worked all my life to keep him, and to the end I loved him dearly. On the evening when Mr Roach was supposed to have left for Glasgow, my father was brought home sadly injured about the head in some disgraceful racecourse quarrel. Blood still poured profusely from his wounds and, in applying bandages to these cuts, my waistcoat became saturated with the blood. My wardrobe was so scantily furnished that I had to wash this waistcoat that same night, so as to be able to wear it at the office the next day. Now you can understand why I was so upset when you called my attention to the odour of blood which the fire drew out of the half-dried garment. Some days afterwards my father managed to totter out again. He met some of the gang who had previously assaulted him. They once more attacked him, and when he was brought home it was to die. When Mr Roach was murdered, I was nursing my father. But there is no one to prove this but he, and his lips are closed for ever!'

'Your life has been a sad one,' said the sympathetic detective.

'Indeed it has. You see, I could never have married Daisy so long as my father lived.'

'Tell me,' said Jules, with a resumption of his quaint, abrupt way. 'do you ever eat musk lozenges?'

'Never. Why do you ask such an odd question?'

'I will tell you. The key—the key so stained with blood, which fitted the door of the strongroom in which the remains of Mr Roach were found—this key, I say, which was said to have been found in your desk, had still a strong flavour of musk about it when it was shown to me.'

'I cannot account for that at all,' declared Rupert.

'Then I must discover for myself why this was so. Now my time is up, and I must go.'

'What do you think of my case, Mr Jules Gervaise? Will they convict me?'

'Undoubtedly, if you are guilty. If you are innocent, I have already promised to save you, and I will!'

'When I want you I will send for you, and you will come.' Jules had said to Julia Barretti, and she remained in her hotel, waiting for his sign.

For some days the detective disappeared from the resorts where he was usually to be found, and even at his own lodgings scarcely anything was seen of him. Some of his acquaintances had met him in the City, going in and out of business premises with which it did not seem probable he could have anything in common.

One man declared positively that he had come across Jules Gervaise in the neighbourhood of Hampstead, carrying on his back the outfit of a travelling glazier; and it is certainly a fact that when a rude-mannered boy was brought before the local magistrate, charged with breaking windows belonging to Mr Felix Sark, it was the detective who paid the fine inflicted.

At last Julia Barretti received a communication from Gervaise, and, on the same night, he visited the house of Saul Lynn, and found that gentleman in very much better spirits than might have been looked for.

'Fate is proving most kind to me, after all,' said he. 'It is an extraordinary thing, but Mr Felix Sark has suddenly taken a wonderful fancy to Daisy. To be quite candid with you, Jules, he is anxious to marry her, just as soon as this disagreeable murder business is forgotten. It seems that poor George Roach always left Mr Sark with a power-of-attorney, authorizing him to carry on the business should Mr Roach be taken suddenly ill or detained in some distant part. Sark says it is as good as a will, and that he is quite justified in constituting himself owner of the concern.'

'Mr Sark is a little wrong in his law,' said Gervaise quietly, with an air of indifference. 'Practically no deed survives death, except a man's final testament. But we can let that pass. You make me very tired of human nature, Saul,' the detective added, placidly. 'If you would only hide your selfishness a little, it would be a kindness to your friends. I do not think we shall ever take that house together we once spoke of.'

'And why not?' queried Saul, his red face growing more crimson.

'Because, my friend, there would not be room for me in it. You would want it all.'

'You are a queer fellow, Jules,' said Saul, not in the best of humours. Then, as Daisy came into the room, he left it, suddenly determining that it might be well to buy an evening paper.

'Oh, Mr Gervaise, I am so thankful to see you!' cried the golden-haired little woman. 'I do hope you have brought me good news.'

'Poor little girl! Poor little girl!' said the detective sympathizingly, 'How sorrow has thinned your pretty cheeks. Yes, I hope to have good news for you soon, but not today—not today!'

'I did as you told me,' said Daisy, 'and I was quite civil to Mr Sark after you had gone; but it has been a hard task to keep it up, for I do dislike him so. There! I do believe this is his knock!'

'Let us hope so!' The detective spoke so fervently that Daisy regarded him in a bewildered way.

'You appear to be upset, Mr Sark,' was his comment, as that gentleman joined them.

'Upset? I should think so, indeed!' was the vicious reply. 'And I daresay you would be if a thievish glazier had ransacked your rooms, and broken open your desk and most secret places! Upset is not the word for it, Mr Gervaise! Why, the rascal hires a boy to break glass when he himself finds work slack. He absolutely creates business, which seems to me to consist mainly of robbery. Ah! but I must not forget a little present I have for you, Miss Lynn.'

'What a pretty box!' cried the girl, as she opened the packet he presented her with.

'Musk lozenges,' said Jules reflectively. 'Are you very fond of them, Mr Sark?'

'If I ever buy anything in that way,' was the answer, 'I get musk lozenges from the chemist.'

'They have a remarkably strong scent,' said Jules. 'It clings to everything, even to steel.'

'What are you going to do with the light, Mr Gervaise?' cried Daisy, as she saw the detective lift the lamp from the table.

'I am going to put it on the sideboard, if you don't mind,' he said blandly. 'That is higher than the table, where it hurts my eyes. Now, I am sure that is better. Did you ever see so old a sixpence as this before?' he added, addressing Mr Sark, compelling that gentleman to cross the room between the light and the blind to examine the coin.

Mr Sark saw nothing at all remarkable in the thin piece of silver offered for his inspection. His own private opinion was that Jules Gervaise was afflicted with an eccentricity which perilously bordered on madness. The detective took Felix Sark's contemptuous comments in good part, and very soon after this left the house to join Julia Barretti, who was waiting for him outside.

The little twisted street wherein stood the warehouse of George Roach and Co. was made still narrower by the erection of complicated scaffolding outside the murdered man's premises, for they were being repainted, and the brickwork generally was undergoing repairs. The thoroughfare was made impassable by the roadway being denuded of its granite blocks to make way for less noisy ones of wood.

In connection with the new foundation for these a huge cauldron of boiling asphalt stood under the planks, and close to the doorway of the murdered man's busy office. Jules Gervaise observed how the black smoke curled heavenwards from this as he conducted a select party of gentlemen into the presence of Felix Sark, who received them with the sulky inquisitiveness characteristic of him.

'My business, though of a particularly delicate nature from one point of view, cannot be kept private,' said the great detective blandly; 'but, if you prefer it, I will disclose the matter in hand to you in your own room, if you do not care for me to speak openly here.'

'Go on,' said Mr Sark, with an air of indifference, perching himself on a high stool, and looking from one to the other of Jules Gervaise's companions sharply and interrogatively.

'Very good,' said the detective. 'I am here, Mr Sark, to tell you the story of a crime. I will not torture you with suspense, so I will tell you at once that two of these gentlemen come from Scotland Yard. They hold a warrant for your arrest, and they are bent on taking you away with them.'

Mr Sark's face assumed a deeper hue, but he regarded Jules defiantly, and did his utmost to preserve a calm exterior.

'Now, Mr Sark, perhaps you will be so good as to let these gentlemen look at your cash-book for last year?'

'I shall do nothing of the kind,' answered the cashier, with a perceptible start.

'Of course you won't,' said Jules pleasantly, 'because you can't. The cash-book is here.'

The detective rested a large square bag on a bale of goods, and drew out a portly white-bound volume.

'You villain!' cried Sark thoughtlessly. 'It is you, then, who broke into my rooms and stole my goods. You shall suffer for it, you rascal!'

'But,' continued the placid Jules, 'this book is not complete. It wants pages 29 and 30. They are here.'

He now produced the ashes he had taken from the grate of the house at Canonbury. They had been cleverly arranged between two sheets of thin glass, and, by a chemical process, a brilliant red ink followed every trace of writing which was on them, so that each entry in the cash columns could be deciphered with the utmost ease.

'Yes, Mr Sark, they are here; and they show, in your own handwriting, that Messrs Fellow and Mark paid into your hands, on Thursday, the fifth day of May, one hundred and fifteen pounds ten shillings. That's all plain enough, isn't it? Unfortunately for you, Mr Sark, it chances that Messrs Fellow and Mark paid you five hundred and fifteen pounds ten shillings, and it is for this amount they hold your receipt. You put down in this book the one hundred odd and pocketed four hundred pounds, Mr Sark. Not your first defalcation, by any means, sir.'

By this time the guilty man had turned green and evil-looking, but his composure was perfect.

'The day poor Mr Roach was summoned to Glasgow he chanced to meet Mr Fellow, whom you see before you, ready to corroborate all I say. He mentioned the account, the bulk of which he believed to be still due from that gentleman to him. Your receipt in full was shown to your employer; his suspicions were aroused, and, to your consternation, he took home with him the cash-book containing the fraudulent entry, determined to go carefully through every item in it at the first opportunity. It was the most unfortunate thing George Roach ever did. It signed his death-warrant!

'The agents from whom your master had taken the house at Canonbury had handed you two sets of keys for the premises, but you only gave up one. So, when you fondly fancied Mr Roach was being whirled northward, you entered his house, and commenced to destroy the incriminating cash-book. Naturally enough, you burned the two most damning pages, but you see that even fire refuses to hide your guilt. In the midst of your work, when you were exultant and fearless, who should suddenly appear before you but your too-trusting master himself. A desperate struggle ensued, but finally you killed him—and with this!'

From the detective's bag came a heavy bar of iron.

'You carried away the book and kept it at your lodgings,' continued Jules quietly, 'because, as you had made up your mind to seize this business, you knew it would be useful to you. But why you should have preserved this murderous piece of metal is best known to yourself. The blood-stained key of the strongroom, which you pretended to find in Rupert Peel's desk, came from your own pocket. The flavour of your musk lozenges still clings to it. You were anxious to marry Miss Lynn because you were well aware Mr Roach had bequeathed her, by a legally attested will, which is at present in my possession, every penny he died possessed of. Now, Mr Sark, I think I have brought my story of your crime to a convincing conclusion.'

'It is all an infamous concoction!' cried the wretched man, his eyes blood-red and furtive. He had not yet abandoned all hope; he would escape them yet, if he could. 'It is a malignant series of lies. I am innocent of this crime. If my dear dead master could rise from his grave he would himself declare that to the end I was faithful and true to him.'

'You lie, Felix Sark, you lie!' declared Julia Barretti, coming among them at that moment. 'I saw you strike the fatal blow! The shadow I observed on the blind of the house at Canonbury I saw again last night at Saul Lynn's house in Kennington, and your shadow has condemned you!'

A look of wild terror changed the entire aspect of his face as he gazed at this woman. Had a spectre confronted him he could not have been more staggered.

He stared hopelessly, first to the right then to the left of him. His eyes caught sight of the stairs leading to the rooms above, and he made a dart for them.

'After him!' cried Jules, to the plain-clothes men from Scotland Yard. 'He will climb that scaffolding, get on to the roof, and we may miss him altogether. Don't hesitate to follow him wherever he goes!'

The moment Felix reached the upper apartment, he made a plunge for the window, and reached the planks outside.

Taking the detective's advice, one of the young officers dashed through the same opening on to the scaffolding. He was just in time to see the fugitive seize the heavy hanging chain, and then a dreadful thing happened.

It may be presumed that Felix's intention was to reach the street by this means, but he had not observed that it dangled immediately over the great cauldron in which seethed and smoked the boiling pitch.

The murderer's weight brought the chain down with a rasping rush, and he completely disappeared in the molten substance, only to be rescued when life was extinct, and his body most horribly disfigured.

Though there was no question about the guilt of Felix Sark, it took a little time to procure the release of Rupert Peel. It need hardly be said that he married Daisy Peel after a short lapse of time, but it should be mentioned that he now carries on the business of George Roach and Co., as may be seen by anyone who searches for the premises in the street we have described.

Jules Gervaise was very proud of his success in this case, because it made Daisy happy. It brought him such fame, too, that he was compelled to abandon his idea of retiring, until he had, at any rate, solved one more mystery, and about that we may have something to write another day.

The Ivy Cottage Mystery

ARTHUR MORRISON

I had been working double tides for a month: at night on my morning paper, as usual; and in the morning on an evening paper as locum tenens for another man who was taking a holiday. This was an exhausting plan of work, although it only actually involved some six hours' attendance a day, or less, at the two offices. I turned up at the headquarters of my own paper at ten in the evening, and by the time I had seen the editor, selected a subject, written my leader, corrected the slips, chatted, smoked, and so on, and cleared off, it was very usually one o'clock. This meant bed at two, or even three, after supper at the club.

This was all very well at ordinary periods, when any time in the morning would do for rising, but when I had to be up again soon after seven, and round at the evening paper office by eight, I naturally felt a little worn and disgusted with things by midday, after a sharp couple of hours' leaderette scribbling and paragraphing, with attendant sundries.

But the strain was over, and on the first day of comparative comfort I indulged in a midday breakfast and the first undisgusted glance at a morning paper for a month. I felt rather interested in an inquest, begun the day before, on the body of a man whom I had known very slightly before I took to living in chambers.

His name was Gavin Kingscote, and he was an artist of a casual and desultory sort, having, I believe, some small private means of his own. As a matter of fact, he had boarded in the same house in which I had lodged myself for a while, but as I was at the time a late homer and a fairly early riser, taking no regular board in the house, we never became much acquainted. He had since, I understood, made some judicious Stock Exchange speculations, and had set up house in Finchley.

Now the news was that he had been found one morning murdered in his smoking-room, while the room itself, with others, was in a state of confusion. His pockets had been rifled, and his watch and chain were gone, with one or two other small articles of value. On the night of the tragedy a friend had sat smoking with him in the room where the murder took place, and he had been the last person to see Mr Kingscote alive. A jobbing gardener, who kept the garden in order by casual work from time to time, had been arrested in consequence of footprints exactly corresponding with his boots, having been found on the garden beds near the French window of the smoking-room.

I finished my breakfast and my paper, and Mrs Clayton, the housekeeper, came to clear my table. She was sister of my late landlady of the house where Kingscote had lodged, and it was by this connection that I had found my chambers. I had not seen the housekeeper since the crime was first reported, so I now said:

'This is shocking news of Mr Kingscote, Mrs Clayton. Did you know him yourself?'

She had apparently only been waiting for some such remark to burst out with whatever information she possessed.

'Yes, sir,' she exclaimed: 'shocking indeed. Pore young feller! I see him often when I was at my sister's, and he was always a nice, quiet gentleman, so different from some. My sister, she's awful cut up, sir, I assure you. And what d'you think 'appened, sir, only last Tuesday? You remember Mr Kingscote's room where he painted the woodwork so beautiful with gold flowers, and blue, and pink? He used to tell my sister she'd always have something to remember him by. Well, two young fellers, gentlemen I can't call them, come and took that room (it being to let), and went and scratched off all the paint in mere wicked mischief, and then chopped up all the panels into sticks and bits! Nice sort o' gentlemen them! And then they bolted in the morning, being afraid, I s'pose, of being made to pay after treating a pore widder's property like that. That was only Tuesday, and the very next day the pore young gentleman himself's dead, murdered in his own 'ouse, and him goin' to be married an' all! Dear, dear! I remember once he said——'

Mrs Clayton was a good soul, but once she began to talk some one else had to stop her. I let her run on for a reasonable time, and then rose and prepared to go out. I remembered very well the panels that had been so mischievously destroyed. They made the room the showroom of the house, which was an old one. They were indeed less than half finished when I came away, and Mrs Lamb, the landlady, had shown them to me one day when Kingscote was out. All the walls of the room were panelled and painted white, and Kingscote had put upon them an eccentric but charming decoration, obviously suggested by some of the work of Mr Whistler. Tendrils, flowers, and butterflies in a quaint convention wandered thinly from panel to panel, giving the otherwise rather uninteresting room an unwonted atmosphere of richness and elegance. The lamentable jackasses who had destroyed this had certainly selected the best feature of the room whereon to inflict their senseless mischief.

I strolled idly downstairs, with no particular plan for the afternoon in my mind, and looked in at Hewitt's offices. Hewitt was reading a note, and after a little chat he informed me that it had been left an hour ago, in his absence, by the brother of the man I had just been speaking of.

'He isn't quite satisfied,' Hewitt said, 'with the way the police are investigating the case, and asks me to run down to Finchley and look round. Yesterday I should have refused, because I have five cases in progress already, but today I find that circumstances have given me a day or two. Didn't you say you knew the man?'

'Scarcely more than by sight. He was a boarder in the house at Chelsea where I stayed before I started chambers.'

'Ah, well; I think I shall look into the thing. Do you feel particularly interested in the case? I mean, if you've nothing better to do, would you come with me?'

'I shall be very glad,' I said. 'I was in some doubt what to do with myself. Shall you start at once?'

'I think so. Kerrett, just call a cab. By the way, Brett, which paper has the fullest report of the inquest yesterday? I'll run over it as we go down.'

As I had only seen one paper that morning, I could not answer Hewitt's question. So we bought various papers as we went along in the cab, and I found the reports while Martin Hewitt studied them. Summarized, this was the evidence given—

Sarah Dodson, general servant, deposed that she had been in service at Ivy Cottage, the residence of the deceased, for five months, the only other regular servant being the housekeeper and cook. On the evening of the previous Tuesday both servants retired a little before eleven, leaving Mr Kingscote with a friend in the smoking or sitting room. She never saw her master again alive. On coming downstairs the following morning and going to open the smoking-room windows, she was horrified to discover the body of Mr Kingscote lying on the floor of the room with blood about the head. She at once raised an alarm, and, on the instructions of the housekeeper, fetched a doctor, and gave information to the police. In answer to questions, witness stated she had heard no noise of any sort during the night, nor had anything suspicious occurred.

Hannah Carr, housekeeper and cook, deposed that she had been in the late Mr Kingscote's service since he had first taken Ivy Cottage—a period of rather more than a year. She had last seen the deceased alive on the evening of the previous Tuesday, at half-past ten, when she knocked at the door of the smoking-room, where Mr Kingscote was sitting with a friend, to ask if he would require anything more. Nothing was required, so witness shortly after went to bed. In the morning she was called by the previous witness, who had just gone downstairs, and found the body of deceased lying as described. Deceased's watch and chain were gone, as also was a ring he usually wore, and his pockets appeared to have been turned out. All the ground floor of the house was in confusion, and a bureau, a writing-table, and various drawers were open—a bunch of keys usually carried by deceased being left hanging at one keyhole. Deceased had drawn some money from the bank on the Tuesday, for current expenses; how much she did not know. She had not heard or seen anything suspicious during the night. Besides Dodson and herself, there were no regular servants; there was a charwoman, who came occasionally, and a jobbing gardener, living near, who was called in as required.

Mr James Vidler, surgeon, had been called by the first witness between seven and eight on Wednesday morning. He found the deceased lying on his face on the floor of the smoking-room, his feet being about eighteen inches from the window, and his head lying in the direction of the fireplace. He found three large contused wounds on the head, any one of which would probably have caused death. The wounds had all been inflicted, apparently, with the same blunt instrument—probably a club or life preserver, or other similar weapon. They could not have been done with the poker. Death was due to concussion of the brain, and deceased had probably been dead seven or eight hours when witness saw him. He had since examined the body more closely, but found no marks at all indicative of a struggle having taken place; indeed, from the position of the wounds and their severity, he should judge that the deceased had been attacked unawares from behind, and had died at once. The body appeared to be perfectly healthy.

Then there was police evidence, which showed that all the doors and windows were found shut and completely fastened, except the front door, which, although shut, was not bolted. There were shutters behind the French windows in the smoking-room, and these were found fastened. No money was found in the bureau, nor in any of the opened drawers, so that if any had been there, it had been stolen. The pockets were entirely empty, except for a small pair of nail scissors, and there was no watch upon the body, nor a ring. Certain footprints were found on the garden beds, which had led the police to take certain steps. No footprints were to be seen on the garden path, which was hard gravel.

Mr Alexander Campbell, stockbroker, stated that he had known deceased for some few years, and had done business for him. He and Mr Kingscote frequently called on one another, and on Tuesday evening they dined together at Ivy Cottage. They sat smoking and chatting till nearly twelve o'clock, when Mr Kingscote himself let him out, the servants having gone to bed. Here the witness proceeded rather excitedly: 'That is all I know of this horrible business, and I can say nothing else. What the police mean by following and watching me——'

The Coroner: 'Pray be calm, Mr Campbell. The police must do what seems best to them in a case of this sort. I am sure you would not have them neglect any means of getting at the truth.'

Witness: 'Certainly not. But if they suspect me, why don't they say so? It is intolerable that I should be——'

The Coroner: 'Order, order, Mr Campbell. You are here to give evidence.'

The witness then, in answer to questions, stated that the French windows of the smoking-room had been left open during the evening, the weather being very warm. He could not recollect whether or not deceased closed them before he left, but he certainly did not close the shutters. Witness saw nobody near the house when he left.

Mr Douglas Kingscote, architect, said deceased was his brother. He had not seen him for some months, living as he did in another part of the country. He believed his brother was fairly well off, and he knew that he had made a good amount by speculation in the last year or two. Knew of no person who would be likely to owe his brother a grudge, and could suggest no motive for the crime except ordinary robbery. His brother was to have been married in a few weeks. Questioned further on this point, witness said that the marriage was to have taken place a year ago, and it was with that view that Ivy Cottage, deceased's residence, was taken. The lady, however, sustained a domestic bereavement, and afterwards went abroad with her family: she was, witness believed, shortly expected back to England.

William Bates, jobbing gardener, who was brought up in custody, was cautioned, but elected to give evidence. Witness, who appeared to be much agitated, admitted having been in the garden of Ivy Cottage at four in the morning, but said that he had only gone to attend to certain plants, and knew absolutely nothing of the murder. He however admitted that he had no order for work beyond what he had done the day before. Being further pressed, witness made various contradictory statements, and finally said that he had gone to take certain plants away.

The inquest was then adjourned.

This was the case as it stood—apparently not a case presenting any very striking feature, although there seemed to me to be doubtful peculiarities in many parts of it. I asked Hewitt what he thought.

'Quite impossible to think anything, my boy, just yet; wait till we see the place. There are any number of possibilities. Kingscote's friend, Campbell, may have come in again, you know, by way of the window or he may not. Campbell may have owed him money or something—or he may not. The anticipated wedding may have something to do with it—or, again, *that* may not. There is no limit to the possibilities, as far as we see from this report—a mere dry husk of the affair. When we get closer we shall examine the possibilities by the light of more detailed information. One *probability* is that the wretched gardener is innocent. It seems to me that his was only a comparatively blameless manœuvre not unheard of at other times in his trade. He came at four in the morning to steal away the flowers he had planted the day before, and felt rather bashful when questioned on the point. Why should he trample on the beds, else? I wonder if the police thought to examine the beds for traces of rooting up, or questioned the housekeeper as to any plants being missing? But we shall see.'

We chatted at random as the train drew near Finchley, and I mentioned *inter alia* the wanton piece of destruction perpetrated at Kingscote's late lodgings. Hewitt was interested.

'That was curious,' he said, 'very curious. Was anything else damaged? Furniture and so forth?'

'I don't know. Mrs Clayton said nothing of it, and I didn't ask her. But it was quite bad enough as it was. The decoration was really good, and I can't conceive a meaner piece of tomfoolery than such an attack on a decent woman's property.'

Then Hewitt talked of other cases of similar stupid damage by creatures inspired by a defective sense of humour, or mere love of mischief. He had several curious and sometimes funny anecdotes of such affairs at museums and picture exhibitions, where the damage had been so great as to induce the authorities to call him in to discover the offender. The work was not always easy, chiefly from the mere absence of intelligible motive; nor, indeed, always successful. One of the anecdotes related to a case of malicious damage to a picture—the outcome of blind artistic jealousy—a case which had been hushed up by a large expenditure in compensation. It would considerably startle most people, could it be printed here, with the actual names of the parties concerned.

Ivy Cottage, Finchley, was a compact little house, standing in a compact little square of garden, little more than a third of an acre, or perhaps no more at all. The front door was but a dozen yards or so back from the road, but the intervening space was well treed and shrubbed. Mr Douglas Kingscote had not yet returned from town, but the housekeeper, an intelligent, matronly woman, who knew of his intention to call in Martin Hewitt, was ready to show us the house.

'*First*,' Hewitt said, when we stood in the smoking-room, 'I observe that somebody has shut the drawers and the bureau. That is unfortunate. Also, the floor has been washed and the carpet taken up, which is much worse. That, I suppose, was because the police had finished their examination, but it doesn't help me to make one at all. Has *anything*—anything *at all*—been left as it was on Tuesday morning?'

'Well, sir, you see everything was in such a muddle,' the housekeeper began, 'and when the police had done——'

'Just so. I know. You "set it to rights", eh? Oh, that setting to rights! It has lost me a fortune at one time and another. As to the other rooms, now, have they been set to rights?'

'Such as was disturbed have been put right, sir, of course.'

'Which were disturbed? Let me see them. But wait a moment.'

He opened the French windows, and closely examined the catch and bolts. He knelt and inspected the holes whereinto the bolts fell, and then glanced casually at the folding shutters. He opened a drawer or two, and tried the working of the locks with the keys the housekeeper carried. They were, the housekeeper explained, Mr Kingscote's own keys. All through the lower floors Hewitt examined some things attentively and closely, and others with scarcely a glance, on a system unaccountable to me. Presently, he asked to be shown Mr Kingscote's bedroom which had not been disturbed, 'set to rights', or slept in since the crime. Here, the housekeeper said, all drawers were kept unlocked but two—one in the wardrobe and one in the dressing-table, which Mr Kingscote had always been careful to keep locked. Hewitt immediately pulled both drawers open without difficulty. Within, in addition to a few odds and ends, were papers. All the contents of these drawers had been turned over confusedly, while those of the unlocked drawers were in perfect order.

'The police,' Hewitt remarked, 'may not have observed these matters. Any more than such an ordinary thing as *this*,' he added, picking up a bent nail lying at the edge of a rug.

The housekeeper doubtless took the remark as a reference to the entire unimportance of a bent nail, but I noticed that Hewitt dropped the article quietly into his pocket.

We came away. At the front gate we met Mr Douglas Kingscote, who had just returned from town. He introduced himself, and expressed surprise at our promptitude both of coming and going.

'You can't have got anything like a clue in this short time, Mr Hewitt?' he asked.

'Well, no,' Hewitt replied, with a certain dryness, 'perhaps not. But I doubt whether a month's visit would have helped me to get anything very striking out of a washed floor and a houseful of carefully cleaned-up and "set-to-rights" rooms. Candidly, I don't think you can reasonably expect much of me. The police have a much better chance—they had the scene of the crime to examine. I have seen just such a few rooms as any one might see in the first well-furnished house he might enter. The trail of the housemaid has overlaid all the others.'

'I'm very sorry for that; the fact was, I expected rather more of the police; and, indeed, I wasn't here in time entirely to prevent the clearing up. But still, I thought your well-known powers——'

'My dear sir, my "well-known powers" are nothing but common sense assiduously applied and made quick by habit. That won't enable me to see the invisible.'

'But can't we have the rooms put back into something of the state they were in? The cook will remember——'

'No, no. That would be worse and worse: that would only be the housemaid's trail in turn overlaid by the cook's. You must leave things with me for a little, I think.'

'Then you don't give the case up?' Mr Kingscote asked anxiously.

'Oh, no! I don't give it up just yet. Do you know anything of your brother's private papers—as they were before his death?'

'I never knew anything till after that. I have gone over them, but they are all very ordinary letters. Do you suspect a theft of papers?'

Martin Hewitt, with his hands on his stick behind him, looked sharply at the other, and shook his head. 'No,' he said, 'I can't quite say that.'

We bade Mr Douglas Kingscote good-day, and walked towards the station. 'Great nuisance, that setting to rights,' Hewitt observed, on the way. 'If the place had been left alone, the job might have been settled one way or another by this time. As it is, we shall have to run over to your old lodgings.'

'My old lodgings?' I repeated, amazed. 'Why my old lodgings?'

Hewitt turned to me with a chuckle and a wide smile. 'Because we can't see the broken panel-work anywhere else,' he said. 'Let's see— Chelsea, isn't it?'

'Yes, Chelsea. But why—you don't suppose the people who defaced the panels also murdered the man who painted them?'

'Well,' Hewitt replied, with another smile, 'that would be carrying a practical joke rather far, wouldn't it? Even for the ordinary picture damager.'

'You mean you *don't* think they did it, then? But what *do* you mean?'

'My dear fellow, I don't mean anything but what I say. Come now, this is rather an interesting case despite appearances, and it *has* interested me: so much, in fact, that I really think I forgot to offer Mr Douglas Kingscote my condolence on his bereavement. You see a problem is a problem, whether of theft, assassination, intrigue, or anything else, and I only think of it as one. The work very often makes me forget merely human sympathies. Now, you have often been good enough to express a very flattering interest in my work, and you shall have an opportunity of exercising your own common sense in the way I am always having to exercise mine. You shall see all my evidence (if I'm lucky enough to get any) as I collect it, and you shall make your own inferences. That will be a little exercise for you; the sort of exercise I should give a pupil if I had one. But I will give you what information I have, and you shall start fairly from this moment. You know the inquest evidence, such as it was, and you saw everything I did in Ivy Cottage?'

'Yes; I think so. But I'm not much the wiser.'

'Very well. Now I will tell you. What does the whole case look like? How would you class the crime?'

'I suppose as the police do. An ordinary case of murder with the object of robbery.'

'It is *not* an ordinary case. If it were, I shouldn't know as much as I do, little as that is; the ordinary cases are always difficult. The assailant did not come to commit a burglary, although he was a skilled burglar, or one of them was, if more than one were concerned. The affair has, I think, nothing to do with the expected wedding, nor had Mr Campbell anything to do in it—at any rate, personally—nor the gardener. The criminal (or one of them) was known personally to the dead man, and was well-dressed: he (or again one of them, and I think there were two) even had a chat with Mr Kingscote before the murder took place. He came to ask for something which Mr Kingscote was unwilling to part with—perhaps hadn't got. It was not a bulky thing. Now you have all my materials before you.'

'But all this doesn't look like the result of the blind spite that would ruin a man's work first and attack him bodily afterwards.'

'Spite isn't always blind, and there are other blind things besides spite; people with good eyes in their heads are blind sometimes, even detectives.'

'But where did you get all this information? What makes you suppose that this was a burglar who didn't want to burgle, and a well-dressed man, and so on?'

Hewitt chuckled and smiled again.

'I saw it—saw it, my boy, that's all,' he said 'But here comes the train.'

On the way back to town, after I had rather minutely described Kingscote's work on the boarding-house panels, Hewitt asked me for the names and professions of such fellow lodgers in that house as I might remember. 'When did you leave yourself?' he ended.

'Three years ago, or rather more. I can remember Kingscote himself; Turner, a medical student—James Turner, I think; Harvey Challitt, diamond merchant's articled pupil—he was a bad egg entirely, he's doing five years for forgery now; by the by he had the room we are going to see till he was marched off, and Kingscote took it—a year before I left; there was Norton—don't know what he was; "something in the City", I think; and Carter Paget, in the Admiralty Office. I don't remember any more at this moment; there were pretty frequent changes. But you can get it all from Mrs Lamb, of course.'

'Of course; and Mrs Lamb's exact address is—what?'

I gave him the address, and the conversation became disjointed. At Farringdon station, where we alighted, Hewitt called two hansoms. Preparing to enter one, he motioned me to the other, saying, 'You get straight away to Mrs Lamb's at once. She may be going to burn that splintered wood, or to set things to rights, after the manner of her kind, and you can stop her. I must make one or two small enquiries, but I shall be there half an hour after you.'

'Shall I tell her our object?'

'Only that I may be able to catch her mischievous lodgers—nothing else yet.' He jumped into the hansom and was gone.

I found Mrs Lamb still in a state of indignant perturbation over the trick served her four days before. Fortunately, she had left everything in the panelled room exactly as she had found it, with an idea of the being better able to demand or enforce reparation should her lodgers return. 'The room's theirs, you see, sir,' she said, 'till the end of the week, since they paid in advance, and they may come back and offer to make amends, although I doubt it. As pleasant-spoken a young chap as you might wish, he seemed, him as come to take the rooms. "My cousin," says he, "is rather an invalid, havin' only just got over congestion of the lungs, and he won't be in London till this evening late. He's comin' up from Birmingham," he ses, "and I hope he won't catch a fresh cold on the way, although of course we've got him muffled up plenty." He took the rooms, sir, like a gentleman, and mentioned several gentlemen's names I knew well, as had lodged here before; and then he put down on that there very table, sir'—Mrs Lamb indicated the exact spot with her hand, as though that made the whole thing much more wonderful—'he put down on that very table a week's rent in advance, and ses, "That's always the best sort of reference, Mrs Lamb, I think," as kind-mannered as anything— and never 'aggled about the amount nor nothing. He only had a little black bag, but he said his cousin had all the luggage coming in the train, and as there was so much, p'r'aps they wouldn't get it here till next day. Then he went out and came in with his cousin at eleven that night—Sarah let 'em in her own self—and in the morning they was gone—and this!' Poor Mrs Lamb, plaintively indignant, stretched her arm towards the wrecked panels.

'If the gentleman as you say is comin' on, sir,' she pursued, 'can do anything to find 'em, I'll prosecute 'em, that I will, if it costs me ten pound. I spoke to the constable on the beat, but he only looked like a fool, and said if I knew where they were I might charge 'em with wilful damage, or county court 'em. Of course I know I can do that if I knew where they were, but how can I find 'em? Mr Jones he said his name was; but how many Joneses is there in London, sir?'

I couldn't imagine any answer to a question like this, but I condoled with Mrs Lamb as well as I could. She afterwards went on to express herself much as her sister had done with regard to Kingscote's death, only as the destruction of her panels loomed larger in her mind, she dwelt primarily on that. 'It might almost seem,' she said, 'that somebody had a deadly spite on the pore young gentleman, and went breakin' up his paintin' one night, and murderin' him the next!'

I examined the broken panels with some care, having half a notion to attempt to deduce something from them myself, if possible. But I could deduce nothing. The beading had been taken out, and the panels, which were thick in the centre but bevelled at the edges, had been removed and split up literally into thin firewood, which lay in a tumbled heap on the hearth and about the floor. Every panel in the room had been treated in the same way, and the result was a pretty large heap of sticks, with nothing whatever about them to dis- tinguish them from other sticks, except the paint on one face, which I observed in many places had been scratched and scraped away. The rug was drawn half across the hearth, and had evidently been used to deaden the sound of chopping. But mischief—wanton and stupid mischief—was all I could deduce from it all.

Mr Jones's cousin, it seemed, only Sarah had seen, as she admitted him in the evening, and then he was so heavily muffled that she could not distinguish his features, and would never be able to identify him. But as for the other one, Mrs Lamb was ready to swear to him anywhere.

Hewitt was long in coming, and internal symptoms of the approach of dinner-time (we had had no lunch) had made themselves felt before a sharp ring at the doorbell foretold his arrival. 'I have had to wait for answers to a telegram,' he said in explanation, 'but at any rate I have the information I wanted. And these are the mysterious panels, are they?'

Mrs Lamb's true opinion of Martin Hewitt's behaviour as it proceeded would have been amusing to know. She watched in amazement the antics of a man who purposed finding out who had been splitting sticks by dint of picking up each separate stick and staring at it. In the end he collected a small handful of sticks by themselves and handed them to me, saying, 'Just put these together on the table, Brett, and see what you make of them.'

I turned the pieces painted side up, and fitted them together into a complete panel, joining up the painted design accurately. 'It is an entire panel,' I said.

'Good. Now look at the sticks a little more closely, and tell me if you notice anything peculiar about them—any particular in which they differ from all the others.'

I looked. 'Two adjoining sticks,' I said, 'have each a small semi-circular cavity stuffed with what seems to be putty. Put together it would mean a small circular hole, perhaps a knot-hole, half an inch or so in diameter, in the panel, filled in with putty, or whatever it is.'

'A *knot-hole?*' Hewitt asked, with particular emphasis.

'Well, no, not a knot-hole, of course, because that would go right through, and this doesn't. It is probably less than half an inch deep from the front surface.'

'Anything else? Look at the whole appearance of the wood itself. Colour, for instance.'

'It is certainly darker than the rest.'

'So it is.' He took the two pieces carrying the puttied hole, threw the rest on the heap, and addressed the landlady. 'The Mr Harvey Challitt who occupied this room before Mr Kingscote, and who got into trouble for forgery, was the Mr Harvey Challitt who was himself robbed of diamonds a few months before on a staircase, wasn't he?'

'Yes, sir,' Mrs Lamb replied in some bewilderment. 'He certainly was that, on his own office stairs, chloroformed.'

'Just so, and when they marched him away because of the forgery, Mr Kingscote changed into his rooms?'

'Yes, and very glad I was. It was bad enough to have the disgrace brought into the house, without the trouble of trying to get people to take his very rooms, and I thought——'

'Yes, yes, very awkward, very awkward!' Hewitt interrupted rather impatiently. 'The man who took the rooms on Monday, now—you'd never seen him before, had you?'

'No, sir.'

'Then is *that* anything like him?' Hewitt held a cabinet photograph before her.

'Why—why—law, yes, that's *him*!'

Hewitt dropped the photograph back into his breast pocket with a contented 'Um', and picked up his hat. 'I think we may soon be able to find that young gentleman for you, Mrs Lamb. He is not a very respectable young gentleman, and perhaps you are well rid of him, even as it is. Come, Brett,' he added, 'the day hasn't been wasted, after all.'

We made towards the nearest telegraph office. On the way I said, 'That puttied-up hole in the piece of wood seems to have influenced you. Is it an important link?'

'Well—yes,' Hewitt answered, 'it is. But all those other pieces are important, too.'

'But why?'

'Because there are no holes in them.' He looked quizzically at my wondering face, and laughed aloud. 'Come,' he said, 'I won't puzzle you much longer. Here is the post office. I'll send my wire, and then we'll go and dine at Luzatti's.'

He sent his telegram, and we cabbed it to Luzatti's. Among actors, journalists, and others who know town and like a good dinner, Luzatti's is well known. We went upstairs for the sake of quietness, and took a table standing alone in a recess just inside the door. We ordered our dinner, and then Hewitt began:

'Now tell me what *your* conclusion is in this matter of the Ivy Cottage murder.'

'Mine? I haven't one. I'm sorry I'm so very dull, but I really haven't.'

'Come, I'll give you a point. Here is the newspaper account (torn sacrilegiously from my scrap-book for your benefit) of the robbery perpetrated on Harvey Challitt a few months before his forgery. Read it.'

'Oh, but I remember the circumstances very well. He was carrying two packets of diamonds belonging to his firm downstairs to the office of another firm of diamond merchants on the ground floor. It was a quiet time in the day, and halfway down he was seized on a dark landing, made insensible by chloroform, and robbed of the diamonds—five or six thousand pounds' worth altogether, of stones of various smallish individual values up to thirty pounds or so. He lay unconscious on the landing till one of the partners, noticing that he had been rather long gone, followed and found him. That's all, I think.'

'Yes, that's all. Well, what do you make of it?'

'I'm afraid I don't quite see the connection with this case.'

'Well, then, I'll give you another point. The telegram I've just sent releases information to the police, in consequence of which they will probably apprehend Harvey Challitt and his confederate, Henry Gillard, alias Jones, for the murder of Gavin Kingscote. Now, then.'

'Challitt! But he's in gaol already.'

'Tut, tut, consider. Five years' penal was his dose, although for the first offence, because the forgery was of an extremely dangerous sort. You left Chelsea over three years ago yourself, and you told me that his difficulty occurred a year before. That makes four years, at least. Good conduct in prison brings a man out of a five years' sentence in that time or a little less, and, as a matter of fact, Challitt was released rather more than a week ago.'

'Still, I'm afraid I don't see what you are driving at.'

'Whose story is this about the diamond robbery from Harvey Challitt?'

'His own.'

'Exactly. His own. Does his subsequent record make him look like a person whose stories are to be accepted without doubt or question?'

'Why, no. I think I see—no, I don't. You mean he stole them

himself? I've a sort of dim perception of your drift now, but still I can't fix it. The whole thing's too complicated.'

'It is a little complicated for a first effort, I admit, so I will tell you. This is the story. Harvey Challitt is an artful young man, and decides on a theft of his firm's diamonds. He first prepares a hiding-place somewhere near the stairs of his office, and when the opportunity arrives he puts the stones away, spills his chloroform, and makes a smell—possibly sniffs some, and actually goes off on the stairs, and the whole thing's done. He is carried into the office—the diamonds are gone. He tells of the attack on the stairs, as we have heard, and he is believed. At a suitable opportunity he takes his plunder from the hiding-place, and goes home to his lodgings. What is he to do with those diamonds? He can't sell them yet, because the robbery is publicly notorious, and all the regular jewel buyers know him.

'Being a criminal novice, he doesn't know any regular receiver of stolen goods, and if he did would prefer to wait and get full value by an ordinary sale. There will always be a danger of detection so long as the stones are not securely hidden, so he proceeds to hide them. He knows that if any suspicion were aroused his rooms would be searched in every likely place, so he looks for an unlikely place. Of course, he thinks of taking out a panel and hiding them behind that. But the idea is so obvious that it won't do; the police would certainly take those panels out to look behind them. Therefore he determines to hide them *in* the panels. See here'—he took the two pieces of wood with the filled hole from his tail pocket and opened his penknife—'the putty near the surface is softer than that near the bottom of the hole; two different lots of putty, differently mixed, perhaps, have been used, therefore, presumably, at different times.

'But to return to Challitt. He makes holes with a centre-bit in different places on the panels, and in each hole he places a diamond, embedding it carefully in putty. He smooths the surface carefully flush with the wood, and then very carefully paints the place over, shading off the paint at the edges so as to leave no signs of a patch. He doesn't do the whole job at once, creating a noise and a smell of paint, but keeps on steadily, a few holes at a time, till in a little while the whole wainscoting is set with hidden diamonds, and every panel is apparently sound and whole.'

'But, then—there was only one such hole in the whole lot.'

'Just so, and that very circumstance tells us the whole truth. Let me tell the story first—I'll explain the clue after. The diamonds lie hidden for a few months—he grows impatient. He wants the money, and he can't see a way of getting it. At last he determines to make a bolt and go abroad to sell his plunder. He knows he will want money for expenses, and that he may not be able to get rid of his diamonds at once. He also expects that his suddenly going abroad while the robbery is still in people's minds will bring suspicion on him in any case, so, in for a penny in for a pound, he commits a bold forgery, which, had it been successful, would have put him in funds and enabled him to leave the country with the stones. But the forgery is detected, and he is haled to prison, leaving the diamonds in their wainscot setting.

'Now we come to Gavin Kingscote. He must have been a shrewd fellow—the sort of man that good detectives are made of. Also he must have been pretty unscrupulous. He had his suspicions about the genuineness of the diamond robbery, and kept his eyes open. What indications he had to guide him we don't know, but living in the same house a sharp fellow on the look-out would probably see enough. At any rate, they led him to the belief that the diamonds were in the thief's rooms, but not among his movables, or they would have been found after the arrest. Here was his chance. Challitt was out of the way for years, and there was plenty of time to take the house to pieces if it were necessary. So he changed into Challitt's rooms.

'How long it took him to find the stones we shall never know. He probably tried many other places first, and, I expect, found the diamonds at last by pricking over the panels with a needle. Then came the problem of getting them out without attracting attention. He decided not to trust to the needle, which might possibly leave a stone or two undiscovered, but to split up each panel carefully into splinters so as to leave no part unexamined. Therefore he took measurements, and had a number of panels made by a joiner of the exact size and pattern of those in the room, and announced to his landlady his intention of painting her panels with a pretty design. This to account for the wet paint, and even for the fact of a panel being out of the wall, should she chance to bounce into the room at an awkward moment. All very clever, eh?'

'Very.'

'Ah, he was a smart man, no doubt. Well, he went to work, taking out a panel, substituting a new one, painting it over, and chopping up the old one on the quiet, getting rid of the splinters out of doors when the booty had been extracted. The decoration progressed and the little heap of diamonds grew. Finally, he came to the last panel, but found that he had used all his new panels and hadn't one left for a substitute. It must have been at some time when it was difficult to get hold of the joiner—Bank Holiday, perhaps, or Sunday, and he was impatient. So he scraped the paint off, and went carefully over every part of the surface—experience had taught him by this that all the holes were of the same sort—and found one diamond. He took it out, refilled the hole with putty, painted the old panel and put it back. *These* are pieces of that old panel—the only old one of the lot.

'Nine men out of ten would have got out of the house as soon as possible after the thing was done, but he was a cool hand and stayed. That made the whole thing look a deal more genuine than if he had unaccountably cleared out as soon as he had got his room nicely decorated. I expect the original capital for those Stock Exchange operations we heard of came out of those diamonds. He stayed as long as suited him, and left when he set up housekeeping with a view to his wedding. The rest of the story is pretty plain. You guess it, of course?'

'Yes,' I said, 'I think I can guess the rest, in a general sort of way—except as to one or two points.'

'It's all plain—perfectly. See here! Challitt, in gaol, determines to get those diamonds when he comes out. To do that without being suspected it will be necessary to hire the room. But he knows that he won't be able to do that himself, because the landlady, of course, knows him, and won't have an ex-convict in the house. There is no help for it; he must have a confederate, and share the spoil. So he makes the acquaintance of another convict, who seems a likely man for the job, and whose sentence expires about the same time as his own. When they come out, he arranges the matter with this confederate, who is a well-mannered (and pretty well-known) housebreaker, and the latter calls at Mrs Lamb's house to look for rooms. The very room itself happens to be to let, and of course it is taken, and Challitt (who is the invalid cousin) comes in at night muffled and unrecognizable.

'The decoration on the panel does not alarm them, because, of course, they suppose it to have been done on the old panels and over the old paint. Challitt tries the spots where diamonds were left—

there are none—there is no putty even. Perhaps, think they, the panels have been shifted and interchanged in the painting, so they set to work and split them all up as we have seen, getting more desperate as they go on. Finally they realize that they are done, and clear out, leaving Mrs Lamb to mourn over their mischief.

'They know that Kingscote is the man who has forestalled them, because Gillard (or Jones), in his chat with the landlady, has heard all about him and his painting of the panels. So the next night they set off for Finchley. They get into Kingscote's garden and watch him let Campbell out. While he is gone, Challitt quietly steps through the French window into the smoking-room, and waits for him, Gillard remaining outside.

'Kingscote returns, and Challitt accuses him of taking the stones. Kingscote is contemptuous—doesn't care for Challitt, because he knows he is powerless, being the original thief himself; besides, knows there is no evidence, since the diamonds are sold and dispersed long ago. Challitt offers to divide the plunder with him—Kingscote laughs and tells him to go; probably threatens to throw him out, Challitt being the smaller man. Gillard, at the open window, hears this, steps in behind, and quietly knocks him on the head. The rest follows as a matter of course. They fasten the window and shutters, to exclude observation; turn over all the drawers, etc., in case the jewels are there; go to the best bedroom and try there, and so on. Failing (and possibly being disturbed after a few hours' search by the noise of the acquisitive gardener), Gillard, with the instinct of an old thief, determines they shan't go away with nothing, so empties Kingscote's pockets and takes his watch and chain and so on. They go out by the front door and shut it after them. *Voilà tout.*'

I was filled with wonder at the prompt ingenuity of the man who in these few hours of hurried enquiry could piece together so accurately all the materials of an intricate and mysterious affair such as this; but more, I wondered where and how he had collected those materials.

'There is no doubt, Hewitt,' I said, 'that the accurate and minute application of what you are pleased to call your common sense has become something very like an instinct with you. What did you deduce from? You told me your conclusions from the examination of Ivy Cottage, but not how you arrived at them.'

'They didn't leave me much material downstairs, did they? But in the bedroom, the two drawers which the thieves found locked were ransacked—opened probably with keys taken from the dead man. On the floor I saw a bent French nail; here it is. You see, it is twice bent at right angles, near the head and near the point, and there is the faint mark of the pliers that were used to bend it. It is a very usual burglars' tool, and handy in experienced hands to open ordinary drawer locks. Therefore, I knew that a professional burglar had been at work. He had probably fiddled at the drawers with the nail first, and then had thrown it down to try the dead man's keys.

'But I knew this professional burglar didn't come for a burglary, from several indications. There was no attempt to take plate, the first thing a burglar looks for. Valuable clocks were left on mantelpieces, and other things that usually go in an ordinary burglary were not disturbed. Notably, it was to be observed that no doors or windows were broken, or had been forcibly opened; therefore, it was plain that the thieves had come in by the French window of the smoking-room, the only entrance left open at the last thing. *Therefore*, they came in, or one did, knowing that Mr Kingscote was up, and being quite willing—presumably anxious—to see him. Ordinary burglars would have waited till he had retired, and then could have got through the closed French window as easily almost as if it were open, notwithstanding the thin wooden shutters, which would never stop a burglar for more than five minutes. Being anxious to see him, they—or again, *one* of them—presumably knew him. That they had come to *get* something was plain, from the ransacking. As, in the end, they *did* steal his money and watch, but did *not* take larger valuables, it was plain that they had no bag with them—which proves not only that they had not come to burgle, for every burglar takes his bag, but that the thing they came to get was not bulky. Still, they could easily have removed plate or clocks by rolling them up in a table-cover or other wrapper, but such a bundle, carried by well-dressed men, would attract attention—therefore it was probable that they were well dressed. Do I make it clear?'

'Quite—nothing seems simpler now it is explained—that's the way with difficult puzzles.'

'There was nothing more to be got at the house. I had already in my mind the curious coincidence that the panels at Chelsea had been broken the very night before that of the murder, and determined to look at them in any case. I got from you the name of the man who had lived in the panelled room before Kingscote, and at once remembered it (although I said nothing about it) as that of the young man who had been chloroformed for his employer's diamonds. I keep things of that sort in my mind, you see—and, indeed, in my scrapbook. You told me yourself about his imprisonment, and there I was with what seemed now a hopeful case getting into a promising shape.

'You went on to prevent any setting to rights at Chelsea, and I made enquiries as to Challitt. I found he had been released only a few days before all this trouble arose, and I also found the name of another man who was released from the same establishment only a few days earlier. I knew this man (Gillard) well, and knew that nobody was a more likely rascal for such a crime as that at Finchley. On my way to Chelsea I called at my office, gave my clerk certain instructions, and looked up my scrap-book. I found the news-paper account of the chloroform business, and also a photograph of Gillard—I keep as many of these things as I can collect. What I did at Chelsea you know. I saw that one panel was of old wood and the rest new. I saw the hole in the old panel, and I asked one or two questions. The case was complete.'

We proceeded with our dinner. Presently I said: 'It all rests with the police now, of course?'

'Of course. I should think it very probable that Challitt and Gillard will be caught. Gillard, at any rate, is pretty well known. It will be rather hard on the surviving Kingscote, after engaging me, to have his dead brother's diamond transactions publicly exposed as a result, won't it? But it can't be helped. *Fiat justitia*, of course.'

'How will the police feel over this?' I asked. 'You've rather cut them out, eh?'

'Oh, the police are all right. They had not the information I had, you see; they knew nothing of the panel business. If Mrs Lamb had gone to Scotland Yard instead of to the policeman on the beat, perhaps I should never have been sent for.'

The same quality that caused Martin Hewitt to rank as mere 'common-sense' his extraordinary power of almost instinctive deduc-tion, kept his respect for the abilities of the police at perhaps a higher level than some might have considered justified.

We sat some little while over our dessert, talking as we sat, when there occurred one of those curious conjunctions of circumstances that we notice again and again in ordinary life, and forget as often, unless the importance of the occasion fixes the matter in the memory. A young man had entered the dining-room, and had taken his seat at a corner table near the back window. He had been sitting there for some little time before I particularly observed him. At last he happened to turn his thin, pale face in my direction, and our eyes met. It was Challitt—the man we had been talking of!

I sprang to my feet in some excitement.

'That's the man!' I cried. 'Challitt!'

Hewitt rose at my words, and at first attempted to pull me back. Challitt, in guilty terror, saw that we were between him and the door, and turning, leaped upon the sill of the open window, and dropped out. There was a fearful crash of broken glass below, and everybody rushed to the window.

Hewitt drew me through the door, and we ran downstairs. 'Pity you let out like that,' he said, as he went. 'If you'd kept quiet we could have sent out for the police with no trouble. Never mind—can't help it.'

Below, Challitt was lying in a broken heap in the midst of a crowd of waiters. He had crashed through a thick glass skylight and fallen, back downward, across the back of a lounge. He was taken away on a stretcher unconscious, and, in fact, died in a week in hospital from injuries to the spine.

During his periods of consciousness he made a detailed statement, bearing out the conclusions of Martin Hewitt with the most surprising exactness, down to the smallest particulars. He and Gillard had parted immediately after the crime, judging it safer not to be seen together. He had, he affirmed, endured agonies of fear and remorse in the few days since the fatal night at Finchley, and had even once or twice thought of giving himself up. When I so excitedly pointed him out, he knew at once that the game was up, and took the one desperate chance of escape that offered. But to the end he persistently denied that he had himself committed the murder, or had even thought of it till he saw it accomplished. That had been wholly the work of Gillard, who, listening at the window and perceiving the drift of the conversation, suddenly beat down Kingscote from behind with a life-preserver. And so Harvey Challitt ended his life at the age of twenty-six.

Gillard was never taken. He doubtless left the country, and has probably since that time become 'known to the police' under another name abroad. Perhaps he has even been hanged, and if he has been, there was no miscarriage of justice, no matter what the charge against him may have been.

The Azteck Opal

RODRIGUES OTTOLENGUI

'Mr Mitchel,' began Mr Barnes, the detective, after exchanging greetings, 'I have called to see you upon a subject which I am sure will enlist your keenest interest, for several reasons. It relates to a magnificent jewel; it concerns your intimate friends; and it is a problem requiring the most analytical qualities of the mind in its solution.'

'Ah! Then you have solved it?' asked Mr Mitchel.

'I think so. You shall judge. I have today been called in to investigate one of the most singular cases that has fallen in my way. It is one in which the usual detective methods would be utterly valueless. The facts were presented to me, and the solution of the mystery could only be reached by analytical deduction.'

'That is to say, by using your brains?'

'Precisely! Now, you have admitted that you consider yourself more expert in this direction than the ordinary detective. I wish to place you for once in the position of a detective, and then see you prove your ability.

'Early this morning I was summoned, by a messenger, to go aboard of the steam yacht *Idler*, which lay at anchor in the lower bay.'

'Why, the *Idler* belongs to my friend Mortimer Gray,' exclaimed Mr Mitchel.

'Yes!' replied Mr Barnes. 'I told you that your friends are interested. I went immediately with the man who had come to my office, and in due season I was aboard of the yacht. Mr Gray received me very politely, and took me to his private room adjoining the cabin. Here he explained to me that he had been off on a cruise for a few weeks, and was approaching the harbour last night, when, in accordance with his plans, a sumptuous dinner was served, as a sort of farewell feast, the party expecting to separate today.'

'What guests were on the yacht?'

'I will tell you everything in order, as the facts were presented to me. Mr Gray enumerated the party as follows. Besides himself and his wife, there were his wife's sister, Mrs Eugene Cortlandt, and her husband, a Wall Street broker. Also, Mr Arthur Livingstone, and his sister, and a Mr Dennett Moore, a young man supposed to be devoting himself to Miss Livingstone.'

'That makes seven persons, three of whom are women. I ought to say, Mr Barnes, that, though Mr Gray is a club friend, I am not personally acquainted with his wife, nor with the others. So I have no advantage over you.'

'I will come at once to the curious incident which made my presence desirable. According to Mr Gray's story, the dinner had proceeded as far as the roast, when suddenly there was a slight shock as the yacht touched, and at the same time the lamps spluttered and then went out, leaving the room totally dark. A second later the vessel righted herself and sped on, so that before any panic ensued, it was evident to all that the danger had passed. The gentlemen begged the ladies to resume their seats, and remain quiet until the lamps were lighted; this, however, the attendants were unable to do, and they were ordered to bring fresh lamps. Thus there was almost total darkness for several minutes.'

'During which, I presume, the person who planned the affair readily consummated his design?'

'So you think that the whole series of events was pre-arranged? Be that as it may, something did happen in that dark room. The women had started from their seats when the yacht touched, and when they groped their way back in the darkness some of them found the wrong places, as was seen when the fresh lamps were brought. This was considered a good joke, and there was some laughter, which was suddenly checked by an exclamation from Mr Gray, who quickly asked his wife, 'Where is your opal?'

'Her opal?' asked Mr Mitchel, in tones which showed that his greatest interest was now aroused. 'Do you mean, Mr Barnes, that she was wearing the Azteck opal?'

'Oh! You know the gem?'

'I know nearly all gems of great value; but what of this one?'

'Mrs Gray and her sister, Mrs Cortlandt, had both donned *décolleté* costumes for this occasion, and Mrs Gray had worn this opal as a pendant to a thin gold chain which hung round her neck. At Mr Gray's question, all looked towards his wife, and it was noted that the clasp was open, and the opal missing. Of course it was supposed that it had merely fallen to the floor, and a search was immediately instituted. But the opal could not be found.'

'That is certainly a very significant fact,' said Mr Mitchel. 'But was the search thorough?'

'I should say extremely thorough, when we consider it was not conducted by a detective, who is supposed to be an expert in such matters. Mr Gray described to me what was done, and he seems to have taken every precaution. He sent the attendants out of the salon, and he and his guests systematically examined every part of the room.'

'Except the place where the opal really was concealed, you mean.'

'With that exception, of course, since they did not find the jewel. Not satisfied with this search by lamplight, Mr Gray locked the salon, so that no one could enter it during the night, and another investigation was made in the morning.'

'The pockets of the seven persons present were not examined, I presume?'

'No! I asked Mr Gray why this had been omitted, and he said that it was an indignity which he could not possibly show to a guest. As you have asked this question, Mr Mitchel, it is only fair for me to tell you that when I spoke to Mr Gray on the subject he seemed very much confused. Nevertheless, however unwilling he may have been to search those of his guests who are innocent, he emphatically told me that if I had reasonable proof that any one present had purloined the opal, he wished that individual to be treated as any other thief, without regard to sex or social position.'

'One can scarcely blame him, because that opal was worth a fabulous sum. I have myself offered Gray twenty-five thousand dollars for it, which was refused. This opal is one of the eyes of an Azteck Idol, and if the other could be found, the two would be as interesting as any jewels in the world.'

'That is the story which I was asked to unravel,' continued Mr Barnes, 'and I must now relate to you what steps I have taken towards that end. It appears that, because of the loss of the jewels, no person has left the yacht, although no restraint was placed upon any one by Mr Gray. All knew, however, that he had sent for a detective, and it was natural that no one should offer to go until formally dismissed by the host. My plan, then, was to have a private interview with each of the seven persons who had been present at the dinner.'

'Then you exempted the attendants from your suspicions?'

'I did. There was but one way by which one of the servants could have stolen the opal, and this was prevented by Mr Gray. It was possible that the opal had fallen on the floor, and, though not found at night, a servant might have discovered and have appropriated it on the following morning, had he been able to enter the salon. But Mr Gray had locked the doors. No servant, however bold, would have been able to take the opal from the lady's neck.'

'I think your reasoning is good, and we will confine ourselves to the original seven.'

'After my interview with Mr Gray, I asked to have Mrs Gray sent in to me. She came in, and at once I noted that she placed herself on the defensive. Women frequently adopt that manner with a detective. Her story was very brief. The main point was that she was aware of the theft before the lamps were relighted. In fact, she felt some one's arms steal around her neck, and knew when the opal was taken. I asked why she had made no outcry, and whether she suspected any special person. To these questions she replied that she supposed it was merely a joke perpetrated in the darkness, and therefore had made no resistance. She would not name any one as suspected by her, but she was willing to tell me that the arms were bare, as she detected when they touched her neck. I must say here, that although Miss Livingstone's dress was not cut low in the neck, it was, practically, sleeveless; and Mrs Cortlandt's dress had no sleeves at all. One other significant statement made by this lady was that her husband had mentioned to her your offer of twenty-five thousand dollars for the opal, and had urged her to permit him to sell it, but she had refused.'

'So! It was Madam that would not sell. The plot thickens!'

'You will observe, of course, the point about the naked arms of the thief. I therefore sent for Mrs Cortlandt next. She had a curious story to tell. Unlike her sister, she was quite willing to express her suspicions. Indeed, she plainly intimated that she supposed that Mr Gray himself had taken the jewel. I will endeavour to repeat her words:

' "Mr Barnes," said she, "the affair is very simple. Gray is a miserable old skinflint. A Mr Mitchel, a crank who collects gems, offered to buy that opal, and he has been bothering my sister for it ever since. When the lamps went out, he took the opportunity to steal it. I do not think this, I know it. How? Well, on account of the confusion and darkness, I sat in my sister's seat when I returned to the table. This explains his mistake, but he put his arms round my neck, and deliberately felt for the opal. I did not understand his purpose at the time, but now it is very evident."

' "Yes, madam," said I, "but how do you know it was Mr Gray?"

' "Why, I grabbed his hand, and before he could pull it away I felt the large cameo ring on his little finger. Oh! there is no doubt whatever."

'I asked her whether Mr Gray had his sleeves rolled up, and though she could not understand the purport of the question, she said "No". Next I had Miss Livingstone come in. She is a slight, tremulous young lady, who cries at the slightest provocation. During the interview, brief as it was, it was only by the greatest diplomacy that I avoided a scene of hysterics. She tried very hard to convince me that she knew absolutely nothing. She had not left her seat during the disturbance; of that she was sure. So how could she know anything about it? I asked her to name the one whom she thought might have taken the opal, and at this her agitation reached such a climax that I was obliged to let her go.'

'You gained very little from her I should say.'

'In a case of this kind, Mr Mitchel, where the criminal is surely one of a very few persons, we cannot fail to gain something from each person's story. A significant feature here was that though Miss Livingstone assures us that she did not leave her seat, she was sitting in a different place when the lamps were lighted again.'

'That might mean anything or nothing.'

'Exactly! but we are not deducing values yet. Mr Dennett Moore came to me next, and he is a straightforward, honest man if I ever saw one. He declared that the whole affair was a great mystery to him, and that, while ordinarily he would not care anything about it, he could not but be somewhat interested because he thought that one of the ladies, he would not say which one, suspected him. Mr Livingstone also impressed me favourably in spite of the fact that he did not remove his cigarette from his mouth throughout the whole of my interview with him. He declined to name the person suspected by him, though he admitted that he could do so. He made this significant remark:

' "You are a detective of experience, Mr Barnes, and ought to be able to decide which man amongst us could place his arms around Mrs Gray's neck without causing her to cry out. But if your imagination fails you, suppose you enquire into the financial standing of all of us, and see which one would be most likely to profit by thieving? Ask Mr Cortlandt." '

'Evidently Mr Livingstone knows more than he tells.'

'Yet he told enough for one to guess his suspicions, and to understand the delicacy which prompted him to say no more. He, however, gave me a good point upon which to question Mr Cortlandt. When I asked that gentleman if any of the men happened to be in pecuniary difficulties, he became grave at once. I will give you his answer.

' "Mr Livingstone and Mr Moore are both exceedingly wealthy men, and I am a millionaire, in very satisfactory business circumstances at present. But I am very sorry to say, that though our host, Mr Gray, is also a distinctly rich man, he has met with some reverses recently, and I can conceive that ready money would be useful to him. But for all that, it is preposterous to believe what your question evidently indicates. None of the persons in this party is a thief, and least of all could we suspect Mr Gray. I am sure that if he wished his wife's opal, she would give it to him cheerily. No, Mr Barnes, the opal is in some crack, or crevice, which we have overlooked. It is lost, not stolen." '

'That ended the interviews with the several persons present, but I made one or two other enquiries, from which I elicited at least two significant facts. First, it was Mr Gray himself who had indicated the course by which the yacht was steered last night, and which ran her over a sand-bar. Second, some one had nearly emptied the oil from the lamps, so that they would have burned out in a short time, even though the yacht had not touched.'

'These, then, are your facts? And from these you have solved the problem? Well, Mr Barnes, who stole the opal?'

'Mr Mitchel, I have told you all I know, but I wish you to work out a solution before I reveal my own opinion.'

'I have already done so, Mr Barnes. Here! I will write my suspicion on a bit of paper. So! Now tell me yours, and you shall know mine afterwards.'

'Why, to my mind it is very simple. Mr Gray, failing to obtain the opal from his wife by fair means, resorted to a trick. He removed the oil from the lamps, and charted out a course for his yacht which would take her over a sand-bar, and when the opportune moment came he stole the jewel. His actions since then have been merely to cover his crime, by shrouding the affair with mystery. By insisting upon a thorough search, and even sending for a detective, he makes it impossible for those who were present to accuse him hereafter. Undoubtedly Mr Cortlandt's opinion will be the one generally adopted. Now what do you think?'

'I think I will go with you at once, and board the yacht *Idler*.'

'But you have not told me whom you suspect,' said Mr Barnes, somewhat irritated.

'Oh! That's immaterial,' said Mr Mitchel, calmly preparing for the street. 'I do not suspect Mr Gray, so if you are correct you will have shown better ability than I. Come! Let us hurry!'

On their way to the dock, from which they were to take the little steam launch which was waiting to carry the detective back to the yacht, Mr Barnes asked Mr Mitchel the following questions:

'Mr Mitchel,' said he, 'you will note that Mrs Cortlandt alluded to you as a "crank who collects gems". I must admit that I have myself harboured a great curiosity as to your reasons for purchasing jewels, which are valued beyond a mere conservative commercial price. Would you mind explaining why you began your collection?'

'I seldom explain my motives to others, especially when they relate to my more important pursuits in life. But in view of all that has passed between us, I think your curiosity justifiable, and I will gratify it. To begin with, I am a very wealthy man. I inherited great riches, and I have made a fortune myself. Have you any conception of the difficulties which harass a man of means?'

'Perhaps not in minute detail, though I can guess that the lot of the rich is not as free from care as the pauper thinks it is.'

'The point is this: the difficulty with a poor man is to get rich, while with the rich man the greatest trouble is to prevent the increase of his wealth. Some men, of course, make no effort in that direction, and those men are a menace to society. My own idea of the proper use of a fortune is to manage it for the benefit of others, as well as one's self, and especially to prevent its increase.'

'And is it so difficult to do this? Cannot money be spent without limit?'

'Yes; but unlimited evil follows such a course. This is sufficient to indicate to you that I am ever in search of a legitimate means of spending my income, provided that I may do good thereby. If I can do this, and at the same time afford myself pleasure, I claim that I am making the best use of my money. Now I happen to be so constructed, that the most interesting studies to me are social problems, and of these I am most entertained with the causes and environments of crime. Such a problem as the one you brought to me today is of immense attractiveness to me, because the environment is one which is commonly supposed to preclude rather than to invite crime. Yet we have seen that despite the wealth of all concerned, some one has stooped to the commonest of crimes—theft.'

'But what has this to do with your collection of jewels?'

'Everything! Jewels—especially those of great magnitude—seem to be a special cause of crime. A hundred-carat diamond will tempt a man to theft, as surely as the false beacon on a rocky shore entices the mariner to wreck and ruin. All the great jewels of the world have murder and crime woven into their histories. My attention was first called to this by accidentally overhearing a plot in a ballroom to rob the lady of the house of a large ruby which she wore on her breast. I went to her, taking the privilege of an intimate friend, and told her enough to persuade her to sell the stone to me. I fastened it into my scarf, and then sought the presence of the plotters, allowing them to see what had occurred. No words passed between us, but by my act I prevented a crime that night.'

'Then am I to understand that you buy jewels with that end in view?'

'After that night I conceived this idea. If all the great jewels in the world could be collected together, and put in a place of safety, hundreds of crimes would be prevented, even before they had been conceived. Moreover, the search for, and acquirement of these jewels would necessarily afford me abundant opportunity for studying the crimes which are perpetrated in order to gain possession of them. Thus you understand more thoroughly why I am anxious to pursue this problem of the Azteck opal.'

Several hours later Mr Mitchel and Mr Barnes were sitting at a quiet table in the corner of the dining-room at Mr Mitchel's club. On board the yacht Mr Mitchel had acted rather mysteriously. He had been closeted a while with Mr Gray, after which he had had an interview with two or three of the others. Then when Mr Barnes had begun to feel neglected, and tired of waiting alone on deck, Mr

Mitchel had come towards him, arm-in-arm with Mr Gray, and the latter said:

'I am very much obliged to you, Mr Barnes, for your services in this affair, and I trust the enclosed cheque will remunerate you for your trouble.'

Mr Barnes, not quite comprehending it all, had attempted to protest, but Mr Mitchel had taken him by the arm, and hurried him off. In the cab which bore them to the club the detective asked for an explanation, but Mr Mitchel only replied:

'I am too hungry to talk now. We will have dinner first.'

The dinner was over at last, and nuts and coffee were before them, when Mr Mitchel took a small parcel from his pocket, and handed it to Mr Barnes, saying:

'It is a beauty, is it not?'

Mr Barnes removed the tissue paper, and a large opal fell on the tablecloth, where it sparkled with a thousand colours under the electric lamps.

'Do you mean that this is——,' cried the detective.

'The Azteck opal, and the finest harlequin I ever saw,' interrupted Mr Mitchel. 'But you wish to know how it came into my possession? Principally so that it may join the collection and cease to be a temptation to this world of wickedness.'

'Then Mr Gray did not steal it?' asked Mr Barnes, with a touch of chagrin in his voice.

'No, Mr Barnes! Mr Gray did not steal it. But you are not to consider yourself very much at fault. Mr Gray tried to steal it, only he failed. That was not your fault, of course. You read his actions aright, but you did not give enough weight to the stories of the others.'

'What important point did I omit from my calculation?'

'I might mention the bare arms which Mrs Gray said she felt round her neck. It was evidently Mr Gray who looked for the opal on the neck of his sister-in-law, but as he did not bare his arms, he would not have done so later.'

'Do you mean that Miss Livingstone was the thief?'

'No! Miss Livingstone being hysterical, she changed her seat without realizing it, but that does not make her a thief. Her excitement when with you was due to her suspicions, which, by the way, were correct. But let us return for a moment to the bare arms. That was the clue from which I worked. It was evident to me that the thief was a man, and it was equally plain that in the hurry of the few moments of darkness, no man would have rolled up his sleeves, risking the return of the attendants with lamps, and the consequent discovery of himself in such a singular disarrangement of costume.'

'How do you account for the bare arms?'

'The lady did not tell the truth, that is all. The arms which encircled her neck were not bare. Neither were they unknown to her. She told you that lie to shield the thief. She also told you that her husband wished to sell the Azteck opal to me, but that she had refused. Thus she deftly led you to suspect him. Now, if she wished to shield the thief, yet was willing to accuse her husband, it followed that the husband was not the thief.'

'Very well reasoned, Mr Mitchel. I see now where you are tending, but I shall not get ahead of your story.'

'So much I had deduced, before we went on board the yacht. When I found myself alone with Gray I candidly told him of your suspicions, and your reasons for harbouring them. He was very much disturbed, and pleadingly asked me what I thought. As frankly I told him that I believed that he had tried to take the opal from his wife—we can scarcely call it stealing since the law does not but that I believed he had failed. He then confessed; admitted emptying the lamps, but denied running the boat on the sand-bar. But he assured me that he had not reached his wife's chair when the lamps were brought in. He was, therefore, much astonished at missing the gem. I promised him to find the jewel upon condition that he would sell it to me. To this he most willingly acceded.'

'But how could you be sure that you would recover the opal?'

'Partly by my knowledge of human nature, and partly because of my inherent faith in my own abilities. I sent for Mrs Gray, and noted her attitude of defence, which, however, only satisfied me the more that I was right in my suspicions. I began by asking her if she knew the origin of the superstition that an opal brings bad luck to its owner. She did not, of course, comprehend my tactics, but she added that she "had heard the stupid superstition, but took no interest in such nonsense". I then gravely explained to her that the opal is the engagement stone of the Orient. The lover gives it to his sweetheart, and the belief is that should she deceive him even in the most trifling manner, the opal will lose its brilliancy and become cloudy. I then suddenly asked her if she had ever noted a change in her opal. "What do you mean to insinuate?" she cried out angrily. "I mean," said I, sternly, "that if an opal has changed colour in accordance with the superstition this one should have done so. I mean that though your husband greatly needs the money which I have offered him you have refused to allow him to sell it, and yet you have permitted another to take it from you tonight. By this act you might have seriously injured if not ruined Mr Gray. Why have you done it?" '

'How did she receive it?' asked Mr Barnes, admiring the ingenuity of Mr Mitchel.

'She began to sob, and between her tears she admitted that the opal had been taken by the man I suspected, but she earnestly declared that she had harboured no idea of injuring her husband. Indeed, she was so agitated in speaking upon this point, that I believe that Gray never thoroughly explained to her why he wished to sell the gem. She urged me to recover the opal if possible, and purchase it, so that her husband might be relieved from his pecuniary embarrassment. I then sent for the thief, Mrs Gray told me his name; but would you not like to hear how I had picked him out before we went aboard? I still have that bit of paper upon which I wrote his name, in confirmation of what I say.'

'Of course, I know now that you mean Mr Livingstone, but would like to hear your reasons for suspecting him'.

'From your account Miss Livingstone suspected some one, and this caused her to be so agitated that she was unaware of the fact that she had changed her seat. Women are shrewd in these affairs, and I was confident that the girl had good reason for her conduct. It was evident that the person in her mind was either her brother or her sweetheart. I decided between these two men from your account of your interviews with them. Moore impressed you as being honest, and he told you that one of the ladies suspected him. In this he was mistaken, but his speaking to you of it was not the act of a thief. Mr Livingstone, on the other hand, tried to throw suspicion upon Mr Gray.'

'Of course that was sound reasoning after you had concluded that Mrs Gray was lying. Now tell me how you recovered the jewel?'

'That was easier than I expected. I simply told Mr Livingstone when I got him alone, what I knew, and asked him to hand me the opal. With a perfectly imperturbable manner, understanding that I promised secrecy, he quietly took it from his pocket and gave it to me, saying:

' "Women are very poor conspirators. They are too weak." '

'What story did you tell Mr Gray?'

'Oh, he would not be likely to enquire too closely into what I should tell him. My cheque was what he most cared for. I told him nothing definitely, but I inferred that his wife had secreted the gem during the darkness, that he might not ask her for it again; and that she had intended to find it again at a future time, just as he had meant to pawn it and then pretend to recover it from the thief by offering a reward.'

'One more question. Why did Mr Livingstone steal it?'

'Ah! The truth about that is another mystery worth probing, and one which I shall make it my business to unravel. I will venture two prophecies. First—Mr Livingstone did not steal it at all. Mrs Gray simply handed it to him in the darkness. There must have been some powerful motive to lead her to such an act; something which she was weighing, and decided impulsively. This brings me to the second point. Livingstone used the word conspirator, which is a clue. You will recall what I told you that this gem is one of a pair of opals, and that with the other, the two would be as interesting as any jewels in the world. I am confident now that Mr Livingstone knows where that other opal is, and that he has been urging Mrs Gray to give or lend him hers, as a means of obtaining the other. If she hoped to do this, it would be easy to understand why she refused to permit the sale of the one she had. This, of course, is guesswork, but I'll promise that if any one ever owns both it shall be your humble servant, Leroy Mitchel, Jewel Collector.'

The Long Arm

MARY E. WILKINS

I

(From notes written by Miss Sarah Fairbanks immediately after the report of the Grand Jury.)

As I take my pen to write this, I have a feeling that I am in the witness-box—for, or against myself, which? The place of the criminal in the dock I will not voluntarily take. I will affirm neither my innocence nor my guilt. I will present the facts of the case as impartially and as coolly as if I had nothing at stake. I will let all who read this judge me as they will.

This I am bound to do since I am condemned to something infinitely worse than the life-cell or the gallows. I will try my own self in lieu of judge and jury; my guilt or my innocence I will prove to you all, if it be in mortal power. In my despair I am tempted to say, I care not which it may be, so something be proved. Open condemnation could not overwhelm me like universal suspicion.

Now, first, as I have heard is the custom in the courts of law, I will present the case. I am Sarah Fairbanks, a country school-teacher, twenty-nine years of age. My mother died when I was twenty-three. Since then, while I have been teaching at Digby, a cousin of my father's, Rufus Bennett, and his wife have lived with my father. During the long summer vacation they returned to their little farm in Vermont, and I kept house for my father.

For five years I have been engaged to be married to Henry Ellis, a young man whom I met in Digby. My father was very much opposed to the match, and has told me repeatedly that if I insisted upon marrying him in his lifetime he would disinherit me. On this account Henry never visited me at my own home. While I could not bring myself to break off my engagement, finally I wished to avoid an open rupture with my father. He was quite an old man, and I was the only one he had left of a large family.

I believe that parents should honour their children, as well as children their parents, but I had arrived at this conclusion: in nine-tenths of the cases wherein children marry against their parents' wishes, even when the parents have no just grounds for opposition, the marriages are unhappy.

I sometimes felt that I was unjust to Henry, and resolved that if ever I suspected that his fancy turned toward any other girl, I would not hinder it, especially as I was getting older and, I thought, losing my good looks.

A little while ago, a young and pretty girl came to Digby to teach the school in the south district. She boarded in the same house with Henry. I heard that he was somewhat attentive to her, and I made up my mind I would not interfere. At the same time it seemed to me that my heart was breaking. I heard her people had money, too, and she was an only child. I had always felt that Henry ought to marry a wife with money, because he had nothing himself, and was not very strong.

School closed five weeks ago, and I came home for the summer vacation. The night before I left, Henry came to see me, and urged me to marry him. I refused again; but I never before had felt that my father was so hard and cruel as I did that night. Henry said that he should certainly see me during the vacation, and when I replied that he must not come, he was angry, and said—but such foolish things are not worth repeating. Henry has really a very sweet temper, and would not hurt a fly.

The very night of my return home Rufus Bennett and my father had words about some maple sugar which Rufus made on his Vermont farm, and sold to father, who made a good trade for it to some people in Boston. That was father's business. He had once kept a store, but had given it up, and sold a few articles that he could make a large profit on here and there at wholesale. He used to send to New Hampshire and Vermont for butter, eggs, and cheese. Cousin Rufus thought father did not allow him enough of his profit on the maple sugar, and in the dispute father lost his temper, and said that Rufus had given him underweight. At that, Rufus swore an oath, and seized father by the throat. Rufus's wife screamed, 'Oh, don't! don't! oh, he'll kill him!'

I went up to Rufus and took hold of his arm.

'Rufus Bennett,' said I, 'you let my father go!'

But Rufus's eyes glared like a madman's, and he would not let go. Then I went to the desk-drawer where father had kept a pistol since some houses in the village were broken into; I got out the pistol, laid hold of Rufus again, and held the muzzle against his forehead.

'You let go of my father,' said I, 'or I'll fire!'

Then Rufus let go, and father dropped like a log. He was purple in the face. Rufus's wife and I worked a long time over him to bring him to.

'Rufus Bennett,' said I, 'go to the well and get a pitcher of water.' He went, but when father had revived and got up Rufus gave him a look that showed he was not over his rage.

'I'll get even with you yet, Martin Fairbanks, old man as you are!' he shouted out, and went into the outer room.

We got father to bed soon. He slept in the bedroom downstairs, out of the sitting-room. Rufus and his wife had the north chamber, and I had the south one. I left my door open that night, and did not sleep. I listened; no one stirred in the night. Rufus and his wife were up very early in the morning, and before nine o'clock left for Vermont. They had a day's journey, and would reach home about nine in the evening. Rufus's wife bade father goodbye, crying, while Rufus was getting their trunk downstairs, but Rufus did not go near father nor me. He ate no breakfast; his very back looked ugly when he went out of the yard.

That very day, about seven in the evening, after tea, I had just washed the dishes and put them away, and went out on the north doorstep, where father was sitting, and sat down on the lowest step. There was a cool breeze there; it had been a very hot day.

'I want to know if that Ellis fellow has been to see you any lately,' said father all at once.

'Not a great deal,' I answered.

'Did he come to see you the last night you were there?' said father.

'Yes, sir,' said I, 'he did come.'

'If you ever have another word to say to that fellow while I live, I'll kick you out of the house like a dog, daughter of mine though you be!' said he. Then he swore a great oath and called God to witness. 'Speak to that fellow again, if you dare, while I live!' said he.

I did not say a word; I just looked up at him as I sat there. Father turned pale, and shrank back, and put his hand to his throat, where

Rufus had clutched him. There were some purple finger-marks there.

'I suppose you would have been glad if he had killed me,' father cried out.

'I saved your life,' said I.

'What did you do with that pistol?' he asked.

'I put it back in the desk-drawer.'

I got up and went around and sat on the west doorstep, which is the front one. As I sat there, the bell rang for the Tuesday evening meeting, and Phœbe Dole and Maria Woods, two old maiden ladies, dressmakers, our next-door neighbours, went past on their way to meeting. Phœbe stopped and asked if Rufus and his wife were gone. Maria went around the house. Very soon they went on, and several other people passed. When they had gone it was as still as death.

I sat alone a long time, until I could see by the shadows that the full moon had risen. Then I went to my room and went to bed.

I lay awake a long time, crying. It seemed to me that all hope of marriage between Henry and me was over. I could not expect him to wait for me. I thought of that other girl; I could see her pretty face wherever I looked. But at last I cried myself to sleep.

At about five o'clock I awoke, and got up. Father always wanted his breakfast at six o'clock, and I had to prepare it now.

When father and I were alone, he always built the fire in the kitchen stove, but that morning I did not hear him stirring as usual, and I fancied that he must be so out of temper with me, that he would not build the fire.

I went to my closet for a dark blue calico dress which I wore to do housework in. It had hung there during all the school term. As I took it off the hook, my attention was caught by something strange about the dress I had worn the night before. This dress was made of thin summer silk; it was green in colour, sprinkled over with white rings. It had been my best dress for two summers, but now I was wearing it on hot afternoons at home, for it was the coolest dress I had. The night before, too, I had thought of the possibility of Henry's driving over from Digby and passing the house. He had done this sometimes during the last summer vacation, and I wished to look my best if he did.

As I took down the calico dress I saw what seemed to be a stain on the green silk. I threw on the calico hastily and then took the green silk and carried it over to the window. It was covered with spots—horrible great splashes and streaks down the front. The right sleeve, too, was stained, and all the stains were wet.

'What have I got on my dress?' said I.

It looked like blood. Then I smelled of it, and it was sickening in my nostrils, but I was not sure what the smell of blood was like. I thought I must have got the stains by some accident the night before.

'If that is blood on my dress,' I said, 'I must do something to get it off at once, or the dress will be ruined.'

It came to my mind that I had been told that blood-stains had been removed from cloth by an application of flour paste on the wrong side. I took my green silk, and ran down the back stairs, which lead—having a door at the foot—directly into the kitchen.

There was no fire in the kitchen stove, as I had thought. Everything was very solitary and still, except for the ticking of the clock on the shelf. When I crossed the kitchen to the pantry, however, the cat mewed to be let in from the shed. She had a little door of her own by which she could enter or leave the shed at will, an aperture just large enough for her Maltese body to pass at ease beside the shed door. It had a little lid, too, hung upon a leathern hinge. On my way I let the cat in; then I went to the pantry and got a bowl of flour. This I mixed with water into a stiff paste, and applied to the under surface of the stains on my dress. I then hung the dress up to dry in the dark end of a closet leading out of the kitchen, which contained some old clothes of father's.

Then I made up the fire in the kitchen stove. I made coffee, baked biscuits, and poached some eggs for breakfast.

Then I opened the door into the sitting-room and called, 'Father, breakfast is ready.' Suddenly I started. There was a red stain on the inside of the sitting-room door. My heart began to beat in my ears. 'Father!' I called out—'father!'

There was no answer.

'Father!' I called again, as loud as I could scream. 'Why don't you speak? What is the matter?'

The door of his bedroom stood open. I had a feeling that I saw a red reflection in there. I gathered myself together and went across the sitting-room to father's bedroom door. His little looking-glass hung over his bureau opposite his bed, which was reflected in it.

That was the first thing I saw, when I reached the door. I could see father in the looking-glass and the bed. Father was dead there; he had been murdered in the night.

II

I think I must have fainted away, for presently I found myself on the floor, and for a minute I could not remember what had happened. Then I remembered, and an awful, unreasoning terror seized me. 'I must lock all the doors quick,' I thought; 'quick, or the murderer will come back.'

I tried to get up, but I could not stand. I sank down again. I had to crawl out of the room on my hands and knees.

I went first to the front door; it was locked with a key and a bolt. I went next to the north door; and that was locked with a key and bolt. I went to the north shed door, and that was bolted. Then I went to the little-used east door in the shed, beside which the cat had her little passageway, and that was fastened with an iron hook. It has no latch.

The whole house was fastened on the inside. The thought struck me like an icy hand, 'The murderer is in this house!' I rose to my feet then; I unhooked that door, and ran out of the house, and out of the yard, as for my life.

I took the road to the village. The first house, where Phœbe Dole and Maria Woods live, is across a wide field from ours. I did not intend to stop there, for they were only women, and could do nothing; but seeing Phœbe looking out of the window I ran into the yard.

She opened the window.

'What is it?' said she. 'What is the matter, Sarah Fairbanks?'

Maria Woods came and leaned over her shoulder. Her face looked almost as white as her hair, and her blue eyes were dilated. My face must have frightened her.

'Father—father is murdered in his bed!' I said.

There was a scream, and Maria Woods' face disappeared from over Phœbe Dole's shoulder—she had fainted. I do not know whether Phœbe looked paler—she is always very pale—but I saw in her black eyes a look which I shall never forget. I think she began to suspect me at that moment.

Phœbe glanced back at Maria, but she asked me another question.

'Has he had words with anybody?' said she.

'Only with Rufus,' I said; 'but Rufus is gone.'

Phœbe turned away from the window to attend to Maria, and I ran on to the village.

A hundred people can testify what I did next—can tell how I called for the doctor and the deputy sheriff; how I went back to my own home with the horror-stricken crowd; how they flocked in and looked at poor father; but only the doctor touched him, very carefully, to see if he were quite dead; how the coroner came, and all the rest.

The pistol was in the bed beside father, but it had not been fired; the charge was still in the barrel. It was bloodstained, and there was one bruise on father's head which might have been inflicted by the pistol, used as a club. But the wound which caused his death was in his breast, and made evidently by some cutting instrument, though the cut was not a clean one; the weapon must have been dull.

They searched the house, lest the murderer should be hidden away. I heard Rufus Bennett's name whispered by one and another. Everybody seemed to know that he and father had had words the night before; I could not understand how, because I had told nobody except Phœbe Dole, who had had no time to spread the news, and I was sure that no one else had spoken of it.

They looked in the closet where my green silk dress hung, and pushed it aside, to be sure nobody was concealed behind it, but they did not notice anything wrong about it. It was dark in the closet, and besides, they did not look for anything like that until later.

All these people—the deputy sheriff, and afterwards the high sheriff, and other out-of-town officers, for whom they had telegraphed, and the neighbours—all hunted their own suspicion, and that was Rufus Bennett. All believed he had come back, and killed my father. They fitted all the facts to that belief. They made him do the deed with a long, slender screwdriver, which he had recently borrowed from one of the neighbours and had not returned. They made his finger-marks, which were still on my father's throat, fit the red prints of the sitting-room door. They made sure that he had returned and stolen into the house by the east door shed, while father and I sat on the doorsteps the evening before; that he had hidden himself away, perhaps in that very closet where my dress hung, and afterwards stolen out and killed my father, and then escaped.

They were not shaken when I told them that every door was bolted and barred that morning. They themselves found all the windows fastened down, except a few which were open on account of the heat, and even these last were raised only the width of the sash, and fastened with sticks, so that they could be raised no higher. Father was very cautious about fastening the house, for he sometimes had considerable sums of money by him. The officers saw all these difficulties in the way, but they fitted them somehow to their theory, and two deputy sheriffs were at once sent to apprehend Rufus.

They had not begun to suspect me then, and not the slightest watch was kept on my movements. The neighbours were very kind, and did everything to help me, relieving me altogether of all those last offices—in this case so much sadder than usual.

An inquest was held, and I told freely all I knew, except about the blood-stains on my dress. I hardly knew why I kept that back. I had no feeling then that I might have done the deed myself, and I could not bear to convict myself, if I was innocent.

Two of the neighbours, Mrs Holmes and Mrs Adams, remained with me all that day. Towards evening, when there were very few in the house, they went into the parlour to put it in order for the funeral, and I sat down alone in the kitchen. As I sat there by the window I thought of my green silk dress, and wondered if the stains were out. I went to the closet and brought the dress out to the light. The spots and streaks had almost disappeared. I took the dress out into the shed, and scraped off the flour paste, which was quite dry; I swept up the paste, burned it in the stove, took the dress upstairs to my own closet, and hung it in its old place. Neighbours remained with me all night.

At three o'clock in the afternoon of the next day, which was Thursday, I went over to Phœbe Dole's to see about a black dress to wear to the funeral. The neighbours had urged me to have my black silk dress altered a little, and trimmed with crape.

I found only Maria Woods at home. When she saw me she gave a little scream, and began to cry. She looked as if she had already been weeping for hours. Her blue eyes were bloodshot.

'Phœbe's gone over to—Mrs Whitney's to—try on her dress,' she sobbed.

'I want to get my black silk dress fixed a little,' said I.

'She'll be home—pretty soon,' said Maria.

I laid my dress on the sofa and sat down. Nobody ever consults

Maria about a dress. She sews well, but Phœbe does all the planning.

Maria Woods continued to sob like a child, holding her little soaked handkerchief over her face. Her shoulders heaved. As for me, I felt like a stone; I could not weep.

'Oh,' she gasped out finally, 'I knew—I knew! I told Phœbe—I knew just how it would be, I—knew!'

I roused myself at that.

'What do you mean?' said I.

'When Phœbe came home Tuesday night and said she heard your father and Rufus Bennett having words, I knew how it would be,' she choked out. 'I knew he had a dreadful temper.'

'Did Phœbe Dole know Tuesday night that father and Rufus Bennett had words?' said I.

'Yes,' said Maria Woods.

'How did she know?'

'She was going through your yard, the short cut to Mrs Ormsby's, to carry her brown alpaca dress home. She came right home and told me; and she overheard them.'

'Have you spoken of it to anybody but me?' said I.

Maria said she didn't know; she might have done so. Then she remembered hearing Phœbe herself speak of it to Harriet Sargent when she came in to try on her dress. It was easy to see how people knew about it.

I did not say any more, but I thought it was strange that Phœbe Dole had asked me if father had had words with anybody when she knew it all the time.

Phœbe came in before long. I tried on my dress, and she made her plan about the alterations, and the trimming. I made no suggestions. I did not care how it was done, but if I had cared it would have made no difference. Phœbe always does things her own way. All the women in the village are in a manner under Phœbe Dole's thumb. Their garments are visible proofs of her force of will.

While she was taking up my black silk on the shoulder seams, Phœbe Dole said, 'Let me see—you had a green silk dress made at Digby three summers ago, didn't you?'

'Yes,' I said.

'Well,' said she, 'why don't you have it dyed black? those thin silks dye quite nice. It would make you a good dress.'

I scarcely replied, and then she offered to dye it for me herself.

She had a recipe which she used with great success. I thought it was very kind of her, but did not say whether I would accept her offer or not. I could not fix my mind upon anything but the awful trouble I was in.

'I'll come over and get it tomorrow morning,' said Phœbe.

I thanked her. I thought of the stains, and then my mind seemed to wander again to the one subject.

All the time Maria Woods sat weeping. Finally Phœbe turned to her with impatience. 'If you can't keep calmer, you'd better go upstairs, Maria,' said she. 'You'll make Sarah sick. Look at her! she doesn't give way—and think of the reason she's got.'

'I've got reason too, ' Maria broke out; then, with a piteous shriek, 'Oh, I've got reason.'

'Maria Woods, go out of the room!' said Phœbe. Her sharpness made me jump, half dazed as I was.

Maria got up without a word, and went out of the room. bending almost double with convulsive sobs.

'She's been dreadfully worked up over your father's death,' said Phœbe, calmly, going on with the fitting. 'She's terribly nervous. Sometimes I have to be real sharp with her, for her own good.'

I nodded. Maria Woods has always been considered a sweet, weakly, dependent woman, and Phœbe Dole is undoubtedly very fond of her. She has seemed to shield her, and take care of her nearly all her life. The two have lived together since they were young girls.

Phœbe is tall, and very pale and thin; but she never had a day's illness. She is plain, yet there is a kind of severe goodness and faithfulness about her colourless face, with the smooth bands of white hair over her ears.

I went home as soon as my dress was fitted. That evening Henry Ellis came over to see me. I do not need to go into details concerning that visit. It seemed enough to say that he tendered the fullest sympathy and protection, and I accepted them. I cried a little, for the first time, and he soothed and comforted me.

Henry had driven over from Digby and tied his horse in the yard. At ten o'clock he bade me good-night on the doorstep, and was just turning his buggy around, when Mrs Adams came running to the door.

'Is this yours?' said she, and she held out a knot of yellow ribbon.

'Why, that's the ribbon you have around your whip, Henry,' said I.

He looked at it. 'So it is,' he said. 'I must have dropped it.' He put it into his pocket and drove away.

'He didn't drop that ribbon tonight!' said Mrs Adams. 'I found it Wednesday morning out in the yard. I thought I remembered seeing him have a yellow ribbon on his whip.'

III

When Mrs Adams told me she had picked up Henry's whip-ribbon Wednesday morning, I said nothing, but thought that Henry must have driven over Tuesday evening after all, and even come up into the yard, although the house was shut up and I in bed, to get a little nearer to me. I felt conscience-stricken because I could not help a thrill of happiness, when my father lay dead in the house.

My father was buried as privately and as quietly as we could bring it about. But it was a terrible ordeal. Meantime word came from Vermont that Rufus Bennett had been arrested on his farm. He was perfectly willing to come back with the officers, and, indeed, had not the slightest trouble in proving that he was at his home in Vermont when the murder took place. He proved by several witnesses that he was out of the State long before my father and I sat on the steps together that evening, and that he proceeded directly to his home as fast as the train and stage-coach could carry him.

The screwdriver with which the deed was supposed to have been committed was found, by the neighbour from whom it had been borrowed, in his wife's bureau drawer. It had been returned, and she had used it to put a picture-hook in her chamber. Bennett was discharged and returned to Vermont.

Then Mrs Adams told of the finding of the yellow ribbon from Henry Ellis's whip, and he was arrested, since he was held to have a motive for putting my father out of the world. Father's opposition to our marriage was well known, and Henry was suspected also of having had an eye to his money. It was found, indeed, that my father had more money than I had known myself.

Henry owned to having driven into the yard that night, and to having missed the ribbon from his whip on his return; but one of the hostlers in the livery stable in Digby, where he kept his horse and buggy, came forward and testified to finding the yellow ribbon in the carriage room that Tuesday night before Henry returned from his drive. There were two yellow ribbons in evidence, therefore, and the one produced by the hostler seemed to fit Henry's whip-stock the more exactly.

Moreover, nearly the exact minute of the murder was claimed to be proved by the post-mortem examination; and by the testimony of the stableman as to the hour of Henry's return and the speed of his horse, he was further cleared of suspicion; for if the opinion of the medical experts was correct, Henry must have returned to the livery stable too soon to have committed the murder.

He was discharged, at any rate, although suspicion still clung to him. Many people believe now in his guilt—those who do not, believe in mine; and some believe we were accomplices.

After Henry's discharge I was arrested. There was no one else left to accuse. There must be a motive for the murder; I was the only person left with a motive. Unlike the others, who were discharged after preliminary examination, I was held to the grand jury and taken to Dedham, where I spent four weeks in jail, awaiting the meeting of the grand jury.

Neither at the preliminary examination, nor before the grand jury, was I allowed to make the full and frank statement that I am making here. I was told simply to answer the questions that were put to me, and to volunteer nothing, and I obeyed.

I know nothing about law. I wished to do the best I could—to act in the wisest manner, for Henry's sake and my own. I said nothing about the green silk dress. They searched the house for all manner of things, at the time of my arrest, but the dress was not there—it was in Phœbe Dole's dye-kettle. She had come over after it one day when I was picking beans in the garden, and had taken it out of the closet. She brought it back herself, and told me this, after I had returned from Dedham.

'I thought I'd get it and surprise you,' said she. 'It's taken a beautiful black.'

She gave me a strange look—half as if she would see into my very soul, in spite of me, half as if she were in terror of what she would see there, as she spoke. I do not know just what Phœbe Dole's look meant. There may have been a stain left on that dress after all, and she may have seen it.

I suppose if it had not been for that flour-paste which I had learned to make, I should have hung for the murder of my father. As it was, the grand jury found no bill against me because there was absolutely no evidence to convict me; and I came home a free woman. And if people were condemned for their motives, would there be enough hangmen in the world?

They found no weapon with which I could have done the deed. They found no blood-stains on my clothes. The one thing which told against me, aside from my ever-present motive, was the fact that on the morning after the murder the doors and windows were fastened. My volunteering this information had of course weakened its force as against myself.

Then, too, some held that I might have been mistaken in my terror and excitement, and there was a theory, advanced by a few, that the murderer had meditated making me also a victim, and had locked the doors that he might not be frustrated in his designs, but had lost heart at the last and had allowed me to escape, and then fled himself. Some held that he had intended to force me to reveal the whereabouts of father's money, but his courage had failed him.

Father had quite a sum in a hiding-place which only he and I knew. But no search for money had been made, as far as any one could see—not a bureau drawer had been disturbed, and father's gold watch was ticking peacefully under his pillow; even his wallet in his vest pocket had not been opened. There was a small roll of banknotes in it, and some change; father never carried much money. I suppose if father's wallet and watch had been taken, I should not have been suspected at all.

I was discharged, as I have said, from lack of evidence, and have returned to my home—free, indeed, but with this awful burden of suspicion on my shoulders. That brings me up to the present day. I returned yesterday evening. This evening Henry Ellis has been over to see me; he will not come again, for I have forbidden him to do so. This is what I said to him:

'I know you are innocent, you know I am innocent. To all the world beside we are under suspicion—I more than you, but we are both under suspicion. If we are known to be together that suspicion is increased for both of us. I do not care for myself, but I do care for you. Separated from me the stigma attached to you will soon fade away, especially if you should marry elsewhere.'

Then Henry interrupted me. 'I will never marry elsewhere,' said he.

I could not help being glad that he said it, but I was firm.

'If you should see some good woman whom you could love, it will be better for you to marry elsewhere,' said I.

'I never will!' he said again. He put his arms around me, but I had strength to push him away.

'You never need, if I succeed in what I undertake before you meet the other,' said I. I began to think he had not cared for that pretty girl who boarded in the same house, after all.

'What is that?' he said. 'What are you going to undertake?'

'To find my father's murderer,' said I.

Henry gave me a strange look; then, before I could stop him, he took me fast in his arms, and kissed my forehead.

'As God is my witness, Sarah, I believe in your innocence,' he said; and from that minute I have felt sustained and fully confident of my power to do what I have undertaken.

My father's murderer I will find. Tomorrow I begin my search. I shall first make an exhaustive examination of the house, such as no officer in the case has yet made, in the hope of finding a clue. Every room I propose to divide into square yards, by line and measure, and every one of these square yards I will study as if it were a problem in algebra.

I have a theory that it is impossible for any human being to enter any house, and commit in it a deed of this kind, and not leave behind traces which are the known quantities in an algebraic equation to those who can use them.

There is a chance that I shall not be quite unaided. Henry has promised not to come again until I bid him, but he is to send a detective here from Boston—one whom he knows. In fact, that man is a cousin of his, or else there would be small hope of our securing him, even if I were to offer him a large price.

The man has been remarkably successful in several cases, but his health is not good; the work is a severe strain upon his nerves, and he is not driven to it from any lack of money. The physicians have forbidden him to undertake any new case, for a year at least, but Henry is confident that we may rely upon him for this.

I will now lay this aside and go to bed. Tomorrow is Wednesday; my father will have been dead seven weeks. Tomorrow morning I commence the work, in which, if it be in human power, aided by a higher wisdom, I shall succeed.

IV

(The pages which follow are from Miss Fairbanks' journal, begun after the conclusion of the notes already given to the reader.)

Wednesday night.—I have resolved to record carefully each day the progress I make in my examination of the house. I began today at the bottom—that is, with the room least likely to contain any clue, the parlour. I took a chalk line and a yardstick, and divided the floor into square yards, and every one of these squares I examined on my hands and knees. I found in this way literally nothing on the carpet but dust, lint, two common white pins, and three inches of blue sewing-silk.

At last I got the dustpan and brush, and yard by yard swept the floor. I took the sweepings in a white pasteboard box out into the yard in the strong sunlight, and examined them. There was nothing but dust and lint and five inches of brown woollen thread—evidently a ravelling of some dress material. The blue silk and the brown thread are the only possible clues which I found today, and they are hardly possible. Rufus's wife can probably account for them. I have written to her about them.

Nobody has come to the house all day. I went down to the store this afternoon to get some necessary provisions, and people stopped talking when I came in. The clerk took my money as if it were poison.

Thursday night.—Today I have searched the sitting-room, out of which my father's bedroom opens. I found two bloody footprints on the carpet which no one had noticed before—perhaps because the carpet itself is red and white. I used a microscope which I had in my school work. The footprints, which are close to the bedroom door, pointing out into the sitting-room, are both from the right foot; one is brighter than the other, but both are faint. The foot was evidently either bare or clad only in a stocking—the prints are so widely spread. They are wider than my father's shoes. I tried one in the brightest print.

I found nothing else new in the sitting-room. The blood-stains on the doors which have been already noted are still there. They had not been washed away, first by order of the sheriff, and next by mine. These stains are of two kinds: one looks as if made by a bloody garment brushing against it; the other, I should say, was made in the first place by the grasp of a bloody hand, and then brushed over with a cloth. There are none of these marks upon the door leading to the bedroom—they are on the doors leading into the front entry and the china closet. The china closet is really a pantry, although I use it only for my best dishes and preserves.

Friday night.—Today I searched the closet. One of the shelves, which is about as high as my shoulders, was blood-stained. It looked to me as if the murderer might have caught hold of it to steady himself. Did he turn faint after his dreadful deed? Some tumblers of jelly were ranged on that shelf and they had not been disturbed. There was only that bloody clutch on the edge.

I found on this closet floor, under the shelves, as if it had been rolled there by a careless foot, a button, evidently from a man's clothing. It is an ordinary black enamelled metal trousers-button: it had evidently been worn off and clumsily sewn on again, for a quantity of stout white thread is still clinging to it. This button must have belonged either to a single man or to one with an idle wife.

If one black button had been sewn on with white thread, another is likely to be. I may be wrong, but I regard this button as a clue.

The pantry was thoroughly swept—cleaned, indeed, by Rufus's wife, the day before she left. Neither my father nor Rufus could have dropped it there, and they never had occasion to go to that closet. The murderer dropped the button.

I have a white pasteboard box which I have marked 'clues'. In it I have put the button.

This afternoon Phœbe Dole came in. She is very kind. She had re-cut the dyed silk, and she fitted it to me. Her great shears clicking in my ears made me nervous. I did not feel like stopping to think about clothes. I hope I did not appear ungrateful, for she is the only soul beside Henry who has treated me as she did before this happened.

Phœbe asked me what I found to busy myself about, and I replied, 'I am searching for my father's murderer.' She asked me if I thought I should find a clue, and I replied, 'I think so.' I had found the button then, but I did not speak of it. She said Maria was not very well.

I saw her eyeing the stains on the doors, and I said I had not washed them off, for I thought they might yet serve a purpose in detecting the murderer. She looked closely at those on the entry-door—the brightest ones—and said she did not see how they could help, for there were no plain finger-marks there, and she should think they would make me nervous.

'I'm beyond being nervous,' I replied.

Saturday.—Today I have found something which I cannot understand. I have been at work in the room where my father came to his dreadful end. Of course some of the most startling evidences have been removed. The bed is clean, and the carpet washed, but the worst horror of it all clings to that room. The spirit of murder seemed to haunt it. It seemed to me at first that I could not enter that room, but in it I made a strange discovery.

My father, while he carried little money about his person, was in the habit of keeping considerable sums in the house; there is no bank within ten miles. However he was wary; he had a hiding-place which he had revealed to no one but myself. He had a small stand in his room near the end of his bed. Under this stand, or rather under the top of it, he had tacked a large leather wallet. In this he kept all his spare money. I remember how his eyes twinkled when he showed it to me.

'The average mind thinks things have either got to be in or on,' said my father. 'They don't consider there's ways of getting around gravitation and calculation.'

In searching my father's room, I called to mind that saying of his, and his peculiar system of concealment, and then I made my discovery. I have argued that in a search of this kind I ought not only to search for hidden traces of the criminal, but for everything which had been for any reason concealed. Something which my father himself had hidden, something from his past history, may furnish a motive for someone else.

The money in the wallet under the table, some five hundred dollars, had been removed and deposited in the bank. Nothing more was to be found there. I examined the bottom of the bureau, and the undersides of the chair seats. There are two chairs in the room, besides the cushioned rocker—green-painted wooden chairs, with flag seats. I found nothing under the seats.

Then I turned each of the green chairs completely over, and examined the bottoms of the legs. My heart leaped when I found a bit of leather tacked over one. I got the tack-hammer and drew the tacks. The chair-leg had been hollowed out, and for an inch the hole was packed tight with cotton. I began picking out the cotton, and soon I felt something hard. It proved to be an old-fashioned gold band, quite wide and heavy, like a wedding-ring.

I took it over to the window and found this inscription on the inside: 'Let love abide forever.' There were two dates—one in August, forty years ago, and the other in August of the present year.

I think the ring had never been worn; while the first part of the inscription is perfectly clear, it looks old, and the last is evidently freshly cut.

This could not have been my mother's ring. She had only her wedding-ring, and that was buried with her. I think my father must have treasured up this ring for years; but why? What does it mean? This can hardly be a clue; this can hardly lead to the discovery of a motive, but I will put it in the box with the rest.

Sunday night.—Today, of course, I did not pursue my search. I did not go to church. I could not face old friends that could not face me. Sometimes I think that everybody in my native village believes in my guilt. What must I have been in my general appearance and demeanour all my life? I have studied myself in the glass, and tried to discover the possibilities of evil that they must see in my face.

This afternoon, about three o'clock, the hour when people here have just finished their Sunday dinner, there was a knock on the north door. I answered it, and a strange young man stood there with a large book under his arm. He was thin and cleanly shaved, with a clerical air.

'I have a work here to which I would like to call your attention,' he began; and I stared at him in astonishment, for why should a book agent be peddling his wares upon the Sabbath?

His mouth twitched a little.

'It's Biblical Cyclopædia,' said he.

'I don't think I care to take it,' said I.

'You are Miss Sarah Fairbanks, I believe?'

'That is my name,' I replied stiffly.

'Mr Henry Ellis, of Digby, sent me here,' he said next. 'My name is Dix—Francis Dix.'

Then I knew it was Henry's first cousin from Boston—the detective who had come to help me. I felt the tears coming to my eyes.

'You are very kind to come,' I managed to say.

'I am selfish, not kind,' he returned, 'but you had better let me come in, or any chance of success in my book agency is lost, if the neighbours see me trying to sell it on a Sunday. And, Miss Fairbanks, this is a bona fide agency. I shall canvass the town.'

He came in. I showed him all that I have written, and he read it carefully. When he had finished he sat still for a long time, with his face screwed up in a peculiar meditative fashion.

'We'll ferret this out in three days at the most,' said he finally, with a sudden clearing of his face and a flash of his eyes at me.

'I had planned for three years, perhaps,' said I.

'I tell you, we'll do it in three days,' he repeated. 'Where can I get board while I canvass for this remarkable and interesting book under my arm? I can't stay here, of course, and there is no hotel. Do you think the two dressmakers next door, Phœbe Dole and the other one, would take me in?'

I said they had never taken boarders.

'Well, I'll go over and enquire,' said Mr Dix; and he had gone, with his book under his arm, almost before I knew it.

Never have I seen any one act with the strange noiseless soft speed that this man does. Can he prove me innocent in three days? He must have succeeded in getting board at Phœbe Dole's, for I saw him go past to meeting with her this evening. I feel sure he will be over very early tomorrow morning.

V

Monday night.—The detective came as I expected. I was up as soon as it was light, and he came across the dewy fields, with his Cyclopædia under his arm. He had stolen out from Phœbe Dole's back door.

He had me bring my father's pistol; then he bade me come with him out into the back yard. 'Now, fire it,' he said, thrusting the pistol into my hands. As I have said before, the charge was still in the barrel.

'I shall arouse the neighbourhood,' I said.

'Fire it,' he ordered.

I tried; I pulled the trigger as hard as I could.

'I can't do it,' I said.

'And you are a reasonably strong woman, too, aren't you?'

I said I had been considered so. Oh, how much I heard about the strength of my poor woman's arms, and their ability to strike that murderous weapon home!

Mr Dix took the pistol himself, and drew a little at the trigger. 'I could do it,' he said, 'but I won't. It would arouse the neighbourhood.'

'This is more evidence against me,' I said despairingly.

'The murderer had tried to fire the pistol and failed.'

'It is more evidence against the murderer', said Mr Dix.

We went into the house, where he examined my box of clues long and carefully. Looking at the ring, he asked whether there was a jeweller in this village, and I said there was not. I told him that my father oftener went on business to Acton, ten miles away, than elsewhere.

He examined very carefully the button which I had found in the closet, and then asked to see my father's wardrobe. That was soon done. Beside the suit in which father was laid away there was one other complete one in the closet in his room. Besides that, there were in this closet two overcoats, an old black frock coat, a pair of pepper-and-salt trousers, and two black vests. Mr Dix examined all the buttons; not one was missing.

There was still another old suit in the closet off the kitchen. This was examined, and no button found wanting.

'What did your father do for work the day before he died?' he then asked. I reflected and said that he had unpacked some stores which had come down from Vermont, and done some work out in the garden.

'What did he wear?'

'I think he wore the pepper-and-salt trousers and the black vest. He wore no coat, while at work.'

Mr Dix went quietly back to father's room and his closet, I following. He took out the grey trousers and the black vest, and examined them closely.

'What did he wear to protect these?' he asked.

'Why, he wore overalls!' I said at once. As I spoke I remembered seeing father go around the path to the yard, with those blue overalls drawn up high under his arms.

'Where are they?'

'Weren't they in the kitchen closet?'

'No.'

We looked again, however, in the kitchen closet; we searched the shed thoroughly. The cat came in through her little door, as we stood there, and brushed around our feet. Mr Dix stooped and stroked her. Then he went quickly to the door, beside which her little entrance was arranged, unhooked it, and stepped out. I was following him, but he motioned me back.

'None of my boarding mistress's windows command us,' he said, 'but she might come to the back door.'

I watched him. He passed slowly around the little winding footpath, which skirted the rear of our house and extended faintly through the grassy fields to the rear of Phœbe Dole's. He stopped, searched a clump of sweetbriar, went on to an old well, and stopped there. The well had been dry many a year, and was choked up with stones and rubbish. Some boards are laid over it, and a big stone or two, to keep them in place.

Mr Dix, glancing across at Phœbe Dole's back door, went down on his knees, rolled the stones away, then removed the boards and peered down the well. He stretched far over the brink, and reached down. He made many efforts; then he got up and came to me, and asked me to get for him an umbrella with a crooked handle, or something that he could hook into clothing.

I brought my own umbrella, the silver handle of which formed an exact hook. He went back to the well, knelt again, thrust in the umbrella and drew up, easily enough, what he had been fishing for. Then he came bringing it to me.

'Don't faint,' he said, and took hold of my arm. I gasped when I saw what he had—my father's blue overalls, all stained and splotched with blood!

I looked at them, then at him.

'Don't faint,' he said again. 'We're on the right track. This is where the button came from—see, see!' He pointed to one of the straps of the overalls, and the button was gone. Some white thread clung to it. Another black metal button was sewed on roughly with the same white thread that I found on the button in my box of clues.

'What does it mean?' I gasped out. My brain reeled.

'You shall know soon,' he said. He looked at his watch. Then he laid down the ghastly bundle he carried. 'It has puzzled you to know how the murderer went in and out and yet kept the doors locked, has it not?' he said.

'Yes.'

'Well, I am going out now. Hook that door after me.'

He went out, still carrying my umbrella. I hooked the door.

Presently I saw the lid of the cat's door lifted, and his hand and arm thrust through. He curved his arm up towards the hook, but it came short by half a foot. Then he withdrew his arm, and thrust in my silver-handled umbrella. He reached the door-hook easily enough with that.

Then he hooked it again. That was not so easy. He had to work a long time. Finally he accomplished it, unhooked the door again, and came in.

'That was how!' I said.

'No, it was not,' he returned. 'No human being, fresh from such a deed, could have used such patience as that to fasten the door after him. Please hang your arm down by your side.'

I obeyed. He looked at my arm, then at his own.

'Have you a tape measure?' he asked.

I brought one out of my work-basket. He measured his arm, then mine, and then the distance from the cat-door to the hook.

'I have two tasks for you today and tomorrow,' he said. I shall come here very little. Find all your father's old letters, and read them. Find a man or woman in this town whose arm is six inches longer than yours. Now I must go home, or my boarding-mistress will get curious.'

He went through the house to the front door, looked all ways to be sure no eyes were upon him, made three strides down the yard, and was pacing soberly up the street, with his Cyclopædia under his arm.

I made myself a cup of coffee, then I went about obeying his instructions. I read old letters all the forenoon; I found packages in trunks in the garret; there were quantities in father's desk. I have selected several to submit to Mr Dix. One of them treats of an old episode in father's youth, which must have years since ceased to interest him. It was concealed after his favourite fashion—tacked under the bottom of his desk. It was written forty years ago, by Maria Woods—two years before my father's marriage—and it was a refusal of an offer of his hand. It was written in the stilted fashion of that day; it might have been copied from a 'Complete Letter-writer'.

My father must have loved Maria Woods as dearly as I love Henry to keep that letter so carefully all these years. I thought he cared for my mother. He seemed as fond of her as other men of their wives, although I did use to wonder if Henry and I would ever get to be quite so much accustomed to each other.

Maria Woods must have been as beautiful as an angel when she was a girl. Mother was not pretty; she was stout, too, and awkward, and I suppose people would have called her rather slow and dull. But she was a good woman, and tried to do her duty.

Tuesday night.—This evening was my first opportunity to obey the second of Mr Dix's orders. It seemed to me the best way to compare the average length of arms was to go to the prayer-meeting. I could not go about the town with my tape measure, and demand of people that they should hold out their arms. Nobody knows how I dreaded to go to the meeting, but I went, and I looked not at my neighbour's cold altered faces, but at their arms.

I discovered what Mr Dix wished me to, but the discovery can avail nothing, and it is one he could have made himself. Phœbe Dole's arm is fully seven inches longer than mine. I never noticed it before, but she has an almost abnormally long arm. But why should Phœbe Dole have unhooked that door?

She made a prayer—a beautiful prayer. It comforted even me a little. She spoke of the tenderness of God in all the troubles of life, and how it never failed us.

When we were all going out I heard several persons speak of Mr Dix and his Biblical Cyclopædia. They decided that he was a theological student, book-canvassing to defray the expenses of his education.

Maria Woods was not at the meeting. Several asked Phœbe how she was, and she replied, 'Not very well.'

It is very late. I thought Mr Dix might be over tonight, but he has not been here.

Wednesday.—I can scarcely believe what I am about to write. Our investigations seem to point all to one person, and that person—— It is incredible! I will not believe it. Mr Dix came, as before, at dawn. He reported, and I reported. I showed Maria Woods' letter. He said he had driven to Acton, and found that the jeweller there had engraved the last date in the ring about six weeks ago.

'I don't want to seem rough, but your father was going to get married again,' said Mr Dix.

'I never knew him to go near any woman since mother died,' I protested.

'Nevertheless, he had made arrangements to be married,' persisted Mr Dix.

'Who was the woman?'

He pointed at the letter in my hand.

'Maria Woods?'

He nodded.

I stood looking at him—dazed. Such a possibility had never entered my head.

He produced an envelope from his pocket, and took out a little card with blue and brown threads neatly wound upon it.

'Let me see those threads you found,' he said.

I got the box and we compared them. He had a number of pieces of blue sewing-silk and brown woollen ravellings, and they matched mine exactly. 'Where did you find them?' I asked.

'In my boarding-mistress's piecebag.'

I stared at him. 'What does it mean?' I gasped out.

'What do you think?'

'It is impossible!'

VI

Wednesday continued.—When Mr Dix thus suggested to me the absurd possibility that Phœbe Dole had committed the murder, he and I were sitting in the kitchen. He was near the table; he laid a sheet of paper upon it, and began to write. The paper is before me.

'First'—said Mr Dix, and he wrote rapidly as he talked—'Whose arm is of such length that it might unlock a certain door of this house from the outside?—Phœbe Dole's.

'Second, who had in her piecebag bits of the same threads and ravellings found upon your parlour floor, where she had not by your knowledge entered?—Phœbe Dole.

'Third, who interested herself most strangely in your blood-stained green silk dress, even to dyeing it?—Phœbe Dole.

'Fourth, who was caught in a lie, while trying to force the guilt of the murder upon an innocent man?—Phœbe Dole.'

Mr Dix looked at me. I had gathered myself together. 'That proves nothing,' I said. 'There is no motive in her case.'

'There is a motive.'

'What is it?'

'Maria Woods shall tell you this afternoon.'

He then wrote.

'Fifth, who was seen to throw a bundle down the old well, in the rear of Martin Fairbanks's house, at one o'clock in the morning?— Phœbe Dole.'

'Was she—seen?' I gasped. Mr Dix nodded. Then he wrote.

'Sixth, who had a strong motive, which had been in existence many years ago?—Phœbe Dole.'

Mr Dix laid down his pen, and looked at me again. 'Well, what have you to say?' he asked.

'It is impossible!'

'Why?'

'She is a woman.'

'A man could have fired that pistol, as she tried to do.'

'It would have taken a man's strength to kill with the kind of weapon that was used,' I said.

'No, it would not. No great strength is required for such a blow.'

'But she is a woman!'

'Crime has no sex.'

'But she is a good woman—a church member. I heard her pray yesterday afternoon. It is not in character.'

'It is not for you, nor for me, nor for any mortal intelligence, to know what is, or is not in character,' said Mr Dix.

He arose and went away. I could only stare at him in a half-dazed manner.

Maria Woods came this afternoon, taking advantage of Phœbe's absence on a dressmaking errand. Maria has aged ten years in the last few weeks. Her hair is white, her cheeks are fallen in, her pretty colour is gone.

'May I have the ring he gave me forty years ago?' she faltered.

I gave it to her; she kissed it, and sobbed like a child. 'Phœbe took it away from me before,' she said; 'but she shan't this time.'

Maria related with piteous sobs the story of her long subordination to Phœbe Dole. This sweet child-like woman had always been completely under the sway of the other's stronger nature. The subordination went back beyond my father's original proposal to her; she had, before he made love to her as a girl, promised Phœbe she would not marry; and it was Phœbe who, by representing to her that she was bound by this solemn promise, had led her to write a letter to my father declining his offer, and sending back the ring.

'And after all, we were going to get married, if he had not died,' she said. 'He was going to give me this ring again, and he had had the other date put in. I should have been so happy!'

She stopped and stared at me with horror-stricken enquiry. 'What was Phœbe Dole doing in your back-yard at one o'clock that night?' she cried.

'What do you mean?' I returned.

'I saw Phœbe come out of your back shed-door at one o'clock that very night. She had a bundle in her arms. She went along the path about as far as the old well, then she stooped down, and seemed to be working at something. When she got up she didn't have the bundle. I was watching at our back-door. I thought I heard her go out a little while before, and went downstairs, and found that door unlocked. I went in quick, and up to my chamber, and into my bed, when she started home across the fields. Pretty soon I heard her come in, then I heard the pump going. She slept downstairs; she went on to her bedroom. What was she doing in your back-yard that night?'

'You must ask her,' said I. I felt my blood running cold.

'I've been afraid to,' moaned Maria Woods. 'She's been dreadful strange lately. I wish that book-agent was going to stay at our house.'

Maria Woods went home in about an hour. I got a ribbon for her, and she has my poor father's ring concealed in her withered bosom. Again I cannot believe this.

Thursday.—It is all over; Phœbe Dole has confessed! I do not know now in exactly what way Mr Dix brought it about—how he accused her of her crime. After breakfast I saw them coming across the fields; Phœbe came first, advancing with rapid strides like a man; Mr Dix followed, and my father's poor old sweetheart tottered behind, with her handkerchief at her eyes. Just as I noticed them the front-door bell rang; I found several people there, headed by the high sheriff. They crowded into the sitting-room just as Phœbe Dole came rushing in, with Mr Dix and Maria Woods.

'I did it!' Phœbe cried out to me. 'I am found out, and I have made up my mind to confess. She was going to marry your father—I found it out. I stopped it once before. This time I knew I couldn't unless I killed him. She's lived with me in that house for over forty years. There are other ties as strong as the marriage one, that are just as sacred. What right had he to take her away from me and break up my home?

'I overheard your father and Rufus Bennett having words. I thought folks would think he did it. I reasoned it all out. I had watched your cat go in that little door, I knew the shed-door hooked, I knew how long my arm was; I thought I could undo it. I stole over here a little after midnight. I went all around the house to be sure nobody was awake. Out in the front-yard I happened to think my shears were tied on my belt with a ribbon, and I untied them. I thought I put the ribbon in my pocket—it was a piece of yellow ribbon—but I suppose I didn't, because they found it afterwards, and thought it came off your young man's whip.

'I went round to the shed-door, unhooked it, and went in. The moon gave light enough. I got out your father's overalls from the kitchen closet; I knew where they were. I went through the sitting-room to the parlour. In there I slipped off my dress and skirts and put on the overalls. I put a handkerchief over my face, leaving only my eyes exposed. I crept out then into the sitting-room; there I pulled off my shoes and went into the bedroom.

'Your father was fast asleep; it was such a hot night, the clothes were thrown back and his chest was bare. The first thing I saw was that pistol on the stand beside his bed. I suppose he had had some fear of Rufus Bennett coming back after all. Suddenly I thought I'd better shoot him. It would be surer and quicker; and if you were aroused I knew that I could get away, and everybody would suppose that he had shot himself.

'I took up the pistol and held it close to his head. I had never fired a pistol, but I knew how it was done. I pulled. but it would not go off. Your father stirred a little—I was mad with terror—I struck at his head with the pistol. He opened his eyes and cried out; then I dropped the pistol, and took these—Phœbe Dole pointed to the great shining shears hanging at her waist—'for I am strong in my wrists. I only struck twice, over his heart.

'Then I went back into the sitting-room. I thought I heard a noise in the kitchen—I was full of terror then—and slipped into the sitting-room closet. I felt as if I were fainting, and clutched the shelf to keep from falling.

'I felt that I must go upstairs to see if you were asleep, to be sure you had not waked up when your father cried out. I thought if you had I should have to do the same by you. I crept upstairs to your chamber. You seemed sound asleep, but, as I watched, you stirred a little; but instead of striking at you I slipped into your closet. I heard nothing more from you. I felt myself wet with blood. I caught something hanging in your closet, and wiped myself over with it. I knew by the feeling it was your green silk. You kept quiet, and I saw you were asleep, so crept out of the closet, and down the stairs, got my clothes and shoes, and, out in the shed, took off the overalls and dressed myself. I rolled up the overalls, and took a board away from the old well and threw them in as I went home. I thought if they were found it would be no clue to me. The handkerchief, which was not much stained, I put to soak that night, and washed it out next morning, before Maria was up. I washed my hands and arms carefully that night, and also my shears.

'I expected Rufus Bennett would be accused of the murder, and, maybe, hung. I was prepared for that, but I did not like to think I had thrown suspicion upon you by staining your dress. I had nothing against you. I made up my mind I'd get hold of that dress—before anybody suspected you—and dye it black. I came in and got it, as you know. I was astonished not to see any more stains on it. I only found two or three little streaks that scarcely anybody would have noticed. I didn't know what to think; I suspected, of course, that you had found the stains and got them off, thinking they might bring suspicion upon you.

'I did not see how you could possibly suspect me in any case. I was glad when your young man was cleared. I had nothing against him. That is all I have to say.'

I think I must have fainted away then. I cannot describe the dreadful calmness with which that woman told this—that woman with the good face, whom I had last heard praying like a saint in meeting. I believe in demoniacal possession after this.

When I came to, the neighbours were around me, putting camphor on my head, and saying soothing things to me, and the old friendly faces had returned. But I wish I could forget!

They have taken Phœbe Dole away—I only know that. I cannot bear to talk any more about it when I think there must be a trial, and I must go!

Henry has been over this evening. I suppose we shall be happy after all, when I have had a little time to get over this. He says I have nothing more to worry about. Mr Dix has gone home: I hope Henry and I may be able to repay his kindness some day.

A month later: I have just heard that Phœbe Dole has died in prison! This is my last entry. May God help all other innocent women in hard straits as He has helped me!

The Case of Euphemia Raphash

M. P. SHIEL

> Man's goings are of God: how can a man then understand his own way?
>
> *Proverbs*

'Oh, Mr Parker, he is coming at last, sir!'

'Good heavens! you mean the Doctor?'

'The Doctor, sir—saw him with my own eyes—he is on foot—must have passed through the north park gates, and is at this moment coming up the drive!'

I ran to the lawn; saw him slowly coming in the old frock-coat of thin stuff, his eyes studying the ground.

'Ah, Parker'—he glanced up and held out a limp hand—'that you? Well, I hope?'

'*I* am well enough, thank you, Doctor.'

'And why the accented *I*? My sister, Parker?'

I was simply astounded.

'You have not then heard?'

'Heard? I have heard nothing.'

'Merciful heavens! in what land have you then wandered?'

'Parker, in a land far away.'

I said nothing more, nor he. For the first time in his life he felt fear—fear to ask the question which I felt fear to answer.

We passed into the gloomy half-ruined pile, an ancient place, the home of a race most ancient. In the little room we called 'study', he seated himself on the divan, and with perfect composure said:

'Now, Parker—my sister.'

'Miss Euphemia, Doctor, is no more.'

His face was stone; but he sallowed. After a time I distinctly heard him mutter:

'I thought as much—so it happened once before.'

What? I was all wonder; but only added:

'Three weeks ago, Doctor.'

'Of what?'

'She was——'

'Go on.'

'Doctor, she was——'

'Say it, man—she was murdered.'

'She was murdered, Doctor.'

I see him now; spare and small, mighty in forehead, which at the top was thinly covered with a cropped iron-grey scrub: thick, tight lips; sallow, shaven face; and those eyes, grey, so unquiet, never for an instant of life ceasing the internal inquisition in which they wandered fro and to, down, and up, and round.

A name high in the view of the world was his—as an apostle of science, as hierophant among the arch-priests of learning. During the fifteen years I had acted as his secretary, we had produced nine books, each monumental in its way. His activities in the domain of thought were, in fact, immeasurable—though I will not say that they were continuous; or, at least, not continuous so far as *I* was concerned; for the doctor would ever and anon leave me, perhaps in the midst of some work, and without warning snatch himself wholly for long weeks from Raphash Towers; nor could I then determine whether sarcophagi of old Egyptian dynasties had lured him overseas, or excavations at Mycenæ, or the enticements of Khorsabad and Balbec. I knew only that he had quietly and mysteriously disappeared; that he as quietly returned in due course to his labours; and that his taciturnity was so inveterate as to seem brutish.

An old housekeeper and myself, beside the Doctor and Miss Euphemia, were the only inmates of the old mansion. We occupied an insignificant portion of the ground floor of one of the immense wings. Never visitor broke our solitude, except a gentleman whose calls always corresponded with the Doctor's absences. The lengthy tête-à-têtes of this personage with Miss Euphemia led me to suspect an old flame, to which the Doctor had had known objections.

Miss Euphemia was a lady of forty-five years, taller than her brother, but remarkably like him. She, too, had become learned by dint of reading the Doctor's books. For the life of me I cannot now say how it was, for they hardly ever exchanged a word, but I had gradually arrived at the conviction that each of these two lives was as necessary to the other as the air it breathed.

Yet for three weeks the newspapers had been discussing her singular disappearance, and he, of all others, knew not one word of the matter! He looked at me through half-closed lids, and said, with that utter dryness of tone which was his:

'Tell me the circumstances.'

I answered: 'I was away in London on business connected with your Shropshire seat, and can only repeat the depositions of old Mrs Grant. Miss Raphash had, strange to say, been persuaded to attend the funeral of a lady, known to her in youth, at Ringlethorpe; and, staying afterwards with the mourning friends, did not return till midnight. She wore, it seems, some old family jewels. By one, however, the house was in darkness; and it was an hour later that a scream shrilled through the night. Mrs Grant was able to light a candle, and had opened her door, when she dimly saw a man rushing towards her with some singular weapon in his hand which flashed vividly in the half-dark—a small, wiry man, she thinks. She had but time to slam her door, when he dashed himself frantically against it, where-upon she fancies she heard the angry remonstrance of another voice. Here, however, her evidence is vague; hours later when she woke to consciousness, she rushed to her mistress' room, and found it empty.'

'Of the jewels?'

'Of Miss Raphash herself.'

'And the jewels?'

'They lay on the dressing-table where they had been placed, untouched.'

'Clearly the murderer was not a burglar.'

'Clearly he was. He, or they, took other things, valuables from your room and mine to the amount of four hundred pounds.'

'But some of these have been traced?'

'Not one. Some have been found—none "traced".'

'Where found?'

'In a clump of bushes immediately beneath the balcony of the south wing.'

'They were singular burglars. And my sister's body was found——'

'Nowhere.'

'It was buried in the park.'

'Quite certainly not. The park has been subjected to too minute a scrutiny for that.'

'It was burned.'

'Not in the house, and again not in the grounds. It was for some ghastly reason conveyed away.'

'It is not *now* in the house, for instance?'

'No—if the most recondite search in the darkest recesses of the mansion are of any value.'

'There were blood-stains?'

'A few on the bed.'

'No clue?'

'One. It would seem that the assassin, or one of them, before gaining entrance, drew off his boots, and on running away left them, for some undreamable reason, behind him.'

'It is very simple. He went in a pair of yours or mine.'

'No. Had his foot, as measured by his boot, been one-third as small, it could never have been urged into a boot of yours or mine.'

'And yet Mrs Grant says he was a small man; it is peculiar he should have so immense a foot.'

'It is clear then that there were more than one.'

'Yet I incline to the one-man theory; for through some failure of courage or memory, one might leave the jewels, but hardly two. Mrs Grant, distracted, may have mistaken his stature; and in the course of my anthropological experience, I have even come across that very discrepancy between man and foot—an occasional survival of simian traits in human beings.'

'There is another point,' I said, 'the boots were found to be odd.'

'But that is a clue!' he said. 'I have the man in my grasp. Have you now told me everything?'

'Except that a gentleman had called to see Miss Raphash that afternoon.'

'Ah—what sort of man?'

'Tall, black-dressed, middle-aged, with side-whiskers. I have seem him here when you have been away. Mrs Grant says that Miss Raphash spoke to him with some show of anger, though no words could be made out.'

'Ah!' said the Doctor, and resumed a restless walk.

'It is not impossible,' he continued after a while, 'that deeps, black to the eye of a policeman, may lighten to the eye of a thinker. Let us go over the house.'

Science had taught the Doctor to labour without the stimulus of expectancy. On this hopeless search we spent several hours in the mouldy vastnesses of the house; in the solemn silence of old Tudor wings which perhaps no foot had set a-barking with echoes for centuries; deep down in the nitre-crusted vaults. We came at length to an old room on the second floor of the south wing overlooking a patch of garden, rank now with shrubs. The chamber was very damp and gloomy; its tapestries of Arras had mouldered to grey shreds. The Doctor had partly used it as a depository: here were stacked bones of mammoths, embrya in flasks, fossils, spongiadæ, implements of stone, iron, and bronze. Along one side was a vast oaken chest, carved, black with centuries of age. It, as well as a secret recess behind a panel in the wall, contained piles of bones methodically labelled.

The lock of the door was of peculiar construction, and the Doctor had the key always about him. I could not therefore but smile, when on entering, I said to him:

'Here, at least, our search is fantastic.'

He glanced at me, and passed in doggedly. Through the grime of the window light hardly entered. Here a piece of old armour, there a cinerary urn of Etruria showed in the gloom its grey freckles of fungus; a dank dust was over all.

'Some one has been here,' said the Doctor.

'Doctor!'

'The catch of the window seems awry: notice the dust on the floor; does it not look——'

'But if it is impossible, it is impossible, and there an end,' I answered.

He opened the window. Below was the stone balcony of the first floor of the wing; and from it to a point near the window a tin rain-spout ran up. It was among the bushes of the garden beneath the balcony that the stolen valuables had been found.

'He climbed up, you see, by the spout,' said the Doctor. 'The feat seems superhuman: but there is the spout, and here is the turned window-catch. We must confront phenomena as we find them.'

'But at least, Doctor, he did not climb up with a dead body in his arms?'

'No; you are right.'

'And he did not enter by the door.'

'No.'

'Then our search here is absurd.'

'Doubtless. You might look behind the panelling.'

I looked and saw only the dust-grown bones of old monsters.

'She is not in *here*, now?' he said, and tapped the oaken chest with his knuckles.

I smiled.

'No, Doctor, she is not in there. The man does not live who could force the century-old secret of *that* riveted lid.'

'Come then, Parker. Come—we shall find her.'

We went out, and he locked the old silences and solitudes within the room once more.

Men of great minds undertake tasks which, from their very vastness, seem nothing less than silly to men of smaller gauge. The region of the impossible, indeed, is the true sphere-of-action of genius. But, on the other hand, the crowd may be excused if, observing this, they become sometimes incredulous, resentful, and even cachinatory.

And, I confess, it was not without resentment that I listened to Doctor Raphash as he said to me:

'Let us find *him*, Parker—the murderer of my sister—the secreter of her body. This is a task we must not leave to the crude intellects of the recognized authorities. Let us hunt *him* down—and, *after* that, we shall resume our consideration of the science of Comparative Mythology.'

But his method, at least, was singular. To acquire personal intimacy with the whole criminal class of London is an undertaking, if possible, at all events far from light. Yet this was his notion. In a few months we had learned a new language, become acclimatized denizens of a new world—the language and the world of the East of London. Our dress was the dress of the 'navvy'; our habits those of the ne'er-do-well.

And now most wondrously were revealed to me ineffable deeps in Doctor Raphash's character. The intensity of this hatred of an unknown man to me seemed hellish. 'Let us hunt *him* down.' His life became the incarnation of that sentence. It was the man of science turned beast of prey, but retaining the perfect scientific calm; an intensity bordering on lunacy shrouding itself behind the serenity of ocean-depths; the avenging angel *without* the flashing eye and flaming sword.

Days and nights we spent in public houses, gambling-hells, cells of pawnbrokers, with roughs at slum-corners, stormy crowds at music-hall doors. We were boon companions of men who related to one another without secrecy or shame-blush their achievements in every species of crime. In the morning we parted; to compare late at night notes of the day's haps. Then far into the morning hours I would hear the slow soft tread of that divine patience to and fro in his room near mine. This, and a heightened glare in his eyes, were all the indication of the mania fretting at his heart.

One day I heard something.

In a gin-palace two women, dissolute of face, stood at the bar.

'And how about your old man, then?' I heard.

'Oh, he must fish for hisself, he must. I took his boots, the last thing I've got, to the pawn this morning, and they wouldn't take them.'

'Ain't they no good, then?'

'They're sound enough, but they're odd.'

'Go on!'

'S'help me. I nearly tore his eyes out over them same boots. I buys my lord a seven-and-eleven pair in the summer and sends him hop-picking in them; two months ago he turns up with his own boot on the right foot and somebody else's on the other.'

'And what accounts did he give of hisself?'

'There's where the provoking part of it comes in. Every time I asks him about it, it's "Drop it, mate", and "Drop it, I tell you, mate." He was on the job, you may bet, got into some scrape, and now dursn't say nothink about it.'

I need not mention the steps by which, in half-an-hour, I had become the bosom friend of these two women. The time, place, and circumstances of the boots profoundly impressed me, and when I parted from them I felt assured that the name and address I had obtained were those of the man we sought. When Doctor Raphash returned, haggard and pallid, to our little garret that night, I pressed his hand.

'You have news for me, Parker.'

'I have heard something that may have some bearing on the case.' I told him the incident.

'Undoubtedly—it has some bearing. Let us go.'

'You look tired tonight, tomorrow perhaps——'

'Not at all! Tonight, man—now—*now*—is the time to find what we seek'—and he stamped on the floor.

I glanced, startled, at him. The action seemed like a sign of the break-up of that supernal serenity which characterized him.

We passed out, I taking the precaution to bring with me a Colt's revolver. When, by the way of endless labyrinths, we reached the address the Doctor at last spoke:

'There is no light, you see; he is, probably, still out. Suppose you wait till he comes; then speak, take him under the lamp there, see the boots, and ask him to drink with you. I, waiting at yonder corner, will then join you.'

Flakes of snow drifted downwards. I walked sentinel-wise; the Doctor crouched still at his post. From a Swedish chapel I heard the strokes of twelve, and at the same moment a working-man approached me.

'Cold tonight, mate,' I said, carelessly.

'Ah, that it is,' he answered.

His teeth chattered—his face wore a blue hue. Turned-up coat-collar, and buried hands, and forward pose, spoke of his shivering agonies.

'You look frozen. Come and have a drink along with me.'

'I could do with one, mate. I haven't tasted grub this day.'

'What—broke?'

'Dead broke!'

'Come along then—the "Brown Bear".'

He followed me. Under the lamp I stopped.

'Do you like the "Brown Bear"? If not——'

The light fell upon him. A sense of contempt and disappointment overcame me at the sight of his weak face, sheepish blue eyes. But there, at any rate, were the counterparts of the odd boots I had handed over to the authorities.

The Doctor had slowly approached us, and was in the middle of the road when Hardy, glancing, saw him.

The change in the man's face was sudden and wonderful.

His eyes glared; he tottered, livid, against a railing; then, suddenly taking to his heels, fled, as for dear life, down a turning.

The Doctor followed, and then I. And now powers of physique, as unexpected as previously depths of soul in my old friend, stood visible to me. He distanced me. His feet grew winged. Hardy, indeed, had an advantage in his knowledge of the intricate grimy courts down which he dodged. Sometimes for a moment he disappeared. But the Doctor slowly gained upon him, 'hunting him down'. The streets were all but deserted.

Suddenly Hardy dashed into a cul-de-sac. The house at the end was empty, every window broken. If the fugitive, then, could gain an entrance his escape by the back was safe. I judged that this was the house for which he had all along been making. On reaching it, Hardy dashed down the area steps to a basement below the street-level.

'Shoot!' cried the Doctor, looking back. 'Shoot with the revolver—shoot!'

This I was far from willing to do, but it was already too late; for Hardy had disappeared. A minute afterwards we, too, had rushed down the steps, and through a gate-like door passed into a low, wide, damp cellar of which the ground was a soft, powdery earth covering our ankles. There was no other visible means of egress, and I was looking about for Hardy, when the gate-door banged suddenly behind us, and a bar clanged down into a staple in the outer wall.

So that we were prisoners. That the man had entered the cellar was certain, and also that he had found some means of leaving it other than the door. But here our knowledge ended. The darkness was Erebus itself; whole clouds rose with every step and choked us; and the intensity of damp cold, after our run, hardly made speech possible. I groped round the walls, fired my revolver; but the flash revealed nothing but a portion of unhewn wall and low ceiling; I shouted at the door; but the neighbouring houses were ruins—an echo answered me.

Towards the early morning I received, I confess, a thrilling shock of horror from Doctor Raphash. That he was not himself, that he suffered far more than I, became apparent. Once or twice only had he spoken through the night, sitting crouched in the dust of a corner, his knees bent up, his head buried in his arms. By palpation I knew him in this position.

Once I said in alarm:

'Doctor, do not sleep! This cold——'

The doctor laughed aloud.

'No, no,' he said bitterly; 'I won't sleep; small fear of that—tonight.'

I walked for warmth to and fro, treading warily on the dust. A deep groan drew me to him: my cold fingers touched his forehead with the sensation of contact with a heated plate.

'You are suffering greatly,' I said.

'Leave me alone, Parker! Go from me!'

An hour, and I knew that he was stalking swiftly up and down the whole length of the cellar; swiftly! filling it with a continuous convolute reek of the brown incense of the dust. Long I stood, noting his faint sounds as he came near, losing them, following in fancy his cloudy progress, determining that now he was here, now there, now yonder. His disjointed mutterings guided me. He seemed oblivious of my presence.

When the air had finally become unbreatheable, I moved to go to him. My head came into contact with something, which on seizing I found to be a rope pendant from the ceiling. Unable to guess its purpose, I succeeded after many efforts in climbing it. My head struck the ceiling. Groping round with my hand, I encountered what seemed like the inner panels of a trapdoor. The means of Hardy's escape flashed upon me. I pushed with my knuckles, and a thin stream of light entered. In another minute I was free on the other side—it was already day.

A strange, pallid face looked up at me, rolling wild eyes. I drew him up, and together we passed out to the street.

Here he suddenly seized my hand.

'Parker!' his breath came in gasps—'be a leech in your tenacity—as you love me, man! Hunt him down! Goodbye.... Madman! do not follow! Good-bye....'

And before I could surge from the depths of maze and stupor into which the hissed words had plunged me, he had rushed furiously down the street, and vanished into a passing cab.

After Dr Raphash's mysterious desertion of our quest when success seemed near, I simply returned to the Towers, and waited. I now, in fact, considered my duty done when I had described to the police the fellow with the odd boots, who at this time was in hiding.

It was a month later that I observed one evening, as I walked about the grounds, that a man, hearing my approaching footsteps, had ducked his head from my sight in a clump of bushes—the very bushes, by the way, in which the stolen articles had been discovered.

I was accompanied by a large mastiff. Coming closer to the spot, I said aloud:

'Do not run, simply rise, and hold your hands over your head. I happen to be armed—and you see the dog.'

The crack of a pistol would have much less surprised me than the hang-dog air with which he rose before me. I recognized at once the insipid face of Hardy.

'No offence, master,' he said, touching his hat, trembling like an aspen.

'Ah, we have met before, Hardy.'

He scrutinized my face, but shook his head.

'You know me better 'n I know you, sir.'

'Well, Charles, you must come with me.' I said. I led him by the arm into a room of the house, instructing Mrs Grant at the entrance to send for a couple of the rather distant local police. I then closed the door, and proceeded to examine my prisoner. The creature wept!

'Now, Hardy,' I said, 'dry your tears, and tell me how came you in those bushes tonight.'

'I was looking for the rings and things. It was hunger drove me—they've been hunting me like an animal for the last month, and I give myself up.'

'What rings?'

'The rings I dropped in those bushes. I thought that, anyway, one of them might by chance be left there still.'

'You admit the burglary, then?'

'Yes, master, I admit it. It was my first, and it will be my last. I haven't had a moment's peace since. I even put up a rope in an old cellar to hang myself, only I'm a coward——'

'And you admit the murder?'

'Murder, master?' he cried with scared face—'murder! Why, it wasn't *me* who did the murder, it was one of the other two, and didn't I nearly drop dead with fright when I see it done?'

'There were, then, two others?'

'Yes, sir, a working man such as myself, and an old gent.'

'Tell me about it.'

'I and a mate of mine, sir, came down hop picking. He was a wild chap, and hops was too slow for him; so he says to me as how some of these country houses was mere child's play, with plenty to be got, and not much danger, besides. He was one of those chaps it's no use saying "no" to, so one night here we stood behind the old shed on the other side, waiting till the old lady was well asleep, when all of a sudden, as if he'd sprung from the ground, this old gent stood between us. I started running; he looked like a spirit to me; but Jim, who was more bolder like than me, he stands his ground; soon he whistles to me, and when I come up, he ses, "'Ere's a lark, Charlie," ses he, "the old chap's on the job hisself!" "Partnership's a leaky ship, Jim," ses I; but he only ses, "Oh, bother, live and let live." Well, pretty soon I and Jim take our boots off, and we all get inside. No sooner inside, than the old man takes the lead, showing the way, telling us what to do, and me and Jim does everything he tells us, quite nat'ral like. He knew every crick of the place; and first he takes us into a room, and ses he, quite wild like, "Plunder now! raven and harry! to your souls' content!" And then he reaches down a case from a shelf, and takes out a strange, shiny knife, locks the case again—I believe he had keys to every lock in the place—and rushes out of the room into the one opposite. "Queer chap, that," ses Jim, looking queer hisself, "makes me feel shivery all over", and before I could tell him I felt sure the man was a devil or a ghost, we hear a struggle in the opposite room—a gasping for breath—and then a long shriek which I ain't ever going to forget while I live. Immediately after, out he flies with blazing eyes, and dashes hisself against the other old woman's door yonder. Jim, sweating cold, plucks up courage to reason with him a bit, and at last he runs back to the murdered lady, and dashes out again with her in his arms, light as a feather, a gash showing right across her chest, her grey hair trailing on the ground. And now he comes up to us, and quite lofty like ses he, "Marshal yourselves before me—march! march! and I will lead you where trophies and treasures lie thick-heaped for yer 'arvesting!" His words is branded into my brain. And then he makes us walk before him right across the building into the other wing and up two flights of stairs, till we come to a dusty room with a lot of bones of dead people—and there, oh great God! hide me! there—there—*there he is*! He will kill me, as he killed my mate—he will kill you, too——'

He started wildly about, rushed behind my chair, and crouched down there. The man's shriek of panic horror thrilled me through, and as the ponderous door swung slowly wide on its hinges, and Dr Raphash calmly entered the room, I clung paralysed to my seat.

'Well, Parker,' he said in the old callous dry voice, 'here I am again, you see. But whom have we . . . the murderer caught at last, surely!' and triumph lighted his eyes as they rested on Hardy, who, pale and panting, now leaned against the tapestries.

'Yes, the murderer!' gasped Hardy, 'but that's not me! Oh, there's plenty of proofs if it comes to that! That long coat is the very one you wore—have you washed out the blood-splash on the sleeve yet?'

Dr Raphash sat, barely smiling, examining the face of Hardy. Presently he looked at his arm.

'It is a remarkable thing,' he said, speaking to himself: 'I *have* noticed a stain here on my sleeve; it cannot be blood; Parker, see, it looks not like blood, man—eh?'

But, as for me, a red mist hung thick before my eyes; I could see nothing.

'It *is* blood,' continued Hardy, gaining courage from the Doctor's calm—'you know it is, or perhaps you were too mad that night to know anything. Who but a madman would have carried the lady's body all the distance to that old chest; and there, didn't you chase Jim round and round the room and stab him like a dog, because you said one body wasn't enough to fill the chest? And if I hadn't slipped down to the balcony by a spout, wouldn't you have killed me, too; and didn't you look out of the window and tell me to prepare myself because you was coming, and didn't I have to jump from the balcony to the ground, rolling over, and dropping all the things I had; and didn't I just have time to draw on two of the boots when you came down and started after me?'

I was looking at Dr Raphash; during this categorical charge, no sound had issued from his lips; gradually a yellow pallor as of death had overspread his features, and the muscles of his face became tense and fixed; his head drooped forward, and his arms and legs stretched stiffly from his body; the cold stony glare in his eyes lent to his face a look of rhadamanthine sternness awful to see.

I ran and seized the clammy fingers in mine; but he did not recognize me. So he remained for several minutes, no sound breaking the silence of the room.

Then, still rigid in all his limbs, he raised his head, and let it drop heavily over the back of the chair; and, with the action, there burst from his blanched lips—higher and higher, peal on peal, in horrid articulation, in shrillest staccato—a carillon of maniac laughter. When this had passed, his whole face slowly settled into the vacant smile of idiocy.

With creeping flesh, I seized Hardy by the arm, rushed—faint—from the room, and locked the door upon the ruin within.

In this way Dr Arnot Raphash hunted down the murderer of his sister; and so, with him, fell the Jewish House of Raphash in the county of Kent.

Some days later I received a letter, of which the following are a few extracts:

When I tell you that I am the proprietor of the private asylum from which this letter is dated, and a cousin of Dr Raphash, you will at once conjecture that his (to you) unaccountable absences from home always corresponded with his voluntary sojourns in my establishment. He well knew the warning symptoms—head pains, a high temperature, etc.—and he usually had two or three days grace before the definite onset of the malady. Sometimes, again, the attack was more sudden, especially when preceded by any excitement; thus, when he reached my establishment a month ago he was already mad, and I at once guessed some previous violent agitation.... His first paroxysm occurred at the age of thirty, when he destroyed a just-married wife by locking her in a room filled by him with a poisonous gas. In the sane state he had no recollection of his insane acts, which were distinguished by their cunning and a strongly marked homicidal mania, directed chiefly against those for whom he most cared. He never knew of his wife's fate, for he was at once placed under my care, and on returning home found her buried.... When he was leaving me, 'cured', after the death of his sister, I deemed it prudent to say nothing to him of the tragedy, preferring that the journey to the Towers should intervene before the shock of the news fell on his newly restored powers; hence his ignorance of the matter.... You have probably seen me on my visits to Miss Raphash when the Doctor was away from home; their object was to give that minute report of her brother which alone could satisfy her. On the very day of the tragedy I had a somewhat angry dispute with her respecting the expediency of putting her brother into irons, she deprecating, I insisting. Unfortunately, I allowed her to influence me, and her death was the result.... It is now beyond all doubt that the Doctor escaped from my establishment on that night, though how he contrived to pass out of the house and grounds and into them again without detection is yet unexplained; but to his cunning, as I have hinted, there were positively no bounds.... I need only add that I shall soon have—I may almost say the pleasure—of announcing to you the death of Dr Raphash. He may still, indeed, linger for a few weeks; but the end, in any case, cannot be distant.

The Tin Box

HERBERT KEEN

'If I were you, Perkins,' said Mr Booth one evening in the smoking-room, 'I should take care what I was about with that little widow.'

'You mean Mrs Williams?' I enquired.

'Oh! Is that her name?' remarked my friend, carelessly, refilling his pipe with deliberation.

'Why, you know it is!' I returned, rather sharply.

'I have a bad memory for names,' said Mr Booth, with a slight shrug; 'you seem to be getting quite intimate.'

'I'm decently civil to her,' I replied, significantly.

'And I have avoided her? Yes; that's quite true,' said Mr Booth, smiling. 'Perhaps I instinctively share Mr Weller senior's antipathy to widows. Anyhow, I don't like the face of this one.'

I was astonished and rather disturbed at this. I had great confidence in my friend's judgement, but when I recalled to mind the refined and delicate features, the soft trustful brown eyes, the gentle voice, and the timid shrinking manner of the unfortunate lady he referred to, I was filled with indignation at his cynical attitude. Mrs Williams had resided at Elvira House for about a week or ten days, with her only child, a pretty little girl of five years old, and, owing to the accident of being placed next to her at the dinner-table, I had struck up an acquaintance with her. But she was neither remarkably good-looking nor particularly young, and my predilection was rather due to sympathy and good-nature than to admiration for her personal charms. Besides, she was apparently the last person to court attention, for her whole thoughts seemed centred upon her child, whom she evidently adored.

'I fancy she manœuvred a little to get put next to you at table,' said Mr Booth, watching me quietly.

'You wouldn't say that if you knew her better,' I retorted, hotly.

'You think it was an accident? Well, perhaps!' said my companion, in his enigmatical way.

'I'm sure of it,' I said, emphatically. 'Mrs Nix arranged it.'

'All right, old fellow. It's no concern of mine,' said Mr Booth, good-humouredly. 'Only I shouldn't lend her any more money if I were you.'

'How do you know I have done so?' I enquired, reddening.

'You asked me to change you a cheque the other day. It is a mere guess, but putting two and two together——'

'You happen to be right for once,' I interrupted, with some vexation. 'I lent her ten pounds, till her dividends fall due on Tuesday next. I suppose you are going to suggest that the money is lost?'

'It depends upon her circumstances,' he replied, nodding his head.

'Well, do you know anything about her? Come, Booth! Out with it!' I exclaimed, irritably.

'I? How should I?' said he, raising his eyebrows. 'I've never seen her before in my life.'

'She is the widow of a Mr John Williams, who died about two years ago. He lived at Gateshead, and was a wholesale tobacconist. He left everything to her by his will,' I explained, to show that I was not wholly ignorant of the lady's affairs.

'How do you know?' enquired Mr Booth.

'She showed me a probate,' I replied. 'I didn't ask her, but when she requested me to accommodate her with that trifle of money, she volunteered to explain how she was situated.'

'I see,' observed Mr Booth, apparently impressed.

'Unfortunately the poor lady was left very badly off,' I went on, mollified by the change in my friend's manner, which was now more sympathetic, 'and that is what now brings her up to town. She has a fixed belief that her husband, who seems to have been somewhat eccentric in his later days, deposited some money or securities at some bank in London or elsewhere.'

'Has she any clue?' enquired Mr Booth, manifestly interested.

'Not that I know of. She is very reticent,' I replied.

'She hasn't asked your assistance then?' said my friend.

'No. Of course I should be pleased to help if I could,' I said, with a touch of defiance in my tone.

Mr Booth did not gainsay me this time; either he was tired of the subject or else he perceived that I rather resented his interference. At all events he relapsed into one of those silent moods in which he was wont to indulge, and sat puffing at his pipe with his eyes fixed on the fire for the remainder of the evening, without joining in the general conversation which presently ensued as other guests strolled in.

I was annoyed with him because I thought that his opinion of poor little Mrs Williams was unreasonably prejudiced and very unjust; nevertheless, his warning was not quite thrown away upon me, for I determined to observe her with closer attention. The only result of this, however, was to convince me more firmly than ever of her absolute good faith, though I confess that I began to realize that her refinement of speech and manner was partly assumed. In unguarded moments, she occasionally dropped an aspirate, and when she grew a little excited in speaking of her efforts to trace her husband's missing estate, she sometimes made use of expressions which were suggestive of a humble origin.

But these slight solecisms were hardly perceptible, and of course a defective education is, at most, a misfortune. For the rest, she continued to interest me greatly and when, punctually on the appointed day, she repaid me the ten pounds with many fervent expressions of gratitude, I could not forbear exulting over my friend.

'That is all right,' he said, laughingly, on hearing the news, but looking a little shamefaced, as I thought. 'You needn't tell her I gave you a friendly warning.'

'Of course not', I replied, indignantly.

'Any news about her husband's property?' he asked, carelessly.

'None. She has looked up all his London friends, and done everything she can,' I answered.

'Why doesn't she advertise in the newspapers?'

'She did so more than a year ago in *The Times* and other journals. Have you anything to suggest?' I enquired, anxiously.

'No. Don't for goodness' sake, my dear fellow, ask me to mix myself up in the lady's affairs,' he said, with more temper than he usually displayed. 'I would rather you didn't even tell her you have consulted me about them.'

I promised this the more readily because I suddenly remembered having once suggested to Mrs Williams that she should ask the advice of a friend of mine—having Mr Booth in my mind—in her difficulty, and had been met by a decided and emphatic refusal. The incident had made no impression on me at the time, but the idea now occurred to me that perhaps Mrs Williams had guessed whom I referred to, and had been moved by resentment at the marked coldness which Mr Booth always displayed towards her.

I had assured him, quite truthfully, that Mrs Williams had never asked me to assist her in her search, nor had I foreseen that she would do so. But a few mornings afterwards, the youth who did the valeting of the male portion of the establishment, entered my room while I was shaving with an urgent message from the lady that she was waiting for me in the drawing-room, and would be obliged if I would descend there as soon as possible.

I found the little widow looking very pale and excited, with an open letter in her hand, which had arrived by the early post. Directly I appeared she flourished triumphantly a slip of blue paper, exclaiming eagerly:

'See, Mr Perkins, what I have received this morning! My sister, who is taking charge of my house at Gateshead, found it between the leaves of a book, *Boswell's Life of Johnson*, which she took out quite by chance from the bookcase in the dining-room. My poor husband was devoted to that work, and was constantly reading it during his illness. I am not much of a reader myself, and if it hadn't been for my sister, the paper might have remained undiscovered for years.'

While Mrs Williams was thus breathlessly explaining, I glanced at the document, which was a form of receipt or acknowledgment from Messrs Drake, Crump & Co., Bankers, of Fleet Street, for a tin box deposited with them by her husband for safe custody on a specified date.

'I congratulate you,' I replied, thinking how attractive she looked in her excitement. 'It is indeed a fortunate discovery.'

'I knew it! I was sure that he had done something of the kind!' exclaimed Mrs Williams, joyfully. 'But he was very secretive about his affairs latterly—it became quite a mania with him—I shouldn't be surprised to find the box contains property of great value.'

'The receipt, I see, is dated about six months before your husband died,' I observed.

'Yes. We were up in town then, staying in lodgings in Edwardes Square, Kensington,' replied Mrs Williams, reflectively. 'I brought him up to see a physician, though nobody suspected at the time the serious nature of his symptoms. He used frequently to go out alone; and I suppose he got the box from his brokers or from some lawyer.'

'Anyhow, he deposited it with Drake, Crump & Co.; there is no doubt about that,' I remarked, feeling quite carried away by the widow's satisfaction. 'I suppose you will call upon them and claim it at once?'

'Yes, unless—I really feel quite ashamed to ask such a favour of you, Mr Perkins—but I was going to say, unless you would mind calling upon them in the first instance? The fact is, my little girl is not very well today, and besides, this delightful surprise has rather upset me; my head aches dreadfully,' said Mrs Williams, putting her white hand to her brow, but smiling bravely.

'Oh! I shall be very pleased,' I answered, readily. 'You had better give me the probate of your husband's will. The bankers will probably want to see that.'

'Certainly, I will go and fetch it. I am so very much obliged to you, Mr Perkins,' said the widow, grasping my hand as she left the room.

Our interview thus terminated. Mrs Williams brought down the official parchment, and armed with this, I hastened after breakfast to call upon Messrs Drake, Crump & Co., feeling quite interested and excited about the affair. I did not have an opportunity of telling Mr Booth of my errand; he was late for breakfast, I remember, and I was impatient to be off so as to look in at the bank on my way to business. I merely mention this because, as will appear later, he afterwards blamed me for not having confided in him at this juncture.

The banking establishment of Messrs Drake, Crump & Co., was a small private concern which has long since been absorbed by one of the big joint-stock undertakings. In those days its affairs were conducted in a dingy old house with barred windows about halfway down Fleet Street, in a leisurely, sleepy kind of way. The cashier's office was in the front room, the staff consisting of only three or four elderly clerks, and on presenting my card I was ushered into a gloomy little apartment at the back, where sat a quaint white-headed old gentleman in knee-breeches, who was evidently one of the partners.

'Dear me! That is very strange,' he exclaimed, when I had explained my business. 'Mr Williams is dead, is he? Well, well, we were wondering! We haven't heard anything of him for quite a long time.'

'He has been dead more than two years,' I replied.

'Two years, eh? Let me see,' he observed, as he rang a hand-bell upon the table. 'Mr Jameson,' he added, as a clerk appeared, 'when did we last hear from Mr John Williams?'

'He has not drawn on his account for upwards of two years. His pass-book is here,' answered the Clerk.

'Oh! then he had a current account as well?' I exclaimed.

'A small one—yes,' replied the old gentleman. 'What is the balance, Mr Jameson?'

'About £130,' said the clerk.

'You see, the pass-book being here, and the receipt for the box mislaid, his widow had no clue,' I explained, eagerly.

'Quite so! Quite so! And this is the probate of his will, eh?' said the old gentleman, taking it up, and holding it close to his nose.

'I wonder you didn't see the advertisements in the papers,' I remarked. 'His widow knew he had property somewhere, and she advertised.'

'Extraordinary that they should have escaped us. We always keep a lookout,' said the old gentleman, glancing through the probate. 'When did the advertisements appear?'

'I cannot tell you the date. Mrs Williams will,' I answered.

'And you are a friend of the widow's,' enquired the old gentleman, looking at me pretty keenly over his spectacles.

'Yes.'

'H'm! The probate seems all right. She is the sole executrix, I see. Of course, if she wants to withdraw the money and take away the box, she must attend in person. You can identify her, I suppose, and verify her signature?'

'Certainly.'

'H'm! You are Mr John Perkins, of the Monarchy Insurance Office?' he said, scrutinizing my card. 'Who is your present manager?'

'Mr Middleton.'

'To be sure. I have the pleasure of knowing him. Make him my compliments,' said the old gentleman, quaintly.

'I will. I suppose Mrs Williams can draw on the account, and have access to the box when she chooses?' I enquired.

'H'm! H'm! I see the testator was described in his will as of Gateshead,' said the old gentleman, doubtfully. 'That isn't the address in our books.'

'He lived there, and his widow lives there still,' I replied. 'Mrs Williams tells me that at the date of that deposit receipt they were residing in lodgings in Edwardes Square, Kensington.'

'Quite right. That is the address be gave. Well, sir,' he added, replying to my former question; 'as everything seems satisfactory, if you will leave the probate for registration, and call here with the lady any time after twelve o'clock tomorrow, the box can be given up. Good morning!'

I was very pleased, for Mrs William's sake, to find that everything was straightforward; and the fact of there being a substantial sum of money to the dead man's credit, which the widow evidently knew nothing about, would, I thought, be some compensation in case the contents of the box should turn out to be less valuable than she anticipated. Later in the day, my chief, Mr Middleton, surprised me by coming up to my desk at the office, and saying:

'Mr Perkins, I have just answered an enquiry about you.'

'An enquiry!' I exclaimed, rather startled.

'Yes, from Messrs Drake, Crump & Co., of Fleet Street. Have you some private business with them?' he asked, curiously.

'Not of my own, sir. A lady in whose affairs I am interested——'

'All right, Mr Perkins. I don't wish to enquire details,' he said, smiling at my embarrassment. 'I was of course pleased to vouch for your respectability and integrity.'

'Thank you, sir,' I replied, secretly annoyed at the banker's inquisitiveness.

I now perceived that I had been of more service to Mrs Williams than I had anticipated, having unconsciously acted as a sort of reference for her, and thereby saved her, perhaps, some little trouble with regard to identification. This gave an additional zest to the pleasure of being able to make such a satisfactory report to her on my return, and I am bound to say that the widow was duly grateful. She overwhelmed me with expressions of thanks, and was really disposed to exaggerate my small civility. I wrote a letter, at her request, to Messrs Drake, Crump & Co., fixing an appointment with them for two o'clock on the following afternoon, and appending a specimen of Mrs Williams' signature; and of course I rapidly agreed to accompany her.

When I told Mr Booth all this, he manifested considerable irritation which, in my surprise, I was foolish enough to attribute to a sort of jealousy, since I could imagine no other possible cause for his ill-humour.

'What the deuce do you want to go meddling with this woman's affairs for, Perkins?' he said, sharply.

'What harm have I done!' I exclaimed.

'Harm! H'm! That remains to be seen,' he growled, puffing angrily at his pipe.

'I cannot understand your prejudice against this poor lady' I said, getting angry in my turn.

'I take no interest in her whatever,' said Mr Booth.

'That's no reason why I shouldn't,' I retorted.

'Oh! Go your own way, only remember that I warned you,' said Mr Booth, dismissing the subject with an impatient shrug.

We might almost have quarrelled, but I was really more amused than angry, and my friend soon recovered his temper. Nothing more was said between us about Mrs Williams, and I attached so little importance to Mr Booth's vague warnings, that it never even occurred to me to cancel the appointment I had made.

Accordingly the next day, at two o'clock, I was waiting for the widow at the door of Messrs Drake, Crump & Co.'s bank as arranged, and, being rather pressed to get back to my office, I began to grow impatient as she did not appear. Ten, twenty, forty minutes passed without any sign of her, and I was on the point of leaving, thinking the lady had made some mistake, when I suddenly espied her on the opposite side of the way; coming up the street from the direction of St Paul's. She looked pale and fatigued, and, as I hastened to her assistance, I saw her glance nervously over her shoulder at a slouching, white-bearded, ragged old beggar man who appeared to be following her.

'What is the matter? Has anything happened?' I enquired.

'Oh no! I lost my way, that's all,' said Mrs Williams, with a nervous laugh.

'Has that fellow been annoying you?' I asked, lowering my voice as the old beggar slunk by hurriedly.

'That man!' exclaimed Mrs Williams, glancing after him, 'Oh no! I hadn't noticed him.'

I gave her my arm, and escorted her across the crowded road into the bank. In the parlour at the back we found old Mr Crump awaiting us, and on a side table was a good-sized tin box with Mrs Williams' name inscribed upon it on a paper label.

'There it is,' exclaimed the widow, as her eyes sparkled. 'I remember it now! I always wondered what had become of it.'

'Have you the key, madam?' enquired Mr Crump, after greeting us with old-fashioned courtesy, and bowing very low to my companion.

'I think so; at least I have one or two keys here, which I haven't been able to account for,' said Mrs Williams, producing her purse eagerly.

She selected one of the keys, and, crossing over to the box, succeeded in opening it immediately. I only had a glimpse of the contents before Mrs Williams shut down the lid and relocked it; and as they were done up in brown paper parcels or packages I could form no idea of their nature or value.

'I have prepared a cheque so that you can draw out the money if you wish,' said Mr Crump.

'Thank you,' replied Mrs Williams, seating herself at his desk, and affixing her signature to the draft.

'Will you take it in cash?' asked Mr Crump.

'Yes, please. In notes and £20 in gold? said the widow, with business-like promptitude, as she drew on her glove again.

Mr Crump summoned a cashier, to whom he handed the draft, with the necessary directions, to which I added a request that the porter might be permitted to call a cab. During the absence of the clerk Mr Crump observed, in course of conversation which naturally turned on the late Mr Williams' eccentric conduct with regard to his property:

'By the way, I've looked through the files of *The Times* for the advertisement but I couldn't find it.'

'What advertisement?' enquired Mrs Williams.

'I understood from Mr Perkins that you had advertised in the papers for information about your husband's missing estate,' said Mr Crump, looking at me.

'Oh, yes, so I did,' answered the widow colouring slightly.

'What was the date?' asked Mr Crump.

'Really, I cannot at the moment recollect. I can send you a copy of it when I get back, if it is of any moment,' said Mrs Williams, rather sharply.

'It is of no consequence, of course,' replied the old gentleman, evidently perturbed at seeing that the lady showed signs of resentment. 'I merely asked out of curiosity.'

Mrs Williams appeared, from her manner to resent Mr Crump's enquiry as insinuating some doubt upon the accuracy of her statement, but, fortunately, the return of the cashier with her money caused a welcome diversion. While she was stowing away the notes and gold in her purse, the cashier looked at me and said:

'There is a cab at the door, sir. Shall I ask the porter to carry the box down?'

'I think I can manage it; it is not heavy,' I replied, as I prepared to lift it.

'I've been thinking, Mr Perkins,' said Mrs Williams, reflectively, while putting her purse away, 'that perhaps it would be wiser to leave the box here for a day or two till I return to Gateshead. That is,' she added, turning to the old gentleman with her pleasantest smile, 'if Mr Crump will kindly allow me?'

'You are welcome to leave it, madam—at your own risk, of course,' replied Mr Crump, a little stiffly.

'You see, I have nowhere to keep it while I am in town,' the lady explained. 'It would be safer here.'

'It is a little irregular, as you are no longer a customer,' said Mr Crump; 'but still——'

'Oh! but if I find I can afford it I shall probably come to live in London, and in that case I should certainly keep my account here,' interrupted Mrs Williams, graciously.

'In any case I am very pleased to oblige you, madam,' said the old gentleman more politely.

Though surprised that Mrs Williams was able to restrain her curiosity about the contents of the box, it was obvious that her suggestion was prudent, and, therefore, we left the box in charge of the bank. Mr Crump bowed us out of his room very civilly, and the porter ushered us to the street door, in front of which was a four-wheeled cab. Just as we reached it the old grey-bearded beggar man, whom I had before noticed, rushed forward and obsequiously turned the handle. Mrs Williams sprang lightly into the vehicle, and again, I thought, she glanced nervously at the cadging old rascal.

'Here, you be off, my man,' I said to him, sharply.

'No, no! Here, my poor fellow, is something for you,' said Mrs Williams, and before I could prevent her she put her hand over my shoulder and gave the beggar a sixpence.

'You shouldn't be so foolish,' I said, laughing, as the old fellow shuffled off with his prize.

'Think of my good luck, Mr Perkins,' laughed the widow.

I gave the cabman the address of Elvira House, and lifted my hat to Mrs Williams from the pavement as she drove away, little imagining that she would have left London before I returned in the evening. But so it happened, for when I reached Elvira House at the end of the day, I learnt that the widow had received a telegram an hour or so previously summoning her down to Bath on account of the illness of her mother.

'She left many kind messages for you,' added Mrs Nix, when she gave me the information. 'She said she would write to you in the course of a day or two. She was dreadfully upset, poor thing, at the sad news.'

'I did not even know she had a mother living,' I remarked.

'You were the only person she confided in,' said Mrs Nix, playfully.

'I suppose the little girl has gone too?' I observed, a trifle abashed.

'Yes. A sweet child. Everyone is so sorry to lose them. Mrs Williams was a universal favourite,' said Mrs Nix.

This was evidently the case, to judge from the expressions of regret which were uttered at the dinner-table when her departure became generally known. We had rather a reduced company that evening, there being several vacant places. The Major had gone to attend some races at York, whither Mr Booth was understood to have accompanied him; and two or three of our guests were dining out. I was surprised to hear of my friend having yielded to the Major's persuasions, for when the latter had broached the subject of the expedition in the smoking-room on the previous evening, Mr Booth had flatly refused the invitation. But horse-racing was a form of sport which seemed to possess extraordinary attractions for him; and I supposed he had been partly influenced by the desire to keep his companion out of mischief.

I must confess that I felt a little depressed at the widow's unexpected absence. It was quite untrue that I admired her, but her confidences had heightened my platonic regard, and her personality undoubtedly attracted me. I therefore awaited the promised letter with some impatience, and she was good enough not to leave me long in suspense, for by the next evening's post I received from her the following epistle, dated from Lower Pultenay Street, Bath.

My Dear Mr Perkins,

Alas! my poor dear mother is dying! So shocking, and so totally unexpected! Of course I must remain by her side till the end, and she may yet linger for some weeks, the doctor says!

I hope Mrs Nix gave you my message. I can never thank you sufficiently for all your kindness dear Mr Perkins, and yet I have a further favour to ask of you!

You know what sick people are! I told my dear mother, who is perfectly conscious, about the box at the bank. Nothing will satisfy her but to know what it contains, as she is anxious to be assured that my little girl and I are sufficiently provided for.

How I regret that I did not examine the contents that day at the bank! And now, what am I to do? I dare not leave my poor mother, even for an hour. I wonder whether you would undertake a journey here and bring the box with you?

I know it is *too* much to ask, yet I have ventured to write to the bank to say that you might call. I am sure your kind heart with prompt you to do this if you possibly can.

Yours most faithfully and sincerely, Dear Mr Perkins,

AMELIA WILLIAMS

I was rather startled by this request and yet—well, in short, I decided to comply with it. I wonder at myself now; most of us have experienced similar astonishment at past foolish actions.

My chief objection, at the time, was that I could not very well get away from the office. However, on consulting a railway timetable, I found that Bath was a much more accessible place than I had imagined. A half-holiday would be all that I required, for I could travel down there and return the same evening. The next day was a Saturday, so that all the indulgence I need ask of my employers was a single hour in order that I might get to the bank before two o'clock to obtain the box.

I therefore wrote immediately to Mrs Williams to say that I would travel down by the train which left Paddington at 3 o'clock, arriving at Bath at 5.15, and that I should return by the express which would bring me back to town about nine. I had no reason for remaining at Bath, and I thought I might accomplish my journey before Mr Booth came back. I think I must have had a vague idea of keeping my trip a secret, both from him and from the other guests, for I was a little sensitive of remarks which had been made about my attentions to the widow.

I duly carried out my programme; the box was handed over to me at the bank without the slightest demur, in consequence of a letter they had received from Mrs Williams; and I arrived at Bath punctually at the time named. I hired a fly, and drove straight to the widow's address in Lower Pultenay Street, but the servant who opened the door said, to my surprise, that the lady was out, and handed to me a brief pencilled note from her, saying that she had been called away unexpectedly owing to her mother's condition, and asking me to leave the box.

'The poor old lady is not in the house, then,' I remarked, casually.

'What old lady, sir?' enquired the girl, opening her eyes.

'Mrs Williams' mother. Do you know where she lives?'

'No, sir, I don't. Never heard her mention she had a mother here, in Bath, sir,' added the girl.

'But Mrs Williams is in constant attendance upon her mother, who is dying,' I exclaimed.

'Mrs Williams has hardly left the house since she has been here, sir,' said the girl, evidently struck by my surprise. 'She and her little girl went for a drive in a fly about an hour ago. I don't know where they went to. She said if a gentleman came and left a tin box, I was to take great care of it.'

'Did Mrs Williams say when she would return?' I enquired, with an uneasy feeling.

'She said I was to have tea ready at six o'clock sir,' replied the girl, glancing back at the clock.

'I will come in and wait,' I said, with sudden resolution, as I stepped inside the hall.

The servant, whose good faith was manifest, ushered me into a neat parlour, and then left me, after again asseverating, in answer to pressing enquiries, that Mrs Williams was certainly not in attendance on an invalid. Indeed, it was impossible to doubt, from the girl's detailed account of the widow's movements since her arrival in Bath, that the story of the dying mother was a complete fiction.

I felt very much like a person who has unexpectedly received a douche of cold water. At first sight it seemed as though the story had been merely a device to work upon my feelings in order to induce me to bring the box down to Bath. Even so, however, it was extraordinary behaviour on Mrs Williams' part to absent herself just at the hour of my arrival. She had evidently counted upon my leaving the box, and returning at once to London, as I had planned; but why this sudden reluctance to meet me, to say nothing of the ungrateful discourtesy?

I grimly resolved to await an explanation, and when I recalled to mind that Mrs Williams had given the alleged illness of her mother as an excuse for a hurried departure from Elvira House, my mystification increased. The repeated warnings of Mr Booth rose unpleasantly to my mind, and I had worked myself into a state of mingled indignation and resentment, when a ring at the street door bell announced, as I imagined, the return of Mrs Williams.

I awaited her with considerable trepidation, for I felt that my position was both painful and embarrassing. I heard the servant respond to the summons, and the next moment the room door was thrown open, and who should walk in but—Mr Booth!

I started, and stared at him as though I had seen a ghost; while he seemed equally surprised at seeing me, though he recovered himself quickly. He glanced at the box on the table, and his eyes twinkled.

'Hullo! I thought you were at York!' I gasped.

'And I thought you were in London,' he said, smiling at my astonishment.

'I'm waiting to see Mrs Williams,' I explained.

'She's a very clever little woman,' he said emphatically. 'You came down by the 5.15 train, I suppose, with that?'

'Yes.'

'While she, to put me off the scent, seeks to lead me a wild goose chase, so as to leave the coast clear,' he added, nodding his head.

'I found a note from her asking me to leave the box,' I said resentfully.

'Yes. She didn't mean to be impolite to you,' said Mr Booth, slyly. 'The fact is, she has been so closely shadowed that if she had stayed at home for you, your arrival with the box would have been noticed. I suspected a trick, though I must own that my calling here in her absence was nothing short of an inspiration,' he added with great satisfaction.

'Perhaps you'll kindly explain it all,' I exclaimed, with a show of indignation which was intended to disguise my increasing confusion.

'Not now,' he said, coolly taking possession of the box, 'unless you want an awkward scene with the woman which might end in my having to call in the police. In that case, my friend, you would figure somewhat unpleasantly before the public, as an innocent accomplice in an awkward affair. We had better clear out before she returns.'

'But the box belongs to Mrs Williams!' I exclaimed, horrified.

'Well, it does and it doesn't! I'll explain going along. Meanwhile, possession is nine points of the law,' he said, putting the box under his arm and moving to the door.

I was scared by the suggestion of a public scandal, and I had complete faith in my friend. I, therefore, put on my hat and followed him, and by rushing through the streets until we met a fly which drove us at full speed to the station, we just contrived to catch the 6.5 train back to town as it was beginning to move away.

'Well?' I enquired eagerly, as soon as I had recovered my breath.

We had, fortunately, and quite by chance, secured an empty first-class compartment. Mr Booth was leaning back with an air of calm triumph, lighting a cigar, with his feet resting on the tin box.

'Mrs Williams,' he said quietly, 'is the wife of an accomplished forger and swell-mobsman, who is at present undergoing the felicity of fourteen years penal servitude.'

'The wife!' I gasped.

'Yes; his real name is Bolton, but he called himself Williams among other aliases. In that name he opened an account at Drake's Bank, and deposited the box, a few months before he was arrested.'

'It *was* her husband's property then?' I exclaimed, slightly relieved.

'It contains the proceeds of a very ingenious robbery in Hatton Garden. He was known to have hidden a good bit away somewhere, but he kept his mouth shut, and the police were nonplussed. So was his clever little wife, whose ingenuity and pluck I can't help admiring.'

'Didn't he tell her?' I enquired, interested in spite of my unenviable feelings.

'Yes; but she couldn't get at it. It was lodged at the bank in the name of Williams for safety, and she dared not claim it. But she bided her time, and at length she heard of the death of a Mr John Williams at Gateshead, which showed her husband's prudence in having adopted a common name. Of course, this was her opportunity. The dead man, a complete stranger, was made to represent the actual depositor, and Mrs Williams pretended to be the widow.'

'How did she get hold of the probate of another man's will?' I asked.

'Probably bribed the clerk of the solicitor who had the custody of it. You see, probates are no good when once an estate is wound up. This one was probably kicking about the office, and wouldn't be missed.'

'What of the real Mrs Williams of Gateshead?'

'She is dead.'

'And the advertisements said to have been inserted in the papers?'

'All a lie. There were no advertisements. My dear fellow, she made you serve her purpose beautifully,' laughed Mr Booth.

'It was very unfriendly of you not to have given me a hint,' I exclaimed, furiously indignant.

'My dear Perkins, didn't I warn you over and over again?'

'Yes, but you didn't tell me what you knew.'

'Because at first I knew absolutely nothing. I simply mistrusted her from a kind of instinct. But when you told me the woman's story I went round to Scotland Yard, where I have a friend,' said Mr Booth, delicately flicking the ash from his cigar with his little finger, 'and was shown some photographs. That same evening you told me you had been to the bank on her behalf. You may remember that I was annoyed with you?'

'Even then you might have been more explicit,' I replied angrily.

'Well, the fact is, my dear Perkins, as you had already committed yourself, I couldn't resist the temptation of undertaking this little coup. You played into my hands as it were. But there is no harm done,' he added, laughing at my discomfiture. 'It is entirely a private venture of my own, carried out single-handed.'

'Why didn't she take the box away from the bank that day?' I enquired, after a sulky silence.

'Because she discovered she was being watched,' replied Mr Booth, with imperturbable good-humour. 'Do you remember an old grey-bearded man?'

'Yes.'

'She spotted him, and that sent her out of London.'

'You followed, I suppose?'

'Yes; I knew she would contrive to get the box sent down to her. I thought she would probably have it brought down by one of the bank messengers. I never thought she would have the cheek to——' Mr Booth checked himself abruptly, evidently out of consideration for my feelings; then, after puffing at his cigar for a few moments, he added in a conciliatory tone, 'You mustn't mind, my dear fellow. Only two people besides yourself will ever have even a suspicion of how it has all come about. *I* shan't tell, and you may be sure *she* won't.'

'You forget the grey-bearded man,' I groaned despondently.

'True! Yes, I forgot him,' said Mr Booth, smiling; 'but I'll answer for his discretion as I would for my own.'

'I wouldn't have had it happen for a thousand pounds!' I exclaimed in deep dejection, after we had travelled for twenty miles in complete silence.

Mr Booth looked at me for a few moments with friendly concern; then he leant forward and touched me lightly on the arm.

'My dear fellow, since it *has* happened, I can offer you half the sum you mention as compensation.'

'What do you mean?'

'The owner of the property in this box will no doubt be glad to pay me £500 as a reward. I am sufficiently repaid by the satisfaction of having accomplished a very neat job, entirely off my own bat. As a matter of fact, I owe my success entirely to you.'

'Thanks, no! I'm not a detective,' I interrupted, more rudely I dare say than I was conscious of.

'At least let me offer you a little memento to hang on your watch chain,' he said. wincing at the rebuff but not the least resenting it.

He produced as he spoke, from his pocket, a six-penny piece, and handed it to me.

'What is this?' I asked.

'The identical coin which the fair widow bestowed upon the grey-bearded beggar,' he replied.

'How did you come by it, then?' I asked.

But Mr Booth only smiled, and I then recollected how he had boasted that he had managed his part of the business single-handed.

I have only to add that though my friend always declared that the 'widow' did not entertain the least suspicion of his identity, she never came to Elvira House again, nor even wrote a line of remonstrance or enquiry to me; and as I have heard nothing whatever from that day to this, I conclude she made no complaint but accepted philosophically her bitter disappointment, probably considering herself lucky to have escaped worse consequences.

Murder by Proxy

M. McDONNELL BODKIN

At two o'clock precisely on that sweltering 12th of August, Eric Neville, young, handsome, *débonnaire*, sauntered through the glass door down the wrought-iron staircase into the beautiful, old-fashioned garden of Berkly Manor, radiant in white flannel, with a broad-brimmed Panama hat perched lightly on his glossy black curls, for he had just come from lazing in his canoe along the shadiest stretches of the river, with a book for company.

The back of the Manor House was the south wall of the garden, which stretched away for nearly a mile, gay with blooming flowers and ripening fruit. The air, heavy with perfume, stole softly through all the windows, now standing wide open in the sunshine, as though the great house gasped for breath.

When Eric's trim, tan boot left the last step of the iron staircase it reached the broad gravelled walk of the garden. Fifty yards off the head gardener was tending his peaches, the smoke from his pipe hanging like a faint blue haze in the still air that seemed to quiver with the heat. Eric, as he reached him, held out a petitionary hand, too lazy to speak.

Without a word the gardener stretched for a huge peach that was striving to hide its red face from the sun under narrow ribbed leaves, plucked it as though he loved it, and put it softly in the young man's hand.

Eric stripped off the velvet coat, rose-coloured, green, and amber, till it hung round the fruit in tatters, and made his sharp, white teeth meet in the juicy flesh of the ripe peach.

BANG!

The sudden shock of sound close to their ears wrenched the nerves of the two men; one dropped his peach, and the other his pipe. Both stared about them in utter amazement.

'Look there, sir,' whispered the gardener, pointing to a little cloud of smoke oozing lazily through a window almost directly over their head, while the pungent spice of gunpowder made itself felt in the hot air.

'My uncle's room,' gasped Eric. 'I left him only a moment ago fast asleep on the sofa.'

He turned as he spoke, and ran like a deer along the garden walk, up the iron steps, and back through the glass door into the house, the old gardener following as swiftly as his rheumatism would allow.

Eric crossed the sitting-room on which the glass door opened, went up the broad, carpeted staircase four steps at a time, turned sharply to the right down a broad corridor, and burst straight through the open door of his uncle's study.

Fast as he had come, there was another before him. A tall, strong figure, dressed in light tweed, was bending over the sofa where, a few minutes before, Eric had seen his uncle asleep.

Eric recognized the broad back and brown hair at once.

'John,' he cried—'John, what is it?'

His cousin turned to him a handsome, manly face, ghastly pale now even to the lips.

'Eric, my boy,' he answered falteringly, 'this is too awful. Uncle has been murdered—shot stone dead.'

'No, no; it cannot be. It's not five minutes since I saw him quietly sleeping,' Eric began. Then his eyes fell on the still figure on the sofa, and he broke off abruptly.

Squire Neville lay with his face to the wall, only the outline of his strong, hard features visible. The charge of shot had entered at the base of the skull, the grey hair was all dabbled with blood, and the heavy, warm drops still fell slowly on to the carpet.

'But who can have——' Eric gasped out, almost speechless with horror.

'It must have been his own gun,' his cousin answered. 'It was lying there on the table, to the right, barrel still smoking, when I came in.'

'It wasn't suicide—was it?' asked Eric, in a frightened whisper.

'Quite impossible, I should say. You see where he is hit.'

'But it was so sudden. I ran the moment I heard the shot, and you were before me. Did you see any one?'

'Not a soul. The room was empty.'

'But how could the murderer escape?'

'Perhaps he leapt through the window. It was open when I came in.'

'He couldn't do that, Master John.' It was the voice of the gardener at the door. 'Me and Master Eric was right under the window when the shot came.'

'Then how in the devil's name did he disappear, Simpson?'

'It's not for me to say, sir.'

John Neville searched the room with eager eyes. There was no cover in it for a cat. A bare, plain room, panelled with brown oak, on which hung some guns and fishing-rods—old-fashioned for the most part, but of the finest workmanship and material. A small bookcase in the corner was the room's sole claim to be called 'a study'. The huge leather-covered sofa on which the corpse lay, a massive round table in the centre of the room, and a few heavy chairs completed the furniture. The dust lay thick on everything, the fierce sunshine streamed in a broad band across the room. The air was stifling with heat and the acrid smoke of gunpowder.

John Neville noticed how pale his young cousin was. He laid his hand on his shoulder with the protecting kindness of an elder brother.

'Come, Eric,' he said softly, 'we can do no good here.'

'We had best look round first, hadn't we, for some clue?' asked Eric, and he stretched his hand towards the gun; but John stopped him.

'No, no,' he cried hastily, 'we must leave things just as we find them. I'll send a man to the village for Wardle and telegraph to London for a detective.'

He drew his young cousin gently from the room, locked the door on the outside, and put the key in his pocket.

'Who shall I wire to?' John Neville called from his desk with pencil poised over the paper, to his cousin, who sat at the library table with his head buried in his hands. 'It will need a sharp man—one who can give his whole time to it.'

'I don't know any one. Yes, I do. That fellow with the queer name that found the Duke of Southern's opal—Beck. That's it. Thornton Crescent, WC, will find him.'

John Neville filled in the name and address to the telegram he had already written—

Come at once. Case of murder. Expense no object. John Neville, Berkly Manor, Dorset.

Little did Eric guess that the filling in of that name was to him a matter of life or death.

John Neville had picked up a timetable and rustled through the leaves. 'Hard lines, Eric,' he said; 'do his best, he cannot get here before midnight. But here's Wardle already, anyhow; that's quick work.'

A shrewd, silent man was Wardle, the local constable, who now came briskly up the broad avenue; strong and active too, though well over fifty years of age.

John Neville met him at the door with the news. But the groom had already told of the murder.

'You did the right thing to lock the door, sir,' said Wardle, as they passed into the library where Eric still sat apparently unconscious of their presence, 'and you wired for a right good man. I've worked with this here Mr Beck before now. A pleasant spoken man and a lucky one. "No hurry, Mr Wardle," he says to me, "and no fuss. Stir nothing. The things about the corpse have always a story of their own if they are let tell it, and I always like to have the first quiet little chat with them myself."'

So the constable held his tongue and kept his hands quiet and used his eyes and ears, while the great house buzzed with gossip. There was a whisper here and a whisper there, and the whispers patched themselves into a story. By slow degrees dark suspicion settled down and closed like a cloud round John Neville.

Its influence seemed to pass in some strange fashion through the closed doors of the library. John began pacing the room restlessly from end to end.

After a little while the big room was not big enough to hold his impatience. He wandered out aimlessly, as it seemed, from one room to another; now down the iron steps to gaze vacantly at the window of his uncle's room, now past the locked door in the broad corridor.

With an elaborate pretence of carelessness Wardle kept him in sight through all his wanderings, but John Neville seemed too self-absorbed to notice it.

Presently he returned to the library. Eric was there, still sitting with his back to the door, only the top of his head showing over the high chair. He seemed absorbed in thought or sleep, he sat so still.

But he started up with a quick cry, showing a white, frightened face, when John touched him lightly on the arm.

'Come for a walk in the grounds, Eric?' he said. 'This waiting and watching and doing nothing is killing work; I cannot stand it much longer.'

'I'd rather not, if you don't mind,' Eric answered wearily; 'I feel completely knocked over.'

'A mouthful of fresh air would do you good, my poor boy; you do look done up.'

Eric shook his head.

'Well, I'm off,' John said.

'If you leave me the key, I will give it to the detective, if he comes.'

'Oh, he cannot be here before midnight, and I'll be back in an hour.'

As John Neville walked rapidly down the avenue without looking back, Wardle stepped quietly after, keeping him well in view.

Presently Neville turned abruptly in amongst the woods, the constable still following cautiously. The trees stood tall and well apart, and the slanting sunshine made lanes of vivid green through the shade. As Wardle crossed between Neville and the sun his shadow fell long and black on the bright green.

John Neville saw the shadow move in front of him and turned sharp round and faced his pursuer.

The constable stood stock still and stared.

'Well, Wardle, what is it? Don't stand there like a fool fingering your baton! Speak out, man—what do you want of me?'

'You see how it is, Master John,' the constable stammered out, 'I don't believe it myself. I've known you twenty-one years—since you were born, I may say—and I don't believe it, not a blessed word of it. But duty is duty, and I must go through with it; and facts is facts, and you and he had words last night, and Master Eric found you first in the room when——'

John Neville listened, bewildered at first. Then suddenly, as it seemed to dawn on him for the first time that he *could* be suspected of this murder, he kindled a sudden hot blaze of anger.

He turned fiercely on the constable. Broad-chested, strong limbed, he towered over him, terrible in his wrath; his hands clenched, his muscles quivered, his strong white teeth shut tight as a rat-trap, and a reddish light shining at the back of his brown eyes.

'How dare you! how dare you!' he hissed out between his teeth, his passion choking him.

He looked dangerous, that roused young giant, but Wardle met his angry eyes without flinching.

'Where's the use, Master John?' he said soothingly. 'It's main hard on you, I know. But the fault isn't mine, and you won't help yourself by taking it that way.'

The gust of passion appeared to sweep by as suddenly as it arose. The handsome face cleared and there was no trace of anger in the frank voice that answered. 'You are right, Wardle, quite right. What is to be done next? Am I to consider myself under arrest?'

'Better not, sir. You've got things to do a prisoner couldn't do handy, and I don't want to stand in the way of your doing them. If you give me your word it will be enough.'

'My word for what?'

'That you'll be here when wanted.'

'Why, man, you don't think I'd be fool enough—innocent or guilty—to run away. My God! run away from a charge of murder!'

'Don't take on like that, sir. There's a man coming from London that will set things straight, you'll see. Have I your word?'

'You have my word.'

'Perhaps you'd better be getting back to the house, sir. There's a deal of talking going on amongst the servants. I'll keep out of the way, and no one will be the wiser for anything that has passed between us.'

Half-way up the avenue a fast-driven dog-cart overtook John Neville, and pulled up so sharply that the horse's hoofs sent the coarse gravel flying. A stout, thick-set man, who up to that had been in close chat with the driver, leapt out more lightly than could have been expected from his figure.

'Mr John Neville, I presume? My name is Beck—Mr Paul Beck.'

'Mr Beck! Why, I thought you couldn't have got here before midnight.'

'Special train,' Mr Beck answered pleasantly. 'Your wire said "Expense no object". Well, time is an object, and comfort is an object too, more or less, in all these cases; so I took a special train, and here I am. With your permission, we will send the trap on and walk to the house together. This seems a bad business, Mr Neville. Shot dead, the driver tells me. Any one suspected?'

'I'm suspected.' The answer broke from John Neville's lips almost fiercely.

Mr Beck looked at him for a minute with placid curiosity, without a touch of surprise in it.

'How do you know that?'

'Wardle, the local constable, has just told me so to my face. It was only by way of a special favour he refrained from arresting me then and there.'

Mr Beck walked on beside John Neville ten or fifteen paces before he spoke again.

'Do you mind,' he said, in a very insinuating voice, 'telling me exactly why you are suspected?'

'Not in the very least.'

'Mind this,' the detective went on quickly, 'I give you no caution and make you no pledge. It's my business to find out the truth. If you think the truth will help you, then you ought to help me. This is very irregular, of course, but I don't mind that. When a man is charged with a crime there is, you see, Mr Neville, always one witness who knows whether he is guilty or not. There is very often only that one. The first thing the British law does by way of discovering the truth is to close the mouth of the only witness that knows it. Well, that's not my way. I like to give an innocent man a chance to tell his own story, and I've no scruple in trapping a guilty man if I can.'

He looked John Neville straight in the eyes as he spoke.

The look was steadily returned. 'I think I understand. What do you want to know? Where shall I begin?'

'At the beginning. What did you quarrel with your uncle about yesterday?'

John Neville hesitated for a moment, and Mr Beck took a mental note of his hesitation.

'I didn't quarrel with him. He quarrelled with me. It was this way: There was a bitter feud between my uncle and his neighbour, Colonel Peyton. The estates adjoin, and the quarrel was about some shooting. My uncle was very violent—he used to call Colonel Peyton "a common poacher". Well, I took no hand in the row. I was rather shy when I met the Colonel for the first time after it, for I knew my uncle had the wrong end of the stick. But the Colonel spoke to me in the kindest way. "No reason why you and I should cease to be friends, John," he said. "This is a foolish business. I would give the best covert on my estate to be out of it. Men cannot fight duels in these days, and gentlemen cannot scold like fishwives. But I don't expect people will call me a coward because I hate a row."

' "Not likely," I said.

'The Colonel, you must know, had distinguished himself in a

dozen engagements, and has the Victoria Cross locked up in a drawer of his desk. Lucy once showed it to me. Lucy is his only daughter and he is devoted to her. Well, after that, of course, the Colonel and I kept on good terms, for I liked him, and I liked going there and all that. But our friendship angered my uncle. I had been going to the Grange pretty often of late, and my uncle heard of it. He spoke to me in a very rough fashion of Colonel Peyton and his daughter at dinner last night, and I stood up for them.

'"By what right, you insolent puppy," he shouted, "do you take this upstart's part against me?"

'"The Peytons are as good a family as our own, sir," I said—that was true—"and as for right, Miss Lucy Peyton has done me the honour of promising to be my wife."

'At that he exploded in a very tempest of rage. I cannot repeat his words about the Colonel and his daughter. Even now, though he lies dead yonder, I can hardly forgive them. He swore he would never see or speak to me again if I disgraced myself of such a marriage. "I cannot break the entail," he growled, "worse luck. But I can make you a beggar while I live, and I shall live forty years to spite you. The poacher can have you a bargain for all I care. Go, sell yourself as dearly as you can, and live on your wife's fortune as soon as you please."

'Then I lost my temper, and gave him a bit of my mind.'

'Try and remember what you said; it's important.'

'I told him that I cast his contempt back in his face; that I loved Lucy Peyton, and that I would live for her, and die for her, if need be.'

'Did you say "it was a comfort he could not live for ever"? You see the story of your quarrel has travelled far and near. The driver told me of it. Try and remember—did you say that?'

'I think I did. I'm sure I did now, but I was so furious I hardly knew what I said. I certainly never meant——'

'Who was in the room when you quarrelled?'

'Only Cousin Eric and the butler.'

'The butler, I suppose, spread the story?'

'I suppose so. I'm sure Cousin Eric never did. He was as much pained at the scene as myself. He tried to interfere at the time, but his interference only made my uncle more furious.'

'What was your allowance from your uncle?'

'A thousand a year.'

'He had power to cut it off, I suppose?'

'Certainly.'

'But he had no power over the estate. You were heir-apparent under the entail, and at the present moment you are owner of Berkly Manor?'

'That is so; but up to the moment you spoke I assure you I never even remembered——'

'Who comes next to you in the entail?'

'My first cousin, Eric. He is four years younger than I am.'

'After him?'

'A distant cousin. I scarcely know him at all; but he has a bad reputation, and I know my uncle and he hated each other cordially.'

'How did your uncle and your cousin Eric hit it off?'

'Not too well. He hated Eric's father—his own youngest brother—and he was sometimes rough on Eric. He used to abuse the dead father in the son's presence, calling him cruel and treacherous, and all that. Poor Eric had often a hard time of it. Uncle was liberal to him so far as money went—as liberal as he was to me—had him to live at the Manor and denied him nothing. But now and again he would sting the poor lad by a passionate curse or a bitter sneer. In spite of all, Eric seemed fond of him.'

'To come now to the murder; you saw your uncle no more that night, I suppose?'

'I never saw him alive again.'

'Do you know what he did next day?'

'Only by hearsay.'

'Hearsay evidence is often first-class evidence, though the law doesn't think so. What did you hear?'

'My uncle was mad about shooting. Did I tell you his quarrel with Colonel Peyton was about the shooting? He had a grouse moor rented about twelve miles from here, and he never missed the first day. He was off at cock-shout with the head gamekeeper, Lennox. I was to have gone with him, but I didn't, of course. Contrary to his custom he came back about noon and went straight to his study. I was writing in my own room and heard his heavy step go past the door. Later on Eric found him asleep on the great leather couch in his study. Five minutes after Eric left I heard the shot and rushed into his room.'

'Did you examine the room after you found the body?'

'No. Eric wanted to, but I thought it better not. I simply locked the door and put the key in my pocket till you came.'

'Could it have been suicide?'

'Impossible, I should say. He was shot through the back of the head.'

'Had your uncle any enemies that you know of?'

'The poachers hated him. He was relentless with them. A fellow once shot at him, and my uncle shot back and shattered the man's leg. He had him sent to hospital first and cured, and then prosecuted him straight away, and got him two years.'

'Then you think a poacher murdered him?' Mr Beck said blandly.

'I don't well see how he could. I was in my own room on the same corridor. The only way to or from my uncle's room was past my door. I rushed out the instant I heard the shot, and saw no one.'

'Perhaps the murderer leapt through the window?'

'Eric tells me that he and the gardener were in the garden almost under the window at the time.'

'What's your theory, then, Mr Neville?'

'I haven't got a theory.'

'You parted with your uncle in anger last night?'

'That's so.'

'Next day your uncle is shot, and you are found—I won't say caught—in his room the instant afterwards.'

John Neville flushed crimson; but he held himself in and nodded without speaking.

The two walked on together in silence.

They were not a hundred yards from the great mansion—John Neville's house—standing high above the embowering trees in the glow of the twilight, when the detective spoke again.

'I'm bound to say, Mr Neville, that things look very black against you, as they stand. I think that constable Wardle ought to have arrested you.'

'It's not too late yet,' John Neville answered shortly, 'I see him there at the corner of the house and I'll tell him you said so.'

He turned on his heel, when Mr Beck called quickly after him: 'What about that key?'

John Neville handed it to him without a word. The detective took it as silently and walked on to the entrance and up the great stone steps alone, whistling softly.

Eric welcomed him at the door, for the driver had told of his coming.

'You have had no dinner, Mr Beck?' he asked courteously.

'Business first; pleasure afterwards. I had a snack in the train. Can I see the gamekeeper, Lennox, for five minutes alone?'

'Certainly. I'll send him to you in a moment here in the library.'

Lennox, the gamekeeper, a long-limbed, high-shouldered, elderly man, shambled shyly into the room, consumed by nervousness in the presence of a London detective.

'Sit down, Lennox—sit down,' said Mr Beck kindly. The very sound of his voice, homely and good-natured, put the man at his ease. 'Now, tell me, why did you come home so soon from the grouse this morning?'

'Well, you see, sir, it was this ways. We were two hours hout when the Squire, 'e says to me, "Lennox," 'e says, "I'm sick of this fooling. I'm going 'ome."'

'No sport?'

'Birds wor as thick as blackberries, sir, and lay like larks.'

'No sportsman, then?'

'Is it the Squire, sir?' cried Lennox, quite forgetting his shyness in his excitement at this slur on the Squire. 'There wasn't a better sportsman in the county—no, nor as good. Real, old-fashioned style, 'e was. "Hang your barnyard shooting," 'e'd say when they'd ask him to go kill tame pheasants. 'E put up 'is own birds with 'is own dogs, 'e did. 'E'd as soon go shooting without a gun very near as without a dog any day. Aye and 'e stuck to 'is old "Manton" muzzle-loader to the last. "'Old it steady, Lennox," 'ed say to me oftentimes, "and point it straight. It will hit harder and further than any of their telescopes, and it won't get marked with rust if you don't clean it every second shot."

'"Easy to load, Squire," the young men would say, cracking up their hammerless breech-loaders.

'"Aye," he'd answer them back, "and spoil your dog's work. What's the good of a dog learning to 'down shot', if you can drop in your cartridges as quick as a cock can pick corn."

'A dead shot the Squire was, too, and no mistake, sir, if he wasn't flurried. Many a time I've seen him wipe the eyes of gents who thought no end of themselves with that same old muzzle-loader that shot himself in the long run. Many a time I seen——'

'Why did he turn his back on good sport yesterday?' asked Mr Beck, cutting short his reminiscences.

'Well, you see, it was scorching hot for one thing, but that wasn't it, for the infernal fire would not stop the Squire if he was on for sport. But he was in a blazing temper all the morning, and temper tells more than most anything on a man's shooting. When Flora sprung a pack—she's a young dog, and the fault wasn't hers either—for she came down the wind on them—but the Squire had the gun to his shoulder to shoot her. Five minutes after she found another pack and set like a stone. They got up as big as haycocks and as lazy as crows, and he missed right and left—never touched a feather—a thing I haven't seen him do since I was a boy.

'"It's myself I should shoot, not the dog," he growled and he flung me the gun to load. When I'd got the caps on and had shaken the powder into the nipples, he ripped out an oath that 'e'd have no more of it. 'E walked right across country to where the trap was. The birds got up under his feet, but divil a shot he'd fire, but drove straight 'ome.

'When we got to the 'ouse I wanted to take the gun and fire it off, or draw the charges. But 'e told me to go to——, and carried it up loaded as it was to his study, where no one goes unless they're sent for special. It was better than an hour afterwards I heard the report of the "Manton"; I'd know it in a thousand. I ran for the study as fast as——'

Eric Neville broke suddenly into the room, flushed and excited.

'Mr Beck,' he cried, 'a monstrous thing has happened. Wardle, the local constable, you know, has arrested my cousin on a charge of wilful murder of my uncle.'

Mr Beck, with his eyes intent on the excited face, waved his big hand soothingly.

'Easy,' he said, 'take it easy, Mr Neville. It's hurtful to your feelings, no doubt; but it cannot be helped. The constable has done no more than his duty. The evidence is very strong, as you know, and in such cases it's best for all parties to proceed regularly.'

'You can go,' he went on, speaking to Lennox, who stood dumfoundered at the news of John Neville's arrest, staring with eyes and mouth wide open.

Then turning again very quietly to Eric: 'Now, Mr Neville, I would like to see the room where the corpse is.'

The perfect placidity of his manner had its effect upon the boy, for he was little more than a boy, calming his excitement as oil smooths troubled water.

'My cousin has the key,' he said; 'I will get it.'

'There is no need,' Mr Beck called after him, for he was half-way out of the room on his errand: 'I've got the key if you will be good enough to show me the room.'

Mastering his surprise, Eric showed him upstairs, and along the corridor to the locked door. Half unconsciously, as it seemed, he was following the detective into the room, when Mr Beck stopped him.

'I know you will kindly humour me, Mr Neville,' he said, 'but I find that I can look closer and think clearer when I'm by myself. I'm not exactly shy you know, but it's a habit I've got.'

He closed the door softly as he spoke, and locked it on the inside, leaving the key in the lock.

The mask of placidity fell from him the moment he found himself alone. His lips tightened, and his eyes sparkled, and his muscles seemed to grow rigid with excitement, like a sporting dog's when he is close upon the game.

One glance at the corpse showed him that it was not suicide. In this, at least, John Neville had spoken the truth.

The back of the head had literally been blown in by the charge of heavy shot at close quarters. The grey hair was clammy and matted, with little white angles of bone protruding. The dropping of the blood had made a black pool on the carpet, and the close air of the room was fœtid with the smell of it.

The detective walked to the table where the gun, a handsome, old-fashioned muzzle-loader, lay, the muzzle still pointed at the corpse. But his attention was diverted by a water-bottle, a great globe of clear glass quite full, and perched on a book a little distance from the gun, and between it and the window. He took it from the table and tested the water with the tip of his tongue. It had a curious, insipid, parboiled taste, but he detected no foreign flavour in it. Though the room was full of dust there was almost none on the cover of the book where the water-bottle stood, and Mr Beck noticed a gap in the third row of the bookcase where the book had been taken.

After a quick glance round the room Mr Beck walked to the

window. On a small table there he found a clear circle in the thick dust. He fitted the round bottom of the water-bottle to this circle and it covered it exactly. While he stood by the window he caught sight of some small scraps of paper crumpled up and thrown into a corner. Picking them up and smoothing them out he found they were curiously drilled with little burnt holes. Having examined the holes minutely with his magnifying glass, he slipped these scraps folded on each other into his waistcoat pocket.

From the window he went back to the gun. This time he examined it with the minutest care. The right barrel he found had been recently discharged, the left was still loaded. Then he made a startling discovery. *Both barrels were on half cock.* The little bright copper cap twinkled on the nipple of the left barrel, from the right nipple the cap was gone.

How had the murderer fired the right barrel without a cap? How and why did he find time in the midst of his deadly work to put the cock back to safety?

Had Mr Beck solved this problem? The grim smile deepened on his lips as he looked, and there was an ugly light in his eyes that boded ill for the unknown assassin. Finally he carried the gun to the window and examined it carefully through a magnifying glass. There was a thin dark line, as if traced with the point of a red-hot needle, running a little way along the wood of the stock and ending in the right nipple.

Mr Beck put the gun back quietly on the table. The whole investigation had not taken ten minutes. He gave one look at the still figure on the couch, unlocked the door, locking it after him, and walked out through the corridor, the same cheerful, imperturbable Mr Beck that had walked into it ten minutes before.

He found Eric waiting for him at the head of the stairs. 'Well?' he said when he saw the detective.

'Well,' replied Mr Beck, ignoring the interrogation in his voice, 'when is the inquest to be? That's the next thing to be thought of; the sooner the better.'

'Tomorrow, if you wish. My cousin John sent a messenger to Mr Morgan, the coroner. He lives only five miles off, and he has promised to be here at twelve o'clock tomorrow. There will be no difficulty in getting a jury in the village.'

'That's right, that's all right,' said Mr Beck, rubbing his hands;

'the sooner and the quieter we get those preliminaries over the better.'

'I have just sent to engage the local solicitor on behalf of my cousin. He's not particularly bright, I'm afraid, but he's the best to be had on a short notice.'

'Very proper and thoughtful on your part—very thoughtful indeed. But solicitors cannot do much in such cases. It's the evidence we have to go by, and the evidence is only too plain, I'm afraid. Now, if you please,' he went on more briskly, dismissing the disagreeable subject, as it were, with a wave of his big hand, 'I'd be very glad of that supper you spoke about.'

Mr Beck supped very heartily on a brace of grouse—the last of the dead man's shooting—and a bottle of ripe Burgundy. He was in high good-humour, and across 'the walnuts and the wine' he told Eric some startling episodes in his career, which seemed to divert the young fellow a little from his manifest grief for his uncle and anxiety for his cousin.

Meanwhile John Neville remained shut close in his own room, with the constable at the door.

The inquest was held at half-past twelve next day in the library.

The Coroner, a large, red-faced man, with a very affable manner, had got to his work promptly.

The jury 'viewed the body' steadily, stolidly, with a kind of morose delectation in the grim spectacle.

In some unaccountable way Mr Beck constituted himself a master of the ceremonies, a kind of assessor to the court.

'You had best take the gun down,' he said to the Coroner as they were leaving the room.

'Certainly, certainly,' replied the Coroner.

'And the water-bottle,' added Mr Beck.

'There is no suspicion of poison, is there?'

'It's best not to take anything for granted,' replied Mr Beck sententiously.

'By all means if you think so,' replied the obsequious Coroner. 'Constable, take that water-bottle down with you.'

The large room was filled with people of the neighbourhood, mostly farmers from the Berkly estate and small shopkeepers from the neighbouring village.

A table had been wheeled to the top of the room for the Coroner, with a seat at it for the ubiquitous local newspaper correspondent. A double row of chairs were set at the right hand of the table for the jury.

The jury had just returned from viewing the body when the crunch of wheels and hoofs was heard on the gravel of the drive, and a two-horse phaeton pulled up sharp at the entrance.

A moment later there came into the room a handsome, soldier-like man, with a girl clinging to his arm, whom he supported with tender, protecting fondness that was very touching. The girl's face was pale, but wonderfully sweet and winsome; cheeks with the faint, pure flush of the wild rose, and eyes like a wild fawn's.

No need to tell Mr Beck that here were Colonel Peyton and his daughter. He saw the look—shy, piteous, loving—that the girl gave John Neville as she passed close to the table where he sat with his head buried in his hands; and the detective's face darkened for a moment with a stern purpose, but the next moment it resumed its customary look of good-nature and good-humour.

The gardener, the gamekeeper, and the butler were briefly examined by the Coroner, and rather clumsily cross-examined by Mr Waggles, the solicitor whom Eric had thoughtfully secured for his cousin's defence.

As the case against John Neville gradually darkened into grim certainty, the girl in the far corner of the room grew white as a lily, and would have fallen but for her father's support.

'Does Mr John Neville offer himself for examination?' said the Coroner, as he finished writing the last words of the butler's deposition describing the quarrel of the night before.

'No, sir,' said Mr Waggles. 'I appear for Mr John Neville, the accused, and we reserve our defence.'

'I really have nothing to say that hasn't been already said,' added John Neville quietly.

'Mr Neville,' said Mr Waggles pompously, 'I must ask you to leave yourself entirely in my hands.'

'Eric Neville!' called out the Coroner. 'This is the last witness, I think.'

Eric stepped in front of the table and took the Bible in his hand. He was pale, but quiet and composed, and there was an unaffected grief in the look of his dark eyes and in the tone of his soft voice that touched every heart—except one.

He told his story shortly and clearly. It was quite plain that he was most anxious to shield his cousin. But in spite of this, perhaps because of this, the evidence went horribly against John Neville.

The answers to questions criminating his cousin had to be literally dragged from him by the Coroner.

With manifest reluctance he described the quarrel at dinner the night before.

'Was your cousin very angry?' the Coroner asked.

'He would not be human if he were not angry at the language used.'

'What did he say?'

'I cannot remember all he said.'

'Did he say to your uncle: "Well, you will not live for ever"?'

No answer.

'Come, Mr Neville, remember you are sworn to tell the truth.'

In an almost inaudible whisper came the words: 'He did.'

'I'm sorry to pain you, but I must do my duty. When you heard the shot you ran straight to your uncle's room, about fifty yards, I believe?'

'About that.'

'Whom did you find there bending over the dead man?'

'My cousin. I am bound to say he appeared in the deepest grief.'

'But you saw no one else?'

'No.'

'Your cousin is, I believe, the heir to Squire Neville's property; the owner I should say now?'

'I believe so.'

'That will do; you can stand down.'

This interchange of question and answer, each one of which seemed to fit the rope tighter and tighter round John Neville's neck, was listened to with hushed eagerness by the room full of people.

There was a long, deep drawing-in of breath when it ended. The suspense seemed over, but not the excitement.

Mr Beck rose as Eric turned from the table, quite as a matter of course, to question him.

'You say you *believe* your cousin was your uncle's heir—don't you *know* it?'

Then Mr Waggles found his voice.

'Really, sir,' he broke out, addressing the Coroner, 'I must protest.

This is grossly irregular. This person is not a professional gentleman. He represents no one. He has no *locus standi* in court at all.'

No one knew better than Mr Beck that technically he had no title to open his lips; but his look of quiet assurance, his calm assumption of unmistakable right, carried the day with the Coroner.

'Mr Beck,' he said, 'has, I understand, been brought down specially from London to take charge of this case, and I certainly shall not stop him in any question he may desire to ask.'

'Thank you, sir,' said Mr Beck, in the tone of a man whose clear right has been allowed. Then again to the witness: 'Didn't you know John Neville was next heir to Berkly Manor?'

'I know it, of course.'

'And if John Neville is hanged you will be the owner?'

Every one was startled at the frank brutality of the question so blandly asked. Mr Waggles bobbed up and down excitedly; but Eric answered, calmly as ever—

'That's very coarsely and cruelly put.'

'But it's true?'

'Yes, it's true.'

'We will pass from that. When you came into the room after the murder, did you examine the gun?'

'I stretched out my hand to take it, but my cousin stopped me. I must be allowed to add that I believe he was actuated, as he said, by a desire to keep everything in the room untouched. He locked the door and carried off the key. I was not in the room afterwards.'

'Did you look closely at the gun?'

'Not particularly.'

'Did you notice that both barrels were at half cock?'

'No.'

'Did you notice that there was no cap on the nipple of the right barrel that had just been fired?'

'Certainly not.'

'That is to say you did not notice it?'

'Yes.'

'Did you notice a little burnt line traced a short distance on the wood of the stock towards the right nipple?'

'No.'

Mr Beck put the gun into his hand.

'Look close. Do you notice it now?'

'I see it now for the first time.'

'You cannot account for it, I suppose?'

'No.'

'Sure?'

'Quite sure.'

All present followed this strange, and apparently purposeless cross-examination with breathless interest, groping vainly for its meaning.

The answers were given calmly and clearly, but those that looked closely saw that Eric's nether lip quivered, and it was only by a strong effort of will that he held his calmness.

Through the blandness of Mr Beck's voice and manner a subtle suggestion of hostility made itself felt, very trying to the nerves of the witness.

'We will pass from that,' said Mr Beck again. 'When you went into your uncle's room before the shot why did you take a book from the shelf and put it on the table?'

'I really cannot remember anything about it.'

'Why did you take the water-bottle from the window and stand it on the book?'

'I wanted a drink.'

'But there was none of the water drunk.'

'Then I suppose it was to take it out of the strong sun.'

'But you set it in the strong sun on the table?'

'Really I cannot remember those trivialities.' His self-control was breaking down at last.

'Then we will pass from that,' said Mr Beck a third time.

He took the little scraps of paper with the burnt holes through them from his waistcoat pocket, and handed them to the witness.

'Do you know anything about these?'

There was a pause of a second. Eric's lips tightened as if with a sudden spasm of pain. But the answer came clearly enough—

'Nothing whatever.'

'Do you ever amuse yourself with a burning glass?'

This seeming simple question was snapped suddenly at the witness like a pistol-shot.

'Really, really,' Mr Waggles broke out, 'this is mere trifling with the Court.'

'That question does certainly seem a little irrelevant, Mr Beck,' mildly remonstrated the Coroner.

'Look at the witness, sir,' retorted Mr Beck sternly. 'He does not think it irrelevant.'

Every eye in court was turned on Eric's face and fixed there.

All colour had fled from his cheeks and lips; his mouth had fallen open, and he stared at Mr Beck with eyes of abject terror.

Mr Beck went on remorselessly: 'Did you ever amuse yourself with a burning glass?'

No answer.

'Do you know that a water-bottle like this makes a capital burning glass?'

Still no answer.

'Do you know that a burning glass has been used before now to touch off a cannon or fire a gun?'

Then a voice broke from Eric at last, as it seemed in defiance of his will; a voice unlike his own—loud, harsh, hardly articulate; such a voice might have been heard in the torture chamber in the old days when the strain on the rack grew unbearable.

'You devilish bloodhound!' he shouted. 'Curse you, curse you, you've caught me! I confess it—I was the murderer!' He fell on the ground in a fit.

'And you made the sun your accomplice!' remarked Mr Beck, placid as ever.

The Duchess of Wiltshire's Diamonds

GUY BOOTHBY

To the reflective mind the rapidity with which the inhabitants of the world's greatest city seize upon a new name or idea and familiarize themselves with it, can scarcely prove otherwise than astonishing. As an illustration of my meaning let me take the case of Klimo—the now famous private detective, who has won for himself the right to be considered as great as Lecocq, or even the late lamented Sherlock Holmes.

Up to a certain morning London had never even heard his name, nor had it the remotest notion as to who or what he might be. It was as sublimely ignorant and careless on the subject as the inhabitants of Kamtchatka or Peru. Within twenty-four hours, however, the whole aspect of the case was changed. The man, woman, or child who had not seen his posters, or heard his name, was counted an ignoramus unworthy of intercourse with human beings.

Princes became familiar with it as their trains bore them to Windsor to luncheon with the Queen; the nobility noticed and commented upon it as they drove about the town; merchants, and business men generally, read it as they made their ways by omnibus or Underground, to their various shops and counting-houses; street boys called each other by it as a nickname; music hall artistes introduced it into their patter, while it was even rumoured that the Stock Exchange itself had paused in the full flood tide of business to manufacture a riddle on the subject.

That Klimo made his profession pay him well was certain, first from the fact that his advertisements must have cost a good round sum, and, second, because he had taken a mansion in Belverton Street, Park Lane, next door to Porchester House, where, to the dismay of that aristocratic neighbourhood, he advertised that he was prepared to receive and be consulted by his clients. The invitation was responded to with alacrity, and from that day forward, between the hours of twelve and two, the pavement upon the north side of the street was lined with carriages, every one containing some person desirous of testing the great man's skill.

I must here explain that I have narrated all this in order to show the state of affairs existing in Belverton Street and Park Lane when Simon Carne arrived, or was supposed to arrive in England. If my memory serves me correctly, it was on Wednesday, the 3rd of May, that the Earl of Amberley drove to Victoria to meet and welcome the man whose acquaintance he had made in India under such peculiar circumstances, and under the spell of whose fascination he and his family had fallen so completely.

Reaching the station, his lordship descended from his carriage, and made his way to the platform set apart for the reception of the Continental express. He walked with a jaunty air, and seemed to be on the best of terms with himself and the world in general. How little he suspected the existence of the noose into which he was so innocently running his head.

As if out of compliment to his arrival, the train put in an appearance within a few moments of his reaching the platform. He immediately placed himself in such a position that he could make sure of seeing the man he wanted, and waited patiently until he should come in sight. Carne, however, was not among the first batch, indeed, the majority of passengers had passed before his lordship caught sight of him.

One thing was very certain, however great the crush might have been, it would have been difficult to mistake Carne's figure. The man's infirmity and the peculiar beauty of his face rendered him easily recognizable. Possibly, after his long sojourn in India, he found the morning cold, for he wore a long fur coat, the collar of which he had turned up round his ears, thus making a fitting frame for his delicate face. On seeing Lord Amberley he hastened forward to greet him.

'This is most kind and friendly of you,' he said as he shook the other by the hand. 'A fine day and Lord Amberley to meet me. One could scarcely imagine a better welcome.'

As he spoke, one of his Indian servants approached and salaamed before him. He gave him an order, and received an answer in Hindustani, whereupon he turned again to Lord Amberley.

'You may imagine how anxious I am to see my new dwelling,' he said. 'My servant tells me that my carriage is here, so may I hope that you will drive back with me and see for yourself how I am likely to be lodged.'

'I shall be delighted,' said Lord Amberley, who was longing for the opportunity, and they accordingly went out into the station yard together to discover a brougham drawn by two magnificent horses, and with Nur Ali, in all the glory of white raiment and crested turban, on the box, waiting to receive them. His lordship dismissed his Victoria, and when Jowur Singh had taken his place beside his fellow servant upon the box, the carriage rolled out of the station yard in the direction of Hyde Park.

'I trust her ladyship is quite well,' said Simon Carne politely, as they turned into Gloucester Place.

'Excellently well, thank you,' replied his lordship. 'She bade me welcome you to England in her name as well as my own, and I was to say that she is looking forward to seeing you.'

'She is most kind, and I shall do myself the honour of calling upon her as soon as circumstances will permit,' answered Carne. 'I beg you will convey my best thanks to her for her thought of me.'

While these polite speeches were passing between them they were rapidly approaching a large hoarding on which was displayed a poster setting forth the name of the now famous detective, Klimo.

Simon Carne, leaning forward, studied it, and when they had passed, turned to his friend again.

'At Victoria and on all the hoardings we meet I see an enormous placard, bearing the word "Klimo". Pray, what does it mean?'

His lordship laughed.

'You are asking a question which, a month ago, was on the lips of nine out of every ten Londoners. It is only within the last fortnight that we have learned who and what "Klimo" is.'

'And pray what is he?'

'Well, the explanation is very simple. He is neither more nor less than a remarkably astute private detective, who has succeeded in attracting notice in such a way that half London has been induced to patronize him. I have had no dealings with the man myself. But a friend of mine, Lord Orpington, has been the victim of a most audacious burglary, and, the police having failed to solve the mystery, he has called Klimo in. We shall therefore see what he can do before many days are past. But, there, I expect you will soon know more about him than any of us.'

'Indeed! And why?'

'For the simple reason that he has taken No. 1, Belverton Terrace, the house adjoining your own, and sees his clients there.'

Simon Carne pursed up his lips, and appeared to be considering something.

'I trust he will not prove a nuisance,' he said at last. 'The agents who found me the house should have acquainted me with the fact. Private detectives, on however large a scale, scarcely strike one as the most desirable of neighbours—particularly for a man who is so fond of quiet as myself.'

At this moment they were approaching their destination. As the carriage passed Belverton Street and pulled up, Lord Amberley pointed to a long line of vehicles standing before the detective's door.

'You can see for yourself something of the business he does,' he said. 'Those are the carriages of his clients, and it is probable that twice as many have arrived on foot.'

'I shall certainly speak to the agent on the subject,' said Carne, with a shadow of annoyance upon his face. 'I consider the fact of this man's being so close to me a serious drawback to the house.'

Jowur Singh here descended from the box and opened the door in order that his master and his guest might alight, while portly Ram Gafur, the butler, came down the steps and salaamed before them with oriental obsequiousness. Carne greeted his domestics with kindly condescension, and then, accompanied by the ex-Viceroy, entered his new abode.

'I think you may congratulate yourself upon having secured one of the most desirable residences in London,' said his lordship ten minutes or so later, when they had explored the principal rooms.

'I am very glad to hear you say so,' said Carne. 'I trust your lordship will remember that you will always be welcome in the house as long as I am its owner.'

'It is very kind of you to say so,' returned Lord Amberley warmly. 'I shall look forward to some months of pleasant intercourse. And now I must be going. Tomorrow, perhaps, if you have nothing better to do, you will give us the pleasure of your company at dinner. Your fame has already gone abroad, and we shall ask one or two nice people to meet you, including my brother and sister-in-law, Lord and Lady Gelpington, Lord and Lady Orpington, and my cousin, the

Duchess of Wiltshire, whose interest in china and Indian Art, as perhaps you know, is only second to your own.'

'I shall be most glad to come.'

'We may count on seeing you in Eaton Square, then, at eight o'clock?'

'If I am alive you may be sure I shall be there. Must you really go? Then goodbye, and many thanks for meeting me.'

His lordship having left the house Simon Carne went upstairs to his dressing room, which it was to be noticed he found without enquiry, and rang the electric bell, beside the fireplace, three times. While he was waiting for it to be answered he stood looking out of the window at the long line of carriages in the street below.

'Everything is progressing admirably,' he said to himself. 'Amberley does not suspect any more than the world in general. As a proof he asks me to dinner tomorrow evening to meet his brother and sister-in-law, two of his particular friends, and above all Her Grace of Wiltshire. Of course I shall go, and when I bid Her Grace goodbye it will be strange if I am not one step nearer the interest on Liz's money.'

At this moment the door opened, and his valet, the grave and respectable Belton, entered the room. Carne turned to greet him impatiently.

'Come, come, Belton,' he said, 'we must be quick. It is twenty minutes to twelve and if we don't hurry, the folk next door will become impatient. Have you succeeded in doing what I spoke to you about last night?'

'I have done everything, sir.'

'I am glad to hear it. Now lock that door and let us get to work. You can let me have your news while I am dressing.'

Opening one side of a massive wardrobe that completely filled one end of the room, Belton took from it a number of garments. They included a well worn velvet coat, a baggy pair of trousers—so old that only a notorious pauper or a millionaire could have afforded to wear them—a flannel waistcoat, a Gladstone collar, a soft silk tie, and a pair of embroidered carpet slippers upon which no old clothes man in the most reckless way of business in Petticoat Lane would have advanced a single halfpenny. Into these he assisted his master to change.

'Now give me the wig, and unfasten the straps of this hump,' said Carne, as the other placed the garments just referred to upon a neighbouring chair.

Belton did as he was ordered, and then there happened a thing the like of which no one would have believed. Having unbuckled a strap on either shoulder, and slipped his hand beneath the waistcoat, he withdrew a large papier-mâché hump, which he carried away and carefully placed in a drawer of the bureau. Relieved of his burden, Simon Carne stood up as straight and well-made a man as any in Her Majesty's dominions. The malformation, for which so many, including the Earl and Countess of Amberley, had often pitied him, was nothing but a hoax intended to produce an effect which would permit him additional facilities of disguise.

The hump discarded, and the grey wig fitted carefully to his head in such a manner that not even a pinch of his own curlylocks could be seen beneath it, he adorned his cheeks with a pair of *crépu*-hair whiskers, donned the flannel vest and the velvet coat previously mentioned, slipped his feet into the carpet slippers, placed a pair of smoked glasses upon his nose, and declared himself ready to proceed about his business. The man who would have known him for Simon Carne would have been as astute as, well, shall we say, as the private detective—Klimo himself.

'It's on the stroke of twelve,' he said, as he gave a final glance at himself in the pier-glass above the dressing-table, and arranged his tie to his satisfaction. 'Should anyone call, instruct Ram Gafur to tell them that I have gone out on business, and shall not be back until three o'clock.'

'Very good, sir.'

'Now undo the door and let me go in.'

Thus commanded, Belton went across to the large wardrobe which, as I have already said, covered the whole of one side of the room, and opened the middle door. Two or three garments were seen inside suspended on pegs, and these he removed, at the same time pushing towards the right the panel at the rear. When this was done a large aperture in the wall between the two houses was disclosed. Through this door Carne passed drawing it behind him.

In No. 1, Belverton Terrace, the house occupied by the detective, whose presence in the street Carne seemed to find so objectionable, the entrance thus constructed was covered by the peculiar kind of confessional box in which Klimo invariably sat to receive his clients, the rearmost panels of which opened in the same fashion as those in the wardrobe in the dressing-room. These being pulled aside, he had but to draw them to again after him, take his seat, ring the electric bell to inform his housekeeper than he was ready, and then welcome his clients as quickly as they cared to come.

Punctually at two o'clock the interviews ceased, and Klimo, having reaped an excellent harvest of fees, returned to Porchester House to become Simon Carne once more.

Possibly it was due to the fact that the Earl and Countess of Amberley were brimming over with his praise, it may have been the rumour that he was worth as many millions as you have fingers upon your hand that did it; one thing, however, was self evident, within twenty-four hours of the noble Earl's meeting him at Victoria Station, Simon Carne was the talk, not only of fashionable, but also of unfashionable, London.

That his household were, with one exception, natives of India, that he had paid a rental for Porchester House which ran into five figures, that he was the greatest living authority upon china and Indian art generally, and that he had come over to England in search of a wife, were among the smallest of the canards set afloat concerning him.

During dinner next evening Carne put forth every effort to please. He was placed on the right hand of his hostess and next to the Duchess of Wiltshire. To the latter he paid particular attention, and to such good purpose that when the ladies returned to the drawing-room afterwards Her Grace was full of his praises. They had discussed china of all sorts, Carne had promised her a specimen which she had longed for all her life, but had never been able to obtain, and in return she had promised to show him the quaintly carved Indian casket in which the famous necklace, of which he had, of course, heard, spent most of its time. She would be wearing the jewels in question at her own ball in a week's time, she informed him, and if he would care to see the case when it came from her bankers on that day, she would be only too pleased to show it to him.

As Simon Carne drove home in his luxurious brougham afterwards, he smiled to himself as he thought of the success which was attending his first endeavour. Two of the guests, who were stewards of the Jockey Club, had heard with delight his idea of purchasing a horse in order to have an interest in the Derby. While another, on hearing that he desired to become the possessor of a yacht, had offered to propose him for the RCYC. To crown it all, however, and much better than all, the Duchess of Wiltshire had promised to show him her famous diamonds.

'By this time next week,' he said to himself, 'Liz's interest should be considerably closer. But satisfactory as my progress has been hitherto it is difficult to see how I am to get possession of the stones. From what I have been able to discover they are only brought from the bank on the day the Duchess intends to wear them, and they are taken back by His Grace the morning following.

'While she has got them on her person it would be manifestly impossible to get them from her. And as, when she takes them off, they are returned to their box and placed in a safe, constructed in the wall of the bedroom adjoining, and which for the occasion is occupied by the butler and one of the under footmen, the only key being in the possession of the Duke himself, it would be equally foolish to hope to appropriate them. In what manner therefore I am to become their possessor passes my comprehension. However, one thing is certain, obtained they must be, and the attempt must be made on the night of the ball if possible. In the meantime I'll set my wits to work upon a plan.'

Next day Simon Carne was the recipient of an invitation to the ball in question, and two days later he called upon the Duchess of Wiltshire at her residence in Belgrave Square with a plan prepared. He also took with him the small vase he had promised her four nights before. She received him most graciously, and their talk fell at once into the usual channel. Having examined her collection and charmed her by means of one or two judicious criticisms, he asked permission to include photographs of certain of her treasures in his forthcoming book, then little by little he skilfully guided the conversation on to the subject of jewels.

'Since we are discussing gems, Mr Carne,' she said, 'Perhaps it would interest you to see my famous necklace. By good fortune I have it in the house now, for the reason that an alteration is being made to one of the clasps by my jewellers.'

'I should like to see it immensely,' answered Carne. 'At one time and another I have had the good fortune to examine the jewels of the leading Indian Princes, and I should like to be able to say that I had seen the famous Wiltshire necklace.'

'Then you shall certainly have that honour,' she answered with a smile. 'If you will ring that bell I will send for it.'

Carne rang the bell as requested, and when the butler entered he was given the key of the safe and ordered to bring the case to the drawing-room.

'We must not keep it very long,' she observed while the man was absent. 'It is to be returned to the bank in an hour's time.'

'I am indeed fortunate,' Carne replied, and turned to the description of some curious Indian wood carving, of which he was making a special feature in his book. As he explained, he had collected his illustrations from the doors of Indian temples, from the gateways of palaces, from old brass work, and even from carved chairs and boxes he had picked up in all sorts of odd corners. Her Grace was most interested.

'How strange that you should have mentioned it,' she said. 'If carved boxes have any interest for you, it is possible my jewel case itself may be of use to you. As I think I told you during Lady Amberley's dinner, it came from Benares, and has carved upon it the portraits of nearly every god in the Hindu Pantheon.'

'You raise my curiosity to fever heat,' said Carne.

A few moments later the servant returned, bringing with him a wooden box, about sixteen inches long, by twelve wide, and eight deep, which he placed upon a table beside his mistress, after which he retired.

'This is the case to which I have just been referring,' said the Duchess, placing her hand on the article in question. 'If you glance at it you will see how exquisitely it is carved.'

Concealing his eagerness with an effort, Simon Carne drew his chair up to the table, and examined the box.

It was with justice she had described it as a work of art. What the wood was of which it was constructed Carne was unable to tell. It was dark and heavy, and, though it was not teak, closely resembled it. It was literally covered with quaint carving, and of its kind was a unique work of art.

'It is most curious and beautiful,' said Carne when he had finished his examination. 'In all my experience I can safely say I have never seen its equal. If you will permit me I should very much like to include a description and an illustration of it in my book.'

'Of course you may do so; I shall be only too delighted,' answered

Her Grace. 'If it will help you in your work I shall be glad to lend it to you for a few hours in order that you may have the illustration made.'

This was exactly what Carne had been waiting for, and he accepted the offer with alacrity.

'Very well, then,' she said. 'On the day of my ball, when it will be brought from the bank again, I will take the necklace out and send the case to you. I must make one proviso, however, and that is that you let me have it back the same day.'

'I will certainly promise to do that,' replied Carne.

'And now let us look inside,' said his hostess.

Choosing a key from a bunch she carried in her pocket, she unlocked the casket, and lifted the lid. Accustomed as Carne had all his life been to the sight of gems, what he saw before him then almost took his breath away. The inside of the box, both sides and bottom, was quilted with the softest Russia leather, and on this luxurious couch reposed the famous necklace. The fire of the stones when the light caught them was sufficient to dazzle the eyes, so fierce was it.

As Carne could see, every gem was perfect of its kind, and there were no fewer than three hundred of them. The setting was a fine example of the jeweller's art, and last, but not least, the value of the whole affair was fifty thousand pounds, a mere fleabite to the man who had given it to his wife, but a fortune to any humbler person.

'And now that you have seen my property, what do you think of it?' asked the Duchess as she watched her visitor's face.

'It is very beautiful,' he answered, 'and I do not wonder that you are proud of it. Yes, the diamonds are very fine, but I think it is their abiding place that fascinates me more. Have you any objection to my measuring it?'

'Pray do so, if it is likely to be of any assistance to you,' replied Her Grace.

Carne thereupon produced a small ivory rule, ran it over the box, and the figures he thus obtained he jotted down in his pocket book.

Ten minutes later, when the case had been returned to the safe, he thanked the Duchess for her kindness and took his departure, promising to call in person for the empty case on the morning of the ball.

Reaching home he passed into his study, and, seating himself at his writing table, pulled a sheet of note paper towards him and began to sketch, as well as he could remember it, the box he had seen. Then he leant back in his chair and closed his eyes.

'I have cracked a good many hard nuts in my time,' he said reflectively, 'but never one that seemed so difficult at first sight as this. As far as I see at present, the case stands as follows: the box will be brought from the bank where it usually reposes to Wiltshire House on the morning of the dance. I shall be allowed to have possession of it, without the stones of course, for a period possibly extending from eleven o'clock in the morning to four or five, at any rate not later than seven, in the evening. After the ball the necklace will be returned to it, when it will be locked up in the safe, over which the butler and a footman will mount guard.

'To get into the room during the night is not only too risky, but physically out of the question; while to rob Her Grace of her treasure during the progress of the dance would be equally impossible. The Duke fetches the casket and takes it back to the bank himself, so that to all intents and purposes I am almost as far off the solution as ever.'

Half-an-hour went by and found him still seated at his desk, staring at the drawing on the paper, then an hour. The traffic of the streets rolled past the house unheeded. Finally Jowur Singh announced his carriage, and, feeling that an idea might come to him with a change of scene, he set off for a drive in the park.

By this time his elegant mail phaeton, with its magnificent horses and Indian servant on the seat behind, was as well known as Her Majesty's state equipage, and attracted almost as much attention. Today, however, the fashionable world noticed that Simon Carne looked preoccupied. He was still working out his problem, but so far without much success. Suddenly something, no one will ever be able to say what, put an idea into his head. The notion was no sooner born in his brain than he left the park and drove quickly home. Ten minutes had scarcely elapsed before he was back in his study again, and had ordered that Wajib Baksh should be sent to him.

When the man he wanted put in an appearance, Carne handed him the paper upon which he had made the drawing of the jewel case.

'Look at that,' he said, 'and tell me what thou seest there.'

'I see a box,' answered the man, who by this time was well accustomed to his master's ways.

'As thou say'st, it is a box,' said Carne. 'The wood is heavy and thick, though what wood it is I do not know. The measurements are upon the paper below. Within, both the sides and bottom are quilted with soft leather as I have also shown. Think now, Wajib Baksh, for in this case thou wilt need to have all thy wits about thee. Tell me is it in thy power, oh most cunning of all craftsmen, to insert such extra sides within this box that they, being held by a spring, shall lie so snug as not to be noticeable to the ordinary eye? Can it be so arranged that, when the box is locked, they shall fall flat upon the bottom thus covering and holding fast what lies beneath them, and yet making the box appear to the eye as if it were empty. Is it possible for thee to do such a thing?'

Wajib Baksh did not reply for a few moments. His instinct told him what his master wanted, and he was not disposed to answer hastily, for he also saw that his reputation as the most cunning craftsman in India was at stake.

'If the Heaven-born will permit me the night for thought,' he said at last, 'I will come to him when he rises from his bed and tell him what I can do, and he can then give his orders as it pleases him.'

'Very good,' said Carne. 'Then tomorrow morning I shall expect thy report. Let the work be good and there will be many rupees for thee to touch in return. As to the lock and the way it shall act, let that be the concern of Hiram Singh.'

Wajib Baksh salaamed and withdrew, and Simon Carne for the time being dismissed the matter from his mind.

Next morning, while he was dressing, Belton reported that the two artificers desired an interview with him. He ordered them to be admitted, and forthwith they entered the room. It was noticeable that Wajib Baksh carried in his hand a heavy box, which, upon Carne's motioning him to do so, he placed upon the table.

'Have ye thought over the matter?' he asked, seeing that the men waited for him to speak.

'We have thought of it,' replied Hiram Singh, who always acted as spokesman for the pair. 'If the Presence will deign to look he will see that we have made a box of the size and shape such as he drew upon the paper.'

'Yes, it is certainly a good copy,' said Carne condescendingly, after he had examined it.

Wajib Baksh showed his white teeth in appreciation of the compliment, and Hiram Singh drew closer to the table.

'And now, if the Sahib will open it, he will in his wisdom be able to tell if it resembles the other that he has in his mind.'

Carne opened the box as requested, and discovered that the interior was an exact counterfeit of the Duchess of Wiltshire's jewel case, even to the extent of the quilted leather lining which had been the other's principal feature. He admitted that the likeness was all that could be desired.

'As he is satisfied,' said Hiram Singh, 'it may be that the Protector of the Poor will deign to try an experiment with it. See, here is a comb. Let it be placed in the box, so—now he will see what he will see.'

The broad, silver-backed comb, lying upon his dressing-table, was placed on the bottom of the box, the lid was closed, and the key turned in the lock. The case being securely fastened, Hiram Singh laid it before his master.

'I am to open it, I suppose?' said Carne, taking the key and replacing it in the lock.

'If my master pleases,' replied the other.

Carne accordingly turned it in the lock, and, having done so, raised the lid and looked inside. His astonishment was complete. To all intents and purposes the box was empty. The comb was not to be seen, and yet the quilted sides and bottom were, to all appearances, just the same as when he had first looked inside.

'This is most wonderful,' he said. And indeed it was as clever a conjuring trick as any he had ever seen.

'Nay, it is very simple,' Wajib Baksh replied. 'The Heaven-born told me that there must be no risk of detection.'

He took the box in his own hands and, running his nails down the centre of the quilting, divided the false bottom into two pieces; these he lifted out, revealing the comb lying upon the real bottom beneath.

'The sides, as my lord will see,' said Hiram Singh, taking a step forward, 'are held in their appointed places by these two springs. Thus, when the key is turned the springs relax, and the sides are driven by others into their places on the bottom, where the seams in the quilting mask the join. There is but one disadvantage. It is as follows: When the pieces which form the bottom are lifted out in order that my lord may get at whatever lies concealed beneath, the springs must of necessity stand revealed. However, to anyone who knows sufficient of the working of the box to lift out the false bottom, it will be an easy matter to withdraw the springs and conceal them about his person.'

'As you say that is an easy matter,' said Carne, 'and I shall not be likely to forget. Now one other question. Presuming I am in a position to put the real box into your hands for say eight hours, do you think that in that time you can fit it up so that detection will be impossible?'

'Assuredly, my lord,' replied Hiram Singh with conviction. 'There is but the lock and the fitting of the springs to be done. Three hours at most would suffice for that.'

'I am pleased with you,' said Carne. 'As a proof of my satisfaction, when the work is finished you will each receive five hundred rupees. Now you can go.'

According to his promise, ten o'clock on the Friday following found him in his hansom driving towards Belgrave Square. He was a little anxious, though the casual observer would scarcely have been able to tell it. The magnitude of the stake for which he was playing was enough to try the nerve of even such a past master in his profession as Simon Carne.

Arriving at the house he discovered some workmen erecting an awning across the footway in preparation for the ball that was to take place at night. It was not long, however, before he found himself in the boudoir, reminding Her Grace of her promise to permit him an opportunity of making a drawing of the famous jewel case. The Duchess was naturally busy, and within a quarter of an hour he was on his way home with the box placed on the seat of the carriage beside him.

'Now,' he said, as he patted it good-humouredly, 'if only the notion worked out by Hiram Singh and Wajib Baksh holds good, the famous Wiltshire diamonds will become my property before very many hours are passed. By this time tomorrow, I suppose, London will be all agog concerning the burglary.'

On reaching his house he left his carriage and himself carried the box into his study. Once there he rang his bell and ordered Hiram Singh and Wajib Baksh to be sent to him. When they arrived he showed them the box upon which they were to exercise their ingenuity.

'Bring your tools in here,' he said, 'and do the work under my own eyes. You have but nine hours before you, so you must make the most of them.'

The men went for their implements, and as soon as they were ready set to work. All through the day they were kept hard at it, with the result that by five o'clock the alterations had been effected and the case stood ready. By the time Carne returned from his afternoon drive in the Park it was quite prepared for the part it was to play in his scheme. Having praised the men, he turned them out and locked the door, then went across the room and unlocked a drawer in his writing table. From it he took a flat leather jewel case which he opened. It contained a necklace of counterfeit diamonds, if anything a little larger than the one he intended to try to obtain. He had purchased it that morning in the Burlington Arcade for the purpose of testing the apparatus his servants had made, and this he now proceeded to do.

Laying it carefully upon the bottom he closed the lid and turned the key. When he opened it again the necklace was gone, and even though he knew the secret he could not for the life of him see where the false bottom began and ended. After that he reset the trap and tossed the necklace carelessly in. To his delight it acted as well as on the previous occasion. He could scarcely contain his satisfaction. His conscience was sufficiently elastic to give him no trouble. To him it was scarcely a robbery he was planning, but an artistic trial of skill, in which he pitted his wits and cunning against the forces of society in general.

At half-past seven he dined and afterwards smoked a meditative cigar over the evening paper in the billiard room. The invitations to the ball were for ten o'clock, and at nine-thirty he went to his dressing-room.

'Make me tidy as quickly as you can,' he said to Belton when the latter appeared, 'and while you are doing so listen to my final instructions.

'Tonight, as you know, I am endeavouring to secure the Duchess of Wiltshire's necklace. Tomorrow morning all London will resound with the hubbub, and I have been making my plans in such a way as to arrange that Klimo shall be the first person consulted. When the messenger calls, if call he does, see that the old woman next door bids him tell the Duke to come personally at twelve o'clock. Do you understand?'

'Perfectly, sir.'

'Very good. Now give me the jewel case, and let me be off. You need not sit up for me.'

Precisely as the clocks in the neighbourhood were striking ten Simon Carne reached Belgrave Square, and, as he hoped, found himself the first guest.

His hostess and her husband received him in the ante-room of the drawing-room.

'I come laden with a thousand apologies,' he said as he took Her Grace's hand, and bent over it with that ceremonious politeness which was one of the man's chief characteristics. 'I am most unconsciably early, I know, but I hastened here in order that I might personally return the jewel case you so kindly lent me. I must trust to your generosity to forgive me. The drawings took longer than I expected.'

'Please do not apologize,' answered Her Grace. 'It is very kind of you to have brought the case yourself. I hope the illustrations have proved successful. I shall look forward to seeing them as soon as they are ready. But I am keeping you holding the box. One of my servants will take it to my room.'

She called a footman to her and bade him take the box and place it upon her dressing-table.

'Before it goes I must let you see that I have not damaged it either externally or internally,' said Carne with a laugh. 'It is such a valuable case that I should never forgive myself if it had even received a scratch during the time it has been in my possession.'

So saying he lifted the lid and allowed her to look inside. To all appearance it was exactly the same as when she had lent it to him earlier in the day.

'You have been most careful,' she said. And then, with an air of banter, she continued: 'If you desire it I shall be pleased to give you a certificate to that effect.'

They jested in this fashion for a few moments after the servant's departure, during which time Carne promised to call upon her the following morning at eleven o'clock, and to bring with him the illustrations he had made and a queer little piece of china he had had the good fortune to pick up in a dealer's shop the previous afternoon. By this time fashionable London was making its way up the grand staircase, and with its appearance further conversation became impossible.

Shortly after midnight Carne bade his hostess good night and slipped away. He was perfectly satisfied with his evening's entertainment, and if the key of the jewel case were not turned before the jewels were placed in it, he was convinced they would become his property. It speaks well for his strength of nerve when I record the fact that on going to bed his slumbers were as peaceful and untroubled as those of a little child.

Breakfast was scarcely over next morning before a hansom drew up at his front door and Lord Amberley alighted. He was ushered into Carne's presence forthwith, and on seeing that the latter was surprised at his early visit, hastened to explain.

'My dear fellow,' he said as he took possession of the chair the other offered him, 'I have come round to see you on most important business. As I told you last night at the dance, when you so kindly asked me to come and see the steam yacht you have purchased, I had an appointment with Wiltshire at half-past nine this morning. On reaching Belgrave Square, I found the whole house in confusion. Servants were running hither and thither with scared faces, the butler was on the borders of lunacy, the Duchess was well-nigh hysterical in her boudoir, while her husband was in his study vowing vengeance against all the world.'

'You alarm me,' said Carne, lighting a cigarette with a hand that was as steady as a rock. 'What on earth has happened?'

'I think I might safely allow you fifty guesses and then wager a hundred pounds you'd not hit the mark; and yet in a certain measure it concerns you.'

'Concerns me? Good gracious. What have I done to bring all this about?'

'Pray do not look so alarmed,' said Amberley. 'Personally you have done nothing. Indeed, on second thoughts, I don't know that I am right in saying that it concerns you at all. The fact of the matter is, Carne, a burglary took place last night at Wiltshire House, *and the famous necklace has disappeared.*'

'Good Heavens! You don't say so?'

'But I *do*. The circumstances of the case are as follows: When my cousin retired to her room last night after the ball, she unclasped the necklace, and, in her husband's presence, placed it carefully in her jewel case, which she locked. That having been done, Wiltshire took the box to the room which contained the safe, and himself placed it there, locking the iron door with his own key. The room was occupied that night, according to custom, by the butler and one of the footmen, both of whom have been in the family since they were boys.

'Next morning, after breakfast, the Duke unlocked the safe and took out the box, intending to convey it to the Bank as usual. Before leaving, however, he placed it on his study-table and went upstairs to speak to his wife. He cannot remember exactly how long he was absent, but he feels convinced that he was not gone more than a quarter of an hour at the very utmost.

'Their conversation finished, she accompanied him downstairs, where she saw him take up the case to carry it to his carriage. Before he left the house, however, she said: "I suppose you have looked to see that the necklace is all right?" "How could I do so?" was his reply. "You know you possess the only key that will fit it."

'She felt in her pockets, but to her surprise the key was not there.'

'If I were a detective I should say that that is a point to be remembered,' said Carne with a smile. 'Pray, where did she find her keys?'

'Upon her dressing-table,' said Amberley. 'Though she has not the slightest recollection of leaving them there.'

'Well, when she had procured the keys, what happened?'

'Why, they opened the box, and to their astonishment and dismay, *found it empty. The jewels were gone!*'

'Good gracious. What a terrible loss! It seems almost impossible that it can be true. And pray, what did they do?'

'At first they stood staring into the empty box, hardly believing the evidence of their own eyes. Stare how they would, however, they could not bring them back. The jewels had without doubt disappeared, but when and where the robbery had taken place it was impossible to say. After that they had up all the servants and questioned them, but the result was what they might have foreseen, no one from the butler to the kitchenmaid could throw any light upon the subject. To this minute it remains as great a mystery as when they first discovered it.'

'I am more concerned than I can tell you,' said Carne. 'How thankful I ought to be that I returned the case to Her Grace last night. But in thinking of myself I am forgetting to ask what has brought you to me. If I can be of any assistance I hope you will command me.'

'Well, I'll tell you why I have come,' replied Lord Amberley. 'Naturally they are most anxious to have the mystery solved and the jewels recovered as soon as possible. Wiltshire wanted to send to Scotland Yard there and then, but his wife and I eventually persuaded him to consult Klimo. As you know, if the police authorities are called in first he refuses the business altogether. Now, we thought, as you are his next door neighbour, you might possibly be able to assist us.'

'You may be very sure, my lord, I will do everything that lies in my power. Let us go in and see him at once.'

As he spoke he rose and threw what remained of his cigarette into the fireplace. His visitor having imitated his example, they procured their hats and walked round from Park Lane into Belverton Street to bring up at No. 1. After they had rung the bell the door was opened to them by the old woman who invariably received the detective's clients.

'Is Mr Klimo at home?' asked Carne. 'And, if so, can we see him?'

The old lady was a little deaf, and the question had to be repeated before she could be made to understand what was wanted. As soon, however, as she realized their desire she informed them that her master was absent from town, but would be back as usual at twelve o'clock to meet his clients.

'What on earth's to be done?' said the Earl, looking at his companion in dismay. 'I am afraid I can't come back again, as I have a most important appointment at that hour.'

'Do you think you could entrust the business to me?' asked Carne. 'If so, I will make a point of seeing him at twelve o'clock, and could call at Wiltshire House afterwards and tell the Duke what I have done.'

'That's very good of you,' replied Amberley. 'If you are sure it would not put you to too much trouble, that would be quite the best thing to be done.'

'I will do it with pleasure,' Carne replied. 'I feel it my duty to help in whatever way I can.'

'You are very kind,' said the other. 'Then, as I understand it, you are to call upon Klimo at twelve o'clock, and afterwards to let my cousins know what you have succeeded in doing. I only hope he will help us to secure the thief. We are having too many of these burglaries just now. I must catch this hansom and be off. Goodbye, and many thanks.'

'Goodbye,' said Carne, and shook him by the hand.

The hansom having rolled away, Carne retraced his steps to his own abode.

'It is really very strange,' he muttered as he walked along, 'how often chance condescends to lend her assistance to my little schemes. The mere fact that His Grace left the box unwatched in his study for a quarter of an hour may serve to throw the police off on quite another scent. I am also glad that they decided to open the case in the house, for if it had gone to the bankers' and had been placed in the strongroom unexamined, I should never have been able to get possession of the jewels at all.'

Three hours later he drove to Wiltshire House and saw the Duke. The Duchess was far too much upset by the catastrophe to see anyone.

'This is really most kind of you, Mr Carne,' said His Grace when the other had supplied an elaborate account of his interview with Klimo. 'We are extremely indebted to you. I am sorry he cannot come before ten o'clock tonight, and that he makes this stipulation of my seeing him alone, for I must confess I should like to have had someone else present to ask any questions that might escape me. But if that's his usual hour and custom, well, we must abide by it, that's all. I hope he will do some good, for this is the greatest calamity that has ever befallen me. As I told you just now, it has made my wife quite ill. She is confined to her bedroom and quite hysterical.'

'You do not suspect anyone, I suppose.' enquired Carne.

'Not a soul,' the other answered. 'The thing is such a mystery that we do not know what to think. I feel convinced, however, that my servants are as innocent as I am. Nothing will ever make me think them otherwise. I wish I could catch the fellow, that's all. I'd make him suffer for the trick he's played me.'

Carne offered an appropriate reply, and after a little further conversation upon the subject, bade the irate nobleman goodbye and left the house. From Belgrave Square he drove to one of the clubs of which he had been elected a member, in search of Lord Orpington, with whom he had promised to lunch, and afterwards took him to a shipbuilder's yard near Greenwich in order to show him the steam yacht he had lately purchased.

It was close upon dinner time before he returned to his own residence. He brought Lord Orpington with him, and they dined in state together. At nine the latter bade him goodbye, and at ten Carne retired to his dressing-room and rang for Belton.

'What have you to report,' he asked, 'with regard to what I bade you do in Belgrave Square?'

'I followed your instructions to the letter,' Belton replied. 'Yesterday morning I wrote to Messrs Horniblow and Jimson, the house agents in Piccadilly, in the name of Colonel Braithwaite, and asked for an order to view the residence to the right of Wiltshire House. I asked that the order might be sent direct to the house, where the Colonel would get it upon his arrival. This letter I posted myself in Basingstoke, as you desired me to do.

'At nine o'clock yesterday morning I dressed myself as much like an elderly army officer as possible, and took a cab to Belgrave Square. The caretaker, an old fellow of close upon seventy years of age, admitted me immediately upon hearing my name, and proposed that he should show me over the house. This, however, I told him was quite unnecessary, backing my speech with a present of half-a-crown, whereupon he returned to his breakfast perfectly satisfied, while I wandered about the house at my own leisure.

'Reaching the same floor as that upon which is situated the room in which the Duke's safe is kept, I discovered that your supposition was quite correct, and that it would be possible for a man, by opening the window, to make his way along the coping from one house to the other, without being seen. I made certain that there was no one in the bedroom in which the butler slept, and then arranged the long telescope walking stick you gave me, and fixed one of my boots to it by means of the screw in the end. With this I was able to make a regular succession of footsteps in the dust along the ledge, between one window and the other.

'That done, I went downstairs again, bade the caretaker good morning, and got into my cab. From Belgrave Square I drove to the shop of the pawnbroker whom you told me you had discovered was out of town. His assistant enquired my business and was anxious to do what he could for me. I told him, however, that I must see his master personally as it was about the sale of some diamonds I had had left me. I pretended to be annoyed that he was not at home, and muttered to myself, so that the man could hear, something about its meaning a journey to Amsterdam.

'Then I limped out of the shop, paid off my cab, and walking down a by-street, removed my moustache, and altered my appearance by taking off my great coat and muffler. A few streets further on I purchased a bowler hat in place of the old-fashioned topper I had hitherto been wearing, and then took a cab from Piccadilly and came home.'

'You have fulfilled my instructions admirably,' said Carne. 'And if the business comes off, as I expect it will, you shall receive your usual percentage. Now I must be turned into Klimo and be off to Belgrave Square to put His Grace of Wiltshire upon the track of this burglar.'

Before he retired to rest that night Simon Carne took something, wrapped in a red silk handkerchief, from the capacious pocket of the coat Klimo had been wearing a few moments before. Having unrolled the covering, he held up to the light the magnificent necklace which for so many years had been the joy and pride of the ducal house of Wiltshire. The electric light played upon it, and touched it with a thousand different hues.

'Where so many have failed,' he said to himself, as he wrapped it in the handkerchief again and locked it in his safe, 'it is pleasant to be able to congratulate oneself on having succeeded. It is without its equal, and I don't think I shall be overstepping the mark if I say that I think when she receives it Liz will be glad she lent me the money.'

Next morning all London was astonished by the news that the famous Wiltshire diamonds had been stolen, and a few hours later Carne learnt from an evening paper that the detectives who had taken up the case, upon the supposed retirement from it of Klimo, were still completely at fault.

That evening he was to entertain several friends to dinner. They included Lord Amberley, Lord Orpington, and a prominent member of the Privy Council. Lord Amberley arrived late, but filled to over-flowing with importance. His friends noticed his state, and questioned him.

'Well, gentlemen,' he answered, as he took up a commanding position upon the drawing-room hearthrug, 'I am in a position to inform you that Klimo has reported upon the case, and the upshot of it is that the Wiltshire Diamond Mystery is a mystery no longer.'

'What do you mean?' asked the others in a chorus.

'I mean that he sent in his report to Wiltshire this afternoon, as arranged. From what he said the other night, after being alone in the room with the empty jewel case and a magnifying glass for two minutes or so, he was in a position to describe the *modus operandi*, and what is more to put the police on the scent of the burglar.'

'And how *was* it worked?' asked Carne.

'From the empty house next door,' replied the other. 'On the morning of the burglary a man, purporting to be a retired army officer, called with an order to view, got the caretaker out of the way, clambered along to Wiltshire House by means of the parapet outside, reached the room during the time the servants were at breakfast, opened the safe, and abstracted the jewels.'

'But how did Klimo find all this out?' asked Lord Orpington.

'By his own inimitable cleverness,' replied Lord Amberley. 'At any rate it has been proved that he was correct. The man *did* make his way from next door, and the police have since discovered that an individual, answering to the description given, visited a pawnbroker's shop in the city about an hour later and stated that he had diamonds to sell.'

'If that is so it turns out to be a very simple mystery after all,' said Lord Orpington as they began their meal.

'Thanks to the ingenuity of the cleverest detective in the world,' remarked Amberley.

'In that case here's a good health to Klimo,' said the Privy Councillor, raising his glass.

'I will join you in that,' said Simon Carne. 'Here's a very good health to Klimo and his connection with the Duchess of Wiltshire's diamonds. May he always be equally successful!'

'Hear, hear to that,' replied his guests.

The Story of The Spaniards, Hammersmith

E. and H. HERON

Lieutenant Roderick Houston, of HMS *Sphinx*, had practically nothing beyond his pay, and he was beginning to be very tired of the West African station, when he received the pleasant intelligence that a relative had left him a legacy. This consisted of a satisfactory sum in ready money and a house in Hammersmith, which was rated at over £200 a year, and was said in addition to be comfortably furnished. Houston, therefore, counted on its rental to bring his income up to a fairly desirable figure. Further information from home, however, showed him that he had been rather premature in his expectations, whereupon, being a man of action, he applied for two months' leave, and came home to look after his affairs himself.

When he had been a week in London, he arrived at the conclusion that he could not possibly hope single-handed to tackle the difficulties which presented themselves. He accordingly wrote the following letter to his friend, Flaxman Low:

The Spaniards, Hammersmith, 23-3-1892.

DEAR LOW, since we parted some three years ago, I have heard very little of you. It was only yesterday that I met our mutual friend, Sammy Smith ('Silkworm' of our schooldays), who told me that your studies have developed in a new direction, and that you are now a good deal interested in psychical subjects. If this be so, I hope to induce you to come and stay with me here for a few days by promising to introduce you to a problem in your own line. I am just now living at 'The Spaniards', a house that has lately been left to me, and which in the first instance was built by an old fellow named Van Nuysen, who married a great-aunt of mine. It is a good house, but there is said to be 'something wrong' with it. It lets easily, but unluckily the tenants cannot be persuaded to remain above a week or two. They complain that the place is haunted by something—presumably a ghost—because its vagaries bear just that brand of inconsequence which stamps the common run of manifestations.

It occurs to me that you may care to investigate the matter with me. If so, send me a wire when to expect you.

Yours ever,
RODERICK HOUSTON

Houston waited in some anxiety for an answer. Low was the sort of man one could rely on in almost any emergency. Sammy Smith had told him a characteristic anecdote of Low's career at Oxford, where, although his intellectual triumphs may be forgotten, he will always be remembered by the story that when Sands, of Queen's, fell ill on the day before the varsity sports, a telegram was sent to Low's rooms: 'Sands ill. You must do the hammer for us.' Low's reply was pithy: 'I'll be there.' Thereupon he finished the treatise upon which he was engaged, and next day his strong, lean figure was to be seen swinging the hammer amidst vociferous cheering, for that was the occasion on which he not only won the event, but beat the record.

On the fifth day Low's answer came from Vienna. As he read it, Houston recalled the high forehead, long neck—with its accompanying low collar—and thin moustache of his scholarly, athletic friend, and smiled. There was so much more in Flaxman Low than anyone gave him credit for.

MY DEAR HOUSTON, Very glad to hear of you again. In response to your kind invitation, I thank you for the opportunity of meeting the ghost, and still more for the pleasure of your companionship. I came here to enquire into a somewhat similar affair. I hope, however, to be able to leave tomorrow, and will be with you sometime on Friday evening.

Very sincerely yours,
FLAXMAN LOW

P.S. By the way, will it be convenient to give your servants a holiday during the term of my visit, as, if my investigations are to be of any value, not a grain of dust must be disturbed in your house, excepting by ourselves F. L.

'The Spaniards' was within some fifteen minutes' walk of Hammersmith Bridge. Set in the midst of a fairly respectable neighbourhood, it presented an odd contrast to the commonplace dullness of the narrow streets crowded about it. As Flaxman Low drove up in the evening light, he reflected that the house might have come from the back of beyond—it gave an impression of something old world and something exotic.

It was surrounded by a ten-foot wall, above which the upper storey was visible, and Low decided that this intensely English house still gave some curious suggestion of the tropics. The interior of the house carried out the same idea, with its sense of space and air, cool tints and wide-matted passages.

'So you have seen something yourself since you came?' Low said, as they sat at dinner, for Houston had arranged that meals should be sent in for them from an hotel.

'I've heard tapping up and down the passage upstairs. It is an uncarpeted landing which runs the whole length of the house. One night, when I was quicker than usual, I saw what looked like a bladder disappear into one of the bedrooms—your room it is to be, by the way—and the door closed behind it,' replied Houston discontentedly. 'The usual meaningless antics of a ghost.'

'What had the tenants who lived here to say about it?' went on Low.

'Most of the people saw and heard just what I have told you, and promptly went away. The only one who stood out for a little while was old Filderg—you know the man? Twenty years ago he made an effort to cross the Australian deserts—he stopped for eight weeks. When he left he saw the house-agent, and said he was afraid he had done a little shooting practice in the upper passage, and he hoped it wouldn't count against him in the bill, as it was done in defence of his life. He said something had jumped on to the bed and tried to strangle him. He described it as cold and glutinous, and he pursued it down the passage, firing at it. He advised the owner to have the house pulled down; but, of course, my cousin did nothing of the kind. It's a very good house, and he did not see the sense of spoiling his property.'

'That's very true,' replied Flaxman Low, looking round. 'Mr Van Nuysen had been in the West Indies, and kept his liking for spacious rooms.'

'Where did you hear anything about him?' asked Houston in surprise.

'I have heard nothing beyond what you told me in your letter; but I see a couple of bottles of Gulf weed and a lace-plant ornament, such as people used to bring from the West Indies in former days.'

'Perhaps I should tell you the history of the old man,' said Houston doubtfully; 'but we aren't proud of it!' Flaxman Low considered a moment.

'When was the ghost seen for the first time?'

'When the first tenant took the house. It was let after old Van Nuysen's time.'

'Then it may clear the way if you will tell me something of him.'

'He owned sugar plantations in Trinidad, where he passed the greater part of his life, while his wife mostly remained in England—incompatibility of temper it was said. When he came home for good and built this house they still lived apart, my aunt declaring that nothing on earth would persuade her to return to him. In course of time he became a confirmed invalid, and he then insisted on my aunt joining him. She lived here for perhaps a year, when she was found dead in bed one morning—in your room.'

'What caused her death?'

'She had been in the habit of taking narcotics, and it was supposed that she smothered herself while under their influence.'

'That doesn't sound very satisfactory,' remarked Flaxman Low.

'Her husband was satisfied with it anyhow, and it was no one else's business. The family were only too glad to have the affair hushed up.'

'And what became of Mr Van Nuysen?'

'That I can't tell you. He disappeared a short time after. Search was made for him in the usual way, but nobody knows to this day what became of him.'

'Ah, that was strange, as he was such an invalid,' said Low, and straightway fell into a long fit of abstraction, from which he was roused by hearing Houston curse the incurable foolishness and imbecility of ghostly behaviour. Flaxman woke up at this. He was a man with an immense capacity for quiet enthusiasm. He broke a walnut thoughtfully and began in a gentle voice:

'My dear fellow, we are apt to be hasty in our condemnation of the general behaviour of ghosts. It may appear incalculably foolish in our eyes, and I admit there often seems to be a total absence of any apparent object or intelligent action. But remember that what appears to us to be foolishness may be wisdom in the spirit world, since our unready senses can only catch broken glimpses of what is, I have not the slightest doubt, a coherent whole, if we could trace the connection.'

'There may be something in that,' replied Houston indifferently. 'People naturally say that this ghost is the ghost of old Van Nuysen. But what connection can possibly exist between what I have told you of him and the manifestations—a tapping up and down the passage and the drawing about of a bladder like a child at play? It sounds idiotic!'

'Certainly. Yet it need not necessarily be so. These are isolated facts, we must look for the links which lie between. Suppose a saddle and a horseshoe were to be shown to a man who had never seen a horse, I doubt whether he, however intelligent, could evolve the connecting idea! The ways of spirits are strange to us simply because we need further data to help us to interpret them.'

'It's a new point of view,' returned Houston, 'but upon my word, you know, Low, I think you're wasting your time!'

Flaxman Low smiled slowly; his grave, melancholy face brightened.

'I have,' said he, 'gone somewhat deeply into the subject. In other sciences one reasons by analogy. Psychology is unfortunately a science with a future but without a past, or more probably it is a lost science of the ancients. However that may be, we stand today on the frontier of an unknown world, and progress is the result of individual effort; each solution of difficult phenomena forms a step towards the solution of the next problem. In this case, for example, the bladder-like object may be the key to the mystery.'

Houston yawned.

'It all seems pretty senseless, but perhaps you may be able to read reason into it. If it were anything tangible, anything a man could meet with his fists, it would be easier.'

'I entirely agree with you. But suppose we deal with this affair as it stands, on similar lines, I mean on prosaic, rational lines, as we should deal with a purely human mystery.'

'My dear fellow,' returned Houston pushing his chair back from the table wearily, 'you shall do just as you like, only get rid of the ghost!'

For some time after Low's arrival nothing very special happened. The tappings continued, and more than once Low had been in time to see the bladder disappear into the closing door of his bedroom, though, unluckily, he never chanced to be inside the room on these occasions, and however quickly he followed the bladder, he never succeeded in seeing anything further. He made a thorough examination of the house, and left no space unaccounted for in his careful measurements. There were no cellars, and the foundation of the house consisted of a thick layer of concrete.

At length, on the sixth night, an event took place, which, as Flaxman Low remarked, came very near to putting an end to the investigations as far as he was concerned. For the preceding two nights he and Houston had kept watch in the hope of getting a glimpse of the person or thing which tapped so persistently up and down the passage. But they were disappointed, for there were no manifestations. On the third evening, therefore, Low went off to his room a little earlier than usual, and fell asleep almost immediately.

He says he was awakened by feeling a heavy weight upon his feet, something that seemed inert and motionless. He recollected that he had left the gas burning, but the room was now in darkness.

Next he was aware that the thing on the bed had slowly shifted, and was gradually travelling up towards his chest. How it came on the bed he had no idea. Had it leaped or climbed? The sensation he experienced as it moved was of some ponderous, pulpy body, not crawling or creeping, but spreading! It was horrible! He tried to move his lower limbs, but could not because of the deadening weight. A feeling of drowsiness began to overpower him, and a deadly cold, such as he said he had before felt at sea when in the neighbourhood of icebergs, chilled upon the air.

With a violent struggle he managed to free his arms, but the thing grew more irresistible as it spread upwards. Then he became conscious of a pair of glassy eyes, with livid, everted lids, looking into his own. Whether they were human eyes or beast eyes, he could not tell, but they were watery, like the eyes of a dead fish, and gleamed with a pale, internal lustre.

Then he owns he grew afraid. But he was still cool enough to notice one peculiarity about this ghastly visitant—although the head was within a few inches of his own, he could detect no breathing. It dawned upon him that he was about to be suffocated, for, by the same method of extension, the thing was now coming over his face! It felt cold and clammy, like a mass of mucilage or a monstrous snail. And every instant the weight became greater. He is a powerful man, and he struck with his fists again and again at the head. Some substance yielded under the blows with a sickening sensation of bruised flesh.

With a lucky twist he raised himself in the bed and battered away with all the force he was capable of in his cramped position. The only effect was an occasional shudder or quake than ran through the mass as his half-arm blows rained upon it. At last, by chance, his hand knocked against the candle beside him. In a moment he recollected the matches. He seized the box, and struck a light.

As he did so, the lump slid to the floor. He sprang out of bed, and lit the candle. He felt a cold touch upon his leg, but when he looked down there was nothing to be seen. The door, which he had locked overnight, was now open, and he rushed out into the passage. All was still and silent with the throbbing vacancy of night time.

After searching round, he returned to his room. The bed still gave ample proof of the struggle that had taken place, and by his watch he saw the hour to be between two and three.

As there seemed nothing more to be done, he put on his dressing-gown, lit his pipe, and sat down to write an account of the experience he had just passed though for the Psychical Research Society—from which paper the above is an abstract.

He is a man of strong nerves, but he could not disguise from himself that he had been at handgrips with some grotesque form of death. What might be the nature of his assailant he could not determine, but his experience was supported by the attack which had been made on Filderg, and also—it was impossible to avoid the conclusion—by the manner of Mrs Van Nuysen's death.

He thought the whole situation over carefully in connection with the tapping and the disappearing bladder, but, turn these events how he would, he could make nothing of them. They were entirely incongruous. A little later he went and made a shakedown in Houston's room.

'What was the thing?' asked Houston, when Low had ended his story of the encounter.

Low shrugged his shoulders.

'At least it proves that Filderg did not dream,' he said.

'But this is monstrous! We are more in the dark than ever. There's nothing for it but to have the house pulled down. Let us leave today.'

'Don't be in a hurry, my dear fellow. You would rob me of a very great pleasure; besides, we may be on the verge of some valuable discovery. This series of manifestations is even more interesting than the Vienna mystery I was telling you of.'

'Discovery or not,' replied the other, 'I don't like it.'

The first thing next morning Low went out for a quarter of an hour. Before breakfast a man with a barrowful of sand came into the garden. Low looked up from his paper, leant out of the window, and gave some order.

When Houston came down a few minutes later he saw the yellowish heap on the lawn with some surprise.

'Hullo! What's this?' he asked.

'I ordered it,' replied Low.

'All right. What's it for?'

'To help us in our investigations. Our visitor is capable of being felt, and he or it left a very distinct impression on the bed. Hence I gather it can also leave an impression on sand. It would be an immense advance if we could arrive at any correct notion of what sort of feet the ghost walks on. I propose to spread a layer of this sand in the upper passage, and the result should be footmarks if the tapping comes tonight.'

That evening the two men made a fire in Houston's bedroom, and sat there smoking and talking, to leave the ghost 'a free run for once', as Houston phrased it. The tapping was heard at the usual hour, and presently the accustomed pause at the other end of the passage and the quiet closing of the door.

Low heaved a long sigh of satisfaction as he listened.

'That's my bedroom door,' he said; 'I know the sound of it perfectly. In the morning, and with the help of daylight, we shall see what we shall see.'

As soon as there was light enough for the purpose of examining the footprints, Low roused Houston.

Houston was as full of excitement as a boy, but his spirits fell by the time he had passed from end to end of the passage.

'There are marks,' he said, 'but they are as perplexing as everything else about this haunting brute, whatever it is. I suppose you think this is the print left by the thing which attacked you the night before last?'

'I fancy it is,' said Low, who was still bending over the floor eagerly. 'What do you make of it, Houston?'

'The brute has only one leg, to start with,' replied Houston, 'and that leaves the mark of a large, clawless pad! It's some animal—some ghoulish monster!'

'On the contrary,' said Low, 'I think we have now every reason to conclude that it is a man.'

'A man? What man ever left footmarks like these?'

'Look at these hollows and streaks at the sides; they are the traces of the sticks we have heard tapping.'

'You don't convince me,' returned Houston doggedly.

'Let us wait another twenty-four hours, and tomorrow night, if nothing further occurs, I will give you my conclusions. Think it over. The tapping, the bladder, and the fact that Mr Van Nuysen had lived in Trinidad. Add to these things this single pad-like print. Does nothing strike you by way of a solution?'

Houston shook his head.

'Nothing. And I fail to connect any of these things with what happened both to you and Filderg.'

'Ah! now,' said Flaxman Low, his face clouding a little, 'I confess you lead me into a somewhat different region, though to me the connection is perfect.'

Houston raised his eyebrows and laughed.

'If you can unravel this tangle of hints and events and diagnose the ghost, I shall be extremely astonished,' he said. 'What can you make of the footless impression?'

'Something, I hope. In fact, that mark may be a clue—an outrageous one, perhaps, but still a clue.'

That evening the weather broke, and by night the storm had risen to a gale, accompanied by sharp bursts of rain.

'It's a noisy night,' remarked Houston; 'I don't suppose we'll hear the ghost, supposing it does turn up.'

This was after dinner, as they were about to go into the smoking-room. Houston, finding the gas low in the hall, stopped to turn it higher, at the same time asking Low to see if the jet on the upper landing was also alight.

Flaxman Low glanced up and uttered a slight exclamation, which brought Houston to his side.

Looking down at them from over the banisters was a face—a blotched, yellowish face, flanked by two swollen, protruding ears, the whole aspect being strangely leonine. It was but a glimpse, a clash of meeting glances, as it were, a glare of defiance, and the face was quickly withdrawn as the two men literally leapt up the stairs.

'There's nothing here,' exclaimed Houston, after a search had been carried out through every room above.

'I didn't suppose we'd find anything,' returned Low.

'This fairly knots up the thread,' said Houston. 'You can't pretend to unravel it now.'

'Come down,' said Low briefly; 'I'm ready to give you my opinion, such as it is.'

Once in the smoking-room, Houston busied himself in turning on all the light he could procure, then he saw to securing the windows, and piled up an immense fire, while Flaxman Low, who, as usual, had a cigarette in his mouth, sat on the edge of the table and watched him with some amusement.

'You saw that abominable face?' cried Houston, as he threw himself into a chair. 'It was as material as yours or mine. But where did he go to? He must be somewhere about.'

'We saw him clearly. That is sufficient for our purpose.'

'You are very good at enumerating points, Low. Now just listen to my list. The difficulties grow with every fresh discovery. We're at a deadlock now, I take it? The sticks and the tapping point to an old man, the playing with a bladder to a child; the footmark might be the pad of a tiger minus claws, yet the thing that attacked you at night was cold and pulpy. And, lastly, by way of a wind-up, we see a lion-like, human face! If you can make all these items square with each other, I'll be happy to hear what you have got to say.'

'You must first allow me to ask you a question. I understood you to say that no blood relationship existed between you and old Mr Van Nuysen?'

'Certainly not. He was quite an outsider,' answered Houston brusquely.

'In that case you are welcome to my conclusions. All the things you have mentioned point to one explanation. This house is haunted by the ghost of Mr Van Nuysen, and he was a leper.'

Houston stood up and stared at his companion.

'What a horrible notion! I must say I fail to see how you have arrived at such a conclusion.'

'Take the chain of evidence in rather different order,' said Low. 'Why should a man tap with a stick?'

'Generally because he's blind.'

'In cases of blindness, one stick is used for guidance. Here we have two for support.'

'A man who has lost the use of his feet.'

'Exactly; a man who has from some cause partially lost the use of his feet.'

'But the bladder and the lion-like face?' went on Houston.

'The bladder, or what seemed to us to resemble a bladder, was one of his feet, contorted by the disease and probably swathed in linen, which foot he dragged rather than used; consequently, in passing through a door, for example, he would be in the habit of drawing it in after him. Now, as regards the single footmark we saw. In one form of leprosy, the smaller bones of the extremities frequently fall away. The pad-like impression was, as I believe, the mark of the other foot—a toeless foot which he used, because in a more advanced stage of the disease the maimed hand or foot heals and becomes callous.'

'Go on,' said Houston; 'it sounds as if it might be true. And the lion-like face I can account for myself. I have been in China, and have seen it before in lepers.'

'Mr Van Nuysen had been in Trinidad for many years, as we know, and while there he probably contracted the disease.'

'I suppose so. After his return,' added Houston, 'he shut himself up almost entirely, and gave out that he was a martyr to rheumatic gout, this awful thing being the true explanation.'

'It also accounts for Mrs Van Nuysen's determination not to return to her husband.'

Houston appeared much disturbed.

'We can't drop it here, Low,' he said, in a constrained voice. 'There is a good deal more to be cleared up yet. Can you tell me more?'

'From this point I find myself on less certain ground,' replied Low unwillingly. 'I merely offer a suggestion, remember—I don't ask you to accept it. I believe Mrs Van Nuysen was murdered!'

'What?' exclaimed Houston. 'By her husband?'

'Indications tend that way.'

'But, my good fellow——'

'He suffocated her and then made away with himself. It is a pity that his body was not recovered. The condition of the remains would be the only really satisfactory test of my theory. If the skeleton could even now be found, the fact that he was a leper would be finally settled.'

There was a prolonged pause until Houston put another question.

'Wait a minute, Low,' he said. 'Ghosts are admittedly immaterial. In this instance our spook has an extremely palpable body. Surely this is rather unusual? You have made everything else more or less plain. Can you tell me why this dead leper should have tried to murder you and old Filderg? And also how he came to have the actual physical power to do so?'

Low removed his cigarette to look thoughtfully at the end of it. 'Now I lapse into the purely theoretical,' he answered. 'Cases have been known where the assumption of diabolical agency is apparently justifiable.'

'Diabolical agency?—I don't follow you.'

'I will try to make myself clear, though the subject is still in a stage of vagueness and immaturity. Van Nuysen committed a murder of exceptional atrocity, and afterwards killed himself. Now, bodies of suicides are known to be peculiarly susceptible to spiritual influences, even to the point of arrested corruption. Add to this our knowledge that the highest aim of an evil spirit is to achieve incarnation. If I carried out my theory to its logical conclusion, I should say that Van Nuysen's body is hidden somewhere on these premises—that this body is intermittently animated by some spirit, which at certain periods is forced to re-enact the gruesome tragedy of the Van Nuysens. Should any living person chance to occupy the position of the first victim, so much the worse for him!'

For some minutes Houston made no remark on this singular expression of opinion.

'But have you ever met with anything of the sort before?' he said at last.

'I can recall,' replied Flaxman Low thoughtfully, 'quite a number of cases which would seem to bear out this hypothesis. Among them a curious problem of haunting exhaustively examined by Busner in the early part of 1888, at which I was myself lucky enough to assist. Indeed, I may add that the affair which I have recently been engaged upon in Vienna offers some rather similar features. There, however, we had to stop short of excavation, by which alone any specific results might have been attained.'

'Then you are of opinion,' said Houston, 'that pulling the house to pieces might cast some further light upon this affair?'

'I cannot see any better course,' said Mr Low.

Then Houston closed the discussion by a very definite declaration. 'This house shall come down!'

So 'The Spaniards' was pulled down.

Such is the story of 'The Spaniards', Hammersmith, and it has been given the first place in this series because, although it may not be of so strange a nature as some that will follow it, yet it seems to us to embody in a high degree the peculiar methods by which Mr Flaxman Low is wont to approach these cases.

The work of demolition, begun at the earliest possible moment, did not occupy very long, and during its early stages, under the boarding at an angle of the landing was found a skeleton. Several of the phalanges were missing, and other indications also established beyond a doubt the fact that the remains were the remains of a leper.

The skeleton is now in the museum of one of our city hospitals. It bears a scientific ticket, and is the only evidence extant of the correctness of Mr Flaxman Low's methods and the possible truth of his extraordinary theories.

The Lost Special

SIR ARTHUR CONAN DOYLE

The confession of Herbert de Lernac, now lying under sentence of death at Marseilles, has thrown a light upon one of the most inexplicable crimes of the century—an incident which is, I believe, absolutely unprecedented in the criminal annals of any country. Although there is a reluctance to discuss the matter in official circles, and little information has been given to the Press, there are still indications that the statement of this arch-criminal is corroborated by the facts, and that we have at last found a solution for a most astounding business. As the matter is eight years old, and as its importance was somewhat obscured by a political crisis which was engaging the public attention at the time, it may be as well to state the facts as far as we have been able to ascertain them. They are collated from the Liverpool papers of that date, from the proceedings at the inquest upon John Slater, the engine-driver, and from the records of the London and West Coast Railway Company, which have been courteously put at my disposal. Briefly, they are as follows.

On the 3rd of June, 1890, a gentleman, who gave his name as Monsieur Louis Caratal, desired an interview with Mr James Bland, the superintendent of the Central London and West Coast Station in Liverpool. He was a small man, middle-aged and dark, with a stoop which was so marked that it suggested some deformity of the spine. He was accompanied by a friend, a man of imposing physique, whose deferential manner and constant attention suggested that his position was one of dependence. This friend or companion, whose name did not transpire, was certainly a foreigner, and probably, from his swarthy complexion, either a Spaniard or a South American. One peculiarity was observed in him. He carried in his left hand a small black leather dispatch-box, and it was noticed by a sharp-eyed clerk in the Central office that this box was fastened to his wrist by a strap. No importance was attached to the fact at the time, but subsequent events endowed it with some significance. Monsieur Caratal was shown up to Mr Bland's office, while his companion remained outside.

Monsieur Caratal's business was quickly dispatched. He had arrived that afternoon from Central America. Affairs of the utmost importance demanded that he should be in Paris without the loss of an unnecessary hour. He had missed the London express. A special must be provided. Money was of no importance. Time was everything. If the company would speed him on his way, they might make their own terms.

Mr Bland struck the electric bell, summoned Mr Potter Hood, the traffic manager, and had the matter arranged in five minutes. The train would start in three-quarters of an hour. It would take that time to ensure that the line should be clear. The powerful engine called 'Rochdale' (No. 247 on the company's register) was attached to two carriages, with a guard's van behind. The first carriage was solely for the purpose of decreasing the inconvenience arising from the oscillation. The second was divided, as usual, into four compartments, a first-class, a first-class smoking, a second-class, and a second-class smoking. The first compartment, which was the nearest to the engine, was the one allotted to the travellers. The other three were empty. The guard of the special train was James McPherson, who had been some years in the service of the company. The stoker, William Smith, was a new hand.

Monsieur Caratal, upon leaving the superintendent's office, rejoined his companion, and both of them manifested extreme impatience to be off. Having paid the money asked, which amounted to fifty pounds five shillings, at the usual special rate of five shillings a mile, they demanded to be shown the carriage, and at once took their seats in it, although they were assured that the better part of an hour must elapse before the line could be cleared. In the meantime a singular coincidence had occurred in the office which Monsieur Caratal had just quitted.

A request for a special is not a very uncommon circumstance in a rich commercial centre, but that two should be required upon the same afternoon was most unusual. It so happened, however, that Mr Bland had hardly dismissed the first traveller before a second entered with a similar request. This was a Mr Horace Moore, a gentlemanly man of military appearance, who alleged that the sudden serious illness of his wife in London made it absolutely imperative that he

should not lose an instant in starting upon the journey. His distress
and anxiety were so evident that Mr Bland did all that was possible to
meet his wishes. A second special was out of the question, as the
ordinary local service was already somewhat deranged by the first.
There was the alternative, however, that Mr Moore should share the
expense of Monsieur Caratal's train, and should travel in the other
empty first-class compartment, if Monsieur Caratal objected to having him in the one which he occupied. It was difficult to see any
objection to such an arrangement, and yet Monsieur Caratal, upon
the suggestion being made to him by Mr Potter Hood, absolutely
refused to consider it for an instant. The train was his, he said, and
he would insist upon the exclusive use of it. All argument failed to
overcome his ungracious objections, and finally the plan had to be
abandoned. Mr Horace Moore left the station in great distress, after
learning that his only course was to take the ordinary slow train which
leaves Liverpool at six o'clock. At four thirty-one exactly by the
station clock the special train, containing the crippled Monsieur
Caratal and his gigantic companion, steamed out of the Liverpool
station. The line was at that time clear, and there should have been
no stoppage before Manchester.

The trains of the London and West Coast Railway run over the
lines of another company as far as this town, which should have been
reached by the special rather before six o'clock. At a quarter after six
considerable surprise and some consternation were caused amongst
the officials at Liverpool by the receipt of a telegram from Manchester
to say that it had not yet arrived. An enquiry directed to St Helens,
which is a third of the way between the two cities, elicited the
following reply:

To James Bland, Superintendent, Central L & W C, Liverpool.—Special
passed here at 4.52, well up to time.—Dowser, St Helens.

This telegram was received at 6.40. At 6.50 a second message was
received from Manchester:

No sign of special as advised by you.

And then ten minutes later a third, more bewildering:

Presume some mistake as to proposed running of special. Local train from St
Helens timed to follow it has just arrived and has seen nothing of it. Kindly
wire advices.—Manchester.

The matter was assuming a most amazing aspect, although in some respects the last telegram was a relief to the authorities at Liverpool. If an accident had occurred to the special, it seemed hardly possible that the local train could have passed down the same line without observing it. And yet, what was the alternative? Where could the train be? Had it possibly been side-tracked for some reason in order to allow the slower train to go past? Such an explanation was possible if some small repair had to be effected. A telegram was dispatched to each of the stations between St Helens and Manchester, and the superintendent and traffic manager waited in the utmost suspense at the instrument for the series of replies which would enable them to say for certain what had become of the missing train. The answers came back in the order of questions, which was the order of the stations beginning at the St Helens end:

Special passed here five o'clock.—Collins Green.

Special passed here six past five.—Earlestown.

Special passed here 5.10.—Newton.

Special passed here 5.20.—Kenyon Junction.

No special train has passed here.—Barton Moss.

The two officials stared at each other in amazement.

'This is unique in my thirty years of experience,' said Mr Bland.

'Absolutely unprecedented and inexplicable, sir. The special has gone wrong between Kenyon Junction and Barton Moss.'

'And yet there is no siding, as far as my memory serves me, between the two stations. The special must have run off the metals.'

'But how could the four-fifty parliamentary pass over the same line without observing it?'

'There's no alternative, Mr Hood. It *must* be so. Possibly the local train may have observed something which may throw some light upon the matter. We will wire to Manchester for more information, and to Kenyon Junction with instructions that the line be examined instantly as far as Barton Moss.'

The answer from Manchester came within a few minutes.

No news of missing special. Driver and guard of slow train positive that no accident between Kenyon Junction and Barton Moss. Line quite clear, and no sign of anything unusual.—Manchester.

'That driver and guard will have to go,' said Mr Bland, grimly. 'There has been a wreck and they have missed it. The special has obviously run off the metals without disturbing the line—how it could have done so passes my comprehension—but so it must be, and we shall have a wire from Kenyon or Barton Moss presently to say that they have found her at the bottom of an embankment.'

But Mr Bland's prophecy was not destined to be fulfilled. A half-hour passed, and then there arrived the following message from the station-master of Kenyon Junction:

There are no traces of the missing special. It is quite certain that she passed here, and that she did not arrive at Barton Moss. We have detached engine from goods train, and I have myself ridden down the line, but all is clear, and there is no sign of any accident.

Mr Bland tore his hair in his perplexity.

'This is rank lunacy, Hood!' he cried. 'Does a train vanish into thin air in England in broad daylight? The thing is preposterous. An engine, a tender, two carriages, a van, five human beings—and all lost on a straight line of railway! Unless we get something positive within the next hour I'll take Inspector Collins, and go down myself.'

And then at last something positive did occur. It took the shape of another telegram from Kenyon Junction.

Regret to report that the dead body of John Slater, driver of the special train, has just been found among the gorse bushes at a point two and a quarter miles from the Junction. Had fallen from his engine, pitched down the embankment, and rolled among bushes. Injuries to his head, from the fall, appear to be cause of death. Ground has now been carefully examined, and there is no trace of the missing train.

The country was, as has already been stated, in the throes of a political crisis, and the attention of the public was further distracted by the important and sensational developments in Paris, where a huge scandal threatened to destroy the Government and to wreck the reputations of many of the leading men in France. The papers were full of these events, and the singular disappearance of the special train attracted less attention than would have been the case in more peaceful times. The grotesque nature of the event helped to detract from its importance, for the papers were disinclined to believe the facts as reported to them. More than one of the London journals treated the matter as an ingenious hoax, until the coroner's inquest upon the unfortunate driver (an inquest which elicited nothing of importance) convinced them of the tragedy of the incident.

Mr Bland, accompanied by Inspector Collins, the senior detective officer in the service of the company, went down to Kenyon Junction the same evening, and their research lasted throughout the following day, but was attended with purely negative results. Not only was no trace found of the missing train, but no conjecture could be put forward which could possibly explain the facts. At the same time, Inspector Collins's official report (which lies before me as I write) served to show that the possibilities were more numerous than might have been expected.

'In the stretch of railway between these two points,' said he, 'the country is dotted with ironworks and collieries. Of these, some are being worked and some have been abandoned. There are no fewer than twelve which have small gauge lines which run trolley-cars down to the main line. These can, of course, be disregarded. Besides these, however, there are seven which have or have had proper lines running down and connecting with points to the main line, so as to convey their produce from the mouth of the mine to the great centres of distribution. In every case these lines are only a few miles in length. Out of the seven, four belong to collieries which are worked out, or at least to shafts which are no longer used. These are the Redgauntlet, Hero, Slough of Despond, and Heartsease mines, the latter having ten years ago been one of the principal mines in Lancashire. These four side lines may be eliminated from our inquiry, for, to prevent possible accidents, the rails nearest to the main line have been taken up, and there is no longer any connection. There remain three other side lines leading

(a) to the Carnstock Iron Works;
(b) to the Big Ben Colliery;
(c) to the Perseverance Colliery.

Of these the Big Ben line is not more than a quarter of a mile long, and ends at a dead wall of of coal waiting removal from the mouth of the mine. Nothing had been seen or heard there of any special. The Carnstock Iron Works line was blocked all day upon the 3rd of June by sixteen truck loads of hematite. It is a single line, and nothing could have passed. As to the Perseverance line, it is a large double line, which does a considerable traffic, for the output of the mine is very large. On the 3rd of June this traffic proceeded as usual; hundreds of men, including a gang of railway platelayers, were working along the two miles and a quarter which constitute the total length of the line, and it is inconceivable that an unexpected train could have come down there without attracting universal attention. It may be remarked in conclusion that this branch line is nearer to St Helens than the point at which the engine-driver was discovered, so that we have every reason to believe that the train was past that point before misfortune overtook her.

'As to John Slater, there is no clue to be gathered from his appearance or injuries. We can only say that, as far as we can see, he met his end by falling off his engine, though why he fell, or what became of the engine after his fall, is a question upon which I do not feel qualified to offer an opinion.' In conclusion, the inspector offered his resignation to the Board, being much nettled by an accusation of incompetence in the London papers.

A month elapsed, during which both the police and the company prosecuted their enquiries without the slightest success. A reward was offered and a pardon promised in case of crime, but they were both unclaimed. Every day the public opened their papers with the conviction that so grotesque a mystery would at last be solved, but week after week passed by, and a solution remained as far off as ever. In broad daylight, upon a June afternoon in the most thickly inhabited portion of England, a train with its occupants had disappeared as completely as if some master of subtle chemistry had volatilized it into gas. Indeed, among the various conjectures which were put forward in the public Press there were some which seriously asserted that supernatural, or, at least, preternatural, agencies had been at work, and that the deformed Monsieur Caratal was probably a person who was better known under a less polite name. Others fixed upon his swarthy companion as being the author of the mischief, but what it was exactly which he had done could never be clearly formulated in words.

Amongst the many suggestions put forward by various newspapers or private individuals, there were one or two which were feasible enough to attract the attention of the public. One which appeared in *The Times*, over the signature of an amateur reasoner of some celebrity at that date, attempted to deal with the matter in a critical and semi-scientific manner. An extract must suffice, although the curious can see the whole letter in the issue of the 3rd of July.

It is one of the elementary principles of practical reasoning [he remarked] that when the impossible has been eliminated the residuum, *however improbable*, must contain the truth. It is certain that the train left Kenyon Junction. It is certain that it did not reach Barton Moss. It is in the highest degree unlikely, but still possible, that it may have taken one of the seven available side lines. It is obviously impossible for a train to run where there are no rails, and, therefore, we may reduce our improbables to the three open lines, namely, the Carnstock Iron Works, the Big Ben, and the Perseverance. Is there a secret society of colliers, an English *camorra*, which is capable of destroying both train and passengers? It is improbable, but it is not impossible. I confess that I am unable to suggest any other solution. I should certainly advise the company to direct all their energies towards the observation of those three lines, and of the workmen at the end of them. A careful supervision of the pawnbrokers' shops of the district might possibly bring some suggestive facts to light.

The suggestion coming from a recognized authority upon such matters created considerable interest, and a fierce opposition from those who considered such a statement to be a preposterous libel upon an honest and deserving set of men. The only answer to this criticism was a challenge to the objectors to lay any more feasible explanation before the public. In reply to this two others were forthcoming (*Times*, July 7th and 9th). The first suggested that the train might have run off the metals and be lying submerged in the Lancashire and Staffordshire Canal, which runs parallel to the railway for some hundreds of yards. This suggestion was thrown out of court by the published depth of the canal, which was entirely insufficient to conceal so large an object. The second correspondent wrote calling attention to the bag which appeared to be the sole luggage which the travellers had brought with them, and suggesting that some novel explosive of immense and pulverizing power might have been concealed in it. The obvious absurdity, however, of supposing that the whole train might be blown to dust while the metals remained uninjured reduced any such explanation to a farce. The investigation had drifted into this hopeless position when a new and most unexpected incident occurred, which raised hopes never destined to be fulfilled.

This was nothing less than the receipt by Mrs McPherson of a letter from her husband, James McPherson, who had been the guard of the missing train. The letter, which was dated July 5th, 1890, was dispatched from New York, and came to hand upon July 14th. Some doubts were expressed as to its genuine character, but Mrs McPherson was positive as to the writing, and the fact that it contained a remittance of a hundred dollars in five-dollar notes was enough in itself to discount the idea of a hoax. No address was given in the letter, which ran in this way:

MY DEAR WIFE, I have been thinking a great deal, and I find it very hard to give you up. The same with Lizzie. I try to fight against it, but it will always come back to me. I send you some money which will change into twenty English pounds. This should be enough to bring both Lizzie and you across the Atlantic, and you will find the Hamburg boats which stop at Southampton very good boats, and cheaper than Liverpool. If you could come here and stop at the Johnston House I would try and send you word how to meet, but things are very difficult with me at present, and I am not very happy, finding it hard to give you both up. So no more at present, from your loving husband,

JAMES McPHERSON

For a time it was confidently anticipated that this letter would lead to the clearing up of the whole matter, the more so as it was ascertained that a passenger who bore a close resemblance to the missing guard had travelled from Southampton under the name of Summers in the Hamburg and New York liner *Vistula*, which started upon the 7th of June. Mrs McPherson and her sister Lizzie Dolton went across to New York as directed, and stayed for three weeks at the Johnston House, without hearing anything from the missing man. It is probable that some injudicious comments in the Press may have warned him that the police were using them as a bait. However this may be, it is certain that he neither wrote nor came, and the women were eventually compelled to return to Liverpool.

And so the matter stood, and has continued to stand up to the present year of 1898. Incredible as it may seem, nothing has transpired during these eight years which has shed the least light upon the extraordinary disappearance of the special train which contained Monsieur Caratal and his companion. Careful enquiries into the antecedents of the two travellers have only established the fact that Monsieur Caratal was well known as a financier and political agent in Central America, and that during his voyage to Europe he had betrayed extraordinary anxiety to reach Paris. His companion, whose name was entered upon the passenger lists as Eduardo Gomez, was a man whose record was a violent one, and whose reputation was that of a bravo and a bully. There was evidence to show, however, that he was honestly devoted to the interests of Monsieur Caratal, and that the latter, being a man of puny physique, employed the other as a guard and protector. It may be added that no information came from Paris as to what the objects of Monsieur Caratal's hurried journey may have been. This comprises all the facts of the case up to the publication in the Marseilles papers of the recent confession of Herbert de Lernac, now under sentence of death for the murder of a merchant named Bonvalot. This statement may be literally translated as follows:

It is not out of mere pride or boasting that I give this information, for, if that were my object, I could tell a dozen actions of mine which are quite as splendid; but I do it in order that certain gentlemen in Paris may understand that I, who am able here to tell about the fate of Monsieur Caratal, can also tell in whose interest and at whose request the deed was done, unless the reprieve which I am awaiting comes to me very quickly. Take warning, messieurs, before it is too late! You know Herbert de Lernac, and you are aware that his deeds are as ready as his words. Hasten then, or you are lost!

At present I shall mention no names—if you only heard the names, what would you not think!—but I shall merely tell you how cleverly I did it. I was true to my employers then, and no doubt they will be true to me now. I hope so, and until I am convinced that they have betrayed me, these names, which would convulse Europe, shall not be divulged. But on that day . . . well, I say no more!

In a word, then, there was a famous trial in Paris, in the year 1890, in connection with a monstrous scandal in politics and finance. How monstrous that scandal was can never be known save by such confidential agents as myself. The honour and careers of many of the chief men in France were at stake. You have seen a group of ninepins standing, all so rigid, and prim, and unbending. Then there comes the ball from far away and pop, pop, pop— there are your ninepins on the floor. Well, imagine some of the greatest men in France as these ninepins, and then this Monsieur Caratal was the ball which could be seen coming from far away. If he arrived, then it was pop, pop, pop for all of them. It was determined that he should not arrive.

I do not accuse them all of being conscious of what was to happen. There were, as I have said, great financial as well as political interests at stake, and a syndicate was formed to manage the business. Some subscribed to the syndicate who hardly understood what were its objects. But others understood very well, and they can rely upon it that I have not forgotten their names. They had ample warning that Monsieur Caratal was coming long before he left South America, and they knew that the evidence which he held would certainly mean ruin to all of them. The syndicate had the command of an unlimited amount of money—absolutely unlimited, you understand. They looked round for an agent who was capable of wielding this gigantic power. The man chosen must be inventive, resolute, adaptive—a man in a million. They chose Herbert de Lernac, and I admit that they were right.

My duties were to choose my subordinates, to use freely the power which money gives, and to make certain that Monsieur Caratal should never arrive in Paris. With characteristic energy I set about my commission within an hour of receiving my instructions, and the steps which I took were the very best for the purpose which could possibly be devised.

A man whom I could trust was dispatched instantly to South America to travel home with Monsieur Caratal. Had he arrived in time the ship would never have reached Liverpool; but, alas, it had already started before my agent could reach it. I fitted out a small armed brig to intercept it, but again I was unfortunate. Like all great organizers I was, however, prepared for failure, and had a series of alternatives prepared, one or the other of which must succeed. You must not underrate the difficulties of my undertaking, or imagine that a mere commonplace assassination would meet the case. We must destroy not only Monsieur Caratal, but Monsieur Caratal's documents, and Monsieur Caratal's companions also, if we had reason to believe that he had communicated his secrets to them. And you must remember that they were on the alert, and keenly suspicious of any such attempt. It was a task which was in every way worthy of me, for I am always most masterful where another would be appalled.

I was all ready for Monsieur Caratal's reception in Liverpool, and I was the more eager because I had reason to believe that he had made arrangements by which he would have a considerable guard from the moment that he arrived in London. Anything which was to be done must be done between the moment of his setting foot upon the Liverpool quay and that of his arrival at the London and West Coast terminus in London. We prepared six plans, each more elaborate than the last; which plan would be used would depend upon his own movements. Do what he would, we were ready for him. If he had stayed in Liverpool, we were ready. If he took an ordinary train, an express, or a special, all was ready. Everything had been foreseen and provided for.

You may imagine that I could not do all this myself. What could I know of the English railway lines? But money can procure willing agents all the world over, and I soon had one of the acutest brains in England to assist me. I will mention no names, but it would be unjust to claim all the credit for myself. My English ally was worthy of such an alliance. He knew the London and

West Coast line thoroughly, and he had the command of a band of workers who were trustworthy and intelligent. The idea was his, and my own judgement was only required in the details. We brought over several officials, amongst whom the most important was James McPherson, whom we had ascertained to be the guard most likely to be employed upon a special train. Smith, the stoker, was also in our employ. John Slater, the engine-driver, had been approached, but had been found to be obstinate and dangerous, so we desisted. We had no certainty that Monsieur Caratal would take a special, but we thought it very probable, for it was of the utmost importance to him that he should reach Paris without delay. It was for this contingency, therefore, that we made special preparations—preparations which were complete down to the last detail long before his steamer had sighted the shores of England. You will be amused to learn that there was one of my agents in the pilot-boat which brought that steamer to its moorings.

The moment that Caratal arrived in Liverpool we knew that he suspected danger and was on his guard. He had brought with him as an escort a dangerous fellow, named Gomez, a man who carried weapons, and was prepared to use them. This fellow carried Caratal's confidential papers for him, and was ready to protect either them or his master. The probability was that Caratal had taken him into his counsels, and that to remove Caratal without removing Gomez would be a mere waste of energy. It was necessary that they should be involved in a common fate, and our plans to that end were much facilitated by their request for a special train. On that special train you will understand that two out of the three servants of the company were really in our employ, at a price which would make them independent for a lifetime. I do not go so far as to say that the English are more honest than any other nation, but I have found them more expensive to buy.

I have already spoken of my English agent—who is a man with a considerable future before him, unless some complaint of the throat carries him off before his time. He had charge of all arrangements at Liverpool, whilst I was stationed at the inn at Kenyon, where I awaited a cipher signal to act. When the special was arranged for, my agent instantly telegraphed to me and warned me how soon I should have everything ready. He himself under the name of Horace Moore applied immediately for a special also, in the hope that he would be sent down with Monsieur Caratal, which might under certain circumstances have been helpful to us. If, for example, our great *coup* had failed, it would then have become the duty of my agent to have shot them both and destroyed their papers. Caratal was on his guard, however, and refused to admit any other traveller. My agent then left the station, returned by another entrance, entered the guard's van on the side farthest from the platform, and travelled down with McPherson, the guard.

In the meantime you will be interested to know what my own movements were. Everything had been prepared for days before, and only the finishing touches were needed. The side line which we had chosen had once joined the main line, but it had been disconnected. We had only to replace a few rails to connect it once more. These rails had been laid down as far as could be done without danger of attracting attention, and now it was merely a case of completing a juncture with the line, and arranging the points as they had been before. The sleepers had never been removed, and the rails, fish-plates, and rivets were all ready, for we had taken them from a siding on the abandoned portion of the line. With my small but competent band of workers, we had everything ready long before the special arrived. When it did arrive, it ran off upon the small side line so easily that the jolting of the points appears to have been entirely unnoticed by the two travellers.

Our plan had been that Smith the stoker should chloroform John Slater the driver, and so that he should vanish with the others. In this respect, and in this respect only, our plans miscarried—I except the criminal folly of McPherson in writing home to his wife. Our stoker did his business so clumsily that Slater in his struggles fell off the engine, and though fortune was with us so far that he broke his neck in the fall, still he remained as a blot upon that which would otherwise have been one of those complete masterpieces which are only to be contemplated in silent admiration. The criminal expert will find in John Slater the one flaw in all our admirable combinations. A man who has had as many triumphs as I can afford to be frank, and I therefore lay my finger upon John Slater, and I proclaim him to be a flaw.

But now I have got our special train upon the small line two kilometres, or rather more than one mile in length, which leads, or rather used to lead, to the abandoned Heartsease mine, once one of the largest coal mines in England. You will ask how it is that no one saw the train upon this unused line. I answer that along its entire length it runs through a deep cutting, and that, unless someone had been on the edge of that cutting, he could not have seen it. There *was* someone on the edge of that cutting. I was there. And now I will tell you what I saw.

My assistant had remained at the points in order that he might superintend the switching off of the train. He had four armed men with him, so that if the train ran off the line—we thought it probable, because the points were very rusty—we might still have resources to fall back upon. Having once seen it safely on the side line, he handed over the responsibility to me. I was waiting at a point which overlooks the mouth of the mine, and I was also armed, as were my two companions. Come what might, you see, I was always ready.

The moment that the train was fairly on the side line, Smith, the stoker, slowed-down the engine, and then, having turned it on to the fullest speed again, he and McPherson, with my English lieutenant, sprang off before it was too late. It may be that it was this slowing-down which first attracted the attention of the travellers, but the train was running at full speed again before their heads appeared at the open window. It makes me smile to think how bewildered they must have been. Picture to yourself your own feelings if, on looking out of your luxurious carriage, you suddenly perceived that the lines upon which you ran were rusted and corroded, red and yellow with disuse and decay! What a catch must have come in their breath as in a second it flashed upon them that it was not Manchester but Death which was waiting for them at the end of that sinister line. But the train was running with frantic speed, rolling and rocking over the rotten line, while the wheels made a frightful screaming sound upon the rusted surface. I was close to them, and could see their faces. Caratal was praying, I think—there was something like a rosary dangling out of his hand. The other roared like a bull who smells the blood of the slaughterhouse. He saw us standing on the bank, and he beckoned to us like a madman. Then he tore at his wrist and threw his dispatch-box out of the window in our direction. Of course, his meaning was obvious. Here was the evidence, and they would promise to be silent if their lives were spared. It would have been very agreeable if we could have done so, but business is business. Besides, the train was now as much beyond our control as theirs.

He ceased howling when the train rattled round the curve and they saw the black mouth of the mine yawning before them. We had removed the boards which had covered it, and we had cleared the square entrance. The rails had formerly run very close to the shaft for the convenience of loading the coal, and we had only to add two or three lengths of rail in order to lead to the very brink of the shaft. In fact, as the lengths would not quite fit, our line projected about three feet over the edge. We saw the two heads at the window: Caratal below, Gomez above; but they had both been struck silent by what they saw. And yet they could not withdraw their heads. The sight seemed to have paralysed them.

I had wondered how the train running at a great speed would take the pit into which I had guided it, and I was much interested in watching it. One of my colleagues thought that it would actually jump it, and indeed it was not very far from doing so. Fortunately, however, it fell short, and the buffers of the engine struck the other lip of the shaft with a tremendous crash. The funnel flew off into the air. The tender, carriages, and van were all mashed into one jumble, which, with the remains of the engine, choked for a minute or so the mouth of the pit. Then something gave way in the middle, and the whole mass of green iron, smoking coals, brass fittings, wheels, woodwork, and cushions all crumbled together and crashed down into the mine. We heard the rattle, rattle, rattle, as the debris struck against the walls, and then quite a long time afterwards there came a deep roar as the remains of the train struck the bottom. The boiler may have burst, for a sharp crash came after the roar, and then a dense cloud of steam and smoke swirled up out of the black depths, falling in a spray as thick as rain all round us. Then the vapour shredded off into thin wisps, which floated away in the summer sunshine, and all was quiet again in the Heartsease mine.

And now, having carried out our plans so successfully, it only remained to leave no trace behind us. Our little band of workers at the other end had already ripped up the rails and disconnected the side line, replacing everything as it had been before. We were equally busy at the mine. The funnel and other fragments were thrown in, the shaft was planked over as it used to be, and the lines which led to it were torn up and taken away. Then, without flurry, but without delay, we all made our way out of the country, most of us to Paris, my English colleague to Manchester, and McPherson to Southampton, whence he emigrated to America. Let the English papers of that date tell how thoroughly we had done our work, and how completely we had thrown the cleverest of their detectives off our track.

You will remember that Gomez threw his bag of papers out of the window, and I need not say that I secured that bag and brought them to my employers. It may interest my employers now, however, to learn that out of that bag I took one or two little papers as a souvenir of the occasion. I have no wish to publish these papers; but, still, it is every man for himself in this world, and what else can I do if my friends will not come to my aid when I want them? Messieurs, you may believe that Herbert de Lernac is quite as formidable when he is against you as when he is with you, and that he is not a man to go to the guillotine until he has seen that every one of you is *en route* for New Caledonia. For your own sake, if not for mine, make haste, Monsieur de——, and General——, and Baron ——(you can fill up the blanks for yourselves as you read this). I promise you that in the next edition there will be no blanks to fill.

P.S. As I look over my statement there is only one omission which I can see. It concerns the unfortunate man McPherson, who was foolish enough to write to his wife and to make an appointment with her in New York. It can be imagined that when interests like ours were at stake, we could not leave them to the chance of whether a man in that class of life would or would not give away his secrets to a woman. Having once broken his oath by writing to his wife, we could not trust him any more. We took steps therefore to ensure that he should not see his wife. I have sometimes thought that it would be a kindness to write to her and to assure her that there is no impediment to her marrying again.

The Banknote Forger

C. J. CUTCLIFFE HYNE

We were running down to Aintree for Grand National day, and were taking it easy in a saloon.

O'Malley is a great man for making train journeys comfortable. We kept two rubbers of whist going for a couple of hours, and then, wearying of cards, lounged on the seats of the carriage and talked. Naturally we got on matters of sport, and discussed the varying size of Valentine's Brook, and the way Emperor had broken his neck on an in-and-out of fencing when dropped from the race, and kindred matters of parochial interest. And then we fell to chatting over heroes and idiots of the past, and with a reminiscent laugh Cope's name was chucked upon the carpet.

'There is no doubt,' said Grayson, the QC, 'that Master Willie Cope had been a young fool in the way of frittering away his money. He had been run with a very loose rein all his infancy, and at the age of twenty-two came into a property which yielded him at least nineteen thousand a year in hard cash. He started fair: he cleared away a prosperous crop of post-obits; and then he, so to speak, stripped off his coat and saw how much money a man could spend if he set his mind to it.

'His methods were large-minded and various. He took over a big racing stable, and ran at least one horse for every notable event on the turf. He had villas at Nice, Homburg, and Aix-les-Bains. He went in hot for yacht-racing, and on the strength of pulling off a few events for 10-raters, had a fling at the America Cup. He didn't bring that away with him, as you may recollect; but the attempt cost him something like fifty-four thousand. And, of course, in addition to these trifling expenses, he had to keep up the shooting lodge in Argyleshire, which was tacked on to the deer forest, and a big house near Hyde Park, as well as Castle Cope in Fermanagh, and Bordell Priory in Yorkshire.

'In fact, during the first four years of his reign, he purchased supreme popularity at the mild charge of nine-and-a-half times his income.

'The scandal papers very naturally got a nickname for him. They dubbed him "The Flutterer". He really had a jumpy, nervous manner about him; and so, as the sobriquet seemed happy, it stuck.

'He had got an agent fellow, by name Presse, to dry-nurse him; and I have reason to know that Presse was continually crying aloud against outrunning the constable. But Cope's domestic motto was, "Whilst we live, don't let's have any doubt about it"; and as he thoroughly enjoyed the pace, he didn't feel in the least inclined to clap the brake on. So he got tighter and tighter nipped every rent day.

'Now, when a poor man commences ruining himself on a small scale, nobody out of his own parish pays any particular heed. But when a millionaire starts going a mucker, then proceedings get interesting to the mob at large. In Cope's case the aforesaid scandal papers made four long interesting paragraphs out of him every week. All the British Islanders watched with prim curiosity the pace at which he was going it. That's an amiable way they have. It makes them feel they aren't so bad as they might be; which is a pleasing sensation to anyone.

'It was when, in his own particular line, Cope had created himself the biggest celebrity in the country, that his earthquake arrived. He was accused of systematically uttering forged Bank of England thousand-pound notes. It seemed that he had negotiated at least fifty-four of them, and there might be others which had not yet come in.

'Now, as this is a crime which, in the British decalogue, comes very little short of brutal murder, Cope stood a very good chance of remaining in gaol from the first moment of his arrest; because, at the magistrate's inquiry, the case was proved against him up to the hilt. However, after they committed him for trial, great pressure was brought to bear, and he was released on bail that was simply enormous.

'Barnes was given the case, and he retained me for the defence; a pretty sick sort of defence it was. The principal argument I was bidden to use was, that Master Willie Cope felt quite convinced of his own innocence. It was his habit to make all his bets in thousand-pound notes. This avoided arithmetical calculations, which he was not good at, and also brought him fame. It is very easy to purchase notoriety of that brand in Great Britain—if only your purse is long enough to pay the price.

'The prosecution, on the other hand, could prove beyond argument that the last fifty of these trifling pieces of paper which Cope had drawn from various banks had been carefully and cunningly duplicated; that Cope, with his own fingers, had paid away the reproductions; and that the originals, after being saved up till their number amounted to some fifty odd, had been simultaneously cashed in Constantinople, Moscow, Berlin, Genoa, Monte Carlo, Marseilles, Lyons, and Paris. This pointed to an extensive organization, but none of the confederates could be traced. Bank of England notes are good all the world over; and these which were passed on the Continent were genuine.

'The counterfeits, too, were, paper and all, so artfully made that they passed unchallenged through all the country banks, and for awhile even at the Bank of banks in the City; and it was not until the other pieces of crisp watermarked paper, bearing the signature of Mr May, and the promise to pay bearer £1,000, began to dribble in from Europe, that the trouble commenced. Then it was observed that $\frac{E}{65}$ 16626 had been negotiated before, as had also $\frac{R}{16}$ 23360, and likewise $\frac{P}{84}$ 86162. The documents bore the blue impress of rubber stamps, and the scratchings of pens, which in part traced their circular tours; and the authorities easily collected other records of the hands passed through, because the majestic movements of thousand-pound notes are spied on with far more interest than the rambles of the commoner and more garden fiver.

'When they found that the last comers were undoubtedly orthodox, and the previous series superb forgeries, then there was one of the solidest rows inside that building ever known since Threadneedle Street was paved. The men at the top thundered at the carelessness of those immediately beneath them; the men at the bottom looked preternaturally grave, and hoped for their step; and the wretched tellers who passed the first batch of notes had to bear the brunt of all these bombardments. Most of the notes had been burnt; but enough were left to show—with the more glaring light of after-knowledge—that they were most accurate forgeries.

'Now, savaging your own underlings may, as sheer dissipation and amusement, be very pleasant in its way; but it isn't solid satisfactory vengeance, and it has no connection with the *lex talionis*, both of which are far more businesslike and to the point. So after the preliminary scratching and swearing match, the directors looked round them and demanded blood. Obviously the supply would have to come from Master Willie Cope; and, as no one else appeared to share the brunt, from him alone. He was a very fit and proper person to be made into an awful example, and so they set the mill of the law in motion, and it looked as though he would be mangled up very small indeed before he was done with. The *Morning Post* mentioned this in a most stately leader.

'Now, those are the outlines of the case, and Barnes quite agreed with me that matters for the defence looked very sick indeed. The prosecution would show that Cope was excessively hard up, that he had been losing very heavily on the turf, that he had drawn good thousand-pound notes from various banks, and then with his own fingers passed bogus notes on to the bookies. All this was absolutely true: we admitted it.

'"Look here," said I to Barnes, "we must find how and by whom these spurious notes were manufactured."

'"Precisely," said Barnes, "that's obvious. The only trifle waiting to be discovered is the method of doing this. I confess that beats me, and what's more, it's too big an order for Cope. His inventive faculties are stimulated just now; he's got as good and solid a scare in him as a man can well carry amongst his ribs without tumbling down; but even that hasn't screwed him to the necessary pitch. He no more knows how those notes got into his pocket than Elk, your clerk, does.

'"You see, the young fool was, in a way, most awfully slipshod about his money matters, though there was method in his madness. A thousand-pound Bank of England note isn't a thing an ordinary pickpocket can get rid of like a tenner. In consequence of this, Cope used to leave his money lying about anywhere, confident that it would not be stolen; and forty people might have had complete access to it. He says Presse was constantly blowing him up for his carelessness, and that he was always chaffing Presse for being a nervous old woman. Presse took a big interest in the fellow, there's no doubt about that."

'"Then, do you hint that this officious agent fellow forged the notes?"

'"I hint nothing, Grayson; but I suspect everybody. I might remark, though, that Presse messes about with a hand camera, and photography certainly had something to do with the production of these forged notes."

'"Why on earth didn't you tell me this before?"

'"Because I can add nothing to it. Between making bad amateur photographs with a half-plate camera and turning out perfect thousand-pound notes, there are many lengthy gaps which I can't fill in anyhow. I'm not exactly a fool, Grayson. You can bet your boots I've tried to father the job on Presse."

'"Yet it strikes me it's *aut Presse aut nullus*. Look here; from what you tell me, nearly all these forged notes were passed at Doncaster during the Leger week. Cope was then staying at Bordell Priory. Do you mind my sending Elk down there to see if he can hunt out anything?"

'"You can send a whole menagerie if you like," said Barnes. I could see he didn't like my trying further where he himself had failed; and if I had seen any other chance of bringing Cope off clear, I shouldn't have suggested the thing. But it seemed to me then that our only hope was to shift the blame on to Presse's shoulders, and if anyone could do that, I believed my queer head clerk to be the man.

'I told Elk what I wanted of him, and the fellow's eye brightened up at once.

'"Think you can tear yourself away from the domestic hearth for a day or two?" I asked.

'Elk grinned like a fiend. He's a little man, and he has married into a nest of gaunt sisters. His home life is one continuous harlequinade, with himself as the bobby. When I send him off on any bit of business, he puts all his wits into it, and does it as well as possible in the hope of soon being packed off again on some other job. Of course, it isn't often that he comes into use; but I'll give him credit for working up some cases into a win which would otherwise have turned out an absolute fizzle.

'This matter of Cope's is a very good instance of Elk's nosing powers. He went down to Bordell Priory fully determined to shift the trouble on to Presse's shoulders, and he left no stone unturned to do it. Presse was away at Castle Cope in Fermanagh, and the coast was entirely clear.

'Cope was vastly civil to the little man. "He treated me quite as the gentleman, sir," said Elk, "and gave me a most magnificent dinner. He had had a very bad scare given him that very morning. Some anonymous Fleet Street scoundrel had written an article about the banknote scrape, giving the whole thing, chapter and verse. He gallantly disregarded the Court of Queen's Bench, and pronounced sentence on his own brazen hook. He pointed out that without the least doubt the whole bar could not argue Mr Cope clear, and was kind enough to assure the young gentleman of fourteen years' toil on public works. He said that when a person of his record gets before a jury of upright tradesmen, they weren't in the habit of taking lenient views of his failings; nor is a judge, when passing sentence, able to restrain himself from making an example.

'"Indeed, I think, sir," said Elk, rubbing his hands, "that it was owing to this scare that I banqueted with Mr Cope in the dining-room. Otherwise I might have found myself taking high tea with the upper servants."

'"Yes, yes," said I, "but get to the point. Have you pinned the onus of this affair on Presse?"

'Elk grinned. "I worked to do that, sir, from the very first moment I set foot in the house. Mr Cope didn't like it, but I told him it was the only chance we saw of saving his own skin, and so he went away to his own room, and let me do as I pleased, without interfering. I started by overhauling Mr Presse's photographic tackle.

'"Ye know, sir, I'm a bit of an amateur in that line myself; got a quarter-plate, and do a touch of portrait work amongst friends against the rustic seat in my back garden; and so I could bring expert knowledge to bear on Mr Presse's outfit.

'"It was stowed in a hump-roofed attic which he used as a dark-room, and didn't seem to have been cared for recently. I took up the camera—an early Meagher—and examined it carefully. At first I thought the thing was sound enough, but on looking still more closely I found the bore-hole of a woodworm barely an inch away from the lens. Now that, sir, would have formed a second superimposed picture of its own; and probably fogged everything as well. The wormhole was comparatively old, and I took it for certain that the camera had not been used since it was drilled.

'"This, of course, didn't prove that Mr Presse had no second camera somewhere stowed away. But I fancied he hadn't, for this reason: the developing bottles had not been used for a long time.

Their shoulders were heavy with dust. The pyro solution was black. The hypo bottle had a cauliflower crust round its cork. Of course he might have had a second set of bottles, but that seemed rather far-fetched.

'"The floor was swept, but on the shelves and in the sink there was evidence that the place hadn't been used as a dark-room for many a month. There was thick dust everywhere, except on one thing.

'"Tilted by the side of the sink was an ebonite half-plate developing tray. The upper half was clean and shining: in the lower angle lay a drop or so of dark-brown liquid covered with a faintly opalescent scum. Now, that was pyrogallic developer, recently used; and I took the tray to the window to have a closer look.

'"On one flange was a thumb-mark, faint indeed, but absolutely distinct in all its lines. Now, Mr Presse has large hands, as I have seen from his photograph, he being an enormous gentleman; and Mr Cope has also 'eights', as I noticed from himself. This thumb-mark could have been made by neither of them. It was small, and long, and delicately shaped. I fancied it was the mark of a woman's thumb, and a lady's at that.

'"It puzzled me much. Mr Cope is not a lady's man: he does not get on with the other sex. He told me himself that he has none but men friends to see him, and that the only women under the roof are the kitchen staff. And my thumb-mark seemed too delicate for anyone who could come from these last. But as I could think of no other way out of it, I went down to consult with Mrs Jarrett, the housekeeper.

'"I found Mrs Jarrett a very nice lady, sir; much above her present station in life. She mentioned that before she had had her misfortune, she drove her own pair——"

'"Bother Mrs Jarrett, Elk," said I, "get along with your tale."

'"Certainly, sir. As I was saying, Mrs Jarrett was very kind, and rendered all the information in her power. I wanted to know if she had noticed one of her staff who constantly had stained finger-ends. Mrs Jarrett was on the point at once. There had been an under kitchen-maid whom she was always chiding at for this very fault; a nice, pleasant-spoken young woman she was, Mrs Jarrett said, and—yes—her hands *were* small and nicely shaped, when she came to think about it. But I was rather knocked, sir, when Mrs Jarrett told me she was gone away from the Priory. It seems that for no special cause, except a sudden spasm of temper, the young woman gave her sauce just two days before Mr Cope's misfortune, and was bundled out of the house with a month's wages and no character, there and then. Her place had not been filled, and Mrs Jarrett had no objection to my examining her bedroom, which had been undisturbed since she left. It was a plain enough attic room, sir—bed, chest of drawers, two cane-seated chairs, and the usual utensils; and for a good half-hour I stared about it without seeing anything suspicious. Then I trod on a drawing-pin, which was lying point uppermost on the floor, and on picking it out of my shoe, I noticed the white of plaster on the shank."

'Elk paused, grinned, and then proceeded—

'"There was nothing very remarkable in that, sir, you'll say. Perhaps not; but it made me stare over the walls more closely, and on one of them I saw three other pins driven into the plaster, and the hole where the fourth had been. Now, I didn't know the size of a thousand-pound Bank of England note, but I had with me the fiver you gave me for expenses, and, guessing it would be the same shape, I flattened that out over the drawing-pins on the wall. It fitted exactly. Each of the brass heads clamped a corner without the pins perforating the paper.

'"So, thought I, that's all right. Now, where could it be photographed from? I looked round. The chest of drawers against the opposite wall would make a perfect camera stand; the gas bracket over them would give light in the right direction. I was prepared to stake a good deal that this was the first step in the process by which those fifty thousand-pound notes had been duplicated. But a lot more detailed proof was wanted before I could fill up a brief which you could handle. So I began to reason it out further."

'"I wish you would cut short your beautiful reasonings." I said, "and give me the bare result. To begin with, how are these things forged at all?"

'"Photographed, sir," said Elk, "as I have shown you, from the original note on to a zinc plate covered with sensitized film. That is developed like an ordinary negative, and then placed in a bath of dilute nitric acid. The acid eats away what corresponds to the bare part of the note, leaving the lettering in bold relief. This is inked, placed in a press, and printed from on to specially watered paper in the usual way."

'"I see. Well, did you find the camera, and the press, and the negatives which these notes had been printed from?"

'The little man looked at me with a comical air of reproach. "No, sir. Why, you'd hardly expect a woman who was clever enough to go through all these processes would be sufficiently green to leave the tackle behind. No, sir, when she had finished her job she sauced Mrs Jarrett, and packed the outfit in her boxes, and went. But she did leave one or two mementos behind her. She used another attic at the end of the passage as her dark-room, a windowless, littered place which was never disturbed. Everything was well hidden even there; but, knowing what to look for, I found a good deal. She had developed on the top of a packing-case, which is all stained with her chemicals, and she poured her slops down into a hollow of the walls. She had also dropped into that niche another thing, a spoiled plate—underexposed—of the note marked $\frac{P}{84}$ 86162. On the corner, over the drawing-pin head and a flower of the wallpaper, was a thumb-mark, identically similar line for line with the thumb-mark on the vulcanite developing tray.

'"You have probably heard, sir, that the markings on the thumbs of no two individuals are the same; and on this matter——"

'"Oh, confound you, do get on."

'"Yes, sir. Well, being able to do no more there just then, I ran up to town and gave at Scotland Yard an accurate description of the young person I wanted. They knew her at once—they've a remarkably wide acquaintance with a certain artistic set at the Yard, sir—and within half a dozen hours they'd got her. She was living in comfort in my own neighbourhood, Brixton; and they found in her house a light, handy lithographic press, an extremely good half-plate camera, with a rapid rectilinear lens, and several unexposed zinc plates coated with bromo-iodine emulsion. This property in itself was doubtless innocent, but in the light of what I could bring forward it was very damnatory. And, moreover, an impression of her right thumb taken in wax coincided line for line with the impressions in my possession. These facts were put before the young lady, Mr Grayson, and I am pleased to inform you that she has owned up to making all those notes which Mr Cope so unluckily fingered."

'Elk rambled on a good deal more, because he wanted to go down to Bordell Priory again to gain further holiday from the gaunt sisters.

His excuse was that he wished to complete the evidence. I knew that was rot, but I let him go out of gratitude. I'm afraid that's all he got out of the case, as I naturally gathered in the public kudos myself.'

'Naturally. Then you got your man off all right?' queried O'Malley.

Grayson rubbed his hands. 'Yes, and had a clinking trial of it, a regular *cause célèbre*. There were two counts, Forging and Uttering. There was no question about the Uttering, and we pleaded "guilty as an unconscious instrument". However, expert evidence from the Bank of England showed how marvellous had been the imitation, so I had little fear of sentence on that score. Still, we had a grand fight of it over the Forging, and some of the most headaching inductive evidence ever heard in court. But we got a Not Guilty on it most triumphantly.

'Old Hawkins was on the Bench though, and you know his way. He couldn't resist reading Cope an improving lecture. It was, perhaps, unfair under the circumstances; but it certainly did that enterprising ass no violent harm. Master Willie Cope ripped out the old leaves and ranged himself most wonderfully afterwards; and, thanks to Presse, the estates are pretty nearly on their feet again by now.'

'But what about the girl?'

'Oh, you see, she was a sinner much in request. She'd done time before for the same game, and came of a fine old criminal stock. Consequently she got it hot.'

'Accomplices?'

'Were many, naturally. The whole thing was worked most scientifically by a large gang. But the girl was staunch, and she wouldn't tell. The rest of the crowd are at large today, and we shall probably meet some of them on the racecourse. If any of you chaps can spot one of them out, the Bank would give you more money than you're likely to make in the afternoon over backing gee-gees. Because, you see——'

The grinding of brakes made the QC look out of window.

'Hullo! My faith, here we are at Aintree. How you fellows have kept me babbling. Here, tell me, someone, ought I still to get 25 to 1 about Canoptic for the National? I want him for a long shot.'

A Warning in Red

VICTOR L. WHITECHURCH and E. CONWAY

'Yes,' said the Colonel, as he lit another cheroot, 'many a man when he is in action is simply mad for the time being, and fights like a demon because he sees red.'

'Sees red?' I asked, with a start.

'Don't you know what I mean?'

'No.'

'Ah, it's a curious psychological problem that I've experienced myself. I was leading a cavalry charge at Joonpore, and suddenly the enemy, the country, everything seemed to fade away into a blood-red mist that blinded me with colour—I could see nothing else. And then the mad desire came upon me to slash and slay. They told me afterwards that I behaved like a fury, and I can believe it, for I've seen many a man in the same condition. It only comes in battle, I believe. That's the only time you can "see red".'

'Are you sure?'

'Yes. But what's the matter, Forbes? You look completely startled.'

'Oh, it's nothing,' I replied, 'only a fanciful presentiment I had when I arrived this evening, and you put me in mind of it.'

'What! you don't mean to say you saw red,' asked the Colonel, with a laugh.

'Not in your sense of the word, Colonel; and you'll only laugh at me if I tell you. It's a mere fancy, that's all.'

'Well, drown your fancies in a whisky and soda, and then get a good night's rest after your journey. That's the best thing for you, Forbes. But if you like to tell me what's upset you I won't laugh at you.'

So in the end I told him about the strange effect I had experienced in alighting at the station. I had come down from town to spend a couple of days with Colonel Ward at Manningford. Although I had known him for many years, and had often seen him at his club, it was the first time I had ever been to stay at his country house. He expected me by a late train, but judgement being given in a case in which I was professionally engaged as solicitor rather earlier than I had expected, I was able to get away from town in the afternoon, and reached Manningford station about six o'clock. I had not thought it worth while to wire, as I had determined to take a trap if it was far to walk, and surprise him.

Manningford was a little country station, I was the only passenger who alighted, and one solitary official, who seemed to combine the offices of stationmaster, porter, and ticket-collector, met me on the platform.

'Tickets, please,' he said, gruffly.

I gave him my ticket. As I did so, the train in which I had been travelling glided off the platform, and I caught a glimpse of the red tail-light showing in the fading day.

Grasping my Gladstone bag, I was about to depart, when the idea struck me that I would ask the stationmaster about a conveyance. He had retired to his office and was standing at the ticket-issuing window, which was open. He had lit the lamp inside, as the office was rather dark.

'Can I get a cab anywhere?' I asked.

He looked up. He was a red-faced man with red hair, and the strong light showed his colour vividly. In accordance with the rules of the railway company he served, he was wearing a red tie.

'No,' he said, rather shortly. Perhaps I was staring a little rudely at his illuminated countenance.

'But,' I persisted, 'surely there is some conveyance to be had near, isn't there?'

'You can hire a dog-cart at the Star,' he said.

'Where is that?'

'Cross the line and go out on the other side of the station. Turn to the right, and it's about five minutes' walk.'

And he slammed down the window.

I went on to the platform once more, and slowly crossed the line. I say slowly, because the *red* colour of my surroundings began to grow upon me. The station itself was painted a chocolate colour of a reddish tinge. The tiles bordering the flower beds were of a deep red colour, enclosing for the most part scarlet geraniums. Looking down the line I caught the crimson rays of the setting sun reflected upon the rails, and glancing in the opposite direction noticed that the red light on the up starting signal was burning brightly. It was a strange, indescribable sensation that attacked me, this predominance of blood-red colouring; and I gave a little shiver as I walked to the inn, which was a good quarter of a mile from the station, though apparently the nearest house. A two-mile drive brought me to the Colonel's, and after dinner his mention of 'seeing red' recalled what had happened.

'Well,' said Colonel Ward, as he bid me goodnight, 'I won't laugh at you, because I'll admit that we're none of us accountable for peculiar brain sensations at times. Monk, the stationmaster, isn't exactly a beauty to look at, is he? But he's a capital official. You've been overworking yourself lately, Forbes, and you must take things easy. Goodnight, old chap. Pleasant dreams. I hope your red sensation is not the preliminary to a nightmare.'

The next morning, as we were sitting at breakfast, a servant burst into the room with a very frightened expression, and told the Colonel that a man wanted to see him at once. He was absent for about a quarter of an hour, when he returned in great agitation.

'Great heavens!' he exclaimed, 'my poor friend Geoffrey Anstruthers has been murdered—killed on the line when coming down from town last night. Your blood-red impression had something in it, perhaps, Forbes.'

'Tell me about it, Colonel.'

'I will. It's upset me dreadfully. Poor Anstruthers was my nearest neighbour, living about a mile off in that big white house you noticed between the station and my place. We were the greatest of friends, for although he was a very peculiar man we got on thoroughly. The poor fellow was to have met you at dinner here tonight.'

'How did it happen?'

'Well, they tell me his body was discovered by the side of the line near Barton—about mid-way between London and Manningford. A platelayer found it early this morning. There were marks of a struggle and a couple of knife stabs, and he seems to have been attacked and killed in the train and then thrown out.'

'Have you any idea if there was a motive for the crime?' I asked.

'Unfortunately, yes,' said the Colonel. 'Poor Anstruthers was a man of most eccentric habits, and one of his fads was that he would bank nowhere but at the Bank of England, and that he would pay nobody by cheque. He also settled all his accounts once a quarter only, and the tradesman who asked for an earlier settlement, or the servant or labourer who demanded monthly or weekly wages, was sure to be dismissed by him. Regularly every quarter he went up to London and drew several hundred pounds in gold out of the Bank of England, bringing it back in an ordinary brief bag. I often warned him that he was doing a very foolish thing, but he only laughed at me.

'Yesterday he went up to town for this purpose. His servants thought that as he had not returned last evening by his usual train, which arrives at 10.15 p.m., he was staying the night in town. But evidently some blackguard got hold of his movements. Poor old Anstruthers!'

'Is anything being done yet?' I asked.

'I hardly know,' said the Colonel; 'I think his nearest relations are abroad. At all events I'm the greatest friend he had, and I'm going to take the matter up. I shall go to Barton by the next train.'

'I'll come with you,' I said.

'That's very kind of you, Forbes; your assistance will be most valuable, for I know your hobby—railways. It might help us.'

We finished our breakfast quickly and drove into the station. On my way I asked the Colonel a few particulars concerning the train by which Anstruthers had travelled the night before. It ran as follows:

London (dep.)	8.45 p.m.	
Muggridge (stop)	9.10	"
Barton (stop)	9.37	"
Manningford (stop)	10.15	"
Porthaven (arrive)	10.30	"

So that the only stops between London and Manningford were Muggridge and Barton. The body, so the Colonel had heard, had been found about two miles on the London side of Barton.

The red-faced stationmaster was in his office when we arrived at the station.

'Sad job this, Mr Monk,' said the Colonel.

'Terrible, sir. It regularly upset me when the down train brought the news this morning. Poor Mr Anstruthers! I knew him well, sir. I'd seen him go up in the morning, and wondered why he didn't come back by the 10.15 as usual. Are you going by the up train?'

'Yes. We're going to Barton to enquire into this awful affair. Two first returns, please.'

The stationmaster reached to his rack for the tickets. Now, as often happens in small country stations where the supply of tickets to various stations on the line is limited and becomes exhausted, he did a very common thing. Selecting two blank tickets he dipped the pen into ink and wrote on their respective halves, 'Manningford to Barton', 'Barton to Manningford', and the fare, 7*s*. 8*d*.

Then he passed them through the window and I took them up. He had written the names in *red ink*!

'I hope they'll catch the wretches, sir,' said the stationmaster a few minutes afterwards, as he opened our carriage door for us.

Arrived at Barton, we took a trap and drove to the scene of the tragedy. The body, we were told, had been removed to an inn close by the railway, but at my request we went first to the line, as I was anxious to see the exact spot where Mr Anstruthers had been thrown out of the train. We found a local policeman and two platelayers at the place, which was in a cutting. One of the latter told us that he was the man who had discovered the body.

'He was lyin' just here, gentlemen,' he said, pointing to the six-foot way between the two lines of metals.

'Of course he was dead when you found him?' I asked.

'Yes, sir, but it's my opinion he wasn't altogether dead when they threw him out.'

'Why?'

''Cause he seemed to have moved afterwards. One of his arms was just restin' on the down rail.'

'Well?'

'Well, sir, he couldn't ha' fallen like that in the first place, cause the wheels o' the train would ha' cut his arm.'

'Stop a minute,' I said. 'What time did you find him here?'

''Tween three and four this mornin', sir.'

'And he was thrown out about 9.30 the night before?'

'Yes, sir.'

'Was that train the last down one?'

'The last passenger train, sir.'

'Was there a down goods train after that?'

'Yes, sir, between half-past one and two.'

'Ah, then, why didn't *that* train crush his arm?'

The question staggered the platelayer and the policeman too. They evidently hadn't thought of this.

'I s'pose 'e must ha' bin alive when the goods train passed, and moved afterwards,' said the platelayer presently, and the policeman entered a note to that effect in his pocket-book.

'What are you driving at?' said the Colonel.

'Never mind yet,' I answered. Then, turning to the platelayer again, I said, 'He was stabbed, wasn't he?'

'Yes, sir.'

'Where?'

'In the chest, sir.'

'Any bloodstains?'

'Yes, sir. He was wearin' a white weskitt, and it was quite red when I turned him over.'

'He was lying on his back, then?'

'Yes, sir.'

'Well, where are the blood-marks on the stones here? Have you cleared them up?'

'*There wasn't none,*' said the man.

'Strange!' I murmured to myself, as we left the spot.

'You'd make a good detective, Forbes,' said the Colonel.

'Not a bit of it,' I replied. 'It's simply because there is a mystery connected with my hobby—railways. That's what makes me a little extra sharp.'

'A *mystery*?' said the Colonel.

'Yes,' I replied, 'more than you think. But now let's see the poor fellow.'

Mr Anstruthers was lying on a bed at the inn, just as they had found him. The neighbouring police inspector was there, very imposing and important. The Colonel gave his card, and we were allowed to see the body.

It was a gruesome sight, and my friend turned away to ask some questions of the inspector. I looked at the dead man carefully. There were signs of a struggle. His clothes were torn, and one of his hands was tightly clenched. Then I saw what, apparently, the wily country police had passed undiscovered—a shred of paper clasped in his hand. Without exciting the inspector's attention, I wrested the fingers open and drew from them a tiny scrap of torn paper, evidently clutched by a dying hand. It bore the following in writing: 'ord—on.' It was such a tiny scrap, such an insignificant thing to go upon, but I slipped it into my pocket-book nevertheless.

'Come,' said the Colonel, 'I can't stand this any longer. Well, inspector, I hope you'll get the villain.'

'Ah, we're on the track,' said the officer, sagaciously. 'They got out at Barton, that's about it; and we'll have 'em yet.'

'Do you want to see anything else, Forbes?' asked the Colonel.

'Yes. I should like to see the doctor who examined the body.'

'It's Dr Moore,' said the policeman. 'He lives at Barton.'

So we called on Dr Moore on our way to the station. He declared that he had seen poor Anstruthers at six o'clock in the morning, and was positively certain that he must then have been dead *seven or eight hours*. The mystery was thickening.

Passing on to the platform at Barton, we had to show our tickets. As I took mine back I gazed at it in a listless sort of way, when suddenly I gave a start. The last three letters of 'Manningford'— where had I seen them? That peculiar elongated 'o' and the curiously tailed 'd'—Ah! I remembered!

Hastily I drew the scrap of paper from my pocket-book, and compared it with the ticket. The 'ord' was in the same handwriting! It was part of the words 'Manningford station'.

In a moment a clue flashed across my mind, and I searched for a porter.

'Is there any official about the station with whom I can have a word? It's about an urgent matter.'

'Yes, sir; Mr Smart, the district superintendent is here; he came down about that murder. You'll find him in the stationmaster's office.'

'Come with me, Colonel,' I cried, turning to the office.

Hastily I introduced myself to Mr Smart, telling him my errand was connected with the murder.

'Tell me,' I asked, 'is there any train from Manningford to London after 10.15?'

'Only a goods,' he said.

'Exactly. What time does it leave Manningford?'

'About midnight.'

'And Barton?'

'It stops here for shunting. Generally starts on about 1.45 a.m.'

'Mr Smart, can you lay your hand on the men who worked that train last night?'

He consulted some return sheets.

'Driver Power and fireman Hussey,' he murmured. 'They're on the Slinford branch today—they don't often run on the main line— and brakesman Sutton. He works a goods back to Porthaven today. He'll arrive there in half an hour.'

'Does he always work main line trains?'

'For several months past he has.'

'He's the man then, Mr Smart. It's of the utmost importance that you should wire to Porthaven to have him closely watched. I'll explain presently.'

The district superintendent hastily scribbled a line on an official telegraph form and rushed out with it. When he returned I said—

'Have you any of the company's detectives at hand?'

'Yes, two,' he answered.

'Bring them then, and come along.'

'My dear fellow,' said the Colonel, who had been patiently silent up to this point, '*what* does it all mean?'

'Yes,' said the superintendent, 'I'm in a fog.'

'I hear the down train coming in,' I cried. 'We must all return to Manningford—quick, sir—I'll explain everything in the train.'

A few minutes, and the Colonel, the superintendent, and his two detectives and myself were in the train bound for Manningford.

'Now, sir?' said Mr Smart.

'Well,' I replied, 'we're going to arrest the murderers, or one of them I think, at all events.'

'And who's that?'

'Monk, the stationmaster at Manningford,' I answered.

'*Monk*? Impossible. Why, the murder occurred forty miles away.'

'No,' I replied, 'It occurred at Manningford station last night shortly after 10.15. Listen. Poor Anstruthers came down from town, got out of the train, and was done to death by the stationmaster, who was *alone on the station*, for the sake of his money. In the struggle the murdered man clutched a letter that Monk had written and was probably carrying in his breast pocket. This scrap of it I found in his hand just now. It is in Monk's handwriting. Look!' and I compared it with the ticket.

'But how about the body being found where it was?' asked the Colonel.

'It was taken there afterwards, probably in Sutton's brake van, and thrown out. This would account for two facts: first, that no blood was found on the permanent way, although Anstruthers had bled; and, secondly, that his arm was lying on the down rail. The down goods had passed before he was thrown from the up goods brake van. That's my theory, gentlemen. Here we are at Manningford, and the least you can do is to arrest the stationmaster on suspicion.'

The latter was on the platform when we arrived. I noticed he gave a start as he saw so many of us get out of the train. The superintendent went up to him.

'Mr Monk,' he said, 'a very painful duty brings us here. These two gentlemen are members of our police force, and they will have to detain you on suspicion.'

'Of what?' gasped Monk, his red face growing paler.

'Of participation in the murder of Mr Anstruthers last night.'

'But he was killed in the train,' said the stationmaster.

'That remains to be proved. At all events we are going to detain you, and to search your house.'

'I won't submit to it,' began the man; but he subsided when a pair of handcuffs were slipped over his wrists. Then we all repaired to his little house, just across the road. Again he proved turbulent, but it was no use. With skeleton keys one of the detectives opened a box in his bedroom.

'Ah!' he exclaimed, as he drew out a brief bag, 'this seems rather heavy. No wonder. It's full of money.'

'That's Anstruthers' bag,' exclaimed the Colonel.

The wretched man saw the game was up, but, wretch that he was, he exclaimed—

'It's not me—it's Sutton—the brakesman of the up goods train. He had as much to do with it as I did. He took the body away; and he's got a lot of the gold.'

'All right,' said the superintendent, 'we're seeing after him. You have to thank this gentleman,' pointing to myself, 'for unravelling the mystery.'

'Curse you!' yelled the stationmaster at me.

Sutton turned against Monk, and between the two of them the whole story came out. Monk's accounts were short, and he owed money all round—the usual story—racing. He had half planned to murder Anstruthers several times, and at last the opportunity presented itself. He was the only passenger to alight that night, and Monk noticed that the guard had not observed him. So he asked him to step into his office for a moment under pretence of something, and then went for him. There was a struggle, but Monk was the stronger man. In this struggle Anstruthers had grasped the bit of paper, but without the other's knowledge.

Then came the disposal of the body. Sutton was a man of doubtful character, and Monk knew enough about him to ruin him if he disclosed certain cases of goods stealing. So, when the goods train came along, he gave Sutton twenty pounds, and promised him another thirty to take the body in his van and pitch it out so that people would think Anstruthers had been murdered in the train. It was the easiest thing possible on a dark night to halt the train with the brake van opposite Monk's office, and to slip the body in without driver or fireman knowing anything about it.

The sequel was the gallows for Monk, and fifteen years at Dartmoor for Sutton.

'There was something uncanny after all, Forbes,' said the Colonel, after dinner on that eventful day, 'about your blood-red impression of Manningford station and its master!'

The Fenchurch Street Mystery

BARONESS ORCZY

I

The man in the corner pushed aside his glass, and leant across the table.

'Mysteries!' he commented. 'There is no such thing as a mystery, in connection with any crime, provided intelligence is brought to bear upon its investigation.'

Astonished I looked over the top of my newspaper at him. Had I been commenting audibly upon the article which was interesting me so much? I cannot say; certain it is that the man over there had spoken in direct answer to my thoughts.

His appearance, in any case, was sufficient to tickle my fancy. I don't think I had ever seen any one so pale, so thin, with such funny light-coloured hair, brushed very smoothly across the top of a very obviously bald crown. I smiled indulgently at him. He looked so timid and nervous as he fidgeted incessantly with a piece of string; his long, lean, and trembling fingers tying and untying it into knots of wonderful and complicated proportions.

'And yet,' I remarked kindly, but authoritatively, 'this article, in an otherwise well-informed journal, will tell you that, even within the last year, no fewer than six crimes have completely baffled the police, and the perpetrators of them are still at large.'

'Pardon me,' he said gently, 'I never for a moment ventured to suggest that there were no mysteries to the *police*; I merely remarked that there were none where intelligence was brought to bear upon the investigation of crime.'

'Not even in the Fenchurch Street *mystery*. I suppose,' I asked sarcastically.

'Least of all in the so-called Fenchurch Street *mystery*,' he replied quietly.

Now, the Fenchurch Street mystery, as that extraordinary crime had popularly been called, had puzzled, I venture to say, the brains of every thinking man and woman for the last twelve months. The attitude of that timid man in the corner, therefore, was peculiarly exasperating, and I retorted with sarcasm destined to completely annihilate my self-complacent interlocutor.

'What a pity it is, in that case, that you do not offer your priceless services to our misguided though well-meaning police.'

'Isn't it?' he replied with perfect good-humour. 'Well, you know for one thing, I doubt if they would accept them, and in the second place, my inclinations and my duty would—were I to become an active member of the detective force—nearly always be in direct conflict. As often as not my sympathies go to the criminal who is clever and astute enough to lead our entire police force by the nose.

'I don't know how much of the case you remember,' he went on quietly. 'It certainly, at first, began even to puzzle me. On the 12th of last December a woman, poorly dressed, but with an unmistakable air of having seen better days, gave information at Scotland Yard of the disappearance of her husband, William Kershaw, of no occupation, and apparently of no fixed abode. She was accompanied by a friend—a fat, oily-looking German, and between them they told a tale, which set the police immediately on the move.

'It appears that on the 10th of December, at about three o'clock in the afternoon, Karl Müller, the German, called on his friend, William Kershaw, for the purpose of collecting a small debt—some ten pounds or so—which the latter owed him. On arriving at the squalid lodging in Charlotte Street, Fitzroy Square, he found William Kershaw in a wild state of excitement, and his wife in tears. Müller attempted to state the object of his visit, but Kershaw, with wild gestures, waved him aside, and—in his own words—flabbergasted him by asking him point-blank for another loan of two pounds, which sum, he declared, would be the means of a speedy fortune for himself and the friend who would help him in his need.

'After a quarter of an hour spent in obscure hints, Kershaw, finding the cautious German obdurate, decided to let him into the secret plan, which, he averred, would place thousands into their hands.'

Instinctively I had put down my paper; the mild stranger, with his nervous air and timid, watery eyes, had a peculiar way of telling his tale, which somehow fascinated me.

'I don't know,' he resumed, 'if you remember the story which the German told to the police, and which was corroborated in every detail by the wife or widow. Briefly it was this: some thirty years previously, Kershaw, then twenty years of age, and a medical student at one of the London hospitals, had a chum named Barker, with whom he roomed, together with another.

'The latter, so it appears, brought home one evening a very considerable sum of money, which he had won on the turf, and the following morning he was found murdered in his bed. Kershaw, fortunately for himself, was able to prove a conclusive alibi; he had spent the night on duty at the hospital; as for Barker, he had disappeared, that is to say, as far as the police were concerned, but not as far as the watchful eyes of his friend Kershaw—at least, so the latter said. Barker very cleverly contrived to get away out of the country, and after sundry vicissitudes, finally settled down at Vladivostock, in Eastern Siberia, where, under the assumed name of Smethurst, he built up an enormous fortune, by trading in furs.

'Now mind you, every one knows Smethurst, the Siberian millionaire. Kershaw's story that he had once been called Barker, and had committed a murder thirty years ago was never proved, was it? I am merely telling you what Kershaw said to his friend the German and to his wife on that memorable afternoon of December the 10th.

'According to him, Smethurst had made one gigantic mistake in his clever career; he had on four occasions written to his late friend, William Kershaw. Two of these letters had no bearing on the case, since they were written more than twenty-five years ago, and Kershaw, moreover had lost them—so he said—long ago. According to him, however, the first of these letters was written when Smethurst, alias Barker, had spent all the money he had obtained from the crime, and found himself destitute in New York.

'Kershaw, then in fairly prosperous circumstances, sent him a £10 note for the sake of old times. The second, when the tables had turned, and Kershaw had begun to go downhill, Smethurst, as he then already called himself, sent his whilom friend £50. After that, as Müller gathered, Kershaw had made sundry demands on Smethurst's ever-increasing purse, and had accompanied these demands by various threats, which, considering the distant country in which the millionaire lived, were worse than futile.

'But now the climax had come, and Kershaw after a final moment of hesitation, handed over to his German friend the two last letters purporting to have been written by Smethurst, and which, if you remember, played such an important part in the mysterious story of this extraordinary crime. I have a copy of both these letters, here,' added the man in the corner, as he took out a piece of paper from a very worn-out pocket-book, and, unfolding it very deliberately, he began to read:

SIR, Your preposterous demands for money are wholly unwarrantable. I have already helped you quite as much as you deserve. However, for the sake of old times, and because you once helped me when I was in a terrible difficulty, I am willing to once more let you impose upon my good nature. A friend of mine here, a Russian merchant, to whom I have sold my business, starts in a few days for an extended tour to many European and Asiatic ports in his yacht, and has invited me to accompany him as far as England. Being tired of foreign parts, and desirous of seeing the old country once again after thirty years' absence, I have decided to accept his invitation. I don't know when we may actually be in Europe, but I promise you that as soon as we touch a suitable port I will write to you again, making an appointment for you to see me in London. But remember that if your demands are too preposterous I will not for a moment listen to them, and that I am the last man in the world to submit to persistent and unwarrantable blackmailing.

I am, sir,
Yours truly,
FRANCIS SMETHURST

'The second letter was dated from Southampton,' he went on with absolute calm, 'and, curiously enough, was the only letter which Kershaw professed to have received from Smethurst, of which he had kept the envelope, and which was dated. It was quite brief,' he added, referring once more to his piece of paper.

DEAR SIR, Referring to my letter of a few weeks ago, I wish to inform you that the *Tsarskoe Selo* will touch at Tilbury on Tuesday next, the 10th. I shall land there, and immediately go up to London by the first train I can get. If you like you may meet me at Fenchurch Street Station, in the first-class waiting room in the late afternoon. Since I surmise that after thirty years' absence my face may not be familiar to you, I may as well tell you that you will recognize me by a heavy Astrakhan fur coat, which I shall wear, together with a cap of the same. You may then introduce yourself to me, and I will personally listen to what you may have to say.

Yours faithfully,
FRANCIS SMETHURST

'It was this last letter which had caused William Kershaw's excitement and his wife's tears. In the German's own words, he was walking up and down the room like a wild beast, gesticulating wildly, and muttering sundry exclamations. Mrs Kershaw, however, was full of apprehension. She mistrusted the man from foreign parts—who, according to her husband's story, had already one crime upon his conscience—who might, she feared, risk another, in order to be rid of a dangerous enemy. Woman-like, she thought the scheme a dishonourable one, for the law, she knew, is severe on the blackmailer.

'The assignation might be a cunning trap, in any case it was a curious one; why, she argued, did not Smethurst elect to see Kershaw at his hotel the following day. A thousand whys and wherefores made her anxious, but the fat German had been won over by Kershaw's visions of untold gold, held tantalizingly before his eyes. He had lent the necessary £2, with which his friend intended to tidy himself up a bit before he went to meet his friend the millionaire. Half-an-hour afterwards Kershaw had left his lodgings, and that was the last the unfortunate woman saw of her husband, or Müller, the German, of his friend.

'Anxiously his wife waited that night, but he did not return, the next day she seems to have spent in making purposeless and futile enquiries about the neighbourhood of Fenchurch Street, and on the 12th she went to Scotland Yard, gave what particulars she knew, and placed in the hands of the police the two letters written by Smethurst.'

II

The man in the corner had finished his glass of milk. His watery blue eyes looked across with evident satisfaction at my obvious eagerness and excitement.

'It was only on the 31st,' he resumed after a while, 'that a body, decomposed past all recognition, was found by two lightermen in the bottom of a disused barge. She had been moored at one time at the foot of one of those dark flights of steps which lead down between tall warehouses to the river in the East End of London. I have a photograph of the place here,' he added, selecting one out of his pocket, and placing it before me.

'The actual barge, you see, had already been removed when I took this snapshot, but you will realize what a perfect place this alley is for the purpose of one man cutting another's throat in comfort, and without fear of detection. The body, as I said, was decomposed beyond all recognition; it had probably been there eleven days, but sundry articles such as a silver ring and a tie pin were recognizable and were identified by Mrs Kershaw as belonging to her husband.

'She, of course, was loud in denouncing Smethurst, and the police had no doubt a very strong case against him, for two days after the discovery of the body in the barge, the Siberian millionaire, as he was already popularly called by enterprising interviewers, was arrested in his luxurious suite of rooms at the Hotel Cecil.

'To confess the truth, at this point, I was not a little puzzled. Mrs Kershaw's story, and Smethurst's letters had both found their way into the papers, and following my usual method—mind you, I am only an amateur, I try to reason out a case for the love of the thing—I sought about for a motive for the crime, which the police declared Smethurst had committed. To effectually get rid of a dangerous blackmailer was the generally accepted theory. Well! did it ever strike you how paltry that motive really was?'

I had to confess, however, that it had never struck me in that light.

'Surely a man who had succeeded in building up an immense fortune by his own individual efforts was not the sort of fool to believe that he had anything to fear from a man like Kershaw. He must have *known* that Kershaw held no damning proofs against him—not enough to hang him anyway. Have you ever seen Smethurst?' he added, as he once more fumbled in his pocket-book.

I replied that I had seen Smethurst's picture in the illustrated papers at the time: then he added, placing a small photograph before me:

'What strikes you most about the face?'

'Well, I think its strange, astonished expression, due to the total absence of eyebrows, and the funny foreign cut of the hair.'

'So close that it almost looks as if it had been shaved. Exactly. That is what struck me most when I elbowed my way into the Court that morning and first caught sight of the millionaire in the dock. He was a tall, soldierly looking man, upright in stature, his face very bronzed and tanned. He wore neither moustache nor beard, his hair was cropped quite close to his head like a Frenchman's; but, of course, what was so very remarkable about him was that total absence of eyebrows and even eyelashes, which gave the face such a peculiar appearance—as you say, a perpetually astonished look.

'He seemed, however, wonderfully calm; he had been accommodated with a chair in the dock—being a millionaire—and chatted pleasantly with his lawyer, Sir Arthur Inglewood, in the intervals between the calling of the several witnesses for the prosecution; whilst during the examination of these witnesses he sat quite placidly, with his head shaded by his hand.

'Müller and Mrs Kershaw repeated the story, which they had already told to the police. I think you said that you were not curious enough to go to the Court that day, and hear the case, so perhaps you have no recollection of Mrs Kershaw. No? Ah, well! Here is a snapshot I managed to get of her once. That is her. Exactly as she stood in the box—overdressed—in elaborate crape, with a bonnet which once had contained pink roses, and to which a remnant of pink petals still clung obtrusively amidst the deep black.

She would not look at the prisoner, and turned her head resolutely towards the magistrate. I fancy she had been fond of that vagabond husband of hers: an enormous wedding-ring encircled her finger, and that, too, was swathed in black. She firmly believed that Kershaw's murderer sat there in the dock, and she literally flaunted her grief before him.

'I was indescribably sorry for her. As for Müller, he was just fat, oily, pompous, conscious of his own importance as a witness; his fat fingers, covered with brass rings, gripped the two incriminating letters, which he had identified. They were his passports, as it were, to a delightful land of importance and notoriety. Sir Arthur Inglewood, I think, disappointed him, by stating that he had no questions to ask of him. Müller had been brimful of answers, ready with the most perfect indictment, the most elaborate accusations against the bloated millionaire who had decoyed his dear friend Kershaw, and murdered him in Heaven knows what an out-of-the-way corner of the East End.

'After this, however, the excitement grew apace. Müller had been dismissed, and had retired from the Court altogether, leading away Mrs Kershaw, who had completely broken down.

'Constable D21 was giving evidence as to the arrest, in the meanwhile. The prisoner, he said, had seemed completely taken by surprise, not understanding the cause or history of the accusation against him; however, when put in full possession of the facts, and realizing, no doubt, the absolute futility of any resistance, he had quietly enough followed the constable into the cab. No one at the fashionable and crowded Hotel Cecil had even suspected that anything unusual had occurred.

'Then a gigantic sigh of expectancy came from everyone of the spectators. The "fun" was about to begin. James Buckland, a porter at Fenchurch Street railway station, had just sworn to tell all the truth, etc. After all it did not amount to much. He said that at six o'clock in the afternoon of December the 10th, in the midst of one of the densest fogs he ever remembers, the 5.5 from Tilbury steamed into the station, being just about an hour late. He was on the arrival platform and was hailed by a passenger in a first-class carriage. He could see very little of him beyond an enormous black fur coat and a travelling cap of fur also.

'The passenger had a quantity of luggage, all marked F. S., and he directed James Buckland to place it all upon a four-wheel cab, with the exception of a small handbag, which he carried himself. Having seen that all his luggage was safely bestowed, the stranger in the fur coat paid the porter, and telling the cabman to wait until he returned, he walked away in the direction of the waiting-rooms, still carrying his small handbag.

'"I stayed for a bit," added James Buckland, "talking to the driver about the fog and that, then I went about my business, seeing that the local from Southend had been signalled."

'The prosecution insisted most strongly upon the hour when the stranger in the fur coat, having seen to his luggage, walked away towards the waiting-rooms. The porter was emphatic. "It was not a minute later than 6.15," he averred.

'Sir Arthur Inglewood still had no questions to ask, and the driver of the cab was called.

'He corroborated the evidence of James Buckland as to the hour when the gentleman in the fur coat had engaged him, and having filled his cab in and out with luggage, had told him to wait. And cabby did wait. He waited in the dense fog—until he was tired, until he seriously thought of depositing all the luggage in the lost property office and of looking out for another fare—waited until at last, at a quarter before nine, whom should he see walking hurriedly towards his cab but the gentleman in the fur coat and cap who got in quickly and told the driver to take him at once to the Hotel Cecil. This, cabby declared, had occurred at a quarter before nine. Still Sir Arthur Inglewood made no comment, and Mr Francis Smethurst, in the crowded, stuffy court, had calmly dropped to sleep.

'The next witness, Constable Thomas Taylor, had noticed a shabbily dressed individual, with shaggy hair and beard, loafing about the station and waiting-rooms in the afternoon of December the 10th. He seemed to be watching the arrival platform of the Tilbury and Southend trains.

'Two separate and independent witnesses, cleverly unearthed by the police, had seen this same shabbily dressed individual stroll into the first-class waiting-room at about 6.15 on Wednesday, December the 10th, and go straight up to a gentleman in a heavy fur coat and cap, who had also just come into the room. The two talked together for a while; no one heard what they said, but presently they walked off together. No one seemed to know in which direction.

'Francis Smethurst was rousing himself from his apathy; he whispered to his lawyer, who nodded with a bland smile of encouragement. The employees of the Hotel Cecil gave evidence as to the arrival of Mr Smethurst at about 9.30 p.m. on Wednesday, December the 10th, in a cab, with a quantity of luggage; and this closed the case for the prosecution.

'Everybody in that Court already *saw* Smethurst mounting the gallows. It was uninterested curiosity which caused the elegant audience to wait and hear what Sir Arthur Inglewood had to say. He, of course, is the most fashionable man in the law at the present moment. His lolling attitudes, his drawling speech, are quite the rage, and imitated by the gilded youth of society.

'Even at this moment, when the Siberian millionaire's neck literally and metaphorically hung in the balance, an expectant titter went round the fair spectators, as Sir Arthur stretched out his long loose limbs and lounged across the table. He waited to make his effect— Sir Arthur is a born actor—and there is no doubt that he made it, when in his slowest, most drawly tones he said quietly:

'"With regard to this alleged murder of one William Kershaw, on Wednesday, December the 10th, between 6.15 and 8.45 p.m., your Honour, I now propose to call two witnesses, who saw this same William Kershaw alive on Tuesday afternoon, December the 16th, that is to say, six days after the supposed murder."

'It was as if a bombshell had exploded in the Court. Even his Honour was aghast, and I am sure the lady next to me only recovered from the shock of the surprise in order to wonder whether she need put off her dinner party after all.

'As for me,' added the man in the corner, with that strange mixture of nervousness and self-complacency which I have never seen equalled, 'well, you see, *I* had made up my mind long ago as to where the hitch lay in this particular case, and I was not so surprised as some of the others.

'Perhaps you remember the wonderful development of the case, which so completely mystified the police—and in fact everybody except myself. Torriani and a waiter at his hotel in the Commercial Road both deposed that at about 3.30 p.m. on December the 10th a shabbily dressed individual lolled into the coffee-room and ordered some tea. He was pleasant enough and talkative, told the waiter that his name was William Kershaw, that very soon all London would be talking about him, as he was about, through an unexpected stroke of good fortune, to become a very rich man, and so on, and so on, nonsense without end.

'When he had finished his tea, he lolled out again, but no sooner had he disappeared down a turning of the road, than the waiter discovered an old umbrella, left behind accidentally by the shabby, talkative individual. As is the custom in his highly respectable restaurant, Signor Torriani put the umbrella carefully away in his office, on the chance of his customer calling to claim it when he had discovered his loss. And sure enough nearly a week later, on Tuesday, the 16th, at about 1 p.m. the same shabbily dressed individual called and asked for his umbrella. He had some lunch, and chatted once again to the waiter. Signor Torriani and the waiter gave a description of William Kershaw which coincided exactly with that given by Mrs Kershaw of her husband.

'Oddly enough he seemed to be a very absent-minded sort of person, for on this second occasion, no sooner had he left than the waiter found a pocket-book in the coffee-room, underneath the table. It contained sundry letters and bills, all addressed to William Kershaw. This pocket-book was produced, and Karl Müller, who had returned to the Court, easily identified it as having belonged to his dear and lamented friend "Villiam".

'This was the first blow to the case against the accused. It was a pretty stiff one, you will admit. Already it had begun to collapse like a house of cards. Still, there was the assignation, and the undisputed meeting between Smethurst and Kershaw, and those two and a half hours of a foggy evening to satisfactorily account for.'

The man in the corner made a long pause, keeping me on tenter-hooks. He had fidgeted with his bit of string till there was not an inch of it free from the most complicated and elaborate knots.

'I assure you,' he resumed at last, 'that at that very moment the whole mystery was, to me, as clear as daylight. I only marvelled how his Honour could waste his time and mine by putting what he thought were searching questions to the accused relating to his past. Francis Smethurst, who had quite shaken off his somnolence, spoke with a curious nasal twang, and with an almost imperceptible soupçon of foreign accent. He calmly denied Kershaw's version of his past; declared that he had never been called Barker, and had certainly never been mixed up in any murder case thirty years ago.

'"But you knew this man Kershaw," persisted his Honour, "since you wrote to him?"

'"Pardon me, your Honour," said the accused quietly, "I have never, to my knowledge, seen this man Kershaw, and I can swear that I never wrote to him."

'"Never wrote to him?" retorted his Honour warningly. "That is a strange assertion to make, when I have two of your letters to him in my hands at the present moment."

'"I never wrote those letters, your Honour," persisted the accused quietly, "they are not in my handwriting."

'"Which we can easily prove," came in Sir Arthur Inglewood's drawly tones, as he handed up a packet to his Honour, "here are a number of letters written by my client since he has landed in this country, and some of which were written under my very eyes."

'As Sir Arthur Inglewood had said, this could be easily proved, and the prisoner, at his Honour's request, scribbled a few lines, together with his signature, several times upon a sheet of notepaper. It was easy to read upon the magistrate's astounded countenance, that there was not the slightest similarity in the two handwritings.

'A fresh mystery had cropped up. Who then had made the assignation with William Kershaw, at Fenchurch Street railway station? The prisoner gave a fairly satisfactory account of the employment of his time, since his landing in England.

'"came over on the *Tsarskoe Selo*," he said, "a yacht belonging to a friend of mine. When we arrived at the mouth of the Thames there was such a dense fog that it was twenty-four hours before it was thought safe for me to land. My friend, who is a Russian, would not land at all; he was regularly frightened at this land of fogs. He was going on to Madeira immediately.

'"I actually landed on Tuesday, the 10th, and took a train at once for town. I did see to my luggage and a cab, as the porter and driver told your Honour; then I tried to find my way to a refreshment room, where I could get a glass of wine. I drifted into the waiting-room, and there I was accosted by a shabbily dressed individual, who began telling me a piteous tale. Who he was I do not know. He *said* he was an old soldier who had served his country faithfully, and then been left to starve. He begged of me to accompany him to his lodgings, where I could see his wife and starving children, and verify the truth and piteousness of his tale.

'"Well, your Honour," added the prisoner with noble frankness, "it was my first day in the old country. I had come back after thirty years, with my pockets full of gold, and this was the first sad tale I had heard; but I am a business man, and did not want to be exactly 'done' in the eye. I followed my man through the fog, out into the streets. He walked silently by my side for a time. I had not a notion where I was.

'"Suddenly I turned to him with some question, and realized in a moment that my gentleman had given me the slip. Finding, probably, that I would not part with my money till I *had* seen the starving wife and children, he left me to my fate, and went in search of more willing bait.

'"The place where I found myself was dismal and deserted. I could see no trace of cab or omnibus. I retraced my steps and tried to find my way back to the station, only to find myself in worse and more deserted neighbourhoods. I became hopelessly lost and fogged. I don't wonder that two and a half hours elapsed while I thus wandered on in the dark and deserted streets; my sole astonishment is that I ever found the station at all that night, or rather close to it a policeman, who showed me the way."

'"But how do you account for Kershaw knowing all your movements?" still persisted his Honour, "and his knowing the exact date of your arrival in England? How do you account for these two letters, in fact?"

'"I cannot account for it or them, your Honour," replied the prisoner quietly. "I have proved to you, have I not, that I never wrote those letters, and that the man—er—Kershaw is his name?—was not murdered by me?"

' "Can you tell me of anyone here or abroad who might have heard of your movements, and of the date of your arrival?"

' "My late employees at Vladivostock, of course, knew of my departure, but none of them could have written these letters, since none of them know a word of English.

' "Then you can throw no light upon these mysterious letters? You cannot help the police in any way towards the clearing up of this strange affair?"

' "The affair is as mysterious to me as to your Honour, and to the police of this country."

'Francis Smethurst was discharged, of course; there was no semblance of evidence against him sufficient to commit him for trial. The two overwhelming points of his defence which had completely routed the prosecution were, firstly, the proof that he had never written the letters making the assignation, and secondly, the fact that the man supposed to have been murdered on the 10th was seen to be alive and well on the 16th. But then, who in the world was the mysterious individual who had apprised Kershaw of the movements of Smethurst, the millionaire?'

III

The man in the corner cocked his funny thin head on one side and looked at me; then he took up his beloved bit of string, and deliberately untied every knot he had made in it. When it was quite smooth, he laid it out upon the table.

'I will take you, if you like, point by point, along the line of reasoning which I followed myself, and which will inevitably lead you, as it led me, to the only possible solution of the mystery.

'First take this point,' he said with nervous restlessness, once more taking up his bit of string, and forming with each point raised a series of knots which would have shamed a navigating instructor, 'obviously, it was *impossible* for Kershaw not to have been acquainted with Smethurst, since he was fully apprised of the latter's arrival in England by two letters. Now it was clear to me from the first that *no one* could have written those two letters except Smethurst. You will argue that those letters were proved not to have been written by the man in the dock. Exactly. Remember, Kershaw was a careless man; he had lost both envelopes. To him they were insignificant. Now it was never *disproved* that those letters were written by Smethurst.'

'But——' I suggested.

'Wait a minute,' he interrupted, while knot number two appeared upon the scene, 'it was proved that six days after the murder. William Kershaw was alive, and visiting the Torriani Hotel, where already he was known, and where he conveniently left a pocket-book behind, so that there should be no mistake as to his identity, but it was never questioned where Mr Francis Smethurst, the millionaire, happened to spend that very same afternoon.'

'Surely, you don't mean——?' I gasped.

'One moment, please,' he added triumphantly. 'How did it come about that the landlord of the Torriani Hotel was brought into court at all; how did Sir Arthur Inglewood, or rather his client, know that William Kershaw had on those two memorable occasions visited the hotel and that its landlord could bring such convincing evidence forward that would for ever exonerate the millionaire from the imputation of murder?'

'Surely,' I argued, 'the usual means, the police——'

'The police had kept the whole affair very dark, until the arrest at the Hotel Cecil. They did not put into the papers the usual: "If any one happens to know of the whereabouts etc. etc." Had the landlord of that hotel heard of the disappearance of Kershaw through the usual channels, he would have put himself in communication with the police. Sir Arthur Inglewood produced him. How did Sir Arthur Inglewood come on his track?'

'Surely, you don't mean——?'

'Point number four,' he resumed imperturbably, 'Mrs Kershaw was never requested to produce a specimen of her husband's handwriting. Why? Because the police, clever as you say they are, never started on the right tack. They believed William Kershaw to have been murdered; they looked for William Kershaw.

'On December the 31st, what was presumed to be the body of William Kershaw was found by two lightermen; I have shown you a photograph of the place where it was found. Dark and deserted it is in all conscience, is it not? Just the place where a bully and a coward would decoy an unsuspecting stranger, murder him first, then rob him of his valuables, his papers, his very identity, and leave him there to rot. The body was found in a disused barge which had been moored some time against the wall, at the foot of these steps. It was in the last stages of decomposition, and, of course, could not be identified; but the police would have it, that it was the body of William Kershaw.

'It never entered their heads that it was the body of *Francis Smethurst, and that William Kershaw was his murderer.*

'Ah! it was cleverly, artistically conceived! Kershaw is a genius. Think of it all! His disguise! Kershaw had a shaggy beard, hair, and moustache. He shaved up to his very eyebrows! No wonder that even his wife did not recognize him across the Court; and remember she never saw much of his face while he stood in the dock. Kershaw was shabby, slouchy, he stooped.

'Smethurst, the millionaire, might have served in the Prussian army. Then that lovely trait about going to revisit the Torriani Hotel. Just a few days grace, in order to purchase moustache and beard and wig, exactly similar to what he had himself shaved off. Making up to look like himself! Splendid! The leaving the pocket-book behind! He! He! He! Kershaw was not murdered! Of course not. He called at the Torriani Hotel six days after the murder, whilst Mr Smethurst, the millionaire, hobnobbed in the park with duchesses! Hang such a man! Fie!'

He fumbled for his hat. With nervous, trembling fingers he held it deferentially in his hand, whilst he rose from the table. I watched him as he strode up to the desk, and paid twopence for his glass of milk and his bun. Soon he disappeared through the shop, whilst I still found myself hopelessly bewildered, with a number of snap-shot photographs before me, still staring at a long piece of string, smothered from end to end in a series of knots, as bewildering, as irritating, as puzzling as the man who had lately sat in the corner.

The Green Spider

SAX ROHMER

I find from my notes that Professor Brayme-Skepley's great lecture which was to revolutionize modern medicine should have been delivered upon the fifteenth of March, and many of Europe's leading scientists were during the preceding week to be seen daily in the quaint old streets of Barminster—for the entire world of medical science was waiting agog for the revelation of the Brayme-Skepley treatment.

Many people wondered that Brayme-Skepley should deliver a lecture so vastly important in old-world Barminster rather than in London; but he was not a man to be coerced—so the savants, perforce, came to Barminster.

At twelve, midnight, as nearly as can be ascertained, on the fourteenth of March the porter in charge of the North Gate—by which direct admission can be gained to the quadrangle—was aroused by a loud ringing of his bell.

Hurrying to the door of his little lodge, he was surprised to find at the gate the gaunt figure of Professor Brayme-Skepley, enveloped in a huge fur coat. He hastened to unlock the wicket and admit the great scientist.

'I am sorry to trouble you at so late an hour, Jamieson,' said the Professor, 'but there are some little preparations which I must make for tomorrow's lecture. I shall probably be engaged in the bacteriological laboratory for a couple of hours. You will not mind turning out with the key?'

He slipped a sovereign into the porter's hand as he spoke, and Jamieson only too gladly acquiesced.

The fire in the little sitting-room of the lodge was almost extinct, but the man revived it, and, putting on a shovelful of coal, lighted his pipe, and sat smoking for about an hour. At one o'clock he stepped outside, and glanced across the quadrangle.

The Professor was still working, and, finding the night air chilly,

Jamieson was about to turn in again when a light suddenly appeared in the top window of one of those ancient houses in Spindle Lane. The house was the last of the row, and overlooked the bacteriological laboratory.

'That's old Kragg's house,' muttered the porter; 'but I didn't know anybody lived there since the old man died.'

The light was a vague and flickering one, almost like that of a match; and, as he watched, it disappeared again. There was something uncanny about this solitary light in a house which he believed to be uninhabited, so, with a slight shudder, Jamieson returned to the comforts of his fireside.

Curiously enough, I had been reading upon this particular night in Harborne's rooms; and at something like twenty minutes past two I knocked the ashes from my pipe, and was about to depart—when there came a sudden scuffling on the stairs. We both turned just as the door was flung open, and Jamieson, white-faced and wild-eyed, stumbled, breathless, into the room.

'Thank Heaven I've found somebody up!' he gasped. 'Yours was the only window with a light!'

'Where's the brandy?' I said, for the man seemed inclined to faint upon the sofa.

A stiff glass of cognac pulled him together somewhat, and, with a little colour returning to his face, but still wild of eye, he burst out:

'Professor Brayme-Skepley has been murdered!'

'Murdered!' echoed Harborne.

'And no mortal hand has done the thing, sir!' continued the frightened man. 'Heaven grant I never see the like again!'

'You're raving!' I said with an assumption of severity, for Jamieson's condition verged closely upon that of hysteria. 'Try to talk sense. Where is the Professor?'

'In the bacteriological laboratory, sir.'

'How long has he been there?'

'Since twelve o'clock!'

I glanced at Harborne in surprise.

'What was he doing there?' enquired the latter.

'He said he had some preparations to make for his lecture.'

'Well, get on! Here, have another pull at the brandy. How do you know he's dead?'

'I went to ask him how much longer he was going to be.'

'Well?'

'He didn't answer to my knocking, although there was a light burning. The door was locked from the inside, so I got on to the dust-box, and just managed to reach a window-ledge. I pulled myself up far enough to look inside; and then—I dropped down again!'

'But what did you see, man? What did you see?'

'I saw Professor Brayme-Skepley lying dead on the floor among broken jars by an overturned table. There were only two lamps on—those over the table—and his head came just in the circle of light. His body was in shadow.'

'What else?'

'Blood! His hair all matted!'

'Come on, Harborne!' I cried, seizing my hat. 'You too, Jamieson!'

'For the love of Heaven, gentlemen,' gasped the man, grasping us each by an arm, 'I couldn't! You haven't heard all!'

'Then get on with it!' said Harborne. 'Every second is of importance.'

'I ran for the window ladder, gentlemen; and when I came back with it the electric lamps were out!'

'Out?'

'I ran up the ladder, and looked in at the window; and saw—how can I tell you what I saw?'

'Don't maunder!' shouted Harborne. 'What was it?'

'It was a thing, sir, like a kind of green spider—only with a body twice the size of that football!'

Harborne and I looked at one another significantly.

'You're a trifle overwrought, Jamieson,' I said, laying my hand upon his shoulder. 'Stay here until we come back.'

The man stared at me.

'You don't believe it,' he said tensely; 'and you'll go into that place unprepared. But I'll swear on the Book that there was some awful thing not of this earth creeping in the corner of the laboratory!'

Harborne, with his hand on the doorknob, turned undecidedly.

'Which corner, Jamieson?' he enquired.

'The north-west, sir. I just caught one glimpse of it through the opening in the partition.'

'How could you see it, since all the lights were out?' Harborne asked.

The porter looked surprised. 'That never occurred to me before, sir,' he said; 'but I think it must have shone—something like the bottles of phosphorus, sir!'

'Come on!' said my friend. And without further ado we ran downstairs into the Square.

A cheerful beam of light from the door of the lodge cut the black shadows of the archway as we approached, and served to show that the panic-stricken porter had left the wicket open. As we hurried through and sprinted across the quadrangle we were met by a cold, damp wind from the direction of the river. The night was intensely dark, and the bacteriological laboratory showed against the driving masses of inky cloud merely as a square patch of blackness.

'Here's the ladder,' said Harborne suddenly; and we both paused, undecided how to act.

'Try the door,' I suggested.

We rattled the handle of the door, but it was evidently locked, so that for a moment we were in a quandary. Harborne mounted the ladder and peered into the impenetrable shadows of the laboratory, but reported that there was nothing to be seen.

'We must burst the door in,' I said; 'it hasn't a very heavy lock.'

We accordingly applied our shoulders to the door, and gave a vigorous push. The lock yielded perceptibly. I then crashed my heel against the woodwork just over the keyhole, and the door flew open. We immediately detected a most peculiar odour.

'It's the broken bottles,' muttered Harborne. 'The switch is over against the wall by the bookcase; we must go straight for that.'

Cautiously we stepped into the darkness, and at the third or fourth step there was a crackling of glass underfoot. My boot slipped where some sticky substance lay, and I gave an involuntary shudder. A moment later I heard an exclamation of disgust.

'The wall is all wet!' said Harborne.

Then he found the electric buttons, and turned on the lights in rapid succession.

Heavens! How can I describe the picture revealed! Never have I witnessed such a scene of chaos, fearsome in its indications of an incredible struggle.

At first glance the place gave an impression of having been wantonly wrecked by a madman. Scarcely a jar or bottle remained upon the shelves, all being strewn in fragments upon the floor, which was simply swimming in the spilled spirits and preservatives. The door of the case that had contained the specimens of bacilli was wide open, and the glass completely smashed. The priceless contents were presumably to be sought among the hundred and one objects lying in the liquid on the floor.

Most of the books from the shelf were distributed about the place as though they had been employed as missiles, and one huge volume was wedged up under the frosted glass of the skylight in the centre of the roof. In the wood of the partition a lancet was stuck, and a horribly suggestive streak linked it with a red pool upon the floor. A table was overturned, and the two lamps immediately above it were broken. Of Professor Brayme-Skepley there was no sign, but his hat and fur coat hung upon a hook where he had evidently placed them on entering.

For some time we surveyed the scene in silence. Then Harborne spoke.

'What are these marks on the wall?' he said. 'They are still wet. And where is the Professor?'

The marks alluded to were a series of impressions in the shape of irregular rings passing from the pool on the floor to the four walls and up the walls to where the shadows of the lamp shades rendered it impossible to follow them. I pulled down a lamp, and turned the shade upwards, whereupon was revealed a thing that caused me a sudden nausea.

The marks extended right to the top of the wall, and could furthermore be distinguished upon the ceiling; and on the framework of the skylight was the reddish-brown impression of a human hand!

'Drop it!' said Harborne huskily. 'If we stay here much longer we shall have no pluck left for looking behind the partition.'

The northern end of the laboratory is partitioned off to form a narrow apartment, which runs from side to side of the building, but is only some six feet in width. It is lined with shelves whereon are stored the greater part of the materials used in experiments, and is lighted by a square window at the Spindle Lane end, beneath which is a sink. The partition does not run flush up to the western wall, but only to within three feet of it, leaving an opening connecting the storeroom with the laboratory proper. There are two electric lamps in the place, one over the sink, and the other in the centre; but they cannot be turned on from the laboratory, the switch being behind the partition. Consequently the storeroom was in darkness, and, ignorant of what awful thing might be lurking there, we yet, in justice to the missing man, had no alternative but to enter.

Harborne, whose pallor can have been no greater than my own, strode quickly up the laboratory, and passed through the opening in the partition. I following closely behind. I heard the click of the electric switch; but only one lamp became lighted. That over the sink was broken.

We were both, I think, anticipating some gruesome sight; but, singular to relate, the only abnormal circumstance that at first came under our notice was that of the broken lamp. A sudden draught of air, damp and cold, that set the other shade swinging drew our attention to the fact that the window had been pulled right away from its fastenings and lay flat down against the wall. Then Harborne detected the gruesome tracks right along the centre of the floor; and under the window we made a further discovery.

The wall all round the casement was smeared with blood, and the marks of a clutching hand showed in all directions.

'Good heavens!' I muttered; 'this is horrible! It looks as though he had been dragged——'

There was a queer catch in Harborne's voice as he answered: 'We must get out a party to scour the marshes.'

'Hark!' I said. 'Jamieson has been knocking some of them up. Here they come across the quad.'

A moment later an excited group was surveying the strange scene in the laboratory.

'Clear out and get lanterns, you fellows!' shouted Harborne. 'His body has been dragged through the window!'

'What's this about a green spider?' called several men.

'Don't ask me!' said my friend. 'I am inclined to agree with Jamieson that this is not the doing of a man. We must spread out and examine Spindle Lane and the surrounding country until we find the Professor's body.'

During the remainder of that never-to-be-forgotten night a party which grew in number as the hours wore on to dawn scoured the entire countryside for miles round. Towards five o'clock the rain suddenly broke over the marshes, and drenched us all to the skin, so that it was a sorry gathering that returned at daybreak to Barminster. The local police had taken charge of the laboratory, and urgent messages had been sent off to Scotland Yard; but when the London experts arrived on the scene we had nothing more to tell them than has already been recounted. Harborne, Doctor Davidson, and myself had devoted the whole of our attention to Spindle Lane and the immediate vicinity of the mysterious crime; but our exertions were not rewarded by the smallest discovery.

Such, then, were the extraordinary but inadequate data which were placed in the hands of the London investigators, and upon which they very naturally based a wholly erroneous theory.

This was the condition of affairs upon the night of the 16th, when Harborne suddenly marched into my rooms, and unceremoniously deposited a dripping leather case, bearing the initials J. B. S., in my fender.

'Any news?' I cried, springing up.

'Not likely to be!' he answered. 'You might almost think these detectives have assumed all along that they are dealing with a case of the supernatural, and have, in consequence, overlooked certain clues which, had the circumstances been less bizarre, they would have instantly followed up.'

'You have some theory, then? What is in this bag?'

There was that in Harborne's manner which I could not altogether fathom as he evasively replied:

'Leaving the bag for a moment, let me just place the facts before you as they really are, and not as they appear to be. I must confess that, last night, I was more than half inclined to agree with the detectives; and it is eminently probable that but for one thing I should now be in complete agreement with the other investigators— who believe that some huge and unknown insect entered the laboratory and bore away the Professor! When I left you and Doctor Davidson yesterday morning I immediately went in search of Jamieson, and found him—three-parts intoxicated. As you have probably heard, he has since become wholly so, and the detectives have utterly failed to extract a sane word from him. In this respect, therefore, I was first in the field; and from him I obtained the one additional clue needed. About one a.m.—an hour after Brayme-Skepley had entered the laboratory—Jamieson came to the door of his lodge, and saw a light in the end house of Spindle Lane.'

'But surely the police have questioned all the tenants in Spindle Lane?'

'The end house is empty.'

'Have they examined it?'

'Certainly. But they merely did so as a matter of form: they had no *particular* reason for doing so. As a result they found nothing. What there was to find I had found before their arrival on the scene.'

'I am afraid I don't altogether follow.'

'Wait a minute. When I extracted from the porter the fact that he had seen a light in this house the entire affair immediately assumed a different aspect. The key to the mystery was in my hands. I went round into Spindle Lane, and surveyed the end house from the front. It was evidently empty, for the ground-floor windows were almost without glass.

'As I did not want to take anyone into my confidence at this stage of the proceedings it was impracticable to apply for the key, but upon passing round to the north I found that there was a back door with three stone steps leading up from the water's edge. I looked about for some means of gaining these steps—for I did not wish to excite attention by getting out a college boat. In the end I jumped for it. I got off badly from the muddy ground, for the rain was coming down in torrents, but, nevertheless, I landed on the bottom step—off which I promptly shot into the river!

'As I was already drenched to the skin this mattered little, and, notwithstanding my condition, a thrill of gratification warmed me on finding the door to be merely latched. Just as a party of six which had been scouring the east valley appeared upon the opposite bank I entered, and shut the door behind me.'

'Well—what then?'

'I went up to the room overlooking the laboratory—for, although no one seems to have attached any particular importance to the circumstance, from the window of this room you could, if the laboratory window were bigger, easily spring through.'

'And what did you find there?'

'The origin of the mysterious light.'

'Which was?'

'A match! Now, you will agree with me that green spiders do not use matches. Inference: That some human being had been in the room on the night of the murder, and had struck a match, which had been observed by Jamieson. There were also certain marks which considerably mystified me at first. On the thick grime of the window-ledge—inside—it was evident that a board had rested. That is to say, a board had been, for some reason, placed across the room. The mortar had fallen off the wall in one corner, and here I found on the floor an impression as though a box had stood on end there— evidently to support the other extremity of the board. My next discovery was even more interesting. I found traces of finger marks— which, by the way, I removed before leaving—on the sill and around the inside of the window-frame. Someone had come in by the window!

'But I remembered that, until I opened it to investigate, the window had been closed. Therefore the mysterious visitor had closed it behind him. Since his bloodstained finger marks testified to the state of his hands on entering, how had he opened the window from outside—a somewhat difficult operation—and yet left no traces upon the sash? for there were none. I assumed, by way of argument, that he had opened the window from the inside.

'I had now constructed a hypothetical assassin who had got into the end house in Spindle Lane, entered the bacteriological laboratory, murdered the Professor, returned through the window, and struck a match—for there were traces of blood upon it. Why had he come back to the room, and by what means had he reached the window of the laboratory? It was upon subsequently examining the laboratory (for the local officer in charge, being an acquaintance, raised no objection to my doing so) that two points became clear. First: That the window could never have been opened from outside. Second: The probability that a plank had been placed across—the same plank that had been used for some other mysterious purpose!

'Working, then, upon this theory, it immediately became evident that a plank could only have been placed in position from one of the windows. Here I had an enlightening inspiration. My assassin must have entered the house from the riverside, as I had done! How had he conveyed the plank into the place? A boat! You will mark that this was all pure supposition. Nevertheless, I determined, for the moment, to assume that a plank had been used.

'It was with this idea before me that I made my examination of the laboratory, and the various facts, viewed in this new light, began to assume their proper places. The horrible marks, suggestive of an incredible assailant, which so horrified us when we first observed them, were less inexplicable when regarded as *intentional* and not accidental! To consider the handmark upon the ceiling, for example, as incidental to a struggle for life, pointed to an opponent possessing attributes usually associated with insects; but it was the easiest thing in the world for a tall man, standing upon a table, to imprint such a mark! This startling revelation, taken in conjunction with the locked door and the impossibility of anyone entering the place from the quadrangle, brought me face to face with a plausible solution of the mystery.

'The elaborate nature of the affair pointed to premeditation, and the fact that the missing man had locked the door was most significant. Who could have known that he would be there upon this particular night, and why had he failed to unlock the door? For you will remember that the key was in the lock. Then, again, how did it come about that his cries for assistance did not arouse the people living in Spindle Lane?

'These ideas carried me to the second stage of my theory, and I assumed that a plank had been placed in position for the purpose of exit from, and not of entrance to, the laboratory! My final conclusion was as follows:

'Professor Brayme-Skepley entered the end house in Spindle Lane from a boat—which he obtained at Long's boathouse—bearing a plank and some kind of box or case. The plank he placed from window to window, the case upon the floor of the house in the Lane. He then returned to his boat, and landed beside the house. Entering the quadrangle, as we know, he went into the laboratory, and locked the door. His next proceeding was to smash everything breakable, wrench the window from its fastenings, and imprint the weird tracks and marks which proved so misleading. The book beneath the skylight and the lancet in the woodwork were the artistic touches of a man of genius. By this time it was close upon one o'clock, and, desirous of ascertaining whether his apparatus for bringing about the spider illusion was ready for instant use, he crawled from window to window. It was his match that Jamieson saw from the lodge door, and had Jamieson been a man of mettle the whole plot must have failed.

'He then, probably, grew very impatient whilst awaiting the coming of Jamieson, but he heard him ultimately, and lay in the light of the lamps as we have heard. All fell out as he had planned. Jamieson climbed on to the dust-box and looked into the laboratory; then he ran for the window ladder, as a reasoning mind would have easily foreseen he would do. The Professor, during his absence, broke the lamps, climbed along his plank, and pulled it after him.'

I had listened with breathless interest so far, but I now broke in: 'How about the spider?'

'Perfectly simple!' answered Harborne. 'Allow me.'

He reached down for the leather case and unstrapped it. From within he took . . . a magic lantern!

'What!' I exclaimed. 'A magic lantern?'

'With cinematograph attachment! Here, you see, is the film—not improved by having been in the river. Some kind of South American spider, is it not?—beautifully coloured and on a black ground. The plank, supported upon the window-ledge and the upturned case, did duty for a table, and as Jamieson went up the ladder, and surveyed the place from the south-east, this was directed from the window of the end house across the few intervening yards of Spindle Lane and through the open laboratory window on to the north-west corner of the wall.

'The beam from the lens would be hidden by the partition and only the weird image visible from the porter's point of view—though had he mounted further up the ladder and glanced over the wall he must have observed the ray of light across the lane. The familiar illuminated circle, usually associated with such demonstrations, was ingeniously eliminated by having a *transparent* photograph on an *opaque* ground. The Professor then retreated to the back door and hauled up his boat by the painter—which he would, of course, have attached there. He pulled upstream to return his boat and to sink his apparatus. He was probably already disguised—his fur coat would have concealed this from Jamieson.'

I stared at Harborne in very considerable amazement.

'You are apparently surprised,' he said with a smile; 'but there is really nothing very remarkable in it all. I have not bored you with all the little details that led to the conclusion, nor related how I suffered a second ducking in leaving the end house; but my solution was no more than a plausible hypothesis until a happy inspiration, born of nothing more palpable than my own imaginings, led me to search for and find the cinematograph. You are about to ask where I found it: I answer, in the deep hole above Long's boat-house where Jimmy Baker made his big catch last summer. Brayme-Skepley, being a man of very high reasoning powers, would, I argued, deposit it *up* and not downstream, knowing that the river would be dragged. He would furthermore put it in the hole, so that the current should not carry it below college.

'There are, however, still one or two points that need clearing up. As to the blood, that offered no insurmountable difficulty to a physiologist; and, by Jove!' . . . He suddenly plunged his hand into the case. . . . 'This rubber ring from a soda-water bottle, ingeniously mounted upon a cane handle, accounts for the mysterious tracks. The point to which I particularly allude is the object of the Professor's disappearance.'

'I think,' I said, 'that I can offer a suggestion. He found, too late to withdraw, that his famous theory had a flaw in it, and could devise no less elaborate means of hiding the fact and at the same time of so destroying his apparatus as to leave no trace whereby his great reputation could be marred.'

'That is my own idea,' agreed Harborne. 'For which reason I have carefully covered such very few tracks as he left, and have decided that this handsome case, with its tell-tale inscription—J. B. S.—must be destroyed. My conclusions are not for the world, which is at perfect liberty to believe that Professor Brayme-Skepley was carried off by an unclassified aptera!'

And so, somewhere or other, Professor Brayme-Skepley is pursuing his distinguished career under a new name, while Harborne allows the world to persist in its opinion.

The Clue of the Silver Spoons

ROBERT BARR

When the card was brought in to me, I looked upon it with some misgiving, for I scented a commercial transaction; and although such cases are lucrative enough, nevertheless I, Eugene Valmont, formerly high in the service of the French Government, do not care to be connected with them. They usually pertain to sordid business affairs that present little that is of interest to a man, who, in his time, has dealt with subtle questions of diplomacy upon which the welfare of nations sometimes turned.

The name of Bentham Gibbes is familiar to everyone, connected as it is with the much-advertised pickles, whose glaring announcements in crude crimson and green strike the eye everywhere in England, and shock the artistic taste wherever seen. Me, I have never tasted them, and shall not, so long as a French restaurant remains open in London; but I doubt not they are as pronounced to the palate as their advertisement is distressing to the eye.

If, then, this gross pickle manufacturer expected me to track down those who were infringing upon the recipes for making his so-called sauces, chutneys, and the like, he would find himself mistaken, for I was now in a position to pick and choose my cases, and a case of pickles did not allure me. 'Beware of imitations,' said the advertisement, 'none genuine without a facsimile of the signature of Bentham Gibbes.' Ah, well, not for me were either the pickles or the tracking of imitators. A forged cheque: yes, if you like, but the forged signature of Mr Gibbes on a pickle bottle was not for me. Nevertheless, I said to Armand:

'Show the gentleman in,' and he did so.

To my astonishment there entered a young man, quite correctly dressed in dark frock-coat, faultless waistcoat and trousers, that proclaimed the Bond Street tailor. When he spoke his voice and language were those of a gentleman.

'Monsieur Valmont?' he enquired.

'At your service,' I replied, bowing and waving my hand as Armand placed a chair for him and withdrew.

'I am a barrister, with chambers in the Temple,' began Mr Gibbes, 'and for some days a matter has been troubling me about which I have now come to seek your advice, your name having been suggested by a friend in whom I confided.'

'Am I acquainted with him?' I asked.

'I think not,' replied Mr Gibbes; 'he also is a barrister with chambers in the same building as my own. Lionel Dacre is his name.'

'I never heard of him.'

'Very likely not. Nevertheless, he recommended you as a man who could keep his own counsel; and if you take up this case I desire the utmost secrecy preserved, whatever may be the outcome.'

I bowed, but made no protestation. Secrecy is a matter of course with me.

The Englishman paused for a few moments, as if he expected fervent assurances; then he went on with no trace of disappointment on his countenance at not receiving them.

'On the night of the twenty-third I gave a little dinner to six friends of mine in my own rooms. I may say that so far as I am aware they are all gentlemen of unimpeachable character. On the night of the dinner I was detained later than I expected at a reception, and in driving to the Temple was still further delayed by a block of traffic in Piccadilly, so that when I arrived at my chambers there was barely time for me to dress and receive my guests. My man Johnson had everything laid out ready for me in my dressing-room, and as I passed through to it, I hurriedly flung off the coat I was wearing and carelessly left it over the back of a chair in the dining-room, where neither Johnson nor myself noticed it until my attention was called to it after the dinner was over, and everyone was rather jolly with wine.

'This coat had an inside pocket. Usually any frock-coat I wear at an afternoon reception has not an inside pocket, but I had been rather on the rush all day. My father is a manufacturer, whose name may be familiar to you, and I am on the directors' board of his company. On this occasion I had to take a cab from the city to the reception I spoke of, and had not time to go and change at my rooms. The reception was a somewhat Bohemian affair, extremely interesting, of course, but not too particular as to costume, so I went as I was. In this inside pocket rested a thin package, composed of two pieces of pasteboard, and between them five twenty-pound Bank of England notes, folded lengthways, and held in place between the pasteboards by an elastic rubber band.

'I had thrown the coat over the chair in such a way that the inside pocket was exposed, and the ends of the notes plainly recognizable. Over the coffee and cigars one of my guests laughingly called attention to what he termed my vulgar display of wealth, and Johnson, in some confusion at having neglected to put away the coat, now picked it up and took it to the reception room, where the wraps of my guests lay about promiscuously. He should, of course, have placed it in my wardrobe, but he said afterwards he thought it belonged to the guest who had spoken. You see, he was in my dressing-room when I threw my coat on the chair in making my way thither, and, of course, he had not noticed the coat in the hurry of arriving guests, otherwise he would have put it where it belonged. After everybody had gone, Johnson came to me and said the coat was there, but the package was missing, nor has any trace of it been found since that night.'

'The dinner was fetched in from outside, I suppose?'

'Yes.'

'How many waiters served it?'

'Two. They are men who have often been in my employ before; but, apart from that, they had left my chambers before the incident of the coat happened.'

'Neither of them went into the reception room, I take it?'

'No. I am certain that not even suspicion can attach to either of the waiters.'

'Your man Johnson——'

'Has been with me for years. He could easily have stolen much more than the hundred pounds if he had wished to do so, but I have never known him to take a penny that did not belong to him.'

'Will you favour me with the names of your guests, Mr Gibbes?'

'Viscount Stern sat at my right hand, and at my left Lord Templemore; Sir John Sanclere next to him, and Angus McKeller next to Sanclere. After Viscount Stern was Lionel Dacre, and at his right was Vincent Innis.'

On a sheet of paper I had written the names of the guests, and noted their places at the table.

'Which guest drew your attention to the money?'

'Lionel Dacre.'

'Is there a window looking out from the reception room?'

'Two of them.'

'Were they fastened on the night of the dinner party?'

'I could not be sure; Johnson would know, very likely. You are hinting at the possibility of a thief coming in through a reception room window while we were somewhat noisy over our wine. I think such a solution highly improbable. My rooms are on the third floor, and a thief would scarcely venture to make an entrance when he could not but know there was a company being entertained. Besides this, the coat was there but an hour or so, and it seems to me whoever stole those notes knew where they were.'

'That sounds reasonable,' I had to admit. 'Have you spoken to anyone of your loss?'

'To no one but Dacre, who recommended me to see you. Oh, yes, and to Johnson, of course.'

I could not help noting that this was the fourth or fifth time Dacre's name had come up during our conversation.

'Why to Dacre?' I asked.

'Oh, well, you see, he occupies chambers in the same building, on the ground floor. He is a very good fellow, and we are by way of being firm friends. Then it was he who had called attention to the money, so I thought he should know the sequel.'

'How did he take your news?'

'Now that you call attention to the fact, he seemed slightly troubled. I should like to say, however, that you must not be misled by that. Lionel Dacre could no more steal than he could lie.'

'Did he seem surprised when you mentioned the theft?'

Bentham Gibbes paused a moment before replying, knitting his brows in thought.

'No,' he said at last; 'and, come to think of it, it almost appears as if he had been expecting my announcement.'

'Doesn't that strike you as rather strange, Mr Gibbes?'

'Really, my mind is in such a whirl, I don't know what to think. But it's perfectly absurd to suspect Dacre. If you knew the man you would understand what I mean. He comes of an excellent family, and he is—oh! he is Lionel Dacre, and when you have said that, you have made any suspicion absurd.'

'I suppose you had the rooms thoroughly searched. The packet didn't drop out and remain unnoticed in some corner?'

'No; Johnson and myself examined every inch of the premises.'

'Have you the numbers of the notes?'

'Yes; I got them from the bank next morning. Payment was stopped, and so far not one of the five has been presented. Of course, one or more may have been cashed at some shop, but none have been offered to any of the banks.'

'A twenty-pound note is not accepted without scrutiny, so the chances are the thief may have some difficulty in disposing of them.'

'As I told you, I don't mind the loss of the money at all. It is the uncertainty, the uneasiness, caused by the incident which troubles me. You will comprehend this when I say that if you are good enough to interest yourself in this case, I shall be disappointed if your fee does not exceed the amount I have lost.'

Mr Gibbes rose as he said this, and I accompanied him to the door, assuring him that I should do my best to solve the mystery. Whether he sprang from pickles or not, I realized he was a polished and generous gentleman, who estimated the services of a professional expert like myself at their true value.

I shall not give the details of my researches during the following few days, because the trend of them must be gone over in the remarkable interview I had somewhat later, and there is little use in repeating myself. Suffice it to say, then, that an examination of the rooms and a close cross-questioning of Johnson satisfied me that he and the two waiters were innocent. I was also convinced that no thief made his way through the window, and I came to the conclusion that the notes were stolen by one of the guests.

Further investigation convinced me that the thief was no other than Lionel Dacre, the only one of the six in pressing need of money at that time.

I had Dacre shadowed, and during one of his absences made the acquaintance of his man Hopper, a surly, impolite brute who accepted my golden sovereign quickly enough, but gave me little in exchange for it. But while I conversed with him, there arrived in the passage where we were talking together, a large case of champagne, bearing one of the best-known names in the trade, and branded as being of the vintage of '78. Now, I know that the product of Camelot Frères is not bought as cheaply as British beer, and I also had learned that two short weeks before Mr Lionel Dacre was at his wits' end for money. Yet he was still the same briefless barrister he had ever been.

On the morning after my unsatisfactory conversation with his man Hopper, I was astonished to receive the following note, written on a dainty correspondence card:

> 3 and 4 Vellum Buildings,
> Inner Temple, E.C.

Mr Lionel Dacre presents his compliments to Monsieur Eugene Valmont, and would be obliged if Monsieur Valmont could make it convenient to call upon him in his chambers tomorrow morning at eleven.

Had the man become aware that he was being shadowed, or did the surly servant inform him of the enquiries made? I was soon to know. I called punctually at eleven next morning, and was received with charming urbanity by Mr Dacre himself. The taciturn Hopper had evidently been sent away for the occasion.

'My dear Monsieur Valmont, I am delighted to meet you,' said the young man with more effusiveness than I had ever noticed in an Englishman before, although his very next words supplied an explanation that did not occur to me until afterwards as somewhat far-fetched. 'I believe we are by way of being countrymen, and, therefore, although the hour is early, I hope you will allow me to offer you some of that bottled sunshine of the year '78, from la belle France, to whose prosperity and honour we shall drink together. For such a toast any hour is propitious,' and to my amazement he brought forth from the case I had seen arrive two days before a bottle of that superb vintage.

'Now,' said I to myself, 'it is going to be difficult to keep a clear head if the aroma of that nectar rises to the brain. But, tempting as is the cup, I shall drink sparingly, and hope he may not be so judicious.'

Sensitive, I already experienced the charm of his personality, and well understood the friendship Mr Bentham Gibbes felt for him. But I saw the trap spread before me. He expected, under the influence of champagne and courtesy, to extract a promise from me which I must find myself unable to give.

'Sir, you interest me by claiming kinship with France. I had understood that you belonged to one of the oldest families of England.'

'Ah, England!' he cried, with an expressive gesture of outspreading hands truly Parisian in its significance. 'The trunk belongs to

England, of course, but the root—ah! the root, Monsieur Valmont, penetrated the soil from which this vine of the gods has been drawn.'

Then, filling my glass and his own, he cried:

'To France, which my family left in the year 1066!'

I could not help laughing at his fervent ejaculation.

'1066! Ah, that is a long time ago, Mr Dacre.'

'In years, perhaps; in feelings but a day. My forefathers came over to steal, and, Lord! how well they accomplished it! They stole the whole country—something like a theft, say I—under that Prince of robbers well named the Conqueror. In our secret hearts we all admire a great thief, and if not a great one, then an expert one, who covers his tracks so perfectly that the hounds of justice are baffled in attempting to follow them. Now, even you, Monsieur Valmont—I can see you are the most generous of men, with a lively sympathy found to perfection only in France—even you must suffer a pang of regret when you lay a thief by the heels who has done his task deftly.'

'I fear, Mr Dacre, you credit me with a magnanimity to which I dare not lay claim. The criminal is a danger to society.'

'True, true; you are in the right, Monsieur Valmont. Still, admit there are cases that would touch you tenderly. For example, a man, ordinarily honest; a great need; a sudden opportunity. He takes that of which another has abundance, and he, nothing. What then, Monsieur Valmont? Is the man to be sent to perdition for a momentary weakness?'

His words astonished me. Was I on the verge of hearing a confession? It almost amounted to that already.

'Mr Dacre,' I said, 'I cannot enter into the subtleties you pursue. My duty is to find the criminal.'

'You are in the right, Monsieur Valmont, and I am enchanted to find so sensible a head on French shoulders. Although you are a more recent arrival, if I may say so, than myself, you nevertheless already give utterance to sentiments which do honour to England. It is your duty to hunt down the criminal. Very well. In that I think I can aid you, so have taken the liberty of requesting your attendance here this morning. Let me fill your glass again, Monsieur Valmont.'

'No more, I beg of you, Mr Dacre.'

'What, do you think the receiver is as bad as the thief?'

I was so taken aback at his remark that I suppose my face showed the amazement within me. But the young man merely laughed with apparently free-hearted enjoyment, poured more wine in his own glass, and tossed it off. Not knowing what to say, I changed the trend of conversation.

'Mr Gibbes said you had been kind enough to recommend me to his attention. May I ask how you came to hear of me?'

'Ah, who has not heard of the renowned Monsieur Valmont?' and as he said this, for the first time there began to grow a suspicion in my mind that he was chaffing me, as it is called in England, a procedure which I cannot endure. Indeed, if this young man practised it in my own country he would find himself with a duel on his hands before he had gone far. However, the next instant his voice resumed its original fascination, and I listened to it as to some delicious melody.

'I have only to mention my cousin, Lady Gladys Dacre, and you will at once understand why I recommended you to my friend. The case of Lady Gladys, you will remember, required a delicate touch which is not always to be had in this land of England, except when those who possess the gift do us the honour to sojourn with us.'

I noticed that my glass was again filled, and as I bowed my acknowledgements of his compliment, I indulged in another sip of the delicious wine; and then I sighed, for I began to realize it was going to be difficult for me, in spite of my disclaimer, to tell this man's friend he had stolen the money.

All this time he had been sitting on the edge of the table, while I occupied a chair at its end. He sat there in careless fashion, swinging a foot to and fro. Now he sprang to the floor and drew up a chair, placing on the table a blank sheet of paper. Then he took from the mantelshelf a packet of letters, and I was astonished to see they were held together by two bits of cardboard and a rubber band similar to the combination that had held the folded banknotes. With great nonchalance he slipped off the rubber band, threw it and the pieces of cardboard on the table before me, leaving the documents loose to his hand.

'Now, Monsieur Valmont,' he cried jauntily, 'you have been occupied for several days on this case—the case of my dear friend, Bentham Gibbes, who is one of the best fellows in the world.'

'He said the same of you, Mr Dacre.'

'I am gratified to hear it. Would you mind letting me know to what point your researches have led you?'

'They have led me to a direction rather than to a point.'

'Ah! In the direction of a man, of course?'

'Certainly.'

'Who is he?'

'Will you pardon me if I decline to answer you at the present moment?'

'That means you are not sure.'

'It may mean, Mr Dacre, that I am employed by Mr Gibbes, and do not feel at liberty to disclose to another the results of my quest without his permission.'

'But Mr Bentham Gibbes and I are entirely at one in this matter. Perhaps you are aware that I am the only person with whom he discussed the case besides yourself.'

'That is undoubtedly true, Mr Dacre; still, you see the difficulty of my position.'

'Yes, I do, and so shall not press you further. But I have also been interesting myself, in a purely amateurish way, of course. You would, perhaps, have no disinclination to learn whether my deductions agree with yours.'

'Not in the least. I should be very glad to know the conclusion at which you have arrived. May I ask if you suspect anyone in particular?'

'Yes, I do.'

'Will you name him?'

'No, I shall copy the admirable reticence you yourself have shown. And now let us attack this mystery in a sane and businesslike manner. You have already examined the room. Well, here is a rough sketch of it. There is the table; in this corner the chair on which the coat was flung. Here sat Gibbes at the head of the table. Those on the left-hand side had their backs to the chair. I, being in the centre to the right, saw the chair, the coat, and the notes, and called attention to them. Now our first duty is to find a motive. If it were a murder, our motive might be hatred, revenge, robbery, what you like. As it is simply the stealing of money, the man must have been either a born thief, or else some hitherto innocent person pressed to the crime by great necessity. Do you agree with me, Monsieur Valmont?'

'Perfectly. You follow exactly the line of my own reasoning.'

'Very well. It is unlikely that a born thief was one of Mr Gibbes' guests. Therefore we are reduced to look for a man under the spur of necessity—a man who has no money of his own, but who must raise a certain amount, let us say by a certain date, if we can find such a man in that company. Do you not agree with me that he is likely to be the thief?'

'Yes, I do.'

'Then let us start our process of elimination. Out goes Viscount Stern, a man with twenty thousand acres of land, and nobody quite knows what income. I mark off the name of Lord Templemere, one of His Majesty's judges, entirely above suspicion. Next Sir John Sanclare; he also is rich, but Vincent Innis is still richer, so the pencil obliterates his name. Now we have Angus McKeller, an author of some note, as you are well aware, deriving a good income from his books, and a better one from his plays; a canny Scot, so we may rub his name from our paper and our memory. How do my erasures correspond with yours, Monsieur Valmont?'

'They correspond exactly, Mr Dacre.'

'I am flattered to hear it. There remains one name untouched; Mr Lionel Dacre, the descendant, as we have said, of robbers.'

'I have not said so, Mr Dacre.'

'Ah, my dear Valmont, the politeness of your country asserts itself. Let us not be deluded, but follow our inquiry wherever it leads. I suspect Lionel Dacre. What do you know of his circumstances before the dinner of the twenty-third?'

As I made no reply, he looked up at me with his frank boyish face illumined with a winning smile.

'You know nothing of his circumstances?' he asked.

'It grieves me to state that I do. Mr Lionel Dacre was penniless on the night of the dinner on the twenty-third.'

'Oh, don't exaggerate, Monsieur Valmont,' cried Dacre, with a laugh, 'he had one sixpence, two pennies, and a halfpenny. How did you know he was penniless?'

'I knew he ordered a case of champagne from the London representative of Camelot Frères, and was refused unless he paid the money down.'

'Quite right; and then when you were talking to Hopper you saw the case of champagne delivered. Excellent, excellent, Monsieur Valmont. But will a man steal, think you, to supply himself with even so delicious a wine as this we have been tasting—and, by the way, forgive my neglect. Allow me to fill your glass, Monsieur Valmont.'

'Not another drop, if you will excuse me, Mr Dacre.'

'Ah, yes, champagne should not be mixed with evidence. When we have finished, perhaps. What further proof have you?'

'I have proof that Mr Dacre was threatened with bankruptcy, if on the twenty-fourth he did not pay a bill of seventy-eight pounds that had long been outstanding. I have proof that this was paid, not on the twenty-fourth, but on the twenty-sixth. Mr Dacre had gone to the solicitor and assured him he would have the money on that date, whereupon he was given two days' grace.'

'Ah, well, he was entitled to three, you know, in law. Yes, there, Monsieur Valmont, you touch the fatal point. The threat of bankruptcy will drive a man in Dacre's position to almost any crime. Bankruptcy to a barrister spells ruin. It means a career blighted; it means a life buried with little chance of resurrection. I see you grasp the supreme importance of that bit of evidence. The case of champagne is as nothing compared with it; and this reminds me that in the crisis I shall take another sip, with your permission. Sure you won't join me?'

'Not at this juncture, Mr Dacre.'

'I envy your moderation. Here's to the success of our search, Monsieur Valmont.'

I felt sorry for the gay young fellow as with smiling face he drank the champagne.

'Now, monsieur,' he went on, 'I am amazed to learn how much you have found out. Really, I think tradespeople, solicitors, and all such should keep better guard on their tongues than they do. Nevertheless, these documents I have at my elbow, and which I expected would surprise you, are merely the letters and receipts. Here is the letter from the solicitor threatening me with bankruptcy; here is his receipt dated the twenty-sixth; here is the refusal of the wine merchant, and here is his receipt for the money. Here are smaller bills liquidated. With my pencil we will add them up. Seventy-eight pounds bulks large. We add the smaller items, and it totals ninety-three pounds, seven shillings, and fourpence. Let us now examine my purse. Here is a five-pound note; there is a minted sovereign. Here is twelve and sixpence in silver; here is twopence in coppers. Now the purse is empty. Let us add this to the amount on the paper. Do my eyes deceive me, or is the total exactly a hundred pounds? There is the stolen money accounted for.'

'Pardon me, Mr Dacre,' I said, 'but there is still a sovereign on the mantelpiece.'

Dacre threw back his head, and laughed with greater heartiness than I had yet known him to indulge in during our short acquaintance.

'By Jove!' he cried, 'you've got me there. I'd forgotten entirely about that pound on the mantelpiece, which belongs to you.'

'To me? Impossible!'

'It does, and cannot interfere in the least with our hundred pound calculation. That is the sovereign you gave to my man, Hopper, who, believing me hard pressed, took it that I might have the enjoyment of it. Hopper belongs to our family, or the family belongs to him, I am never sure which. You must have missed in him the deferential bearing of a man-servant in Paris, yet he is true gold, like the sovereign you bestowed upon him, and he bestowed upon me. Now here, monsieur, is the evidence of the theft, together with the rubber band and two pieces of cardboard. Ask my friend Gibbes to examine them minutely. They are all at your disposition, monsieur, and you will learn how much easier it is to deal with the master than with the servant when you wish information. All the gold you possess would not have wrung these incriminating documents from old Hopper. I had to send him away today to the West End, fearing that in his brutal British way he might have assaulted you if he got an inkling of your mission.'

'Mr Dacre,' said I slowly, 'you have thoroughly convinced me——'

'I thought I would,' he interrupted with a laugh.

'——that you did not take the money.'

'Oh, this is a change of wind, surely. Many a man has been hanged through a chain of circumstantial evidence much weaker than this which I have exhibited to you. Don't you see the subtlety of my action? Ninety-nine persons in a hundred would say, "No man could be such a fool as to put Valmont on his track, and then place in Valmont's hands such striking evidence." But there comes in my craftiness. Of course the rock you run up against will be Gibbes' incredulity. The first question he will ask you may be this: "Why did not Dacre come and borrow the money from me?" Now there you have a certain weakness in your chain of evidence. I know perfectly well that Gibbes would lend me the money, and he knew perfectly well that if I were pressed to the wall I should ask him.'

'Mr Dacre,' said I, 'you have been playing with me. I should resent that with most men, but whether it is your own genial manner, or the effect of this excellent champagne, or both together, I forgive you. But I am convinced of another thing. You know who took the money.'

'I don't know, but I suspect.'

'Will you tell me whom you suspect?'

'That would not be fair, but I shall now take the liberty of filling your glass with champagne.'

'I am your guest, Mr Dacre.'

'Admirably answered, monsieur,' he replied, pouring out the wine; 'and now I shall give you the clue. Find out all about the story of the silver spoons.'

'The story of the silver spoons? What silver spoons?'

'Ah, that is the point. You step out of the Temple into Fleet Street, seize by the shoulder the first man you meet, and ask him to tell you about the silver spoons. There are but two men and two spoons concerned. When you learn who those two men are, you will know that one of them did not take the money, and I give you my assurance that the other did.'

'You speak in mystery, Mr Dacre.'

'But certainly, for I am speaking to Monsieur Engene Valmont.'

'I echo your words, sir. Admirably answered. You put me on my mettle, and I flatter myself that I see your kindly drift. You wish me to solve the mystery of this stolen money. Sir, you do me honour, and I drink to your health.'

'To yours, monsieur,' said Lionel Dacre, 'and here is a further piece of information which my friend Gibbes would never have given you. When he told me the money was gone, I cried in the anguish of impending bankruptcy: "I wish to goodness I had it!" Whereupon he immediately compelled me to accept his cheque for a hundred pounds, of which, as I have shown you, alas! only six pounds twelve and eightpence remains.'

On leaving Mr Dacre I took a hansom to a café in Regent Street, which is a passable imitation of similar places of refreshment in Paris. There, calling for a cup of black coffee, I sat down to think. The clue of the silver spoons! He had laughingly suggested that I should take by the shoulders the first man I met, and ask him what the story of the silver spoons was. This course naturally struck me as absurd. Nevertheless, it contained a hint. I must ask somebody, and that the right person, to tell me the tale of the silver spoons.

Under the influence of the black coffee, I reasoned it out in this way. On the night of the twenty-third some one of the six guests there present stole a hundred pounds, but Dacre had said that one of the actors in the silver spoon episode was the actual thief. That person, then, must have been one of Mr Gibbes' guests at the dinner of the twenty-third. Probably two of the guests were the participators in the silver spoon comedy, but be that as it may, it followed that one at least of the men around Mr Gibbes' table knew the episode of the silver spoons.

Perhaps Bentham Gibbes himself was cognizant of it. It followed, therefore, that the easiest plan was to question each of the men who partook of that dinner. Yet if only one knew about the spoons, that one must also have some idea that these spoons formed the clue which attached him to the crime of the twenty-third, in which case he was little likely to divulge what he knew, and that to an entire stranger. Of course I might go to Dacre himself and demand the story of the silver spoons, but this would be a confession of failure on my part, and I rather dreaded Lionel Dacre's hearty laughter when I admitted that the mystery was too much for me. Besides this, I was very well aware of the young man's kindly intentions towards me. He wished me to unravel the coil myself, and so I determined not to go to him except as a last resource.

I resolved to begin with Mr Gibbes, and, finishing my coffee, got again into a hansom and drove back to the Temple. I found Mr Gibbes in his room, and after greeting me, his first enquiry was about the case.

'How are you getting on?' he asked.

'I think I am getting on fairly well,' I replied, 'and expect to finish in a day or two, if you will kindly tell me the story of the silver spoons.'

'The silver spoons?' he echoed, quite evidently not understanding me.

'There happened an incident in which two men were engaged, and this incident related to a pair of silver spoons. I want to get the particulars of that.'

'I haven't the slightest idea what you are talking about,' replied Gibbes, thoroughly bewildered. 'You will have to be more definite, I fear, if you are to get any help from me.'

'I cannot be more definite, because I have already told you all I know.'

'What bearing has all this on our own case?'

'I was informed that if I got hold of the clue of the silver spoons I should be in a fair way of setting our case.'

'Who told you that?'

'Mr Lionel Dacre.'

'Oh, does Dacre refer to his own conjuring?'

'I don't know, I'm sure. What was his conjuring?'

'A very clever trick he did one night at dinner here about two months ago.'

'Had it anything to do with silver spoons?'

'Well, it was silver spoons or silver forks, or something of that kind. I had entirely forgotten the incident. So far as I recollect at the moment, there was a sleight-of-hand man of great expertness in one of the music-halls, and the talk turned upon him. Then Dacre said the tricks he did were easy, and holding up a spoon or a fork, I don't remember which, he asserted his ability to make it disappear before our eyes, to be found afterwards in the clothing of someone there present. Several offered to make him a bet that he could do nothing of the kind, but he said he would bet with no one but Innis, who sat opposite him. Innis, with some reluctance, accepted the bet, and then Dacre, with a great show of the usual conjurer's gesticulations, spread forth his empty hands, and said we should find the spoon in Innis' pocket, and there, sure enough, it was. It was a clever trick, but we were never able to get him to repeat it.'

'Thank you very much, Mr Gibbes; I think I see daylight now.'

'If you do, you are cleverer than I, by a long chalk,' cried Bentham Gibbes, as I took my departure.

I went directly downstairs, and knocked at Mr Dacre's door once more. He opened the door himself, his man not yet having returned.

'Ah, monsieur,' he cried; 'back already? You don't mean to tell me you have so soon got to the bottom of the silver spoon entanglement?'

'I think I have, Mr Dacre. You were sitting at dinner opposite Mr Vincent Innis. You saw him conceal a silver spoon in his pocket. You probably waited for some time to understand what he meant by this, and as he did not return the spoon to its place, you proposed a conjuring trick, made the bet with him, and thus the spoon was returned to the table.'

'Excellent, excellent, monsieur! That is very nearly what occurred, except that I acted at once. I had had experiences with Mr Vincent Innis before. Never did he come to these rooms without my missing some little trinket after he was gone. I am not a man of many possessions, while Mr Innis is a very rich person, and so, if anything is taken, I have little difficulty in coming to a knowledge of my loss. Of course, I never mentioned these disappearances to him. They were all trivial, as I have said, and, so far as the silver spoon was concerned, it was of no great value either. But I thought the bet and the recovery of the spoon would teach him a lesson; it apparently has not done so. On the night of the twenty-third he sat at my right hand, as you will see by consulting your diagram of the table and the guests. I asked him a question twice to which he did not reply, and, looking at him, I was startled by the expression in his eyes. They were fixed on a distant corner of the room, and following his gaze I saw what he was looking at with such hypnotizing concentration.

'So absorbed was he in contemplation of the packet there so plainly exposed, that he seemed to be entirely oblivious of what was going on around him. I roused him from his trance by jocularly calling Gibbes' attention to the display of money. I expected in this way to save Innis from committing the act which he seemingly did commit. Imagine, then, the dilemma in which I was placed when Gibbes confided to me the morning after what had occurred the night before.

'I was positive that Innis had taken the money, yet I possessed no proof of it. I could not tell Gibbes, and I dare not speak to Innis. Of course, monsieur, you do not need to be told that Innis is not a thief in the ordinary sense of the word. He has no need to steal, and yet apparently cannot help doing so. I am sure that no attempt has been made to pass those notes. They are doubtless in his house at Kensington at this present moment. He is, in fact, a kleptomaniac, or a maniac of some sort. And now, Monsieur Valmont, was my hint regarding the silver spoons of any value to you?'

'Of the most infinite value, Mr Dacre.'

'Then let me make another suggestion. I leave it entirely to your bravery; a bravery which I confess I do not myself possess. Will you take a hansom, drive to Mr Innis' house in the Cromwell Road, confront him quietly, and ask for the return of the packet? I am anxious to know what will happen. If he hands it to you, as I expect he will, then you must tell Mr Gibbes the whole story.'

'Mr Dacre, your suggestion shall be immediately acted upon, and I thank you for your compliment to my courage.'

I found that Mr Innis inhabited a very grand house. After a time he

entered the study on the ground floor, to which I had been conducted. He held my card in his hand, and was looking at it with some
surprise.

'I think I have not the pleasure of knowing you, Mr Valmont,' he
said, courteously enough.

'No. I have called on a matter of business. I was once investigator
for the French Government, and now am doing private detective
work here in London.'

'Ah! And how is that supposed to interest me? I have nothing that I
wish investigated. I did not send for you, did I?'

'No, Mr Innis; I merely took the liberty of calling to ask you to let
me have the package you took out of Mr Bentham Gibbes' frock-coat
pocket on the night of the twenty-third.'

'He wishes it returned, does he?'

'Yes.'

Mr Innis calmly went to a desk, which he unlocked and opened,
displaying a veritable museum of trinkets of one sort and another.
Pulling out a small drawer, he took from it the packet containing the
five twenty-pound notes. Apparently it had never been undone. With
a smile he handed it to me.

'You will make my apologies to Mr Gibbes for not returning it
before. Tell him I have been unusually busy of late.'

'I shall not fail to do so,' said I, with a bow.

'Thanks so much. Good morning, Monsieur Valmont.'

'Good morning, Mr Innis.'

And so I returned the packet to Mr Bentham Gibbes, who pulled
the notes from between their pasteboard protection, and begged me
to accept them.

SOURCES

'The Purloined Letter' by Edgar Allan Poe (1809–49). *Tales*, ed. Evert A. Duyckinck (New York: Wiley & Putnam, 1845).

'The Murdered Cousin' by J[oseph] S[heridan] Le Fanu (1814–73). *Ghost Stories and Tales of Mystery* (Dublin and London: James McGlashan, William S. Orr & Co., 1851).

'Hunted Down' by Charles Dickens (1812–70). *New York Ledger* (20/27 Aug., 3 Sept. 1859); it later appeared in *All the Year Round* (4/11 Apr. 1860) but was not reprinted in Dickens's lifetime.

'Levison's Victim' by Mary Elizabeth Braddon (1835–1915). *Belgravia* (Jan. 1870); reprinted in *Weavers and Weft, and other tales* (John Maxwell, 3 vols., 1877).

'The Mystery at Number Seven' by Mrs Henry Wood (*née* Ellen Price, 1814–87). *The Argosy* (Jan.–Feb. 1877). Reprinted in *Johnny Ludlow, Sixth Series* (Macmillan, 1899).

'The Going Out of Alessandro Pozzone' by Richard Dowling (1846–98). *Belgravia* (Aug. 1878).

'Who Killed Zebedee?' by Wilkie Collins (1824–89). *Seaside Library* (26 Jan. 1881); reprinted (as 'Mr Policeman and the Cook') in *Little Novels* (Chatto & Windus, 3 vols., 1887).

'A Circumstantial Puzzle' by R[obert] E[dward] Francillon (1841–1919). From *Romances of the Law* (Chatto & Windus, 1889).

'The Mystery of Essex Stairs' by Sir Gilbert [Edward] Campbell (1838–99). *New Detective Stories* (Ward, Lock, Bowden & Co., n.d. [1891]).

'The Adventure of the Blue Carbuncle' by Sir Arthur Conan Doyle (1859–30). *Strand Magazine* (Jan. 1892); reprinted in *The Adventures of Sherlock Holmes* (George Newnes, 1892).

'The Great Ruby Robbery' by [Charles] Grant [Blairfindie] Allen (1848–99). *Strand Magazine* (Oct. 1892).

'The Sapient Monkey' by Headon Hill (Francis Edward Grainger, 1857–1927). *The Million* (22 Oct. 1892); reprinted in *Clues from a Detective's Camera* (Bristol: J. W. Arrowsmith, and London: Simpkin, Marshall, Hamilton, Kent & Co., n.d. [1893]).

'Cheating the Gallows' by Israel Zangwill (1864–1926). *The Idler* (Feb. 1893); reprinted in *The King of Schnorrers: Grotesques and Fantasies* (Heinemann, 1894).

'Drawn Daggers' by C[atherine] L[ouisa] Pirkis (d. 1910). *Ludgate Monthly* (June 1893); reprinted in *The Experiences of Loveday Brooke, Lady Detective* (Hutchinson, 1894).

'The Greenstone God and the Stockbroker' by Fergus Hume (1859–1932). *The Idler* (Jan. 1894); reprinted in *The Dwarf's Chamber, and other stories* (Ward, Lock, & Bowden, 1896).

'The Arrest of Captain Vandaleur' by L[illie] T[homasina] Meade (pseudonym of Elizabeth Thomasina Meade, later Mrs Toulmin Smith, 1854–1914) and Robert Eustace (pseudonym of Robert Eustace Barton, 1868–1943). *Harmsworth Magazine* (July 1894).

'The Accusing Shadow' by Harry Blyth (1852–98). *The Halfpenny Marvel*, No. 48 (3 Oct. 1894).

'The Ivy Cottage Mystery' by Arthur Morrison (1863–1945). *Windsor Magazine* (Jan. 1895); reprinted in *Chronicles of Martin Hewitt, Investigator* (Ward, Lock, & Bowden, 1895).

'The Azteck Opal' by Rodrigues Ottolengui (?1861–1937). *The Idler* (Apr. 1895); reprinted in *Final Proof* (New York: G. P. Putnam, 1898).

'The Long Arm' by Mary E[leanor] Wilkins (also known as Wilkins-Freeman, 1852–1930). *Chapman's Magazine of Fiction* (Aug. 1895); reprinted in *The Long Arm, and other detective stories*, by Mary E. Wilkins, George Ira Brett, Brander Matthews, and Roy Tellet [pseudonym of Albert Eubule Evans] (Chapman's Story Series No. 1: Chapman & Hall, 1895).

'The Case of Euphemia Raphash' by M[atthew] P[hipps] Shiel (1865–1947). *Chapman's Magazine of Fiction* (Dec. 1895).

'The Tin Box' by Herbert Keen. *The Idler* (Apr. 1896), part of a series of 'Chronicles of Elvira House'—a 'well-known boarding house in Baker Street'. I have been unable to find any information concerning the author, who does not appear in the British Library catalogue.

'Murder by Proxy' by M[atthias] McDonnell Bodkin (1850–1933). *Pearson's Weekly* (6 Feb. 1897), as part of series recounting the exploits of Alfred Juggins; for his appearance in book form the name of the detective was changed to *Paul Beck. The Rule of Thumb Detective* (C. Arthur Pearson, 1898).

'The Duchess of Wiltshire's Diamonds' by Guy Boothby (1867–1905). *Pearson's Magazine* (Feb. 1897); reprinted in *A Prince of Swindlers* (Ward, Lock, n.d. [1900]).

'The Story of The Spaniards, Hammersmith' by E. and H. Heron (Katherine O'Brien Ryall Prichard and [Vernon] Hesketh Prichard, 1876–

1922, mother and son writing team). *Pearson's Magazine* (Jan. 1898); reprinted in *Ghosts* (C. Arthur Pearson, 1899).

'The Lost Special' by Sir Arthur Conan Doyle. *Strand Magazine* (Aug. 1898); reprinted in *Round the Fire Stories* (Smith, Elder, 1908).

'The Banknote Forger' by C[harles] J[ohn] Cutcliffe Hyne (1865–1944). *Harmsworth Magazine* (Sept. 1899).

'A Warning in Red' by Victor L[orenzo] Whitechurch (1868–1933) and E. Conway. *Harmsworth Magazine* (Dec. 1899). Of Conway nothing seems to be known. It has been plausibly suggested to me that he was responsible for providing the plot outline. This seems to be the only instance of collaboration in Canon Whitechurch's prolific career as a short-story writer for the magazines.

'The Fenchurch Street Mystery' by Baroness E[mmuska] Orczy (1865–1947). *Royal Magazine* (May 1901), the first story in a series entitled 'London Mysteries', later reprinted as *The Old Man in the Corner* (Greening, 1909).

'The Green Spider' by Sax Rohmer (Arthur Henry Sarsfield Ward, 1883–1959; also wrote as Michael Furey). *Pearson's Magazine* (Oct. 1904), under the byline 'A. Sarsfield Ward'. Ward is best known as the creator of Fu Manchu.

'The Clue of the Silver Spoons' by Robert Barr (1850–1912). *Pearson's Magazine* (Dec. 1904); reprinted in *The Triumphs of Eugene Valmont* (Hurst & Blackett, 1906).

SELECT BIBLIOGRAPHY

Short-story Collections

Grant Allen, *An African Millionaire, and other stories* (1887)
Robert Barr, *The Triumphs of Eugine Valmont* (1906)
Arnold Bennett, *The Loot of Cities* (1905)
Matthias McDonnell Bodkin, *Paul Beck, the Rule of Thumb Detective* (1898)
—— *Dora Myrl, the Lady Detective* (1900)
Guy Boothby, *A Prince of Swindlers* (n.d. [1900])
Sir Gilbert Campbell, *New Detective Stories* (n.d. [1891])
Wilkie Collins, *The Queen of Hearts* (1859)
—— *Little Novels* (1887)
Hugh Conway [F. J. Fargus], *The Missing Will, and other stories* (1886)
Robert Curtis, *Curiosities of Detection* (1862)
Dick Donovan [J. E. Preston Muddock], *Who Poisoned Hetty Duncan, and other stories* (1890)
—— *A Detective's Triumphs* (1891)
—— *From Clue to Capture. Stories* (1893)
—— *Vincent Trill of the Detective Service* (1899)
—— *The Adventures of Tyler Tatlock* (1900)
Arthur Conan Doyle, *The Adventures of Sherlock Holmes* (1892)
—— *The Memoirs of Sherlock Holmes* (1894)
—— *The Return of Sherlock Holmes* (1905)
—— *His Last Bow* (1917)
—— *The Case-book of Sherlock Holmes* (1927)
—— *Round the Fire Stories* (1908)
Andrew Forrester Jnr, *Revelations of a Private Detective* (1863)
—— *Secret Service; or, Recollections of a City Detective* (1864)
—— *The Female Detective* (1864)
George Griffith, *Knaves of Diamonds* (1899)
Headon Hill [Francis Edward Grainger], *Clues from a Detective's Camera* (1894)
—— *Zambra the Detective* (1894)
E. W. Hornung, *Raffles* (1899)
William Hope Hodgson, *Carnacki, the Ghost-finder* (1913)
Fergus Hume, *The Dwarf's Chamber, and other stories* (1896)
—— *Hagar of the Pawn-shop, the Gypsy Detective* (1898)
J. S. Le Fanu, *Ghost Stories and Tales of Mystery* (1851)
L. T. Meade and Clifford Halifax, *Stories from the Diary of a Doctor* (1894)
Arthur Morrison, *Martin Hewitt, Investigator* (1894)

—— *Chronicles of Martin Hewitt* (1895)
—— *Adventures of Martin Hewitt* (1896)
—— *The Dorrington Deed-box* (1897)
Baroness [Emmuska] Orczy, *The Old Man in the Corner* (1909)
—— *Lady Molly of Scotland Yard* (1910)
Rodrigues Ottolengui, *Final Proof* (1898)
Max Pemberton, *Jewel Mysteries I Have Known* (1894)
Catherine Louisa Pirkis, *The Experiences of Loveday Brooke, Lady Detective* (1894)
Melville Davisson Post, *The Strange Schemes of Randolph Mason* (New York, 1896)
M. P. Shiel, *Prince Zaleski* (1895)
George R. Sims, *Memoirs of a Landlady* (1894)
—— *Dorcas Dene, Detective* (1897)
—— *Dorcas Dene, Detective*, 2nd series (1898)
—— *A Blind Marriage* (1901)
Mary E. Wilkins et al., *The Long Arm, and other detective stories* (1895)

Anthologies

E. F. Bleiler (ed.), *Treasury of Victorian Detective Stories* (1980)
Hugh Carleton Green (ed.), *The Rivals of Sherlock Holmes* (1970)
—— *More Rivals of Sherlock Holmes* (1971)
—— *The Crooked Counties: Further Rivals of Sherlock Holmes* (1973)

Bibliography and Criticism

Jacques Barzun and Wendell Hertig Taylor, *A Catalogue of Crime* (1971)
Bernard Benstock (ed.), *Essays on Detective Fiction* (1983)
T. J. Binyon, *'Murder Will Out'. The detective in fiction* (1989)
John Cawelti, *Adventure, Mystery and Romance* (1976)
Patricia Craig and Mary Cadogan, *The Lady Investigates* (1981)
David I. Grossvogel, *Mystery and its Fictions. From Oedipus to Agatha Christie* (1979)
Howard Haycraft, *Murder for Pleasure. The life and times of the detective story* (1942, 1951)
—— *The Art of the Mystery Story* (1946)
Allen J. Hubin, *Crime Fiction 1749–1980. A comprehensive bibliography* (1984)
H. R. F. Keating (ed.), *Whodunnit? A Guide to Crime, Suspense and Spy Fiction* (1982)
[Eric Osborne], *Victorian Detective Fiction. A catalogue of the collection made by Dorothy Glover and Graham Greene*, introduction by John Carter (1966)
Ian Ousby, *Bloodhounds of Heaven. The detective in English fiction from Godwin to Doyle* (1976)

Ellery Queen [Frederic Dannay and Manfred Bennington Lee], *Queen's Quorum. A history of the detective-crime short story . . . 1845–1967* (1969)

John M. Reilly (ed.), *Twentieth-century Crime and Mystery Writers* (2nd edn., 1985)

Chris Steinbrunner and Otto Penzler, *Encyclopedia of Mystery and Detection* (1976)

R. F. Stewart, . . . *And Always a Detective. Chapters in the history of detective fiction* (1980)

Julian Symons, *Bloody Murder. From the detective story to the crime novel* (rev. edn., 1985)

Colin Watson, *Snobbery with Violence* (1971)

Robin W. Winks (ed.), *Detective Fiction. A collection of critical essays* (1980)

OXFORD

MORE OXFORD PAPERBACKS

This book is just one of nearly 1000 Oxford Paperbacks currently in print. If you would like details of other Oxford Paperbacks, including titles in the World's Classics, Oxford Reference, Oxford Books, OPUS, Past Masters, Oxford Authors, and Oxford Shakespeare series, please write to:

UK and Europe: Oxford Paperbacks Publicity Manager, Arts and Reference Publicity Department, Oxford University Press, Walton Street, Oxford OX2 6DP.

Customers in UK and Europe will find Oxford Paperbacks available in all good bookshops. But in case of difficulty please send orders to the Cash-with-Order Department, Oxford University Press Distribution Services, Saxon Way West, Corby, Northants NN18 9ES. Tel: 0536 741519; Fax: 0536 746337. Please send a cheque for the total cost of the books, plus £1.75 postage and packing for orders under £20; £2.75 for orders over £20. Customers outside the UK should add 10% of the cost of the books for postage and packing.

USA: Oxford Paperbacks Marketing Manager, Oxford University Press, Inc., 200 Madison Avenue, New York, N.Y. 10016.

Canada: Trade Department, Oxford University Press, 70 Wynford Drive, Don Mills, Ontario M3C 1J9.

Australia: Trade Marketing Manager, Oxford University Press, G.P.O. Box 2784Y, Melbourne 3001, Victoria.

South Africa: Oxford University Press, P.O. Box 1141, Cape Town 8000.

OXFORD BOOKS

THE OXFORD BOOK OF ENGLISH GHOST STORIES

Chosen by Michael Cox and R. A. Gilbert

This anthology includes some of the best and most frightening ghost stories ever written, including M. R. James's 'Oh Whistle, and I'll Come to You, My Lad', 'The Monkey's Paw' by W. W. Jacobs, and H. G. Wells's 'The Red Room'. The important contribution of women writers to the genre is represented by stories such as Amelia Edwards's 'The Phantom Coach', Edith Wharton's 'Mr Jones', and Elizabeth Bowen's 'Hand in Glove'.

As the editors stress in their informative introduction, a good ghost story, though it may raise many profound questions about life and death, entertains as much as it unsettles us, and the best writers are careful to satisfy what Virginia Woolf called 'the strange human craving for the pleasure of feeling afraid'. This anthology, the first to present the full range of classic English ghost fiction, similarly combines a serious literary purpose with the plain intention of arousing pleasing fear at the doings of the dead.

'an excellent cross-section of familiar and unfamiliar stories and guaranteed to delight' *New Statesman*

GREYSCALE

BIN TRAVELER FORM

Cut By _____ Qty _____ Date _____

Scanned By _____ Qty _____ Date _____

Scanned Batch IDs _____

_____

Notes / Exception _____

_____

_____

_____

_____